THE ILLUSTRATED ENCYCLOPEDIA OF
HANDGUNS

THE ILLUSTRATED ENCYCLOPEDIA OF
HANDGUNS
Pistols and Revolvers of the World
1870 to the Present

A. B. ZHUK

Translated by N. N. Bobrov

Edited by John Walter

LEWIS
INTERNATIONAL, INC

The Illustrated Encyclopedia of Handguns

Published in the United States in 2000 by
Lewis International
2201 NW 102nd Place, 1
Miami, FL 33172, USA
Tel: 305-436-7984/800-259-5962
Fax: 305-436-7985/800-664-5095

First published in Great Britain in 1995
by Greenhill Books/Lionel Leventhal Limited, Park House,
1 Russell Gardens, London NW11 9NN

A catalogue record for this book is available
from the British Library.

ISBN 1-930983-02-6

Printed and bound in Great Britain
by Butler & Tanner Limited, Frome, Somerset

Contents

Foreword

The Illustrated Encyclopedia of Handguns presents, for the first time in English, the extraordinary life-long work of Aleksandr Zhuk. His original book—*Revolver i Pistolet*—achieved cult status in privileged Western circles once a few copies had been spirited out of the USSR in the 1980s, but remains unknown to many gun collectors.

Aleksandr Borisovich Zhuk was born in 1922 in Zvenigorodka, a small town in the Ukraine. Moving with his family first to Tula and then to Moscow, he was conscripted into a Red Army anti-aircraft unit in 1941. After the war, he worked as an assistant in Grekov's School of Military Painters, then studied at the Moscow Painter's School before graduating from the Polygraphic Institute.

Work as a freelance illustrator for Russian publishing houses led, in 1965, to an official appointment. Zhuk worked in a department responsible for military symbols and rank-badges, producing designs for—amongst others—the armed forces, the customs service, the procurator's office and the transport ministry.

Even as a child, blessed with natural talent, Zhuk drew machinery, steam engines, cars, trams and aeroplanes with great skill. He admits to a particular love of weaponry, being attracted by the elegance of their lines and also by the fact that they could be drawn 'direct from nature'. Trams and railway engines could not be brought into the drawing room!

Aleksandr Zhuk began recording details of small arms before the Second World War, when traces of post-revolutionary civil strife were still evident throughout the Soviet Union. As years passed, his collection of books, drawings and information grew until what had once been simply a childhood hobby became an abiding passion.

Eventually, the artist was persuaded to prepare his work for publication. This was tedious and protracted; not only did many new drawings have to be created, but supporting text had also to be gathered.

The publication of the book was greeted with great acclaim in the USSR, gaining Aleksandr Zhuk the S.I. Mosin Prize and a fellowship of the Association of Armourers of the Soviet Union. At the Moscow International Book Fair in 1983, the original version of *Revolver i Pistolet* was sold to more than thirty countries. Subsequent editions have been enlarged and greatly refined; for *The Illustrated Encyclopedia of Handguns*, therefore, the opportunity has now been taken to add several hundred drawings.

The cornerstone of the book is its detailed illustrations. These fascinated me from the first time I saw them. With first-hand experience of similar work, I could appreciate not only the problems of transferring the details of so many guns to paper, but also the labour of love involved. The work had obviously taken a long time, yet had been presented in amazingly consistent style.

In an era in which computer-assisted techniques have become commonplace, Aleksandr Zhuk is a champion of draughtsmanship as art. His line drawings require skills that range far beyond merely ensuring an accurate outline—note, for example, the subtlety of shading on the many grips. Zhuk's approach echoes traditional engraving skills, seen at their best before photographic techniques swept them away in the period between the world wars.

I once drew a life-size rifle (amusingly, in the context of this introduction, a Soviet Mosin-Nagant) in a painstaking dot-and-line style. The work took forty hours to complete, but could not be justified by commercial yardsticks and the methods have only ever been repeated on a small scale. Not surprisingly, nothing comparable with Aleksandr Zhuk's work has been published in the West in recent years.

Yet accurate drawings possess important merits: they generally reproduce better than photographs, especially in small sizes; are dimensionally true to the guns whereas photographs often distort; and can call attention, whenever necessary, to hidden features.

The late nineteenth century produced men such as Rudolf Schmidt and Konrad von Kromar, who were to be renowned as much for their firearms-designing skills as for their draughtsmanship. And though it is often difficult to assess the part played by engravers who transcribed the illustrations onto printing plates, it is clear from *Die Handfeuerwaffen* (1875–8) that Schmidt, in particular, deserves lasting recognition.

The First World War not only raised popular interest in firearms, but also inspired collection of modern weapons. From this era came James E. Coombes and André Jandot.

Coombes served with US Army Ordnance during the First World War and is best known for the pamphlet *Gewehr 98*, produced in 1921 with the assistance of Captain J.L. Aney. He also contributed many drawings to Bannerman sales catalogues. Jandot, a Frenchman, gained his professional interest in small arms whilst kicking his heels in a German prison camp. He emigrated to the USA after the First World War, illustrated the books of James E. Hicks, then produced a vast number of line drawings for the US Army in 1941–5. No firearms illustrator has attained comparable eminence since 1945, excepting possibly Edward Hoffschmidt and James Triggs. But all of these men are now dead, and the gun-collecting world has been much poorer for the dearth of carefully observed line drawings.

It is with great pleasure, therefore, that I commend the work of Aleksandr Zhuk—not only as peerless, judged from an artistic viewpoint, but also in the knowledge that *The Illustrated Encyclopedia of Handguns* provides the collecting fraternity with a unique and invaluable reference tool.

John Walter, Hove, 1995

Bibliography

Anon.: *Entsiklopediya voennkh i morskikh nauk* ('Encyclopedia of military and naval science'). St Petersburg, 1893.
— *Siravochnik po strelkovomu oruzhiyo inostrannkh armiy* ('Reference book of the firearms of foreign armies'). Voenizdat, Moscow, 1947.
— *Sovetskaya Voennaya Entsiklopediya* ('Soviet military encyclopedia'). Voenizdat, Moscow, eight volumes, 1976–80.
Adamcyzk, M.: *Pistolet P-64*. Warsaw, 1974.

Bady, Donald B.: *Colt Automatic Pistols, 1896–1955*. Borden Publishing Company, Alhambra, California, revised (second) edition, 1973.
Balasz, J., and J. Pongo: *Pisztolyok, revolverek*. Budapest, 1977.
Barnes, Frank C.: *Cartridges of the World* ('The Book for Every Shooter, Collector and Handloader'). DBI Books, Inc., Northbrook, Illinois, fifth edition, 1985.
Beneš, C.: *Palné Zbraně v zbirkach nasich musei*. Pardubice, 1981.
Blagonravov, Arkady A.: *Materialnaya chast strelkovogo oruzhiya* ('Constructional details of firearms'). Voenizdat, Moscow, 1945.
Bock, Gerhard, and Wilhelm Weigel: *Faustfeuerwaffen*. Melsungen, several editions, 1965–74.
Boeheim, Wendelin: *Handbuch der Waffenkunde*. Leipzig, 1890; reprinted by Akademische Druck- und Verlagsanstalt, Graz, 1985.
Bolotin, David N.: *Sovetskoye strelkovoe oruzhiye za 50 let* ('Fifty years of Soviet firearms'). Leningrad, 1967.
— *Sovetskoye strelkovoe oruzhiye* ('Soviet firearms'). Voenizdat, Moscow, 1986.
Breathed, John W., Jr, and Joseph J. Schroeder, Jr: *System Mauser* ('A pictorial history of the Model 1896 self-loading pistol'). Handgun Press, Chicago, 1967.
Bruce, Gordon, and Christian Reinhart: *Webley Revolvers* ('revised from W.C. Dowell's *The Webley Story*'). Verlag Stocker-Schmid, Dietikon-Zürich, 1988.

Cochran, Keith: *Colt Peacemaker Encyclopedia*. Published privately, Rapid City, South Dakota, 1986. A supplement was produced in 1989.

Derby, Harry: *The Hand Cannons of Imperial Japan*. Derby Publishing Company, Charlotte, North Carolina, 1981.
Dowell, William C.: *The Webley Story* ('A History of Webley Pistols and Revolvers and the Development of the Pistol Cartridge'). The Skyrac Press, Kirkgate, Leeds, 1962.
Durdick, Jiri, with Miroslav Mudra and Miroslav Šáda: *Alte Handfeuerwaffen*. Prague, 1977.

Erlmeier, Hans A., and Jacob H. Brandt: *Manual of Pistol & Revolver Cartridges*. Journal-Verlag Schwend GmbH, Schwäbisch Hall, volume 1 (centre-fire, metric calibres) 1967, volume 2 (centre-fire, Anglo-American calibres) 1980.
Ezell, Edward C.: *Handguns of the World* ('Military revolvers and self-loaders from 1870 to 1945'). The Stackpole Company, Harrisburg, Pennsylvania, 1981.
— *Small Arms Today*. Stackpole Books, Harrisburg, Pennsylvania, second edition, 1988.

Federov, Vladimir G.: *Novobbedeinya v vooruzhenii inostrannkh armiy. Avtomaticheskie pistolet* ('Introduction to the armament of foreign armies. Automatic pistols'). Strelkovoy shkol, 1907.
— *Evolyutsiya strelkovogo oruzhiya* ('Evolution of firearms'). Voenizdat, Moscow, two parts, 1938–9.
— *Oruzheynoe delo na grani dvukh epokh* ('Gunnery on the boundary of two epochs'). F.E. Dzerzhinsky Artillery Academy, three parts, 1939.

Gluckman, Colonel Arcadi: *United States Martial Pistols & Revolvers*. The Stackpole Company, Harrisburg, Pennsylvania, 1956.
Gnatovsky, N.I., and P.A. Shorin: *Istoriya razvitiya otechestvennogo strelkovogo oruzhiya* ('Historical catalogue of indigenous firearms'). Voenizdat, Moscow, 1959.
Görtz, Joachim: *Die Pistole 08*. Verlag Stocker-Schmid, Dietikon-Zürich, and Motorbuch-Verlag, Stuttgart, 1985.
— and John D. Walter: *The Navy Luger* ('The 9mm Pistole 1904 and the Imperial German Navy: a concise illustrated history'). The Lyon Press, Eastbourne, and Handgun Press, Chicago, 1988.

Hatch, Alden: *Remington Arms in American History*. Remington Arms Company, Inc., Ilion, New York, revised edition, 1972.
Hatcher, Major General Julian S.: *Hatcher's Notebook* ('A Standard Reference Book for Shooters, Gunsmiths, Ballisticians, Historians, Hunters and Collectors'). The Stackpole Company, Harrisburg, Pennsylvania, third edition, 1962.
Häusler, Fritz: *Schweizer Fastfeuerwaffen — Armes de poing suisses — Swiss Handguns*. Verlag Häusler, Frauenfeld, 1975.
Haven, Charles T., and Frank A. Belden: *A History of the Colt Revolver*. William Morrow & Company, New York, 1940.
Hogg, Ian V.: *German Pistols and Revolvers, 1871–1945*. Arms & Armour Press, London, 1971.
— [Editor]: *Jane's Infantry Weapons*. Jane's Publishing Co. Ltd, London, published annually.
— *Military Pistols & Revolvers*. Arms & Armour Press, London; 1988.
— *The Cartridge Guide* ('The Small Arms Ammunition Identification Manual'). Arms & Armour Press, London; 1982.
— and John S. Weeks: *Military Small Arms of the Twentieth Century*. Arms & Armour Press, London; sixth edition, 1991.
— and John S. Weeks: *Pistols of the World* ("The definitive illustrated guide to the world's pistols and revolvers"). Arms & Armour Press, London, third edition, 1992.

Jinks, Roy G.: *History of Smith & Wesson* ('No Things of Importance Will Come Without Effort'). Beinfeld Publishing Company, North Hollywood, California, 1977.
Johnson, Melvin M., and Charles T. Haven: *Automatic Arms*. William Morrow & Company, New York, 1943.

König, Klaus-Peter; *Faustfeuerwaffen*. Motorbuch Verlag, Stuttgart, 1980.
Kopec, John A., with Ron Graham and Kenneth C. Moore: *A Study of the Colt Single Action Army Revolver*. Published by the authors, La Puente, California, 1976.

Lugs, Jaroslav: *Handfeuerwaffen*. Berlin, 1973, 1980.

Markevich, V.E.: *Ruchnoe ognestrelnoe oruzhiye* ('Manually-operated small arms'). F.E. Dzerzhinsky Artillery Academy, 1937.
Mathews, J. Howard; *Firearms Identification*. Charles C. Thomas, Springfield, Illinois, three volumes, 1962–73.
Müller, H.: *Gewehre, Pistolen, Revolver*. Leipzig, 1979.

Neal, Robert J., and Roy G. Jinks: *Smith & Wesson 1857–1945*. A.S. Barnes & Company, Inc., South Brunswick, New Jersey, 1966.

Parsons, John E.: *Smith & Wesson Revolvers: The Pioneer Single Action Models*. William Morrow & Company, New York, 1957.
— *The Peacemaker and its Rivals*. William Morrow & Company, New York, 1950.

Pastukhov, I.P., and S.E. Plotnikov: *Rasskaz o strelkovom oruzhii* ('Stories of firearms'). DOSAAF, Moscow, 1983.
Ponomarev, P.D.: *Revolver i Pistolet* ('Revolver and pistol'). Voenizdat, Moscow, 1941.

Reinhart, Christian, and Michael am Rhyn: *Faustfeuerwaffen*. Verlag Stocker-Schmid, Dietikon-Zürich, two volumes ('Vorderladerpistolen, Revolver' and 'Selbstladepistolen'), 1974–5.

Šáda, Miroslav: *Československé ruční palné zbraně a kulomety*. Naše Vojsko, Prague, 1971.
Schaal, Dieter: *Suhler Feuerwaffen*. Berlin, 1981.
Serven, James E.: *Colt Firearms from 1836*. The Foundation Press, La Habra, California, seventh printing, 1972.
Smith, Walter H.B.: *Mauser, Walther & Mannlicher Firearms*. The Stackpole Company, Harrisburg, Pennsylvania, 1971.
— *The Book of Pistols & Revolvers*. The Stackpole Company, Harrisburg, Pennsylvania, seventh edition, 1968.
Stammel, H.J.: *Mit gebremster Gewalt (Polizeiwaffen von beute und morgen)*. Stuttgart, 1974.
Stern, Daniel K.: *10 Shots Quick* ('The Fascinating Story of the Savage Pocket Automatics'). Globe Printing Company, San Jose, California, 1967.

Taylerson, Anthony W.F. [with R.A.N. Andrews and J. Firth]: *The Revolver, 1818–1865*. Herbert Jenkins Ltd, London; 1968.
— *The Revolver, 1865–1888*. Herbert Jenkins Ltd, London; 1966.
— *The Revolver, 1889–1914*. Barrie & Jenkins, London; 1970.

Velyaminov, S.P., with V.I. Slavolyubov and S.I. Shestakov: *Strelkovy sport. Chast 2. Strelokovoe oruzhie* ('Shooting sport. Part 2, Firearms'). Osoaviakhim, Moscow, 1928.

Walter, John D.: *German Military Handguns, 1879–1918*. Arms & Armour Press, London; 1980.
— *The Luger Book* ('The encyclopedia of Borchardt and Borchardt-Luger handguns, 1885–1985'). Arms & Armour Press, London; 1986.
— *The Pistol Book*. Arms & Armour Press, London; second edition, 1988.
Wilson, Lieutenant Colonel Robert K. [edited by Ian V. Hogg]: *Textbook of Automatic Pistols*. Arms & Armour Press, London; 1975.
Wilson, R.L.: *The Colt Heritage* ('The Official History of Colt Firearms from 1836 to the Present'). Simon & Schuster, New York, undated (1979).
— *Colt, An American Legend*. Blacksmith Corporation, Chino Valley, 1991.
White, Henry P., with Barton D. Munhall and Ray Bearse: *Centrefire Pistol & Revolver Cartridges*. A.S.Barnes & Company, New York, 1967.

The organisation of this book

The Russian-language editions have all followed the same pattern: grouped text followed by grouped drawings. This construction, though once universally popular, is very difficult to use effectually. *The Illustrated Encyclopedia of Handguns* retains the drawings and the substance of the original Russian text, but the material is integrated so that text appears with the relevant drawings.

Altering the basic layout has led to important changes in the structure of the text. The original format permitted guns to be grouped together, but avoided the necessity to describe or identify individual items in detail. The new format, conversely, draws immediate attention to gaps in coverage. Thus the opportunity has been taken to correct errors and to identify, wherever possible, guns that were previously listed as 'unknown'.

The principle of splitting guns into two basic categories (revolvers and pistols) and then by nationality has been retained. The guns are now numbered in a single sequence instead of chapter by chapter, and data, once included in the captions, have been consolidated in the text.

Within each nation, guns are presented alphabetically by model name or designation. The original work was organised on an approximately chronological basis, but the difficulty of dating some lesser guns and the lengthy periods in which well-known designs have been made (e.g., the Parabellum) created anomalies which the new approach seeks to avoid.

To ease the problems of locating individual guns, the products of the major countries have been split into chronological groups within which they are listed alphabetically by model-name. For example, US products are split into pre-1917, 1917–45 and post-war designs.

Each chronological group, if appropriate, is sub-divided on the basis of construction. Open-frame guns are considered first, followed by solid-frame types, and lastly by hinged-frame or similar patterns.

Handgun origins

Owing to the purpose they serve, revolvers and pistols share many common features and differ fundamentally only in their actions. In the broadest sense, a pistol is a firearm held in one hand when fired. But this definition does not specify construction; a revolver is a pistol, but its structure is such that it is immediately distinguishable. A revolver—by definition, a multi-shot weapon—retains its cartridges in a revolving cylinder. This feature was so important that a new name, derived from the Latin verb *volvere* ('to turn') had to be created to describe it. The revolving cylinder provides the most important means of distinguishing revolvers from their predecessors, the pistols.

Just as the revolver quickly eclipsed its predecessors—it shot faster and certainly much more effactually—so it was itself overtaken by the auto-loading pistol. Excepting flare guns, single-shot target pistols, replicas and some other specialised designs, almost all modern pistols derive their multi-shot capabilities from the power generated in the cartridge on firing. This is then translated into mechanical action necessary to eject and reload. Most of them are more accurately defined as 'semi-automatic', requiring the firer to consciously press the trigger for each shot, but custom—and

the comparative scarcity of commercially available fully-automatic guns—has promoted the term 'automatic' to encompass semi-automatic patterns as well. Unless qualified by terms such as 'single shot', therefore, a modern pistol is invariably assumed to be a (semi-)automatic.

Judged on any absolute time-scale, revolvers and pistols do not have a long history. The first primitive firearms appeared at the beginning of the fourteenth century and guns fired with one hand were in existence by the middle of the sixteenth century. The invention of the true one-hand gun is traditionally ascribed to an Italian gunmaker named Vettelli, working in the town of Pistoia, from where, so the story

1. A typical wheel-lock.
2. A German wheel-lock pistol of the mid-sixteenth century.
3. A German wheel-lock pistol dating from the second half of the sixteenth century.
4. The keys for winding the lock-springs of the guns in figs. 2 and 3; a lever pattern (left) and a socket type (right).
5. A German wheel-lock pistol dating from the end of the sixteenth century.
6. An Italian wheel-lock pistol of the mid-seventeenth century.
7. A French wheel-lock pistol dating from the first half of the seventeenth century.

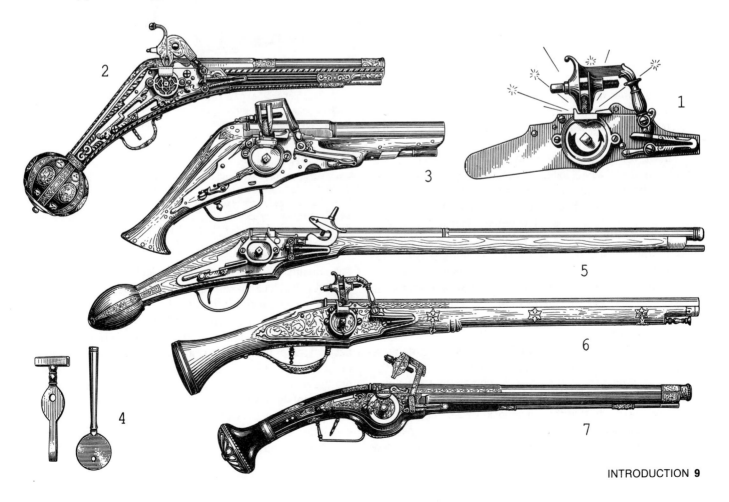

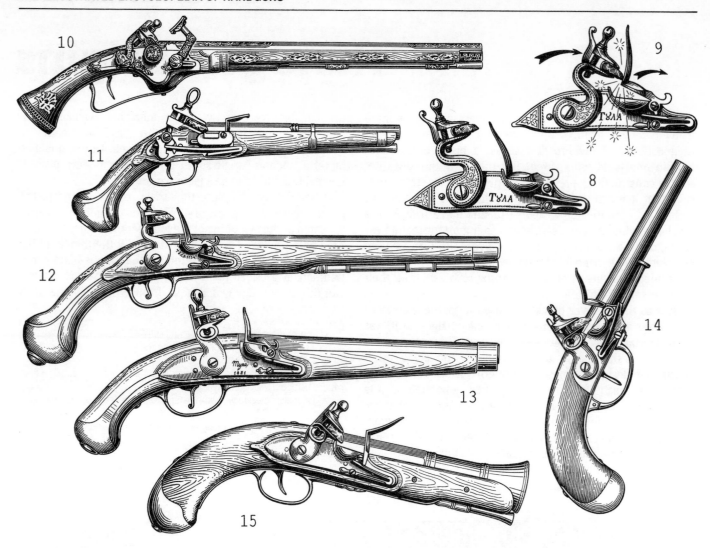

goes, the name of the new cavalry weapon—'pistol'—was corrupted. However, an equally plausible derivation from the Czech *pištala*, a musical instrument better known in English as a 'fife', also has its champions.

The advent of effectual pistols was due largely to the invention of the wheel-lock. Previously, the development of compact firearms had been hindered by the crudity of the slow-match ignition. The wheel-lock relied on a clockwork mechanism to rotate a serrated wheel against a wedge of pyrites held in the jaws of a pivoting cock. The mechanism was wound or 'spanned' with a key, priming powder was placed in the pan, and the cock was thumbed back so that the pyrites rested against the surface of the wheel. When the trigger was pressed, the sparks from the pyrites ignited the priming powder, and the priming powder ignited the main charge in the barrel.

The wheel-lock enjoyed a brief heyday; some guns were adapted so that the cock sprang back into battery and the priming-powder pan sprang open as soon as the trigger was pressed; a few proprietary waterproof guns were even made. There was no doubt that the wheel-lock was an improvement on its predecessors, but it was complicated and expensive to make. This restricted production to a comparatively few

8, 9. The flintlock—shown cocked and ready to fire (8) and just as the flinted cock strikes the frizzen, anvil or battery (9) to produce a shower of sparks which are directed naturally into the priming-powder pan.
10. A Russian flintlock pistol of the early seventeenth century.
11. A Spanish pistol from the end of the seventeenth century.
12. The archetypal European flintlock pistol was made from the end of the seventeenth century to the mid-nineteenth; this Russian example was made in Tula in 1754.
13. A Russian cavalry pistol of 1810.
14. A French cavalry pistol of 1777.
15. A French naval *Trombon* (blunderbuss) of the late eighteenth century. The bell-shaped muzzle increased shot-scatter.

good-quality pieces, many of the lock components being made by the clock makers of central Europe.

Though the lock mechanism improved, the basic design of pistols remained the same for three hundred years. Even the most radical changes were comparatively insignificant: barrel length increased towards the end of the sixteenth century, as calibre simultaneously decreased; flintlocks gradually replaced wheel-locks during the seventeenth century; and the shape of the grip was improved. Once these changes had been made, however, alterations were largely cosmetic. The technical development of the pistol, which awaited the advent of the great changes in production techniques wrought by nineteenth-century industrialisation, was subordinated to aesthetics. The increasing elegance of the pistol, which in time improved balance and shooting capabilities, culminated in the heyday of the single-shot duelling pistol (c.1770–1840).

Apart from uncertainty of ignition, an obvious problem with powder-and-ball charges was the protracted loading process. The most obvious solution was to add more charges, either by alternating them in the bore ('superimposed loads') or by adding self-contained barrels. Virtually every possible combination was tried—barrel clusters, pivoting barrels or fixed barrels with multiple locks—but few found success. The penalties were generally excessive weight and needless complication.

The first true flintlocks appeared in France early in the seventeenth century, though some years elapsed before they supplanted alternative forms of ignition. By the end of the century, however, the perfected flintlock—which combined the frizzen and pan cover*—had eclipsed the match- and wheel-locks. Not only was the flintlock technically superior, but it was also much simpler. Simplicity allowed locks to be made more easily, and at a greatly reduced price. This was particularly attractive from a military viewpoint and led to the near-universal issue of the flintlock musket and pistol throughout the armies of Europe.

---

* The true flint- or French-lock, which combined the frizzen with the pan cover, was rivalled in the early days by systems in which the pan and frizzen were separate components. These are known as 'Snaphaunce' (deriving from Dutch) but required the pan cover to be opened manually and, therefore, did not stand the test of time.

Though the use of multiple barrels did accelerate the rate and efficacy of fire—at least until reloading was required—it had no effect on accuracy, which remained poor. A partial answer was found in the development of patched balls, which were driven down into rudimentary rifling with a mallet. Accuracy improved perceptibly compared with smooth-bores firing sub-calibre projectiles, but loading took much longer. The development of breech-loading promised a better solution, as a lead ball of slightly greater than bore size could be inserted into a slightly tapering chamber ahead of the powder charge and engrave effectually in the rifling when the weapon was fired. Unfortunately, despite widespread experimentation, most early breech-loaders were defeated by shortcomings in contemporary metallurgy. Even though the separate loading chamber was nearly as old as the gun itself, few smiths could make the principles work effectually in a small arm.

16. A pocket pistol of the 1790–1810 period, fitted with a folding bayonet. The gun has an all-metal 'box lock', a typically English construction with the cock on the centre-line of the bore.
17. A typical late eighteenth-century European pocket pistol with a folding trigger.
18. A Russian duelling pistol, 1800–25.
19–22. A Russian powder horn of the seventeenth century (19) and an eighteenth-century powder flask (20); a European powder flask (21) and powder horn (22), both dating from the late eighteenth century.
23, 24. Typical Scottish flintlock pistols dating from the middle of the eighteenth century, showing the characteristic all-metal stocks—in this case, brass.

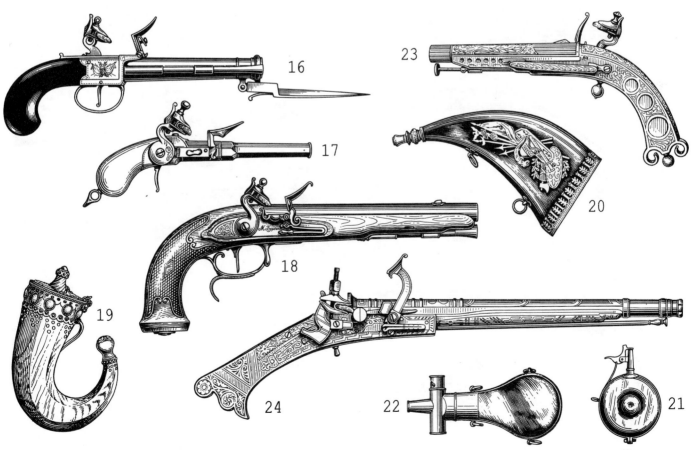

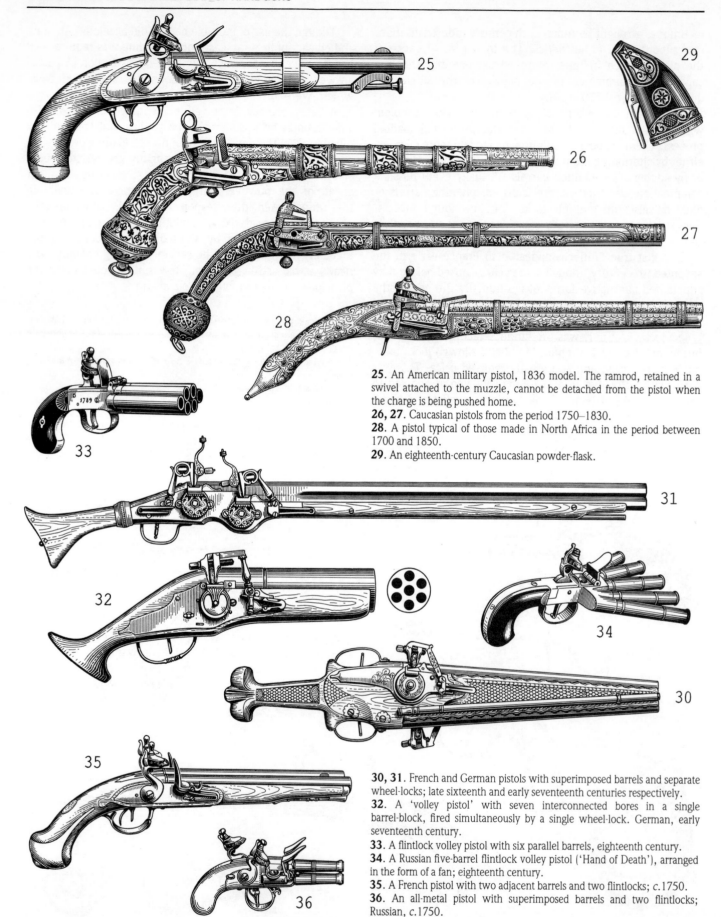

25. An American military pistol, 1836 model. The ramrod, retained in a swivel attached to the muzzle, cannot be detached from the pistol when the charge is being pushed home.

26, 27. Caucasian pistols from the period 1750–1830.

28. A pistol typical of those made in North Africa in the period between 1700 and 1850.

29. An eighteenth-century Caucasian powder-flask.

30, 31. French and German pistols with superimposed barrels and separate wheel-locks; late sixteenth and early seventeenth centuries respectively.

32. A 'volley pistol' with seven interconnected bores in a single barrel-block, fired simultaneously by a single wheel-lock. German, early seventeenth century.

33. A flintlock volley pistol with six parallel barrels, eighteenth century.

34. A Russian five-barrel flintlock volley pistol ('Hand of Death'), arranged in the form of a fan; eighteenth century.

35. A French pistol with two adjacent barrels and two flintlocks; *c*.1750.

36. An all-metal pistol with superimposed barrels and two flintlocks; Russian, *c*.1750.

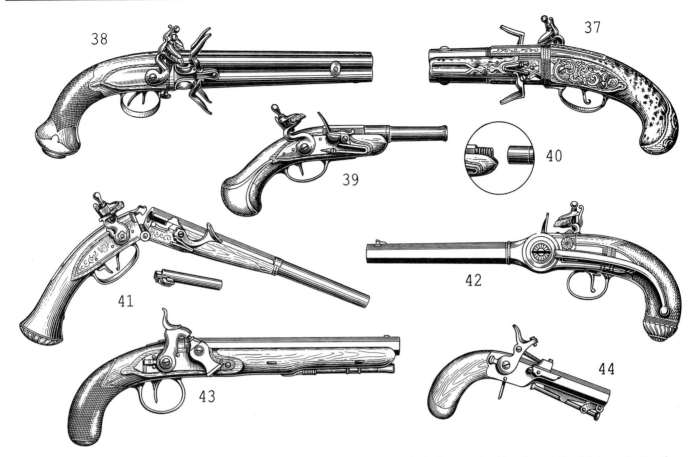

37. A pistol whose two barrels rotate around a longitudinal axis. Each barrel has its own priming-powder pan, but a single cock on the breech suffices; Russian, mid-eighteenth century.

38. A German pistol with four barrels in a revolving cluster; two cocks and four pans enable four shots to be fired for only one turn of the barrel-group.

39, 40. A European 'travelling pistol', c.1720–50; particularly popular in Britain in the first half of the eighteenth century, when the so-called 'Queen Anne' or 'Cannon-Barrel' patterns had their heyday, guns of this type had barrels that unscrewed from the breech.

41. A breech-loading snaphaunce pistol with a detachable chamber, probably dating from 1670–85. The chamber is shown beneath the open breech, which is unlatched by pressing the lever ahead of the trigger.

42. Pistols operating on the Lorenzoni system, originating in Italy in the 1660s, were made by gunsmiths in many European countries. The lever on the left side of the breech could be rotated to feed a bullet and a powder charge into the barrel, and then prime the pan. Bullet and powder magazines were contained in the grip. Success depended on the breech-disc making an effectual seal with the walls of its chamber, and premature explosions were no doubt commonplace.

43. A pistol with a Forsyth lock. The flask-like reservoir contains priming, and is rotated to feed priming compound into a recess beneath the hammer. English, c.1810. Some guns were subsequently altered to accept priming pellets instead of powder.

44. Pistol with a lock for igniting fulminate pellets; Westley Richards, Birmingham, c.1815–20.

The demise of even the most promising of the flintlock breech-loaders was due to dependence on sparks generated from a flint igniting loose priming powder in an open pan. Though improved springs, rollers and special 'waterproof' pan designs had helped to raise the efficiency of the flintlock to its apogee, the basic principle was deeply flawed. The

entire period of spark ignition is not the history, but rather the pre-history of the firearm.

The first signs of more rapid development came with the adaption of metallic fulminates or 'detonating powders' to ignite gunpowder, a process patented in Britain by Alexander Forsyth in 1807. Forsyth initially used a pivoting reservoir, known colloquially as the Scent Bottle, to feed measured charges of his priming powder beneath the hammer for each shot. The gun still loaded conventionally from the muzzle. Though the effects of wear soon proved the weakness of the Forsyth system, the advent of self-contained pills, tubes and caps pointed the way forward. Ultimately, by 1835, the waterproof cap had triumphed.

A rifled barrel and a breech-loading chamber were most important pre-requisites of pistol development. Though both pre-dated the percussion cap by many years, they had been developed in isolation and, lacking a satisfactory system of ignition, had simply lain dormant.

The cap improved both speed and certainty of ignition, tempting pistol designers to seek increases in the rate of fire. The accuracy, range and dimensions of the existing guns, as well as their lethality, all left much to be desired—though each met existing criteria well enough for officialdom in almost all states to discourage experimentation.

Rapid fire presented the greatest problem. The guns of the early nineteenth century still loaded from the muzzle, which took time. Owing to limited range and poor striking energy, the pistol could only be used when the enemy closed

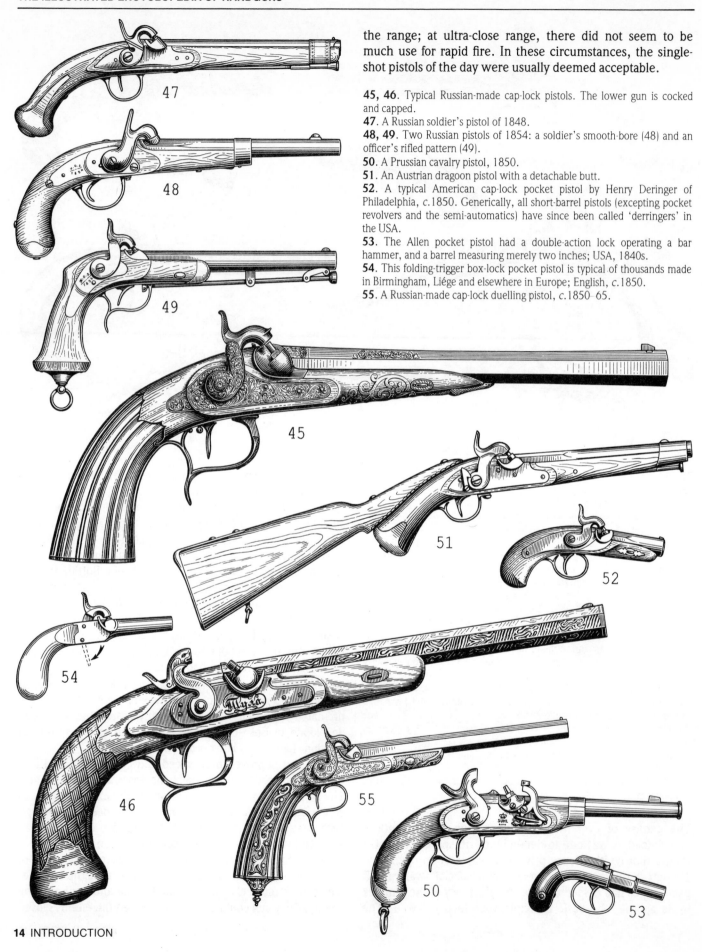

the range; at ultra-close range, there did not seem to be much use for rapid fire. In these circumstances, the single-shot pistols of the day were usually deemed acceptable.

45, 46. Typical Russian-made cap-lock pistols. The lower gun is cocked and capped.

47. A Russian soldier's pistol of 1848.

48, 49. Two Russian pistols of 1854: a soldier's smooth-bore (48) and an officer's rifled pattern (49).

50. A Prussian cavalry pistol, 1850.

51. An Austrian dragoon pistol with a detachable butt.

52. A typical American cap-lock pocket pistol by Henry Deringer of Philadelphia, *c*.1850. Generically, all short-barrel pistols (excepting pocket revolvers and the semi-automatics) have since been called 'derringers' in the USA.

53. The Allen pocket pistol had a double-action lock operating a bar hammer, and a barrel measuring merely two inches; USA, 1840s.

54. This folding-trigger box-lock pocket pistol is typical of thousands made in Birmingham, Liége and elsewhere in Europe; English, *c*.1850.

55. A Russian-made cap-lock duelling pistol, *c*.1850–65.

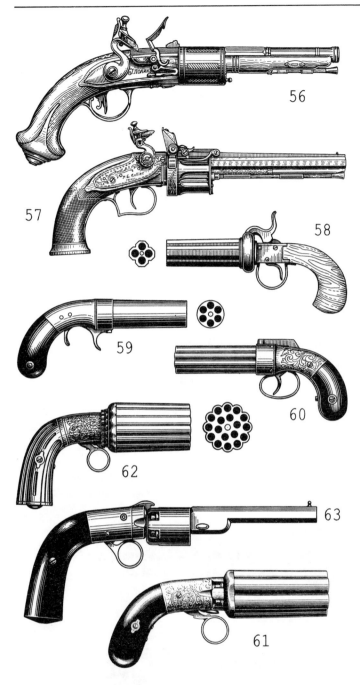

The revolving cylinder

Guns of this type had been made in the seventeenth century, including a few which automatically rotated the cylinder as the cock was retracted. Their greatest weakness lay in the ignition system, particularly as the pans of priming powder on the underside of the cylinder were carried upside down. Rotation tended to displace the priming and misfires were frequent.

The first effectual revolver is generally agreed to have been made by Elisha Collier, though Collier himself credited the American Artemus Wheeler with the basic ideas on which he had drawn. Wheeler's patent was granted in June 1818, whilst the Collier revolver was made in Britain in small numbers into the 1830s. The earliest examples rotated the cylinder through a mechanical linkage, but this complex and comparatively unreliable system was eventually replaced by manual rotation.

Collier's limited achievements were soon eclipsed by Samuel Colt, whose first practicable revolver was made by a Baltimorean mechanic named John Pearson in 1834. Series production of the Paterson Colt—named after the factory in Paterson, New Jersey—began in the late 1830s. Though the Paterson Colt did not make Colt's fortune, and business soon collapsed, it had sown the seeds of later glory. War with Mexico in the late 1840s and the California Gold Rush of 1849 proved turning points: the former because it favoured the enormous Colt cavalry revolvers, and the latter for its promotion of the pocket patterns.

The guns produced by Colt and his rivals found a ready market not only in the United States, but also throughout the world. Revolvers were the first effectual rapid-fire arms, and had great advantages over the conventional single-shot pistols. As the cylinder had several chambers—five or six were the most popular in early designs—it was only necessary to cock the hammer and squeeze the trigger to fire shots in rapid succession. Loading was still tortuous, but the step forward had been immense.

The pepperbox was a short-lived competitor of the earliest revolvers, differing in the substitution of several full-length barrels for the cylinder-and-barrel arrangement. Guns with multi-barrel clusters were appreciably heavier than revolvers of comparable overall dimensions, which usually restricted them to smaller calibres. However, though pepperboxes were unhandy, they did possess some important advantages. Amongst even the earliest of the pepperboxes were self-cocking guns which could be fired simply by pulling through on the trigger. This enabled them to be fired more rapidly than the Colts, which had to be thumb-cocked for each shot. In addition, the cap-lock pepperboxes were less prone than cap-lock revolvers to chain-firing, when flash from the firing chamber radiated across the front surface of the cylinder to ignite some or all of the remaining chambers simultaneously.

Revolvers were easier to handle than pepperboxes and, owing to the longer barrel, usually proved to shoot much

56. A Russian pistol with a six-chamber revolving cylinder, dating from the late eighteenth century.
57. An English-made Collier revolver of 1820–5.
58. An Engholm manually rotated single-action pepperbox; Sweden, c.1845–50.
59. The Bacon underhammer pepperbox; USA.
60. A typical double-action pepperbox; the barrel-cluster rotated automatically as the trigger was pressed. Ethan Allen, USA, c.1840.
61. A Mariette cap-lock six-shot pepperbox of a pattern originating in 1837. Belgian.
62. A Belgian-made ring-trigger Mariette pepperbox, c.1845. Eighteen shots, with concentric rows of twelve (outer) and six (inner). The barrel-cluster was rotated manually.
63. A Belgian proto-revolver by Henri Colleye of Liége. This is basically a short pepperbox fitted with a long barrel wedged to an extension of the barrel-cluster axis pin. These inferior hybrids enjoyed a brief period in vogue in the 1850s before being swept away by perfected revolver designs.

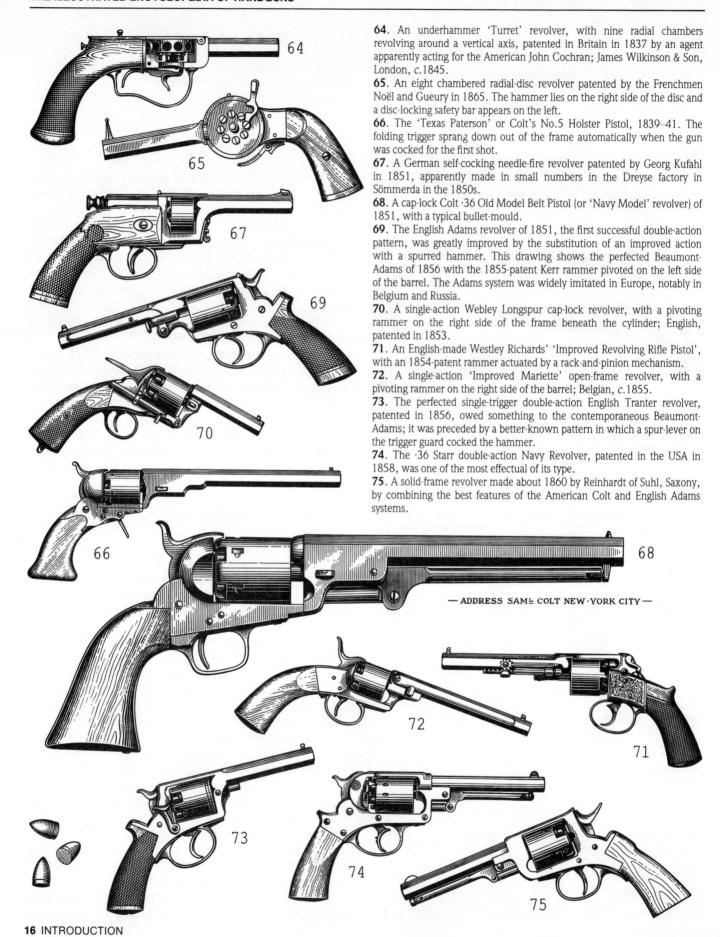

64. An underhammer 'Turret' revolver, with nine radial chambers revolving around a vertical axis, patented in Britain in 1837 by an agent apparently acting for the American John Cochran; James Wilkinson & Son, London, *c*.1845.

65. An eight chambered radial-disc revolver patented by the Frenchmen Noël and Gueury in 1865. The hammer lies on the right side of the disc and a disc-locking safety bar appears on the left.

66. The 'Texas Paterson' or Colt's No.5 Holster Pistol, 1839–41. The folding trigger sprang down out of the frame automatically when the gun was cocked for the first shot.

67. A German self-cocking needle-fire revolver patented by Georg Kufahl in 1851, apparently made in small numbers in the Dreyse factory in Sömmerda in the 1850s.

68. A cap-lock Colt ·36 Old Model Belt Pistol (or 'Navy Model' revolver) of 1851, with a typical bullet-mould.

69. The English Adams revolver of 1851, the first successful double-action pattern, was greatly improved by the substitution of an improved action with a spurred hammer. This drawing shows the perfected Beaumont-Adams of 1856 with the 1855-patent Kerr rammer pivoted on the left side of the barrel. The Adams system was widely imitated in Europe, notably in Belgium and Russia.

70. A single-action Webley Longspur cap-lock revolver, with a pivoting rammer on the right side of the frame beneath the cylinder; English, patented in 1853.

71. An English-made Westley Richards' 'Improved Revolving Rifle Pistol', with an 1854-patent rammer actuated by a rack-and-pinion mechanism.

72. A single-action 'Improved Mariette' open-frame revolver, with a pivoting rammer on the right side of the barrel; Belgian, *c*.1855.

73. The perfected single-trigger double-action English Tranter revolver, patented in 1856, owed something to the contemporaneous Beaumont-Adams; it was preceded by a better-known pattern in which a spur-lever on the trigger guard cocked the hammer.

74. The ·36 Starr double-action Navy Revolver, patented in the USA in 1858, was one of the most effectual of its type.

75. A solid-frame revolver made about 1860 by Reinhardt of Suhl, Saxony, by combining the best features of the American Colt and English Adams systems.

— ADDRESS SAM⸱ COLT NEW·YORK CITY —

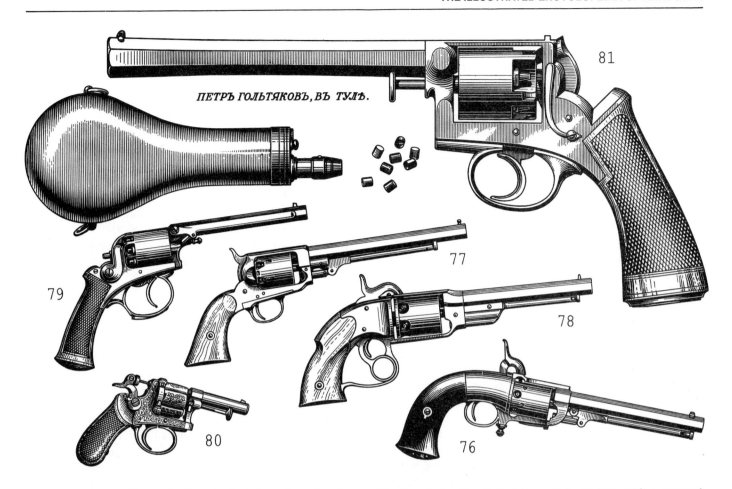

ПЕТРЪ ГОЛЬТЯКОВЪ, ВЪ ТУЛѢ.

more accurately. Firing bullets loaded into the chamber behind a rifled barrel, instead of simply pushing round balls down a smooth-bore barrel from the muzzle, was a crucial advance; it greatly increased effectual range and improved penetrating ability.

Colt cap-lock revolvers were so popular in their heyday that replicas are still being produced to satisfy interest in the Wild West. However, imitations of the Colt revolvers appeared in the United States and Europe almost soon as the genuine articles had been announced.

The success of the Colts inspired the development of guns that were technically more advanced, though the extension until 1855 of Colt's master patent—which protected the mechanical rotation of the cylinder—provided a major stumbling-block. By 1860, however, the double-action cocking mechanism had been perfected and a solid frame had become commonplace. The balance and handling qualities of the average cap-lock gun were excellent.

The development of the cap-lock revolver allowed the power of handguns to increase, even as size and weight decreased. The rapidity and accuracy with which revolvers could fire sharply reduced the significance of 'numerical superiority' in a skirmish.

The self-contained cartridge

The invention of cartridges in which the charge, bullet and primer are united in a waterproof case was crucial in the

76. The single-action Butterfield cap-lock revolver, with a patented automatic cap feed and a rammer beneath the barrel, still embodied features of the transitional proto-revolvers; American, c.1862.

77. A second-pattern Whitney ·36-calibre Navy Belt Model revolver, marked as a product of the 'Western Arms Co.'; a typical solid-frame design of the American Civil War period. USA, c.1861.

78. A single-action ·36 revolver made by the Savage Revolving Fire Arms Company under patents granted in 1856–60 to Henry North. The hammer is cocked by pulling back on the ring-lever with the middle finger of the firing hand. The lever also cams the cylinder forward so that the chamber-mouth enshrouds the barrel-breech to improve the gas seal.

79. A double-action Belgian Comblain-patent revolver, characterised by an external spurless hammer pivoted on the right side of the frame. The trigger guard has a spring device to cock the hammer independent of the trigger, providing effectual single-action fire without the necessity for separate thumb cocking. Mangeot, Bruxelles, c.1855–8.

80. A German Wagner-pattern needle-fire pocket revolver, c.1860.

81. A Russian Adams-type cap-lock revolver made by Petr Goltyakov (sic) in Tula in 1866, together with a powder flask and caps. Note the unusual 'swamped' or reverse-taper barrel, which was intended to reduce the upward jump of the barrel when the gun fired.

development of effectual firearms. It not only helped to ensure the success of the revolver, but also subsequently provided the basis for the development of a new class of one-hand gun—the semi-automatic pistol.

Self-contained combustible cartridges were proposed by Johann Niklaus Dreyse, a German gunsmith, as early as 1827. However, as Dreyse saw their use in relation to his bulky needle-ignition system, the cartridges were more widely used in long arms than handguns. A few needle-fire revolvers were made in the 1850s and 1860s (see figs. 67 and 80), but were unable to compete effectually with the contemporaneous cap-locks.

Allegedly invented in 1836 by Casimir Lefaucheux of Paris, but initially made with a cardboard case, the pinfire cartridge held far greater promise. The first one-piece metal-case design was patented in France in 1846 by Houllier, whereupon a clutch of similar designs appeared in rapid succession. In 1854, Lefaucheux's son Eugène produced the first revolvers chambering pinfire ammunition of this type— so successfully that the cartridges are now often considered as his own invention.

The essence of the Lefaucheux cartridge was a pin, protruding from the body ahead of the rim, which ran vertically down to rest against the primer pellet. The cartridges were inserted into the cylinder so that the pins projected radially. As the firing mechanism was actuated and the cylinder turned, the hammer struck the pins downward to ignite the primer.

Pinfire revolvers had enormous advantages compared with the cap-locks; the ammunition was virtually waterproof, immune to chain ignition, expanded momentarily to seal the chamber-breech, and left much less fouling. Their one great disadvantage was that the exposed pin was vulnerable to damage, allowing the cartridge to be ignited by unexpected blows.* in addition, compared with the most powerful of the cap-locks, the pinfire guns were not particularly hard-hitting. And loading was complicated by the fact that the cartridges had to be inserted in the chambers so that the pins corresponded with their notches.

* Many guns were fitted with projecting rims around the cylinder or, alternatively, with shields attached to the frame or standing breech. These measures undoubtedly reduced the chances of accidental discharge appreciably, but added to the weight, complexity and cost.

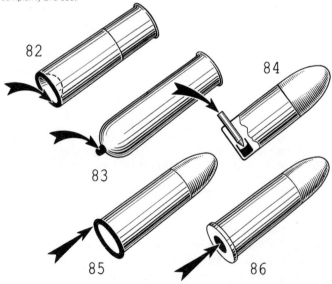

82–86. Ignition in self-contained cartridges (arrows indicate the firing-pin strike): 82 and 83, obsolescent American cup- and teat-fire cartridges inserted into the cylinder from the front; 84, Lefaucheux pinfire; 85, rimfire; 86, centre-fire.

Self-contained cartridges with seamless metallic cases and differing primer positions appeared almost as soon as the first pinfires had been distributed. Rimfire cartridges (fig. 85) are characterised by an annulus of priming compound tucked into the edge of the rim. The hammer-nose was adapted to strike towards the edge of the cartridge-case base. Initially restricted to low-power American revolvers—the Smith & Wesson Model No. 1 of 1857 was the first effectual design— rimfire ammunition has been used ever since. The first true rimfire cartridge was patented in France by the gunsmith Robert in 1831.

Primitive centre-fire cartridges (fig. 86) were patented in France in 1826 by Galy & Cazalat, though the rudiments of the design had been glimpsed in a gun designed by Pauly fifteen years previously. Though years of experimentation elapsed before it could be made strong enough to handle the power needed in military rifle ammunition, the centre-fire pattern has proved the most effectual of all the self-contained designs, contributing immeasurably to the development of handguns. The primer was placed in the centre of the case bottom, facilitating loading whilst also igniting the main charge more evenly in large-capacity cases.

Centre-fire cartridges were also much safer than either pin- or rimfire versions, as they were all but immune to the effects of a blow.

Invention of the modern centre-fire cartridge is usually credited to Pottet, another of the French gunsmiths, but important improvements were made by Colonel Edward Boxer of the British Army and the American General Hiram Berdan, whose names are still attached to differing systems of primer-pocket/anvil construction.

The centre-fire cartridge quickly won universal acclaim, although the advantages of self-contained ammunition had already stimulated the distribution of pinfire cartridges so rapidly that they were still being produced in 1914.

Improved revolver designs

Guns which had originated in America quickly spread throughout Europe, where they developed along their own distinct lines. The first American cartridge revolvers used rimfire ammunition and single-action lockwork, whilst European patterns chambered mainly pin- or centre-fire cartridges and were invariably double action.

As time passed, advances in one group were borrowed by the other, and the differences between them quickly blurred; ideas which won widespread acclaim were eagerly imitated by gunmakers keen to make their fortune. The most important result of this process was that a comparatively small number of designs became established as international standards. The metal-case cartridge had brought revolvers to such perfection that alternative solutions to the problems of attaining rapid fire in a one-hand gun seemed to be doomed.

The advent of smokeless powder in the 1880s was to change the situation appreciably, though many years were to elapse before the importance of the advance became clear. Once perfected, smokeless powder greatly reduced the level

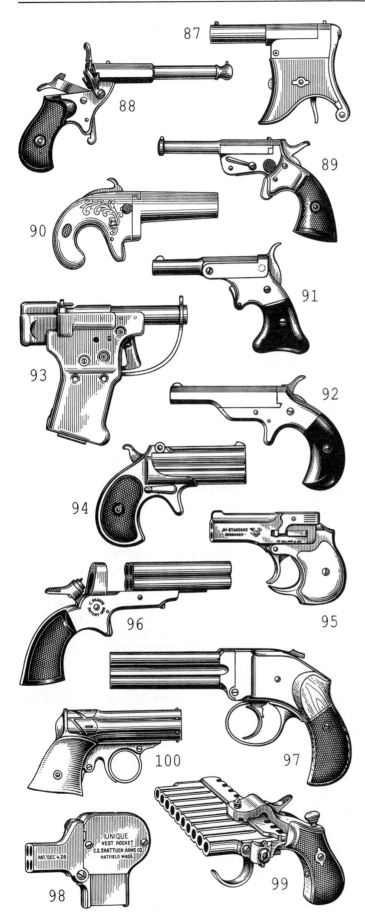

of propellant fouling and, once suitable advances had been made in metallurgy, facilitated the development of weapons that could load and fire automatically. Though some of the most vital advances in revolver design were made late in the nineteenth century—e.g., the yoke-mounted swinging cylinder or the break-open auto-ejector—designers turned their efforts to perfecting a handgun that could load by harnessing the power in its cartridge.

Repeating and automatic pistols

Attempts to automate the revolver, which dated back to 1863 or earlier, were never fruitful. Although the auto-revolvers shot slightly faster, they were never as reliable as the simpler mechanically-actuated patterns. A new approach was clearly needed to avoid the rotational motion inherent in a cylinder-magazine.

Attempts to make effectual repeating pistols also failed. Though multi-barrel and magazine-fed prototypes were produced in quantity, very few achieved more than qualified success. The guns were often much too complicated to be reliable, and the effort required to load cartridges from the magazines was so great that accuracy suffered.

Auto-loading pistols operated by powder-gas energy were patented as early as 1872, by the European Plessner, and in 1873–4 by the American George Luce. Unfortunately, the fouling produced by gunpowder rapidly clogged actions that may have had a far greater effect on firearms history

87. Delvique. Chambers Lefaucheux pinfire cartridges.

88. Flobert 'Monte Cristo', chambered for 6mm or 9mm cartridges. The 6mm pattern—the more common—appeared in 1856. The spherical bullet is forced out of the barrel by the detonation of a charge of priming compound. Barrels may be of differing length, rifled or smooth-bore. The metal safety wedge turns upward to the left when the pistol is being opened. Guns of this general type were made from the 1850s until 1920.

89. A Monte Cristo pistol with a tipping barrel.

90. The National (later Colt) Derringer No. 1 in ·41 rimfire. The barrel drops around the longitudinal hinge above the trigger to facilitate reloading.

91. The ·22 rimfire Stevens Vest Pocket or Kick-Up pistol, patented in 1864. The barrel tips downward to load.

92. The Victor, made in the USA by Marlin in 1875–81. To reload, the barrel is turned laterally around the vertical axis.

93. A ·45 ACP Liberator. More than a million of these single-shot pistols were made in the USA during the Second World War to be air-dropped into Europe to arm the Resistance.

94. A Remington Double Repeating Deringer Pistol, ·41; patented by William Elliot in 1865, this double-barrelled design is still being copied in calibres ranging from ·22 to ·38.

95. High Standard: double barrel, double-action. USA, modern.

96. The Sharps four-shot cluster-barrel derringer was made in the USA from 1859 until 1874. A sequential firing pin on the hammer, turning through 90° with each cocking stroke, fires each of the chambers in turn.

97. Thomas Bland & Sons, ·455. An imitation of the Lancaster system, with a double-action trigger and striker system that fires each of the four chambers in succession.

98. Unique; a four-shot vest-pocket pistol patented in the USA in 1906, by Oscar Mossberg, and made by the Shattuck Arms Company.

99. A harmonica-pistol with a block of ten chambers which moved horizontally as the action was cocked. Patented in 1873 by Parisians A. & P. Jarre, this example shoots Lefaucheux pinfire cartridges.

100. The Remington four-shot 'Zig-Zag Derringer' was patented by William Elliot in 1860. The ring trigger rotated the barrel block.

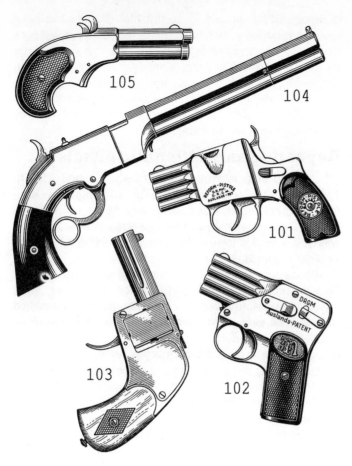

101. A four-shot Reform pistol by August Schüler of Suhl. The barrel-block moves vertically upward, ejecting all but the final spent case by residual gas pressure. The distinctively shaped hammer acts as a rudimentary deflector.
102. A four-shot Regnum, by August Menz of Suhl. This is similar to the Reform design pictured previously, but the barrel-block tips down and forward to load. The gun superficially resembles an auto-loading pistol.
103. The Bär-Pistole, designed by Burkhard Behr, patented in 1899 and made by J.P. Sauer & Sohn of Suhl in the early 1900s; double-barrel, double-action, four shots. After firing the two upper chambers, the flat cartridge block is rotated through 180° around its longitudinal axis to allow the lower pair to be fired.
104. The Volcanic repeating pistol was patented in the USA in 1854 by Horace Smith and Daniel Wesson. The tubular magazine beneath the barrel contains—in the example drawn—nine bullets containing their own charges and caps. The feed mechanism is actuated by a lever in the form of a trigger guard.
105. A Remington Magazine Repeating Pistol, with a five-cartridge tube underneath the barrel. Patented by Joseph Rider in 1871, it is operated by a modification of the popular Rolling Block.

had effectual smokeless powder been available in early 1870s. Real progress had to await the near-contemporaneous emergence of the Maxim machine-gun in Britain and an effectual smokeless propellant in France.

By the end of the nineteenth century, the first true auto-loaders had appeared. Revolvers had spread rapidly almost as soon as they had been perfected, but the progress of the auto-loading pistol was much more protracted. This was largely due to the peak of development reached by the revolvers of 1900, and to the undeniable fact that even the best of the pistols of this period was appreciably less reliable.

By the end of the nineteenth century, dozens of differing pistol systems had been designed. Many of the earliest had consciously followed the layout of revolvers, but this proved an impediment to efficiency as magazines were often placed where the cylinder would have been. The first pistol to contain a detachable magazine within the hand-grip, which would become the standard arrangement within a few years, was the Borchardt (patented in Germany in 1893). Though the Borchardt pistol was clumsy, being designed to double as a light carbine, it eliminated one of the last obstacles to the development of effectual pistols. The Borchardt was soon transformed into the elegant and effectual Borchardt-Luger, known from 1901 as the 'Parabellum', and—in 1897—the first of many pistol-related patents was granted to John Browning.

When the First World War began, great strides to perfect the auto-loading pistol had been made. The best designs had been adopted for military service, traditionally cautious of new ideas, whilst effectual pocket- and personal-defence patterns had been marketed in quantity. The emergence of inexpensive blowbacks was due largely to the persistence of John Browning, Fabrique Nationale d'Armes de Guerre in Belgium, and Colt in the USA. The 6·35mm (·25) 1906-type FN-Browning pistol inspired the production of countless imitations in Spain, and did much to overcome the prejudice of markets used to inexpensive small-calibre pin-, rim- and centre-fire revolvers.

Auto-loading pistols became steadily more compact as the years passed. Some of the earliest FN-Brownings, for example, had their return spring above the barrel whilst later patterns had the springs either concentric with the barrel or beneath it in the bottom of the frame. Changes such as these allowed magazine capacities to increase without altering the overall dimensions of the gun or, alternatively, a reduction in the size of the pistol could be made without affecting the number of shots that could be fired without reloading.

As pistol mechanisms improved, refinements were made in the trigger systems. Effectual double-action triggers were designed prior to the First World War by the Russian Korovin and the Bohemian Tomiška, the latter being embodied in the 'Little Tom' pistol—apparently readied for production in 1914, but not made in quantity until after the end of the First World War. Catches were developed to hold the reciprocating slide open after the last cartridge had been chambered, fired and ejected, indicating to the firer that the magazine was to be changed; indicators were added to show that a round was in the firing chamber. And great effort was expended in the search for simple but effectual safety systems, often to satisfy demands made by cavalrymen.

The modern handgun

Revolvers and pistols reached a high level of perfection many years ago. Consequently, many of today's guns—e.g., the Smith & Wesson Model 10 revolver—have their origins in the nineteenth century. Whether a handgun classifies as 'modern' is usually dependent on the current availability of appropriate ammunition; however, many modern cartridges were also designed prior to 1914, and so many handguns dating from the early years of this century also fall within this

106. Patented in 1887, the Passler & Seidl pistol relies on a ring-tipped operating lever to actuate the sliding bolt. The central magazine is loaded from the bottom with five single cartridges.

107. The Laumann repeater of 1891 was essentially similar to the Passler & Seidl, but locked differently.

108. The Bittner pistol of 1893 was basically a Passler & Seidl action feeding from a clip-loaded magazine.

109. The Gay et Guenot 'Guycot' repeater, patented in 1879, fired Volcanic-type ammunition contained in an endless chain of separate compartments, one of which was moved into position in the breech each time the double-action trigger was pressed.

110. The Francotte repeating pistol had a box-like magazine in the grip. It was loaded and cocked by pressing the spur under the trigger guard.

111. Tested by the German army in the early 1890s, the double-action Schlegelmilch was among the most effectual of the repeating pistols adapted for one-hand operation. As the hammer is drawn back to its farthest position, the bolt swings out to the left and the spent case is ejected. A special magazine follower presents another cartridge to the breech, then the bolt moves back to the right and locks in place.

112. The Protector was patented by Jacques Turbiaux in 1883. Cartridges are held in ten radial chambers in the disc magazine. Squeezing the trigger bar at the rear of the action rotates the disc and fires the gun.

113. An improved Protector, made in the USA in accordance with the Norris patent of 1901; it is similar to the previous model, but the trigger is a double-bar pattern at the front of the disc housing.

114. The Gaulois was a five-shot pistol which was fired simply by holding it tightly in the hand and squeezing inward on the grip.

classification. A typical example is the Parabellum (Luger) pistol, dating back to 1898–9; though production ceased in Germany at the end of the Second World War, and in Switzerland in 1947, work recommenced in Germany in the 1960s. Abandoned again in the 1980s, production has recently recommenced in the USA! Not only has 7·65mm and 9mm Parabellum ammunition been available through the entire period in which the Parabellum pistol has been made, but the 1908-type guns being made in 1994 by Mitchell Arms are virtual facsimiles of those being made for the German army at the beginning of the First World War. 'Modern', therefore, is an elastic term in firearms history.

Truly modern handguns are generally easier to handle, more advanced technologically, and easier to make than their predecessors. However, though these considerations are undeniably important, they have practically no effect on tactical parameters.

Pistols are still being improved in detail, though headway is slow and few truly novel designs are to be found. Many 'new' pistols are fundamentally no different from those produced decades ago, but are instead simply a more effectual combination of well-tried parts.

Much of the stagnation has arisen from the introduction of better and more effectual submachine-guns, leading to the role of the handgun being questioned in many military circles. However, many of the attempts to develop compact automatic weapons combining the power of a submachine-

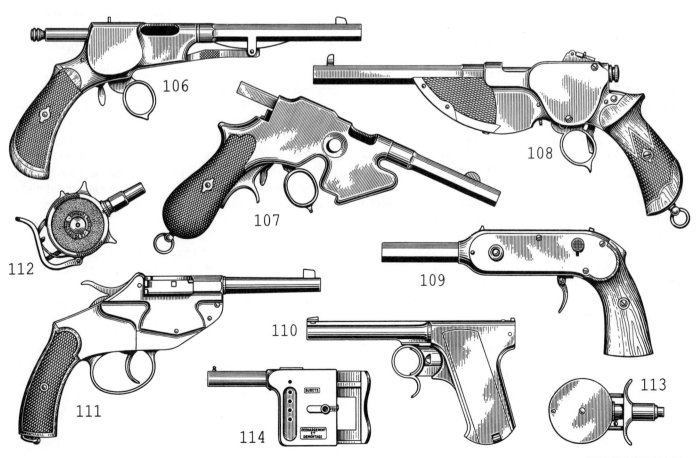

gun within the dimensions of a large pistol have failed; truly automatic fire in such a light weapon is virtually impossible to control unless the cartridge has little real power. The ease with which a conventional handgun can be carried, and efforts to extend its flexibility with ambidexterous controls and better trigger systems, ensures that the modern pistol will survive for many years to come.

Future developments

Can the handgun still be improved? The answer is certainly 'yes', but mechanical advances seem unlikely. Conversely, new materials and new propellants will inevitably promote development. Improvement in one area often effects changes in several others—e.g., if the propellant quality changes, so may cartridge design, calibre, magazine capacity and even the basic shape of the gun. Some specialists believe that the development of an effectual caseless cartridge holds the key to the next generation of handguns, but this would require radical changes in gun design.

As has been seen, a cylinder with chambers for individual cartridges is a characteristic feature of all revolvers. The cylinder revolves around its axis, presenting each chamber successively in line with the bore; but it turns mechanically, and the source of energy is the muscular power of the shooter. This power is conveyed to the cylinder not directly, but through the cocking mechanism. Most of the shooter's energy is used to compress the main spring whilst cocking the hammer, either by pressing the hammer-spur or retracting the trigger. This pressure actuates the cocking mechanism, which includes a means of turning the cylinder. When the cartridges are fired, the spent cases remain in the cylinder. Before reloading, therefore, it is necessary to remove the cases from the cylinder manually.

The design of an automatic pistol differs fundamentally from that of a revolver. A cartridge is fed automatically into the solitary chamber each time the slide or breechblock reciprocates, providing that cartridges remain in the magazine. The moving parts are thrust back automatically by the energy generated in the cartridge when the pistol is fired, then returned by energy stored in a spring which has been compressed during the opening stroke of the breech. The energy of powder gas can also be used to actuate locking devices.

All that the shooter has to do, therefore, is to take aim and press the trigger. Since unlocking, ejecting and reloading are accomplished automatically, shooting is very easy; the cycle is so rapid that the trigger can be pressed to fire another shot almost as soon as one has been fired. The spent case is ejected from the pistol after each shot. Once the last shot has been fired, the pistol can be reloaded much more rapidly than a revolver.

Although revolvers and pistols differ greatly in their construction, they share many common features befitting a handgun. These include the ballistic qualities necessary to strike effectively at short distances; acceptable short-range accuracy; the features necessary to carry a loaded weapon in perfect safety; good handling characteristics; and the ability to fire sufficiently rapidly when necessary.

However, revolvers and pistols also have their own specific features, often inherent in the differing operation of their mechanisms. These can influence the effort applied by the shooter, which is generally greater in a revolver than an auto-loading pistol; the ease of reloading; and the effects of fouling or cartridge design on the operation of the mechanism (on which the reliability of the entire weapon depends).

Handgun performance

Alone amongst the commonalities listed previously, ballistic qualities are independent of structural features. The muzzle velocity of handgun bullets is not great in comparison with other types of firearms, but their trajectory is flat enough for the effects of projectile-drop to be ignored at short range.

The striking power of bullets fired from pistols or revolvers differs greatly from those fired from rifles, in which flight-time, distance travelled and residual kinetic energy are vitally important parameters. Energy figures derive from the velocity and the mass of the bullet, but present an arbitrary result that is not an infallible indicator of performance. Assessments of 'stopping power', conversely, rely more on the sectional density of the bullet—i.e., the ratio of mass to cross-sectional area.

At short range, the velocity of a rifle bullet is high, and its pointed tip encourages a shock wave to move outward when a target is struck. A vessel containing liquid will burst when struck at short range, as the kinetic energy of the bullet is sufficient to rupture the container walls by displacing the liquid outward.

At long range, however, the velocity of the rifle bullet diminishes until the outward-moving component of the shock wave is either greatly weakened or lost altogether. Sufficient striking energy remains in the projectile to incapacitate, even at extreme distances, owing to the comparatively large mass of the bullet and its high sectional density. The effect on an animate target at long range is comparatively unimportant; as the primary goal is simply to hit, it is not essential to disable an enemy immediately.

Expectations of a handgun are quite different. Under normal conditions, it is vital to disable a target instantly to ensure that—for example—an armed opponent cannot continue to pose a threat, even if the hit is not immediately life-threatening.

The muzzle velocities of most handgun-cartridge bullets, owing to constraints of size and recoil, are generally low. Consequently, the use of large calibres has proved to be the simplest and most effectual means of achieving adequate stopping power. Such bullets are capable of transmitting the greatest possible kinetic energy to the target whilst penetrating minimally.

A small-calibre bullet with a kinetic energy of 500 joules (about 50 kgm) can easily pierce bodily tissue without harming vital organs. Expending, say, 50 joules during its passage, the bullet emerges to continue its flight with its kinetic energy diminished only minimally. Conversely, if the same tissue is struck by a large-diameter bullet offering greater stopping power but lesser theoretical striking energy, the bullet may be brought to a halt and give up all its 200 joules. This imparts a stunning, often immediately paralysing blow—an important quality in short-range weapons.

Sectional density is generally reduced by increases in calibre, to ensure that the cartridges do not become too powerful to be fired in a hand-held gun. Ballistic qualities are also impaired when the sectional density decreases, though the effects are not usually detectable at the short ranges accessible to handguns. The calibres of military rifles rarely exceed 8mm (·315), yet those of handguns are usually far greater. The most common calibres are 9mm and ·38, though the lethality of bullets in these groups—particularly military-style jacketed patterns—is still widely questioned. Many authorities advocate bullet diameters as large as 11·4mm (·45), which, assuming an adequate velocity is maintained, can have a beneficial effect on stopping power.

Calibre is determined largely by optimal handgun size, particularly in relation to the role for which the gun has been designed. If too large a bullet is selected, it may be necessary to enlarge the gun or reduce the number of cartridges it can hold. Conversely, if the gun needs to be small and light (e.g., to aid concealment), or must have a large-capacity magazine, only a comparatively small-diameter bullet can be adopted. Selection of calibre requires careful balancing of stopping-power potential with cartridge size.

Calibres smaller than 9mm are rarely encountered in military handguns, though some have been adopted primarily out of financial considerations. Selecting a single calibre cuts production costs by allowing rifling machinery to produce barrels for a wide range of weapons. An extreme view was taken in the Soviet Union, where 7·62mm-calibre weapons were standardised in the 1930s. During the Second World War, therefore, two submachine-gun or four handgun barrels could often be cannibalised from a single defective rifle pattern.

In the first half of the nineteenth century, the calibres of European military rifles and pistols—then still single-shot—were often the same. The introduction of machine-made rifle-muskets in the 1850s was accompanied by a notable reduction in calibre, which the pistols of the time eventually followed. By the early 1870s, and the universal issue of single-shot breech-loading rifles, calibres of 10–12mm were standardised.

The introduction of smokeless propellant caused another wholesale reduction in calibre to 6–8mm. The changes in the rifles were mirrored in most of the contemporaneous service revolvers and the first auto-loading pistols. However, heed had not been taken of the differing power of long arms and handguns, and some armies—most notably those of colonial powers required to fight against native tribesmen—quickly replaced small-calibre revolvers with weapons of much larger calibre.

The armies of countries which were more peaceable, or less wealthy, often retained the small-calibre guns and simply increased the propellant charge. Unfortunately, the desired results could not be attained: the initial velocities of bullets could not be raised far enough to compensate for the reduction in cross-sectional area. Though the kinetic energy of these small high-velocity bullets was high, allowing them to retain a surprising amount of energy to several hundred metres, the guns were not adapted to shoot accurately at such distances. Moreover, powerful charges gave a robust recoil which actually reduced accuracy still further.

The calibre of handguns intended for police or civil use was often governed by a need to make the weapons as compact as practicable, on the premise that stopping power was not as important as in a military pistol. For many years, ·32 (7·65mm) cartridges were deemed acceptable in self-defence roles—though the ineffectual ·25 (6·35mm) was also popular. That smaller bullets fired at comparatively low velocity inevitably reduced both effective range and tissue-damaging ability passed unacknowledged for many years.

The recent trend is towards personal-defence guns of larger calibre—e.g., ·357 or ·44. Handguns chambering cartridges of 6·35mm-calibre or smaller can hardly be regarded as effectual. It is little wonder that the most inferior small-calibre revolvers and pistols have been known as 'Suicide Specials', presenting a greater threat to the firer than the intended target.

Attempts have been made to make handguns in calibres as small as 2·7mm (e.g., the Kolibri) or 4·25mm (Menz Liliput), producing so-called lady's or vest-pocket models. None of these are of any real value.

If the commercial trend is towards increased calibres, then recent military opinion has often supported a reduction. The assumption is that the potential inadequacy of small calibres can be compensated by semi-jacketed expansive bullets, which deform when they hit the target to enhance stopping power. Alternatively, an increase in velocity and a projectile designed on the limits of stability can suffice, by causing the bullet to tumble as it penetrates an obstacle.

Cartridge design

In the search for a more effectual bullet, preference was initially given to enhancement of muzzle velocity. This generally increased penetrative ability, which was most important militarily when protective clothing began to be used. Raising the velocity of small-calibre bullets required a more powerful propellant charge, which in turn necessitated enlarging the cartridge. Slender narrow cases predictably proved to be weak, so the case-diameter was increased instead. This required a reduced-diameter neck to accept the bullet, creating a style of cartridge that is now universal in military small arms.

The classical cast-lead projectiles were unable to cope with the friction generated in the bore at high velocities, and were replaced by bullets with hard metal jackets—usually nickel—over a core made from lead and antimony.

By 1900, powerful 5·5mm centre-fire cartridges with elongated cylindrical cases and jacketed bullets were being used in extremely short-barrelled Velo-Dog revolvers, which lacked accuracy and had a miserable effective range; consequently, cartridges and revolvers of this type gradually fell into oblivion. Similar cartridges such as the ·22 Winchester Magnum Rimfire are currently employed in revolvers intended for target shooting or self-defence, depending on the size of the barrel. The ammunition is still an ineffectual man-stopper.

Powerful necked small-calibre cartridges, now confined largely to handguns intended for target shooting, will probably be improved and may gain greater acceptance in commercial, police and military models. However, only the Soviet PSM currently chambers ammunition of this pattern.

Strengths and weaknesses

The modern revolver is simple, reliable and almost always works properly when it is fired. It is unusual that a revolver will misfire more than once in a thousand shots, and its mechanically-actuated design is such that the next cartridge can be fired simply by pulling the trigger again. The chance of a second misfire is extremely remote. Consequently, the delay in firing is rarely serious. Another advantage of the revolver is that, being mechanical, it is not especially dangerous in inexperienced hands: the state of cocking, or the presence of cartridges in the chambers, can be seen at a glance.

Double-action revolvers with an enclosed hammer cannot fire when the trigger is pulled accidentally, e.g. in a pocket, because of the effort that must be exerted to operate the double-action mechanism. Such a revolver can be fired only by holding the grip and deliberately squeezing the trigger with the finger.

The revolver is always ready for use, which is one of its most important features. No preliminary operations are required before firing a double-action revolver, and the speed with which the first shot can be fired meets one of the most important requirements of a self-defence weapon.

An important advantage is that a revolver, depending on purely mechanical means to operate its action, can fire cartridges of differing type or power indiscriminately. It is even possible to use cartridges containing gunpowder, which is far less susceptible to decomposition than smokeless propellant. Gunpowder fouling is far less likely to jam a revolver than an auto-loader.

Disadvantages include the limited capacity of the cylinder in comparison with the detachable box magazines of many modern auto-loaders; a slower rate of fire arising from the muscular pressure necessary to cycle the action; a protruding cylinder; a grip that extends backward from the frame; and, most importantly, the lengthy time required to reload. The last disadvantage pertains to revolvers in general, but particularly those in which the spent cases can only be extracted successively through a hinged gate on the frame. As it is almost impossible to reload weapons of this type in the heat

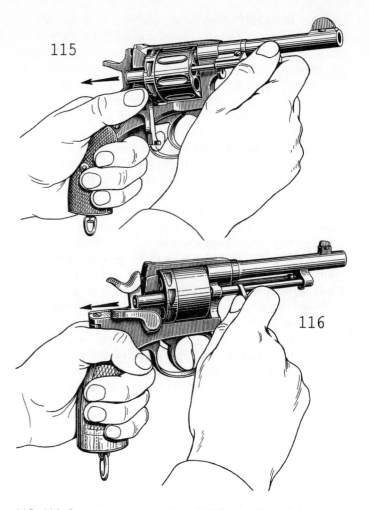

115, 116. Successive case extraction—115 (Russian Nagant), by a yoke-mounted ejector which is rotated into position in front of a chamber; 116 (Austro-Hungarian Rast & Gasser), by an offset ejector which is always in position. Fig. 116 shows an open Abadie-type gate.

of combat, so they offer little real advance on the old cap-lock patterns.

Efforts to enhance the firing capacity of revolvers have been made, either by increasing the number of chambers or by changing the design to give access to all the chambers simultaneously. Aberrant designs containing as many as thirty cartridges were made in the nineteenth century, but the guns became so cumbersome that they ceased to be useful; even a ten-chambered cylinder was too bulky. A better solution lay in forward-moving cylinders, hinged frames and swing-out cylinders, which allowed cases to be extracted simultaneously. In addition to ejecting effectually, some of these guns could accommodate effectual speed-loading systems. But even the best of them is inferior to a box-magazine pistol if reloading time is the principal yardstick.

Auto-loading pistols hold several important advantages. They are generally more powerful than revolvers of the same weight, fire more rapidly, carry more cartridges and require less effort on the part of the firer. Most importantly, they can be reloaded much more quickly, as an empty magazine can be simply be replaced with a full one. Therefore, attempts to increase cartridge capacity are far less important in pistol design than in a revolver. This is partly because pistol actions are generally arranged so that a larger number of cartridges can be carried in the magazine than in a revolver cylinder, but there is no real need to increase the capacity of magazines if they can be replaced so rapidly. Unusually capacious magazines only make the pistol heavier and bulkier, whilst the ability to replace the magazine simply gives a cartridge capacity limited only by the supply of magazines. If two magazines with eight cartridges apiece are being carried, the pistol can be regarded as a sixteen-shot firearm; if there are three such magazines, then it is a 24-shot pattern.

The practical fire-rate—the speed with which a gun can be fired over a protracted period—is undoubtedly greater for pistols than even the most advanced revolver. Pistols, therefore, are widely favoured for military service.

Cartridges loaded with smokeless propellant are obligatory in auto-loaders, owing partly to the lack of the

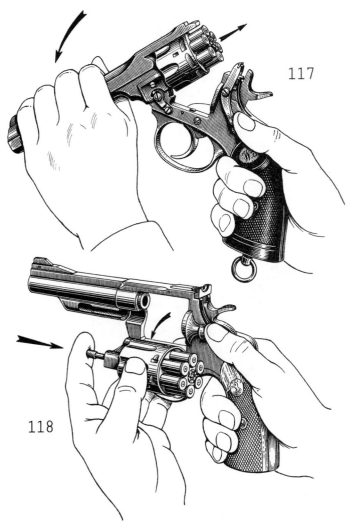

117

118

117, 118. Simultaneous case extraction—117 (Webley), where the barrel and cylinder unit is tipped downward at the muzzle; 118 (Colt), when the cylinder is swung out on a yoke.

fouling that would otherwise clog the mechanism but also to the greater velocity that can be generated compared with black powder. Owing to the lack of tell-tale smoke on firing, cartridges of this type are ideally suited to military use, as they neither hinder aim nor attract the attention of the enemy unduly.

The disadvantages of automatic pistols include somewhat inferior reliability, as their mechanism is largely dependent on the quality of the ammunition. Shooting is inhibited in cases of misfire—e.g. when the pistol mechanism fails owing to too little recoil—and, though problems of this type are often cleared by retracting the slide, there will be occasions when the problems arise from a distorted cartridge; a mis-feed from the magazine; fouling in the mechanism; excessively thick lubricant; or inferior ammunition.

Some jams can be so complicated that considerable time may be needed to clear them, a worrying factor in combat. However, when an auto-loading pistol works effectually, jams are so infrequent that they can be disregarded in favour of the many advantages mentioned previously.

The best examples of the current generation of auto-loaders are almost as reliable as revolvers. Modern pistols generally embody constructional features that outweigh the perceived advantages of revolvers. Previously, the champions of the latter opined that pistols were dangerous in inexperienced hands, simply because the state of loading was impossible to determine externally. Some modern pistols have loaded chamber indicators in addition to hammers or similar devices from which the state of cocking can be seen (or felt) at a glance. Typical are the extractor of the perfected Parabellums, which doubled as a loaded-chamber indicator, or the signal pin above the hammers of Walther PP/PPK series.

Promoters of revolvers have often maintained that pistols could not be used with one hand alone, and that the hand holding the firearm could not also load a cartridge into the chamber. It was certainly safer for the inexperienced to carry a pistol with an empty chamber, but the gun then lost one of the most important features of handgun: the ability to fire immediately when required. To load a pistol in this condition, the slide had to be retracted—and this could be done only with the other hand. But the proponents of revolvers were correct in their claims only when, for safety reasons, the pistol had no cartridge in its chamber; otherwise, it is easier to use a loaded pistol with one hand than a revolver.

The use of the firing hand to retract the slide was not considered in the design of most auto-loaders, though there have been exceptions to this general rule. One-hand cocking systems were not as convenient to use as their promoters were apt to claim, particularly if the return spring was strong. Consequently, they have been largely confined to small-calibre personal defence pistols such as the Chylewski or the Lignose Einhand.

Most modern automatic pistols have reliable safeties, making them safe to carry when loaded. This is particularly true of the current double-action-only designs with hammer-blocking safety units.

A pistol should always be loaded if it is required for immediate use (in some systems with integral charger-loaded magazines, a cartridge is even put into the chamber when the magazine is being filled). In these cases, it is enough to move the finger of the hand holding the pistol to unlock the safety and cock the hammer, allowing fire to be opened as soon as necessary. Some guns have grip safeties that unlock the mechanism once the grip is held in the firing hand.

Double-action mechanisms have proved to be the best way of reducing the time required for the first shot, which can be fired in same manner as a double-action revolver—i.e., without cocking the hammer manually. As pistols improved, therefore, they have acquired some of the best features of the revolvers.

Pocket pistols have considerable advantages over pocket revolvers, as they are more compact, flat, and have virtually no protrusions. In addition, they are generally more powerful than revolvers of comparable dimensions and hold a greater number of cartridges. Many auto-loading pocket or so-called waistcoat-pocket ('vest pocket') pistols have been marketed successfully since the early years of the twentieth century. Revolvers which were similarly small and light proved to be greatly inferior and were abandoned soon after the end of the First World War.

In sum, therefore, in many respects, the best of today's pistols are better weapons than the best of the revolvers. The latter, however, still retain favourable features which remain characteristic of them alone. In addition to many individuals, some countries continue to provide revolvers not only for police forces but also the army. The USA, Germany, France, Italy, Spain, Japan and elsewhere are still all committed to revolver production.

119–123. Loading aids for revolvers—119, metallic 'Half Moon' clips for rimless cartridges; 120, a rubber truncated cone which releases the cartridges inserted into the chamber when its top is pressed; 121, a charger which releases cartridges when the head is turned; 122, a band which releases the cartridges once their heads are in the chambers; and 123, a flat elastic clip to insert cartridges into chambers in pairs when the strip is bent sharply backward.

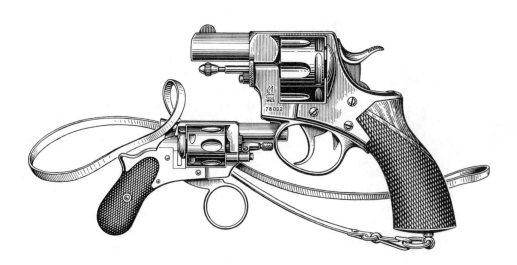

Revolver construction

Revolvers differ from one another mainly in the methods of extracting fired cases; consequently, there is also variety in the construction of their frames. They are divided here into several groups (figs. 124–131) on the basis of the way in which extraction is performed.

Successive extraction

These guns generally have a solid fixture closing the cylinder from the rear, preventing the chambered rounds sliding backward. The simplest guns are reloaded by removing the cylinder, punching spent cases out of the chambers and then inserting fresh rounds before replacing the cylinder in the frame. However, this was not especially effectual. A better solution was provided by a special gate, usually on the rear right side of the frame. This could usually be pivoted to give access to an individual chamber. The spent case was expelled by a reciprocating ejector rod, a new round was inserted, and the cylinder turned to bring the next chamber into line. This process continued until all the chambers were filled with cartridges, whereupon the loading gate could be closed.

The cartridge-ejector was usually fixed on the side of the barrel—from where it simply slid backward—or could be attached to the barrel lug, where it was held by a spring catch and had to be swung laterally outward until it aligned with the chamber. This was achieved by a crane or yoke. And though the yokes were often light and compact, they were a manufacturing complication and required an additional movement before extraction could begin. A shortcoming in some designs (especially the earliest ones) was the exposed and easily damaged extractor. In some systems, therefore, the extractor was sheathed or kept in a hollow stem of the cylinder-axis pin.

Many of the revolvers made in Europe prior to 1914 featured the so-called Abadie Gate, which was perfected in Belgium and was particularly common on guns made by Nagant. The hammer disengaged when the gate was opened, allowing the cylinder to be turned by the trigger. Alternately pressing the trigger and the extractor-head caused the cylinder to revolve and fired cases to be ejected, greatly facilitating reloading.

Some systems lacked extractors, relying on any convenient rod to force cases out of the chambers. This was occasionally undertaken without removing the cylinder from the frame, but the detachable method was much more popular. A detachable ejector could be carried (fig. 124) or, alternatvely, a fixed spigot was provided (fig. 125).

Simultaneous extraction

This proved to be an excellent way of accelerating the reloading process. The first Smith & Wesson cartridge revolvers, produced during the American Civil War (1861–5), had a barrel that could be pivoted upward to release the cylinder. By the end of the 1860s, the company had refined the system so that the cylinder was attached to the barrel unit (e.g., figs. 788, 793). When the breech was unlatched, the barrel/cylinder unit could be pressed downward, pivoting around a transverse bolt on the lower front of the frame. As the action opened, a cam forced the extractor (which slid inside the hollow cylinder-axis pin) to project from the face of the cylinder and expel the spent cases. The extractor then sprang back into the cylinder to allow fresh cartridges to be inserted in the chambers.

The Smith & Wesson was the best system of its day, largely because cases were extracted automatically as soons as the revolver was opened. This greatly assisted loading. However, owing to wear, the hinge eventually wore excessively and the action became loose.

In the late 1880s, Colt developed an effectual system in which the cylinder and extractor unit could be swung laterally out of the solid frame. Cases were easily and quickly extracted by pressing the head of the rod passing through the cylinder axis, which was linked with the

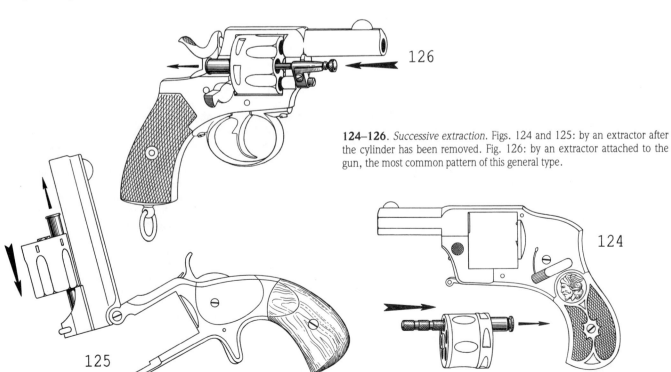

124–126. *Successive extraction.* Figs. 124 and 125: by an extractor after the cylinder has been removed. Fig. 126: by an extractor attached to the gun, the most common pattern of this general type.

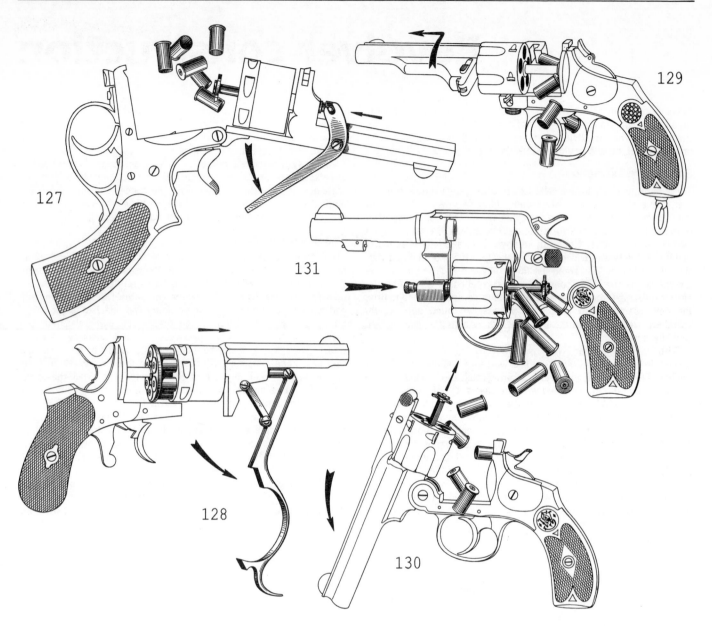

127–131. *Simultaneous extraction.* Fig. 127: when the barrel is tipped upward and a lever acts on the extractor. Fig. 128: when the barrel and cylinder are cammed forward. Fig. 129: when the barrel and cylinder move forward after rotating around the cylinder axis. Fig. 130: when the barrel tips downward. Fig 131: by pressing the extractor head after the cylinder has been swung laterally outward.

rims of the cartridges by a star-shaped extractor. The extractor was returned to its rest position by a spring.

By the end of the nineteenth century, Colt and Smith & Wesson had proved the potential of the swinging-cylinder system, which widespread copying in Belgium and Spain rapidly confirmed. As handgun cartridges became increasingly powerful, these effectual solid-frame guns entirely eclipsed weaker hinged-frame types. The British Webley remained in production into the 1970s, but was never offered in Magnum chamberings.

Revolvers with swinging cylinders are slower to reload than the best of the hinged-frame patterns, largely because extraction requires an additional manual operation. Nevertheless, the advantages of a solid frame—principally lightness and durability—more than offset the loss of a few extra seconds whilst reloading.

Accelerated reloading generally requires a reduction in the operations needed to fill the cylinder with cartridges. The US M1917 service revolvers, made by Colt and Smith & Wesson during the First World War, chambered rimless pistol cartridges with the help of a special three-round clip (fig. 119). Though the clips were developed specifically to allow standard cartridges to be used, it was soon obvious that they also facilitated reloading. In the 1920s, therefore, the first of the quick-loaders appeared. The Mollo pattern (fig. 122), for instance, was an elastic band wrapped around the cartridges in such a way that they were held in alignment with the cylinder chambers.

The noses of the cartridges were simply positioned behind the cylinder and inserted in the chamber-mouths; the clasp was released, the elastic band was removed, and the cartridges were pushed fully home. With practice, this could be completed in a simple movement.

The most common quick-loaders are currently rubber cylinders or cones (figs. 120, 121). The cartridges are inserted simultaneously into the chambers, once the revolver cylinder has been swung outward, then released simply by pressing the end of the quick-loader body. Simpler systems hold cartridges in a row (fig. 123), allowing them to be pressed into the chambers one by one; a modification allows two chambers to be loaded simultaneously.

Trigger systems

Depending on the design of the cocking mechanism, revolvers are classed as 'single action', 'double action' or 'double-action only'.

A shot can be fired from a single-action revolver only after cocking the hammer manually, which must be done for each shot. Cocking the hammer turns the cylinder automatically to align a chamber with the barrel. The hammer drops when the trigger is pressed, causing a shot to be fired.

The single-action trigger, exemplified by the earliest Colts, is simple and very sturdy. However, it is comparatively awkward to use and cannot be operated quickly. The need for rapid fire promoted the double-action trigger that, in addition to thumb-cocking, can also fire simply by a single pull on the trigger. This retracts the hammer and turns the cylinder until the next chamber is aligned with the barrel. Once it reaches the backward limit of its travel, however, the hammer is not held on the sear; instead, it flies forward to hit the primer of the chambered cartridge. To fire another shot, the trigger must be released to return to its initial position before the cycle can begin again.

Double-action fire is faster but less accurate than single action, owing to the greater effort needed to operate the trigger. This pressure has also to rotate the cylinder and compress the main spring. However, a double-action revolver allows the firer to select either accuracy—when the hammer is thumb-cocked for each shot—or rapidity, by simply pressing through on the trigger.

The 'double-action-only' systems, which have become increasingly popular in recent years, cannot be thumb cocked. As they can be fired only by a pull on the trigger, many feature enclosed hammers.

The term 'triple action' is sometimes encountered in old literature. It is usually applied to otherwise conventional double-action revolvers with a rebounding hammer (see below). In a few cases, however, triple-action revolvers were simply what would now be termed double-action designs. In accordance with this classification, 'single action' applied to manually-cocked guns whilst 'double action' applied to a mechanism which required two operations to fire—e.g., preliminary cocking of the hammer and then a subsequent pull of the trigger. Developed in the 1850s for cap-lock revolvers, notably by the Englishman William Tranter, this was achieved either with two successive pulls on a single trigger lever (see fig. 754) or by using two levers (fig. 379).

Half-cocking hammers were popular on single-action revolvers. The hammer could be retracted far enough to prevent the firing pin reaching the primer, usually also allowing the cylinder to turn freely to assist loading. As the hammer could not be released by the trigger from the half-cock position, this feature is sometimes called 'safety cocking'.

Several double-action revolvers also had this system, a characteristic feature often being a long leaf spring on the right side of the frame between the cylinder and the trigger (e.g., figs. 232, 234).

Virtually all modern revolvers are fitted with rebounding hammers, though the concept dates back to the nineteenth century. In essence, the hammer bounces back after firing, allowing the cylinder to turn freely whilst the gun is being loaded. The partially retracted hammer does not press directly on the primer of a chambered round or, alternatively, on the head of the firing pin. And though this was not a foolproof guarantee of safety in older revolvers, most modern guns have additional 'transfer bars' or safety blocks to prevent the hammer reaching the firing position unless the trigger is being pulled back

Gas-seal patterns

A small portion of the propellant gas inevitably escapes through the gap between the revolver cylinder and the barrel as each shot is fired. However, this is not a serious shortcoming as the ballistic performance and handling characteristics are not seriously affected. Most manufacturers simply minimise the gap between the front face of the cylinder and the rear of the barrel.

Attempts have been made to entirely eliminate the gas-escape problem. In the Nagant and Pieper systems, for instance, complete obturation was attained by means of a elongated cartridge case with a neck protruding 1·5–2mm from the front face of the cylinder. As the hammer is cocked, a camming lever not only turns the cylinder, but also moves it slightly forward until the neck of the case enters the bore. When a shot is fired, the case expands outward to close the gap between the barrel and the cylinder, pressing tightly against the bore wall to prevent escape of gas.

Complete obturation may also be achieved by moving an individual cartridge forward instead of the entire cylinder. Remaining cartridges are prevented from moving by special plates abutting the cylinder face.

Constructional features

The internal design of the many revolver systems is often most distinctive. Externally, individual parts can be even more diverse. Frames differ greatly—some guns have solid straps above the cylinder, others are simply left open—whilst grips may be wood, plastic, rubber, metal, horn or ivory. Sights may be fixed or adjustable. The surface of the cylinders, notably between the chambers, may be plain, fluted, ribbed or recessed.

Some guns may incorporate separate safety catches to minimise the chance of firing accidentally, though these are less common on revolvers than automatic pistols. As the cocking systems of revolvers are generally safe enough, additional safety catches often merely hinder efficient shooting.

Many revolvers, especially the smallest pocket models, may lack a trigger guard. The trigger may then be protected by a sheath (e.g., fig. 206) or, alternatively, can fold either into or against the frame (figs. 146, 154). A folding trigger is often regarded as a safety feature in itself, as it cannot be accidentally pulled. However, the trigger can easily be snagged in the lining of a pocket and may present considerable danger to the firer.

Folding-trigger guns are particularly compact, but extra time may be lost unfolding the trigger for firing . . . even though some levers spring open when the hammer is thumbed back.

The barrel may be cylindrical, tapered, faceted, or virtually any combination of shapes. Many guns—especially those with adjustable sights—have ribs along the top surface of the barrel, partly to increase rigidity but also to provide a base for accessories. The top surfaces of the ribs are often chequered or roughened to prevent reflected light interfering with the sight-picture; some are even ventilated, to save weight but also to dissipate barrel heat.

Revolver directory

Pinfire patterns

The earliest successful pinfire handguns—made in France about 1850—were pepperboxes made by the Parisian gunsmith Casimir Lefaucheux, to whom the invention of their self-contained cartridge (c.1836) is generally credited. His son Eugène made the first revolvers in 1854, allegedly for the French army, by copying the construction of the Mariette cap-lock which was in its turn inspired by the contemporaneous Colts. The Lefaucheux revolver was subsequently adopted in October 1857 by the French Navy, improved by a double-action firing mechanism patented by Chaineux in 1853. Pinfire revolvers are generically known as 'Lefaucheux', acknowledging the parentage of their cartridge (but see also remarks made in the Introduction).

Soon after the introduction of the earliest pinfire revolvers, Lefaucheux advertised improved double-action models; the standing breech was constructed differently, and the pocket models acquired folding triggers. The archetypal Lefaucheux pinfire revolver was finally established; the shape of the grip, hammer and many other parts had characteristic shapes, making the guns not only distinctive but also easily recognisable.

Lefaucheux revolvers were copied in many countries, most notably in Austria-Hungary, Belgium, Germany and Spain. They were produced in such great numbers in Liége that many people still mistakenly believe that the origins of the Lefaucheux system lie in Belgium.

The advent, development and rapid distribution of the centre-fire revolver had no immediate impact on the European-made pinfire—even though the latter was much less effectual. This was partly due to the fact that the pinfire cartridges were cheaper and more easily made than their centre-fire equivalents. Manufacture of pinfire revolvers continued in many countries, and improvements were still being made. Inspired by centre-fire patterns, these changes included a sturdier standing breech incorporated with a solid frame; loading gates of better design; and fluted cylinders. Some guns could even utilise pin- or centre-fire cartridges at will.

Even the newest pinfire revolvers were still popularly called 'Lefaucheux', though the considerable structural changes deviated so greatly from the classical pattern. Indeed, the Lefaucheux system was so popular that many new centre-fire revolvers acquired many of its features. An interesting situation was thus created: pinfire revolvers acquired features of centre-fire patterns, whilst the centre-fire examples sometimes assumed the mantle of a pinfire. The construction of the centre-fire Gasser revolvers was typically Lefaucheux, therefore, whereas many British-made pinfires resembled Webley centre-fire designs.

Rim- or centre-fire revolvers incorporating the basic Lefaucheux characteristics are discussed in a later section. Guns chambering pinfire cartridges—classical Lefaucheux and improved patterns alike—are listed here.

By the 1860s and 1870s, a particular type of double-action Lefaucheux revolver was developed (e.g., figs. 138, 139, 143–5 or 149). Its characteristics included an octahedral barrel or, alternatively, a cylindrical barrel with only the breech portion faceted. The barrel lug was screwed onto the cylinder axis pin, which was rigidly fixed in the standing breech. The extractor rod generally ran through the barrel lug, offset to the right so that spent cases could be punched out through the loading gate, and was usually retained by a spring catch. The lower end of the barrel lug was attached to the frame with a screw. The cylinder surface was smooth, excepting for the cylinder-pawl notches

which kept it in position after every turn. The spring-catch gate opened upward. The grip projected behind the hammer and flared at the base. An elevated front sight, frequently topped by a bead, was screwed into the barrel; alternatively, the sight was crimped into a lateral groove in the form of a swallow-tail. The back sight, if fitted, was either a small V-block or a slot in the hammer.

The 12mm Belgian revolvers shown here are typical of the large-calibre patterns. The classical small-calibre Lefaucheux had all the features described previously, but also featured folding triggers without a trigger guard. Typical of these are figs. 159 and 160. Revolvers of the Lefaucheux system produced by individual companies often deviated from the standard patterns. The grips could take a particular shape—e.g., fig. 140, 141, 162 or 169—whilst loading gates often rotated down instead of upward (figs. 147 and 150). The cylinder could have an annular shield to protect the vulnerable cartridge pins from an external blow (fig. 134 or 155). Ejector rods were usually contained in the grip or, more rarely, carried under the barrel; they were detached from the revolver when it was necessary to push out the cases from the cylinder chambers (e.g., figs. 153 and 158). Cylinder flutes were often noteworthy (cf., fig. 167, 175 or 177), but other distinguishing features were rare. However, some revolvers had hammer-blocking safety levers, and others had sliding-bar safety catches on the standing breech near the hammer (e.g., fig. 192). Belgian Arendt revolvers had a remarkable grip shape (fig. 153); Francotte revolvers had standing breeches fabricated of several parts, characteristic grips and hammers with a cocking safety (fig. 155); Renault revolvers had swing-down loading gates with knobs and flat springs (fig. 150).

Unfortunately, few of these features now provide a foolproof identifier, as they were soon copied elsewhere. Moreover, although some guns incorporated distinctive parts of their own, most shared a commonplace design that had evolved surprisingly quickly.

Guns that were adapted to handle pin- and centre-fire cartridges interchangeably generally had a special hammer with a flat striker—characteristic of pinfires—and a dart-like projection to crush a centre-fire primer (e.g., fig. 210).

The barrels of some pinfire revolvers made towards the end of their period in vogue—e.g., Figs. 187 or 189—had an extension of the barrel reaching back to upper rear part of the standing breech, where it was held by screws to provide a closed frame. Guns embodying this construction are undoubtedly sturdier than open-frame equivalents. The solid-frame designs, however, were the strongest of all.

Pinfire pocket revolvers include barrelless models inspired by the earliest cap-lock pepperboxes. Made by an assortment of gunmakers, these were easier to make than conventional revolvers, allowing each chamber of an elongated cylinder block to double as a barrel.

Manufacturers of Lefaucheux revolvers were often reluctant to mark their wares, hindering identification and accurate dating of pinfires. Consequently, the numerous double-action six-shot revolvers are grouped here according to calibre.

132. Casimir Lefaucheux, Paris. Exhibited at the Great Exhibition, London, in 1851, this pepperbox chambers cartridges with a paper case.

133. Eugène Lefaucheux, Paris. 12·7mm. A commercial version of the Mle. 1858 N French navy revolver of 1862. Its distinguishing features include a single-action trigger system, an extended barrel which reaches backward beneath the cylinder, and a characteristic grip lacking the projection behind the hammer to support the hand.

134, 135. Lefaucheux type; Fabrique d'Armes Lepage, Liége.

136, 137. Lefaucheux type; maker unknown, Belgium. These single-action guns, dating later than those in figs. 134 and 135, differ principally in the use of a screw on the lower front surface of the barrel-lug to attach the lug to the frame.

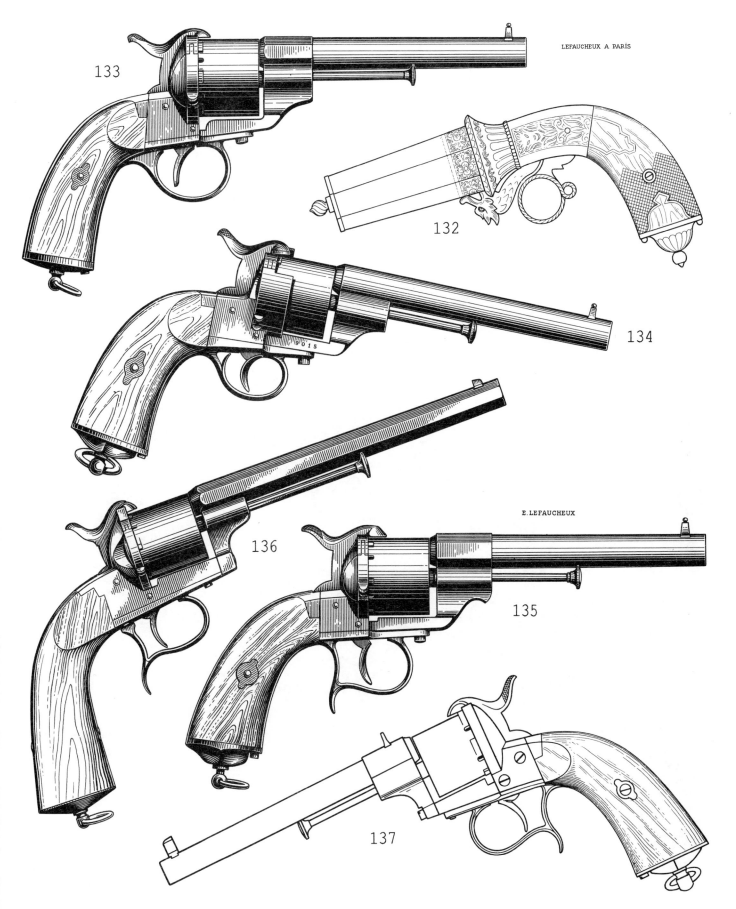

133

LEFAUCHEUX A PARIS

132

134

E. LEFAUCHEUX

136

135

137

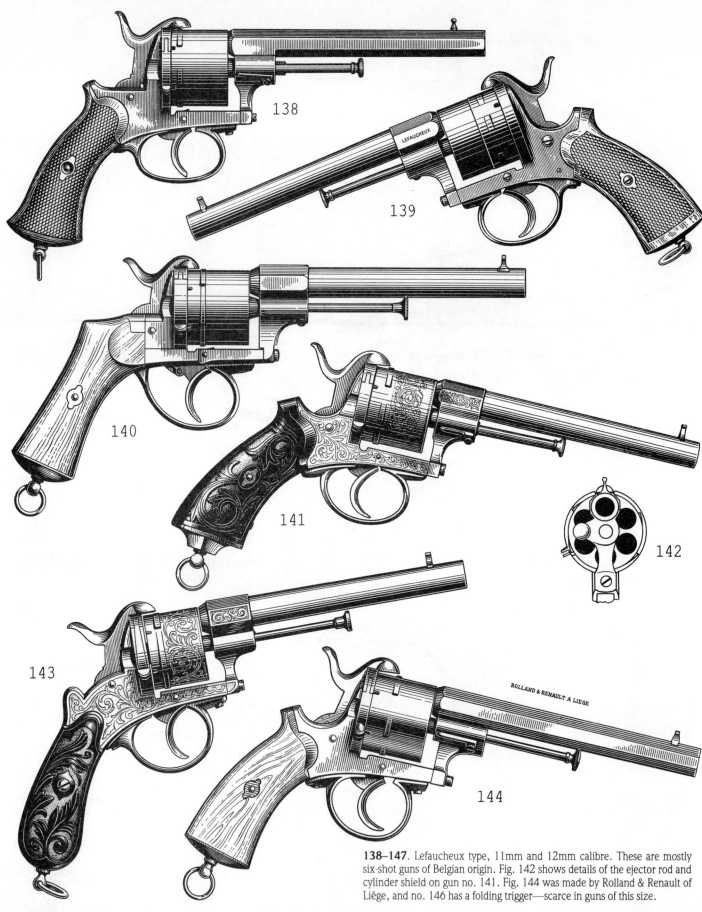

138–147. Lefaucheux type, 11mm and 12mm calibre. These are mostly six-shot guns of Belgian origin. Fig. 142 shows details of the ejector rod and cylinder shield on gun no. 141. Fig. 144 was made by Rolland & Renault of Liége, and no. 146 has a folding trigger—scarce in guns of this size.

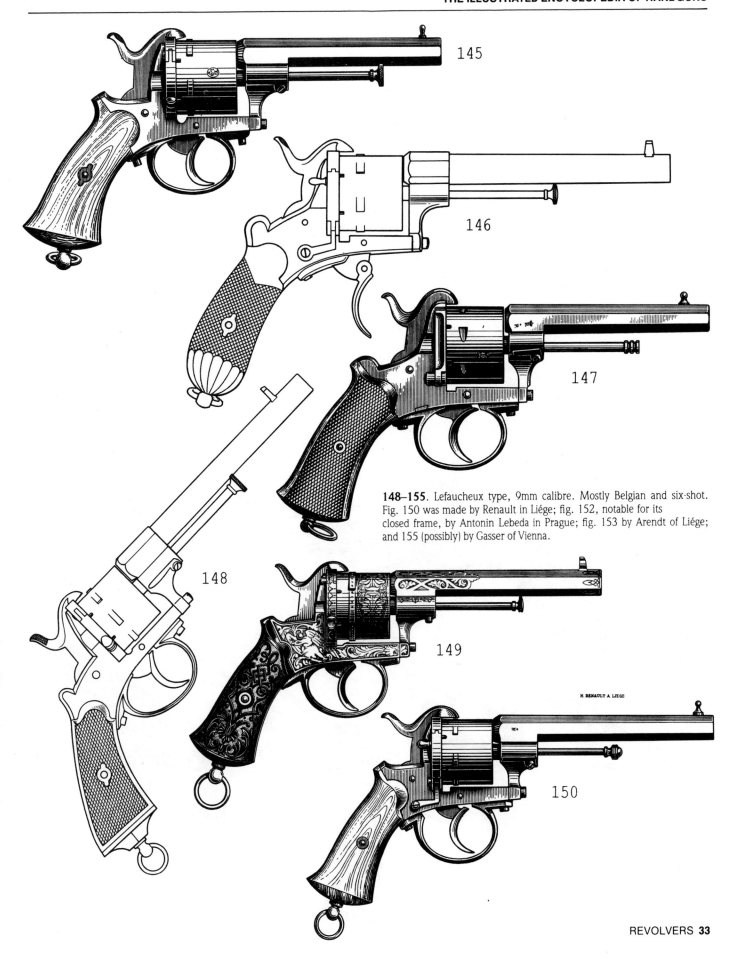

148–155. Lefaucheux type, 9mm calibre. Mostly Belgian and six-shot.
Fig. 150 was made by Renault in Liége; fig. 152, notable for its
closed frame, by Antonin Lebeda in Prague; fig. 153 by Arendt of Liége;
and 155 (possibly) by Gasser of Vienna.

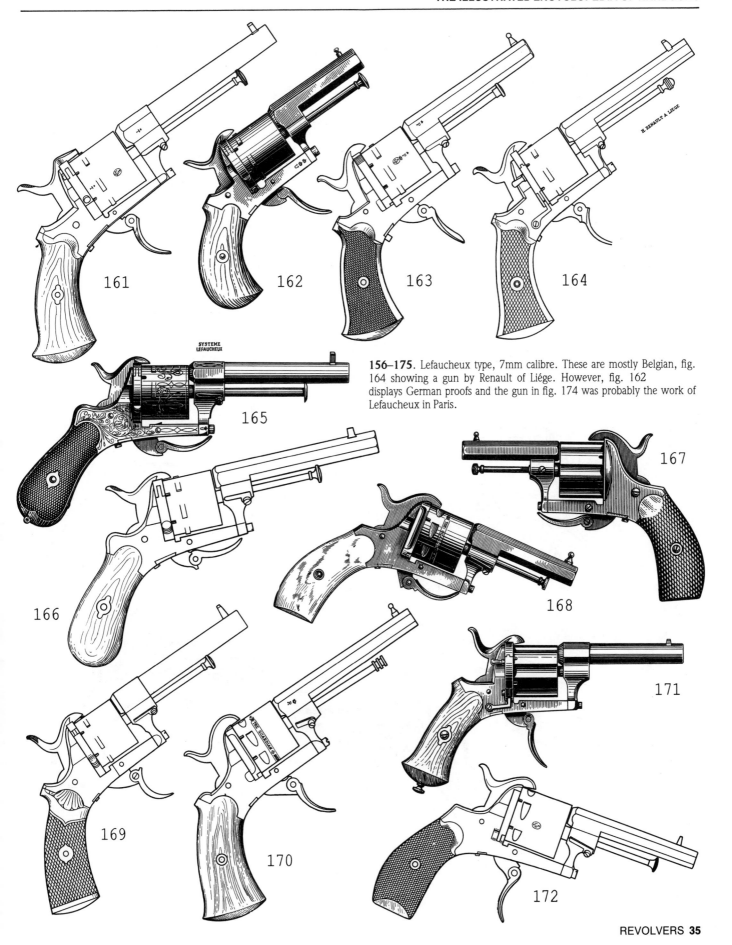

156–175. Lefaucheux type, 7mm calibre. These are mostly Belgian, fig. 164 showing a gun by Renault of Liége. However, fig. 162 displays German proofs and the gun in fig. 174 was probably the work of Lefaucheux in Paris.

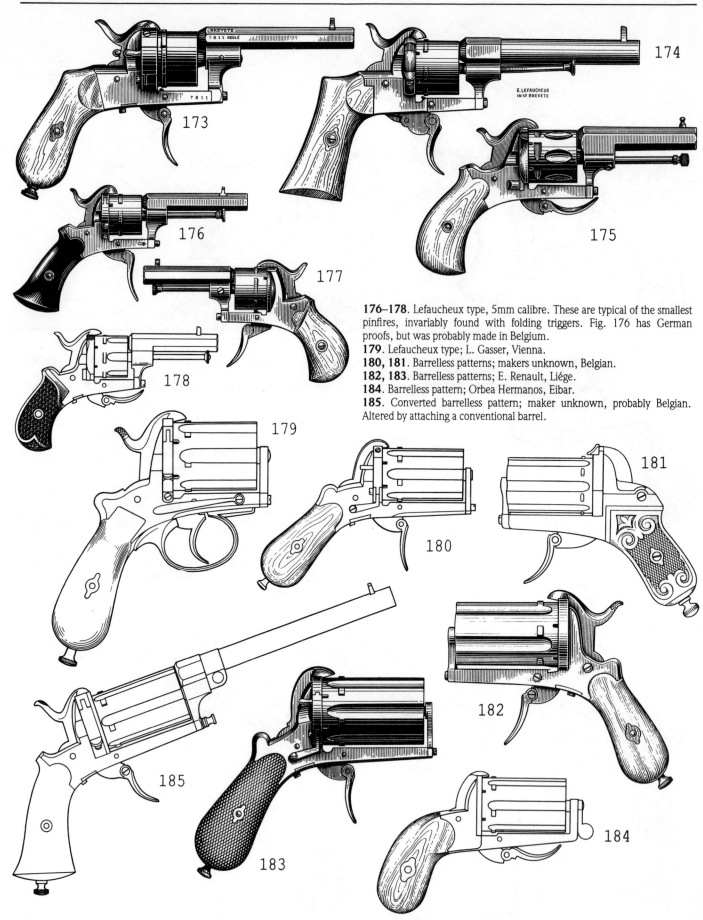

176–178. Lefaucheux type, 5mm calibre. These are typical of the smallest pinfires, invariably found with folding triggers. Fig. 176 has German proofs, but was probably made in Belgium.
179. Lefaucheux type; L. Gasser, Vienna.
180, 181. Barrelless patterns; makers unknown, Belgian.
182, 183. Barrelless patterns; E. Renault, Liége.
184. Barrelless pattern; Orbea Hermanos, Eibar.
185. Converted barrelless pattern; maker unknown, probably Belgian. Altered by attaching a conventional barrel.

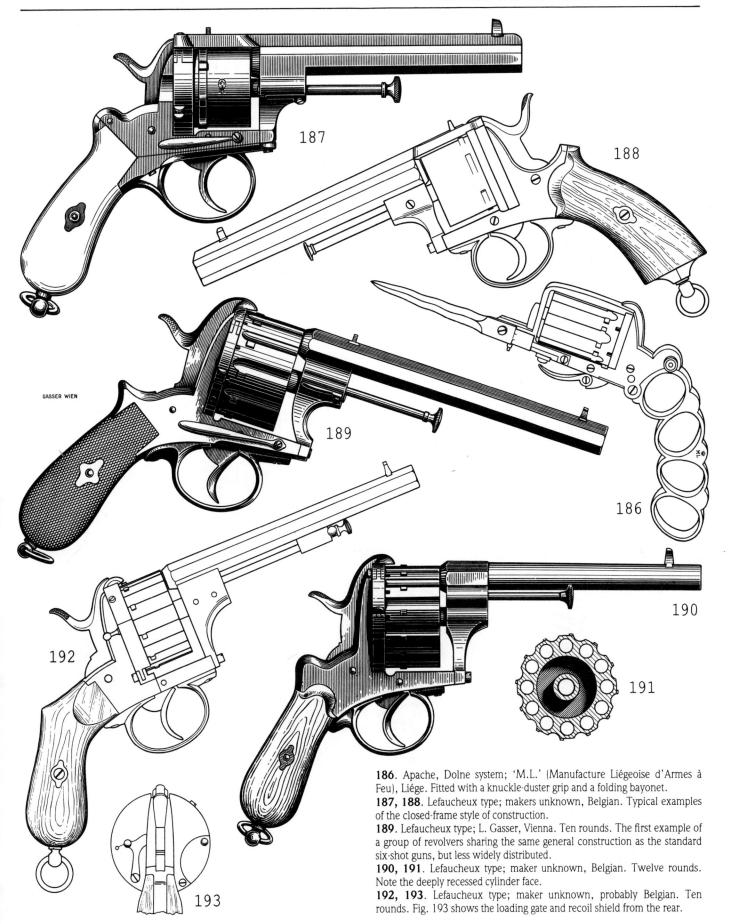

GASSER WIEN

186. Apache, Dolne system; 'M.L.' (Manufacture Liégeoise d'Armes à Feu), Liége. Fitted with a knuckle-duster grip and a folding bayonet.

187, 188. Lefaucheux type; makers unknown, Belgian. Typical examples of the closed-frame style of construction.

189. Lefaucheux type; L. Gasser, Vienna. Ten rounds. The first example of a group of revolvers sharing the same general construction as the standard six-shot guns, but less widely distributed.

190, 191. Lefaucheux type; maker unknown, Belgian. Twelve rounds. Note the deeply recessed cylinder face.

192, 193. Lefaucheux type; maker unknown, probably Belgian. Ten rounds. Fig. 193 shows the loading gate and recoil shield from the rear.

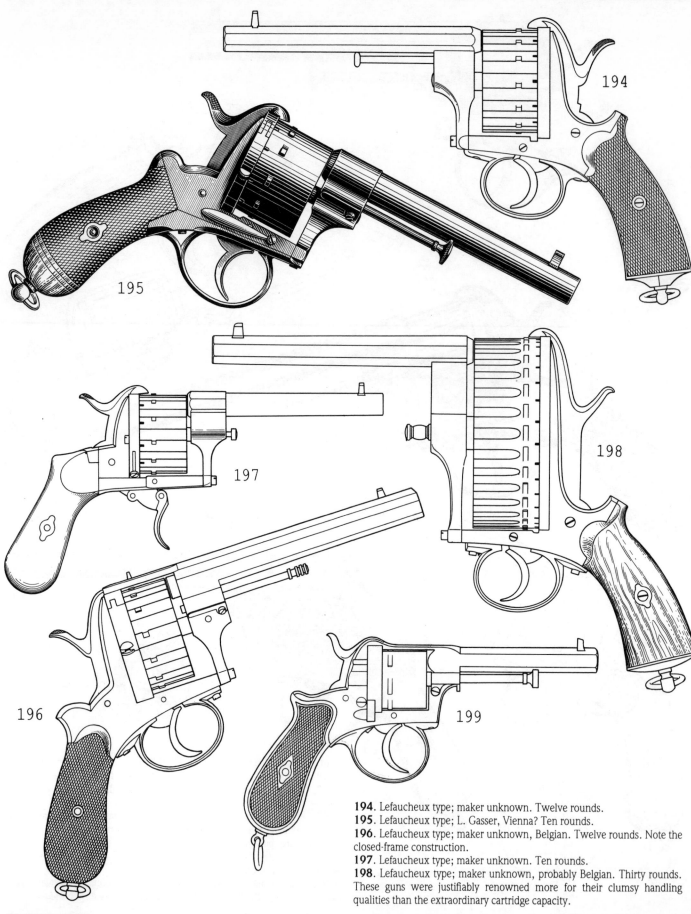

194. Lefaucheux type; maker unknown. Twelve rounds.
195. Lefaucheux type; L. Gasser, Vienna? Ten rounds.
196. Lefaucheux type; maker unknown, Belgian. Twelve rounds. Note the closed-frame construction.
197. Lefaucheux type; maker unknown. Ten rounds.
198. Lefaucheux type; maker unknown, probably Belgian. Thirty rounds. These guns were justifiably renowned more for their clumsy handling qualities than the extraordinary cartridge capacity.

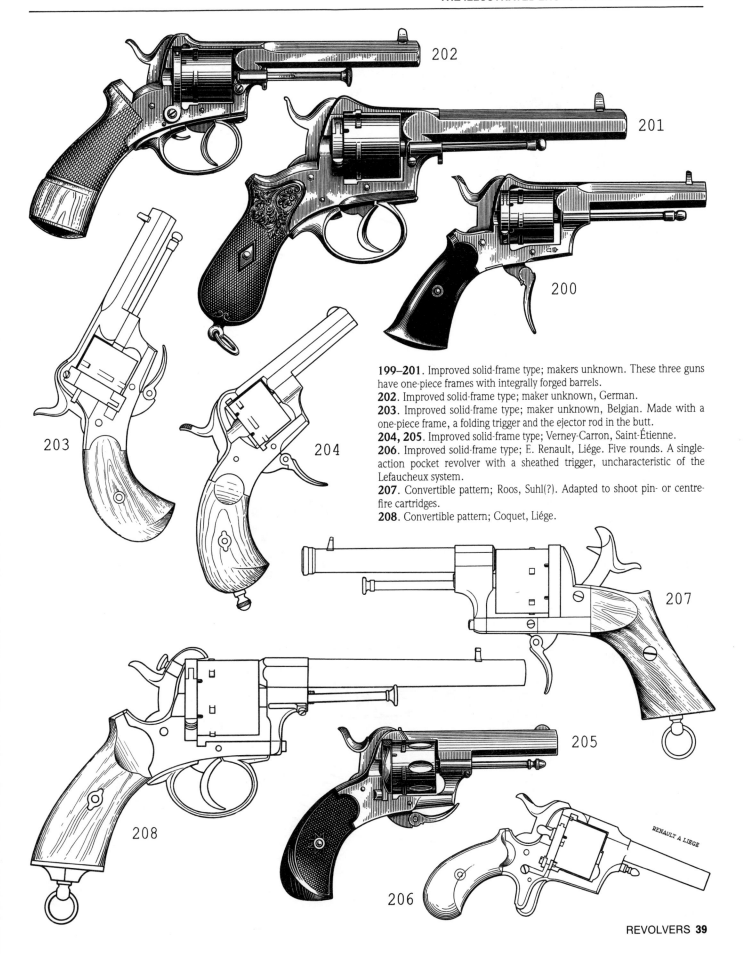

199–201. Improved solid-frame type; makers unknown. These three guns have one-piece frames with integrally forged barrels.

202. Improved solid-frame type; maker unknown, German.

203. Improved solid-frame type; maker unknown, Belgian. Made with a one-piece frame, a folding trigger and the ejector rod in the butt.

204, 205. Improved solid-frame type; Verney-Carron, Saint-Étienne.

206. Improved solid-frame type; E. Renault, Liége. Five rounds. A single-action pocket revolver with a sheathed trigger, uncharacteristic of the Lefaucheux system.

207. Convertible pattern; Roos, Suhl(?). Adapted to shoot pin- or centre-fire cartridges.

208. Convertible pattern; Coquet, Liége.

RENAULT A LIEGE

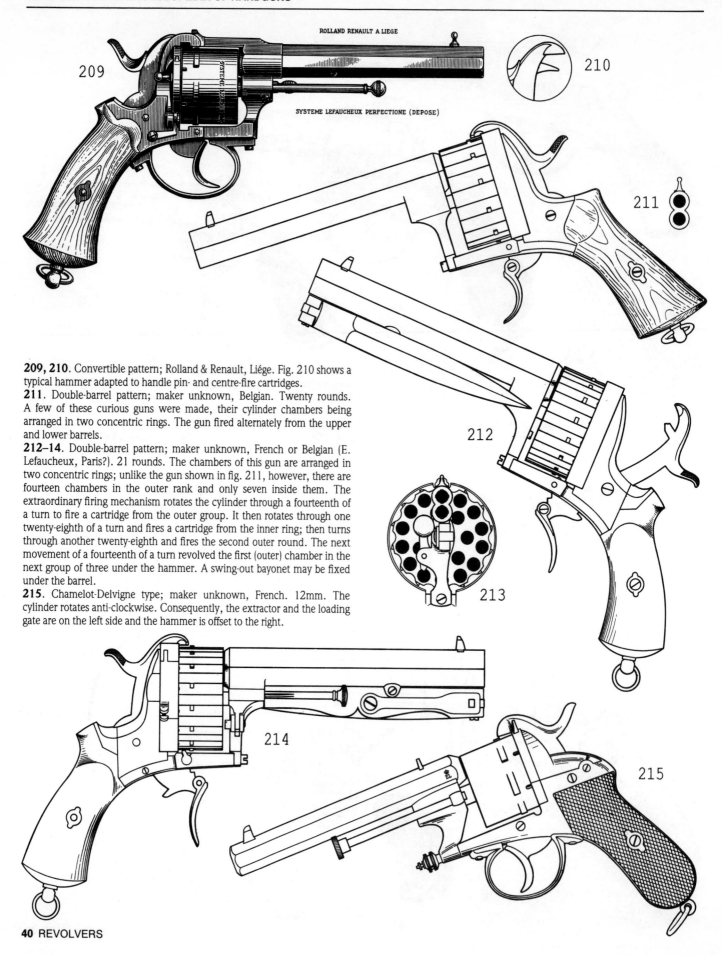

ROLLAND RENAULT A LIEGE

SYSTEME LEFAUCHEUX PERFECTIONE (DEPOSE)

209, 210. Convertible pattern; Rolland & Renault, Liége. Fig. 210 shows a typical hammer adapted to handle pin- and centre-fire cartridges.

211. Double-barrel pattern; maker unknown, Belgian. Twenty rounds. A few of these curious guns were made, their cylinder chambers being arranged in two concentric rings. The gun fired alternately from the upper and lower barrels.

212–14. Double-barrel pattern; maker unknown, French or Belgian (E. Lefaucheux, Paris?). 21 rounds. The chambers of this gun are arranged in two concentric rings; unlike the gun shown in fig. 211, however, there are fourteen chambers in the outer rank and only seven inside them. The extraordinary firing mechanism rotates the cylinder through a fourteenth of a turn to fire a cartridge from the outer group. It then rotates through one twenty-eighth of a turn and fires a cartridge from the inner ring; then turns through another twenty-eighth and fires the second outer round. The next movement of a fourteenth of a turn revolved the first (outer) chamber in the next group of three under the hammer. A swing-out bayonet may be fixed under the barrel.

215. Chamelot-Delvigne type; maker unknown, French. 12mm. The cylinder rotates anti-clockwise. Consequently, the extractor and the loading gate are on the left side and the hammer is offset to the right.

216. Maker unknown, probably Belgian. The barrel of this gun tips upward to facilitate reloading once the catch in front of the trigger guard has been released.

217. Le Mat; maker unknown, probably French. This is among the most unusual of the designs shown here, with a rifled barrel above a large-calibre single-shot smoothbore pattern. (See also fig. 417.)

218. Lefaucheux type; F. Jung & Söhne, Suhl, c.1870. 9mm. Five rounds? The barrel and cylinder can be detached from the frame to facilitate loading. The barrel is retained by a version of the simplified Galand system (see figs. 412–14).

219, 220. Auto-ejecting pattern; Begueldre, Liége. A lever pivoted on the barrel lug can be used to pull the barrel lug and the cylinder forward along the elongated cylinder axis pin (fig. 220). An annular ring around the cylinder catches the cartridge-pins and extracts all spent cases simultaneously.

221. Lefaucheux type; maker unknown, Belgian, c.1870–80. 9mm.

222, 223. Guerriero or 'Système Italien'; maker unknown, Belgian. To reload, the cylinder was swung out to the right and then a disc-like gate fixed to the cylinder could be opened. The ejection system was patented in 1865 by Alessandro Guerriero of Genoa.

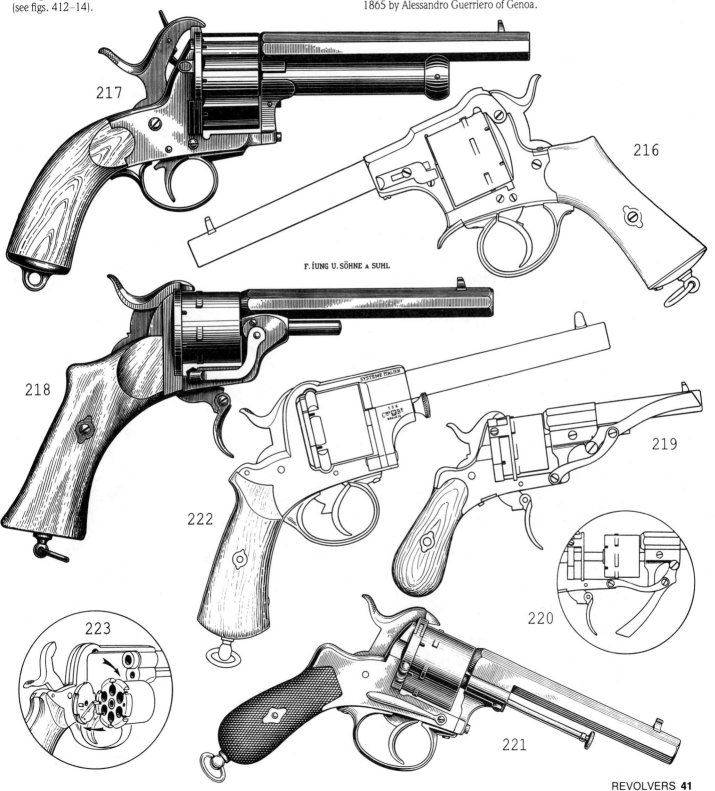

F. ÏUNG U. SÖHNE A SUHL

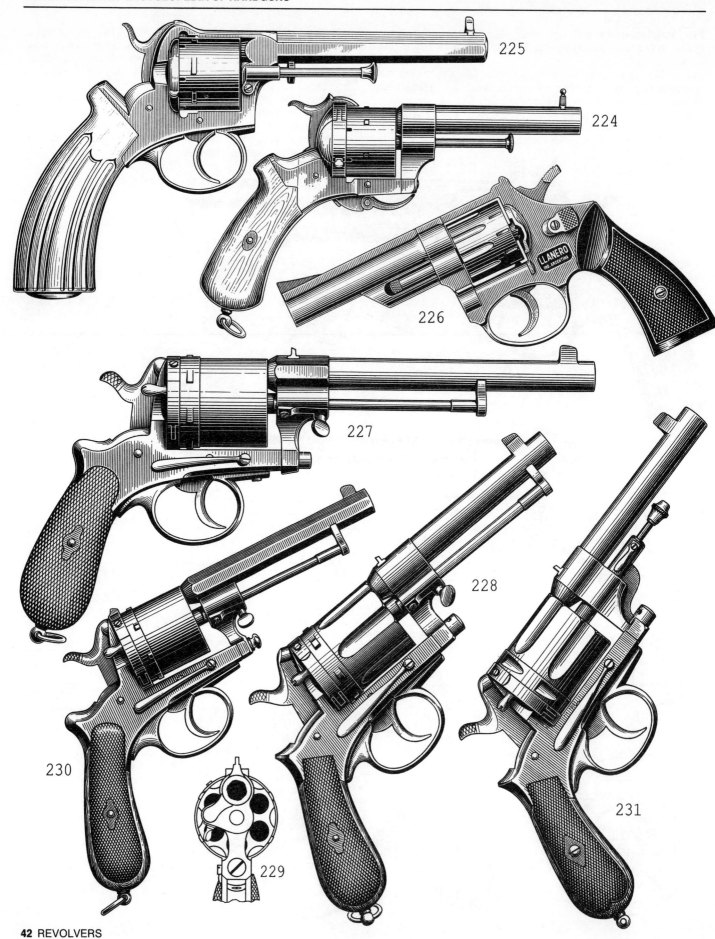

224. Lefaucheux type; maker unknown, French. 9mm; 102mm barrel.
225. Lefaucheux type; maker unknown, Suhl (?), c.1870. 9mm; 137mm barrel. Note the solid frame and ejector rod.

Argentina

226. Llanero; ·22 LR rimfire; nine-shot.
Not shown. Sheriff. ·22 LR rimfire, ·22 Magnum rimfire, ·357 Magnum or ·44 Magnum; 5·5in barrel. The marks of the US importer—FIE, Inc., of Miami—lies on the right side of the frame. A modern copy of the Colt Peacemaker (q.v.).

Austria-Hungary

In addition to the indigenous Gasser and Rast & Gasser products, other types of revolver (e.g., Lefaucheux pinfires) were also produced from 1867 until the demise of the Dual Monarchy in 1918.

Open-frame designs

227–229. Gasser army models, 1870 and 1870/74; L. or J. Gasser, Vienna. 11mm; 375mm overall, 235mm barrel. Five-shot. Double-action. The hammer can be cocked even when the safety catch is applied. The barrel is attached similarly to a conventional Lefaucheux design—i.e., the barrel-lug is screwed onto the cylinder axis-pin and retained by a screw connecting the lug with the frame. The ejector is offset to the right of the barrel on a fixed yoke. Ejection: see fig. 126. Barrel length was subsequently changed to 185mm and then 127mm (overall lengths being 325mm and 267mm respectively). The frame of the earliest guns was made of wrought iron, but steel was substituted on the 1870/74 model (figs. 228–9).

230. Gasser army infantry officer's model, 1870; L. or J. Gasser, Vienna. 9mm; 235mm overall, 770gm. Five-shot. Known as the 'Gasser-Kropatschek', this differed from the army revolver (figs. 227 and 228) only in dimensions.
231. Gasser 'Montenegrin Model'; J. Gasser, Vienna. 11mm; five-shot. This differs from the 1870/74 pattern (fig. 228) largely in the design of the ejector, which pivots outward when required but is usually housed beneath the barrel as an extension of the cylinder axis. This made the gun easier to carry under the belt, customary in Montenegro.
232. Gasser type; maker unknown, Belgian. Many guns sold in Austria-Hungary, owing to the limited production capacity of the Gasser factory in Vienna, were actually made in Liége.

Solid-frame designs

233. Eigner & Co., Vienna. 7·2mm rimfire; seven-shot. A single-action design, with a sheathed trigger but lacking an ejector. The frame is bronze, the other parts being steel.
234. Gasser gendarmerie model; J. Gasser, Vienna. 9mm; 187mm overall, 84mm barrel. Double-action trigger mechanism with a rebounding hammer. No ejector.
235. Gasser improved military model, 1873; J. Gasser, Vienna. 11mm; 242mm overall, 127mm barrel. Five-shot. The yoke-mounted ejector pivots laterally to the right when required.
236. Gasser police model; J. or A. Gasser, Vienna. 9mm; 225mm overall, 112mm barrel. The spring-loaded ejector is offset to the right of the barrel, and acts in conjunction with an Abadie-type loading gate. Ejection is sequential in accordance with fig. 126.
237. Rast & Gasser army model, 1898; Rast & Gasser, Vienna. 8mm; 225mm overall, 114mm barrel, 850gm. Eight-shot. Together with the auto-loading pistols of 1907 (Roth-Steyr) and 1912 (Steyr-Hahn), this well-

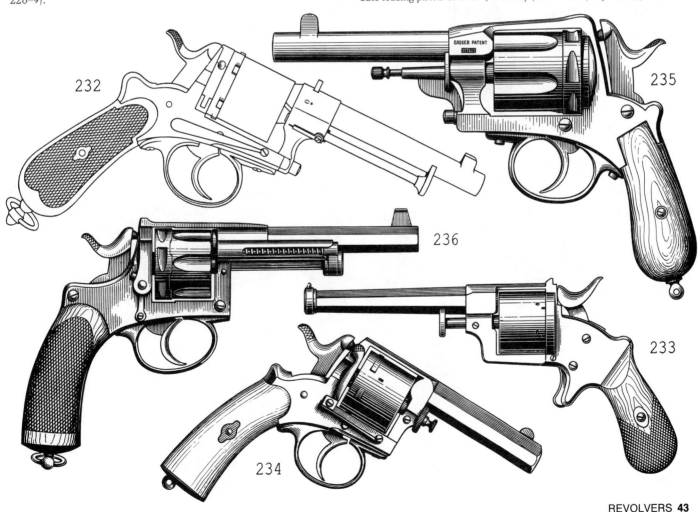

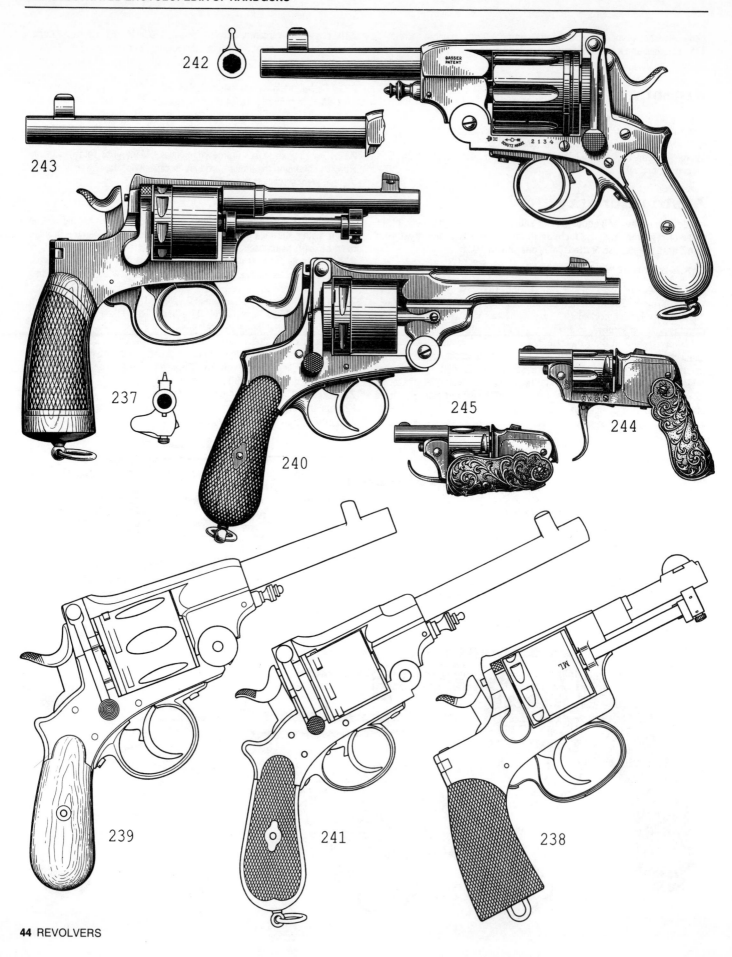

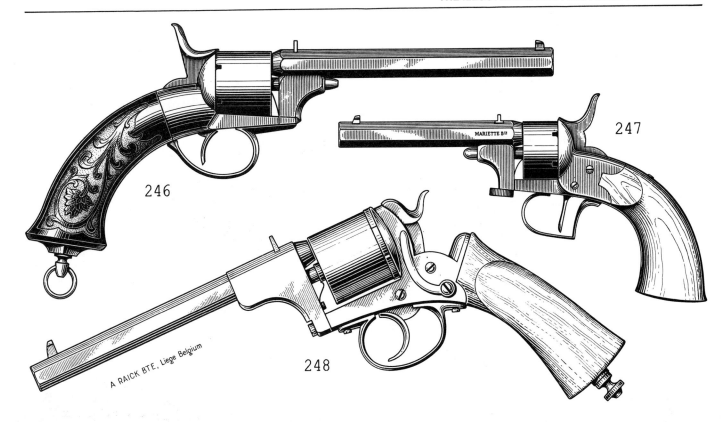

balanced and easily handled weapon, specifically designed for smokeless cartridges, equipped the Austro-Hungarian army during the First World War. The double-action lock has a rebounding hammer, whilst the striker is a separate component in the breech. The spring-loaded ejector, mounted on a fixed yoke on the right side of the frame, operates in conjunction with an Abadie gate in accordance with fig. 126. An interesting feature is the lack of screws, enabling the gun to be stripped and reassembled without tools.

238. Rast & Gasser type; Manufacture Liégeoise d'Armes à Feu ('ML'), Liége. 7·62mm Nagant. This is basically an alteration of the Austro-Hungarian Rast & Gasser army revolver of 1898 (above), adapted to fire Nagant cartridges. The barrel and cylinder have been replaced, the butt has been shortened and the overall dimensions are reduced.

Hinged-frame designs

239. Gasser auto-ejecting pattern; J. Gasser, Vienna. 9mm. The spent rounds are withdrawn from the chambers by a star-shape extractor and then ejected simultaneously when the barrel is tipped open. The locking latch lies only on the right side of the frame.

240, 241. Gasser auto-ejecting patterns; makers unknown, Belgian. These are conventional revolvers emanating from Liége. They display minor changes in the design of the parts, but will often be found with Austro-Hungarian proofmarks.

242, 243. Gasser military or 'Montenegrin' model, 1880; J. Gasser, Vienna. 11·3mm; 133mm or 235mm barrel. This gun—particularly the long-barrelled version—gained its popular name because the Montenegrin militia (effectively the adult male population) carried it from 1889 onward. The Montenegrin ruler, Prince Nicholas, also represented the Gasser Company and presumably promoted these revolvers personally. He is also said to have participated in the introduction of this auto-ejector, though it utilises a version of the Francotte double-lever latch. Simultaneous ejection in accordance with fig. 130; the extractor is basically a pierced disc.

Belgium

Throughout the period from the middle of the ninteenth century to 1914, Belgian gunmakers—Auguste Francotte, for example—made huge quantities of revolvers of the most diverse construction, calibre and size; most, however, were imitations of other well-known systems. The lesser patterns, therefore, are included in the sections devoted to the Bulldog, Velo-Dog and hybrid models.

In addition to original designs, Henri Pieper & Companie and Anciens Établissements Pieper produced excellent copies of Smith & Wesson revolvers, with swing-out cylinders and simultaneous spent-case ejection. Many of these will be found with the Pieper brand name, 'Bayard'. Auguste Francotte made similar guns.

Open-frame designs

244, 245. Le Novo; Charles F. Galand, Paris (made in Liége). An original pattern of pocket revolver, with a folding trigger and a pivoting metallic grip. The barrel and cylinder must be detached from the frame to reload. The long Galand-type barrel latch lies on the right of the frame.

246. Mariette; maker unknown. 8mm rimfire. One of the first European revolvers to fire self-contained cartridges. Its single-action trigger system, construction and general appearance resemble a cap-lock.

247. Mariette; maker unknown. 9mm rimfire. Similar to the preceding gun, but chambered for differing ammunition.

248. Raick Frères, Liége. 11mm.

Solid-frame designs

249, 250. Barracuda; FN Herstal SA, Herstal (Liége). ·38 Special and 9mm Parabellum; 75mm or 100mm barrel. This was introduced in the late 1970s, featuring a Smith & Wesson-type swinging cylinder—which can be detached simply by pressing a button on the lower front right side of the frame. Substitute cylinders allow the use of either rimmed ·357 Magnum/·38 Special or rimless 9mm Parabellum ammunition, the 9mm variety requiring a star-like clip to function effectually. The trigger guard is shaped to support the forefinger of the left hand if a two-hand grip is used.

251. Bayard; Henri Pieper & Companie (Anciens Établissements Pieper), Herstal-lèz-Liége. 8mm; seven-shot. Spent cases are automatically ejected when the cylinders of these guns are swung out to the left (see fig. 131), the Colt-type release latch appearing on the left side of frame behind the cylinder.

In 1890, the Pieper company introduced a revolver similar to the gun drawn here, but which embodied a camming system that moved a single cartridge forward to improve obturation before each shot was fired. This method was apparently originated by the American Daniel Wesson in 1878. A characteristic feature of this 'gas-seal' design was that a spent case was ejected automatically after every shot from the second one onward. The extractor gripped the head of the case as the hammer was retracted, then forcibly ejected it as the hammer fell. This facilitated reloading, but was not especially reliable and was found to promote misfiring.

Pieper also made small numbers of the revolver patented in 1895 by Garcia Reynoso, an Argentine army officer. They incorporated elements of the 1890-type gas-seal guns, but had an additional quick-loading system. The Reynoso cylinder held five cartridges, but another five were carried in a feed-case on the rear left side of the frame. The cylinder could be loaded by inserting a five-round clip into the feed case; by pressing the trigger, a single cartridge was thrust forward into the cylinder-chamber whilst the hammer remained at rest. By pressing the trigger five times, the cylinder could be completely filled. Another cartridge-clip was then inserted into the feed-case and the revolver was ready for use.

The trigger system permitted double- or single-action operation. Once two shots had been fired, fired cases were forcibly ejected. And when an empty chamber revolved to a suitable position in front of the feed-case, a fresh round was inserted. When the feed-case had been emptied—the cylinder still contained five rounds—another clip could be inserted. The revolver did not reload in the conventional sense, and could be shot continuously simply by inserting a new clip every five shots. However, the Reynoso system was much too complex and insufficiently reliable to encounter lasting success.

252. Bayard; Henri Pieper & Companie (later Anciens Établissements Pieper), Herstal-lèz-Liége. ·32 or ·38; 100mm, 115mm, 140mm or 150mm barrel. This is a copy of the 1905-type Smith & Wesson revolver. The grips of long-barrel revolvers are generally elongated.

253. Chamelot-Delvigne type, 1871 pattern; maker unknown. 10·4mm.

254. Chamelot-Delvigne type; maker unknown. This gun has a distinctive ejection system, which revolves a new chamber into position each time a spent case is expelled.

255. Clément; Charles P. Clément, Liége. A manual safety lies on the left side of the frame above the grip. Similar guns were made in Liége by William Grah. See fig. 286.

256. Colt type; Henrion, Dassy & Heuschen ('HDH'), Liége. ·32 or ·38; six-shot. In addition to a selection of lesser patterns, HDH made a copy of the swinging-cylinder Colt New Navy revolver.

257. Excelsior; Simonis, Janssen & Dumoulin ('S.J. & D.'), Liége. 9·1mm Abadie; 222mm overall, 113mm barrel, 790gm. An Abadie-type revolver of c.1886. When the loading gate is open, the trigger is disconnected from the hammer and can rotate the cylinder either to present the chambers for loading or facilitate ejection. To aid field-stripping, the left side of the frame opens outward around a vertical axis in the upper rear part of the grip. The

253

250

249

255
similar to fig. 286

254

251

252

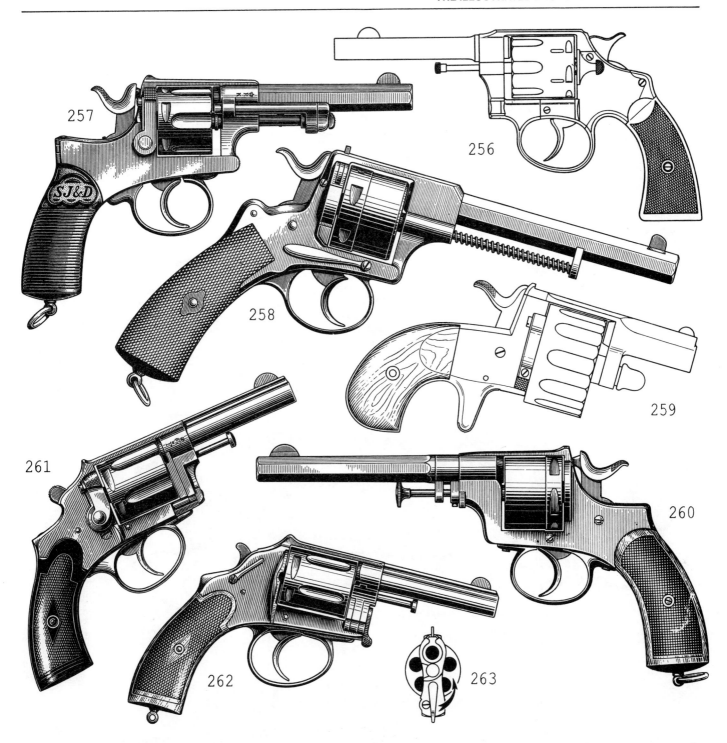

side-plate is held shut by the sprung trigger guard. Similar devices are found on Abadie revolvers issued in the Portuguese army, the Austro-Hungarian Rast & Gasser revolver of 1898 (fig. 237), and the Japanese Meiji 26th Year Type (fig. 533).

258. Francotte; Auguste Francotte & Companie, Liége. 11mm; five-shot. The spring-loaded ejector rod returns automatically to its initial position after use. The double-action trigger system incorporates a cocking safety.

259. Francotte; Auguste Francotte & Companie, Liége. 12mm; ten-shot. A most distinctive 'Travelling Pattern' revolver, with a single-action mechanism, a sheathed trigger and a bronze frame.

260. Francotte; Auguste Francotte & Companie, Liége. A double-action gun with a Nagant-type 'cylinder axis' ejector in a pivoting crane.

261. Francotte; Auguste Francotte & Companie, Liége. 7·5mm, 7·62mm Nagant or 8mm Lebel; five-shot. The cylinder of this gun swings out to the right to reload, and the double-action mechanism has a partially-shrouded rebounding hammer. These were advertised as the 'Bogatyr' or 'Nagant' in catalogues published in Russia prior to 1917. They were also marketed as the 'Puppy' or ''French Officer's Model''. Similar revolvers were produced in Liége by Établissements Lebeaux and Manufacture Liégeoise d'Armes à Feu, distinguished by the shape of individual parts, the method of locking the cylinder, and the arrangement of the firing mechanism — e.g., some guns had a fixed striker whilst others had hinged patterns. This gun uses a swing-back loading gate to lock the cylinder.

262, 263. Francotte; Auguste Francotte & Companie, Liége. A variant of fig. 261 in which the cylinder is opened by pivoting the lever on the front of the frame laterally to the left (see inset).

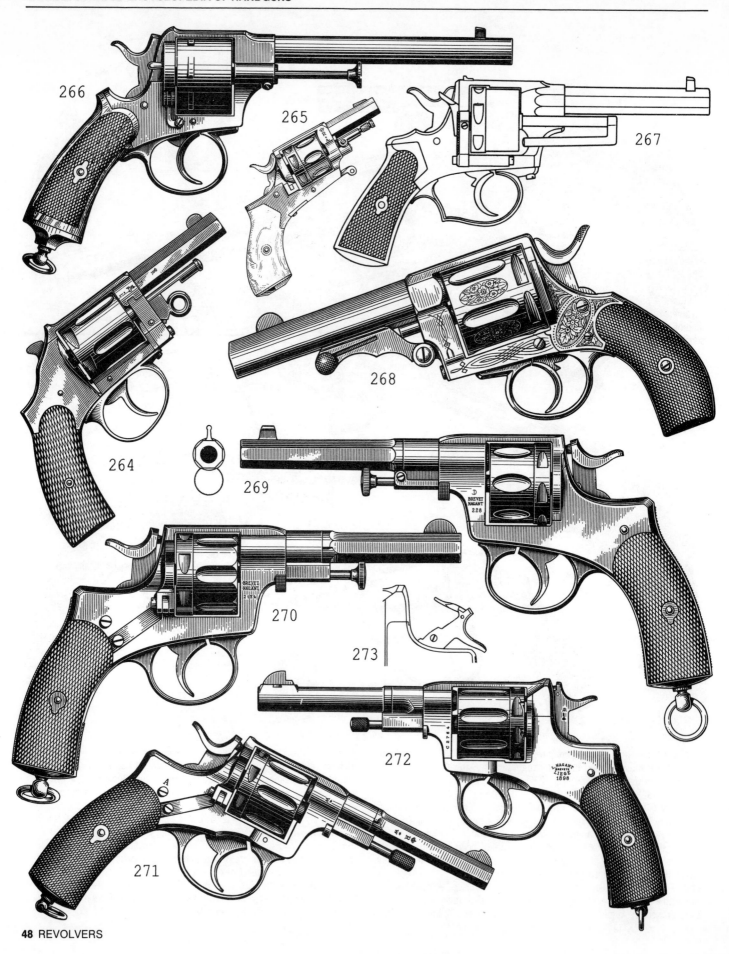

264. Francotte; Auguste Francotte & Companie, Liége. An alternative type of gun shown in fig. 261. The cylinder is opened by pulling the ejector rod forward, allowing the locking ring projecting from the frame to drop.

265. "Lady's Model"; maker unknown. ·22 Short rimfire; six-shot.

266. Lefaucheux type, improved; Jean-Mathieu Deprez, Liége. 11mm. Ejection is successive, in accordance with fig. 126. The gun is marked DEPREZ. BREVETE.

267. Levaux; Établissements Levaux, Liége. Spent cases are extracted successively once the cylinder has been swung out of the frame to the right. The latch lies on the right side of the frame alongside the hammer. The cylinder can be moved forward along its axis, allowing the ejector rod to force a case out of a chamber. The cylinder must then be returned to its original position, turned one-sixth of a revolution, and the process repeated. This continues until all the chambers have been emptied. The gun can then be reloaded and the cylinder locked back into the frame.

268. Montenegrin model; L. & J. Warnant Frères, Hognée. 11mm; five-shot. Spent cases are ejected simultaneously when the cylinder is swung out to the right.

269, 270. Nagant army officer's model, 1878; L. & E. Nagant, Liége. 9mm. An NCO's pattern, introduced in 1883, had a smooth-surfaced cylinder. A similar gun served the Norwegian army (q.v.). Nagant-type revolvers were very popular. They were characterised by a solid frame, the loading gate was retained by a leaf-spring, and the barrel was tightly screwed into the frame. Yoked to the barrel was a tube containing the ejector rod, which entered the cylinder-axis pin when not in use. The highly successful Nagant-type construction was widely imitated in Belgium, Germany and Spain. Nagants made for commercial sale were essentially similar to the contemporaneous Bulldogs (see fig. 1068).

271. Nagant army model, 1887; L. & E. Nagant, Liége. 7·5mm Nagant. Developed to fire smokeless ammunition, this pattern was adopted by the armies of Sweden (1887, fig. 609) and Norway (1893). A copy was made under licence in Sweden by Husqvarna Våpenfabriks Ab.

272, 273. Nagant army or 'Gas-seal' model, 1895; L. & E. Nagant, Liége. 7·62mm Nagant; seven-shot. The detachable side-plates on the frames are noteworthy, whilst the cylinders are cammed forward during the firing cycle to prevent gas escaping through the gap between the barrel and the chamber mouth. Revolvers of this pattern were made in Russia prior to 1917, and then in Poland and the USSR after the October Revolution.

274. Nagant army model, 1910; L. Nagant, Liége. 7·62mm Nagant; seven-shot. This is similar to the earlier or 1895 pattern, but the cylinder swings out to the right to facilitate ejection. The release catch lies on the right side of the frame behind the cylinder.

275. Nagant type; Lepage & Co., Liége.

276. Nagant type; Anciens Établissements Pieper, Herstal-lèz-Liége.

277. Nagant type; Auguste Francotte & Companie, Liége.

278. Perfectionne; Henri Pieper & Companie (later Anciens Établissements Pieper), Herstal-lèz-Liége. 8mm Lebel; six-shot. A smaller and lighter version of the gun drawn in fig. 279.

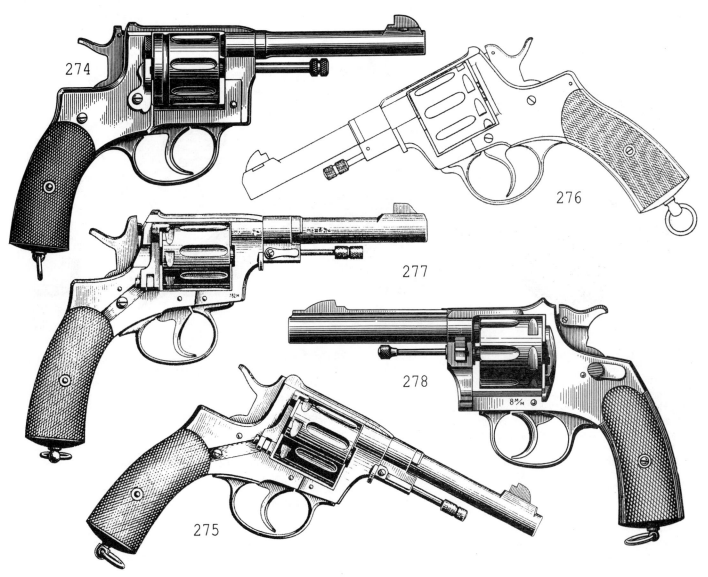

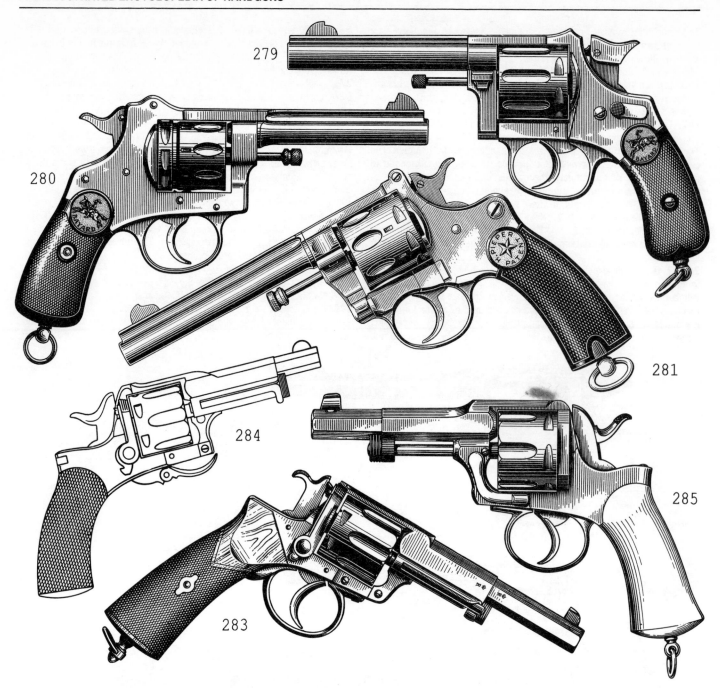

279. Pieper, or Bayard; Henri Pieper & Companie (Anciens Établissements Pieper), Herstal-lèz-Liége. 7·62mm Nagant; 240mm overall, 860gm. Seven-shot. The cylinder-release catch lies on the yoke on the front left side of the frame ahead of the cylinder.

280. Pieper, or Bayard; Henri Pieper & Companie (Anciens Établissements Pieper), Herstal-lèz-Liége. 8mm Nagant; 235mm overall, 115mm barrel. Seven-shot. Made in accordance with a patent of 1889, the cylinder of this gun moved forward to facilitate obturation.

281. Pieper, or Bayard; Henri Pieper & Companie (Anciens Établissements Pieper), Herstal-lèz-Liége. 7·62mm Nagant; seven-shot. A gas-seal revolver with a cylinder which is cammed forward at the instant of firing.

282. Rongé; J.B. Rongé Fils, Liége. 6·35mm Auto; eight-shot. An original design, lacking an ejector. The bulky acorn-shaped striker is accompanied by a hammer with a vestigial spur. The firing system is double-action only.

283. 'Saint-Étienne', Chamelot-Delvigne type; maker unknown. 9·3mm; six-shot. Inspired by the French service revolvers of the late nineteenth century.

284. 'Saint-Étienne', Chamelot-Delvigne type; maker unknown. 7·3mm.

285. 'Saint-Étienne', Chamelot-Delvigne type; maker unknown. 11mm.

286. Saint George; William Grah, Liége. Similar to the Pieper and Clément revolvers (q.v.).

Hinged, pivoting and other frame designs

287. Bernard; maker unknown. 10·6mm; six-shot. This Warnant-type revolver—marked V. BERNARD BREVETE—is latched by a press-button on the left side of the frame behind the cylinder. It ejects simultaneously in accord with fig. 130.

288. Brazilian Model, Gérard type; Lepage & Companie, Liége. ·380; six-shot. Cases are ejected simultaneously when the barrel/cylinder unit is swung upward (see fig. 127). Lepage revolvers included a wide selection of Lefaucheux, Bulldogs and Velo-Dogs, discussed in the appropriate sections.

289. Deville. Probably made in Liége, this revolver utilises a system of levers above the barrel to move the barrel/cylinder unit forward to eject the spent cases simultaneously.

290. Francotte; Auguste Francotte & Companie, Liége. 7·65mm; six-shot. There is a folding trigger, and only a single locking-latch on the left side of the frame instead of the customary two (see fig. 292).

291, 292. Francotte; Auguste Francotte & Companie, Liége. 7·65mm. The most notable feature of these revolvers, patented by Philippe Counet, was the twin barrel-latches placed vertically on the frame behind the cylinder. When the lower tips of the levers were pressed, the upper ends sprang outward to allow the breech to open. Guns of this type were made throughout the 1890s in calibres ranging from ·320 to ·577. Though they were fundamentally identical, they differed in details: smooth or fluted cylinders, spurred or plain trigger guards, folding triggers, or differently shaped grips.

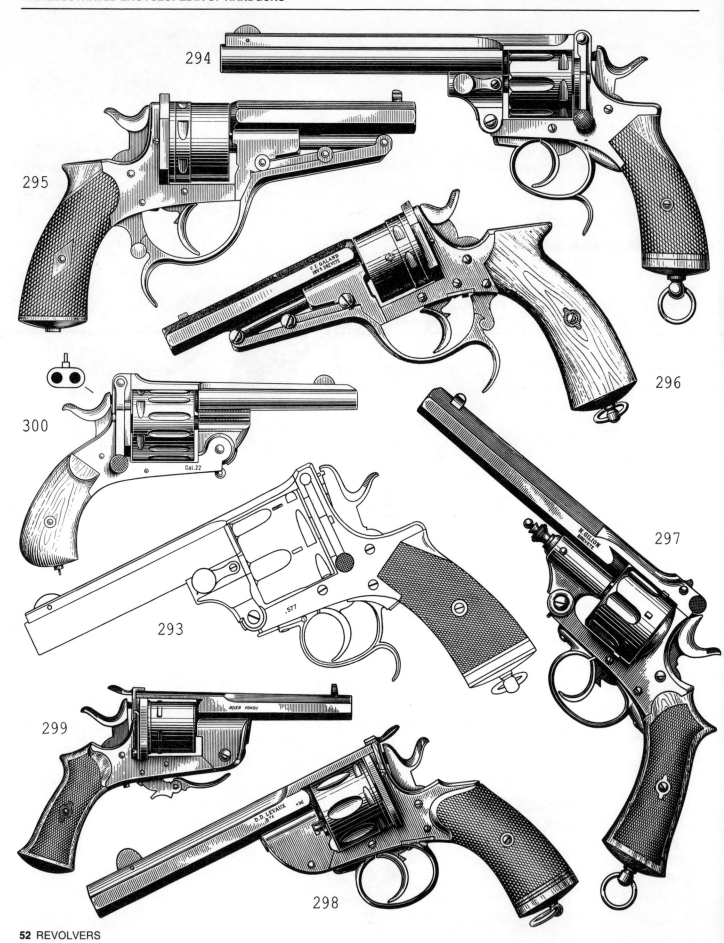

293, 294. Francotte; Auguste Francotte & Companie, Liége. ·577 (fig. 293, five-shot) and ·450 (fig. 294, six-shot).

295. Galand navy model, 1868; Charles F. Galand, Paris (made in Liége). 12mm; six-shot. Galand was a Frenchman, but his distinctive revolver (patented in 1868) was made exclusively in Belgium. It was adopted for the Russian navy, serving as the '4½-Line Galand Revolver' until eventually displaced by the gas-seal Nagants. The barrel and cylinder assembly slides longitudinally away from the standing breech as the actuating lever (which forms the trigger guard) is pulled downward; see fig. 128. Spent cases are withdrawn by a disc-like extractor as the action opens.

296. Galand, 1872 pattern; Charles F. Galand, Paris (made in Liége). 11mm Perrin; 260mm overall, 124mm barrel, about 950gm.

297. Gilion; Nicholas Gilion, Liége. 11mm; six-shot. The spent cases are extracted simultaneously in accordance with fig. 130 once the press-button barrel/cylinder latch has been released.

298. Levaux; Établissements Levaux, Liége. ·38; six-shot. A simultaneous ejector in accordance with fig. 130. The disc-like extractor moves out from the cylinder as the revolver is opened, then springs back when the barrel reaches its lowest position. The latch on top of the frame ahead of the hammer must be drawn back to release the barrel/cylinder unit. Similar guns were made in larger calibres.

299. Levaux; Établissements Levaux, Liége. ·32; six-shot.

300. Maker unknown. ·22 rimfire; 95mm barrel. Twelve-shot. This gun can only fire six times, as both barrels discharge simultaneously.

301. Martin & Companie, Liége. 7·65mm. The barrel hinges upward so that the cylinder can be detached for reloading.

302. Mercenier. ·380; six-shot. The ejection system of this gun, probably made in Liége, relies on the ball-ended lever on the front of the frame being turned laterally to the left to swing the cylinder out to the right. The lever is then pivoted forward to eject spent cases simultaneously by way of a disc-like extractor.

303. Pryse type; Auguste Francotte & Companie, Liége, 1870s. ·450; six-shot. Simultaneous ejection in accordance with fig. 130, the breech latches being the double Francotte pattern. These English-style revolvers were made by Francotte and other Belgian manufacturers for distribution in Britain. Consequently, they will often bear the marks of well-known gunsmiths—e.g., Isaac Hollis & Sons of Birmingham and London—and care is necessary to distinguish these from the actual manufacturers.

304. Pryse type; Auguste Francotte & Companie, Liége. ·38 S&W; six-shot.

305. Puppy; Henrion, Dassy & Heuschen ('HDH'), Liége. ·22 Short rimfire or 6·35mm Auto; five- or six-shot. A Smith & Wesson imitation, with a folding trigger.

306. Russian Model; L. & J. Warnant Frères, Hognée. ·44 S&W Russian; six-shot.

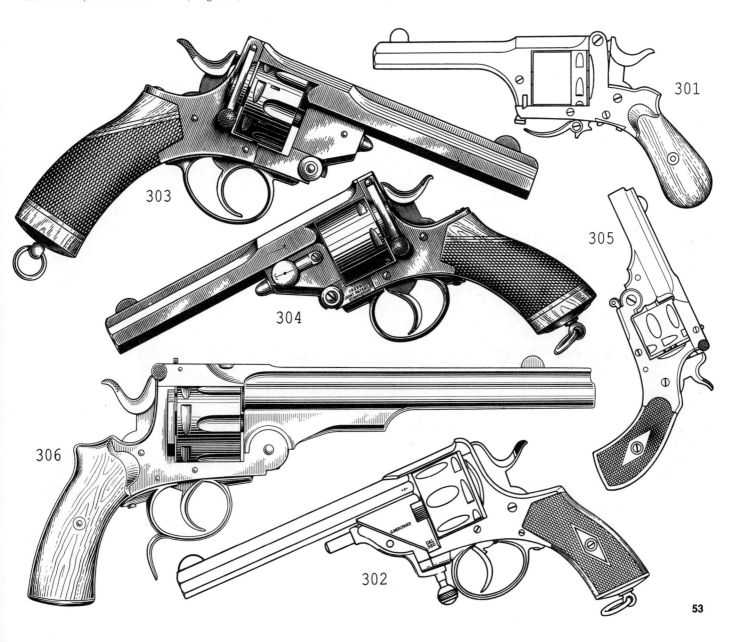

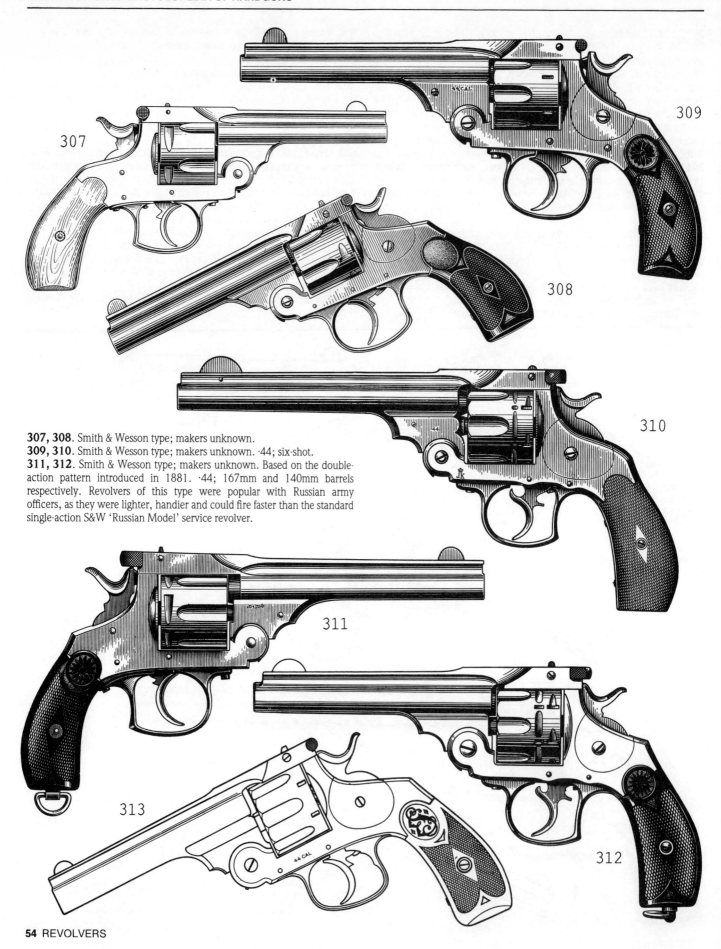

307, 308. Smith & Wesson type; makers unknown.
309, 310. Smith & Wesson type; makers unknown. ·44; six-shot.
311, 312. Smith & Wesson type; makers unknown. Based on the double-action pattern introduced in 1881. ·44; 167mm and 140mm barrels respectively. Revolvers of this type were popular with Russian army officers, as they were lighter, handier and could fire faster than the standard single-action S&W 'Russian Model' service revolver.

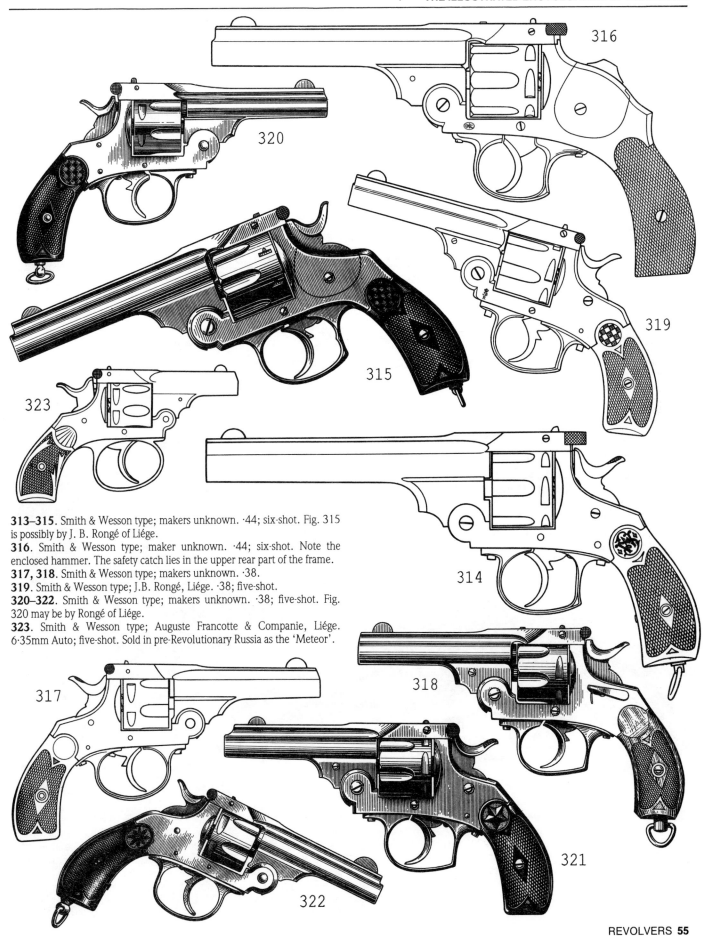

313–315. Smith & Wesson type; makers unknown. ·44; six-shot. Fig. 315 is possibly by J. B. Rongé of Liége.

316. Smith & Wesson type; maker unknown. ·44; six-shot. Note the enclosed hammer. The safety catch lies in the upper rear part of the frame.

317, 318. Smith & Wesson type; makers unknown. ·38.

319. Smith & Wesson type; J.B. Rongé, Liége. ·38; five-shot.

320–322. Smith & Wesson type; makers unknown. ·38; five-shot. Fig. 320 may be by Rongé of Liége.

323. Smith & Wesson type; Auguste Francotte & Companie, Liége. 6·35mm Auto; five-shot. Sold in pre-Revolutionary Russia as the 'Meteor'.

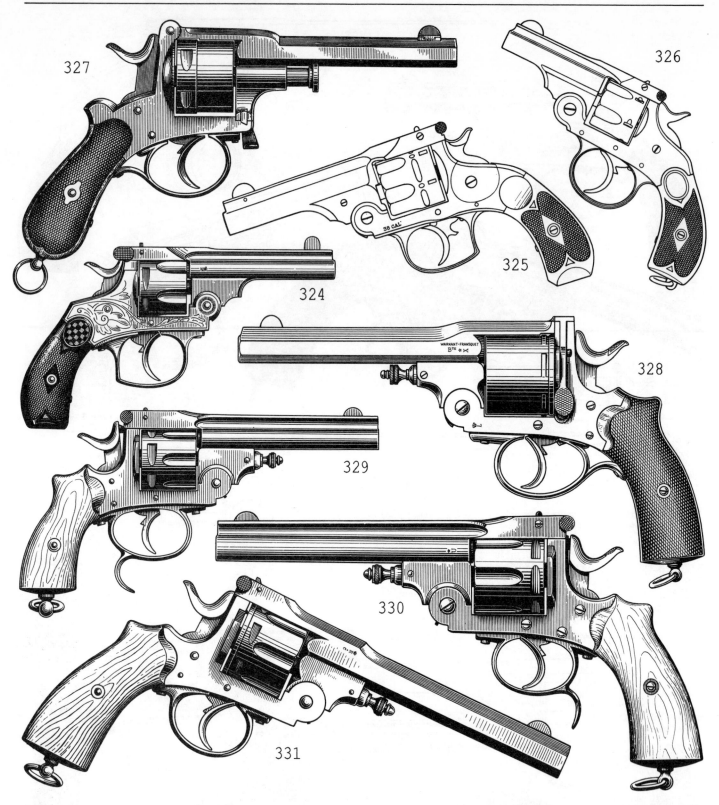

324. Smith & Wesson type; maker unknown. ·32; five-shot.

325. Smith & Wesson type; Auguste Francotte, Liége. 7·65mm; five-shot.

326. Smith & Wesson type; maker unknown. ·22 Long rimfire; five-shot.

327. Spirlet, 1869 pattern. 11·5mm; five-shot. Once the catch on the frame ahead of the trigger guard has been released, the barrel/cylinder unit can be pivoted upward around the hinge on the rear of the frame ahead of the hammer. Pressing the cylinder-axis pin backward then allows a star-like extractor to expel the cases simultaneously, in accordance with fig. 127.

328. Warnant; L. & J. Warnant Frères, Hognée. 9–11mm; five- or six-shot. This gun has a Francotte-type locking latch on the left side of the frame, but others had them on both sides of the breech. The upper rear portion of the grips usually has a characteristic protrusion. Spent cases were ejected simultaneously when the breech was opened (fig. 130).

329–31. Warnant; L. & J. Warnant Frères, Hognée. 9–11mm; five- or six-shot. These guns have Smith & Wesson push-button latches set into the barrel extension. Warnant also made Gasser patterns (figs. 240 and 241).

Brazil

The guns made in Brazil since the end of the Second World War are virtually straightforward copies of the Smith & Wesson Hand Ejector.

332. Rossi Ladysmith type; Amadeo Rossi SA, São Leopoldo. ·22 LR rimfire; seven-shot.

333–335. Rossi Model 68; Amadeo Rossi SA, São Leopoldo. ·38 Special; 50mm or 75mm barrel. Five-shot. The Model 88 is identical, but made of stainless steel. The ·32 S&W Model 69 and ·22 LR rimfire Model 70 are also similar to the Model 68, but the latter is six-shot. A variant of the Model 70 in ·22 Magnum rimfire has a 150mm barrel.

Models 27, 87 and 881 (·38 Special, five-shot) are all copied from the S&W Model 36. The Models 27 and 87 have a 50mm barrel, but the former is made of ordinary blued steel whilst the latter is bright-finished stainless steel. The six-shot ·22 LR rimfire Model 43 has a 75mm barrel; Model 87A is similar to the Model 87 described previously, but has an American Bianchi-type grip.

Models 851, 853, 951 and 953 are six-shot ·38 Special patterns with ejector shrouds, ventilated barrel ribs, adjustable sights, and target-pattern grips; '8'-prefix guns are stainless steel, '9'-prefix versions are blued carbon steel. The last numeral indicates a 10cm barrel (1) or a 15cm pattern (3).

336. Rossi Model 87; Amadeo Rossi SA, São Leopoldo. ·38 Special; 180mm overall, 50mm barrel, 650gm. Five-shot.

337. Rossi Model 511; Amadeo Rossi SA, São Leopoldo. ·22 LR rimfire.

338. Rossi Model 851; Amadeo Rossi SA, São Leopoldo. ·38 Special.

339. Rossi Model 971; Amadeo Rossi SA, São Leopoldo. ·357 Magnum.

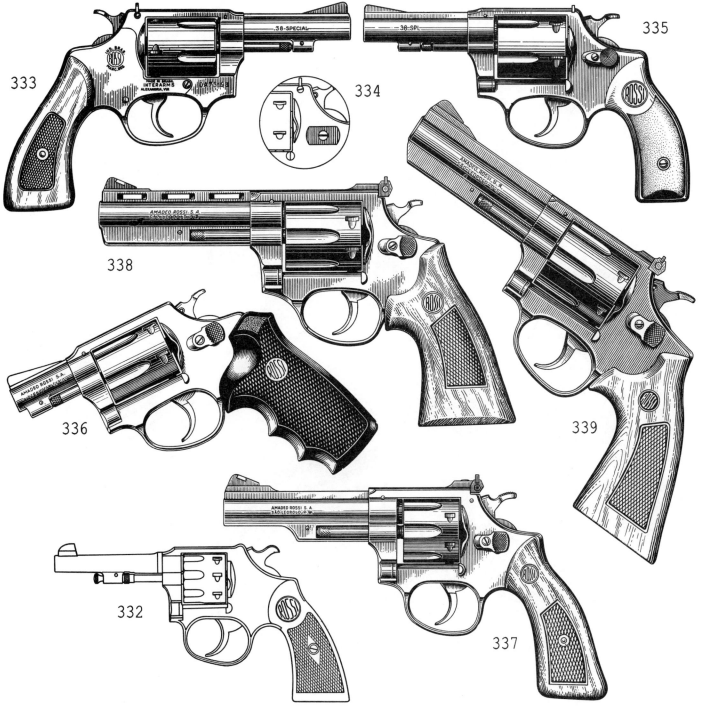

340. Taurus Model 66; Forjas Taurus SA, Porto Alegre. ·357 Magnum; 100mm barrel.

341. Taurus Model 74; Forjas Taurus SA, Porto Alegre. ·32 S&W Long; 75mm barrel.

342, 343. Taurus Model 82; Forjas Taurus SA, Porto Alegre. ·38 Special and '+P'; 75mm or 100mm barrel. Model 80 is similar, but lacks the barrel-rib.

344, 345. Taurus Model 85; Forjas Taurus SA, Porto Alegre. ·38 Special; 75mm or 100mm barrel. Five-shot. The hammer may be partly shrouded. The Model 73 is similar, but chambers the ·32 S&W Long round.

346. Taurus Model 85 SN; Forjas Taurus SA, Porto Alegre. ·38 Special; 50mm barrel. Five-shot.

347. Taurus Model 94; Forjas Taurus SA, Porto Alegre. ·22 LR rimfire; 100mm barrel. Nine-shot.

348. Taurus Model 669; Forjas Taurus SA, Porto Alegre. ·357 Magnum; 100mm barrel.

349. Taurus Pocket model; Forjas Taurus SA, Porto Alegre. ·38 Special; 50mm or 63mm barrel. Five-shot. Revolvers with a 75mm barrel are known as 'Boxer', and those with a 10cm barrel as 'Target'. A ·22 LR rimfire version with a 75mm barrel is the 'Fox'.

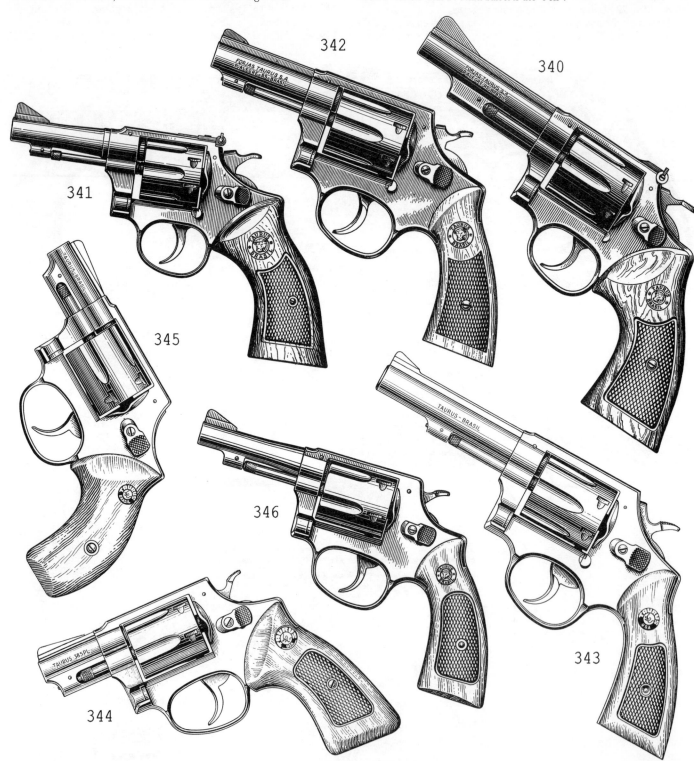

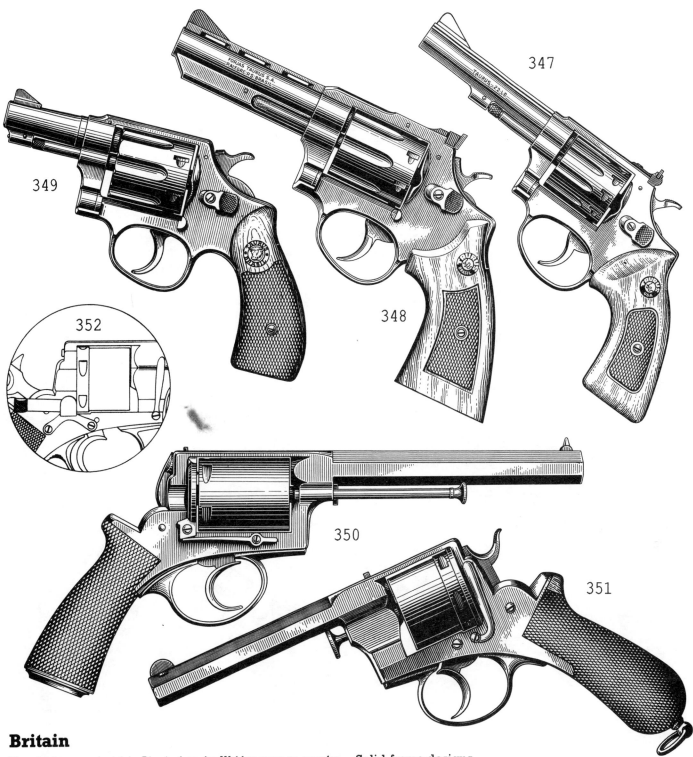

Britain

The revolvers produced in Birmingham by Webley were so popular that they soon became regarded as the archetypal British handgun. Consequently, the auto-loading pistol made much less of an impact on the British market than it did in Continental Europe.

In addition to domestic patterns, foreign models—mainly Smith & Wessons—were used by the British armed forces. During the First World War, owing to a universal shortage of serviceable handguns, Smith & Wesson-type hinged-frame revolver were produced in Spain (fig. 553), and swinging-cylinder S&W or Colt guns were procured in the USA (figs. 657, 709). They differed from American revolvers only in that they chambered ·455 cartridges and had British proofmarks.

Solid-frame designs

350. Adams type; Deane, Adams & Deane, London. ·440; 6·5in barrel. Five-shot. This is a conversion from an original cap-lock revolver made in the early 1850s.

351, 352. Adams; Adams Patent Small Arms Co. Ltd, London. ·450; five-shot. Though a backward-pivoting loading gate is fitted, the gun lacks an ejector. It is assumed that the rod was carried separately, possibly in an accompanying case.

353, 354. Adams army model, 1867; Adams Patent Small Arms Co. Ltd, London. ·450 Boxer; five-shot. The cylinder is much longer than necessary

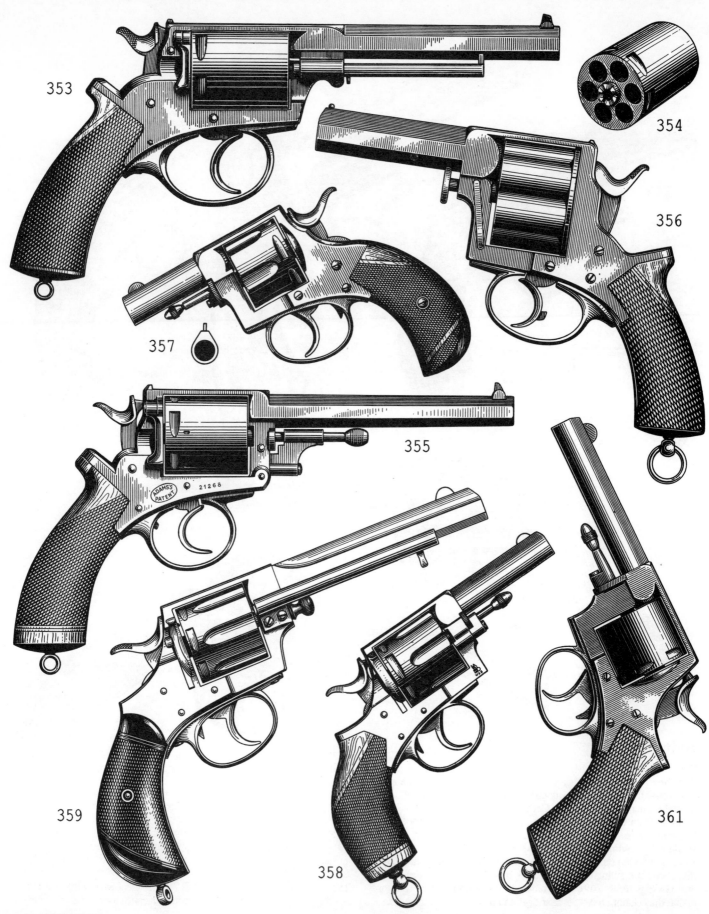

for the comparatively short cartridge, as the frame-design was inherited from the preceding cap-locks. The ejector rod is offset to the right of the barrel, whilst the loading gate behind the cylinder opens to the side and then upward.

355. Adams army model, 1872; Adams Patent Small Arms Co. Ltd, London. This is similar in size and chambering to the preceding pattern, but was newly made and thus has a shorter cylinder. The head of the ejector rod retracts into the cylinder axis-pin stem, though a fixed rod—offset to the right—is sometimes encountered instead. Guns of this type served the British army until the 1880s.

356. Boxer or Bulldog, 1866; Philip Webley & Son, Birmingham. ·577; five-shot. This gun fired a cartridge loaded with a lead ball. Spent cases were extracted by removing the cylinder from the frame and punching them out with the cylinder axis-pin.

357. Bulldog No. 2; Philip Webley & Son (Webley & Scott Revolver & Arms Co. Ltd after 1897, then Webley & Scott Ltd from 1906), Birmingham. ·455; 2·5in barrel. Five-shot. Often called the 'Sherlock Holmes' pattern.

358. Express No. 5; Philip Webley & Son (Webley & Scott Revolver & Arms Co. Ltd after 1897, then Webley & Scott Ltd from 1906), Birmingham. ·360; 7·5in or 9in overall, 3in or 4·5in barrel, 28–31oz. Six-shot.

359. Frontier or Army Express; Philip Webley & Son (Webley & Scott Revolver & Arms Co. Ltd after 1897, then Webley & Scott Ltd from 1906), Birmingham. ·450 or ·45 Long Colt; 10·85in overall, 5·5in barrel, 35oz. Six-shot. The spring-loaded ejector is offset on the right side of the barrel.

360. M.P. ('Metropolitan Police'); Philip Webley & Son (Webley & Scott Revolver & Arms Co. Ltd after 1897, then Webley & Scott Ltd from 1906), Birmingham. ·450; 7in overall, 2·5in barrel, 27oz. Six-shot. Issued to the police from 1883 onward.

361. R.I.C. ('Royal Irish Constabulary'), 1867; Philip Webley & Son, Birmingham. ·442 Boxer; 9in overall, 4·5in barrel, 30oz. Six-shot.

362. R.I.C. No. 2 Model; Philip Webley & Son, Birmingham. ·450; 8·6in overall, 3·5in barrel, 28·5oz. Six-shot. Also made in ·320 and ·380, these guns being smaller and lighter than the ·442 type.

363, 364. R.I.C. type; Philip Webley & Son (Webley & Scott Revolver & Arms Co. Ltd after 1897, then Webley & Scott Ltd from 1906 onward), Birmingham. ·450, ·455 and other chamberings; generally five-shot. These are typical commercial variants of the standard pattern. Spent cases are ejected successively through a pivoting gate on the right side of the frame behind the cylinder, in accordance with fig. 126.

365, 366. Sterling; Sterling Armament Co. Ltd, Dagenham. ·357 Magnum and ·38 Special, interchangeably; 9·5in overall (4in barrel), 2in or 4in barrel, 38·8oz. Production of these Smith & Wesson-type revolvers, based on the guns previously made in Germany by J.P. Sauer & Sohn (see figs. 483 and 506), began tentatively in 1984. In 1991, however, operations closed down before series production had begun. Sterling revolvers were distinguished by twin full-length coil-type main springs inside the grip.

367. Thomas type; Tipping & Lawden, Birmingham. ·450; five shot. Patented in 1869, this revolver ejects spent cases simultaneously when the barrel and cylinder are pushed forward together.

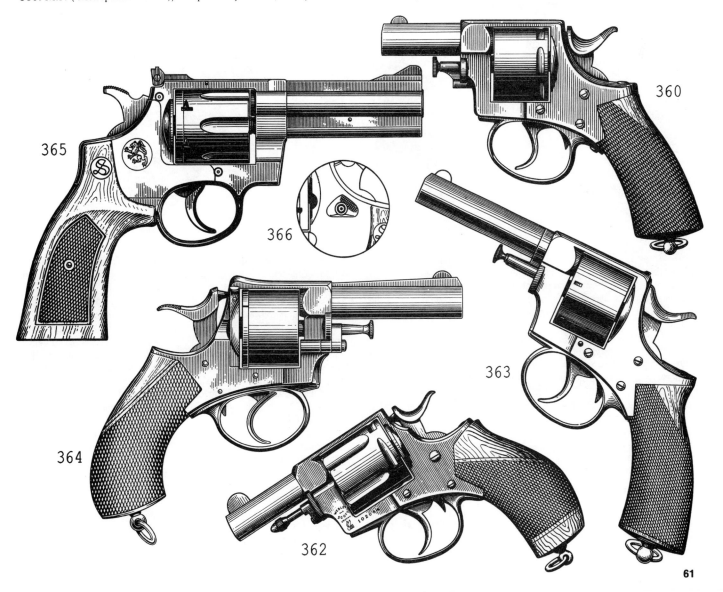

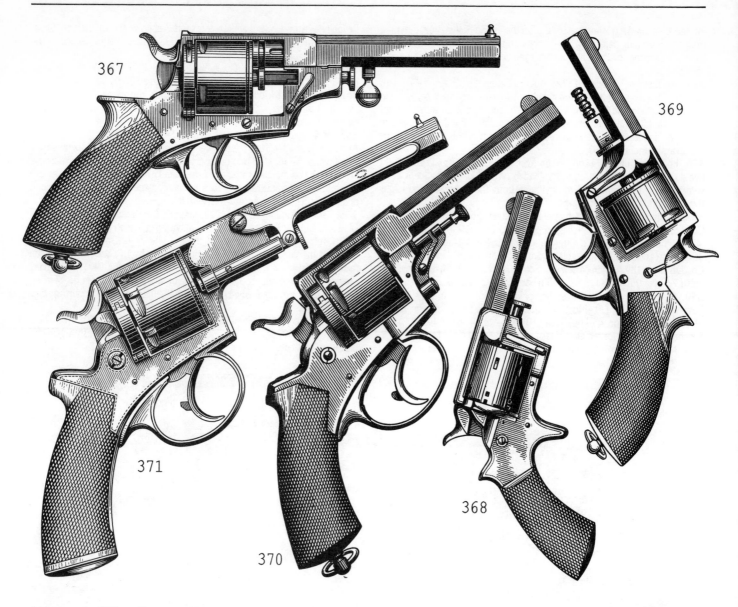

368. Tranter; William Tranter & Company, Birmingham. ·320 rimfire; 3·38in barrel. Seven-shot. A single-action revolver with a sheathed trigger, doubtless influenced by contemporaneous US practice. The cylinder must be removed before spent cases can be extracted, in accordance with fig. 124. The cylinder axis-pin can then double as the ejector. The frame, barrel and grip are forged as a single piece.

369. Tranter; William Tranter & Company, Birmingham. ·380; six-shot. A typical English-made gun of the 1860s. Double-action firing mechanism.

370. Tranter; William Tranter & Company, Birmingham. ·450; five-shot. Otherwise similar to the gun pictured in fig. 369.

371. Tranter; William Tranter & Company, Birmingham. ·45; 6·5in barrel. Five-shot. A pivoting ejector rod lies on the right side of the barrel.

372. Tranter army revolver, model 1878; William Tranter & Company, Birmingham. ·450; six-shot.

373. Webley; Philip Webley & Son, Birmingham. The first of these solid-frame guns was made in 1865. They had a single-action firing mechanism and ejected spent cases successively in accordance with fig. 126.

Hinged, pivoting and other frame designs

374. Enfield Mark II, 1882; Royal Small Arms Factory, Enfield Lock, Middlesex. ·476; six-shot. Designed by an American, Owen Jones, this service revolver had a most distinctive extraction system. The spent cases were withdrawn simultaneously by tipping the barrel downward to draw the cylinder forward from the standing breech. Enfields equipped the British Army and the Royal Canadian Mounted Police, but were soon replaced by the Webley Mark I.

375–377. Enfield No. 2 Mark I; Royal Small Arms Factory, Enfield Lock. ·38–200; 5in barrel. Introduced in 1931, this was a minor adaption of the ·38 Webley Mk IV, sharing similar automatic ejection. The grips were wood or plastic. No. 2 Mk I* and I**, differing from each other in minor details, were double-action only and lacked hammer spurs. Guns of this type were made by Albion Motors in Glasgow during the Second World War, whilst the Singer Sewing Machine Co. Ltd of Clydebank made parts. Essentially similar ·38 Mk IV revolvers were ordered from Webley & Scott in 1940–4. The barrels of some Enfields were subsequently cut to 2in or 3in, apparently unofficially.

378. Hill's Patent Revolver; William Hill & Company, Birmingham and Wolverhampton, c.1876–80. ·320; 3·75in barrel. The spent cases are ejected automatically when the barrel is tipped upward (see fig. 127). Hill-type revolvers were also made in Belgium, by Braendlin and Francotte, and will be encountered in a number of differing sizes.

379. Kynoch army model; The Kynoch Gun Factory, Aston Cross, Birmingham, 1885–7. ·455; 6in barrel. Patented by Henry Schlund in 1885–6. The enclosed hammer can be cocked by the spur-lever beneath the trigger guard, reminiscent of the 1853-patent cap-lock Tranter. A later version had the lever within the guard.

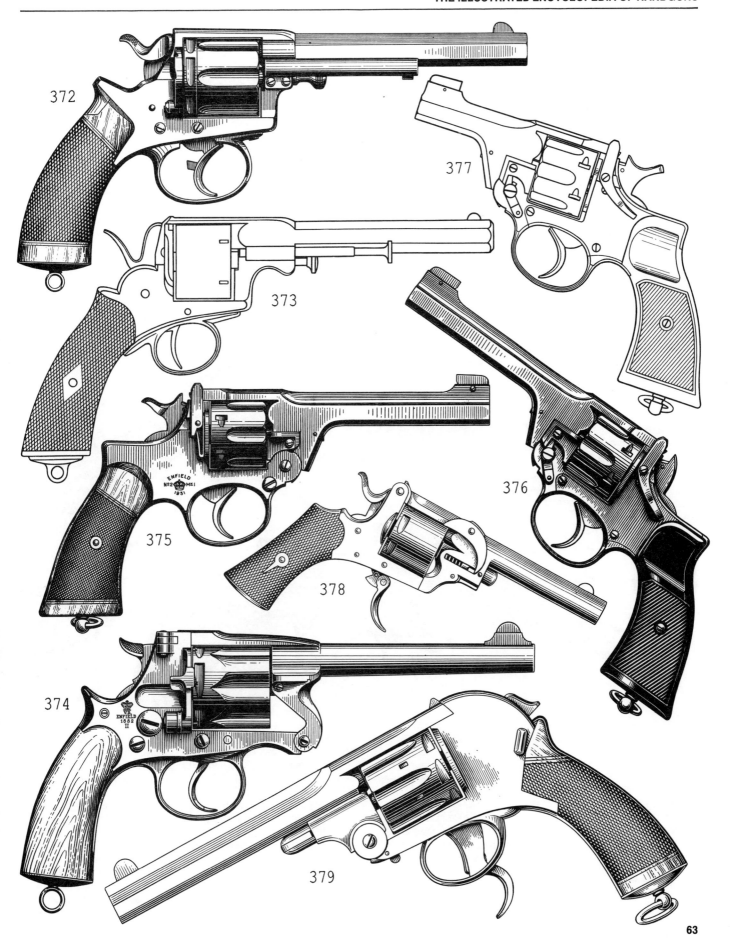

372

373

377

376

375

378

374

379

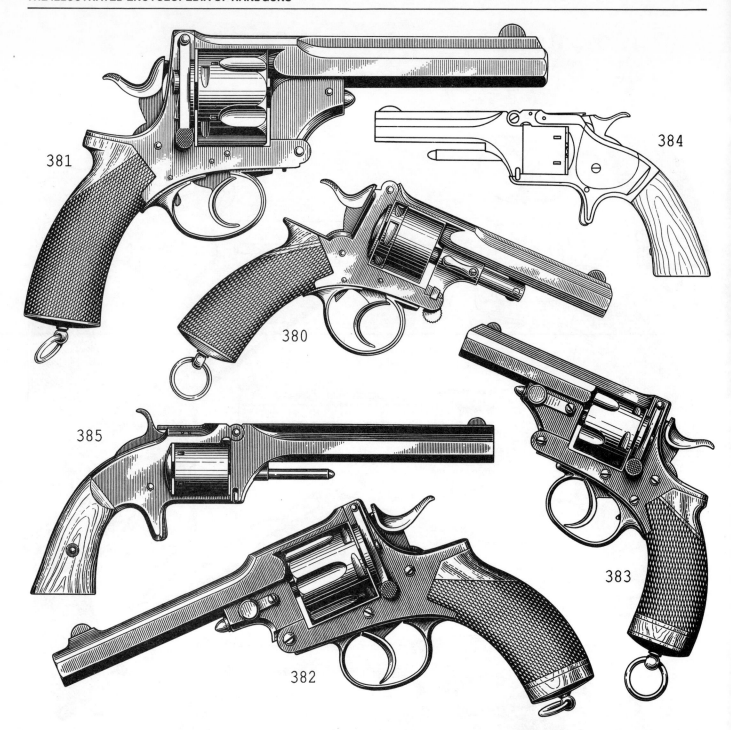

380. Maker unknown, probably in Birmingham. ·380; 4in barrel. The barrel tips upward.

381. Pryse type; Thomas Bland & Sons, London. ·577; 5·8in barrel. Five-shot. Made to the 1876 patent granted to Charles Pryse the Younger, also exploited by Webley.

382, 383. Pryse type; Philip Webley & Son (Webley & Scott Revolver & Arms Co. Ltd after 1897), Birmingham. These guns were made to patents granted to Charles Pryse the Younger in 1876, others being made elsewhere in Britain as well as in Belgium. Spent cases were ejected simultaneously in accordance with fig. 130, the breech being latched by a characteristically Francotte-type catch on each side of the frame.

384. Smith & Wesson type; John Calvert, Leeds. ·30. A copy of the S&W No. 1 (q.v.), probably made about 1863–5. The ejection system functions in accordance with fig. 125.

385. Smith & Wesson type; Philip Webley & Son, Birmingham. The very first Webley revolvers chambering self-contained cartridges were copies of S&W No.1 and No. 2 (q.v.), with upward-pivoting barrels.

386. Tranter army model; William Tranter & Company, Birmingham. ·450; 6in barrel. Six-shot. Believed to have been patented in 1879 and made in small numbers for about five years. A transverse rib on the barrel extension enters a groove across the hammer face as the latter falls, helping to secure the breech.

387. Webley-Fosbery; Webley & Scott Revolver & Arms Co. Ltd (Webley & Scott Ltd from 1906), Birmingham. ·38 or ·455; eight- or six-shot respectively. Introduced in 1896, the recoil of this 'automatic revolver' is used to propel the barrel, cylinder and upper-frame unit backward along rails in the top of the lower frame, cocking the hammer and simultaneously indexing the cylinder. Loading is effected in the same way

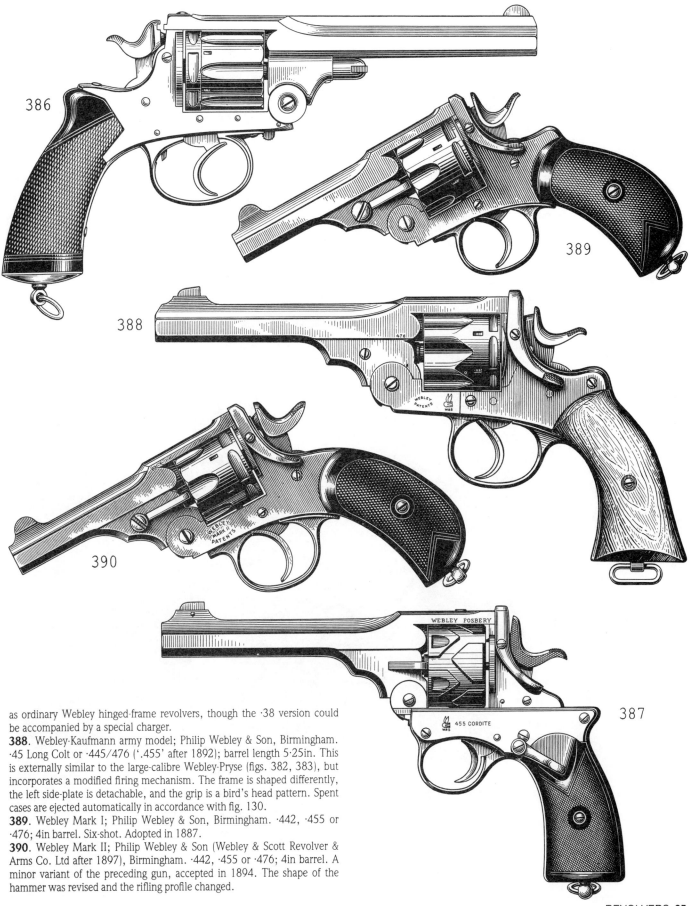

386

389

388

390

387

as ordinary Webley hinged-frame revolvers, though the ·38 version could be accompanied by a special charger.

388. Webley-Kaufmann army model; Philip Webley & Son, Birmingham. ·45 Long Colt or ·445/476 ('.455' after 1892); barrel length 5·25in. This is externally similar to the large-calibre Webley-Pryse (figs. 382, 383), but incorporates a modified firing mechanism. The frame is shaped differently, the left side-plate is detachable, and the grip is a bird's head pattern. Spent cases are ejected automatically in accordance with fig. 130.

389. Webley Mark I; Philip Webley & Son, Birmingham. ·442, ·455 or ·476; 4in barrel. Six-shot. Adopted in 1887.

390. Webley Mark II; Philip Webley & Son (Webley & Scott Revolver & Arms Co. Ltd after 1897), Birmingham. ·442, ·455 or ·476; 4in barrel. A minor variant of the preceding gun, accepted in 1894. The shape of the hammer was revised and the rifling profile changed.

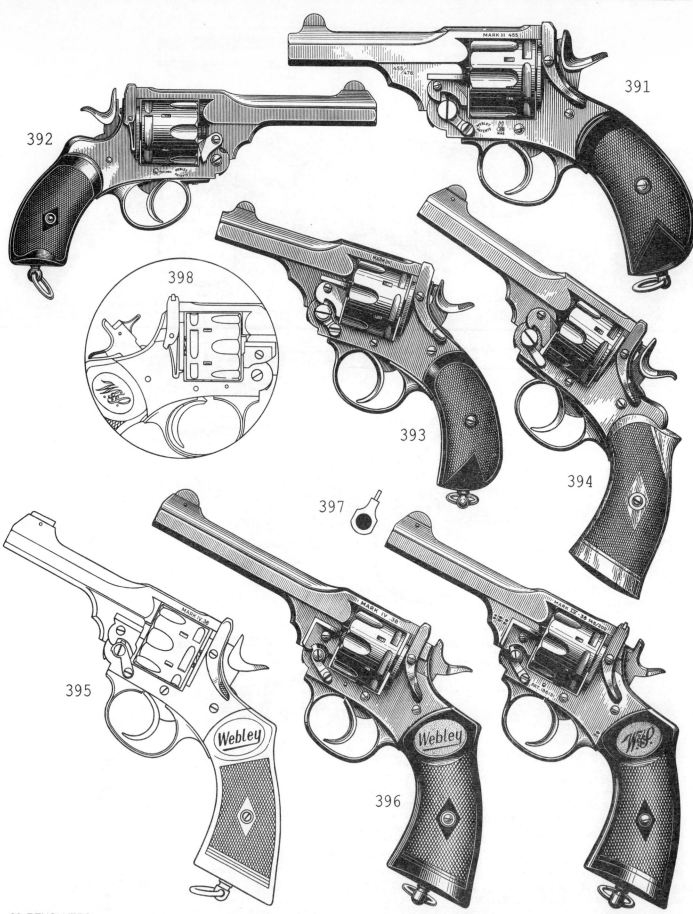

391. Webley Marks III, IV and V; Webley & Scott Revolver & Arms Co. Ltd (Webley & Scott Ltd from 1906), Birmingham. ·455; 4in barrel. Essentially similar to the preceding Mark II, the Mark III (·442, ·455 or ·476) was adopted in 1897. It was followed by the Mark IV of 1899 (·455, black powder cartridge) and, after alterations in detail, by the Mark V of 1913 (·455, cordite). During the First World War, a few Mark V Webleys were adapted to shoot rimless ·45 ACP cartridges with the assistance of half-moon clips.

392–394. Webley Mark III; Webley & Scott Revolver & Arms Co. Ltd (Webley & Scott Ltd from 1906), Birmingham. ·38. Similar to the military models, but smaller, these civilian and police revolvers were manufactured until 1945.

395–398. Webley Mark IV; Webley & Scott Ltd, Birmingham. ·38 S&W and ·38–200 Webley, interchangeably. The insert shows the Webley catch as viewed from the right.

399. Webley Mark IV, new pattern; Webley & Scott Ltd, Birmingham. ·38 S&W; 6in barrel. This differs from the 'old' Mk IV in the design of the frame—which is integral with the trigger guard—and the addition of detachable plate on the left side.

400, 401. Webley Mark IV, pocket model; Webley & Scott Ltd, Birmingham. ·32 S&W Long or ·38 S&W; 3in barrel, about 22oz. Guns of this type were still being produced in the 1970s.

402. Webley Mark VI; Webley & Scott Ltd, Birmingham. ·455; 6in barrel. Adopted in 1915, more than 300,000 of these revolvers were made during the First World War. Some were adapted for shooting ·45 ACP cartridges, requiring half-moon clips. The Mark VI remained in use throughout the Second World War alongside the ·38 Enfields and their Webley-made equivalents.

403. Webley-Wilkinson; Philip Webley & Son (Webley & Scott Revolver & Arms Co. Ltd after 1897, then Webley & Scott Ltd from 1906),

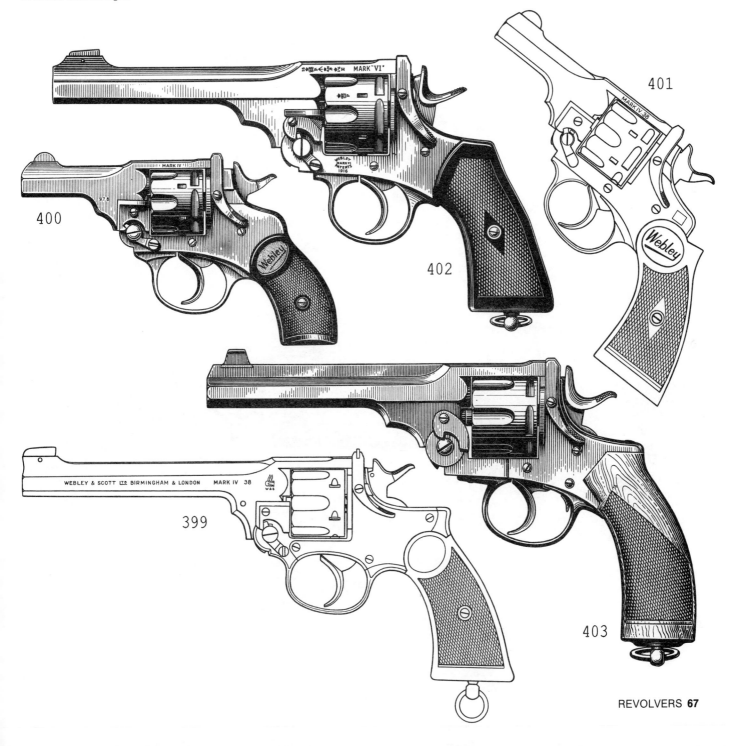

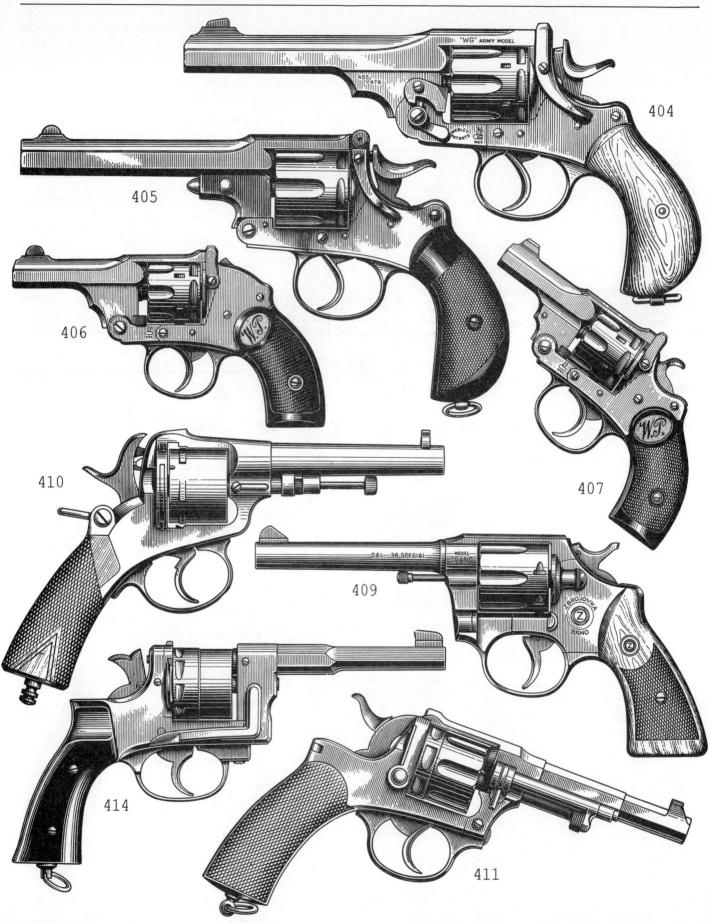

Birmingham. ·455; 6in barrel, Six-shot. Made for the Wilkinson Sword Co. Ltd of London for sale to army officers alongside Wilkinson-made edged weapons. Many differing types were made prior to the First World War.

404. W.G. (Webley-Green) army model, 1889; Philip Webley & Son, Birmingham. ·45 Long Colt or ·455/476; 11·75in overall, 6in barrel, 40oz. Six-shot. This powerful weapon was greatly favoured by British Army officers. Spent cases were ejected simultaneously in accordance with fig. 130 but—compared with the Pryse and Kaufmann patterns—the hinge, the extractor and the design of the catch were improved. Situated on the left side of the frame behind the recoil shield, the catch was a curved spring-steel stirrup. When the tip of the lever was pressed, the stirrup pivoted back and away from the barrel extension, allowing the breech to open. The system was retained for virtually all subsequent Webley revolvers.

405. W.G. (Webley-Green) target model, 1892; Philip Webley & Son, Birmingham. ·450; 13·25in overall, 7·5in barrel, 44·3oz. Six-shot. Note the bird's head butt.

406. W.P. (Webley Pocket), hammerless pattern; Webley & Scott Revolver & Arms Co. Ltd (Webley & Scott Ltd from 1906), Birmingham. ·320; 6in or 7in overall, 2in or 3in barrel, 16–18oz. Six-shot. Introduced in 1901; discontinued c.1937.

407. W.P. (Webley Pocket), new or hammer model; Webley & Scott Ltd, Birmingham. Similar to the preceding gun, apart from the exposed hammer. Introduced about 1906 and discontinued in the late 1930s.

Chile

408. FAMAE; Fabricaciones Materiales del Ejercito, Santiago. ·38 Special; 225mm overall, 82mm barrel, 630gm. Five-shot. A copy of the Colt swinging-cylinder system.

Czechoslovakia

409. ZKR-590 or Grand; Československá Zbrojovka, Brno. ·22 LR rimfire, ·357 Magnum or ·38 Special; 50mm, 100mm or 125mm barrels (·357 and ·38), or 125mm and 150mm barrels (·22). A copy of the Colt swinging-cylinder system. The Mayor (or 'Major') is virtually identical with the

long-barrelled ·22 Grand but has adjustable target-pattern sights. Production apparently ceased in the 1970s.

Denmark

410. Army officer's revolver, M1880; Haerens Tøjhus, Copenhagen. 9mm; 231mm overall, 112mm barrel, 780gm. Six-shot. Similar in many respects to the French Mle. 1873 (q.v.).

411. Army revolver, M1865/97; Kronborg Geværfabrik (originally). 11·45mm centre-fire; 270mm overal, 125mm barrel, 915gm. Six-shot. Converted from the M1865 Lefaucheux-type pinfire pattern, this could still chamber pinfire ammunition in an emergency.

France

The armed forces of France were the first to issue revolvers firing self-contained metal-case ammunition, when the Lefaucheux pinfires (q.v.) were adopted by the navy in 1857. The general design was retained for the first centre-fire pattern, accepted in 1870. French gunsmiths were most active prior to 1914, pursuing many original ideas. These included the first Velo-Dog (q.v.), developed by the Parisian gunmaker Charles Galand to capitalise on the introduction of smokeless propellant.

Open-frame designs

412. Galand, simplified model; Charles Galand & Companie, Paris and Liége. 9mm. To reload this revolver, which appeared in c.1880, the barrel/cylinder unit can be detached by pivoting the lever on the front right side of the frame downward. Spent cases can then be ejected from the chambers by the tip of the cylinder axis-pin. The firing mechanism is single action.

413. Galand, simplified model; Charles Galand & Companie, Paris & Liége. 7mm. A pocket version of the preceding gun, with a folding trigger.

414. Galand type; maker unknown, possibly Asian. 8mm Lebel. This is similar to the other simplified Galands, but is greatly improved in detail.

415. Lagieze (or 'Lagreze'), Paris. 10·9mm; 298mm overall, 159mm barrel. Made to the patents of Pidault and Cordier.

415

408

413

412

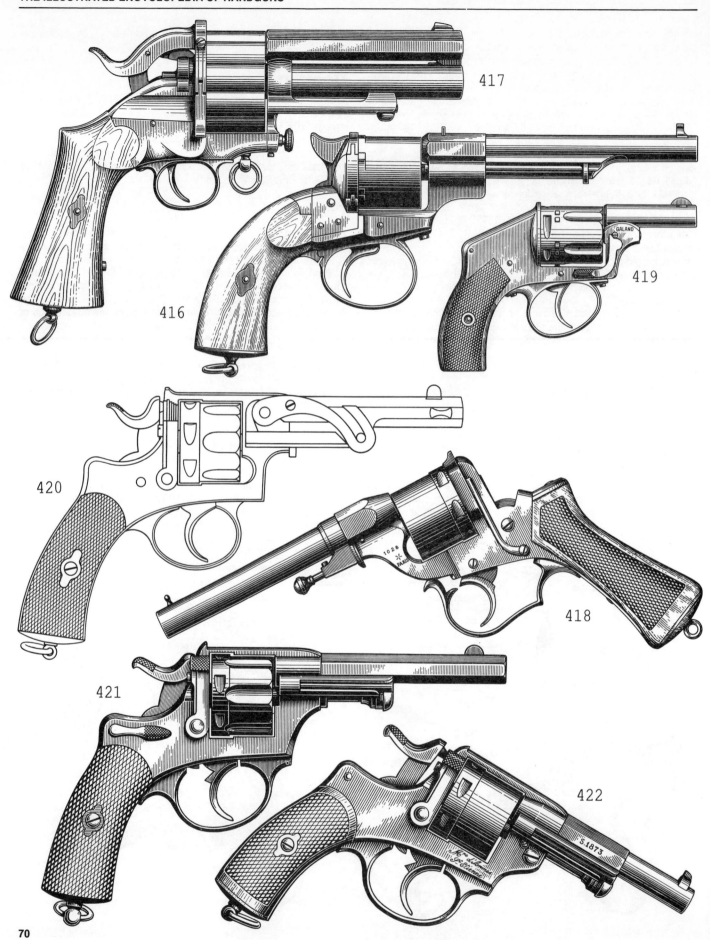

416. Lefaucheux navy revolver, M1858 T; Manufacture Impériale de Saint-Étienne. 11mm. This is a post-1873 centre-fire conversion of the original pinfire M1858 (1857–62). Single-action firing mechanism. Spent cases are ejected successively in accordance with fig. 126.

417. Le Mat; Girard & Fils, Paris. ·44 and ·65; nine-plus-one shots. This was produced on the basis of the cap-locks patented in the United States by Jean François Alexandre Le Mat in 1856–9. Patents protecting the centre-fire version were granted in 1868–9. Fed by the revolving cylinder, the upper barrel is rifled; it is accompanied by a single-shot smooth-bore barrel doubling as the cylinder axis. The firing pin on the hammer could be set to fire either barrel. Cap-lock Le Mats were made in the United States, Belgium and Britain; the later centre-fire guns were made in France or Belgium.

418. Perrin; L. Perrin & Companie, Paris. 10·4mm, ·41 rimfire or 12mm Thick Rim. Patented by Perrin and Delmas in 1859–65, these revolvers are usually distinguished by the shape of their trigger guard and their odd thick-rimmed cartridge, though pin-, rim- and centre-fire versions are known. Later guns had solid frames and spur hammers (see below).

419. Teuf-Teuf. Charles Galand & Companie, Paris and Liége. ·320, 7·65mm or 8mm Galand. A version of figs. 412 and 413 with a double-action firing mechanism.

Solid-frame designs

420. Aumond. 11mm; six-shot. A military-type revolver with a lever extractor. It is marked INVTION DE L'ESPEE AUMOND BTE, and was probably made in either Paris or Saint-Étienne.

421. Chamelot-Delvigne, 1872. 11mm. Spent cases are expelled by an ejector rod offset on the right side of the barrel, in accordance with fig. 126. The head of the ejector rod also locks the cylinder axis-pin in place.

422. Chamelot-Delvigne army revolver, M1873; Manufacture d'Armes de Saint-Étienne, 1873–85. 11mm; 240mm overall, 115mm barrel, 1225gm. Six-shot. An improved version of the M1872. The guns were often called 'Saint-Étienne' after the factory in which they were made.

423. Chamelot-Delvigne army officer's revolver, M1874; Manufacture d'Armes de Saint-Étienne, 1875–86. 11mm; 240mm overall, 115mm barrel, 1050gm. This is identical with the M1873 (q.v.), excepting for the fluted cylinder and reduced weight.

424. Galand type; probably made by Charles Galand & Companie of Paris and Liége. 11mm; six-shot.

425. L'Agent, Nagant type; Manufacture Française d'Armes et Cycles, Saint-Étienne. 8mm Lebel; five-shot.

426. Lebel-type army revolver, 1887; Manufacture d'Armes de Saint-Étienne. 8mm; 240mm overall, 118mm barrel, 900gm. Six-shot. An experimental predecessor of the better-known M1892.

427. Lebel-type army revolver, M1892; Manufacture d'Armes de Saint-Étienne. 8mm Lebel (smokeless loading); 240mm overall, 117mm barrel, 840gm. Six-shot. Popular for many years, this sturdy revolver was unloaded by opening the Abadie-type gate and swinging the cylinder out to the right, when a star-extractor could be used to expel the spent cases simultaneously. The mechanism was then closed and loaded singly through the open gate, using the trigger to turn the cylinder.

428. 'Le Brigadier Municipal', Lebel type; Manufacture Française d'Armes

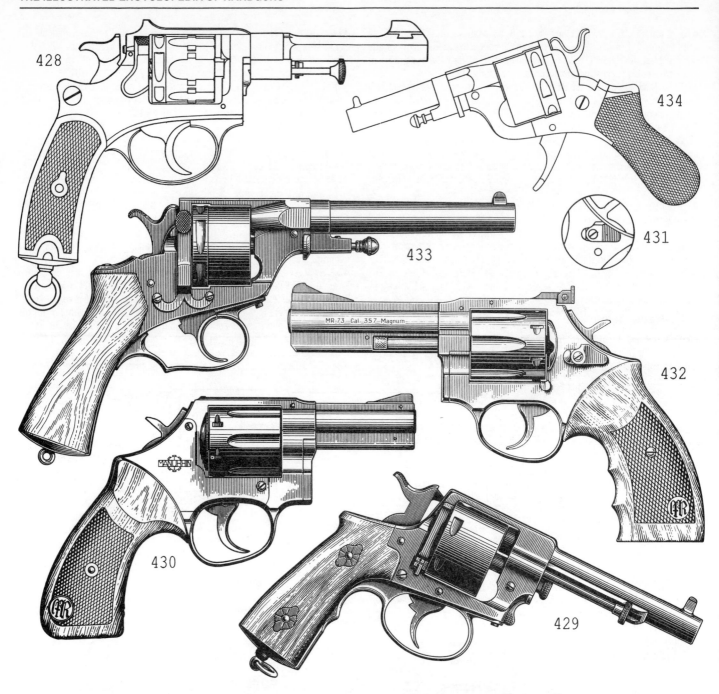

et Cycles, Saint-Étienne. 8mm Lebel; six shot. This commercially distributed gun retains the Abadie gate, but the Nagant-inspired ejector rod pivots laterally to the right when required (see fig. 126). The firing pin is mounted in the frame.

429. Lefaucheux navy revolver, M1870 N; Eugène Lefaucheux, Paris. 11mm. An improved version of the original open-frame pattern (fig. 416) with a double-action firing mechanism and a rebounding hammer.

430, 431. Manurhin MR-73, Version Police et Défense; Manurhin SA (Manufacture de Machines du Haut-Rhin), Mulhouse, 1973 to date. ·357 Magnum or 9mm Parabellum; 50mm, 75mm or 100mm barrels, 860gm, 890gm or 950gm respectively. Six-shot. This is essentially similar to the Smith & Wesson revolvers, but has a proprietary firing mechanism. An exchangeable cylinder is required to accommodate the rimless 9mm Parabellum cartridges. Long-barrel but otherwise similar revolvers are made for target shooting—e.g., MR-32 and MR-73 Sport.

432. Manurhin MR-73, Version Sport; Manurhin SA (Manufacture de

Machines du Haut-Rhin), Mulhouse, 1973 to date. ·357 Magnum; 100mm barrel. Fitted with adjustable sights.

433. Perrin; L. Perrin & Companie, Paris. 10·4mm, ·41 rimfire or 12mm Thick Rim. Originally patented by Perrin & Delmas in 1859–65, this is an improved version of the original open-frame pattern (fig. 418) with a strap extending back to the standing breech and a spurred hammer.

434. Perrin; L. Perrin & Companie, Paris. 9mm. These guns were made in small numbers, usually with folding triggers. Cartridges were distinguished by unusually thick rims and were ejected successively (see fig. 126).

435. Pocket Police Model, Nagant type; Manufacture Française d'Armes et Cycles, Saint-Étienne. 8mm Lebel; six-shot.

436. 'Réglementaire Stand', Lebel type; Manufacture Française d'Armes et Cycles, Saint-Étienne. 6mm rimfire; twelve-shot. Essentially similar to the 1892-type army revolver, this was intended for marksmanship training. It was also advertised as a self-defence weapon.

437. 'Revolver de Poche', Chamelot-Delvigne type; Manufacture

Française d'Armes et Cycles, Saint-Étienne. 7·5mm; six-shot. These French-pattern revolvers were made in large numbers in France and Belgium during the late nineteenth and early twentieth centuries.

438. 'Revolver de Poche', Lebel type; Manufacture Française d'Armes et Cycles, Saint-Étienne. 7·65mm; six-shot. A variant with a folding trigger was also made.

439. RMR Special Police; Manurhin SA (Manufacture de Machines du Haut-Rhin), Mulhouse. ·357 and 9mm Parabellum (exchangeable cylinders); 75mm barrel, 940gm. Introduced in 1981, this police model is based on the Ruger Speed Six (q.v.). It was replaced in 1984 by the MR-F1 Special Police.

440. 'Saint-Etienne', Lebel type; probably made by Manufacture Française d'Armes & Cycles of Saint-Étienne.

441. Verney-Carron Frères, Saint-Étienne and Paris. ·320; six-shot.

Hinged, pivoting and other frame designs

442. Devisme; J.-B. Devisme, Paris. 11mm; six-shot. Single action. The barrel/cylinder unit (patented in France in 1869) tips downward around a transverse pivot ahead of the trigger-guard when the latch on the frame-front is released. This also tips the barrel sideways until the ejector rod can enter a chamber. Returning the lever aligns the cylinder and barrel, then locks the breech.

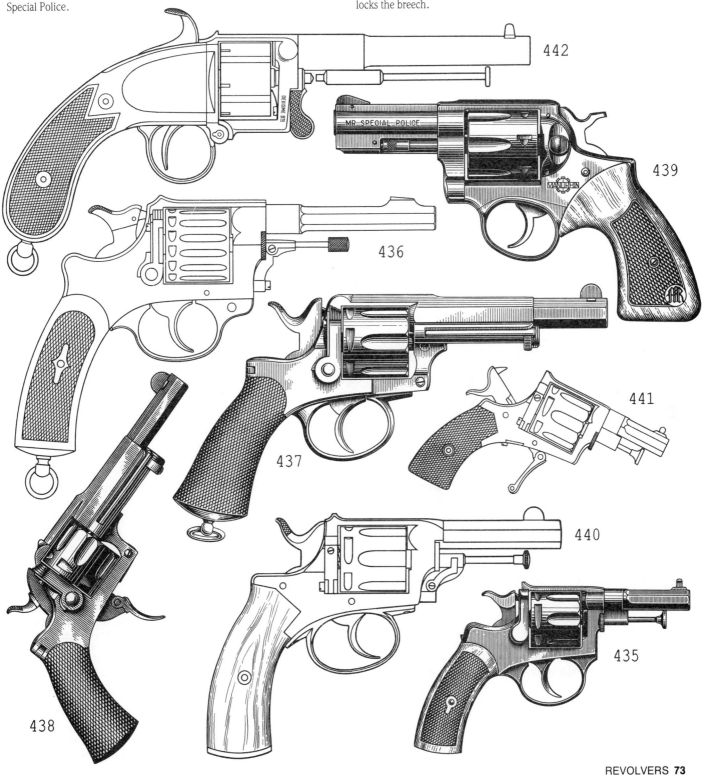

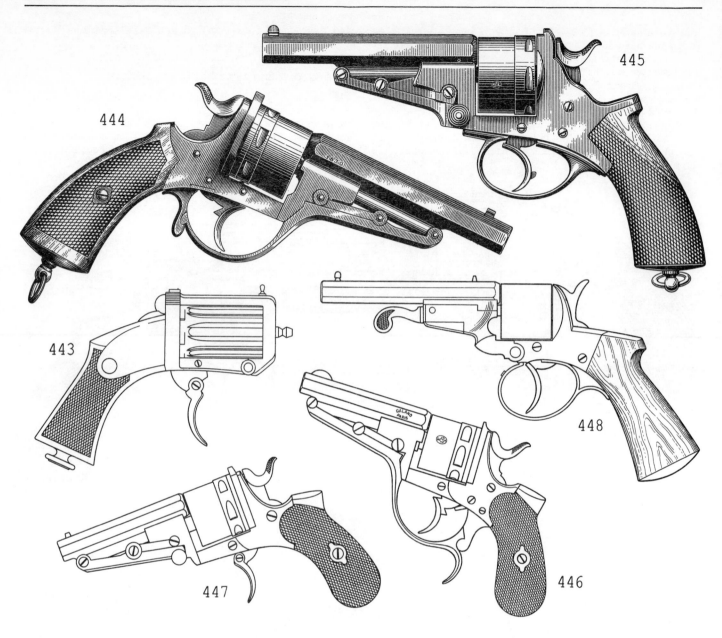

443. Devisme; J.-B. Devisme, Paris. 7·65mm. Typically pepperbox-type construction. The barrel unit tips up and forward when the latch is released.

444. Galand, 1870 type; Charles Galand & Companie, Paris and Liége. 12mm. This system was patented by Galand and Sommerville in 1868. When the lever doubling as a trigger guard is pulled downward, the barrel/cylinder unit slides forward along the cylinder-axis pin (which is fixed in the standing breech) in accordance with fig. 128. This allows a disc-like extractor to pull all the spent cases from the cylinder simultaneously, until they fall free. Most Galand auto-extracting revolvers have special ratchet-pattern rifling.

445. Galand, improved type; Charles Galand & Companie, Paris and Liége. Guns of this pattern were usually made in Belgium. This is a later version with a conventional trigger guard and a shortened actuating lever.

446. Galand pocket revolver; Charles Galand & Companie, Paris and Liége. ·32; six-shot. Note that the gun is marked GALAND. PARIS, but bears Liége proofmarks on the cylinder. The actuating lever is combined with the trigger guard.

447. Galand pocket revolver; Charles Galand & Companie, Paris and Liége. ·32; six-shot. Similar to fig. 446, but with a shorter actuating lever and a folding trigger.

448. Javelle, Saint-Étienne. 9mm; six-shot. This pocket revolver is opened by turning the lever beneath the barrel laterally and then tipping the barrel/cylinder unit downward.

Germany

The rapid development and burgeoning distribution of the revolver had little effect on Germany, which was still a multitude of separate kingdoms, principalities and duchies in the 1860s. The manufacture of firearms—even in Suhl, its traditional centre—was hamstrung by the low levels of industrialisation. The first indigenous military, police and self-defence revolvers appeared only after the Franco-Prussian war of 1870–1 and the formation of the Deutsches Reich (German empire).

Prior to 1870, differing revolvers had been popular in individual states—Adams-type and Stahl cap-locks, Dreyse (Kufahl) and Wagner needle-revolvers, Lefaucheux-type Jung pinfires, and adaptions of the Austro-Hungarian Gasser.

Manufacture of military revolvers ceased when the Parabellum (Luger) pistol was adopted by the army in 1908. However, production of police and personal-defence revolvers continued until 1918, and then recommenced in the early 1920s even though the comparatively small-scale indigenous production was often supplemented by guns imported from Spain and the USA. Revolvers are still being made.

Guns produced in Germany prior to 1939 included many imitations of Lefaucheux and Smith & Wesson designs, in addition to a wide assortment of Bulldogs and Velo-Dogs. These are described in the relevant sections.

After the end of the Second World War, Weihrauch of Mellrichstadt began to make the first of an extensive range of revolvers marketed either as 'H.W.' or 'Arminius', the pre-1945 owner of the latter brand name, Friedrich Pickert of Zella-Mehlis, having ceased trading. Many pre-1945 Pickert Arminius revolvers were Velo-Dog (q.v.) patterns.

Pre-1945. Solid-frame designs

449, 450. Decker; Walter Decker, Zella St Blasii. 6·35mm Auto; six-shot. Patented in Britain in 1912, this double-action pocket revolver was an original design. The trigger lies under the barrel, at the end of the rod which runs back inside the frame beneath the cylinder. The backward movement of the rod indexes the cylinder, cocks and then releases the striker. Spent cases are ejected sequentially by a rod carried separately. A

safety lever will be found on the left side of the frame. The Decker revolver is very convenient to hold, but a special shield on the right side of the frame was necessary; owing to the shape of the grip and the unusual position of the trigger, the base of the index finger would otherwise interfere with the cylinder.

451, 452. Dreyse; Waffenfabrik Franz von Dreyse, Sömmerda. 10·6mm; six-shot. Said to date from c.1890–3, this double-action enclosed hammer revolver shares some of the constructional features (e.g., the barrel) of the Reichsrevolver of 1883. A safety lever on the left side of the frame can be used to hold the hammer at full-cock, whilst the cylinder moves forward on firing to improve obturation.

453. Geco; Gustav Genschow & Co. ·38; six-shot. A good-quality copy of the Colt swinging-cylinder system made, possibly in Spain, in a selection of chamberings and sizes. Smith & Wesson imitations were also available.

454. Haenel; C.G. Haenel, Suhl. 9mm; six-shot. This combines features of the Nagant system and Reichsrevolvers. Ejection is performed sequentially, in accordance with fig. 126.

455, 456. Mauser; Gebrüder Mauser & Co., Oberndorf. 11mm; six-shot. Single action, solid frame; sequential ejection in accordance with fig. 126.

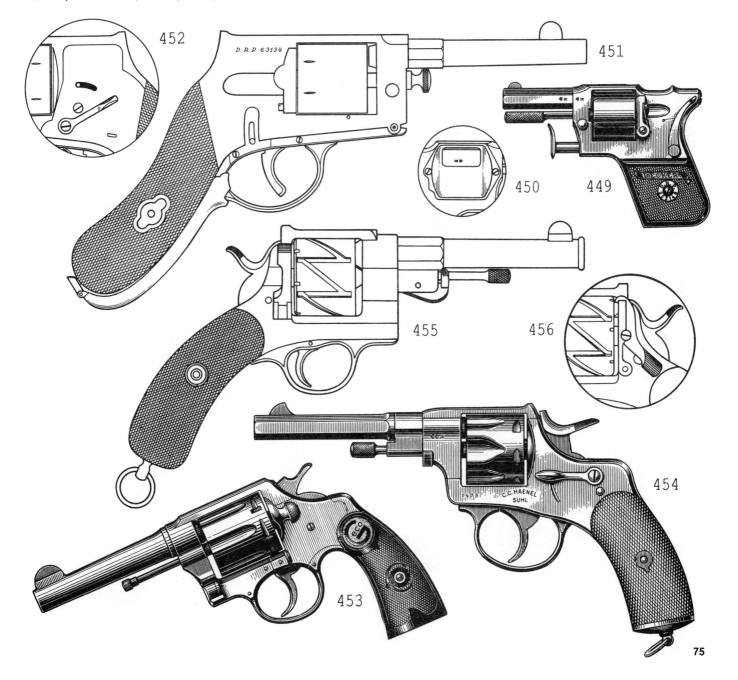

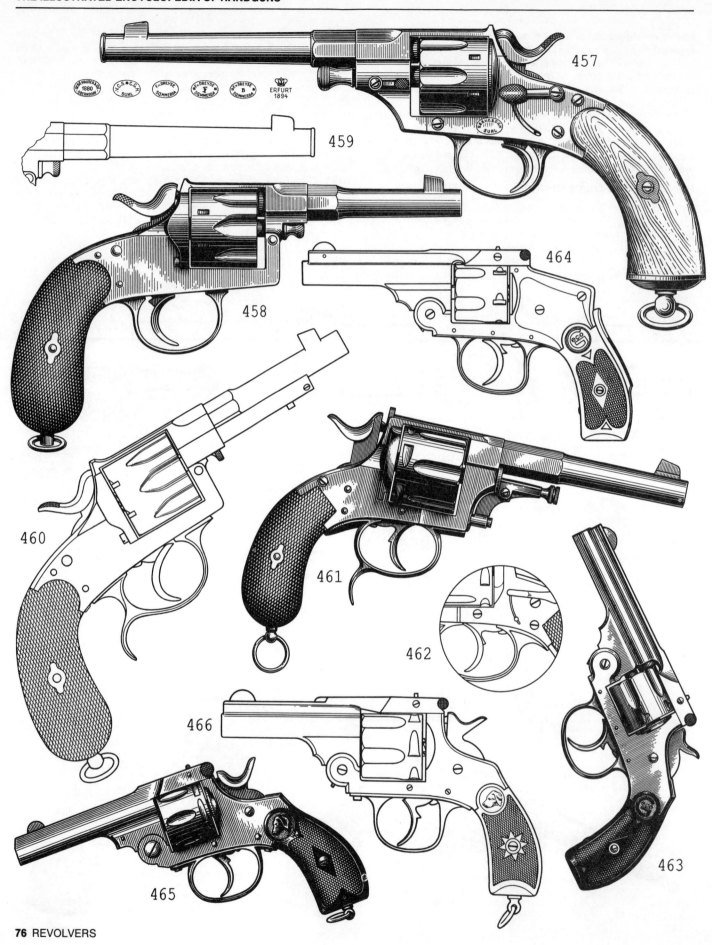

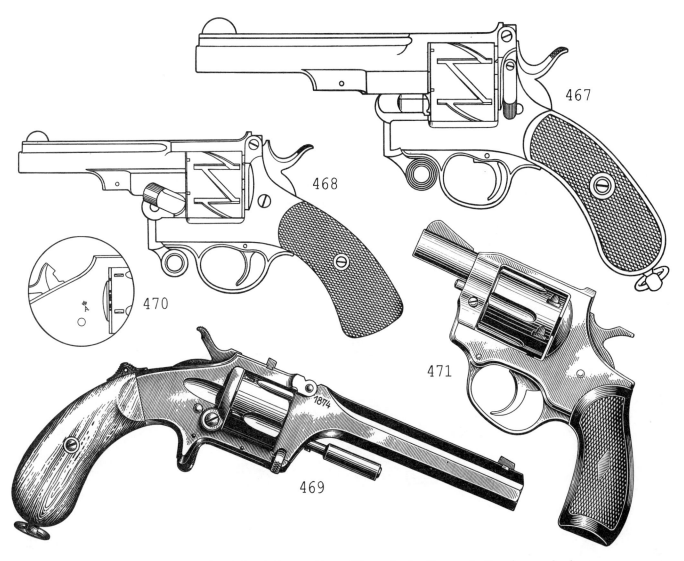

7mm- and 9mm-calibre versions were also produced, though the quantities involved were small.

457. Reichsrevolver M1879. 10·6mm; 340mm overall, 182mm barrel, 1310gm. Single action, no ejection system; a radial safety lever lies on the left side of the frame beneath the hammer. The guns were made by the Prussian government arsenal in Erfurt, by Mauser, by the Dreyse factory in Sömmerda, and by a selection of private manufacturers in Thuringia—Schilling, Haenel and Sauer.

458, 459. Reichsrevolver M1879/83 or M1883. 10·6mm; 255mm overall, 118mm, 950gm. This was a short version of the M1879, intended for infantry and dismounted units. Variations are occasionally encountered with 174mm barrels, which give an overall length of about 311mm and a weight of 1025gm.

460. Reichsrevolver M1879/83; Waffenfabrik Franz von Dreyse, Sömmerda. 10·6mm. This is a modified version of the standard military pattern, intended for commercial sale; many were acquired by army officers, as they chambered the standard military cartridge. Some guns will be found with double-action firing systems and others have ejector rods on the right side of the barrel. Similar models were also made in Belgium.

461, 462. Reichsrevolver type; Karl Burgsmüller, Kreiensen. 10·6mm; six-shot. Made about 1890, this is basically a modified 1879/83 Reichsrevolver intended for commercial sale. The extractor pivots laterally when required, but normally locks into the tip of the cylinder axis-pin; the firing mechanism is double action; and the radius of the grip has been tightened to improve handling qualities. Many guns of this type were purchased by army officers.

Hinged, pivoting and other frame designs

463. Geco; Gustav Genschow & Companie. ·32; five-shot. A Smith & Wesson-type gun probably made in Spain in the 1920s.

464. Geco; Gustav Genschow & Companie. Similar to the preceding gun, but with an enclosed hammer.

465. Maker unknown, German proofmarks. ·32; six-shot.

466. Maker unknown, German proofmarks. ·38; five-shot. Another of the many Smith & Wesson copies.

467, 468. Mauser; Gebrüder Mauser & Co. (Waffenfabrik Mauser AG after 1884), Oberndorf. 7mm, 9mm or 10·6mm. Patented in Germany in 1878, the barrel of this single-action gun opens upward to allow spent cases to be ejected simultaneously in accordance with fig. 127. The coil-type main spring lies in the lower front part of the frame. The spring acts on a block which moves forward directly under the cylinder. The block is in turn connected with the hammer; when the latter is being cocked, the block moves forward to compress the main spring and revolve the cylinder.

469, 470. Smith & Wesson type, M1873 and M1874. 10·75mm (rim-, later centre-fire); 140mm barrel. Five-shot. Issued to the Saxon army, this is a copy of the Smith & Wesson No. 2 with improvements—e.g., a safety catch was added behind the hammer and a lanyard ring to the butt. The 1874 pattern had a fluted cylinder, a better-shaped hammer, an improved grip, and (ultimately) a hinged loading gate.

Post-1945. Solid-frame designs

471. Arminius FIE; Hermann Weihrauch KG, Mellrichstadt. ·22 LR rimfire, ·22 Magnum rimfire or ·38 Special; 51mm or 102mm barrel, 710–850gm. Made for FIE, Inc (Firearms Import–Export, Inc.) of Miami and Hialeah, Florida.

472. Arminius HW-3; Hermann Weihrauch KG, Mellrichstadt. ·22 LR rimfire, ·22 Magnum rimfire or ·32 S&W Long; 178mm overall, 70mm barrel, 700gm. Seven-shot (·32) or eight-shot (·22). These revolvers have swing-out cylinders latched by a sleeve, coaxial with the ejector rod, which can be pulled forward to release the cylinder yoke. Most guns have streamlined frames and ventilated barrel ribs.

The Arminius HW-5 is similar to the HW-3, but has a longer barrel and a larger grip. It is 220mm overall, has a 100mm barrel and weighs 750gm. HW-7S and HW-9 are ·22 rimfire target models with longer barrels, adjustable sights, and better grips.

The Arminius HW-68 (170mm overall, 64mm barrel) is much like the HW-3, excepting that the butt is squared and the back sight does not protrude. The frame is aluminium alloy instead of steel. The ·22 LR rimfire version has an eight-cartridge cylinder, whilst the ·22 Magnum rimfire and ·32 S&W Long patterns are seven-shot.

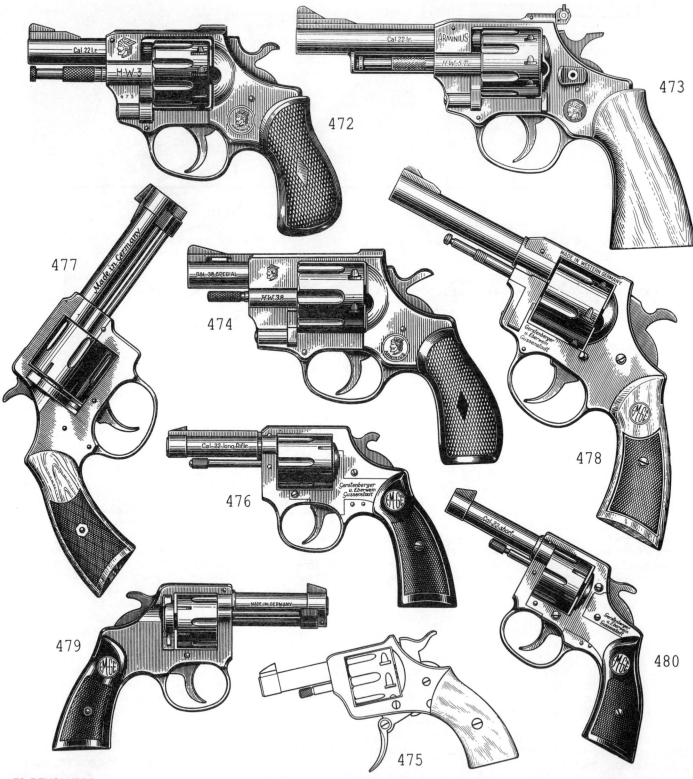

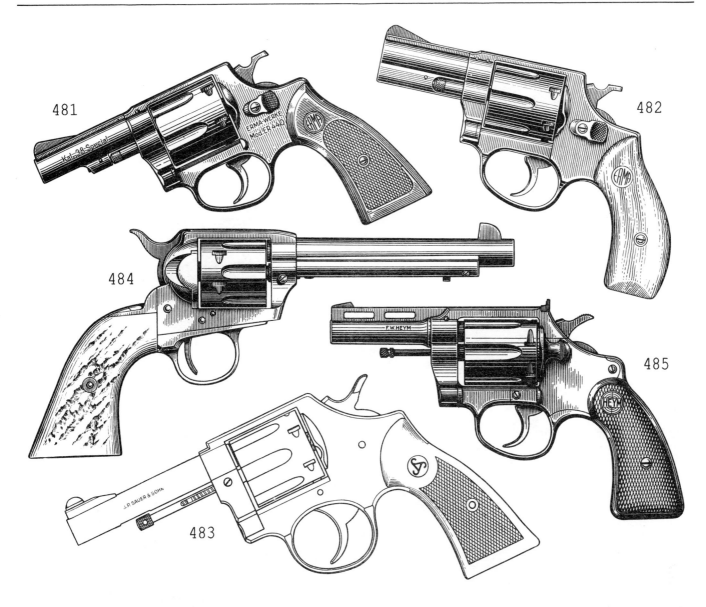

The HW-357 (·357 Magnum, six-shot) is the most powerful of the series, with a steel frame, a 100mm barrel and a larger grip.

473. Arminius HW5T; Hermann Weihrauch KG, Mellrichstadt. ·22 LR rimfire, ·22 Magnum rimfire or ·32 S&W; 102mm barrel. Eight (·22) or seven (·32) shots.

474. Arminius HW-38; Hermann Weihrauch KG, Mellrichstadt. ·38 Special; 180mm or 225mm overall, 63·5mm or 100mm barrel, 765gm or 875gm. The grip of the longer-barrelled version is customarily like that of the HW-5.

475. Chicago Cub or Recky; Karl Arndt Reck Sportwaffenfabrik KG, Lauf bei Nürnberg. ·22 Short rimfire; 135mm overall, 51mm barrel. No ejection system is fitted.

476. Em-Ge Model 200-KS; Gerstenberger & Eberwein (Em-Ge Sportgeräte GmbH & Co. KG), Gerstetten-Gussenstadt. ·22 LR rimfire; 63–150mm barrel, 410–473gm.

477. Em-Ge Model 32-KS; Gerstenberger & Eberwein (Em-Ge Sportgeräte GmbH & Co. KG), Gerstetten-Gussenstadt. ·32 S&W Long; 63–150mm barrel, 530–587gm. Sequential ejection in accordance with fig. 126.

478. Em-Ge Models 223 and 323; Gerstenberger & Eberwein (Em-Ge Sportgeräte GmbH & Co. KG), Gerstetten-Gussenstadt. ·22 LR rimfire or ·32 S&W Long; 76mm, 102mm or 152mm barrel. Simultaneous ejection (fig. 131).

479, 480. Em-Ge Model 22-KS; Gerstenberger & Eberwein (Em-Ge Sportgeräte GmbH & Co. KG), Gerstetten-Gussenstadt. ·22 Short rimfire; 63–150mm barrels, 350–413gm. The ·22 Flobert Model 220-FL is similar, but fitted with an ejector. Its barrel meaures 63mm or 100mm.

481. Erma-Revolver Model 440 (ER-440); Erma-Werke GmbH, München-Dachau. ·38 Special; 51mm or 76mm barrels, 550gm or 570gm. Five-shot. The near-identical six-shot ·22 LR rimfire ER-423 has an 86mm barrel and weighs 615gm. Simultaneous ejection in accordance with fig. 131.

482. Erma-Revolver Model 442 (ER-442); Erma-Werke GmbH, München-Dachau. ·22 LR rimfire or ·22 Magnum rimfire (exchangeable cylinders). Made of stainless steel.

483. Ferteidigungsrevolver Model 4 (FR-4); J.P. Sauer & Sohn GmbH, Eckenförde/Holstein. Similar to the TR-6 pattern (fig. 506), but chambered for ·22 LR rimfire or ·38 Special ammunition; 75mm, 100mm or 150mm barrel, 1000gm (150mm barrel).

484. Frontier or Western Model 2/59; J.P. Sauer & Sohn GmbH, Eckenförde/Holstein. ·22 LR rimfire or ·22 Magnum rimfire; 140mm barrel, 1100gm. Copied from the Colt Peacemaker, this gun has exchangeable cylinders. Model 2/61 is identical, but chambered for ·357 Magnum, ·44 Magnum or ·45 Colt, and fitted with a 165mm barrel. Model 2/64 is simply a Model 2/61 with adjustable sights.

485. Heym; Friedr. Wilh. Heym GmbH & Co. KG, Münnerstadt. ·22 LR rimfire, ·22 Magnum rimfire or ·38 Special; 50mm, 75mm or 100mm barrel, 700gm, 740gm and 780gm respectively.

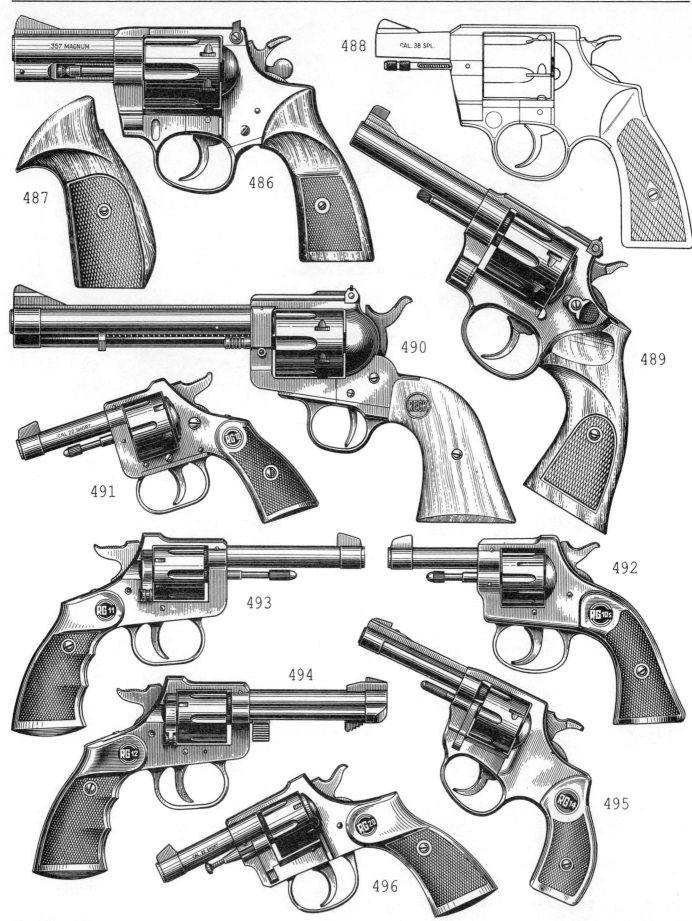

486, 487. Korth-Combat, 1972 pattern; W. Korth GmbH, Ratzeburg/Holstein. ·357 Magnum; 76mm barrel, 950gm. Six-shot. These guns have a distinctive latch, to the right of the hammer, which is pushed forward to release the cylinder yoke. In addition to short-barrelled personal defence weapons, Korth revolvers include target models with ventilated ribs, improved sights and special grips. The guns are renowned for their excellent quality.

488. Korth-Revolver; W. Korth GmbH, Ratzeburg/Holstein. ·38 Special. Introduced in 1965, these police-type revolvers had a simplified cylinder latch doubling as an ejector rod.

489. Reck R-15; Karl Arndt Reck Sportwaffenfabrik KG, Lauf bei Nürnberg. 5mm Flobert, ·22 LR rimfire, ·22 Magnum rimfire, ·32 S&W or ·38 Special; 63mm, 100mm or 150mm barrel. Simultaneous ejection in accordance with fig. 131.

490. Reck R-18; Karl Arndt Reck Sportwaffenfabrik KG, Lauf bei Nürnberg. ·357 Magnum, ·38 Special or 9mm Parabellum; 150mm barrel. A near-facsimile of the Colt Peacemaker.

491. Röhm RG-10; Röhm GmbH, Sontheim an der Brenz. ·22 Short rimfire; 155mm overall, 63mm barrel, 330gm. A typically inexpensive design, lacking an ejection system.

492. Röhm RG-10S; Röhm GmbH, Sontheim an der Brenz. ·22 Short rimfire; 170mm overall, 63mm barrel.

493. Röhm RG-11; Röhm GmbH, Sontheim an der Brenz. ·22 LR rimfire; 210mm overall, 93mm barrel.

494. Röhm RG-12; Röhm GmbH, Sontheim an der Brenz. ·22 LR rimfire; 210mm overall, 92mm barrel, 460gm. A variant of the RG-11 with a rod ejector similar to that of the Colt Peacemaker.

495. Röhm RG-14; Röhm GmbH, Sontheim an der Brenz. ·22 LR rimfire; 175mm overall, 78mm barrel, 450gm. Simultaneous ejection.

496. Röhm RG-20; Röhm GmbH, Sontheim an der Brenz. ·22 Short rimfire; 170mm overall, 63mm barrel, 420gm. Sequential case ejection.

497. Röhm RG-23; Röhm GmbH, Sontheim an der Brenz. ·22 LR rimfire; 190mm overall, 89mm barrel, 480gm.

498. Röhm RG-24; Röhm GmbH, Sontheim an der Brenz. ·22 LR rimfire; 210mm overall, 92mm barrel, 550gm.

499. Röhm RG-30; Röhm GmbH, Sontheim an der Brenz. ·22 LR rimfire and ·32 S&W. A typical swinging-cylinder design.

500, 501. Röhm RG-34; Röhm GmbH, Sontheim an der Brenz. ·22 LR rimfire; six-shot. The RG-35 is similar, but the cylinder holds eight rounds; the RG-36 is available in ·32 S&W only. Distinguished by a ventilated rib above the barrel (see fig. 501), the ·38 Special RG-38 can be obtained with barrels of 53mm, 89mm or 102mm, and weighs 860–960gm.

502. Röhm RG-57; Röhm GmbH, Sontheim an der Brenz. ·357 Magnum; 102mm barrel, 1250gm.

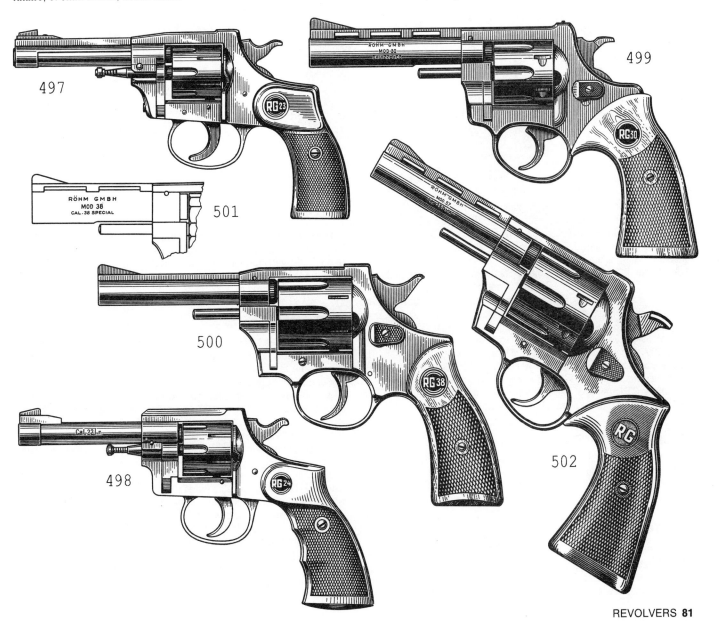

503. Röhm RG-63; Röhm GmbH, Sontheim an der Brenz. ·22 LR rimfire, ·22 Magnum rimfire, ·32 Short, ·32 Long or ·38 Special; 127mm barrel. Five-, six- or eight-shot (·22 LR, ·22 Magnum/·32 and ·38 respectively). This revolver resembles the Colt Peacemaker externally, but embodies a double-action firing mechanism.

504. Röhm RG-66M; Röhm GmbH, Sontheim an der Brenz. ·22 LR rimfire or ·22 Magnum rimfire; 120mm barrel. Six-shot. Based on the Colt Peacemaker. The 'Liberty Mustang' was a similar ·22 LR gun with an eight-cartridge cylinder, a 127mm barrel and smooth walnut grips.

505. Röhm RG-88; Röhm GmbH, Sontheim an der Brenz. ·357 Magnum; six-shot. Spent cases are ejected simultaneously in accord with fig. 131.

506, 507. Taschenrevolver Model 6 (TR-6); J.P. Sauer & Sohn GmbH, Eckenförde/Holstein. ·38 Special; 100mm barrel, 560gm. Based on the swinging-cylinder Smith & Wesson. Also made with a 50mm barrel.

Not shown. Facsimiles of the Colt Peacemaker revolvers are also made by H. Schmidt GmbH of Ostheim/Rhön as the Model 21 (·22 LR rimfire) and Model 121 (·357 Magnum).

Hinged-frame design

508, 509. Model MS or 'M & S'; Mayer & Söhne, Arnsberg. ·22 LR rimfire or ·22 Magnum, 7·65mm Auto or ·32 S&W Long; 170mm or 195mm overall, 75mm or 100mm barrel, 680–780gm. The barrel tips downward, ejecting spent cases automatically in accordance with fig. 130.

Israel

510. Military Model; Israeli Military Industries ('IMI'), Ramat ha-Sharon. 9mm Parabellum. Dating from the 1950s, this copy of the swinging-cylinder Smith & Wesson Model 10 Military & Police revolver shoots rimless cartridges with the assistance of two three-round half-moon clips.

Italy

Revolvers of the Smith & Wesson hinged-frame system were made in Spain for the Italian armed forces during the First World War (fig. 600). In addition, gunsmiths in the major production centres of Brescia and Gardone Val Trompia have copied swinging-cylinder Colts and Smith & Wessons.

Solid-frame patterns

511, 512. Bodeo type; maker unknown. 10·35mm. A distinctive pocket revolver with an enclosed hammer, this incorporates a Bodeo-type firing mechanism. Extraction is sequential, and a radial safety lever lies on the left side of the frame (fig. 512).

513. Bodeo type; maker unknown. 7·65mm. Marked BREVETTO BASTON BODEO, this gun has a distinctively shrouded hammer, an improved ejector mechanism, and a safety lever on the left side of the frame. It is said to have equipped the Neapolitan national guard.

514–516. Nuovo-Revolver; Fabbrica d'Armi Vincenzo Bernardelli SpA, Brescia. ·32 Long Colt; 50mm, 63mm, 110mm and 150mm barrels, 490–565gm. Production of these guns started in the early 1950s, an improved 'Nuovo' form being introduced in 1958 with a trigger-bar safety system. Manufacture continues as the 'VB-Revolver', in standard target (MR) and pocket (Tascabile) versions.

517. RF-83 Service Model; Luigi Franchi SpA, Fornaci/Brescia. ·38 Special. Standard models have 63mm, 75mm or 100mm barrels and full-length ejector-rod shrouds; Target and Super Target models have barrels of 100mm or 150mm respectively, adjustable sights, and ventilated ribs. The RF-83 is simply good-quality copy of the standard Colt swinging-cylinder system.

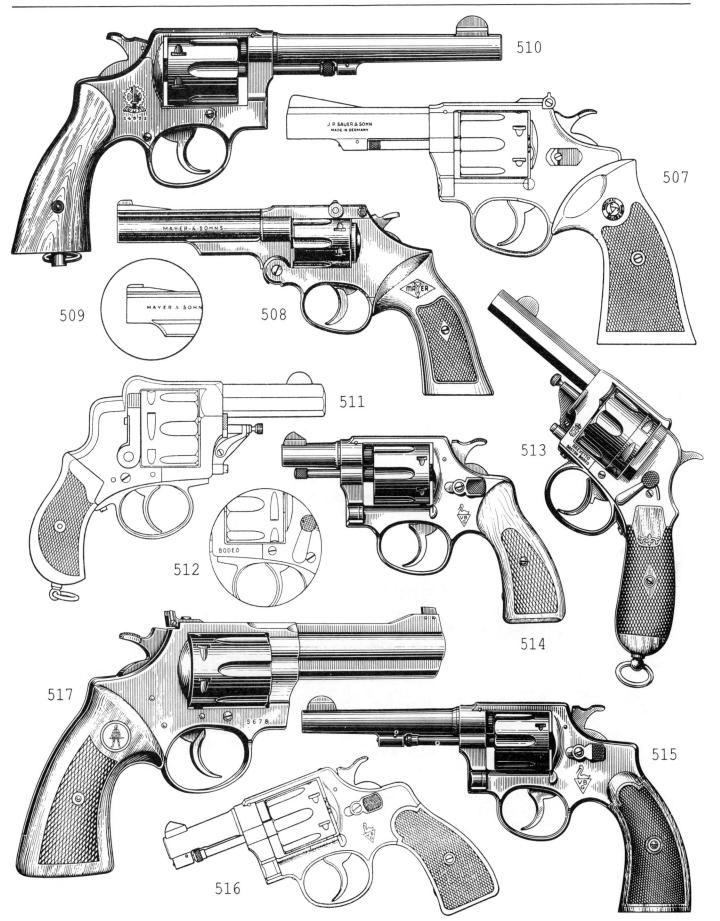

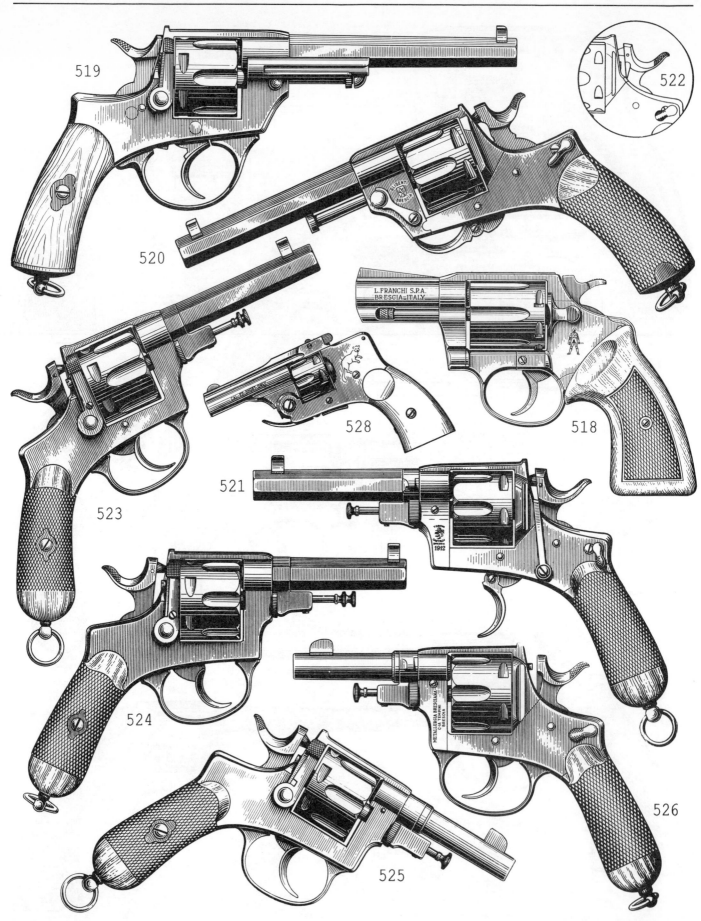

518. RF-83 Compact (or, alternatively, 'Extra Small'); Luigi Franchi SpA, Fornaci/Brescia. ·38 Special; 50mm barrel.

519. Service revolver, Chamelot-Delvigne type, M1872; Pirlot Frères, Liége 10·35mm; 280mm overall, 160mm barrel, 1110gm. This is similar to the M1872/78 Swiss pattern (fig. 612). Minor variants were subsequently made by the state arsenal (Reale Fabbrica d'Armi) and Società Siderugica Glisenti in Brescia, possibly as the 'M1874'.

520. Service revolver, Chamelot-Delvigne type, M1886; Società Siderugica Glisenti, Brescia. 10·35mm. This differs from the previous pattern largely in the substitution of a folding trigger for the conventional trigger and guard. It is said to have been issued to NCOs and enlisted men from 1888 onward.

521–523. Service revolver, Bodeo type, M1889; Società Siderugica Glisenti, Brescia, and others. 10·35mm; 235mm overall, 115mm barrel, 880 and 850gm respectively. Issued from 1891 onward, this was a simplified version of the original Italian Chamelot-Delvigne army revolvers credited to technician Carlo Bodeo of the Brescia arms factory, though now widely known as 'Glisenti' after the principal manufacturer. Officer's revolvers had a conventional trigger guard; those destined for NCOs and enlisted men had a folding trigger. The earliest guns had an external hammer-block bar on the left side of the frame (fig. 521), but this was later substituted by an internal pattern (fig. 522). Spent cases were expelled sequentially by a rod beneath the barrel, which could be swung laterally on a Nagant-type yoke and retracted into the cylinder-axis pin when not required. An Abadie-type loading gate was also used. The barrel was octahedral, whilst the distinctive grip was unofficially called a "lamb's foot". The revolvers were made by several contractors, including Castelli and Società Metallurgica Bresciana gia Tempini.

524. Service revolver, Bodeo type, M1889. The last officer's revolvers made before 1918 had a 95mm barrel.

525, 526. Service revolver, Bodeo type, M1889; Società Metallurgica Bresciana gia Tempini, Brescia. 10·35mm; 85mm barrel. Production of M1889 revolvers resumed in the early 1920s. In c.1923, however, a new version appeared with a short round barrel and a separate firing-pin mounted in the frame. These guns are known as 'Modern' or 'Tempini' patterns, after the principal manufacturer. They were made until 1927.

527. Trident; Armi Renato Gamba SpA, Gardone Val Trompia. ·38 Special; 63mm (Trident) or 100mm barrel (Trident Super). A copy of the ubiquitous Colt swinging-cylinder system.

Hinged-frame pattern

528. Sable; Pietro Beretta SpA, Gardone Val Trompia. ·22 Short; six-shot. A folding-trigger pocket revolver produced shortly after the end of the Second World War.

Japan

Solid-frame patterns

529. Miroku pocket model; Miroku Firearms Manufacturing Company, Kochi. ·38 Special; five-shot. A copy of the Colt swinging-cylinder design.

530. Miroku police model; Miroku Firearms Manufacturing Company, Kochi. ·38 Special; six-shot. A Colt copy.

531. New Nambu Model 58; Shin Chuo Kogyo KK, Tokyo. ·38 Special; 170mm overall, 50mm barrel, about 625gm. Five-shot. An imitation of the Smith & Wesson swinging-cylinder system (fig. 131).

532. New Nambu Type 60; Shin Chuo Kogyo KK, Tokyo. ·38 Special; 197mm overall, 75mm barrel, 680gm. Five-shot. Adopted by the Japanese police and coast guard, this is similar to the Model 58 but has a lanyard ring on the butt and better grips.

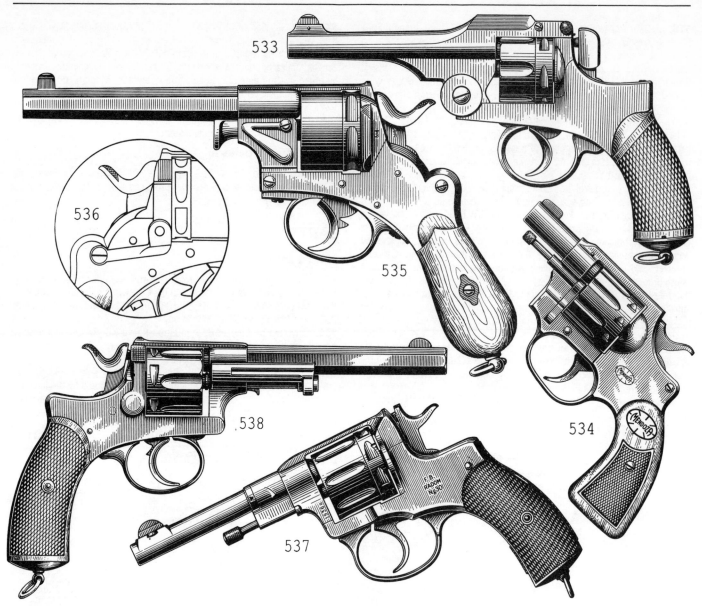

Hinged-frame pattern

533. Meiji 26th Year Type; imperial artillery arsenal, Koishikawa, Tokyo, 1894–1935. 9mm; 230mm overall, 120mm barrel, 935gm. Six-shot. Designed in the 26th year of the reign of the emperor Meiji (1893), though not adopted until 1894, the firing mechanism of this interesting weapon is double-action only. Spent cases are extracted simultaneously as the revolver is opened and the barrel tips downward. The plate on the left side of the frame can be unlatched by pulling down on the trigger guard, then swung laterally around a vertical axis above the grip. A similar system was embodied in the Austro-Hungarian Rast & Gasser of 1898 (fig. 237).

Mexico

534. Mendoza RM-22; Productos Mendoza SA, Mexico City. ·22 LR rimfire; eight-shot. Spent cases are ejected simultaneously after the yoked cylinder has been swung out to the left. A similiar six-shot ·38 Special RM-38 version has also been made.

Netherlands

Details of a 9·4mm-calibre gendarmerie revolver (fig. 965) will be found in the section devoted to the Bulldogs.

535, 536. Service revolver, M1873 O.M.; E. de Beaumont, Maastricht. 9·4mm; 283mm overall, 161mm barrel, 1285gm. Six-shot. Based on a combination of Chamelot-Delvigne and Nagant features, these revolvers have a pivoting loading gate on the right side of the frame behind the cylinder (fig. 536), but lack an ejector. A suitable rod was carried separately. The O.M. or 'Old Model' had an octahedral barrel; the improved N.M. ('New Model') had a lightened cylindrical barrel; and the five-shot Kl.M., or small model, was apparently intended for officers.

Norway

The standard service revolvers were basically Nagants. The M1878 fired a 9mm cartridge loaded with black powder, whereas the M1883 was intended for smokeless 7·5mm Swiss Schmidt-type ammunition. These guns were made in Belgium and Sweden (figs. 271 and 609 respectively).

Philippines

The Bingham Model 100 revolver (·38 Special), made by Squires, Bingham & Co., has a 4in barrel and weighs about 30oz. It resembles the Colt Diamondback, but lacks the full-length ejector shroud and the barrel-rib has small recesses rather than true vents. The front sight is dovetailed directly into the top surface of the rib, the cylinder flutes are narrower, and the grip is more like that shown in fig. 870.

Poland

537. Ng.30 (Nagant, 1895 type); Fabryka Bronie w Radomiu. 7·62mm Nagant; 235mm overall, 115mm barrel, 775gm. Seven-shot. Made in the Radom factory from 1930 onward, this is identical with the original Russian pattern excepting for markings and a few insignificant details.

Portugal

538. Army revolver M1886, Abadie type; L. Soleil, Liége. 9·1mm; 220mm overall, 115mm barrel, 750gm. This is similar to the Belgian Excelsior pattern (fig. 257), excepting that the firing mechanism incorporated a single-pin leaf spring instead of a double-pin pattern. The detachable plate on the left side of the frame does not pivot around a fixed axis, whilst the arrangement of the ejector also varies. The grips are retained by a single screw. An earlier 1878 pattern had a longer barrel, an Excelsior-type extractor, and a differing method of fastening the grip.

Romania

539, 540. Dimancea; Gatling Arms & Ammunition Co. Ltd, Perry Barr, Birmingham. Patented in Britain in 1885, by a Romanian army officer, the prototypes of this bulky service revolver (fig. 539) were apparently made by the Kynoch Gun Factory of Aston Cross, Birmingham. When Kynoch failed in 1888, production (fig. 540)—never large—switched to the equally short-lived Gatling company, which collapsed in 1890. To extract cases, the hinged barrel/cylinder unit is swung laterally to the left and then drawn forward. The double-action firing mechanism contains a trigger which actuates a six-limbed star-wheel. One limb turns the cylinder whilst another

retracts the hammer. When the revolver is fired, the next pair of limbs repeat the cycle as pressure is taken on the trigger for the next shot.

Russia

The acceptance of revolvers in Tsarist Russia was hindered by the conservatism of high-ranking army officers, even though gendarmerie used Lefaucheux pinfires (made in Belgium and Russia) in the 1860s. In 1871, however, the first 1869-pattern Smith & Wessons began to replace the old single shot cap-lock muzzle-loaders. The new gun was known as the '4·2-Line Revolver, Smith & Wesson System'. For its era, it was a highly effectual product; indeed, the S&W 'Russian model' won a gold medal at the International Exposition in Vienna in 1873.

The principal features of the 4·2-Line (10·67mm) weapon were a single-action firing mechanism and simultaneous spent-case ejection performed automatically as the breech was opened. The centre-fire cartridges were loaded with black powder.*

The 1870-pattern Galand revolver was purchased in small numbers for the Russian Navy; the gun was of French origin, but made in Belgium (fig. 295).

* It has been claimed, notably in Soviet sources, that the Russians were the first to adopt revolvers chambering centre-fire cartridges; however, the British Royal Navy accepted the ·450 Adams in 1868.

Solid-frame patterns

541, 542. 3-Line Nagant, M1895; L. & E. Nagant, Liége, and the imperial small-arms factory, Tula. 7·62mm; 235mm overall, 115mm barrel, 750gm. Seven-shot. Spent-case ejection was sequential, the rod—which locked into the cylinder-axis pin when not required—being mounted on a revolving collar around the barrel. The most important feature was the 'gas seal' achieved by camming the cylinder forward until the chamber mouth enveloped the rear of the barrel, ensuring reliable obturation. The

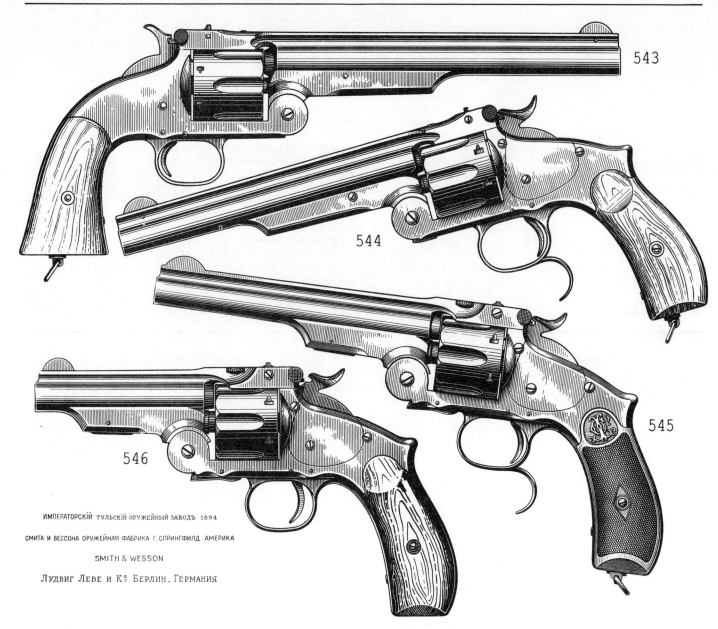

543

544

546

545

ИМПЕРАТОРСКІЙ ТУЛЬСКІЙ ОРУЖЕЙНЫЙ ЗАВОДЪ 1894

СМИТА И ВЕССОНА ОРУЖЕЙНАЯ ФАБРИКА Г. СПРИНГФИЛД АМЕРИКА

SMITH & WESSON

ЛУДВИГ ЛЕВЕ И Кⁿ. БЕРЛИН, ГЕРМАНИЯ

Nagant revolver was sturdy, reliable and surprisingly powerful for such a small-calibre weapon.

Double- and single-action Nagants were issued in the pre-1917 army, the former to officers and the latter to NCOs and enlisted men. The single-action version was made simply by omitting the hammer-rotating pawl from the standard firing mechanism; it was believed that ordinary soldiers would waste ammunition if given 'rapid-fire' weapons, even though the changes reduced the utility of the Nagant appreciably.

Hinged-frame patterns

543. Smith & Wesson Russian Model, first pattern, 1871; Smith & Wesson, Springfield, Massachusetts. 10·67mm; 203mm barrel, about 1220gm. The design of the hammer ensured that the gun could not be fired until the action was securely shut; otherwise, a notch on the hammer could not engage with a lug on the barrel catch and prevented the firing pin reaching the primer of the chambered cartridge. A catch on the ejector could disengage the extractor mechanism, allowing cartridges to remain in the chambers instead of falling to the ground. They could then be removed singly or shaken out into the palm of the hand.

544. Smith & Wesson Russian Model, second ('Infantry') pattern, 1872; Smith & Wesson, Springfield, Massachusetts. 10·67mm; 178mm barrel.

This differed from its predecessor in the shape of the grip, the design of the hammer, and the addition of a finger-spur on the trigger guard for the middle finger. The barrel and frame were connected with a single pinned screw, instead of a screw and lock-screw. After the introduction of the third pattern, the second was retrospectively classed as the infantry version.

545, 546. Smith & Wesson Russian Model, third ('Cavalry') pattern, 1874; Smith & Wesson, Springfield, Massachusetts. 10·67mm; 167mm barrel, about 1100gm. The distinguishing features of this gun included a front sight forged integrally with the barrel; a new extractor gear in a shorter under-barrel housing; and a modified retainer screw to facilitate cylinder removal. Some third-model revolvers were subsequently refurbished and often slightly altered in the Tula factory, where a few were greatly shortened (fig. 546) for uniformed police.

The first-, second- and some of third-pattern S&W Russian revolvers were made in the USA; in all, about 250,000 came from Smith & Wesson. At the time of the war with Turkey, which began in 1877, an emergency order was placed with Ludwig Loewe & Company of Berlin, apparently for 70,000 third-pattern guns. These were virtually identical with Smith & Wesson examples, excepting for a few small details and their barrel marks. Production of revolvers and their cartridges finally began in the Tula factory about 1880–1.

547–549. Smith & Wesson 'Baby Russian' revolvers; Smith & Wesson, Springfield, Massachusetts. ·38 S&W. The first of these guns, the ·38 Single Action First Model (fig. 547) was designed in 1875 around the components of the ·44 Russian Model. It was followed by the Second Model (fig. 548) in 1877, retaining the sheathed trigger but distinguished by an improved ejector system which dispensed with the housing beneath the barrel. These guns were not specifically developed for the Russian market, though doubtless many sold there. The gun in fig. 549, similar to the S&W ·38 Third Model of 1891 (excepting for the addition of a trigger-guard spur), is believed to be a Belgian- or Spanish-made copy.

South Africa

Lynx revolvers are imitation Smith & Wesson Hand Ejectors, made in several differing barrel lengths—2·5in, 4in or 6in—and an assortment of chamberings. Some guns of nominally 9mm/·357 calibre can fire rimmed ·357 Magnum, ·38 Special and ·38 S&W cartridges, as well as rimless ·38 Super, 9mm Short and 9mm Parabellum. Like the American Colt Python, the barrels have ejector-rod shrouds and ventilated ribs. The trigger guard has a finger-support for use with a two-hand grip; the back sight is an adjustable S&W type; and the grips have a distinctive shape. A lynx-head trademark will be found on the right side of the frame.

Spain

The most diverse selection of Bulldog, Velo-Dog, Colt and Nagant-type revolvers was made in Spain from the 1880s until the Spanish Civil War of 1936–9, after which all but a few of the gunsmiths were forcibly deprived of their living. The greatest attention, however, was paid to the Smith & Wessons: hinged-frame and swinging-cylinder alike. Even the most modern solid-frame models—despite ventilated lugs, compensators and adjustable sights—are almost exact duplicates of the Smith & Wesson Hand Ejectors. Details of lesser patterns may be found in the Bulldog, Velo-Dog and Hybrid Revolver sections, the remainder being described below.

During the First World War, many hinged-frame Smith & Wesson-type service revolvers were made in Spain for the Allies, particularly Britain, Italy and Romania. Guns chambering the Italian 10·35mm cartridge, made by Orbea Hermanos, were called 'Model 1916'. They supplemented ·44-calibre weapons made by a selection of Spanish gunmakers in 1914–15. Even though many of these bore '1914' on the butts, they were subsequently assimilated with the 10·35mm M1916 pattern.

Solid-frame patterns

550. Alfa; Armero Especialistas Reunidas, Eibar. ·38 Long Colt. This is almost an exact copy of the Smith & Wesson system of 1899, excepting that the grip is based on the 1905 model. Probably made for Alfa by Orueta Hermanos of Eibar.
551. Alfa; Armero Especialistas Reunidas, Eibar. ·38 Long Colt. A copy of the 1905-pattern Smith & Wesson.
552. Astra Cadix Model 224; Astra-Unceta y Cia, Guernica. ·22 LR rimfire; 100mm barrel. Nine-shot. The Astra revolvers—introduced in 1958—are based on the Smith & Wesson Hand Ejector system, differing

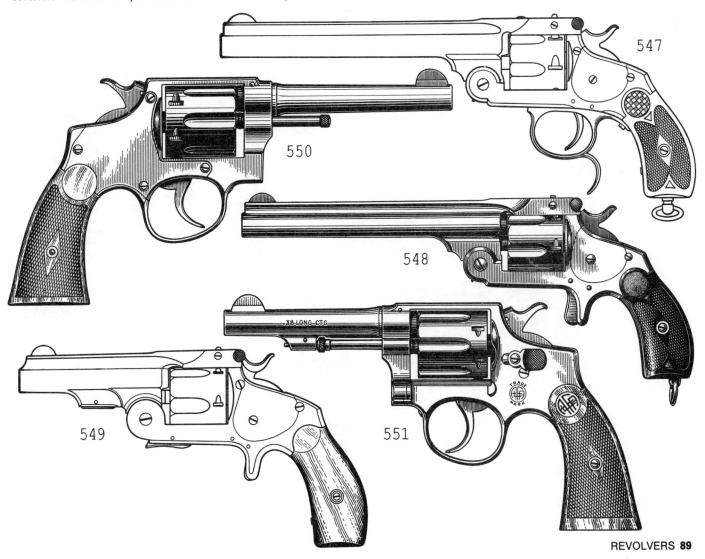

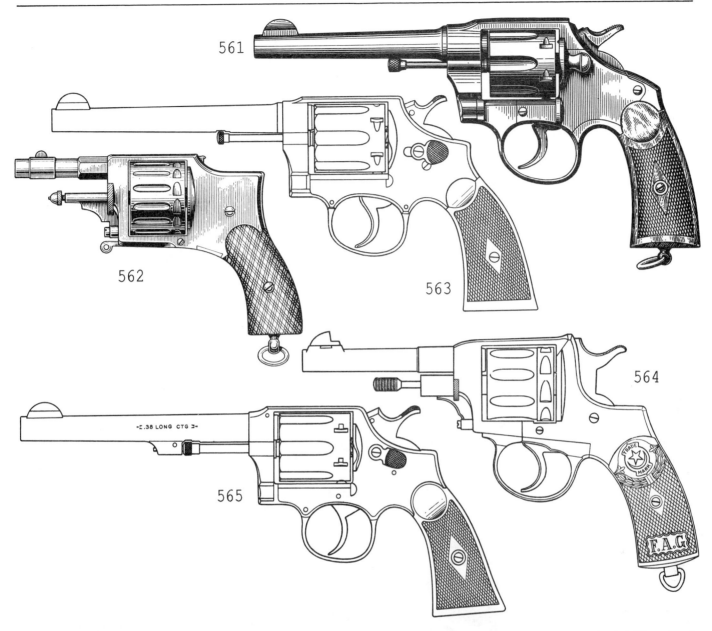

largely in calibre, cylinder capacity and barrel length. The Cadix is made in several versions, each designated by a three-digit code. The first two numerals represent the calibre; the third is the barrel length, also in inches. The three rimfires are numbered 222, 224 and 226.

553. Astra Cadix Model 326; Astra-Unceta y Cia, Guernica. ·32 S&W; 150mm barrel. Six-shot. This group includes Models 322, 324 and 326.

554. Astra Cadix Model 382; Astra-Unceta y Cia, Guernica. ·38 Special; 50mm barrel. The ·38 Cadix variants are the Models 382, 384 and 386.

555. Astra Magnum; Astra-Unceta y Cia, Guernica. ·357 Magnum; 75mm, 100mm or 150mm barrel.

556. Astra Model 44; Astra-Unceta y Cia, Guernica. ·44 Magnum; 150mm or 215mm barrel. Six-shot. Target-style grips and adjustable sights. The Model 45 (.45 Long Colt) is essentially similar to the Model 44 in all respects other than chambering. The Police Model (·357 Magnum or 9mm Parabellum) is identical mechanically, but has a 75mm barrel, a rounded butt and fixed sights.

557. Astra Model 680; Astra-Unceta y Cia, Guernica. ·38 Special.

558. Astra Model 960; Astra-Unceta y Cia, Guernica. ·38 Special; 100mm or 150mm barrel. Mechanically similar to the Model 44 described previously (fig. 556), it has a Magna-type grip.

559. Astra Regent; Astra-Unceta y Cia, Guernica. ·22 LR rimfire; 75mm,

100mm or 150mm barrel. Eight-shot. Based on the Smith & Wesson Hand Ejector, though somewhat different in constructional detail.

560. Automatic Revolver; Zulaica y Cia, Eibar. ·22 LR rimfire. A short-lived attempt to produce an auto-loading revolver. Production, never large, was apparently confined to c.1905–14.

561. Cosmopolite Oscillatore; Garate, Anitua y Cia, Eibar, c.1925–33. ·32 Long Colt. A copy of the Colt Police Positive, excepting that the ejector yoke is unlatched by pulling the ejector-rod head forward. Also made in ·38 Long Colt.

562. Dek-Du or Dek Due; Tómas de Urizar y Cia, Eibar, c.1905–12. 5·5mm Velo-Dog, 6mm Type Française or 6·35mm Auto; 120mm overall, 56mm barrel, 395gm. Twelve shots.

563. El Cano; Arana y Cia, Eibar. ·32 Long Colt; 267mm overall, 150mm barrel. Five-shot. A copy of the Smith & Wesson Hand Ejector of 1899.

564. F.A.G., Nagant type; Francisco Arizmendi y Goenaga, Eibar, pre-1914. 7·62mm Nagant or 8mm Lebel; seven-shot. Though externally similar to the Belgian gas-seal Nagant of 1895 (fig. 272), the F.A.G. has a fixed cylinder. Guns of this type were popular in Africa and South America.

565, 566. Guisasola, Eibar. ·38 Long Colt. These guns are imitations of the Smith & Wesson Hand Ejector. One—usually associated with Benito Guisasola—has a conventional cylinder-yoke latch on the left side of

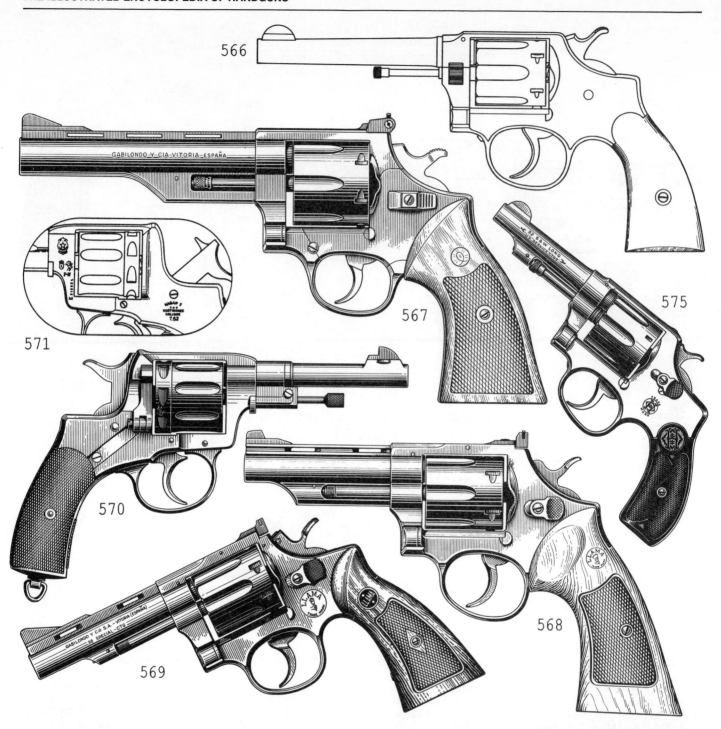

the frame beneath the hammer, whilst the other, marked by Guisasola Hermanos, has a simpler slide-type release on the left side of the yoke ahead of the cylinder.

567. Llama Comanche; Llama-Gabilondo y Cia, Vitoria. This greatly resembles the Smith & Wesson Model 19 (fig. 855), excepting that it has a ventilated rib above the barrel.

568. Llama Comanche III; Llama-Gabilondo y Cia, Vitoria. ·357 Magnum; 100mm or 150mm barrel.

569. Llama Martial; Llama-Gabilondo y Cia, Vitoria. ·38 Special; 50mm, 100mm or 150mm barrel, 820–960gm. This Smith & Wesson swinging-cylinder pattern differs from Ruby Extra Model 12 (q.v.) principally in the addition of a ventilated lug. The ·38 Llama Martial Police revolver is similar; so too are the ·22 LR rimfire Models 26 and 28 (the latter with an alloy frame), the ·32 Model 27, and the ·22 Magnum rimfire Model 30.

570, 571. Nagan, Nagans or Nagant; Francisco Arizmendi y Cia, Eibar, post-1914. 7·62mm Nagant; seven-shot. A newer version of the F.A.G. described above. The cylinder is fixed.

572. O.H.; Orbea Hermanos, Eibar. ·38 Long Colt. A facsimile of the Smith & Wesson ·38 Hand Ejector M&P Second Model of 1902.

573, 574. O.H.; Orbea Hermanos, Eibar. 8mm Lebel or ·38 Long Colt. Copies of the Smith & Wesson ·38 Hand Ejector M&P Third Model of 1905, these were made for the French military cartridge at the beginning of the First World War. The military-contract guns were made in several minor variations (e.g., fig. 574).

575. O.H.; Orbea Hermanos, Eibar. ·32 S&W. Based on the Smith & Wesson ·32 Hand Ejector Second Model of 1903.

576. O.H.; Orbea Hermanos, Eibar. ·22 LR rimfire. A copy of the Smith & Wesson ·22 Hand Ejector (Ladysmith) Third Model of 1909.

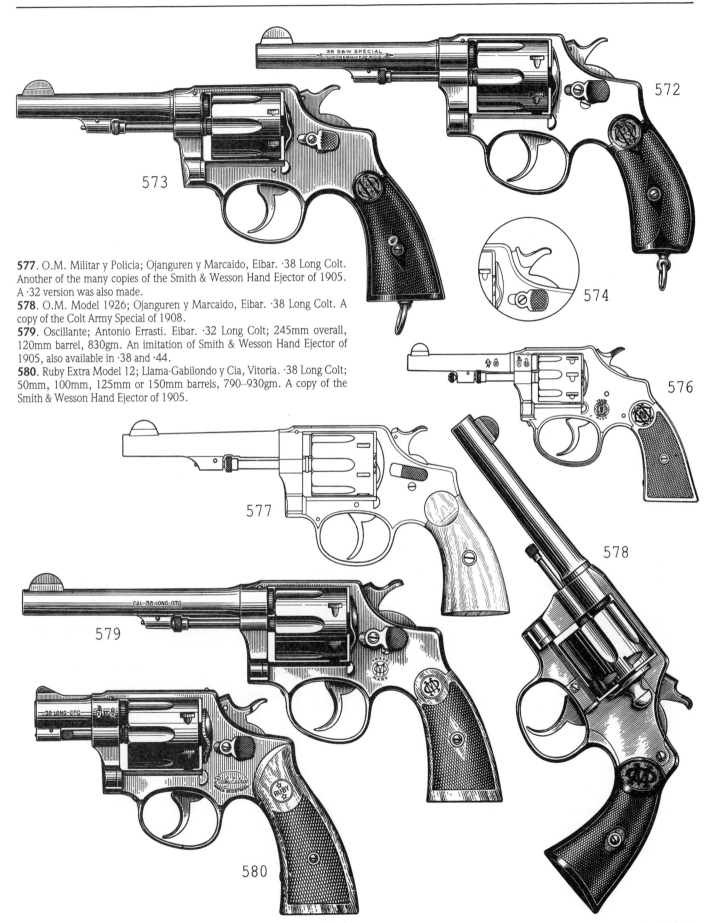

577. O.M. Militar y Policia; Ojanguren y Marcaido, Eibar. ·38 Long Colt. Another of the many copies of the Smith & Wesson Hand Ejector of 1905. A ·32 version was also made.

578. O.M. Model 1926; Ojanguren y Marcaido, Eibar. ·38 Long Colt. A copy of the Colt Army Special of 1908.

579. Oscillante; Antonio Errasti. Eibar. ·32 Long Colt; 245mm overall, 120mm barrel, 830gm. An imitation of Smith & Wesson Hand Ejector of 1905, also available in ·38 and ·44.

580. Ruby Extra Model 12; Llama-Gabilondo y Cia, Vitoria. ·38 Long Colt; 50mm, 100mm, 125mm or 150mm barrels, 790–930gm. A copy of the Smith & Wesson Hand Ejector of 1905.

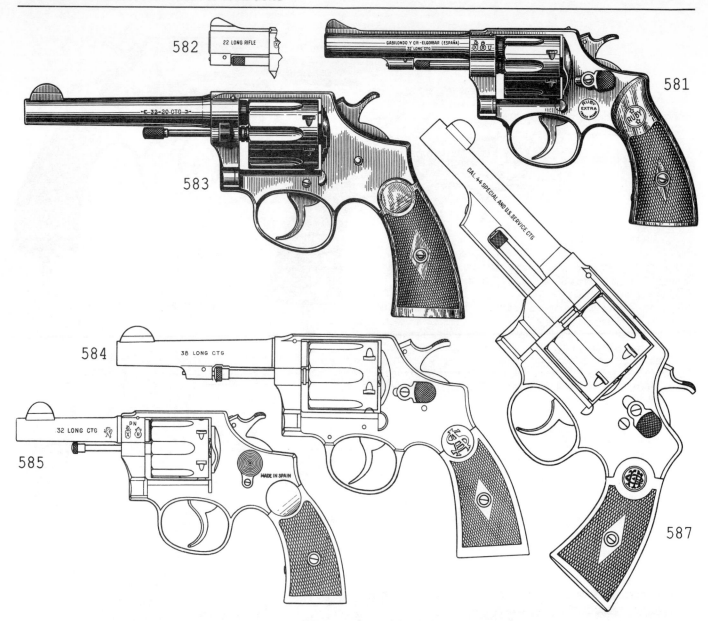

581, 582. Ruby Extra Model 13; Llama-Gabilondo y Cia, Vitoria. ·32 Long Colt; five barrel lengths (50–150mm), 520–580gm. The Model 14 is similar, but chambered ·22 LR rimfire ammunition; Models 23 (·38) and 24 (·22) are target-shooting variants with long barrels, ventilated ribs, improved sights and better grips.

583. Rural Model or M1925; maker unknown, Eibar. ·32–20 WCF. This is similar to Smith & Wesson Hand Ejector of 1905, but the cylinder latch lies on the yoke ahead of the cylinder. An essentially similar ·38 'M1924' revolver marked by Fabrica de Armas Garantizadas is usually credited to Ojanguren y Vidosa.

584. S.A., S&A; Suinaga y Aramperri, Eibar. ·38 Long Colt; 235mm overall, 110mm barrel, 825gm. Six-shot. A conventional Smith & Wesson Hand Ejector copy.

585. T.A.C.; Trocaola, Aranzabal y Cia, Eibar. ·32 Long Colt. An imitation of the Smith & Wesson swinging-cylinder system, distinguished by the shape of the cylinder latch.

586. T.A.C.; Trocaola, Aranzabal y Cia, Eibar. ·38 Special. A copy of the Smith & Wesson ·38 Hand Ejector M&P Third Model of 1905. Similar guns chambering the 8mm Lebel cartridge were made for the French army during the First World War.

587. T.A.C.; Trocaola, Aranzabal y Cia, Eibar. ·44 Special. Another of the many Smith & Wesson copies.

588. T.A.C. Model 333; Trocaola, Aranzabal y Cia, Eibar. ·32–20 WCF. A long-barrelled copy of the Smith & Wesson Hand Ejector. Note the design of the cylinder latch.

589. T.A.C. Modelo Corzo; Trocaola, Aranzabal y Cia, Eibar. ·32 Long Colt. A copy of the Colt Police Positive revolver.

590. T.A.C. Para Bosino (sic); Trocaola, Aranzabal y Cia, Eibar. ·32 Long Colt. A copy of the short-barrelled Colt Police Positive.

591. T.A.C., pocket model; Trocaola, Aranzabal y Cia, Eibar. ·32 S&W. A copy of the Smith & Wesson ·32 Hand Ejector.

Hinged-frame patterns

592. C.H.; Crucelegui Hermanos, Eibar. ·38 S&W; 89mm barrel, Five-shot. A typical Smith & Wesson copy.

593. Euscaro; Orbea Hermanos or Crucelegui Hermanos, Eibar. ·32 S&W or ·38 S&W; five-shot.

594. G.A.C. Model 1916; Garate, Anitua y Cia, Eibar. ·44 S&W. Essentially similar ·455-calibre guns were made during the First World War for Britain, with a 'GAC' monogram on the butt.

595. Maker unknown; Eibar. ·22 Short rimfire; six-shot.

596. Maker unknown; Eibar. ·38 S&W; five-shot.

597. Maker unknown; Eibar, marked '1926'. ·38; five-shot.

598. Maker unknown; Eibar. ·38 S&W; five-shot.

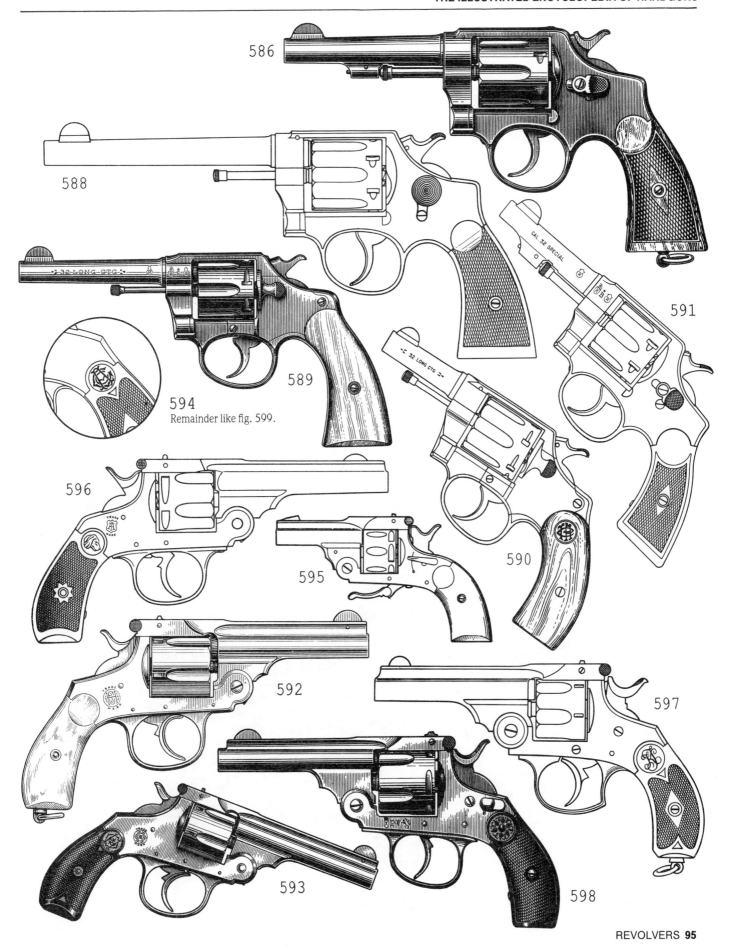

586

588

589

594
Remainder like fig. 599.

591

590

596

595

592

597

593

598

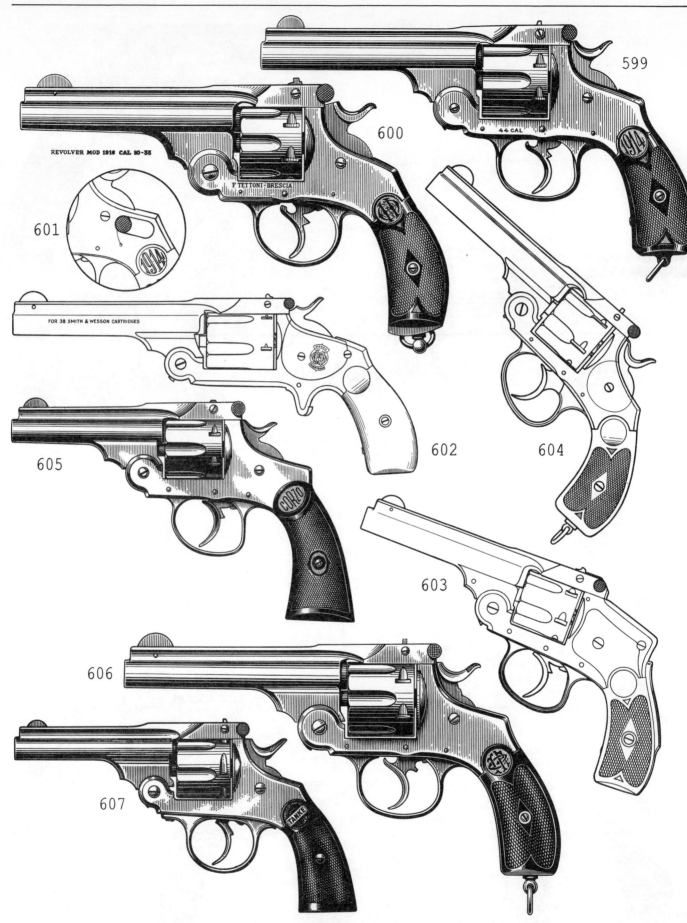

599. O.H. Model 1914, later 'M1916'; Orbea Hermanos, Eibar. ·44 S&W. One grip generally bears the manufacturer's monogram; the other displays the '1914' date

600, 601. O.H. Model 1916; Orbea Hermanos, Eibar. 10·35mm Italian. A variant with a safety lever on the left side of the frame is also shown.

602. O.H.; Orbea Hermanos, Eibar. ·38 S&W; five-shot. A copy of the Smith & Wesson ·38 Single Action Second Model, with a sheathed trigger.

603. Safe Model; maker unknown, Eibar. ·38 S&W; five-shot. A copy of the Smith & Wesson ·38 Safety Hammerless, with an enclosed hammer and a grip safety.

604. Smith Americano; Antonio Errasti or Retolaza Hermanos, Eibar. ·32 S&W, ·38 S&W or ·44 S&W; five-shot.

605. T.A.C. Corzo; Trocaola, Aranzabal y Cia, Eibar. ·38; six-shot. A copy of the double-action Smith & Wesson

606. T.A.C. Model 1914; Trocaola, Aranzabal y Cia, Eibar. ·44 S&W. Made for Romania during the First World War.

607. Tanke (or Tanque) Automatic Model 1A; Orueta Hermanos, Eibar. ·38 S&W; 190mm overall, 90mm barrel. Five-shot.

Sweden

608. Service revolver M1871; Auguste Francotte & Co., Liége. 11mm; 310mm overall, 150mm barrel, 1175gm. Six-shot. A single-action pattern,

with sequential spent-case expulsion. A few were made by Husqvarna Våpenfabriks in c.1877–8. Issued to cavalry and artillerymen.

609. Service revolver, Nagant type, M1887; Husqvarna Våpenfabriks, Huskvarna. 7·5mm; 235mm overall, 115mm barrel, 770gm. Six-shot. Chambered for a Swiss Schmidt-type smokeless cartridge, a slightly modified version of this gun was used by Norway as the 'M1893'. The earliest Swedish guns were made by L. & E. Nagant in Liége.

Switzerland

610, 611. Sauerbrey; Valentin Sauerbrey, Basle. 12·7mm. This gun has a solid frame and a French-type ejector. Behind the rebounding hammer is a catch holding the plate on the left side of the frame—visible in fig. 611—which opens when the revolver is being stripped.

612. Ordonnanzrevolver, Chamelot-Delvigne & Schmidt type, M1872; Pirlot Frères, Liége, 1873–9. 10·4mm; 279mm overall, 150mm barrel, 1020gm. Six-shot. The ejector rod is offset on the right side of the barrel. The M1872 chambers rimfire ammunition; the M1872/78 adaption is centre-fire.

613. Ordonnanzrevolver, Warnant & Schmidt type, M1878; Eidgenössische Waffenfabrik, Bern, 1879–80. 10·4mm; 280mm overall, 150mm barrel, 1000gm. Six-shot. An improved version of the M1872.

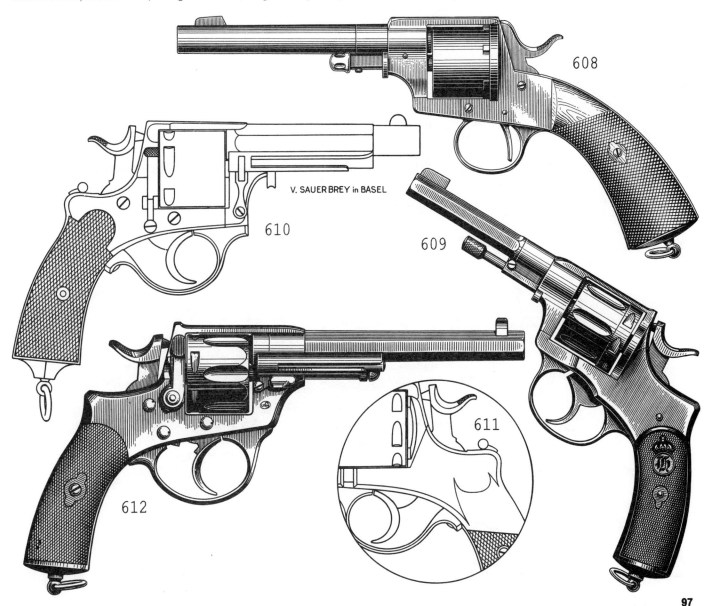

V. SAUERBREY in BASEL

608
610
609
611
612

613

614

616

615

617

620

618

623

619

621

622

614, 615. Ordonnanzrevolver, Schmidt type, M1882; Eidgenössische Waffenfabrik, Bern, 1882–1917. 7·5mm; 235mm overall, 130mm barrel, 755gm. Six-shot. This is similar to the M1878, but smaller and lighter. An Abadie-pattern loading gate lies on the right side of the frame behind the cylinder. Also made by Waffenfabrik Neuhausen (SIG), generally for police use or commercial sale.

616, 617. Ordonnanzrevolver M1929 (or 1882/29); Eidgenössische Waffenfabrik, Bern, 1933–46. 7·5mm; 230mm overall, 115mm barrel, 765gm. A simplified version of the M1882 with a notably squarer butt.

Turkey

618. Russian Model; Smith & Wesson, Springfield, Massachusetts. ·44 rimfire. This gun was basically a second-pattern Russian Model altered to accept rimfire ammunition. The first newly-made guns were ordered in 1874 and another batch followed in 1877–8, converted from centre-fire components. An inscription in Arabic lies on the barrel rib.

Union of Soviet Socialist Republics

619. Nagant revolver M1895; State small-arms factory, Tula. 7·62mm Nagant; 235mm overall, 115mm barrel, 750gm. Seven-shot. The sturdy and dependable ex-Tsarist double-action pattern was standardised after the October Revolution of 1917. It remained in production throughout the period in which the TT auto-loading pistol was being developed, and then on into the Great Patriotic War. The last revolvers were made in 1944. So many had been produced that large numbers remained in the hands of the lesser army units and the reserve into the 1950s, whilst others were converted for target shooting. Only minimal changes were made during the Soviet régime: the back sight notch became semi-circular instead of triangular, and the shape of the front sight was revised.

Training revolvers chambered for the 5·6 (·22 LR) rimfire cartridge were also made. They could be distinguished from the 7·62mm patterns by the smaller front sight.

620. Nagant revolver M1895, shortened; State small-arms factory, Tula. 7·62mm Nagant; 207mm overall, 90mm barrel, 675gm. Seven-shot. Small numbers of these guns were made, differing not only in dimensions but also in the method of stripping and re-assembly.

United States of America

The first revolvers chambering self-contained metal-case rimfire ammunition were made in 1857 by Smith & Wesson in Springfield, Massachusetts, on the basis of patents granted to Rollin White. Many other companies immediately attempted to promote revolvers with bored-through cylinders—e.g., Warner, Plant, Prescott, Moore—but Smith & Wesson successfully sued them for patent infringements. However, the cap-lock Colts were so successful that they were still being made even after rivals introduced revolvers suited to self-contained cartridges. The very first metallic-cartridge Colt designs, therefore, were inferior. The situation changed dramatically with the advent in 1873 of the legendary Single Action Army Revolver.

In 1869, Smith & Wesson began to produce hinged-frame revolvers whose barrel tipped down instead of upward. Spent cases were expelled simultaneously by a star-shaped extractor based on a patent granted to W.C. Dodge in 1865. These revolvers were easier to load, handled appreciably better than conventional solid-frame patterns, and were an instantaneous success. Improved Smith & Wessons soon appeared, inspiring the manufacture of many similar revolvers in Europe as well as the USA.

Smith & Wesson continued to offer these guns into the 1930s, though their day had gone. The solid-frame swinging-cylinder pattern, inspired by the Colt ·38 Army Model of 1889, had become so widely accepted that the perfected Colt and its Smith & Wesson equivalents still form the basis for the guns of the 1990s.

i) Pre-1917. Open-frame patterns

621. Bacon Arms & Manufacturing Company, Norwich, Connecticut. A modification of a cap-lock pattern.

622. Bacon Arms & Manufacturing Company, Norwich, Connecticut. A five-shot pepperbox type.

623. Bacon Arms & Manufacturing Company, Norwich, Connecticut. .32 rimfire.

624. New Model Army Revolver (or M1860), converted; Colt's Patent Fire Arms Manufacturing Company, Hartford, Connecticut. ·44 Thuer or ·44 rimfire. This was originally sold with a quirky cartridge which was inserted from the front of the chamber, but was soon modified to accept a conventional rimfire pattern. A sliding ejector rod has been added on the right side of the barrel.

625. New Model Pocket Revolver of Navy Caliber (or M1862), converted; Colt's Patent Fire Arms Manufacturing Company, Hartford, Connecticut. ·38 rimfire. This was originally a ·36-calibre cap-lock, fitted with a new cylinder and ejector rod.

626. New Model Army Revolver, or Model 1872; Colt's Patent Fire Arms Manufacturing Company, Hartford, Connecticut. ·44; six-shot. This was the first of the purpose-built metallic-cartridge Colts, based on the Army-

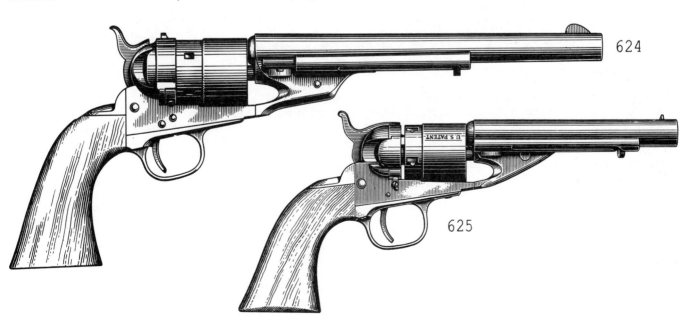

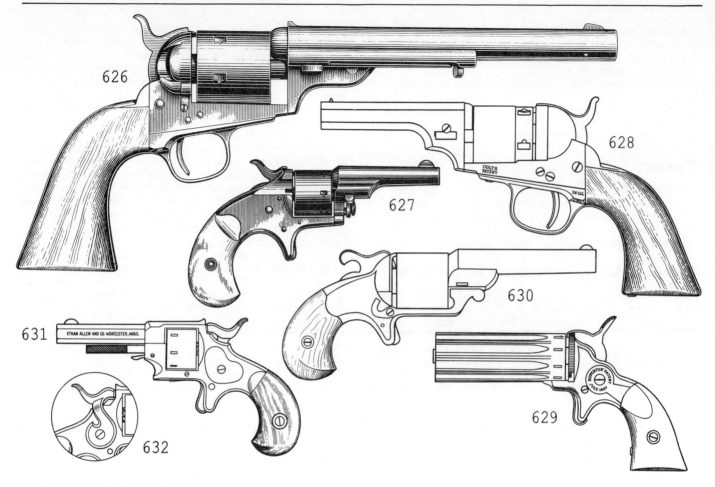

model cap-lock of 1860, but with a new barrel and a spring-loaded ejector rod in a tubular case on the right side. Construction proved to be too weak, so the unsuccessful M1872 was almost immediately replaced by the legendary M1873 Single Action Army Model.

627. Old Line Revolver; Colt's Patent Fire Arms Manufacturing Company, Hartford, Connecticut. ·22 rimfire; 2·4in barrel. Seven-shot. A single-action design with a sheathed trigger and a bronze frame, this tiny revolver lacked an ejector system. The construction of the barrel and frame is similar to the preceding cap-locks. After the introduction of solid-frame patterns—the 'New Line'—this model was called 'Old Line'. It was originally advertised as ''Colt's Breech-Loading Seven Shot Revolving Pistol''.

628. Pocket Revolver (or M1849), converted; Colt's Patent Fire Arms Manufacturing Company, Hartford, Connecticut. ·38 rimfire. This was originally a ·31-calibre cap-lock, adapted to fire metallic ammunition. Note the short barrel and the lack of an ejector.

629. Rupertus Patented Pistol Manufacturing Company, Philadelphia, Pennsylvania. ·22 rimfire; eight-shot. A pepperbox-type revolver patented in 1864.

630. Williamson, 1864; Moore's Patent Fire Arms Company, Brooklyn, New York. ·32 teat-fire. An evasion of patents controlled by Smith & Wesson, this was designed by David Williamson in 1863–4 to chamber seamless metal-case cartridges with a nipple-like protrusion in the centre of the base. The cartridges were inserted from the front of the cylinder, allowing the teats to protrude through small apertures in the rear face where they could be struck obliquely by the nose of the hammer. Some Williamson-pattern revolvers may be found with an ejector rod, designed to push the spent cases forward.

Solid-frame patterns

631, 632. Allen; Ethan Allen Arms Company, Worcester, Massachusetts, c.1863–8. ·22 lip-fire.

633. Allen & Wheelock, Worcester, Massachusetts, c.1859–1863. ·32 lip-fire. The 1858-patent revolvers produced by this company and its successor, the Ethan Allen Arms Company (1863–72), fired a special rimless cylindrical cartridge. A small projection on one side of the case, near the base, contained the priming composition.

634, 635. American Bull Dog; Iver Johnson's Arms & Cycle Works Company, Worcester (prior to 1891) and Fitchburg, Massachusetts, 1882–1900. ·22 rimfire, ·32, ·38 or ·44; 2·5in, 4·5in or 6in barrels. Five-shot. Supplied only in nickel-plate finish. The ·32 and ·38 versions could be chambered for rim- or centre-fire ammunition on request. The Boston Bull Dog of 1887–1900 (·22, ·32 or ·38) was similar, but had a 2·5in barrel.

636. American Model; Harrington & Richardson Arms Company, Worcester, Massachusetts, 1883–1941. ·32; 2·5in barrel. This pattern is similar to many similar guns made by US gunmakers in 1870–1900. They have a solid frame and a double-action firing mechanism, but lack an ejector. To reload, the cylinder-axis pin must be removed (it is held by a spring catch on the front of the frame) to allow the cylinder to fall free. Spent cases are then punched-out singly using the axis-pin as a rod. Alternatively, the cases can be thrust back singly through the loading gate if a suitable rod is available. The Victor was similar, but had a 2·5in cylindrical barrel.

637. Army Model 1875; E. Remington & Sons (to 1886) and the Remington Arms Company, Ilion, New York, 1875–89. ·44 Remington, ·44–40 Winchester or ·45 Long Colt; 7·5in barrel, 44oz. Six-shot. This was based on the perfected solid-frame cap-lock Remingtons of the Civil War, though superficially resembling the Colt Single Action Army revolver of 1873. The web beneath the muzzle is characteristic.

638. Army Model 1890; Remington Arms Company, Ilion, New York. ·45 Long Colt. This was a variant of the Model 1875 (q.v.), though the removal of much of the under-barrel web gave it a similar appearance to the Colt Peacemaker. However, the grip and the back of the frame were typically Remington. The drawing shows a modern Italian-made ·357 Magnum replica, with a 5·5in barrel and a weight of about 38oz.

639, 640. Army Model 1917; Colt's Patent Fire Arms Manufacturing Company, Hartford, Connecticut. ·45 ACP; 10·75in overall, 5·5in barrel, 36·3oz. Six-shot. Ordered when the USA entered the First World War in 1917, this was a New Service Model (fig. 705) adapted to fire rimless ·45 ACP ammunition with the assistance of half-moon clips. A comparable Smith & Wesson was adopted under the same model-date. Short-barrelled versions of the ·45 New Service and M1917 revolvers are occasionally encountered. These usually measure 2·5in or 2·75in.

641. Army Special Model; Colt's Patent Fire Arms Manufacturing Company, Hartford, Connecticut, 1908–27. ·38 Long Colt; 9·65in overall, 4·5in barrel, 34oz. Six-shot. This was essentially similar to the preceding New Army Model (fig. 694), but was built on a larger ·41-type frame and its cylinder rotated to the right instead of leftward. Variants were made in ·32 and ·41 Long Colt, and with 6in barrels. The Army Special was renamed 'Official Police' in 1927 (·22, ·32 or ·38), minor changes were made to the finish and the sights, and manufacture continued until 1969.

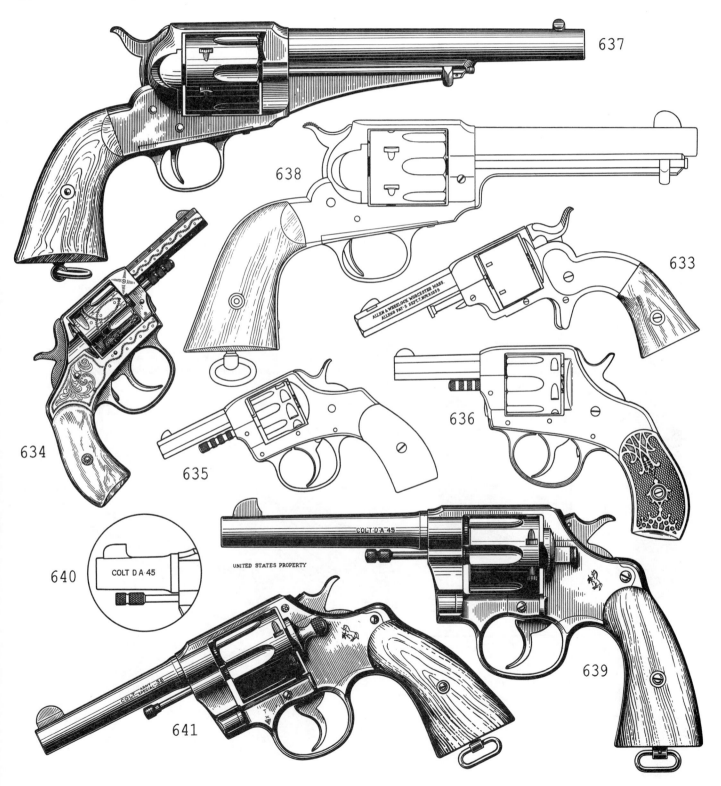

642. Baby Hammerless; Henry Kolb & Company, Philadelphia, Pennsylvania. ·22 Short rimfire; five-shot. From 1892 until 1938, Kolb and his successor R.F. Sedgley made miniature revolvers of the European Puppy type. Spent cases are ejected by removing the cylinder, in accordance with fig. 124. This is apparently the original pattern, with a double row of locking-bolt recesses on the cylinder surface.

643. Baby Hammerless; Henry Kolb & Company, Philadelphia, Pennsylvania. ·22 rimfire; 4·7in overall, 1·7in barrel. Five-shot.

644. Baby Hammerless, 1910 pattern; Henry Kolb & Company, Philadelphia, Pennsylvania. ·32; five-shot. Similar to the ·22 pattern drawn in fig. 643, but with an improved horizontal spring-latch to retain the cylinder-axis pin.

645. Baby Hammerless, 1910 pattern; R.F. Sedgley, Inc., Philadelphia, Pennsylvania, 1930–8. ·22 Long rimfire; five-shot. A version of the Baby Hammerless previously made by Henry Kolb, ejection being undertaken in accordance with fig. 124.

646. Bisley Model; Colt's Patent Fire Arms Manufacturing Company, Hartford, Connecticut, 1894–1915. ·45 Long Colt; 5·5in barrel. Six-shot. This was named after the famous British firing range. Made in many chamberings and barrel lengths, the Bisley was distinguished by a special grip, raised in relation to the frame, and had a lower hammer-spur so that the sights could be seen at all times. The Bisley Target Model (or 'Bisley Flat-Top') of 1894–7 was essentially similar, but had a special back sight on a raised rib.

647. Brooklyn Arms Company, Brooklyn, New York. ·32 Long rimfire. Patented by Frank Slocum in 1863, this gun is distinguished by a cylinder with five longitudinal grooves and sliding sleeves. To load the gun, a chamber is moved forward onto the rod on the right side of the frame ahead of the cylinder, which pushes a spent case back until it can be removed manually. A new cartridge is placed in the open groove and the sleeve is closed. The procedure can be repeated until all the chambers are loaded.

648. British Bulldog; Forehand & Wadsworth, Worcester, Massachusetts. ·32 or ·38; six (·38) or seven (·32) shots. A typical European Bulldog in appearance and construction. Spent cases are ejected singly in accordance with fig. 126.

649. Bulldog; Forehand & Wadsworth, Worcester, Massachusetts. ·32; five-shot. A typical sheathed-trigger non-ejecting pocket revolver, based on a patent granted in 1875.

650. Bulldog; Forehand & Wadsworth, Worcester, Massachusetts, c.1872–80. ·38; 2·5in barrel. Five-shot.

651. Bulldog; Forehand & Wadsworth, Worcester, Massachusetts. ·44; 2·75in barrel. Five-shot. This company also produced ·38-calibre revolvers of the same name, but they usually had sheathed triggers and hexahedral barrels. Spent cases are ejected by removing the cylinder and using its axis pin as a rod.

652. Columbian Double Action; probably made by Foehl & Weeks of Philadelphia, Pennsylvania. ·38, five-shot. This gun dates from the early 1890s; spent cases are extracted by detaching the cylinder in accordance with fig. 124.

653. Connecticut Arms Company, Norfolk, Connecticut. ·28 rimfire. These guns, which fired special cartridges with the priming compound in a hemispherical indentations in the base, were patented by Stephen Wood in 1864. Cartridges were inserted into the chambers from the front, the hammer-nose striking the lower part of the priming chamber obliquely. Spent cases are ejected with a pivoting lever on the right side of the frame beneath the cylinder.

654. Defender Model 89; Hopkins & Allen, Norwich, Connecticut. ·22 rimfire; seven-shot. An improved form of the basic Hopkins & Allen sheath-trigger revolver design, made in c.1889–1900.

655. Defiance; Hopkins & Allen, Norwich, Connecticut. A typical single-action sheathed-trigger pocket revolver, said to have been introduced in the early 1870s.

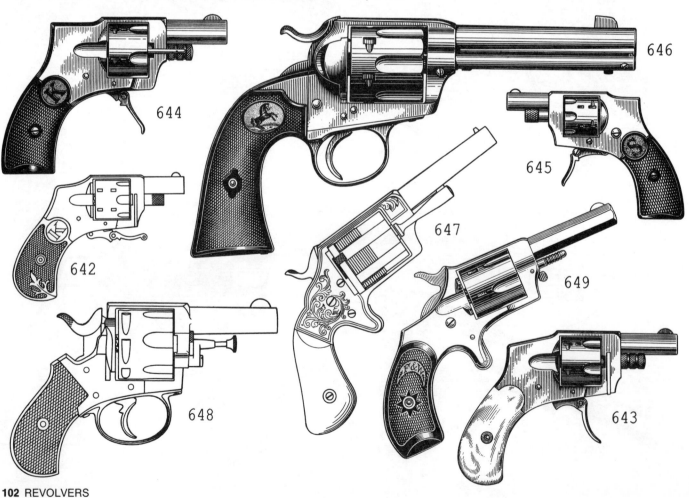

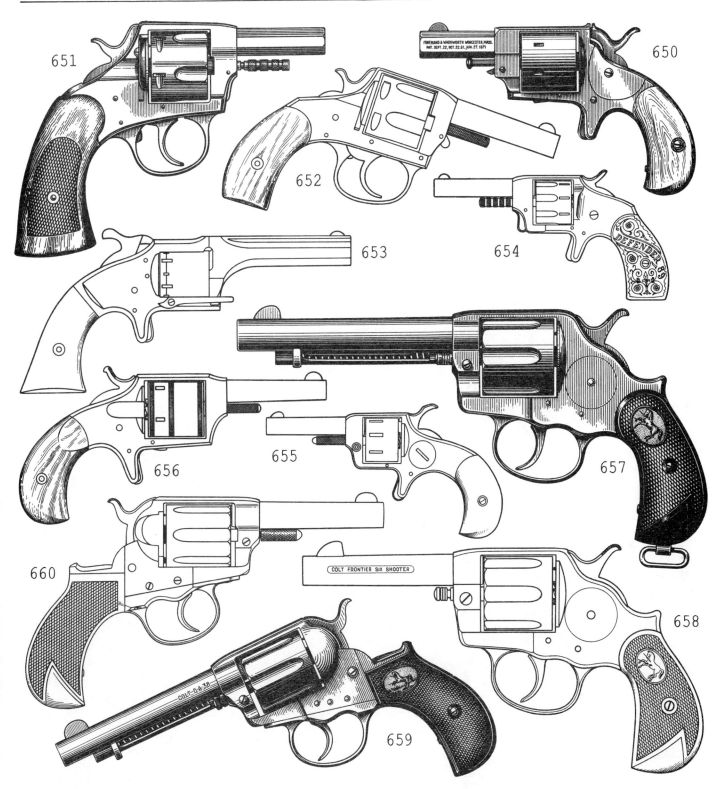

656. Dictator; Hopkins & Allen, Norwich, Connecticut, c.1873–9. ·32. Many large-calibre sheath-trigger single action revolvers were made by this particular company, in addition to a range of pocket patterns.

657, 658. Double Action ·45 Army & Frontier Model, 1878–1905; Colt's Patent Fire Arms Manufacturing Company, Hartford, Connecticut. ·45. This was the first large-calibre double-action military revolver to be made in the USA, though few were acquired by the army until 1902—when several thousand were purchased with specially enlarged trigger guards. These were designed to admit a gloved finger and are generally (if misleadingly)

known as 'Alaska Models'. Many were sent to the Philippines, where the ·45-diameter bullet proved more effectual against Moro fanatics than the regulation ·38.

659, 660. Double Action ·38 Model or Lightning, 1877–1909; Colt's Patent Fire Arms Manufacturing Company, Hartford, Connecticut. ·38 Long Colt; 9·05in overall, 4·5in barrel. Six-shot. Made in a variety of sizes and styles (fig. 660 shows a ''Sheriff's Model''), this was the first Colt to embody a double-action firing mechanism, though otherwise similar to the Single Action Army Model. A ·41 version was sold as the 'Thunderer'.

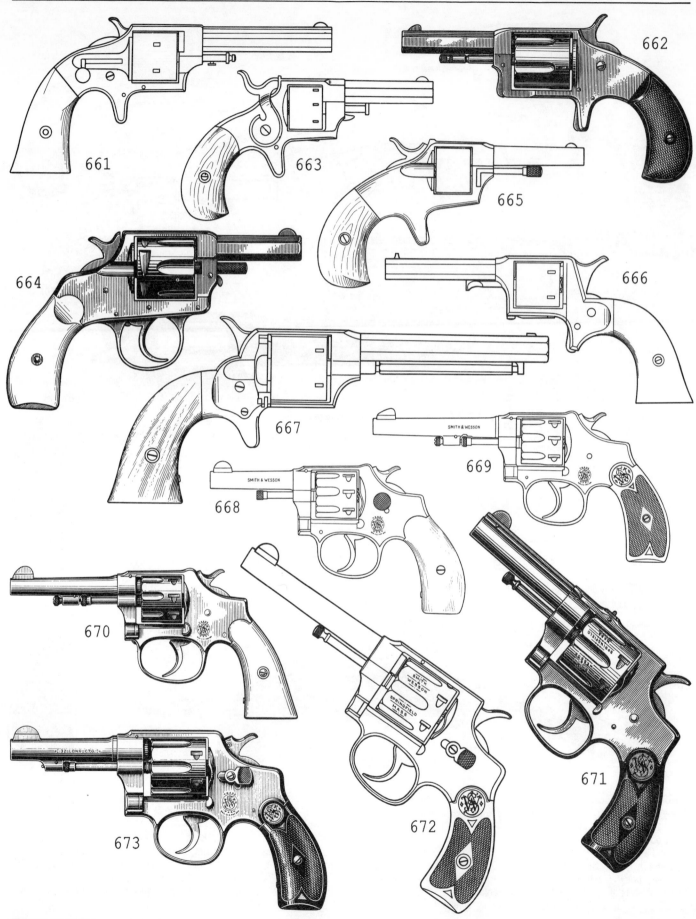

661. Eagle Arms Company, New York. ·28 rimfire. This sales agency sold the Plant revolver (q.v.) from 1865 until about 1870.

662. Etna No. 2; maker unknown (Hopkins & Allen?). ·32 rimfire; five-shot. A typical American revolver of the 1870s, with a single-action firing mechanism and a sheathed trigger. The gun is reloaded by removing the cylinder in accordance with fig. 124.

663. Forehand & Wadsworth, Worcester, Massachusetts. ·22; seven-shot. This is a variation of the single-action sheath trigger revolvers (see fig. 632) made by Ethan Allen & Company, which was superseded by Forehand & Wadsworth in 1872. This gun lacks an ejector.

664. Forehand Arms Company, Worcester, Massachusetts, post-1890. ·32 or ·38; five (·38) or six (·32) shots. This is typical of the double-action non-ejecting pocket revolvers made in the USA in the last quarter of the nineteenth century by gunmakers such as Harrington & Richardson or Hopkins & Allen. The gun is reloaded by removing the cylinder and punching out spent cases with the cylinder-axis pin (see fig. 124).

665. Governor; Bacon Arms & Manufacturing Company, Norwich, Connecticut. ·22 Short rimfire; seven-shot.

666, 667. Grant; possibly made by Grant & Company of Newark, New Jersey, in the late 1860s. ·22 rimfire or ·32 rimfire.

668–670. Hand Ejector, ·22 (Ladysmith or Bicycle Gun); Smith & Wesson, Springfield, Massachusetts. ·22 Long rimfire; 6·5in or 7in overall, 3in or 3·5in barrel, 9–10·5oz. Seven-shot. The first of these tiny swinging-cylinder guns was made in 1902, incorporating a miniature version of the standard press-button cylinder release. This was abandoned in the second model of 1906 in favour of a longitudinally-sliding locking bolt under the barrel; the third model (1909–21) was a minor variant of the preceding pattern with a squared butt. The third model was offered with barrels of 2·25in, 3in and 6in.

671. Hand Ejector, ·32, First or 1896 Model; Smith & Wesson, Springfield, Massachusetts, 1896–1903. ·32 S&W Long; 3·25in, 4·25in or 6in barrel. Six-shot. In 1896, aware of the success of the 1889-pattern Colt, Smith & Wesson introduced a revolver with a swing-out cylinder. The essence was a crane or yoke, which formed the left front portion of the frame, carried the cylinder-axis pin and could pivot outward to the left when released by pulling forward on the extractor-rod head. The opening movement swung the cylinder far enough to clear the frame, whereupon the contents of the chambers could be expelled simply by pressing the head of the star-shape extractor backward. Consequently, the gun became known as the 'Hand Ejector'. The cylinder-lock lay in the frame-strap above the cylinder. Like all Smith & Wessons of this type, the cylinder rotates to the left.

672. Hand Ejector, ·32, hybrid model; Smith & Wesson, Springfield, Massachusetts. ·32 S&W Long; 3·25in, 4·5 or 6in barrel. Six-shot. This embodies some of the changes associated with the second model described below, principally the cylinder-release catch on the left side of the frame beneath the hammer.

673. Hand Ejector, ·32, Second or 1903 Model; Smith & Wesson, Springfield, Massachusetts. ·32 S&W Long. The perfected or second model ·32 Hand Ejector of 1903–11 differed considerably from its immediate predecessor; the barrel was cylindrical instead of ribbed, the cylinder stop was moved to the bottom of the frame, and an auxiliary locking lug was added beneath the barrel to retain the head of the extractor rod. This required an additional button on the left side of the frame, which was pressed forward to release the cylinder. The third model, externally identical with the second model, fifth change, was made until 1942.

674. Hand Ejector, ·38, Military & Police, First or 1899 Model; Smith & Wesson, Springfield, Massachusetts, 1899–1902. ·32–20 WCF or ·38 Long Colt; 4in, 5in, 6in, 6·5in or 8in barrel. This was a larger version of the ·32 Hand Ejector, incorporating the frame-mounted cylinder release catch but lacking the auxiliary lug beneath the barrel. It was adopted by the US Army in 1899; guns were also supplied to the navy, identical but for the grips and the absence of a lanyard ring on the butt.

675. Hand Ejector, ·38, Military & Police, Second or 1902 Model; Smith & Wesson, Springfield, Massachusetts, 1902–5. ·38 S&W Special; 4in, 5in, 6in or 6·5in barrel. Six-shot. This differed from the 1899 pattern principally in the chambering and the addition of a locking lug for the extractor-rod head. The 1902 and the improved third or 1905 models (1905–42) served as prototypes for all the subsequent Smith & Wessons in this calibre-group.

676, 677. Hand Ejector, ·38, Military & Police, Third or 1905 Model; Smith & Wesson, Springfield, Massachusetts. ·38 S&W Special; 4in, 4·5in, 5in or 6in barrel. Six-shot. The perfected version of the ·38 Hand Ejector

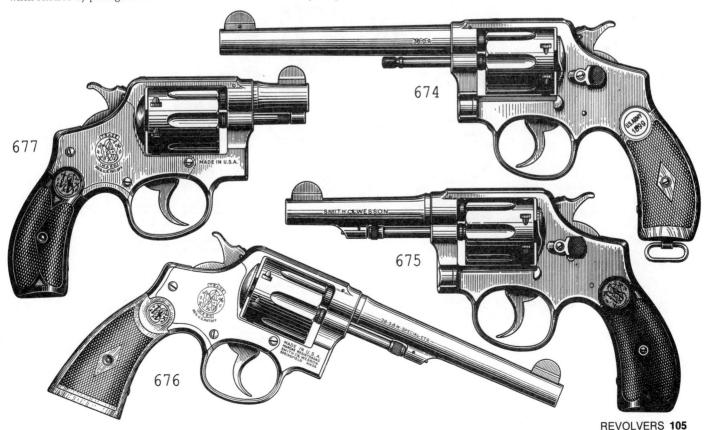

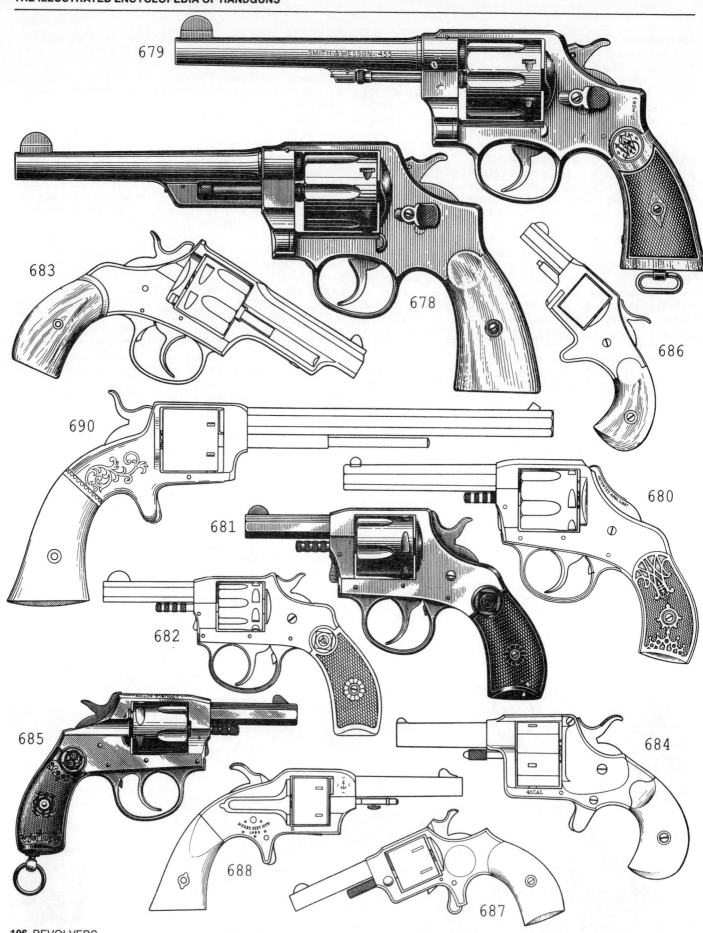

has been outstandingly successful. The millionth gun was made in 1942; by 1965, more than 2,500,000 had been sold. Some examples were offered with 2in barrels, but are uncommon.

678. Hand Ejector, ·44, First Model, also known as the ·44 Military Model 1908; Smith & Wesson, Springfield, Massachusetts, 1908–15. ·38–40 WCF, ·44 S&W Russian, ·44 S&W Special, ·44–40 WCF or ·45 Long Colt; 5in or 6·5in barrel. Six-shot. This was the first of the company's large-calibre swinging-cylinder revolvers, originally embodying a third locking lug between the yoke and the frame. This gave the ·44 Hand Ejector its sobriquet 'Triple Lock', though it was also known as the 'New Century'. The second model (1915–40, all chamberings excepting ·44 S&W Russian), dispensed with the third lug and the under-barrel extractor-rod shroud in an attempt to cut costs. The shroud reappeared on the third or 1926 version (1926–49), though the third locking lug did not.

679. Hand Ejector, ·455; Smith & Wesson, Springfield, Massachusetts. ·455; 6·5in barrel. Six-shot. These were made during the First World War for the British government, initially embodying the additional lock between the yoke and the frame (first version, 1914–15), and then in the simpler two-lug guise (second version, 1915–16). The US ·45 M1917 Smith & Wesson revolver was also essentially similar to the two-lug ·44 Hand Ejector, but had a 5·5in barrel, a lanyard ring on the butt, and chambered rimless ·45 ACP cartridges with the assistance of two half-moon clips. Designed by Joseph Wesson in collusion with Springfield Armory, the clips were necessary to support the rimless cartridges, facilitate loading, and allow the extractor to function effectually.

680. H&R; Harrington & Richardson, Worcester, Massachusetts. ·32, ·38 or ·44; 2·5in or 4in barrel. five (·38, ·44) or six (·32) shots. These were all typical double-action non-ejecting revolvers, fitted with the 1887-patent spurless safety hammer.

681. H&R Model 4 or 1904; Harrington & Richardson, Worcester, Massachusetts, 1904–41. ·32 S&W Long or ·38 S&W; 2·5in, 4·5in or 6in barrel. Five (·38) or six (·32) shots. The ·32 S&W H&R Model 5 (1905–39) was similar, but had a smaller five-cartridge cylinder.

682. H&R Model 6 or 1906; Harrington & Richardson, Worcester, Massachusetts, 1906–41. ·22 LR rimfire; seven-shot.

683. Hyde Model 1879; Iver Johnson's Arms & Cycle Works Company, Worcester, Massachusetts, 1883–7. ·38; five-shot. This peculiar revolver, patented by Andrew Hyde, ejects in a most distinctive way. The tip of the elongated cylinder-axis pin is hinged in the shroud under the barrel, and rigidly connected to a star-shaped extractor recessed in back face of the cylinder. When the gate on the right side of the frame is opened, the cylinder can be swung laterally to the right, then slid along the axis pin to ejects spent cases simultaneously. The action is then closed, whereupon fresh cartridges can be loaded singly through the gate. The Hyde model was not particularly successful and was soon replaced by more effectual designs.

684. Improved Patent House Pistol; Colt's Patent Fire Arms Manufacturing Co., Hartford, Connecticut, c.1874. ·41 rimfire; five-shot. This was a modification of the original Cloverleaf pattern (fig. 708) with a cylinder of more conventional form.

685. Iver Johnson Model 1900; Iver Johnson's Arms & Cycle Works Company, Fitchburg, Massachusetts, 1900–47. ·22 rimfire, ·32 rimfire, ·32 centre-fire, or ·38 centre-fire; 2·5in, 4·5in or 6in barrel. Five-shot (seven in ·22 only). A modernised version of the American Bull Dog.

686. Gem (sic); Bacon Arms & Manufacturing Company, Norwich, Connecticut. ·22 Short rimfire; five-shot.

687. Liberty; Hood Firearms Company, Norwich, Connecticut. ·22; five-shot. Spent cases were ejected by removing the cylinder.

688. Merwin & Bray, Worcester, Massachusetts, c.1865–8. ·22 rimfire. It shoots the same cartridges as the Wood-patent revolver shown in fig. 653.

689. My Friend; James Reid, Catskill, New York, 1866/7–80. ·22 rimfire; seven-shot. Patented in 1865, this single-action revolver has no barrel, relying instead on an elongated cylinder. The peculiar shape of the frame and grip allows it to be used as a knuckle-duster. The frame is bronze, whilst the cylinder and other parts are steel. My Friends were also made in ·32 and ·41. A few even appeared in 1880–4 with short barrels attached to the front of the frame.

690. Navy Model; Bacon Arms & Manufacturing Company, Norwich, Connecticut. ·32 rimfire.

691. Navy Model; Hopkins & Allen, Norwich, Connecticut. ·38; 6in barrel. Six-shot. These guns were made in small numbers in the late 1870s, embodying the detachable side-plate patented in 1877. The general layout is similar to the contemporaneous Forehand & Wadsworth Navy Model.

692. Navy Model; Hopkins & Allen, Norwich, Connecticut. ·38; 7in barrel. Six-shot. This is a refinement of the preceding gun, probably dating from 1880. Refinement is obvious in the shape of the frame and the design of the ejector, but the detachable side-plate is absent. Very few of these guns were made.

693. Navy Model; Edwin Prescott, Worcester, Massachusetts, c.1861–3. ·36 rimfire. An improved version of the original S&W-type Prescott (fig. 719), this is usually found with the name of distributors Merwin & Bray.

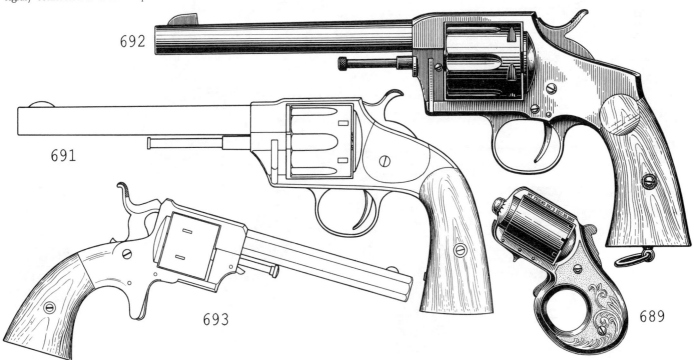

694. New Army Model, 1892; Colt's Patent Fire Arms Manufacturing Company, Hartford, Connecticut. ·38 Long Colt; 11·2in overall, 6in barrel. Six-shot. Adopted by the US Army to replace the Single Action Army Model (Peacemaker), this differs from the New Navy model only in the shape of the grip, which is extended downward and has a lanyard loop on the butt. Variants were made with 3in or 4·5in barrels (8·15in and 9·65in overall respectively), and also in ·41-calibre.

695. New House Pistol; Colt's Patent Fire Arms Manufacturing Company, Hartford, Connecticut. ·32 rim- or centre-fire; five-shot. Introduced in 1880, this is distinguished by a squared butt and a loading gate on the right side of the frame behind the cylinder. It was more commonly encountered in ·38 or ·41.

696. New Line ·38 Breech-Loading Revolving Pistol; Colt's Patent Fire Arms Manufacturing Company, Hartford, Connecticut. ·38 rimfire; five-shot. The drawings represents the improved pattern of 1876, with the locking-bolt notches on the rear of the cylinder instead of its surface. Similar

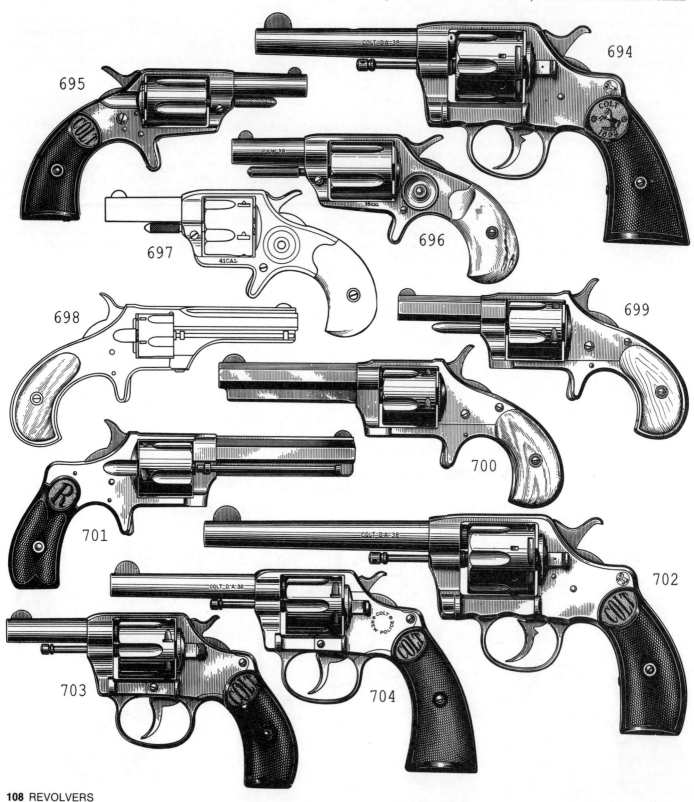

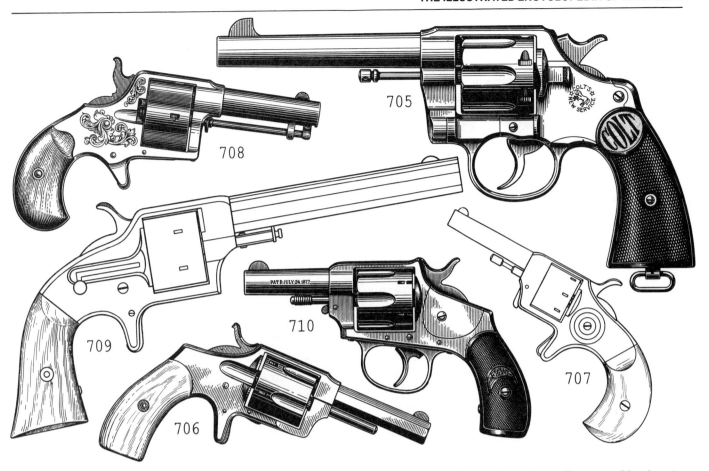

patterns were offered in ·22 rimfire (seven-shot), ·30 rimfire or ·32 rimfire.

697. New Line ·41 Breech-Loading Revolving Pistol; Colt's Patent Fire Arms Manufacturing Company, Hartford, Connecticut. ·41 rimfire; five-shot. This is the original version of the series (1874–6) with the locking-bolt notches on the surface of the cylinder. Guns made after 1876 have longer flutes and the notches on the rear surface of the cylinder.

698. New Line No. 1; E. Remington & Sons, Ilion, New York, 1873–86. ·30 Short rimfire; 2·8in barrel. Five-shot. This is the smallest of a series of single-action sheathed-trigger pocket revolvers introduced by Remington in the 1870s. Ejector rods were carried on the right side of the shroud beneath the barrel.

699. New Line No. 3; E. Remington & Sons, Ilion, New York, 1875–86. ·38 Short rimfire; 3·75in barrel. Five-shot.

700. New Line No. 3, improved or lightened pattern; E. Remington & Sons, Ilion, New York. ·38 Short rimfire or ·38 centre-fire; 2·5in barrel. Five-shot. The barrel may be round or octahedral. Note the absence of the ejector; the cylinder-axis pin is removed to allow the cylinder to be detached from the frame. These guns were probably made in the 1880s.

701. New Line No. 4; E. Remington & Sons, Ilion, New York, 1877–86. ·41 Short rimfire; 2·5in or 3·75in barrel. Five-shot. Also made for ·38 centre-fire cartridges. The No.4 was apparently the only gun in the series to have a prawl on the back strap.

702. New Navy Model, 1892; Colt's Patent Fire Arms Manufacturing Company, Hartford, Connecticut. ·38 Long Colt; 10·85in overall, 6in barrel. Six-shot. The US Navy adopted the original Navy Model in 1889, the first Colt to incorporate a laterally-swinging yoked cylinder and simultaneous spent-case ejection—though a similar system had been patented by the Italian, Arturo Albini, as early as 1869. The M1889 cylinder had long flutes and the locking-bolt notches on its rear face; this was changed in 1892, when a conventional system of short flutes and locking notches on the outer surface reappeared. The recoil shield on the left of the frame is pulled back to release the yoke, immediately distinguishing Colts from the swinging-cylinder Smith & Wessons. Most of the latter group have a separate thumb-piece which moves forward.

703. New Pocket Model; Colt's Patent Fire Arms Manufacturing Company, Hartford, Connecticut, 1893–1905. ·32 Long Colt; 2·5in, 3·5in or 6in barrel. Six-shot.

704. New Police Model; Colt's Patent Fire Arms Manufacturing Company, Hartford, Connecticut, c.1896–1907. ·32 Long Colt, ·32 S&W or ·32 Colt New Police. This was originally a variant of the New Pocket Model with a longer grip.

705. New Service Model; Colt's Patent Fire Arms Manufacturing Company, Hartford, Connecticut, 1897–1943. ·45 Long Colt; 10·75in overall, 5·5in barrel, 38·8oz. This was the first of the large-calibre swinging-cylinder Colts to appear, though it was mechanically similar to the contemporaneous ·38 New Army Model. New Service revolvers were made in a selection of chamberings—including ·44 S&W Special, ·44 S&W Russian, ·38–40 WCF or ·44–40 WCF—and in a variety of barrel lengths. A version known as 'M1917' was acquired by the US Army during the First World War.

706. New Ranger No. 2; Hopkins & Allen, Norwich, Connecticut. ·30 short rimfire. A modernised version of the standard Hopkins & Allen sheathed-trigger designs. The original Ranger No. 2 apparently had a rounded butt and frame.

707. OK Model; J.M. Marlin, New Haven, Connecticut, 1863–70. ·22 rimfire, ·30 rimfire or ·32 Short rimfire; 2·1–3·1in barrel, 6·5oz. Seven-shot (·22). A typical single-action pocket revolver with a sheathed trigger.

708. Patent House Pistol or 'Cloverleaf'; Colt's Patent Fire Arms Manufacturing Company, Hartford, Connecticut, 1871–3. ·41; 14·5oz. Four-shot. This single-action sheathed-trigger gun gained its nickname from the unusual cross-section of the cylinder. It was not particularly successful.

709. Plant's Manufacturing Company, New Haven, Connecticut, c.1863–6. ·28, ·30, ·36 or ·42 teat-fire. These guns were made to patents granted to Ellis and White in 1859–63. An ejector-rod lies in a housing on the right side of the frame behind the cylinder, spent cases being thrust forward. After the Plant factory was burned down, guns were apparently made by Marlin.

710. Pocket Model Double Action; Forehand & Wadsworth, Worcester,

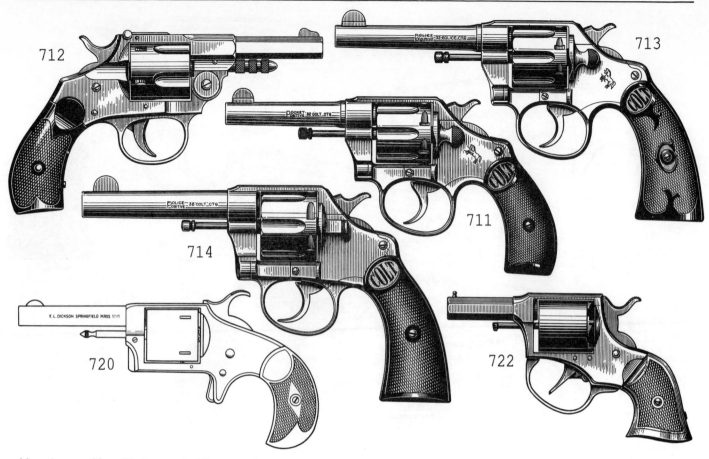

Massachusetts. ·32 or ·38; 7in overall, 2·7in barrel. Five (·38) or six (·32) shots. A conventional double-action non-ejector, patented in 1877 and introduced about 1879–80.

711. Pocket Positive; Colt's Patent Fire Arms Manufacturing Company, Hartford, Connecticut, 1905–40. ·32 Long Colt; 8·5in overall, 4·5in barrel, 16oz. Improved by the introduction of the Positive Lock safety system, this replaced the 1893-vintage New Pocket Model.

712. Police Model 1884; Maltby, Curtiss & Company, New York, prior to 1888. ·32 rimfire; five-shot. The resemblance to a hinged-frame revolver is misleading, as the frame is solid; what appears to be a lateral pivot ahead of the cylinder is an integral part of the dismantling system. The design was apparently patented by Otis and John Smith in 1881.

713. Police Positive ·32; Colt's Patent Fire Arms Manufacturing Company, Hartford, Connecticut, 1907–39. ·32 Long Colt; 6·75–10·25in overall, 2·5, 4in, 5in or 6in barrel, 18–22oz. Introduced to replace the New Police Model of 1896.

714, 715. Police Positive ·38; Colt's Patent Fire Arms Manufacturing Company, Hartford, Connecticut, 1908–43. ·38 Colt New Police or ·38 S&W; 8·5in overall, 4in barrel, 20oz. Six-shot. Introduced to provide a more effectual weapon than the ·32 Police Positive (q.v.), these guns were popular. The short-lived ·38 Colt New Police variant was produced in 1911–14 in response for greater stopping power, but was eclipsed by the more powerful Police Positive Special Model of 1907. The Banker's Special (1928–43) shared the frame and grip of the ·38 Police Positive, but had a 2in barrel, weighed 19oz and lacked the lanyard ring on the butt.

716, 717. Police Positive Special; Colt's Patent Fire Arms Manufacturing Company, Hartford, Connecticut, c.1908–73. ·32, ·32-40 WCF, ·38 S&W or ·38 Special; 1·25–6in barrel. Six-shot. This was the first small-frame swinging-cylinder revolver to be chambered for what, at the time of introduction, was considered to be very powerful ammunition. Guns made towards the end of production had streamlined fronts sights, rounded butts, and insignificant internal improvements.

718. Pond's Improved Model Revolver; Lucius Pond, Worcester, Massachusetts, c.1864–70. ·32 rimfire; five-shot. This gun had removable

chamber liners, which could be loaded with standard rimmed cartridges before being re-inserted (a successful attempt to evade patents controlled by Smith & Wesson). The combination cylinder-axis pin and ejector rod was patented in 1864 by Freeman Hood. A seven-shot ·22 rimfire variant was also made.

719. Prescott, Smith & Wesson type; Edwin Prescott, Worcester, Massachusetts, c.1860–1. ·32 rimfire. Externally similar to the S&W No. 2, this has a solid frame and an 1860-patent cylinder latch.

720. Ranger No. 2; E.L. Dickson, Springfield, Massachusetts. ·32 rimfire; 6·7in overall, 2·8in barrel. Six-shot. Introduced about 1871 and made until c.1880. Hopkins & Allen also marketed a gun of this name, suggesting that Dickson may have been a distributor.

721. Regulation Police; Smith & Wesson, Springfield, Massachusetts, 1917 to date. ·32 S&W Long. This was a minor variant of the ·32 Hand Ejector with a longer walnut butt. A minor modification is currently being made as the Model 31-1.

722. Rider Pocket Revolver or Remington-Rider; E. Remington & Sons, Ilion, New York ·32 Short rimfire; 2in or 3·5in barrel, 10oz. Five-shot. Introduced in 1860 as a cap-lock, but made from about 1870 until 1886 for metallic-case ammunition.

723. Russian Model; Forehand & Wadsworth, Worcester, Massachusetts. ·44 Russian; 12·8in overall, 7·5in barrel, 34·8oz. Six-shot. This large single-action revolver was touted briefly in 1877–9. Spent cases are expelled singly through the loading gate by a laterally-pivoting yoked ejector beneath the barrel.

724–726. Single Action Army Revolver, Model P, Peacemaker or M1873; Colt's Patent Fire Arms Manufacturing Company, Hartford, Connecticut. ·45 Long Colt. Six-shot. After experimenting with an unsuccessful open-frame revolver marketed briefly as the Model 1872, Colt persuaded the US Army to adopt this classic design in 1873. The general arrangement resembles the perfected Colt cap-locks, excepting that the frame is solid. Spent cases are ejected sequentially by a sliding spring-loaded rod in a case on the lower right side of the barrel. The head (or finger piece) of the ejector projects under the barrel to the left, allowing the firer to eject

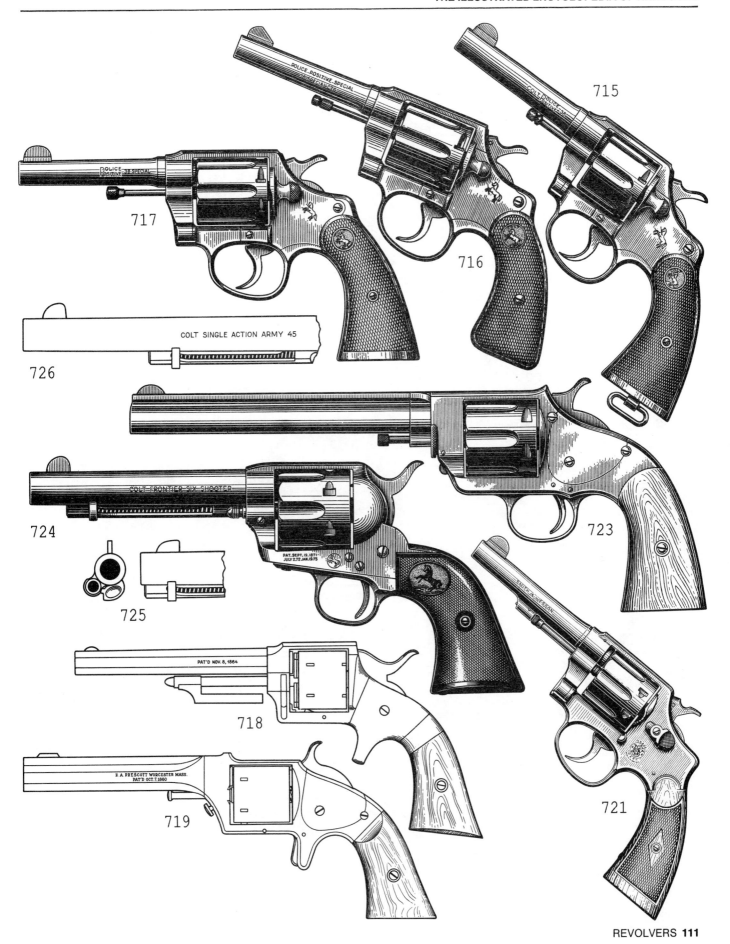

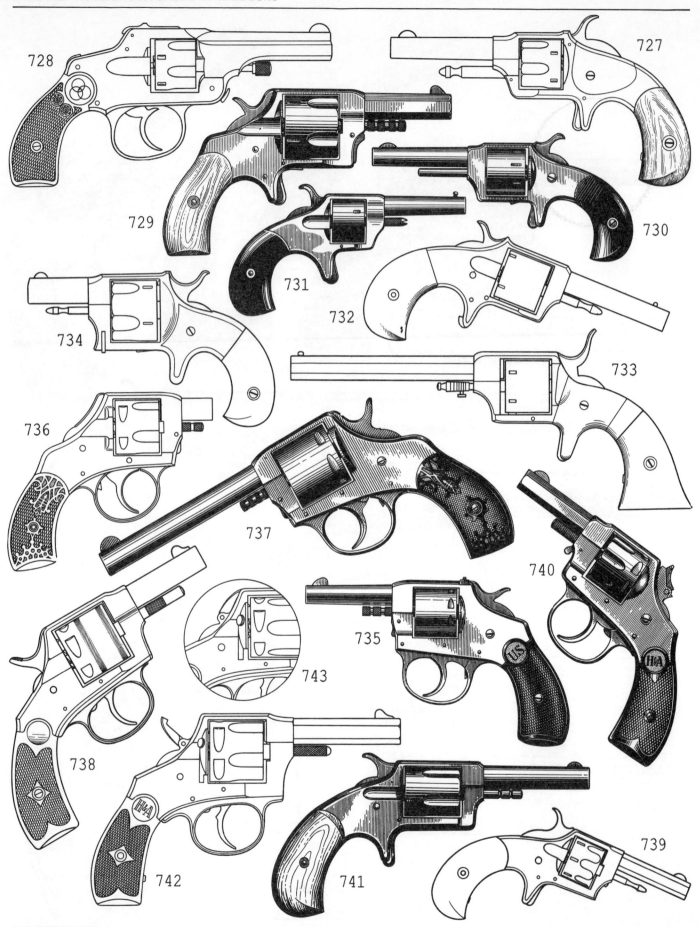

spent cases whilst rotating the cylinder with the firing hand. The single-action firing mechanism has a non-rebounding hammer, a half-cock notch providing a safety feature of dubious efficacy.

Several differing versions of the Single Action Army Model have been made. The US Army bought cavalry patterns with 7·5in barrels and guns for the artillery with 5·5in barrels; these were sold commercially as the Peacemaker and Frontier Models respectively. Revolvers were produced to meet commercial requirements in chamberings from ·22 rimfire to ·476 Eley, and in an assortment of barrel lengths from 2in to 16in.

The Single Action Army revolver soon became universally popular amongst lawmen, pioneers, gold prospectors, farmers and cowboys alike, remaining in service with the US Army until displaced by the first of the ·38-calibre Colts in 1892. Commercial production ceased in 1940, but began again in 1955 in response to public demand and is still underway.

The so-called Sheriff or Bartender Models, based on the Single Action Army frame (more rarely, on the Bisley Model) are distinguished by short barrels—usually 2·5 to 4·75in—and the omission of the ejector mechanism. Detail differences may also be evident in the individual components. In recent years, Colt has offered a ·22 LR rimfire or ·357 Magnum 'House Pistol' of this general type, with a 4in barrel.

The post-1955 New Single Action Army Model has been made by Colt's Patent Fire Arms Manufacturing Company, Colt Industries Firearms Division, and Colt's Manufacturing Co., Inc., in ·32–20 WCF, ·357 Magnum, ·38 Special, ·44 Special or ·45 Long Colt. Barrels measure 4·65in, 5·5in or 7·5in. The New Frontier Model is similar, but carries the front sight on a high ramp whilst the back sight can be adjusted laterally. The New Frontier Buntline Special (·45 Colt only)—based on the original long-barrel guns made in 1878–84—had a 12in barrel, which gave an overall length of 18in and a weight of 43oz. It has an ordinary fixed back sight. 'Ned Buntline' was the pseudonym of Edward Judson, a nineteenth-century American writer/traveller.

Colt-type revolvers have also been made extensively in Europe in recent years, particularly in Italy. Owing to various improvements, imitation Western-style Colts are frequently better than their prototype.

727. Smith; Otis Smith, Rock Fall, Connecticut, 1873–80. ·32; five-shot. The patented rod beneath the barrel, which releases the cylinder from the frame, acts as an ejector once the cylinder has been removed.

728. Smith Hammerless Model 92; Maltby, Henley & Company, New York, c.1892–1900. ·32 or ·38; five-shot. This double-action design, with the general appearance of a hinged-frame revolver, was patented by John Smith in 1888–9 and made by Otis Smith. Maltby, Henley simply acted as distributors.

729. Smoker; Iver Johnson's Arms & Cycle Works Company, Worcester, Massachusetts, 1875–84. ·38 S&W; five-shot. A sheathed-trigger non-ejecting pattern.

730. Sterling; maker unknown. ·22; seven-shot.

731. Tramp's Terror; Hopkins & Allen, Norwich, Connecticut. Production of these guns began in 1871 and continued until c.1880.

732. Tycoon No. 2; Iver Johnson's Arms & Cycle Works Company, Worcester, Massachusetts, 1873–87. ·32 Short rimfire; five-shot. A typical American single-action sheathed trigger revolver, made in a variety of sizes—No. 1 in ·22 Short rimfire; No. 3 in ·38 rimfire; and No. 4 in ·44 Short rimfire.

733. Union Revolver; Union Arms Company, Hartford, Connecticut, c.1860–1. ·32 rimfire; five-shot. A single-action sheathed-trigger gun of primitive form, not unlike the Prescott Navy Model (fig. 693).

734. US Arms Company, Brooklyn, New York, 1873–8. ·41 rimfire; five-shot. Similar to the Etna No. 2 excepting for the catch on the cylinder-axis pin. Also offered in ·22 and ·38 rimfire.

735. US Revolver Company. ·22 Long rimfire; seven-shot. This is basically a second-grade American Bull Dog (fig. 634), sold by Iver Johnson to disguise its origins. Similarly marked versions of the Model 1900 (fig. 685) are also known. The brand name was used until 1940.

736. Vest Pocket Model; Harrington & Richardson Arms Company, Worcester, Massachusetts. ·32; 1·1in or 2in barrel. Five-shot. An ultra-compact version of the Young America (fig. 751).

737. Victor; Harrington & Richardson Arms Company, Worcester, Massachusetts. ·32; 2·5in or 4in barrel. This was similar to the American Model (fig. 636), excepting for the cylindrical barrel and plain-surface cylinder.

738. XL Bulldog; Hopkins & Allen, Norwich, Connecticut. ·32 M&H; six-shot. In the 1880s, Hopkins & Allen introduced a series of double action XL revolvers, which were similar to European Bulldogs but lacked ejectors.

739. XL No. 1; Hopkins & Allen, Norwich, Connecticut, c.1878–90. ·22 rimfire; seven-shot. One of a series of similar guns, made in accordance with patents granted in 1871–7.

740. XL No. 1 Double Action; Hopkins & Allen, Norwich, Connecticut. ·22 rimfire; seven-shot.

741. XL No. 2; Hopkins & Allen, Norwich, Connecticut, c.1878–85. ·30 rimfire; six-shot. The XL Nos. 2½ and 3 were similar, but chambered ·32 Short rimfire and ·32 Long rimfire respectively.

742, 743. XL No. 3 Double Action; Hopkins & Allen, Norwich, Connecticut. ·32; 2·5in barrel. Six-shot. Note the unusual folding cocking-spur on the hammer.

744. XL No. 4; Hopkins & Allen, Norwich, Connecticut, c.1878–85. ·38 rimfire; five-shot.

745. XL No. 6 Double Action; Hopkins & Allen, Norwich, Connecticut. ·38 M&H; five-shot.

746. Warner type; Springfield Arms Company, Springfield, Massachusetts. ·30 Short rimfire; five-shot. Guns of this type were introduced in 1857 as cap-locks. However, small numbers were made for metal-case ammunition in the early 1860s.

747. Wesson & Harrington Arms Company (Harrington & Richardson after 1876), Worcester, Massachusetts, 1874–8. ·32 Short rimfire; six-shot. A conventional sheathed-trigger single-action pocket revolver.

748. White Star; probably made by Hopkins & Allen of Norwich,

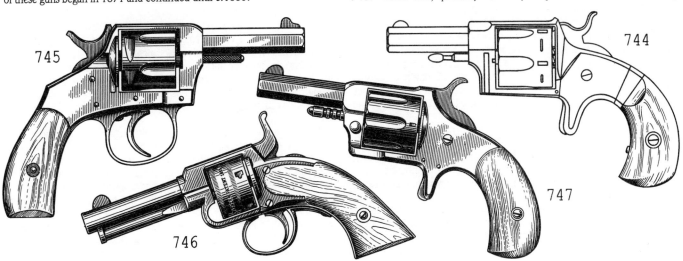

Connecticut. ·32 Short rimfire; 6·55in overall, 2·5in barrel. Five-shot.

749. Whitney Arms Company, Whitneyville, Connecticut. ·38 rimfire; 1·5in, 2·5in or 3·5in barrel. Five-shot. Also offered in ·22 or ·32, with cylinders holding seven and five rounds respectively.

750. Williamson pattern; National Arms Company, Brooklyn, New York. ·45 teat-fire. A large holster pistol made to the 1864 patent of David Williamson. The cases are ejected forward by means of a rod.

751. Young America; Harrington & Richardson Arms Company, Worcester, Massachusetts, 1887–1941. ·32; 2in barrel, Five-shot. Fitted with a spurless safety hammer, patented in 1887 by Homer Caldwell.

Not shown. Hopkins & Allen also made the ·32 Young America and ·38 American, similar in appearance to the Harrington & Richardson revolver shown in fig. 751. Harrington & Richardson made ·22 rimfire seven-shot revolvers with single-action firing mechanisms and sheathed triggers. They were similar to the Hopkins & Allen Ranger No. 2 (fig. 720), but often had ejectors.

Hinged-frame, pivoting frame and similar patterns

752. A.J. Aubrey Model; Meriden Firearms Company, Meriden, Connecticut. ·32; 3in barrel, Six-shot. Made for the distributors Sears, Roebuck & Company in the 1890s. Differing chamberings and barrel lengths may be encountered.

753. American Arms Company, Boston, Massachusetts. ·38; five-shot. A copy of the Smith & Wesson ·38 Single Action or 'Baby Russian' introduced in the late 1870s. Spent cases extract simultaneously when the breech is opened (fig. 130).

754. American Arms Company, Boston, Massachusetts (to 1893), and Milwaukee, Wisconsin, c.1892–1901. ·32, ·38 or ·44; five- or six-shot. This revolver is fitted with a switch allowing a form of double action—in which the trigger is pressed slightly back, released, then pulled back completely—or a means of cocking the hammer with one pull and then releasing it with the next. This was patented in 1890 by Henry Wheeler, but was a needless complexity. The guns may have been made by Iver Johnson (q.v.).

755. American Standard Tool Company, Newark, New Jersey, 1869–73. A copy of the Smith & Wesson No. 1 top-break revolver.

756. Automatic; Hopkins & Allen, Norwich, Connecticut. ·32 or ·38; 3in or 4in barrel. Five-shot. Introduced in 1885, this ejects simultaneously as the action is opened. The latch is generally in the form of two levers, though some of the earliest guns used a Smith & Wesson-type cross-bolt. The double-action firing mechanism includes a rebounding hammer and a floating firing pin in the frame.

757–760. Automatic Ejecting Model; Harrington & Richardson Arms Company, Worcester, Massachusetts. ·32 S&W or ·38 S&W; 3·75in, 4in, 5in or 6in barrel. Five (·38) or six (·32) shot. Introduced in c.1896, this was similar to contemporaneous Smith & Wesson revolvers with simultaneous case extraction. A variant had a spurless hammer (fig. 758), whilst a ·38 Knife Model had a 2·5in folding bayonet (fig. 759) beneath the barrel. Fig. 760 shows a long-barrelled version with extended grips.

761. Automatic Hammerless; Hopkins & Allen, Norwich, Connecticut. ·32 or ·38; five-shot. A version of the standard 'Automatic' model (fig. 756) with an enclosed hammer and a double-action-only firing mechanism.

762. Crispin pattern; Smith Arms Company, New York, 1865–70. Patented by Silas Crispin in 1865, this chambers distinctive ring-fire cartridges with the priming-compound annulus around the case-wall above the base. The frame is hinged ahead of the trigger and the cylinder is made in two parts, the front bored through and the rear portion with six blind recesses. Cartridges are inserted into the chambers through the front part of the cylinder. When the revolver is closed, the priming collars lie at the cylinder joint whilst the bases rest in the recesses. The hammer hits the collar obliquely from the top.

763. Double Action ·32; Smith & Wesson, Springfield, Massachusetts.

·32 S&W; 3·25in, 3·5in, 4in, 6in, 8in or 10in barrel. Five-shot. Like the ·38 pattern (below), the ·32 was made in five versions. Sales of about 328,000 (1880–1919) made it the best known of the company's hinged-frame pocket revolvers. The guns drawn here represent the short-lived third pattern of 1882–3.

764–767. Double Action ·38; Smith & Wesson, Springfield, Massachusetts. ·38 S&W; five-shot. The original pattern (fig. 764) was introduced in 1880, being identified by a detachable plate running the entire depth of the left side of the frame beneath the hammer. This was quickly replaced by the second pattern (1880–4, fig. 765), which had an

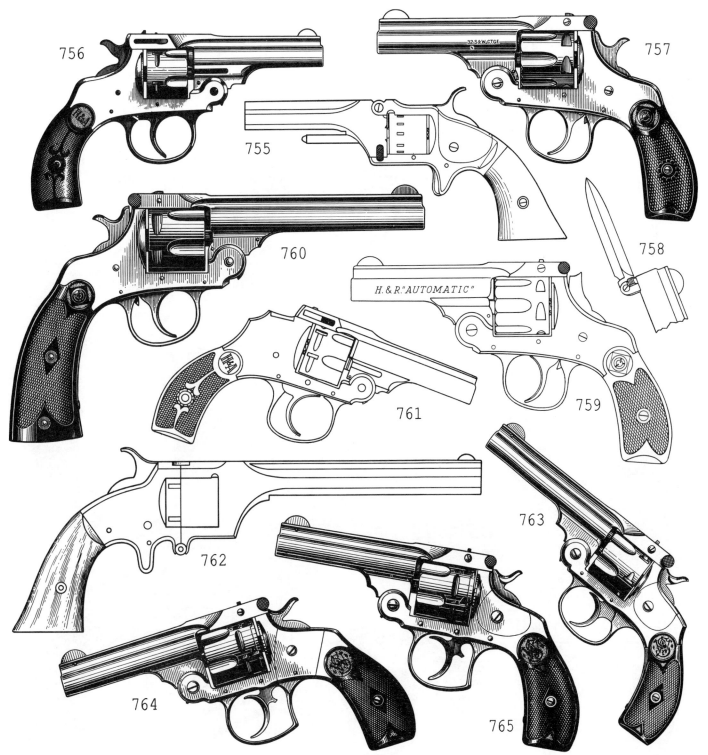

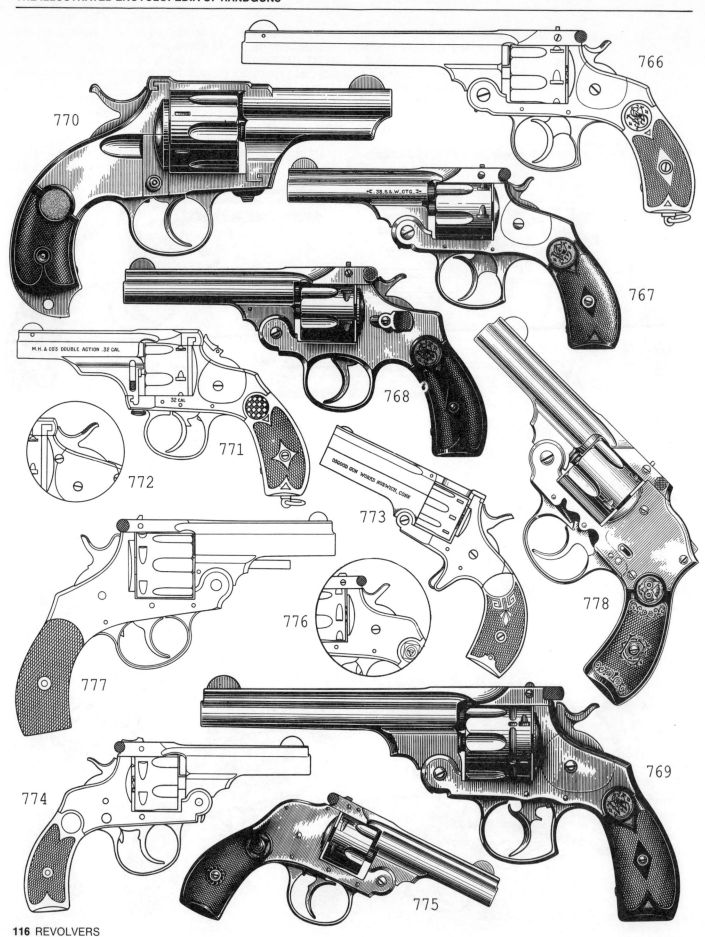

elliptical side plate. The third version of 1884–95 (figs. 766, 767) lacked the circumferential groove on the cylinder between the flutes and the cylinder-stop notches. The fourth (1895–1909) and the fifth patterns (1909–11) were virtually identical externally with the third variant.

768. Double Action ·38 Perfected Model; Smith & Wesson, Springfield, Massachusetts, 1909–20. ·38 S&W or ·38 Colt New Police; 3·25–6in barrel. Five-shot. The frame of this break-open gun was built on the general lines of the ·32 Hand Ejector, with an additional barrel-lock catch on the left side of the frame beneath the hammer.

769. Double Action ·44, or New Model No. 3; Smith & Wesson, Springfield, Massachusetts, 1881–1913. ·44 S&W Russian; 4in, 5in, 5·5in, 6in or 6·5in barrel. Six-shot. This was the first of the company's large-calibre double-action auto-ejectors. The Double Action Frontier (1886–1913) was similar, but had a longer cylinder chambered for ·44–40 WCF ammunition.

770. Double Action Pocket Army Model; Merwin, Hulbert & Company, and (from 1892) Hulbert Brothers & Company, New York. ·44; six-shot, c.1884–96. This is a modified top-strap Pocket Army (fig. 799) with a new firing mechanism. The barrel is linked to frame in two places instead of the previous one.

771, 772. Double Action Pocket Model or Triumph; Merwin, Hulbert & Company, and (from 1892) Hulbert Brothers & Company, New York, c.1885–96. ·32; five-shot. The ·38-calibre model has an ordinary hammer spur (see inset). Made in Norwich, Connecticut, by Hopkins & Allen.

773. Duplex; Osgood Gun Works, Norwich, Connecticut (but possibly made elsewhere), c.1881–3. ·22/·32. Patented by Freeman Hood, this interesting single-action sheathed-trigger revolver contains seven ·22in cartridges in the cylinder and one ·32 round in a barrel doubling as the cylinder axis. The barrels tip downward to load.

774. Fyrberg Arms Company, Hopkinson, Massachusetts, c.1903–10. ·32 or ·38; five-shot. Patented in 1903, this is an imitation of the Smith & Wesson system with an improved locking latch. Manufacture was probably sub-contracted to Iver Johnson.

775, 776. Hammerless; Harrington & Richardson Arms Company, Worcester, Massachusetts. ·32 S&W; 2–6in barrel. Five-shot. Also made as a seven-shot ·22 rimfire.

777. Harrington & Richardson Arms Company, Worcester, Massachusetts. ·32 or ·38; five-shot. These double-action simultaneous ejectors are believed to have been introduced in 1887. Differing from each other in calibre, barrel length and grip, they also had a cylindrical cylinder-axis pin (replaced on later designs by a pentahedral pattern). The star-type extractor was prevented from rotating by splines.

778. Iver Johnson's Arms & Cycle Works Company, Fitchburg, Massachusetts. Another version of the enclosed-hammer Wheeler-trigger system (see fig. 754).

779. Manhattan Fire Arms Company, New York (to 1863) and Newark, New Jersey, c.1861–8. ·22; seven-shot. A near-facsimile of the Smith & Wesson No. 1, with the cylinder-catch on the lower part of the frame instead of the upper portion. The American Standard Tool Company arose from a reorganisation of this company.

780–782. Meriden Fire Arms Company, Meriden, Connecticut, prior to 1909. ·32 or ·38; 3in, 4in or 5in barrels. Five-shot. These are simultaneous-ejection patterns (see fig. 130), often found with enclosed hammers (fig. 781) or a front sight of most unusual form (fig. 782).

783–785. Model No. 1; Smith & Wesson, Springfield, Massachusetts. ·22 Short rimfire; seven-shot. These were the first metal-case cartridge revolvers to be marketed successfully in the USA. The first pattern (made in 1857–60) initially had a flat spring-latch for the barrel, but this was soon replaced by a vertically-sliding sprung block. The second version (1860–8) had a flat brass frame with a detachable plate on the left side beneath the hammer, and other engineering changes. The third pattern (1868–82) had a rounded iron frame, a fluted cylinder and a bird's head butt.

To load the No. 1, the barrel was hinged upward to allow the cylinder to be removed. Spent cases were punched out of the chambers with an under-barrel rod (see fig. 125). The cylinder lock was in the upper rear part of the frame, where it acted in concert with the hammer.

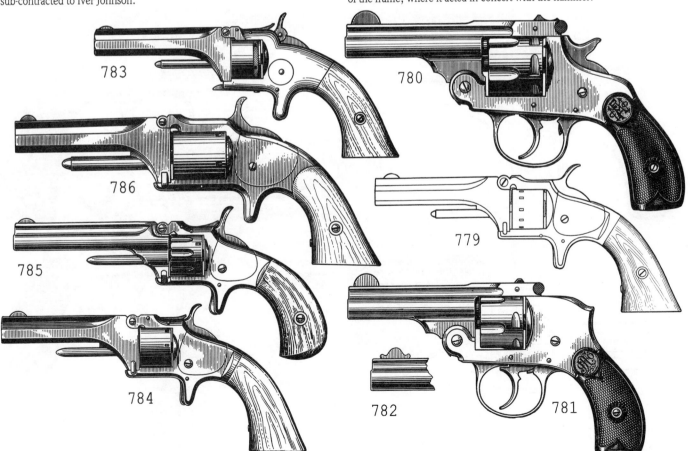

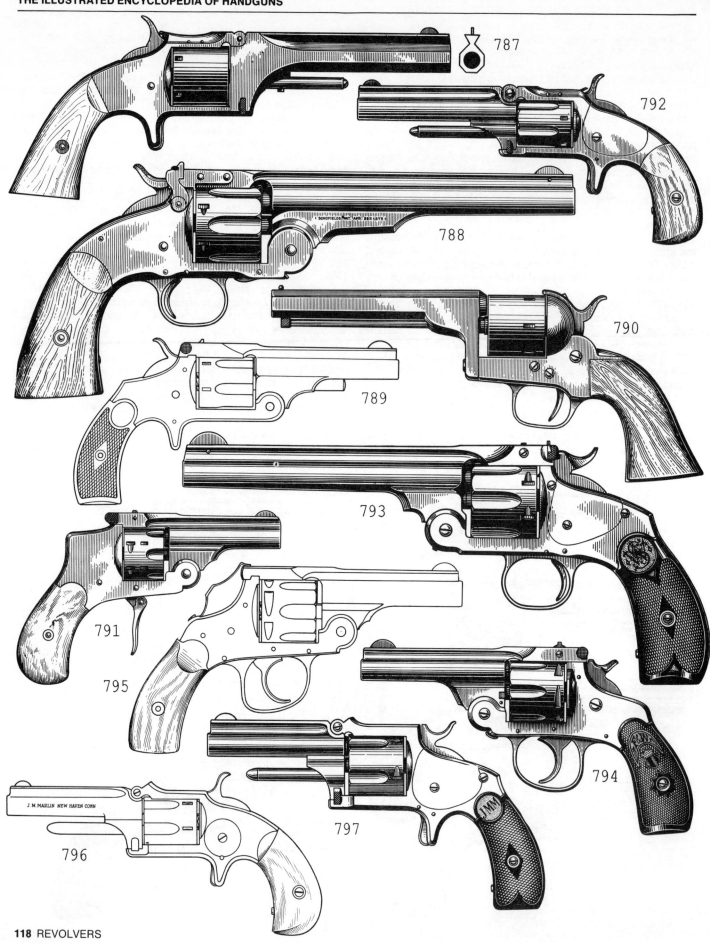

786. Model No. 1½; Smith & Wesson, Springfield, Massachusetts, 1865–75. ·32 Short rimfire; five-shot. This was simply an enlargement of the No. 1.

787. Model No. 2 Army; Smith & Wesson, Springfield, Massachusetts, 1861–72. ·32 Long rimfire; six-shot. This was similar to the No. 1, but was larger, had a six-shot cylinder and chambered more powerful cartridges.

788. Model No. 3 Schofield; Smith & Wesson, Springfield, Massachusetts, 1875–8. ·45; six-shot. This was a variation of the standard No. 3 American, with the barrel latch and an improved extractor mechanism patented in 1871–3 by Major George Schofield of the US Army.

789. Model 83 Shell Ejector; Otis Smith, Rock Fall, Connecticut. ·32 rimfire; five-shot. Patented in 1881, this single-action sheathed-trigger revolver expels spent cases simultaneously when the barrel is tipped downward.

790. Moore's Patent Fire Arms Company, Brooklyn, New York. ·32; seven-shot. The barrel/cylinder of this 1862-patent revolver can be rotated laterally around the pivot at the front of the frame when a catch alongside the hammer is pressed. This served as a prototype of the swinging-cylinder group. Also offered in ·30 or ·44.

791. New Baby Hammerless; Henry Kolb, Philadelphia, Pennsylvania. ·32; five-shot. Spent cases are ejected simultaneously in accordance with fig. 130.

792. New Model No. 1½; Smith & Wesson, Springfield, Massachusetts, 1868–75. ·32 Short rimfire; five-shot. This was a modernised version of the original No. 1½, with a rounded frame and a fluted cylinder. Some guns were apparently made for centre-fire ammunition in the 1870s.

793. New Model No. 3 or Single Action ·44; Smith & Wesson, Springfield, Massachusetts. ·44 S&W Russian; 3·5–8in barrel. Six shot. An adaption of the perfected Russian Model of 1874 (see fig. 543), this single-action auto-ejector was introduced in 1878. Production actually ceased in 1898, though guns were sold from stock until 1912. Variations of the No. 3 included the New Model No. 3 Frontier in ·44–40 WCF (1885–1908) and the New Model No. 3 Target (1887–1910).

794. New Model Double Action; Forehand & Wadsworth, Worcester, Massachusetts, c.1887–90. ·32 or ·38; five (·38) or six (·32) shot.

795. New Model Hammerless; Forehand Arms Company, Worcester, Massachusetts, 1890–1902. ·32; six-shot. A typical hinged-frame pocket revolver with a double-action-only firing mechanism and a shrouded hammer. Ejection is in accordance with fig. 130.

796. No. 32 Standard; J.M. Marlin, New Haven, Connecticut, 1875–87. ·32; 3·25in barrel, 12·5oz. Five-shot. This is similar to the Smith & Wesson No. 2, but the cylinder catch is in the lower part of the frame. The XX and XXX Standard were similar, but in ·22- and ·30-calibre respectively.

797. No. 38 Standard; J.M. Marlin, New Haven, Connecticut, 1878–87. ·38; five-shot. Similar to the No. 32, but with a strengthened frame and a prawled back strap.

798. Plant's Manufacturing Company, Southington and New Haven, Connecticut. This single-action sheathed-trigger revolver was based on the contemporaneous Smith & Wesson system in which the barrel tips upward. The distinctive rimless rimfire cartridges, with a hemispherical indentation in the base, were inserted backward into the chambers once the cylinder had been detached. Spent cases were punched out singly with the assistance of the rod projecting beneath the barrel

799. Pocket Army Model; Merwin, Hulbert & Company, New York, c.1881–2. ·44; 3·25in barrel. This single-action revolver—made by Hopkins & Allen—was an improved version of the Russian Model (fig. 804), but was soon replaced by a stronger version with a top-strap above the cylinder. Pocket Army guns could be converted to long-barrel (5in or 7in) 'Army' form merely by exchanging the barrel.

800. Pocket Model; Merwin, Hulbert & Company, New York, c.1879–85. ·38; five-shot. This Hopkins & Allen-made single-action sheathed-trigger revolver was the first of the series to embody a strengthened frame with a top strap above the cylinder.

801. Pond; Lucius Pond, Worcester, Massachusetts. ·32 rimfire. The cylinder is removed by tipping the barrel upward, after which spent cases can be punched out individually with the cylinder-axis pin.

802. Premier; Harrington & Richardson Arms Company, Worcester, Massachusetts. ·22 Long rimfire; 2–6in barrel. Seven-shot. A five-shot ·32 centre-fire version was also made. Guns with barrels longer than 4in generally also have an extended butt.

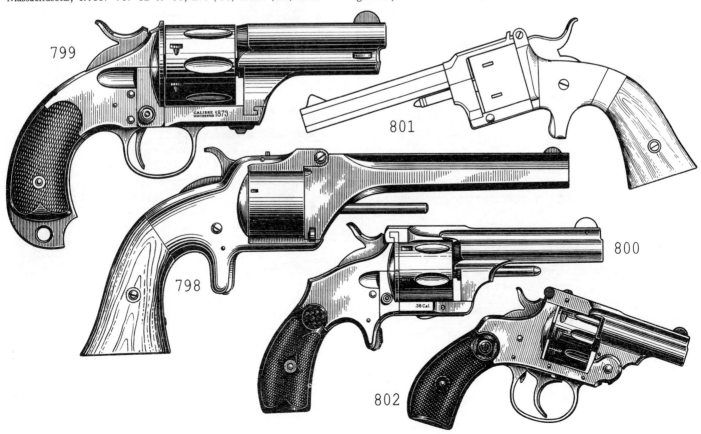

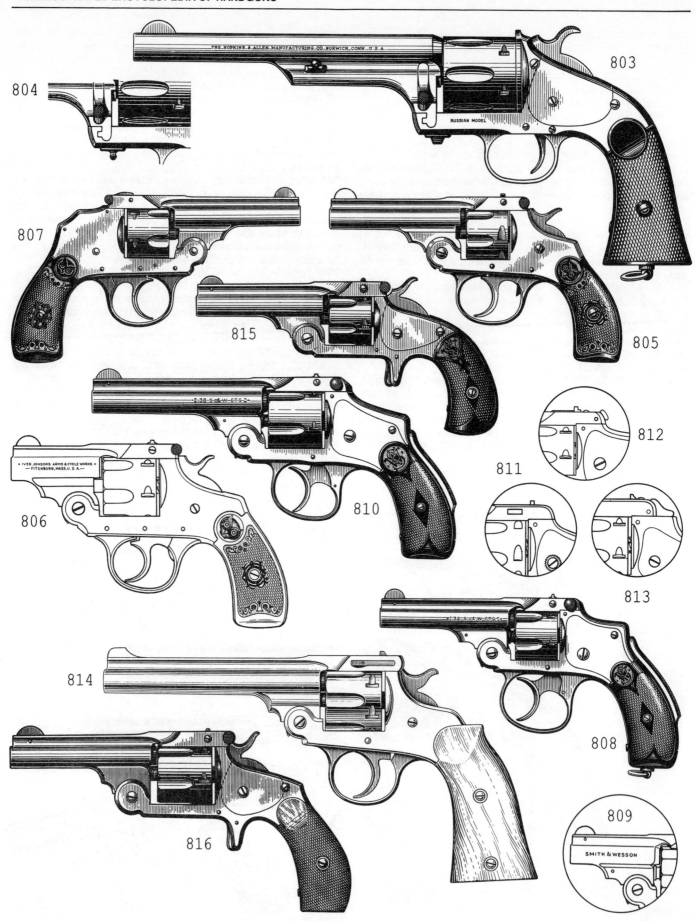

803, 804. Russian model; Merwin, Hulbert & Company, New York, 1877–8. ·44 S&W Russian; 7in barrel. Six-shot. Made by Hopkins & Allen to patents granted in 1874–7, this single-action revolver was distinguished by its quirky simultaneous extraction system. The barrel is released by a catch and then turned a quarter-circle to the right (fig. 129), whereafter spent cases can be extracted simply by moving the barrel and cylinder forward. The action is then replaced. A loading gate on the right side of the frame, partly formed by the upper portion of the safety wedge, pivots outward to give access to the chambers as the cylinder is turned.

805, 806. Safety Automatic; Iver Johnson's Arms & Cycle Works Company, Fitchburg, Massachusetts. ·32 or ·38; 2–6in barrel. Five- or six-shot. Introduced in 1892, these embody the famous 'Hammer-the-Hammer' safety system relying on a separate firing pin in the frame, a flat-face hammer, and a safety or transfer bar. The blow of the hammer is transmitted to the firing pin by way of the raised bar. When the trigger is released, however, the bar moves downward and the hammer can no longer transmit its blow to the firing pin. From 1908 onward, the Safety Automatic revolvers used coil-type main springs with an adjustable-tension system. Production continued until 1950 in an assortment of barrel lengths, finishes and grips.

807. Safety Automatic Hammerless; Iver Johnson's Arms & Cycle Works Company, Fitchburg, Massachusetts, 1894–1950. ·32 or ·38; 2–6in barrel. Five- or six-shot. An enclosed-hammer variant of the standard guns (figs. 801, 802).

808, 809. Safety Hammerless ·32; Smith & Wesson, Springfield, Massachusetts. ·32 S&W; 2–6in barrel. Five-shot. This was little more than a diminution of the ·38 pattern (fig. 810), being made in three patterns. The first (1888–1902) had a barrel-latch of the pattern shown in fig. 811, whereas the others had the perfected button latch. The drawing shows the second version of 1902–9; the third, available until 1937, had the front sight forged integrally with the barrel.

810–813. Safety Hammerless ·38; Smith & Wesson, Springfield, Massachusetts. ·38 S&W; 2–6in barrels. Five-shot. This enclosed-hammer pocket revolver was popular for many years. Five basic variations were made, most of the alterations concerning the barrel-latch. Fig. 810 depicts the fourth-pattern gun (1898–1907), though the fifth, available until 1940, was similar excepting that the front sight was forged integrally with the barrel. The insets show the first three models—1886–7 (fig. 811), 1887–90 (fig. 812) and 1890–8 (fig. 813). The guns were also known as

'New Departure' or, popularly, as the 'Lemon Squeezers'.

814. Safety Police Model; Hopkins & Allen, Norwich, Connecticut. ·32 or ·38; 6in barrel. Five-shot. An example of the large-frame ·38 version.

815. Single Action ·32; Smith & Wesson, Springfield, Massachusetts, 1878–92. ·32 S&W; five-shot. This single-action top-break pattern, distinguished by its sheathed trigger and bird's head grip, superseded the old No. 1½.

816. Single Action ·38, or 'Baby Russian', second pattern; Smith & Wesson, Springfield, Massachusetts. ·38 S&W; five-shot. Introduced in 1876, this was the first of the new-model Smith & Wesson pocket revolvers. The original version had an extractor housing beneath the barrel, but this was replaced by the improved form drawn here in 1877. The third pattern of 1891 is described below.

817. Single Action ·38, third pattern; Smith & Wesson, Springfield, Massachusetts, 1891–1911. ·38 S&W; 3·25in, 4in, 5in or 6in barrel. Five-shot. Introduced to replace the second model (above), this was distinguished by its conventional trigger guard. Target-shooting versions in ·22, ·32 and ·38 were also offered, with barrels of 6in, 8in or 10in.

818. Swift Hammerless (uncertain designation); Iver Johnson's Arms & Cycle Works Company, Fitchburg, Massachusetts, 1890–1910. ·38; 2–6in barrel. Five-shot. A predecessor of the perfected Safety Automatic (figs. 801, 802), lacking the transfer bar system. The barrel locking catch is also different.

819. Union; Union Arms Company, Toledo, Ohio, c.1910–12. ·32 S&W; five-shot. Patented by Charles Lefever in 1909, this auto-loading revolver relied on recoil to cock the hammer and turn the cylinder. Spent cases were ejected by tipping the barrel downward.

Not shown. The Smith & Wesson Model No. 3 American was the first large-frame pattern to incorporate the tipping-barrel auto-ejecting action protected by patents originally granted to W.C. Dodge in 1865. The first guns were made in 1870, but then a slightly altered version was sold in quantity to Russia (see fig. 543). The US Army received a thousand guns in 1871, but the Single Action Army Model (Colt) was eventually judged to be superior.

ii) 1917–45: solid-frame patterns

820, 821. Detective Special; Colt's Patent Fire Arms Manufacturing Company, Colt Industries Firearms Division, and Colt's Manufacturing

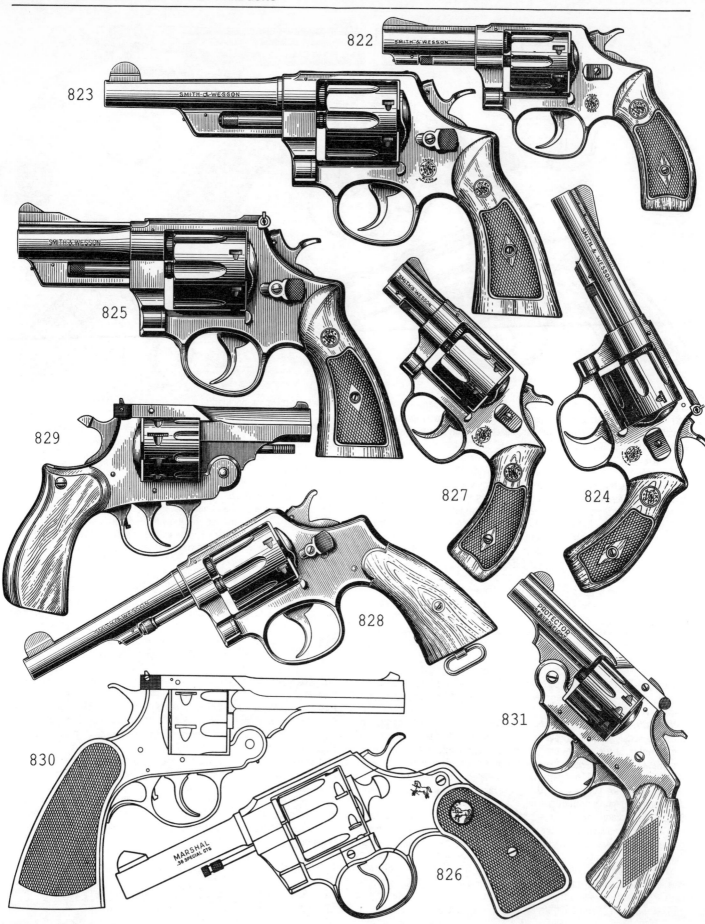

Company, Inc., Hartford, Connecticut, 1927 to date. ·38 Special; six-shot. This was simply a variant of the Police Positive Special (q.v.) with a two-inch barrel. Fig. 821 shows the modern version, with better grips, a low-profile ramped front sight, and a full-length ejector-rod shroud.

822. Hand Ejector ·32 (known from 1957 as the Model 30); Smith & Wesson, Springfield, Massachusetts, 1917–61. ·32 S&W Long; 2in, 3in or 4in barrel (more rarely, 6 inches), 18·7–19·9oz. This was a modernised version of the ·32 Hand Ejector Model 1903, which had been made in several versions from 1903 until 1917. The post-war 'I'-frame ·32 Hand Ejector, production of which began in 1949, had the 1944-type hammer-block mechanism and changes to the extractor rod; the Model 30-1 of 1961–76 was identical, but built on the 'J' frame.

823. Heavy Duty ·38/44 (also known as the Model 20 from 1957); Smith & Wesson, Springfield, Massachusetts, 1930–65. ·38/44 S&W Special; 5in barrel, 40oz. Six-shot. This was basically a ·44 large-frame revolver adapted to handle a special high-pressure cartridge; barrels of differing length are known, though the 5in pattern was supposedly standard. The ·44 Hand Ejector or Military Model, introduced in 1950 and known as the 'Model 21' after 1957, was essentially similar to the ·38/44. It had fixed sights and a similar heavy extractor-rod shroud beneath the barrel, but chambered ·44 Special ammunition.

824. Kit-Gun ·22/32 (Model 34 from 1957 onward), post-war pattern; Smith & Wesson, Springfield, Massachusetts, 1936–60. ·22 LR rimfire; 2in or 4in barrel. This was a simplified version of the ·22/32 Target, built on the frame associated with the ·32-calibre Smith & Wessons. A new series, with an improved frame and better sights, began in 1953. A change to the 'J' frame (Model 34-1) occurred in 1960 and guns of this type are still being made. The word 'kit' is synonymous with the articles carried by sportsmen, travellers or hunters. The original ·22/32 Target revolver of 1911 was improved in 1953, became the 'Model 35' in 1957, gained a 'J' frame (Model 35-1) in 1960, but was discontinued in 1973. It was similar to the Model 34, but had a six-inch barrel, a special ramped front sight, and an extended grip.

825. Magnum ·357 (known after 1957 as the Model 27); Smith & Wesson, Springfield, Massachusetts, 1935 to date. ·357; 3·5in, 5in, 6in, 6·5in or 8·4in barrel. The special Magnum cartridge was developed for Smith & Wesson by Winchester, by elongating the ·38 Special case. The '·357' designation arose from the need to differentiate the new cartridge from the many others in its true ·38-calibre group. The power of the cartridge required the introduction of the strengthened 'N' frame.

826. Marshal; Colt's Patent Fire Arms Manufacturing Company, Hartford, Connecticut, 1942–4. ·38 Special; 4in barrel. Six-shot. This was simply a version of the Official Police revolver with only a single barrel-length option and a matt wartime finish.

827. Terrier ·38/32 (Model 32 from 1957 onward): Smith & Wesson,

Springfield, Massachusetts, 1936–60. ·38 S&W; 2in barrel, 17oz. Five-shot. This was basically a variant of the 1917-vintage ·38 Regulation Police (q.v.) revolver, with a short barrel and a rounded butt. The Model 32-1 of 1960–74 was built on the 'J' frame instead of the original 'I'.

828. Victory Model (Hand Ejector ·38 Military & Police, Victory Model); Smith & Wesson, Springfield, Massachusetts, 1942–5. ·38 S&W Special; 2in or 4in barrel. Six-shot. This was a wartime version of the standard Military & Police pattern, deviating from peacetime products largely in a reduction in barrel-length options and the adoption of a matt parkerized finish. Most examples had plain wood grips and lanyard rings on the butt. An essentially similar 6·5in-barrelled ·38 Hand Ejector M&P was made for the British armed forces in 1940–5, chambered for US ·38 S&W Long or British ·38–200 cartridges (which were interchangeable). It is usually encountered with a matt-grey finish, but is not strictly classifiable as a 'Victory Model'.

Hinged-frame, pivoting frame and similar patterns

829. Defender; Harrington & Richardson Arms Company, Worcester, Massachusetts. ·38; five-shot. The ·22 LR rimfire Model 999 Sportsman is very similar, but has a long barrel and a nine-cartridge cylinder.

830. Defender Special; Harrington & Richardson Arms Company, Worcester, Massachusetts. ·38, five-shot.

831. Protector; Iver Johnson. ·22 LR rimfire; 2·5in barrel. Eight-shot. This gun is typical of the version produced in 1933–49.

iii) Post-1945 solid-frame patterns

The lengthy periods in which some guns have remained in production have meant that many minor changes have been made, particularly in regard to sights, grips and fittings. This is especially true of the Smith & Wessons, which may have 'Magna' grips—initially applied to the distinctive stocks fitted in 1935 to the first ·357 Magnums (fig. 827). Alternatives have included the Target (fig. 849) and the Mustang (fig. 847), whilst auxiliary 'compensators' (fig. 850) were also developed.

832. Agent; Colt's Patent Fire Arms Manufacturing Company, and (from 1964) Colt Industries Firearms Division, Hartford, Connecticut. ·38 Special; 6·75in overall, 2in barrel, 14·5oz. Introduced in 1955, this was basically a Courier frame combined with a Cobra barrel. It was especially popular with female police officers. The original pattern was replaced in 1973 by an alloy-framed 'Agent Lightweight', which lasted until 1985–6.

833, 834. Aircrewman; Colt's Patent Fire Arms Manufacturing Company, Hartford, Connecticut. ·38 Special. Developed in 1951 for the US Air Force, this had a frame and cylinder of aluminium alloy.

835. Bearcat; Sturm, Ruger & Company, Southport, Connecticut, 1966–73. ·22 LR rimfire. This small-scale rimfire derivative of the Colt Peacemaker reappeared in 1993 in modified 'New Super Bearcat' form,

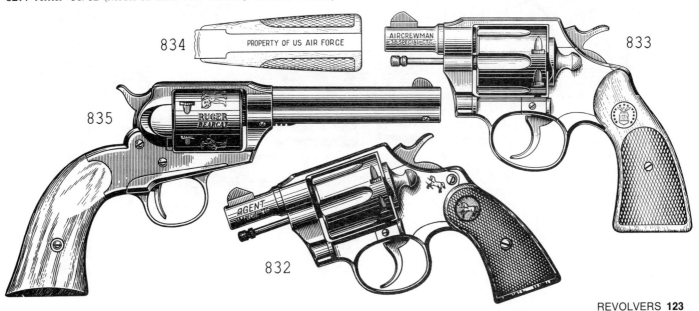

chambering ·22 LR rimfire or ·22 Magnum rimfire rounds interchangeably.

836, 837. Blackhawk and Super Blackhawk; Sturm, Ruger & Company, Southport, Connecticut. ·30 M1 Carbine, ·357 Magnum/·38 Special, ·41 Magnum, ·44 Magnum, ·45 Long Colt; 4·65in, 5·5in, 6·5in, 7·5in or 10in barrel. Introduced in 1955, this centre-fire derivative of the rimfire Single Six (q.v.) was upgraded to 'New Model' standards in 1973 by the addition of an interlocked safety mechanism. The front sight lies on a high ramp and the back sight is adjustable. Fig. 836 shows a five-shot Super Blackhawk derivative made in the early 1990s for a special ·50 cartridge. The Tomahawk was a variant of the standard Blackhawk with a smooth-surface cylinder and a compensator (fig. 837) through which propellant gases escape up and to the side to keep the muzzle down during firing.

838. Bodyguard Airweight ·38 (Model 38 from 1957 onward); Smith & Wesson, Springfield, Massachusetts, 1955 to date. ·38 S&W Special; 2in or 3in barrel, 14·5oz or 16·9oz. Five-shot. Shrouded hammer. The ·38 Model 49 Bodyguard (1959 to date) is identical, but has a steel frame and weighs 20·5oz. The otherwise similar Model 649 is made of stainless steel.

839, 840. Bulldog; Charter Arms Corporation, Stratford, Connecticut. ·44 Special; 2·5in or 3·25in barrel. Five-shot. The Target Bulldog, dating from

1971, is similar but has adjustable sights. ·357 Magnum or ·44 Special; 3in, 4in or 6in barrel. In spite of its name, the gun is intended mainly for self-defence.

841. Bulldog Pug; Charter Arms Corporation, Stratford, Connecticut, and (from 1993) Charco, Inc., Ansonia, Connecticut. ·38 Special; 2·5in barrel. Five-shot. Note the distinctive snubbed hammer.

842, 843. Cadet Model 55C; Iver Johnson's Arms & Cycle Works Company and Iver Johnson's Arms, Inc., Fitchburg, Massachusetts (to 1977) and Middlesex, New Jersey, 1955–84. ·22 LR rimfire; 2·5in barrel. Eight-shot. Cases are extracted by removing the cylinder and punching the spent cases out singly. The rear edge of the cylinder is shrouded to prevent the escape of powder gases or metal fragments should the case-rim rupture. This is particulary useful in shooting galleries, where the long-barrelled derivative was once popular.

844. Cadet Model 55CA; Iver Johnson's Arms & Cycle Works Company and Iver Johnson's Arms, Inc., Fitchburg, Massachusetts (to 1977) and Middlesex, New Jersey. ·22 LR rimfire, ·22 Magnum rimfire, ·32 S&W Long or ·38 S&W Long; five (early ·32 and ·38), six (later ·32) or eight (·22) shots.

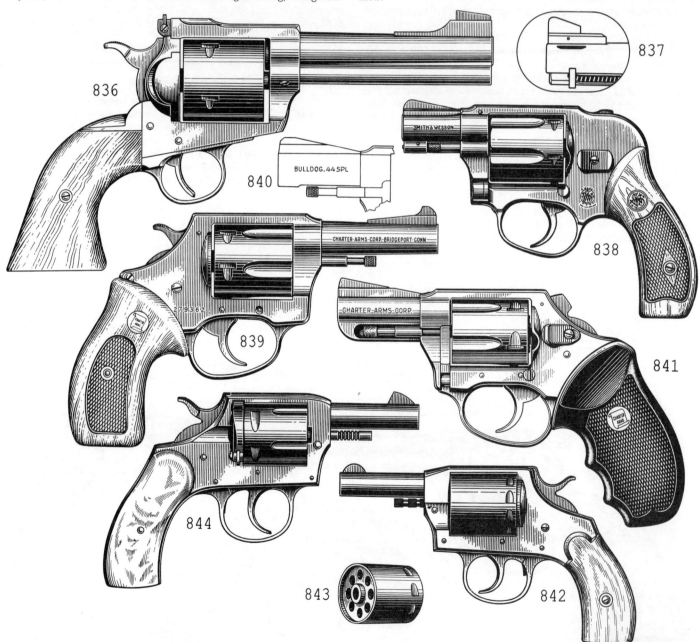

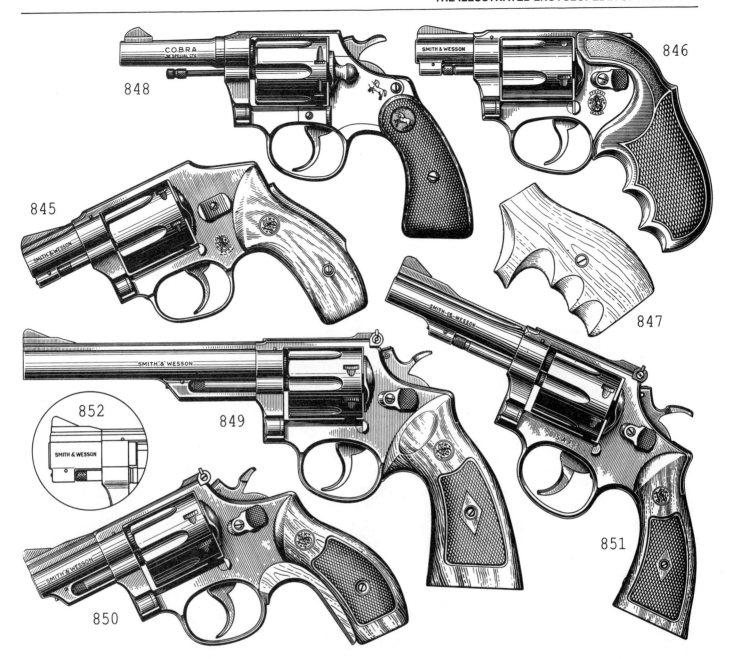

845. Centennial ·38 (Model 40 from 1957 onward); Smith & Wesson, Springfield, Massachusetts, 1952–91. ·38 S&W Special; 2in barrel, 19oz. Five-shot. The most distinctive features are the concealed hammer and an automatic back-strap safety. The ·38 Centennial Airweight or Model 42 (1952 to date) has an alloy frame and weighs merely 13oz.

846, 847. Chief's Special Airweight (Model 37 from 1957 onward); Smith & Wesson, Springfield, Massachusetts, 1952 to date. ·38 S&W Special; 2in or 3in barrel. This is a variant of the ·38 Chief's Special—known from 1957 as the Model 36—which had been introduced in 1950 (2in or 3in barrel, 18·6oz or 20oz). The Airweight had an alloy frame, and weighed 10·8oz with the original alloy cylinder (1952–4) or 12·5oz with the post-1954 steel pattern. Drawing 846 shows a Bianchi grip, whilst 847 is a Mustang type.

848. Cobra; Colt's Patent Fire Arms Manufacturing Company, and Colt Industries Firearms Division, Hartford, Connecticut, 1950–73. ·357 Magnum or ·38 Special; 2in barrel, 15oz. Six-shot. This was a Detective Special with an alloy frame. Versions were made with 3in or 5in barrels. Short-butt but otherwise similar guns in ·22 LR rimfire or ·32 Colt New Police were known as the 'Courier' (q.v.).

849, 850. Combat Magnum ·357, or (after 1957) Model 19; Smith & Wesson, Springfield, Massachusetts, introduced in 1955. ·357 Magnum; 2·5in, 4in or 6in barrel, 30·7–38·8oz. This was created to satisfy demand for a Magnum-power revolver built on the S&W medium 'K' frame, which would thus be smaller and lighter than rival patterns. The Model 53 ·22 Magnum (4in, 6in or 8·5in barrel) was a small-calibre variant of the Model 19, introduced in 1961 for the ·22 Remington Jet cartridge. By exchanging the cylinder and altering the position of the striker, the revolver could be adapted to accept ·22 LR rimfire cartridges. It weighed 39·8oz with a 6in barrel. The Model 66 ·357 Combat Magnum Stainless of 1970 is a duplicate of the Model 19, excepting for the material of the frame.

851, 852. Combat Masterpiece ·38, or (from 1957) Model 15; Smith & Wesson, Springfield, Massachusetts, 1950 to date. ·38 Special; 2in or 4in barrel, 965gm (4in barrel). The Masterpiece series of 1947 originally comprised target revolvers, built on the medium or 'K' frame, but was soon extended to include two 'Combat Models' with streamlined front sights facilitating a holster-draw. The ·22 Combat Masterpiece (4in barrel only) became the Model 18 in 1957. The Model 67 ·38 Stainless Steel Combat Masterpiece, introduced in 1972, is little more than a Model 15 made of

differing material. The original Masterpiece series contained the K-22 (·22 LR rimfire), K-32 (·32 S&W Long) and the K-38 (·38 Special); in 1957, these were designated Models 17, 16 and 14 respectively.

853. Commando; Colt's Patent Fire Arms Manufacturing Company, Hartford, Connecticut, 1954–5. ·38 Special; 2in or 4in barrel. Six-shot. This was a short-lived post-war variant of the Official Police Model.

854, 855. Courier; Colt's Patent Fire Arms Manufacturing Company, Hartford, Connecticut, 1955–7. ·22 LR rimfire or ·32 Colt New Police; 3in barrel. Six-shot. Only a few thousand of this short-butt variant of the Cobra (q.v.) were ever made. During the 1950s, Colt offered special shrouds to streamline the company's smallest revolvers; these enabled the guns to be drawn out of the pocket without snagging the material (fig. 855).

856. Dan Wesson Model 12; Dan Wesson Arms Company, Monson, Massachusetts. ·357 Magnum; 2·5in, 4in, 5in or 6in barrel. Six-shot. This swinging-cylinder pattern, with the locking latch on the yoke, has a unique exchangeable-barrel system.

857, 858. Dan Wesson Model 15; Dan Wesson Arms Company, Monson, Massachusetts, and Wesson Firearms Co., Inc., Palmer, Massachusetts. ·357 Magnum; 2·5–8in barrel. Six-shot. This exchangeable-barrel swinging-cylinder revolver has been offered in several variants—15-2 with a plain barrel; 15-2H with an under-barrel rib; 15-2Y, lacking the rib beneath the barrel but with a ventilated rib above it; and 15-2HY with both ribs. Model 14 is similar to the Model 15, but has a fixed back sight.

859. Deputy; Stoeger Arms Company. ·22 LR rimfire, ·357 Magnum, ·38

Special or ·44 Special; 4·6in, 7·5in or 12in barrel. Introduced to the US market in 1958, but actually made in Italy.

860. Diamondback; Colt's Patent Fire Arms Manufacturing Company, and Colt Industries Firearms Division, Hartford, Connecticut, c.1967–85. ·22 LR rimfire or ·38 Special; 4in or 6in barel, 27·5oz or 31·8oz. Six-shot. this is a medium-frame pattern, with a ventilated barrel rib

861. Frontier Scout Model 62; Colt's Patent Fire Arms Manufacturing Company, and Colt Industries Firearms Division, Hartford, Connecticut. ·22 LR rimfire or ·22 Magnum rimfire; 30oz. Six-shot. This is a reduced-scale version of the Single Action Army Model (fig. 725). The Frontier Scout appeared in 1958, followed by the long-barrelled Buntline Scout in 1959. The original guns (·22 LR only), built on the 'Q' alloy frame, weighed only 24oz. The improved 1962-vintage gun, with a steel 'K' frame, was substantially stronger to handle rimfire magnum ammunition.

862–864. Hand Ejector ·38, Military and Police or (from 1957) Model 10; Smith & Wesson, Springfield, Massachusetts, introduced in 1948 (post-war version). ·38 Special; 2in, 3in, 4in, 5in or 6in barrel. Six-shot. In addition to the standard barrel, a variant (Model 10-1) with a heavy 4in barrel appeared in 1959 (see fig. 907). Introduced in 1952, the Military & Police Airweight (Model 12 from 1957) is similar to the Model 10 but has an alloy frame which reduces its weight to 18·8oz (2in barrel) or 27oz (4in pattern). The Model 64 Military & Police Stainless of 1970 is a stainless-steel Model 10; Model 65 Military & Police (1974) is a heavy-barrel stainless-steel variant chambered for the ·357 cartridge.

865. Hand Ejector, ·45 Military or 1950 Model (redesignated Model 22 in 1957); Smith & Wesson, Springfield, Massachusetts, 1951–66. ·45 ACP/·45 Auto-Rim or ·45 Long Colt; 5·5in barrel, 36·3oz. Six-shot. This was a modernised version of the Model 1917 (q.v.), with an improved hammer mechanism and Magna-pattern grip.

866. H&R Model 504 Ultra Round Butt; Harrington & Richardson, Inc.,

Gardner, Massachusetts, 1984–5. ·32 H&R Magnum; 2·5in or 4in barrel, 22·9oz or 26·1oz. Five-shot.

867. H&R Model 622; Harrington & Richardson, Inc., Worcester and Gardner, Massachusetts, 1957–85. ·22 LR rimfire; 2·5in, 4in or 6in barrel, 25oz or 28·2oz. Nine-shot.

868. H&R Model 649 Convertible; Harrington & Richardson, Inc.,

Gardner, Massachusetts. ·22 LR rimfire or ·22 Magnum rimfire; 5·5in barrel. A Western-style revolver with exchangeable cylinders. The Model 676 Convertible is very similar, but has a trigger guard of the pattern shown in fig. 820 whilst barrel length varies from 4in to 12in.

869. H&R Model 732 Guardsman; Harrington & Richardson, Inc., Gardner, Massachusetts. ·32 S&W Long; 2·5in or 4in barrel. Six-shot. The Model 733 is identical, but chromium plated.

870. H&R Model 900; Harrington & Richardson, Inc., Gardner, Massachusetts. ·22 LR; 2·5in, 4in or 6in. Nine-shot. The long-barrelled revolvers have grips similar to those of the Model 929 (q.v.). To extract spent cases, the cylinder is removed from the frame and the cylinder axis-pin—which became known as the 'push-pin extractor'—is re-inserted into its channel. Pressing the cylinder axis-pin head activates the star-shaped extractor to expel all the cases simultaneously. A flange on the rear of the cylinder prevents a sudden escape of powder gases or small fragments if the rim of a cartridge bursts. The Model 901 is identical, but chromium plated. Model 922 (nine-shot) is also essentially similar.

871. H&R Model 929; Harrington & Richardson, Inc., Gardner, Massachusetts. ·22 LR rimfire; 2·5in, 4in or 10in barrel. Nine-shot. The cylinder swings out to the left to allow simultaneous expulsion of spent cases. The unique safety system is controlled by a key, the slot for which lies is the lower part of the butt.

872. J.C. Higgins Model 88; High Standard Manufacturing Company, Hamden, Connecticut, c.1958–70. ·22 LR rimfire; 4in or 6in barrel. Nine-shot. This is a variation of the Sentinel (q.v.), made for the well-known mail-order distributor Sears, Roebuck. The elegant frame is made of matt-finish aluminium, whilst the barrel, cylinder, hammer and other parts are made of polished steel.

873, 874. King Cobra; Colt Industries Firearms Division, Hartford, Connecticut, 1986–92. ·357 Magnum; 4in barrel. Six-shot. A rugged large-frame design with a heavy barrel, a full-length ejector-rod shroud and a neoprene wraparound grip. The Anaconda (fig. 874, 1990 to date) is a ·44 Magnum variant of the King Cobra with a 6in barrel. It has a distinctive ventilated barrel rib and a full-length ejector-rod shroud.

875. Kit Gun; High Standard Manufacturing Company, Hamden, Connecticut, and High Standard, Inc., East Hartford, Connecticut. ·22 LR rimfire; 4in barrel, 19oz. Nine-shot. Introduced in 1970.

876. Kit-Gun Airweight ·22/32 (Model 43 from 1957 onward); Smith & Wesson, Springfield, Massachusetts, 1955–74. ·22 LR rimfire; 3·5in barrel, 14·1oz. The heavy-duty alloy frame is the same as those of the ·32

S&W revolvers. The Model 51 ·22/32 Kit-Gun Magnum (1960–74) is externally similar to the Model 43, but chambers ·22 Magnum rimfire ammunition, has a steel frame, and weighs 24oz. The Model 63 Stainless Steel (·22 LR rimfire) is also similar, but has a 4in barrel.

877. Lawman Mark III; Colt Industries Firearms Division, Hartford, Connecticut, 1969–87. ·357 Magnum; 2in or 4in barrel. Six-shot. The 'Mark III' series was introduced in 1969. A coil-type main spring replaced the old leaf pattern, and the firing pin was moved from the hammer to the frame. A transfer bar was added so that the blow of the hammer could be transmitted to the striker only when the trigger was squeezed. Revolvers of the Mark III series have chromed-steel springs, a firing pin made of beryllium alloy, a rim around the rear surface of the cylinder—helping to shroud the cartridge rims and close the gap between the cylinder and the rear part of the frame. Rifling has a right-hand twist instead of the previous leftward pattern. The Lawman Mk V of 1982 had an improved firing mechanism with a shorter lock time.

878. Little Ranger; Firearms Import–Export, Inc. (FIE), Miami and Hialeah, Florida, pre-1991. ·22 LR rimfire or ·22 Magnum rimfire; six-shot. An Italian-made replica of the Colt Peacemaker. This particular pattern is a version of the TA-22 made by Tanfoglio of Gardone Val Trompia.

879. Metropolitan Mark III; Colt Industries Firearms Division, Hartford, Connecticut. ·38 Special; 4in barrel. Six-shot. Introduced in 1969, this could be distinguished from the otherwise similar Official Police Mk III by its heavyweight barrel.

880. Mini-Revolver FA-BG ('Boot Gun'); Freedom Arms, Freedom, Wyoming, 1981–9. ·22 LR rimfire; 6·3in overall, 3in barrel, 7·5oz. The ·22 FA-BG Magnum has a longer four-chamber cylinder.

881. Mini-Revolver FA-L; Freedom Arms, Freedom, Wyoming, 1978–89. ·22 LR rimfire; 4·7in overall, 1·8in barrel, 4·8oz. A four-shot ·22 Magnum version has also been made.

882. Mini-Revolver FA-S; Freedom Arms, Freedom, Wyoming, 1978–89. ·22 LR rimfire; 4in overall, 1·1in barrel, 4oz. The FA-S Magnum (·22 Magnum rimfire, four-shot) is similar, but has a longer cylinder.

883. NAA-22L; North American Arms, Spanish Fork, Utah, 1977 to date. ·22 LR rimfire; 3·6in or 4·1in overall, 1·1in or 1·6in barrel, 4oz or 5oz. Five-shot.

884. NAA-22M; North American Arms, Spanish Fork, Utah, 1977 to date. ·22 Magnum rimfire; 4·6in or 5·1in overall, 1·1in or 1·6in barrel, 5·3oz or 6·6oz. Five-shot.

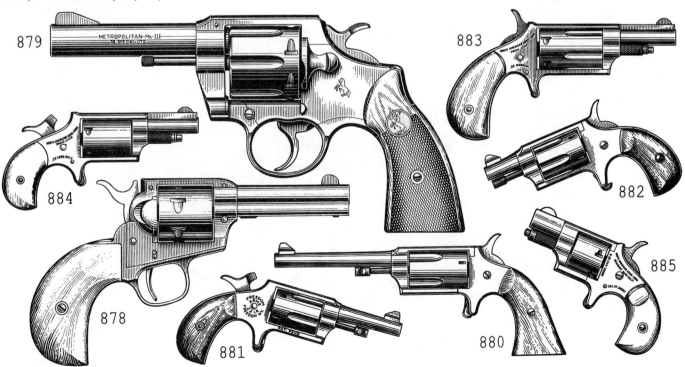

885. NAA-22S; North American Arms, Spanish Fork, Utah, 1977–87. ·22 Short rimfire; 3·6in overall. Five-shot.

886. Off-Duty; Charter Arms Corporation, Stratford, Connecticut, and (from 1993) Charco, Inc., Ansonia, Connecticut. ·22 LR rimfire or ·38 Special; 2in barrel. Five- or six-shot, depending on calibre. The 'Police Undercover'—·32 H&R Magnum or ·38 Special, 2·5in barrel, 17·6oz—is externally similar, excepting that its grip is much like that drawn in fig. 891. The six-shot 'Bonnie' (·32 H&R Magnum) and 'Clyde' (·38 special) patterns are also similar, but are made of blued carbon steel.

887. Official Police Mark III; Colt Industries Firearms Division, Hartford, Connecticut. ·38 Special; 4in, 5in or 6in barrel. Introduced in 1969.

888. Pathfinder; Charter Arms Corporation, Stratford, Connecticut, 1970–92. ·22 LR rimfire or ·22 Magnum rimfire; 3in or 6in barrel. Five-shot.

889. Pocket Pony; ESFAC. ·22 LR; 4·7in overall, 1·75in barrel, 10·6oz. A distinctive reduced-scale 'replica' of the Colt Peacemaker with a bronze frame. Spent cases are ejected by removing the cylinder and punching them out singly.

890, 891. Police Bulldog; Charter Arms Corporation, Stratford, Connecticut, 1976–92. ·357 Magnum, ·38 Special or ·44 Special; 3·5in or 4in barrel, 23·5–27·9oz. Five-shot. Available in carbon or stainless steel. The Pit Bull (9mm Parabellum, 2·5in or 3·5in barrel) is essentially similar, excepting that it is six-shot.

892. 'PPM'; Security Industries of America ('SIA'). ·357 Magnum; 2in or 2·5in barrel. Five-shot. A personal-defence revolver produced in the 1980s. Some versions have spurred hammers and conventional grips.

893. Pussy; High Standard Manufacturing Company, Hamden, Connecticut, and High Standard, Inc., East Hartford, Connecticut. ·22 LR rimfire; 3·5in barrel. Nine-shot. This gun lacks the ejector-rod and case assembly fitted to other models in the range.

894–896. Python; Colt's Patent Fire Arms Manufacturing Company, and Colt Industries Firearms Division, Hartford, Connecticut. ·357 Magnum; 2·5in, 4in, 6in or 8in barrel. Six-shot. This 1953-vintage revolver was the first of the post-war large frame designs, featuring a barrel with a ventilated rib and a full-length ejector-rod shroud.

897, 898. Ruger GP-100; Sturm, Ruger & Company, Southport, Connecticut, 1987 to date. ·357 Magnum or ·38 Special; 3in, 4in or 6in barrel, 35–38oz. Six-shot. A modern design of personal-defence revolver. The current classification system depends on a three-digit number and letter prefixes. Thus the GP-100 Model KGPF-331 is made of stainless steel ('K') and has fixed sights ('F'). It is chambered for ·357 Magnum ammunition (calibre-group '3'), and has a 3in ('3') heavyweight ('1') barrel.

899, 900. Ruger SP-101; Sturm, Ruger & Company, Southport, Connecticut, 1988 to date. ·22 LR rimfire, ·32 H&R Magnum, ·357 Magnum/·38 Special ' + P' or 9mm Parabellum; 2·25in, 3·1in or 4in barrel, 25–29oz. Five (·357/·38, 9mm) or six shots (·22, ·32). A sporting revolver with fixed or adjustable back sights.

901. Security Six; Sturm, Ruger & Company, Southport, Connecticut, 1968–88. ·357 Magnum. ·38 Special; 9·45in overall, 4in barrel, 33·5oz. Ruger made a series of general-purpose and personal-defence revolvers with swing-out cylinders (see fig. 131). Known as Security Six, Service Six and Speed Six, these differed mainly in barrel size, sights and chamberings. The company has used several identification systems in recent years. Thus each differing pattern has been denoted by a three-digit number—e.g., the Security Six was the 'Model 117' and one of the many Speed Sixes was 'Model 737'. Guns have been sold in Europe with 'GA' and 'GS'

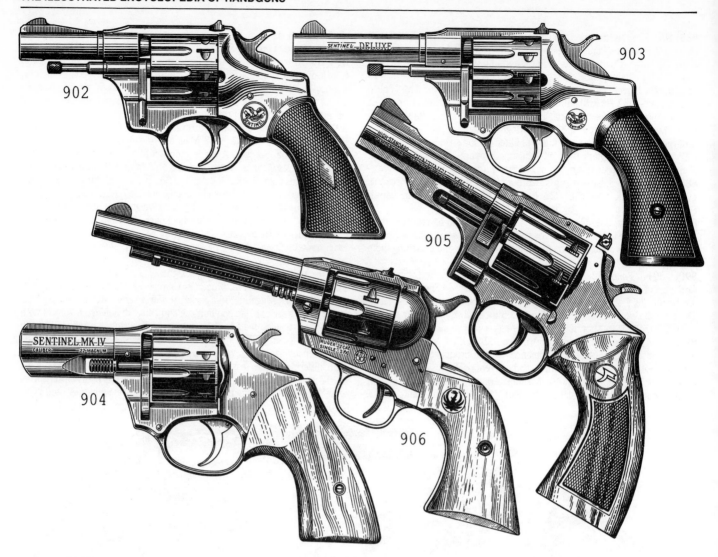

prefixes, 'GS-32' signifying a fixed back sight and a 2in barrel. 'GA' guns had adjustable sights; 'SS' denoted a satin-finish stainless steel. The latest classification system is described under 'Ruger GP-100' (fig. 897).

902. Sentinel; High Standard Manufacturing Company, Hamden, Connecticut, 1954–74. ·22 LR rimfire; 3in, 4in, 5in or 6in barrel, 20–24oz. These swinging-cylinder guns had alloy frames. The Sentinel Snub was similar, but had a 2·5in barrel and a shorter rounded butt.

903. Sentinel Deluxe; High Standard Manufacturing Company, Hamden, Connecticut, 1965–74. ·22 LR rimfire; 4in or 6in barrel. This replaced the Sentinel Imperial (1961–5), which had the front sight on a long ramp.

904. Sentinel Mk I and Mk IV; High Standard Manufacturing Company, Hamden, Connecticut, and High Standard, Inc., East Hartford, Connecticut, c.1969–79. ·22 LR rimfire (Mk I) or ·22 Magnum rimfire; 2in, 3in or 4in barrel. Nine-shot. These steel-frame guns were introduced to supplement and ultimately replace the earlier alloy-frame Sentinels.

905. Sentinel Mk III; High Standard Manufacturing Company and High Standard, Inc., Hamden, Connecticut, c.1969–75. ·357 Magnum; 2·25in, 4in or 6in barrel. Six-shot. The Mark II is similar, but has a fixed back sight.

906. Single Six; Sturm, Ruger & Company, Southport, Connecticut. ·22 LR rimfire; 11·8in overall (6·5in barrel), 4·65in, 5·5in, 6·5in or 9·5in barrel, 32–37oz. Six-shot. This is a modified reduced-scale version of the Colt Single Action Army revolver of 1873, introduced in 1953 and upgraded to 'New Model' standards in 1973. Also offered (from 1985) in ·32 H&R Magnum as the SSM Single Six. The Super Single Six Convertible appeared in 1990 in ·22 LR rimfire and ·22 Magnum rimfire (sold with interchangeable cylinders).

907. S&W Model 13 ·357 Military & Police; Smith & Wesson, Springfield,

Massachusetts, 1974 to date. ·357 Magnum; 3in or 4in barrel. This was originally a heavy-barrel Magnum variant of the Model 10, purchased by the New York State Police. The 'Model 13' designation was adopted when Smith & Wesson made it a standard pattern.

908. S&W Model 16 K-32 Full Lug; Smith & Wesson, Springfield, Massachusetts, 1990 to date. ·32 H&R Magnum; 4in, 6in or 8·4in barrel, 9·15in overall (4in barrel), 42oz (4in barrel). Six-shot. This offers square combat-style grips and an adjustable back sight.

909. S&W Model 28 ·357 Highway Patrolman; Smith & Wesson, Springfield, Massachusetts, 1955–86. ·357 Magnum; 4in or 6in barrel. Six-shot. This is similar to the Model 27 described previously, differing originally in the shaping and finish of the frame, but now largely in the design of the sights.

910. S&W Model 29 ·44 Magnum; Smith & Wesson, Springfield, Massachusetts, 1956 to date. ·44 Magnum; 4in, 6·5in or 8·4in barrel, 43oz, 47oz or 51·5oz respectively. The cartridge was developed by Remington from the ·44 S&W Special, which the Model 29 will also chamber. Owing to the power of the cartridge, a large and very sturdy gun was needed. The Model 629 is simply a '29' with a stainless-steel frame.

911, 912. S&W Model 31 ·32 Regulation Police; Smith & Wesson, Springfield, Massachusetts. ·32 S&W Long; 2in, 3in or 4in barrel. Introduced in 1917 and renamed 'Model 31' in 1957; built on an 'I' frame until 1960, then on a 'J' pattern (Model 31-1) until 1976. Discontinued in 1991. This was virtually identical with the Model 30 excepting for a squared butt. Fig. 911 shows a gun made in the immediate post-war period, whilst that depicted in fig. 912 is a post-1960 version.

913. S&W Model 33 ·38 Regulation Police; Smith & Wesson, Springfield,

Massachusetts. ·38 S&W; 4in barrel, 18oz. Five-shot. Introduced in 1917 and renamed 'Model 33' in 1957; the Model 33-1 of 1960–74 was built on the 'J' frame instead of the earlier 'I' type.

914. S&W Model 57, ·41 Magnum; Smith & Wesson, Springfield, Massachusetts, 1963 to date. ·41 Magnum; 4in, 6in or 8·4in barrel, 44·7oz, 48oz or 52·5oz respectively. The Model 657 of 1986 is identical, but made of stainless steel.

915. S&W Model 58, ·41 Magnum Military and Police; Smith & Wesson, Springfield, Massachusetts, 1964–91. ·41 Magnum; 4in barrel, 41oz. This may be distinguished from the Model 57 by the fixed back sight and the heavyweight cylindrical barrel.

916. S&W Model 60, ·38 Chief's Special Stainless; Smith & Wesson, Springfield, Massachusetts, 1965 to date. ·38 Special; 2in barrel. This is essentially similar to the standard Model 36 Chief's Special (q.v.), but it is made of stainless steel and has only a single barrel-length option.

917. S&W Model 67 ·38 Stainless Steel Combat Masterpiece; Smith & Wesson, Springfield, Massachusetts, 1967 to date. ·38 Special; 2in or 4in barrel. Built on the 'K' frame, this is simply a stainless-steel variant of the ·38 Combat Masterpiece—originally introduced in 1950 and known as the Model 15 from 1957 onward. The 2in-barrel version was originally made for the US Air Force as the 'Model 56' (1962–4) before being assimilated with the standard Model 67.

918. S&W Model 547; Smith & Wesson, Springfield, Massachusetts. 9mm

Parabellum; 3in or 4in barrel, 32·1oz (3in barrel). Six-shot. Specially developed to fire rimless cartridges, this revolver incorporates an extractor with six spring-steel plates. Teeth on the plates enter the extractor grooves on rimless cases, allowing them to be expelled without requiring clips. However, the system did not prove to be as successful as Smith & Wesson had hoped and the Model 547 was discontinued in 1985. The hammer was shortened to prevent the spur being driven back into the thumb-web of the shooter's hand by back-blast from a pierced primer.

919. S&W Model 586 ·357 Distinguished Combat Magnum; Smith & Wesson, Springfield, Massachusetts, 1981 to date. ·357 Magnum; 4in or 6in barrel, 42oz and 45·9oz respectively. This gun introduced the intermediate 'L' frame, midway between the medium 'K' and large 'N'. Model 581 is similar, but has fixed sights and a four-inch barrel.

920, 921. S&W Model 625 Stainless; Smith & Wesson, Springfield, Massachusetts, 1989 to date. ·41 Magnum or ·45 ACP; 3in, 4in or 5in barrel. Built on the large 'N' frame.

922, 923. S&W Model 640 Centennial Stainless; Smith & Wesson, Springfield, Massachusetts, 1990 to date. ·38 Special; 2in or 3in barrel, 6·3in or 7·3in overall, 20oz or 22·5oz. Five-shot. This is a variant of the original Model 40 Centennial, but lacks the automatic safety. The gun in fig. 922 has a special front sight; these are sometimes known as 'Carry/Comp[etition]' patterns

924. S&W Model 686 Distinguished Service Magnum (Carry/

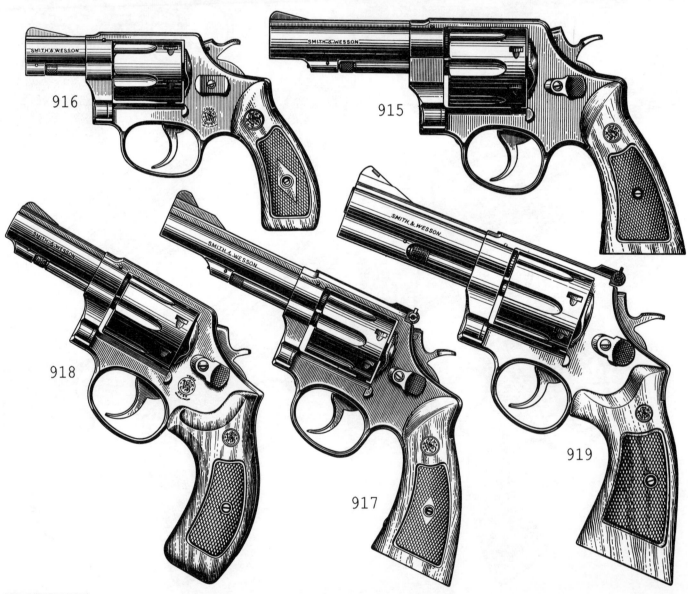

Comp[etition] pattern); Smith & Wesson, Springfield, Massachusetts. ·357 Magnum; 4in, 6in or 8·4in barrel, 44–49oz depending on barrel-length. Six-shot. This is a stainless-steel version of the standard 'L'-frame Model 586 Distinguished Combat Magnum, introduced in 1981. The Model 682 is similar, but has fixed sights and a four-inch barrel.

925, 926. S&W Model 940 Centennial; Smith & Wesson, Springfield, Massachusetts, 1991 to date. 9mm Parabellum; 2in or 3in barrel. Five-shot. This enclosed-hammer gun, derived from the Model 640 Centennial (q.v.), requires a special five-shot clip to chamber the rimless cartridges effectually.

927, 928. Speed Six; Sturm, Ruger & Company, Southport, Connecticut. ·357 Magnum or 9mm Parabellum; six rounds. Discontinued in 1988.

929. 'TDA'; Thermodynamic Associates, Inc. ·357 Magnum; 2·5in or 4in barrel. Six-shot. This swinging-cylinder pattern was made in the mid 1970s in accordance with then-new technology, the frame being a stainless-steel casting and the barrel being a rifled liner. Grips may be of Target or Mustang type.

930. Trooper; Colt's Patent Fire Arms Manufacturing Company, and (from 1964) Colt Industries Firearms Division, Hartford, Connecticut, 1953–69. ·357 Magnum; 4in or 6in barrel. This large-frame revolver—also made in ·22 LR rimfire or ·38 Special—had the front sight on a ramp and an adjustable back sight. It was replaced by the Trooper Mk III.

931. Trooper Mark III; Colt Industries Firearms Division, Hartford, Connecticut, 1969–82. ·357 Magnum; 4in or 6in barel.

932. Trooper Mk V; Colt Industries Firearms Division, Hartford, Connecticut, c.1982–90. ·357 Magnum; 4in or 6in barrel, 39·5 or 46·5oz. Mark V-type Colts were improvements of the Mk III, with a better firing mechanism and a shorter lock-time. They had ventilated barrel ribs and improved grips.

933. Undercover; Charter Arms Corporation, Stratford, Connecticut, and (from 1993) Charco, Inc., Ansonia, Connecticut, 1965 to date. ·38 Special; 2in barrel. Five-shot. A variant chambering ·32 S&W Long appeared in 1970. The hammer acts on the firing pin in the frame by way of a transmitting device, which drops when the trigger returns to its forward position.

934. Viper; Colt's Patent Fire Arms Manufacturing Company, and Colt

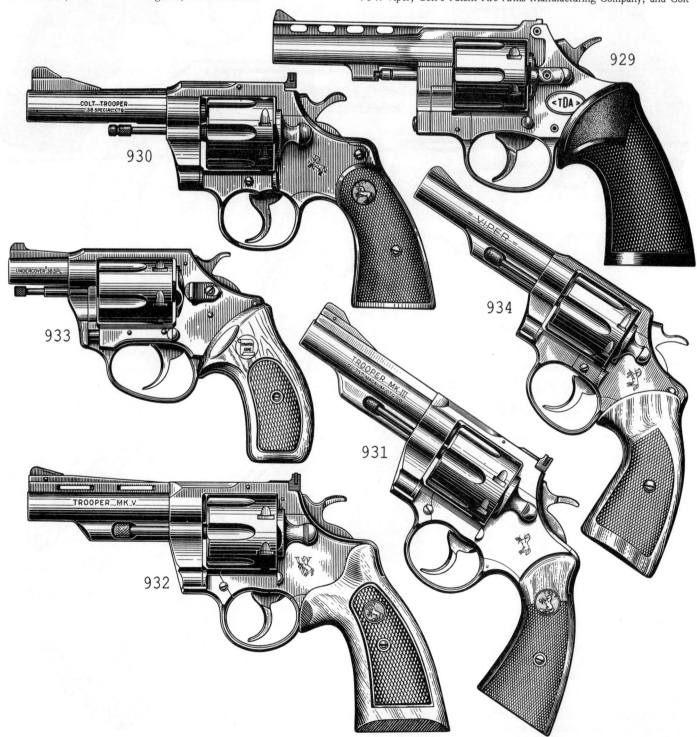

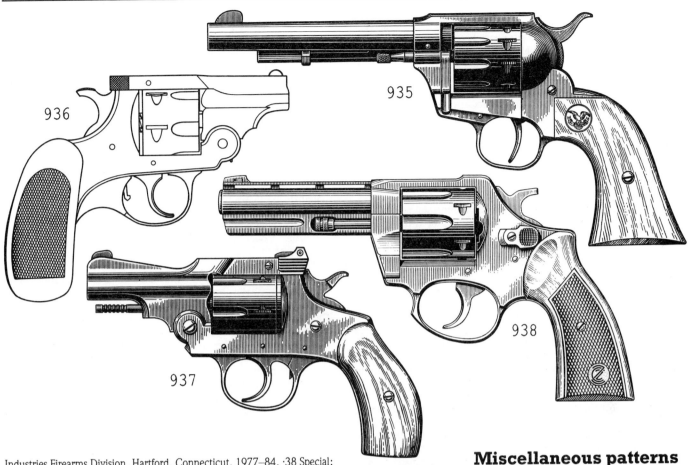

Industries Firearms Division, Hartford, Connecticut, 1977–84. ·38 Special; 4in barrel. Six-shot. A modernised version of the Official Police, with an alloy frame and a half-length ejector-rod shroud.

935. Western; High Standard Manufacturing Company, Hamden, Connecticut, and High Standard, Inc., East Hartford, Connecticut. ·22 LR rimfire; 5·5in barrel. Nine-shot. Based on the Colt Peacemaker of 1873, this gun has a double-action trigger system. The rod ejector is superfluous, though true to Western style, as the cylinder can be swung laterally to expel the spent cases simultaneously. The High Sierra Model is essentially similar, but has a 7in barrel. The Longhorn was also comparable, excepting for the smooth-surface cylinder. The synthetic grips imitate walnut, staghorn or mother-of-pearl. The Durango had a trigger guard and grip-straps of brass. The Double Nine—double-action, nine-shot—had an imitation-ivory grip and a 5·5in barrel.

Not shown. The Savage Model 101 was a reduced-scale ·22 rimfire version of the Colt Peacemaker, but with an adjustable back sight. The barrel measured 5·5in.

Hinged-frame patterns

936. Defender Model 925; Harrington & Richardson, Inc., Gardner, Massachusetts. ·22 LR or ·38 S&W Long; 2·5in or 4in barrel. Five (·38) or nine (·22) shots. Spent cases are ejected simultaneously by opening the action and tipping the barrel downward.

937. Trailsman Model 66 Snub; Iver Johnson's Arms & Cycle Works Company, Fitchburg, Massachusetts, 1959–75. ·22 LR rimfire, ·32 S&W Long or ·38 S&W Long; five (·32, ·38) or eight (·22) shots. The Viking Model 67 was similar, but chambered for ·22 LR rimfire ammunition only. Cases extracted simultaneously as the barrel tipped down (see fig. 130).

Yugoslavia

938. ZCZ Model 1983; Zavodi Crvena Zastava, Kragujevač. ·357 Magnum; 188mm or 230mm overall, 64mm or 102mm barrel, 900gm. Six-shot. A copy of the ubiquitous swinging-cylinder Smith & Wesson.

Miscellaneous patterns

The advent and widespread distribution of revolvers amongst the armies and police forces of the world prior to 1914 was accompanied by an equally rapid increase in the production of guns for commercial sale. Compact guns chambering self-contained cartridges were especially popular, as they were light and easy to handle. They were also inexpensive enough to appeal to virtually everyone. Guns of this general type were made in huge quantities, initially in Belgium but subsequently also in Spain. The best of them were well made and effectual, but the worst—particularly those chambered for small pin- or rimfire cartridges—were weak and of very little real utility.

The cheapest revolvers were generally sold to those who knew least about guns, but had decided to acquire a means of self-defence. The most important criteria, therefore, included small size, ease of use and low price. The concept of 'stopping power' was rarely appreciated. The quality of many pocket revolvers was inferior, largely because their manufacturers were aiming at the cheapest market. Even the so-called 'deluxe' models differed from the mass-produced examples only in the application of nickel plating or clumsily-executed engraving.

Not all of the pocket-revolver class was bad; indeed, there were many guns which offered good-quality material, reliability, and surprisingly good lethality. These were occasionally used by police—particularly plain-clothes men—whilst others were purchased by members of the armed forces for 'off-duty' use. The strongest of them chambered cartridges loaded with smokeless powder.

Revolvers sold commercially were very diverse, though the differences were rarely more than superficial. Few guns exhibited anything original in construction; mechanically, most were based on established principles. Consequently, they can usually be grouped in several classes. Unfortunately, the distinctions between these groups are not always as clear-cut as collectors would like them to be. For example, some of the Bulldogs chamber the 5·5mm Velo-Dog cartridge and thus could be included in the Velo-Dog group. Hybrids may combine Bulldog-like construction with Smith & Wesson-type swinging-cylinder systems. And guns have been deliberately modelled on better-known (and often better quality) designs to capitalise on established markets, though this was often achieved simply by featuring a well-known name—e.g., 'Smith & Wesson', 'Use Only *Colt* Cartridges'—or an approximation of it. Trademarks resembling the Smith & Wesson monogram were particularly favoured by Spansh gunmakers.

Absurdities were often to be found in promotional material. For instance, a gun with typical Bulldog features (see fig. 988) was called 'a revolver of the Nagant system, Lebel, of A. Francotte' in a pre-1917 Russian dealer's catalogue.

There were often more words than data in descriptions: terms such as 'elegant', 'wonderfully burnished', 'has excellent safety features', 'shoots amazingly hard and true' or 'fires with dreadful power' were popular. Many names applied to whole groups of revolvers, e.g. "lady's", 'knuckle-duster' or 'pocket model'. Some guns were designated merely by calibre and the number of shots.

A major problem was created by the advent of the telegraph, which brought with it a series of proprietary telegraphic codes. This persuaded many large wholesalers to apply a range of names to distinguish between their wares. These are not pattern-names in the truest sense, and, with very rare exceptions, never appear on the guns themselves. As virtually no two catalogues are alike, and as individual distributors often applied the same name to differing guns over a period of years, stock-control codes usually have little value in identifying handguns. Sometimes, however, catalogue names are perpetuated on the guns—notably when the weapons were imported in large numbers into specific national markets. As these were often given the importers' names as a condition of the contract, very little extra effort was required to add pattern-names as well.

Among the names suggested by pre-1917 Russian catalogues, therefore, are Antei, Boets, Gerkules, Grozny, Karlik, Mars, Muzhik, Nadezhny, Neptun, Skif, Vityaz and Yermak. Unfortunately, these were given arbitrarily and the same revolvers were distinguished differently in the catalogues of rival traders.

It can also be difficult to establish country of origin. Comparatively few of the cheapest grades of commercially-available revolvers bore makers' marks, though the experienced student can sometimes deduce the manufacturer from details of construction or machining techniques. The appearance of proof marks—which were not always demanded in law—is not necessarily an accurate indicator. The recognition of foreign proof marks varied by country, which meant, for example, that guns made in Spain (where there was no mandatory proof prior to 1925) could not be sold in Britain until they had passed through the proof houses in London or Birmingham.

1. BULLDOG PATTERNS

No sooner had the perfected centre-fire cartridges appeared than the so-called 'British Bulldog' became a major class of pocket personal-defence revolver. Its prototype is generally believed to have been the Webley 'The British Bull Dog, Pattern No. 2',* a compact large-bore weapon introduced in 1878–9 and made until the beginning of the First World War in ·320, ·380, ·442 and ·450. However, the genesis of the gun may be seen in the Royal Irish Constabulary ('RIC') Webley of 1867, or even in the gargantaun ·577 Boxer of the same era.

A classical Bulldog is characterised by a standing breech forged integrally with the one-piece frame/grip. Spent cases are extracted sequentially by a yoke-mounted rod which retracts into the head of the cylinder-axis when not required. The loading gate swings outward to the right. The double-action firing mechanism has an exposed hammer, the barrel is extremely short, and the short bird's head (beaked) butt has a characteristic projection—or 'prawl'—behind the hammer.

---

* A ·41 rimfire version was known as 'The Pug, Pattern No. 1'.

The sturdiness and simplicity of the British Bulldog, and the general inability of the British gun-trade to make guns in great quantity, was immediately noted in Liége. Many Belgian gunmakers began to make Bulldogs to fill the gap that had been created in the market. The earliest examples were virtual facsimiles of the Webley pattern, even to the appearance of the 'Bulldog' name in several forms—e.g., 'British Bull Dog', 'Bul Dog' or 'Belgian Bulldog'. Gradually, however, the guns were produced in greater variety and recognisable sub-classes appeared. Bulldogs with plain bird's head grips, lacking the prawl behind the hammer, were called 'Cobold'; those with metal butt-caps and lanyard rings were called 'Constabulary'. Diminutions of the classical Bulldogs appeared with folding triggers, enclosed or semi-enclosed hammers (the so-called 'hammerless' and 'half-hammer' systems), and an assortment of safety devices. Owing to their restricted dimensions, these pocket revolvers were customarily chambered for tiny rim- or centre-fire cartridges. The smallest of them were often sold as "Ladies' Model" or 'Puppy', and were rarely of much use.

Many of the most characteristic features of the pocket revolvers were soon interchanged with their larger brethren. In addition, many guns were sold by wholesalers who knew little about gunsmithing—but were nevertheless prepared to blur the distinctions until few of the names in their catalogues corresponded with established standards. Thus a revolver with the typical appearance of a Cobold could be called 'Bulldog', or a stubby large-calibre gun could be called a 'Puppy'.

Improvements in the structure of new Bulldog models produced guns that no longer fitted the classical definition of the genre. Features of Velo-Dogs (q.v.) and other sub-groups were soon assimilated with the basic Bulldog ideals, producing constructional hybrids. Simultaneously, some guns of distinctive Velo-Dog appearance were chambered for much larger-calibre cartridges than the original 5·5mm pattern. As these cannot be considered as true Velo-Dogs, they are included here as part of the ubiquitous Bulldog family.

The emergence of pocket-pattern automatic pistols effected changes in the external appearance of the European pocket revolvers that had evolved from the British Bulldog. Revolvers resembling pistols were often to be called 'Browning', either because of their appearance or because they chambered the 6·35mm and 7·65mm semi-rimless pistol cartridges. The largest varieties were comparable with Bulldogs in their basic construction, retaining short barrels, solid standing breeches and sequential spent-case extraction.

Named patterns

Note: unless otherwise stated, details of manufacture are not known.

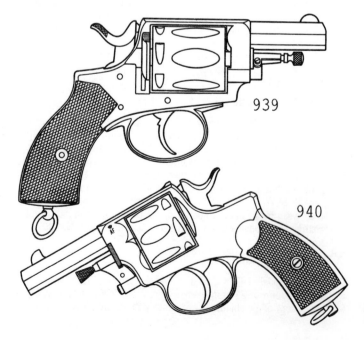

939. 'A.F.'; Auguste Francotte & Companie, Liége. Constabulary type.
940. 'A.F.'; Auguste Francotte & Companie, Liége. ·320; six-shot. A constabulary type.
941. American Model Extra; Belgian. 7·65mm; six-shot. A Bulldog-style gun with an elongated cylinder accepting smokeless cartridges.
942. Belgian Buldog (sic); Belgian. ·320; six-shot.
943. Belgia[n] Bull Dog; Belgian. ·38; six-shot.
944. Belgian Bulldog; Belgian. ·380; six-shot.
945. Belgian Constable; Belgian. ·380.

946. Birmingham; probably Belgian. ·38; five-shot. An imitation of early English-style cartridge revolvers, possibly made for sale in Britain.
947. British Bul-Dog (sic); Belgian. .·320; six-shot.
948. British Buldog (sic); Belgian. ·44; six-shot.
949. British Bul-Dog (sic); Belgian. ·44; five-shot. Similar revolvers chambered for ·450 cartridges were used by the police in Duisburg, Germany, prior to the First World War. They had fluted cylinders similar to fig. 955 and chequered grips; the lanyard ring on the butt-cap was omitted.
950. British Constabulary; Belgian. ·44; six-shot.

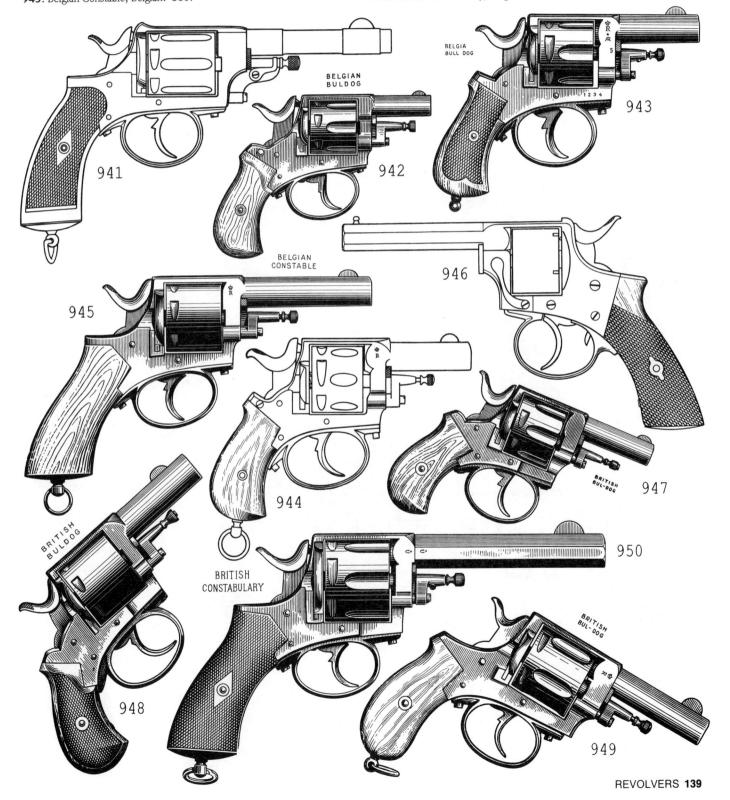

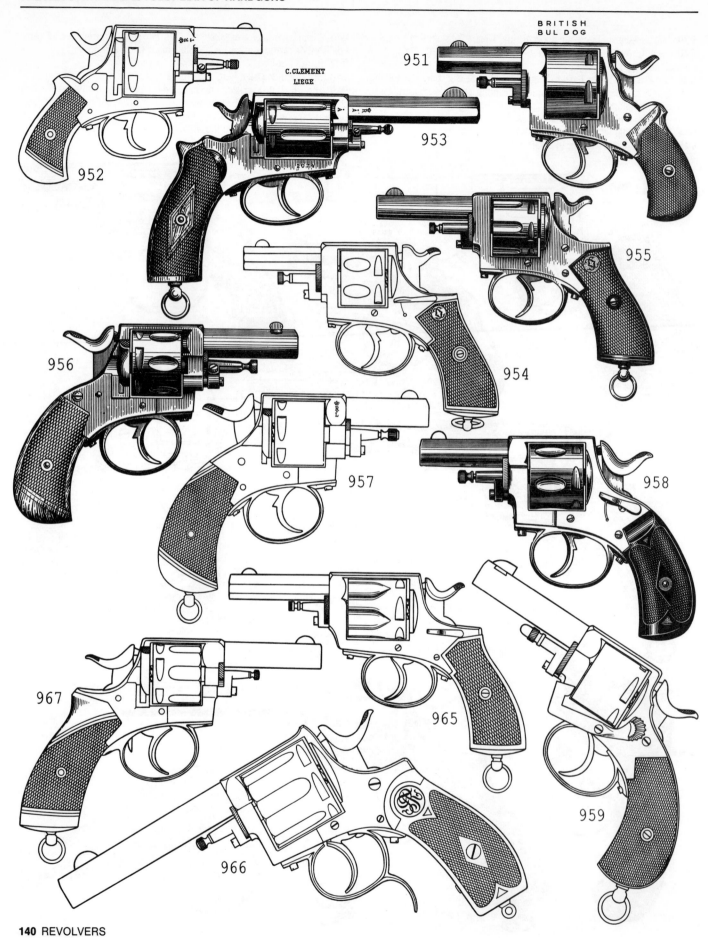

BRITISH
BUL DOG

951

C.CLEMENT
LIEGE

952

953

955

954

956

957

958

967

965

966

959

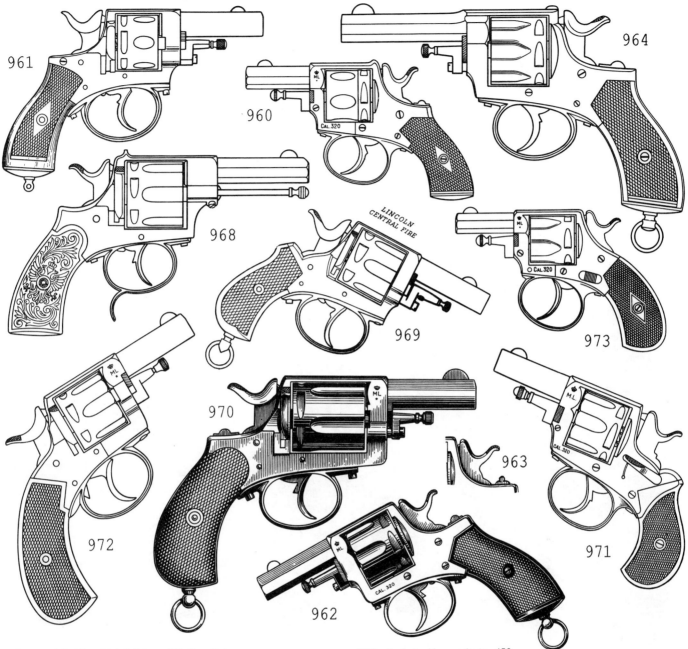

951. British Bul Dog (sic); Belgian. ·440; five-shot.

952. Bull Fighter; Belgian. ·32; six-shot.

953. Clément; Charles Ph. Clément, Liége. 7·62mm Nagant; five-shot. 'Smokeless Bulldog' type.

954, 955. Clément; Charles Ph. Clément, Liége. ·320; five- and six-shot respectively. Constabulary type.

956. Cobold; German proofs but possibly made in Belgium. ·32; six-shot.

957, 958. Cobold; Belgian. ·38; six-shot.

959. Cobold; Henrion, Dassy & Heuschen ('HDH'), Liége. 9·4mm; five-shot. A lever on the left side of the frame, beneath the cylinder, can be pivoted into a chamber mouth to lock the cylinder and firing mechanism.

960. Constable; Manufacture Liégeoise d'Armes à Feu ('M.L.'), Liége. ·320; five-shot. A reduced-scale version of the company's standard constabulary pattern. A sliding safety catch lies behind the hammer.

961. Constable; probably made by Manufacture Liégeoise d'Armes à Feu of Liége. ·320; six-shot.

962, 963. Constable; Manufacture Liégeoise d'Armes à Feu ('M.L.'), Liége. ·320; six-shot. The sliding safety-catch lies behind the hammer.

964. Constable; Manufacture Liégeoise d'Armes à Feu ('M.L.'), Liége.

·380; six-shot. Also made in ·450.

965. Constable-Municipal; Henrion, Dassy & Heuschen ('HDH'), Liége. 8mm; six-shot.

966. Frontier; Belgian. ·42; six-shot.

967. Greener; W.W. Greener, Birmingham. ·320; six-shot. Probably made in Belgium, despite its apparent genesis.

968. L'Avengeur (dated 1886); Belgian, or possibly French. 7·65mm Auto; six-shot.

969. Lincoln; Manufacture Liégeoise d'Armes à Feu ('M.L.'), Liége. ·320; six-shot.

970. Lincoln; Manufacture Liégeoise d'Armes à Feu ('M.L.'), Liége. ·44 S&W Russian or ·450; five-shot. Smaller patterns were made in ·320 and ·380. A safety catch lies behind the hammer.

971. Lincoln B; Manufacture Liégeoise d'Armes à Feu ('M.L.'), Liége. ·320; six-shot.

972. Lincoln C; Manufacture Liégeoise d'Armes à Feu ('M.L.'), Liége. ·320; six-shot.

973. Mylady; Manufacture Liégeoise d'Armes à Feu ('M.L.'), Liége. ·320; five-shot. The safety catch takes the form of a slider.

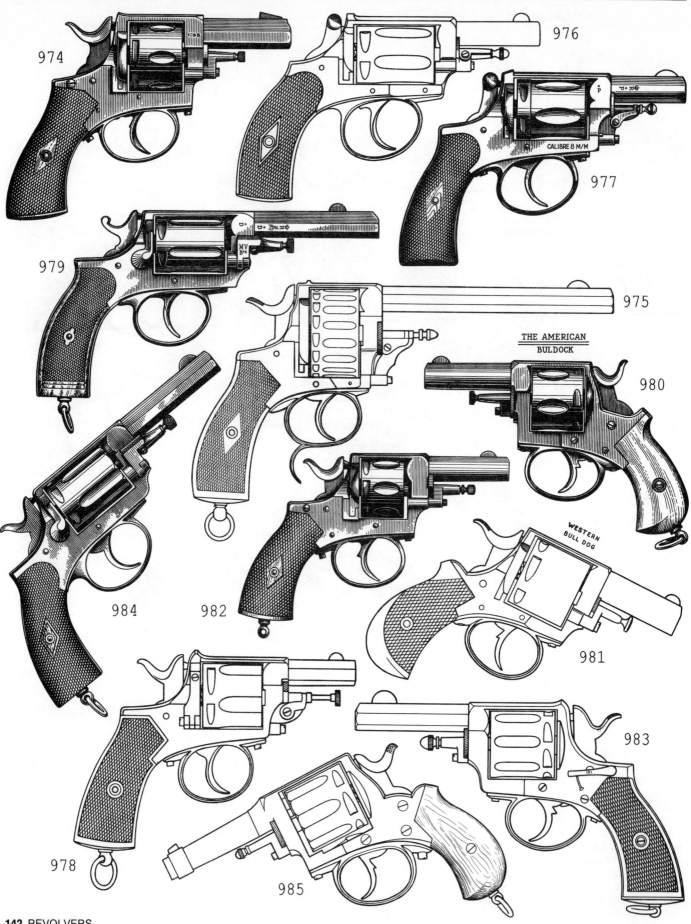

974

976

977

979

975

THE AMERICAN
BULDOCK

980

984

982

WESTERN
BULL DOG

981

978

985

983

974. Pocket Revolver; German proofs. 9mm; six shot. Probably made in Belgium.

975. Puppy; Henrion, Dassy & Heuschen ('HDH'), Liége. ·22 Long or LR rimfire; sixteen-shot.

976, 977. Puppy; Henrion, Dassy & Heuschen ('HDH'), Liége. ·38 Long (fig. 976) or 8mm (fig. 977); five-shot.

978. Puppy-Municipal; Henrion, Dassy & Heuschen ('HDH'), Liége. 8mm; five-shot.

979. Rongé; J.B. Rongé Fils, Liége. 7·62mm Nagant or ·32–20 WCF; five-shot. Sold in Russia prior to 1917 as the 'Tayozhik'. 'Smokeless Bulldog' type.

980. The American Buldock (sic); Belgian. ·380; five-shot.

981. Western Buldog (sic); Belgian. ·44; six-shot.

Anonymous patterns, Belgian

982. 7·5mm; six-shot. Constabulary type.

983. 7·62mm Nagant; seven-shot. Sold in Russia prior to 1917 as the 'Priyatel'. Constabulary type.

984. 7·62mm Nagant; five-shot. 'Smokeless Bulldog' type.

985. 8mm; six-shot.

986, 987. 8mm Lebel; six shot. A 'Lebel type' Bulldog.

988. 8mm Lebel; five-shot. Constabulary type. Sold in Russia prior to 1917 as the 'Lebel'. Possibly made by Auguste Francotte & Companie, Liége.

989. ·32; six-shot. German proofs, but probably Belgian-made.

990. ·32; six-shot. Made for export to Austria-Hungary, where revolvers with short barrels were prohibited. The long barrel complied with the law, but the sight was placed back from the muzzle so that part of the barrel could be cut away once the gun had been delivered. Constabulary type.

991. ·320; six-shot.

992. ·320; six-shot. A lever on the left side of the frame in front of the cylinder can be pivoted into a chamber mouth to lock the action.

993. ·320; six-shot.

994. ·320; six-shot. Constabulary type.

995. ·320; six-shot. German proofs, but probably made in Belgium. Constabulary type.

996, 997. ·320; six-shot. Constabulary type.

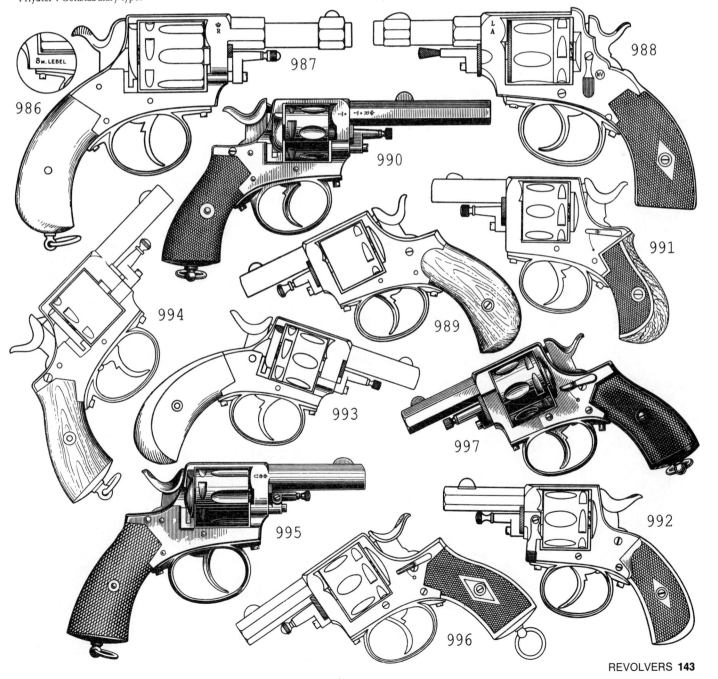

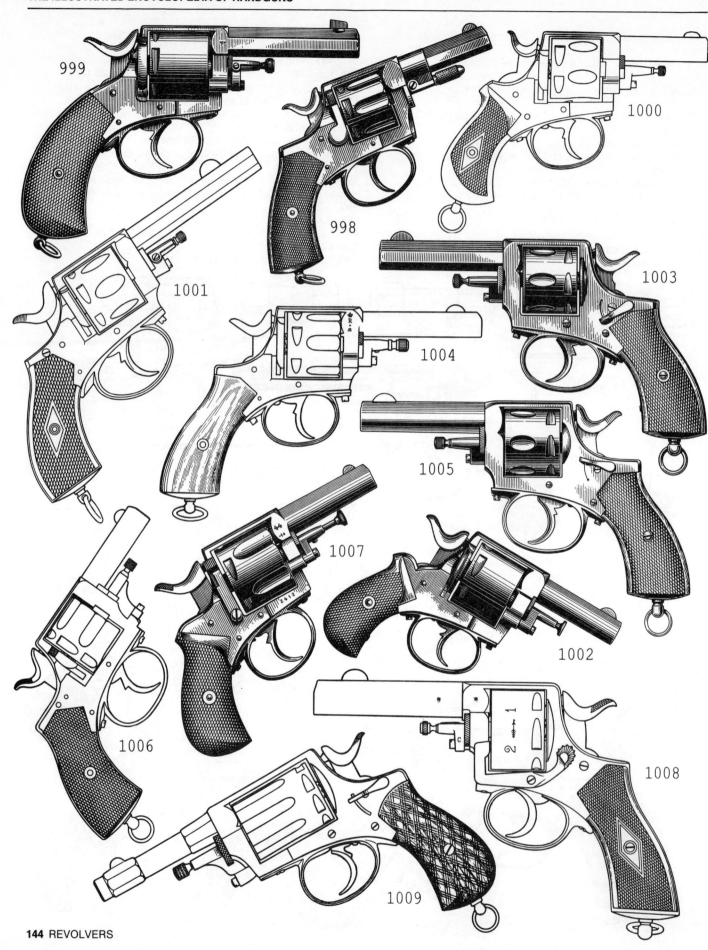

999
998
1000
1001
1003
1004
1005
1007
1006
1002
1008
1009

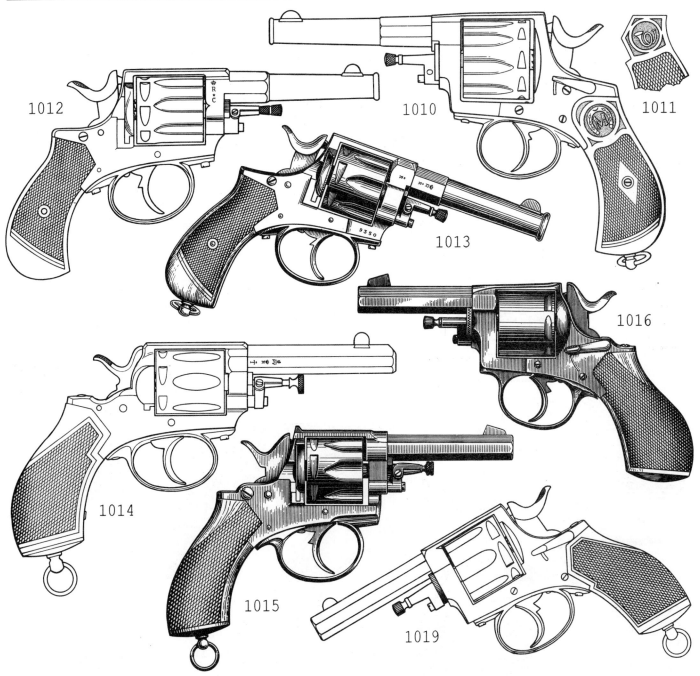

998. ·320; six-shot. The extractor is the same as that of the Nagant system; the gate opens backward. Constabulary type. Possibly made by E. & L. Nagant of Liége.

999. 9·4mm; six-shot. Guns of this type were issued to the army and police in the Netherlands.

1000. ·38; six-shot.

1001. ·38; six-shot. Made for export to Austria-Hungary. Constabulary type. See fig. 990.

1002. ·380; six-shot. British Bulldog type.

1003–1005. ·380; six-shot. Constabulary type.

1006. ·380; five-shot. Constabulary type. German proofs, but probably Belgian-made.

1007. ·44; five-shot. British Bulldog type. The gate opens backward.

1008. ·450; five-shot. A pivoting cylinder-locking lever lies on the left side of the frame. The general appearance is that of a larger version of fig. 959, and this revolver may thus have been a product of Henrion, Dassy & Heuschen. Constabulary type.

1009. 8mm; seven-shot. The elongated cylinder is not characteristic of standard Bulldogs. Possibly made in Spain.

1010–1013. ·320, 7·62mm Nagant, 8mm Lebel or ·380; six-, seven-, eight- or nine-shot. Guns of this type are generally known as 'Service Revolver', 'Police Revolver' or, most popularly, 'Postal [Services] Revolver'. They were also sold in Russia prior to 1917 as the 'Zashchitnik'. Their distinguishing characteristics are merely details—e.g., a round barrel with an annular boss at the muzzle, a short octahedral section at the breech (part of the frame or the barrel), fluted cylinders, distinctive cylinder-stop notches and bird's head grips. Most were made prior to 1914. Similar guns were made in Spain.

Polizei-Revolvers

1014–1020. Owing to common features, these can be separated into their own group. As the guns were once popular amongst German policemen, they are generally known as 'Polizeirevolver' instead of 'Constabulary' patterns. It is a useful distinction. They have a characteristic one-piece

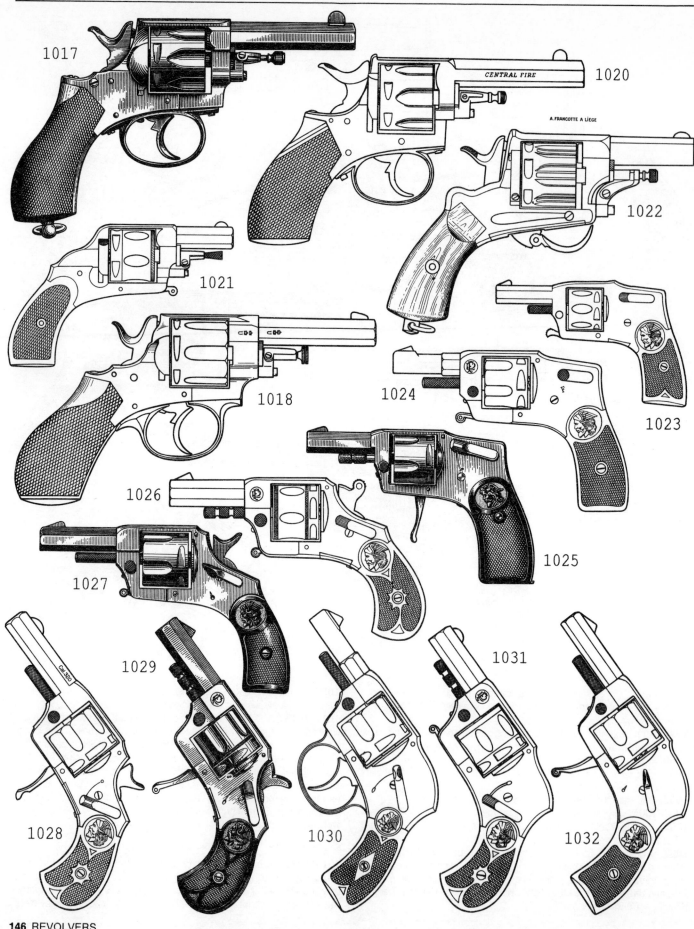

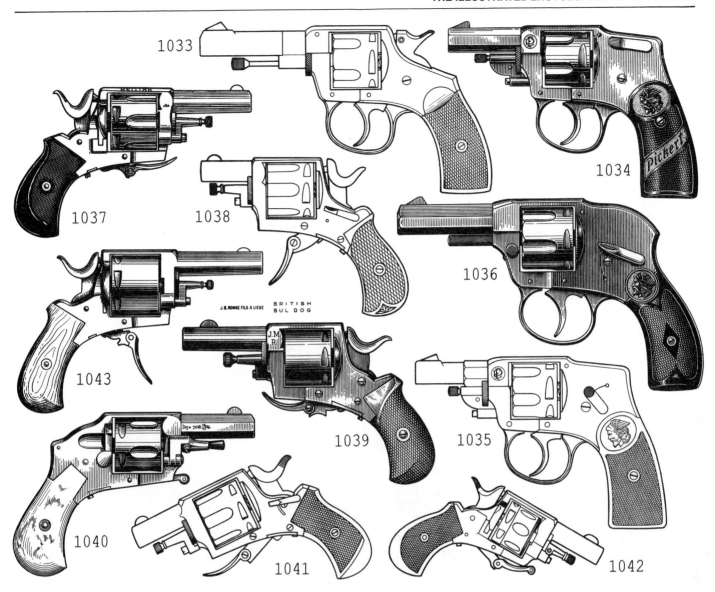

wood grip retained by a solitary vertical screw. The guns drawn here include the so-called 'Berlin police model' of 1886 (fig. 1016). Those shown in figs. 1019 and 1020 were advertised as 'Cobold' in pre-1917 Russian catalogues.

2. POCKET BULLDOG, PUPPY AND OTHER GUNS

Named patterns

1021. 'A.F.'; Auguste Francotte & Companie, Liége. ·320; five-shot. Fitted with a safety hammer.

1022. 'A.F.'; Auguste Francotte & Companie, Liége. ·380; six-shot.

1023. Arminius Model 1; Friedrich Pickert, Zella St Blasii (to 1919) and Zella-Mehlis. ·22 Long rimfire; six-shot. Made from c.1905 until 1939, these pocket revolvers were distinguished by 'FP' and the head of the legendary warrior Arminius. They differed in calibre, size and structure. Their most characteristic features are a solid frame and the customary absence of an ejector. Most guns have folding triggers and a safety lever on the left side of the frame beneath the hammer.

1024, 1025. Arminius Model 3; Friedrich Pickert, Zella St Blasii (to 1919) and Zella-Mehlis. 6·35mm Auto; five-shot. The grip has a cavity in which cartridges can be stored. The Model 4 chambers 5·5mm Velo-Dog rounds (see fig. 1213).

1026–1029. Arminius Model 7; Friedrich Pickert, Zella St Blasii (to 1919) and Zella-Mehlis. 7·65mm Auto or ·320; five-shot. The Arminius Model 5

(7·5mm Swiss, 7·62mm Nagant or 8mm Lebel) is similar to the Model 7, excepting that it is larger and has a conventional trigger guard. The Model 13 is the same as the Model 5, but chambered for ·380 cartridges.

1030–1032. Arminius Model 8; Friedrich Pickert, Zella St Blasii (to 1919) and Zella-Mehlis. 7·65mm; five-shot.

1033. Arminius Model 9; Friedrich Pickert, Zella St Blasii (to 1919) and Zella-Mehlis. 7·65mm Auto; five-shot. Also made in a ·22 LR rimfire version (six shots) with a 142mm barrel.

1034, 1035. Arminius Model 10; Friedrich Pickert, Zella St Blasii (to 1919) and Zella-Mehlis. 7·65mm Auto; five-shot. The grip cavity can hold five cartridges.

1036. Arminius Model 14; Friedrich Pickert, Zella St Blasii (to 1919) and Zella-Mehlis. ·380; five-shot.

1037. British Bulldog; Belgian. ·320; six-shot.

1038. British Bulldog; Gustav Genschow & Company. ·320; six-shot. Possibly made in Belgium, despite apparently German provenance.

1039. British Bul Dog (sic); J.B. Rongé Fils, Liége. ·320; six-shot.

1040. Browning; Auguste Francotte & Companie or Henrion, Dassy & Heuschen ('HDH'), Liége. 7·65mm Auto; five-shot. The name was applied simply because the gun used the Browning cartridge. The gate opens backward, whilst the design of the ejector yoke is distinctive.

1041. Bul Dog; J.B. Rongé Fils, Liége. ·320; six-shot.

1042. Bulldog. ·22 Short rimfire; six-shot.

1043. Bulldog; possibly Belgian. ·320; six-shot.

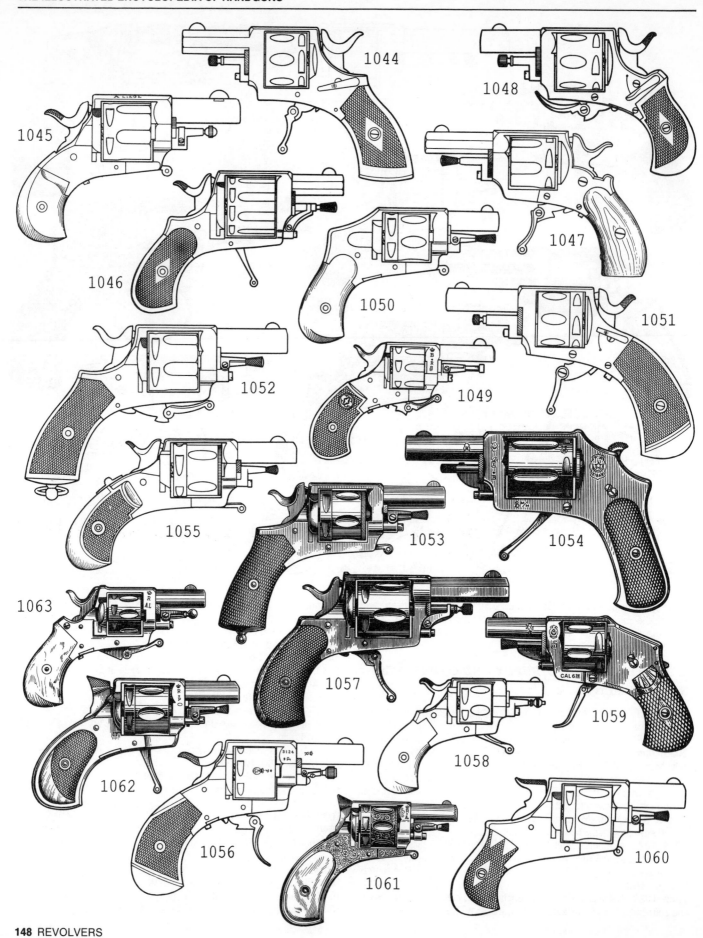

1044. Bulldog; German proofs. ·320; six-shot.

1045. Bulldog; Belgian. ·38; five-shot.

1046. Bulldog; Auguste Francotte & Companie, Liége. ·22 Long rimfire; eight-shot.

1047. Bulldog; Auguste Francotte & Companie, Liége. ·320; five-shot.

1048. Bulldog; Henrion, Dassy & Heuschen ('HDH'), Liége. ·320; six-shot.

1049. Clément; Charles Ph. Clément, Liége. ·22 rimfire; six-shot.

1050. Clément; Charles Ph. Clément, Liége. 6·35mm; five-shot. Sold in pre-Revolutionary Russia as the 'Boyets'.

1051. Cobold; J.B. Rongé Fils, Liége. ·320; six-shot.

1052. Constabulary; Belgian. ·38; five-shot.

1053. Constabulary; A. Francotte & Companie, Liége. ·320; five-shot.

1054. 'F.A.'; Francisco Arizmendi, Eibar. 8mm; five-shot. The semi-enclosed hammer is noteworthy. A similar, but smaller 6·35mm revolver was made by Henrion, Dassy & Heuschen of Liége as the 'Puppy'.

1055. 'F.A.'; Francisco Arizmendi, Eibar. ·320; five-shot.

1056. Faure le Page, Paris. ·320; six-shot. This manufacturer should not be confused with Lepage of Liége—even though the revolver bears Belgian proofs.

1057. Francotte's Bulldog; Auguste Francotte & Companie, Liége. 7·65mm Auto; five-shot.

1058. Geco; Gustav Genschow & Company. ·22 Short rimfire; five-shot. Probably made in Belgium.

1059. Geco Revolver; Francisco Arizmendi, Eibar. 6·35mm Auto; five-shot. Made in Spain, but distributed in Germany. The Belgian Lebeaux company made a similar revolver with a ring-trigger, but no safety catch. It was advertised in pre-1917 Russian catalogues as the 'Adyutant'.

1060. Knuckle-Duster; Belgian. ·380; five-shot.

1061. Knuckle-Duster; Établissements Lebeaux or Manufacture Liégeoise d'Armes à Feu ('M.L.'), Liége. ·22 Short rimfire; six-shot.

1062. Knuckle-Duster; J.B. Rongé Fils, Liége. 6·35mm Auto or 7·65mm Auto; five-shot.

1063. ''Lady's Model''; Établissements Lebeaux, Liége. ·22 Short rimfire; six-shot.

1064. Lebeaux; Établissements Lebeaux, Liége. 6·35mm; five-shot. Sold in pre-Revolutionary Russia as the 'Adyutant'. See fig. 1059, above. Similar guns emanated from other gunmakers in Liége.

1065. L'Eclair; Garate, Anitua y Cia, Eibar. 8mm Lebel; five-shot.

1066. Lepage & Companie, Liége. 6·35mm Auto; five-shot. The safety catch lies on the back of the frame above the grip.

1067. Lepage & Companie, Liége. ·320; five-shot.

1068. Lincoln. ·22 Short rimfire; six-shot. Possibly made by Henrion, Dassy & Heuschen ('HDH') of Liége.

1069. Lincoln; Henrion, Dassy & Heuschen ('HDH'), Liége. ·22 Short rimfire; six-shot.

1070. Lincoln; Manufacture Liégeoise d'Armes à Feu ('M.L.'), Liége. ·230; nine-shot.

1071. Lincoln; Manufacture Liégeoise d'Armes à Feu or Auguste Francotte & Companie, Liége. 6·35mm Auto; six-shot. The hammer axis-pin, which can move laterally, acts as a safety catch.

1072. Lincoln B; Manufacture Liégeoise d'Armes à Feu ('M.L.'), Liége. ·320; six-shot.

1073. Lincoln-Mylady; Manufacture Liégeoise d'Armes à Feu ('M.L.'), Liége. ·320; six-shot.

1074. Mexican Model; Lepage & Companie, Liége. ·320; six-shot. Also made in ·380.

1075. Puppy; Belgian.

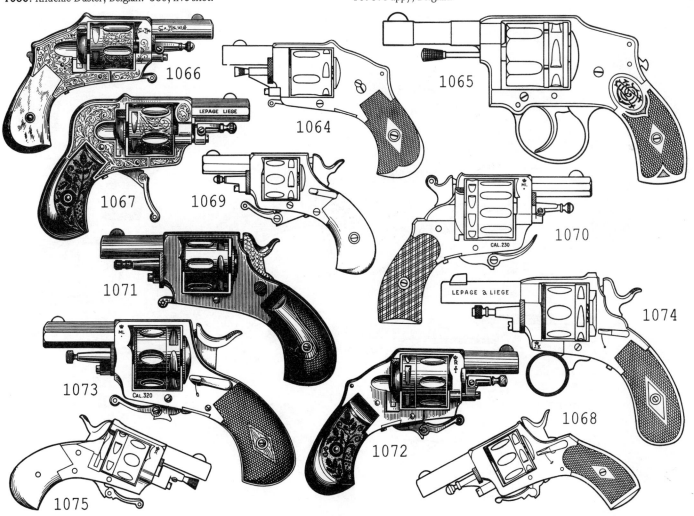

1076. Puppy; Belgian. The safety takes the form of a mobile hammer axis.

1077. Puppy; Belgian. ·22 Short rimfire; five-shot.

1078. Puppy; Spanish. ·22 Short rimfire; five-shot. Note the 'safety hammer'.

1079. Puppy; 6·35mm Auto. German proofs, but possibly Belgian-made.

1080. Puppy; Belgian. 8mm Lebel; five-shot.

1081. Puppy; Henrion, Dassy & Heuschen ('HDH'), Liége. ·22 Short rimfire; six-shot.

1082. Puppy; Ojanguren y Marcaido, Eibar. ·22 Short rimfire; five-shot. The 'safety hammer' does not protrude from the frame when lowered.

1083. Puppy; Manufacture Liégeoise d'Armes à Feu ('M.L.'), Liége.

1084. Puppy-Lincoln; Manufacture Liégeoise d'Armes à Feu ('M.L.'), Liége. ·320; seven-shot.

1085. Radfahrerrevolver (''Bicyclist's revolver''). ·22 Short rimfire; six-shot. No ejector. German proofs.

1086, 1087. Radfahrerrevolver. ·22 Short rimfire; five-shot. German proofs.

1088. Raick; Felix Raick, Liége. ·22 Short rimfire; six-shot.

1089. Revolvelo; French. ·320; five-shot.

1090, 1091. Revolver-Knuckle-Duster; Belgian. ·320; five-shot.

1092, 1093. Revolver-Knuckle-Duster; Auguste Francotte & Companie, Liége. ·320 or 6·35mm Auto; five- or six-shot respectively. Sometimes found with a lateral safety catch similar to that of fig. 1119.

1094. Rongé; J.B. Rongé Fils, Liége. 7·65mm; six-shot. Sold in Tsarist Russia as the 'Privatel'.

1095. Rongé; J.B. Rongé Fils, Liége. ·380; five-shot.

1096. Saint-Étienne. 7·65mm Auto, five-shot. French; maker unknown. The revolver has the so-called 'safety hammer', which lacks a spur.

1097. The Baby Hammerless/America; Belgian. ·38; five-shot. Barrel legend notwithstanding, the gun is neither hammerless nor typically American in construction.

Anonymous patterns, Belgian

1098. ·22 rimfire; six-shot. The hammer can be cocked with the safety catch applied, the ejector is a Lefaucheux type, and the gate opens backward.

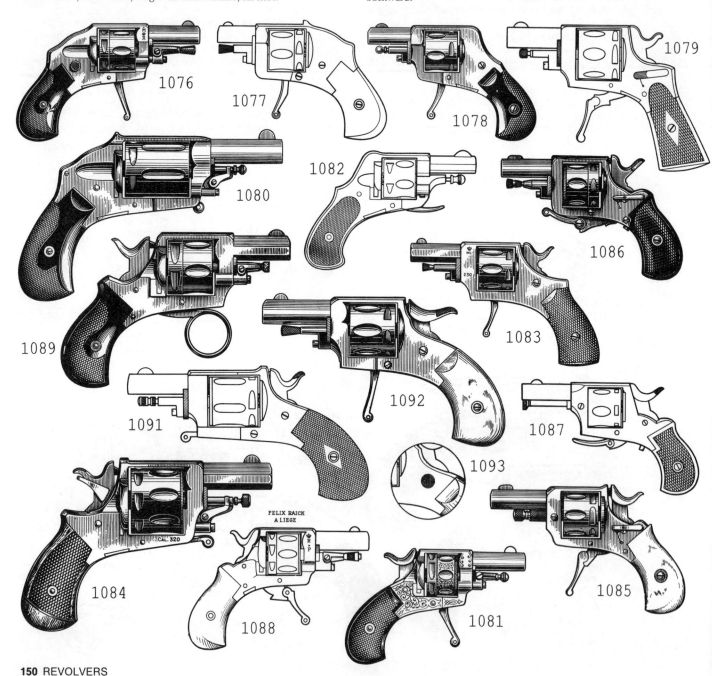

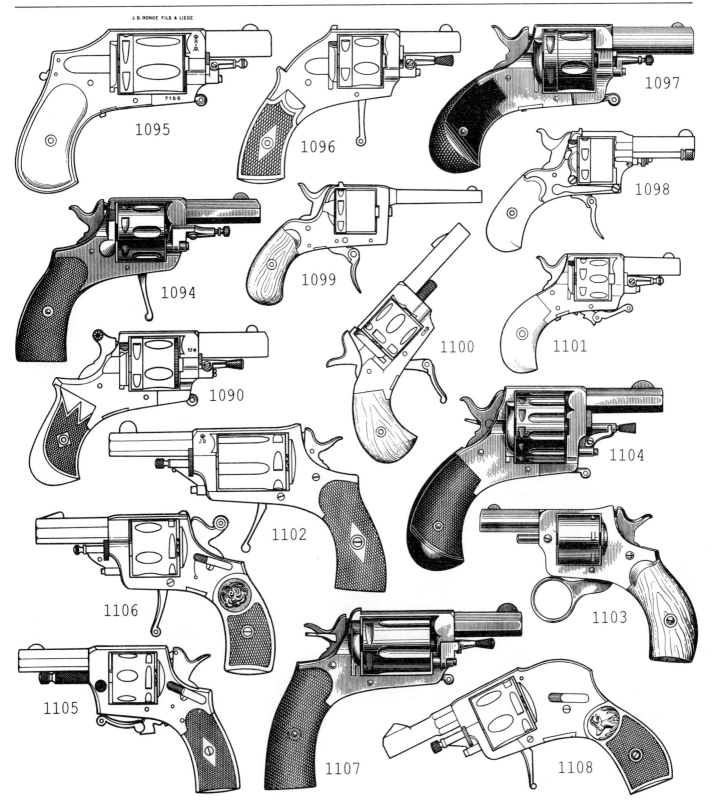

1099. ·22 rimfire; six-shot. This gun has neither loading gate nor ejector.

1100. ·22 rimfire; six-shot. No ejector.

1101. ·22 rimfire; six-shot.

1102. ·22 Extra Long or ·32–20 WCF; five-shot. Sold in Russia prior to 1917 as the 'Tayozhik'. Possibly made by Rongé of Liége.

1103. 6mm Flobert; six-shot. German proofs, but probably made in Belgium. The trigger is in the form of a ring, and an ejector is omitted.

1104. ·230 (6mm); twelve-shot. The safety is attached to the hammer.

Sold in pre-Revolutionary Russia as the 'Karapuz'.

1105. 6·35mm Auto; six-shot. No ejector. German proofs, but probably Belgian-made. Essentially similar to fig. 1109; somewhat larger guns, differing in minor respects, were chambered for 7·65mm Auto cartridges.

1106. 6·35mm Auto or ·320; five-shot. German proofs.

1107. 7·62mm Nagant; five-shot. A safety lever is attached to the hammer and a distinctive ejector is fitted. Possibly made by E. & L. Nagant of Liége.

1108. 7·65mm Auto; five-shot. German proofs.

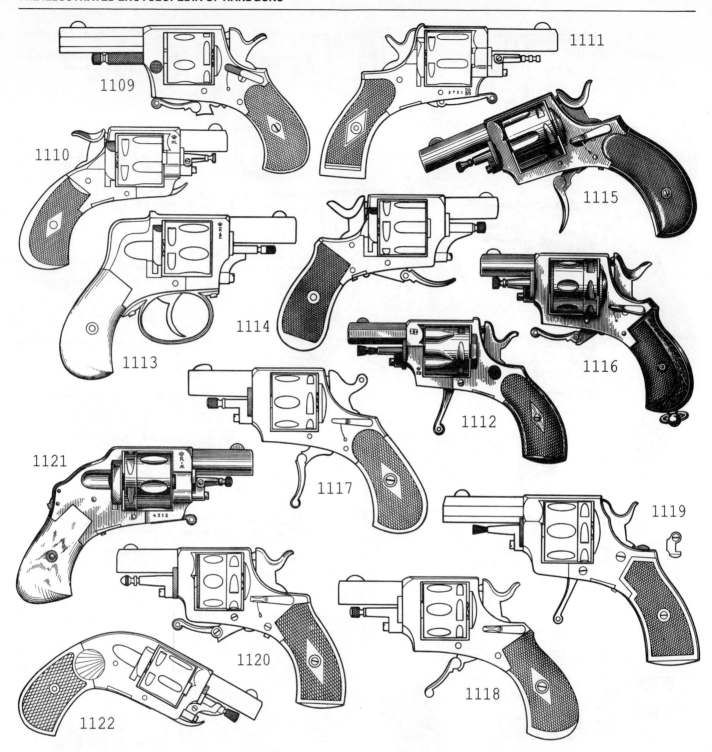

1109. ·320; five-shot. Similar to 1117 and 1118 (below), with German proofs, but lacking an ejector.

1110. ·320; five-shot. Probably made by Manufacture Liégeoise d'Armes à Feu or Établissements Lebeaux, Liége. Sold in pre-1917 Russia as the 'Karlik'.

1111. ·320; five-shot.

1112. ·320; five-shot. The mobile axis of the hammer doubles as a safety catch.

1113. ·320; five-shot. Sold in Tsarist Russia as the 'Strazh' or 'Muzhik'.

1114–1116. ·320; six-shot. All have German proofs, but may have been made in Belgium.

1117, 1118. ·320; six-shot. The guns have German proofs, but were probably made in Belgium.

1119. ·320; six-shot. The safety catch pivots laterally behind the hammer (shown in plan above the back of the frame).

1120. ·320; six-shot.

1121. ·380; five-shot.

Anonymous patterns, others

1122. 6·35mm; five-shot. Spanish.

1123. 7·65mm; five-shot. German proofs (probably made by Friedrich Pickert of Zella St Blasii). To reload the revolver, the cylinder must be removed and the fired cases punched out of the chambers with the cylinder axis-pin.

3. PISTOL-TYPE POCKET REVOLVERS

Belgian patterns

1124. 6·35mm Auto; five-shot.

1125. 6·35mm Auto; five-shot. Sold in Tsarist Russia as the 'Novost'.

1126. 6·35mm Auto or 7·65mm Auto; six-shot. Made by Auguste Francotte & Companie or Henrion, Dassy & Heuschen ('HDH') of Liége.

1127. 7·65mm Auto.

1128. 7·65mm Auto; five-shot.

1129. Browning; Auguste Francotte & Companie, Liége. 7·65mm Auto.

1130. Browning; Auguste Francotte & Companie, Liége. 7·65mm Auto or ·320; five-shot.

1131. Browning; J.B. Rongé Fils, Liége. 7·65mm Auto; five-shot. Similar guns were made by Auguste Francotte & Companie.

1132. Browning Model. A 6·35mm version of fig. 1133.

1133. Browning Model. 7·65mm Auto; five-shot. Fitted with a French-type extractor.

1134. Façon Browning; maker unknown, Belgian. 6·35mm Auto or 7·65mm Auto; five-shot.

1135. Lebeaux; Établissements Lebeaux, Liége. 6·35mm Auto; five-shot.

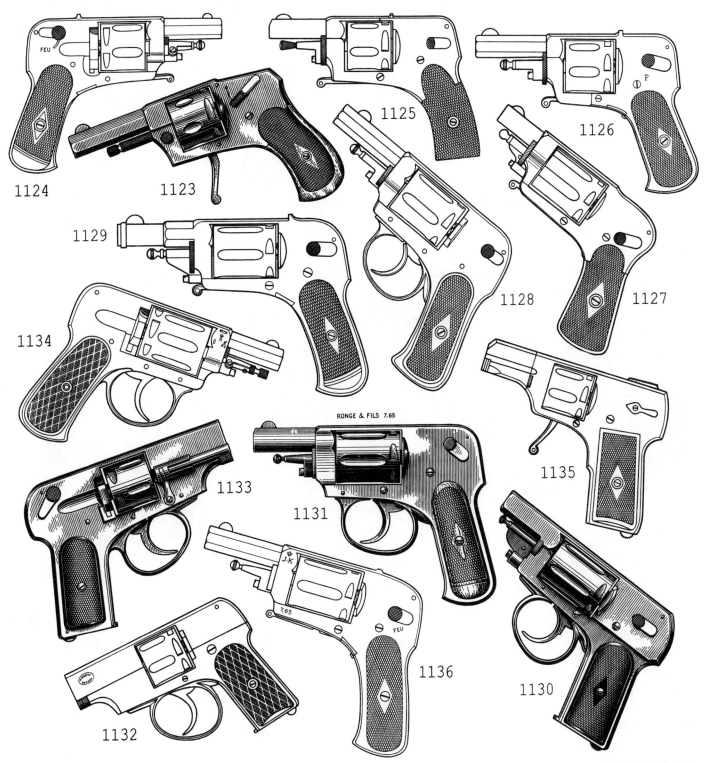

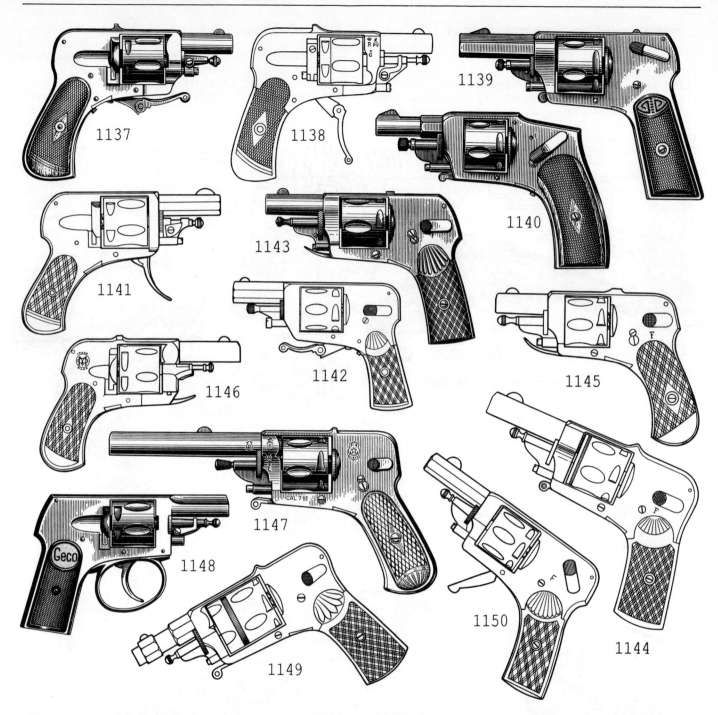

1136. Lepage & Companie, Liége. 7·65mm Auto; five-shot. Sold in pre-Revolutionary Russia as the 'Drug'.

1137, 1138. Lincoln Bossu; possibly made by Manufacture Liégeoise d'Armes à Feu of Liége. 6·35mm Auto; five-shot.

German patterns

1139, 1140. 7·65mm Auto; five-shot. Probably made by Friedrich Pickert of Zella St Blasii (to 1919) and Zella-Mehlis.

Italian pattern

1141. Ufficio Scambi Commerciale. 6·35mm Auto; five-shot. Said to have been made after the end of the Second World War.

Spanish patterns

1142. ·22 rimfire; six-shot. Possibly made by Retolaza Hermanos of Eibar.

1143. Brompetier; Retolaza Hermanos, Eibar. 6·35mm Auto; five-shot.

1144. Brong-Grand; Crucelegui Hermanos, Eibar. 6mm Cartouche Française, 6·35mm Auto or 7·65mm Auto; five-shot.

1145. Brong-Petit; Crucelegui Hermanos, Eibar. 6·35mm Auto; five-shot.

1146. Brow; Ojanguren y Marcaido, Eibar. 6·35mm Auto; five-shot.

1147. 'F.A.'; Francisco Arizmendi, Eibar. 7·65mm Auto; five-shot. This long-barrel gun was intended for export to Austro-Hungary—see remarks accompanying fig. 990.

1148. Geco; Crucelegui Hermanos, Eibar. 6·35mm Auto; five-shot. The revolver was produced in Spain (as the 'Brong-Sport') and sold in Germany by Gustav Genschow & Companie.

1149. Lebrong or Le Brong; Crucelegui Hermanos, Eibar. 8mm Lebel; five-shot.

1150. Lincoln. 6·35mm Auto.

4. VELO-DOG REVOLVERS

The pocket revolvers known as 'Velo-Dogs' (sometimes 'Vele-Dogs' in old advertising literature) first found favour in the 1890s, the design of the distinctive long-case cartridge—among the earliest commercially available smokeless-propellant loadings—being credited to the Parisian gunsmith Galand in 1894. The guns were initially intended to protect 'velocipedists' (cyclists) from dogs, which was much more of a problem at the end of the nineteenth century than it is today. Eventually, however, the guns became classed as self-defence weapons. By 1900, Velo-Dog revolvers were being made throughout Continental Europe in general, but in particular in Belgium, France and Spain.

The true Velo-Dogs were light, small, but more powerful than similar pocket revolvers chambered for small-calibre black powder cartridges. Their streamlined shape enabled them to be pulled out of the pocket without snagging the lining.

Most Velo-Dogs have enclosed hammers, though some exposed-hammer versions exist. Folding triggers are customary—but not obligatory. Most guns have yoke-mounted ejectors which lock into the cylinder axis-pin head when not required. Externally, the typical Velo-Dog has a characteristic streamlined-revolver outline or, alternatively, resembles an automatic pistol. The principal feature distinguishing Velo-Dogs from other types of pocket revolver was the elongated cylinder chambered either for the slender 5·5mm centre-fire Velo-Dog cartridges (sometimes known as '5·75mm') or a similar 6mm rimfire 'Type Française'. Centre-fire cartridges were usually loaded with smokeless propellant and a jacketed lead-core bullet, whilst the rimfires had a plain lead bullet and were often loaded with black powder.

Soon after its introduction, however, the Velo-Dog began to lose its individuality. Consequently, typically Velo-Dog guns were chambered for cartridges other than the 5·5mm long-case type, whilst revolvers of differing designs were adapted for the 5·5mm Velo-Dog cartridge. The former group is excluded from the Velo-Dogs listed here but, as the ultimate determining factor is the cartridge, guns of the latter type are included in the classification.

The Velo-Dog family can be roughly sub-divided into the classical revolvers used to protect cyclists from dogs, and the later (but much more diverse) guns intended for self-defence.

Note: unless stated otherwise, all guns chamber the standard 5·5mm centre-fire Velo-Dog cartridge.

Belgian patterns

1151–1158. Five-shot.
1159. Five-shot. Sold in pre-1917 Russia as the 'Antei'.
1160. Five shot. Spent cases are ejected by tipping the barrel downward.
1161. Five-shot. Shrouded hammer.

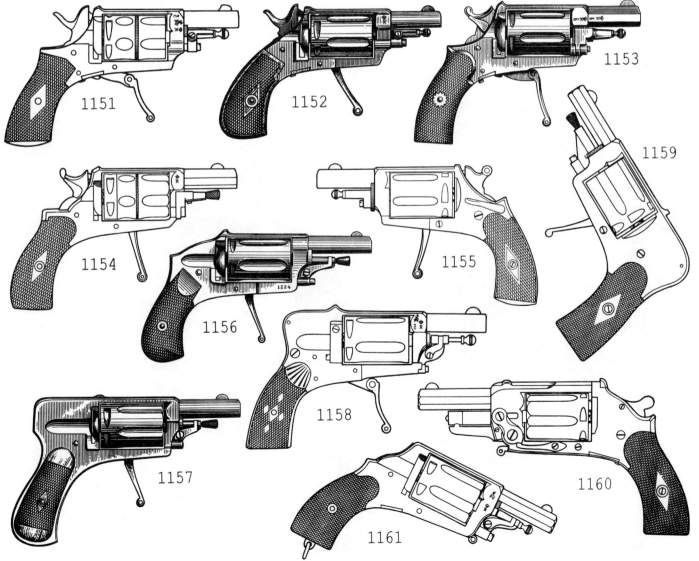

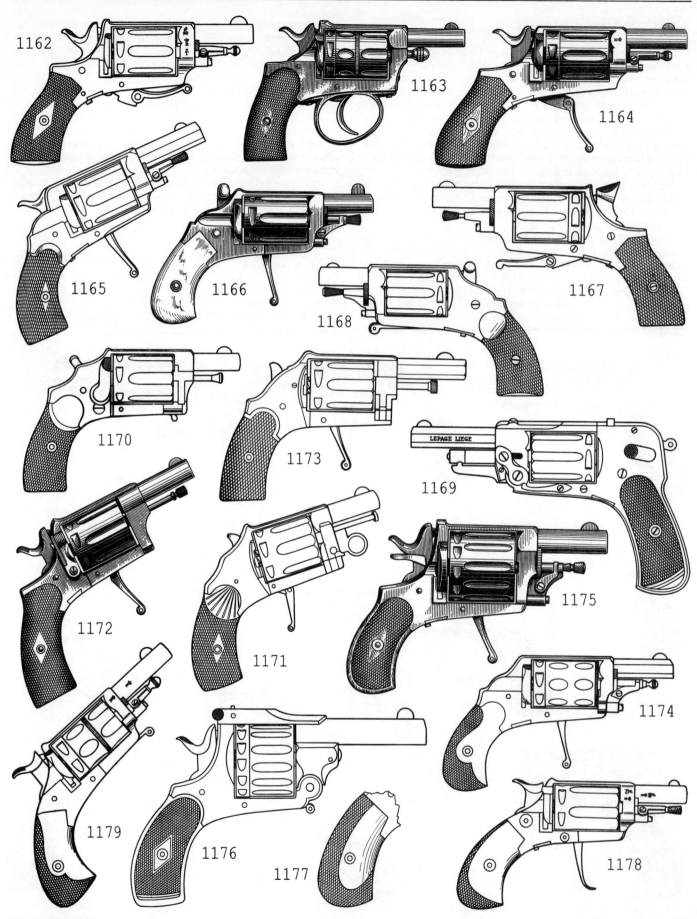

1162

1163

1164

1165

1166

1167

1168

1170

1173

1169

LEPAGE LIEGE

1172

1171

1175

1174

1179

1176

1177

1178

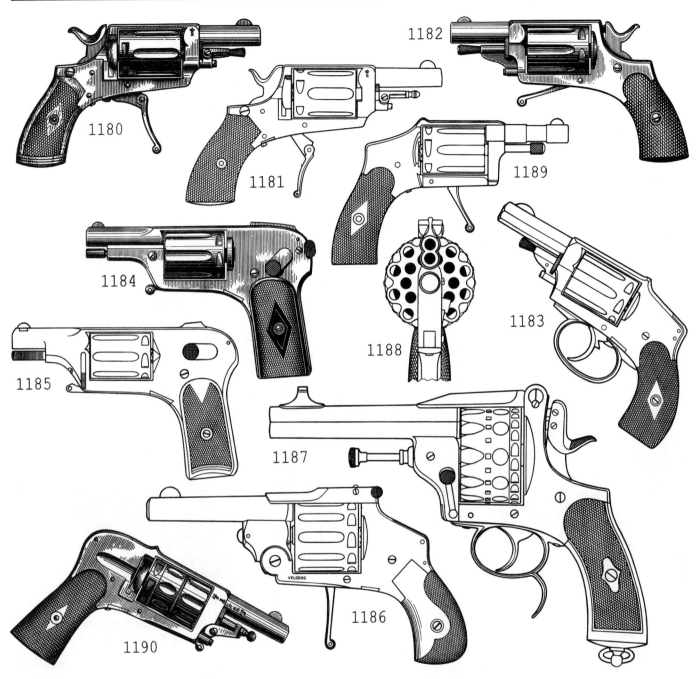

1162–1168. Six-shot.

1169. Six-shot. Spent cases are ejected by tipping the barrel downward in accordance with fig. 130.

1170, 1171. Six-shot. Spent cases are ejected by swinging the cylinder out on its yoke and pressing the extractor-rod head backward (see fig. 131).

1172. Six-shot. A swinging-cylinder pattern sold in Tsarist Russia as the 'Merkuri'.

1173. Six-shot. Sold in Russia prior to 1917 as the 'Nadezhny'. Made by Auguste Francotte & Companie or Établissements Lebeaux of Liége, the gun features a laterally-swinging cylinder.

1174. Six-shot. Shrouded hammer.

1175. Ten-shot.

1176, 1177. Twelve-shot. The grip of a variant with a short barrel—sold in pre-Revolutionary Russia as the 'Karapuz'—is also shown. Cases are expelled by swinging the barrel downward.

1178, 1179. 'A.F.'; Auguste Francotte & Companie, Liége. Five-shot.

1180–1183. 'A.F.'; Auguste Francotte & Companie, Liége. Six-shot.

1184, 1185. Browning Model; Auguste Francotte & Companie, Liége.

1186. 'H.D.H.'; Henrion, Dassy & Heuschen, Liége. Ten-shot. Cases are ejected by swinging the barrel downward.

1187, 1188. 'H.D.H.'; Henrion, Dassy & Heuschen, Liége. Twenty-shot. This revolver is unique among the Velo-Dogs, owing to the unusual cylinder arrangements. Cartridges are held in two concentric rows of ten apiece in an attempt to keep the cylinder diameter within manageable bounds. There are two barrels and two firing pins on the hammer. When the cylinder turns, a chamber on the outer row aligns with the upper barrel; the firing pin then strikes it. For the next shot, the cylinder indexes just far enough to align a chamber in the lower row behind the lower barrel. This is then fired with the lower firing pin. Thus shots are fired from each barrel in turn. Spent cases are extracted simultaneously when the revolver is unlocked and the barrels are tipped upward.

1189. Indispensable. Six-shot. Cases are ejected by swinging the cylinder laterally and pressing the ejector-rod head backward (see fig. 131).

1190. Jupiter; Auguste Francotte & Companie, Liége. Seven-shot.

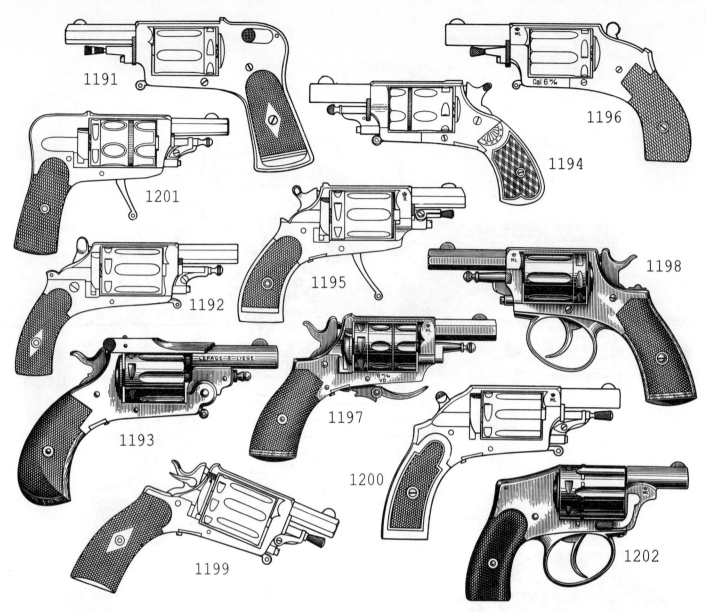

1191. 'L.A.M.'; L. Ancion-Marx, Liége. Five-shot. Also offered in 7·65mm Auto as the 'Auto-Dog'.

1192. 'L.A.M.'; L. Ancion-Marx, Liége. Six-shot.

1193. Lepage & Companie, Liége. Six-shot. This swinging-cylinder pattern was sold in pre-1917 Russia as the 'Lesnik'.

1194. Lincoln. Five-shot.

1195. Little Dog. Six-shot.

1196. 'M.L.'; Manufacture Liégeoise d'Armes à Feu, Liége. Five-shot.

1197, 1198. 'M.L.'; Manufacture Liégeoise d'Armes à Feu, Liége. Six-shot.

1199. 'M.L.'; Manufacture Liégeoise d'Armes à Feu, Liége. Seven-shot.

1200. Puppy; Manufacture Liégeoise d'Armes à Feu ('M.L.'), Liége. Six-shot.

French patterns

1201. Five-shot.

1202. Galand; Charles F. Galand & Companie, Paris. 5·5mm Velo-Dog centre-fire or 6mm 'Type Française' rimfire; six-shot. Galand made the first Velo-Dog. The spent cases can be pushed out of the chambers when the cylinder is detached. To remove the cylinder, the curved lever is pivoted, the barrel is drawn forward off the cylinder axis-pin, and the cylinder can then be removed. Similar revolvers were made in Liége by Auguste

Francotte & Companie and Manufacture Liégeoise d'Armes à Feu. They were advertised as the 'Tovarishch' in catalogues published in Russia before the October Revolution.

1203. Charles F. Galand & Companie, Paris. Six-shot. Cases are extracted by swinging the barrel downward.

1204, 1205. L'Explorateur-Mitraille. Twelve-shot. It has two barrels and two strikers. Although the cylinder has twelve chambers, it only makes a sixth-turn for each pull of the trigger, as it fires two shots simultaneously whenever the hammer strikes. This was intended to improve reliability, as at least one shot was certain to fire for each fall of the hammer. Moreover, the effectiveness of the firearm could be altered by loading either all the chambers (twelve shots, 2 × 6) or each alternate chamber (six shots only). These revolvers were made with solid or hinged frames, spent cases being extracted either sequentially, by a yoke-mounted ejector (fig. 126), or by tipping the barrel downward so that they were expelled simultaneously (fig 130). Guns of this general pattern were advertised as the 'Pulemet' in Russian catalogues before the October Revolution.

1206, 1207. Manufacture Française d'Armes et Cycles, Saint-Étienne. Five-shot. The gun shown in fig. 1207 was sold in pre-1917 Russia as the 'Nansen'.

1208, 1209. Manufacture Française d'Armes et Cycles, Saint-Étienne. Six-shot.

German patterns

1210. Five-shot.

1211. Five-shot. Probably made by Friedrich Pickert of Zella St Blasii and then Zella-Mehlis. Spent cases are extracted by removing the cylinder.

1212. Six-shot. Spent cases are expelled by tipping the barrel downward in accordance with fig. 130.

1213. Arminius Model 4; Friedrich Pickert, Zella St Blasii (to 1919) and Zella-Mehlis. Seven-shot.

Russian patterns, pre-1917

1214–1216. Strelets; Imperial ordnance factory, Tula. 5·5mm Velo-Dog centre-fire or 6mm 'Type Française' rimfire; seven-shot. The safety catch is attached to the hammer.

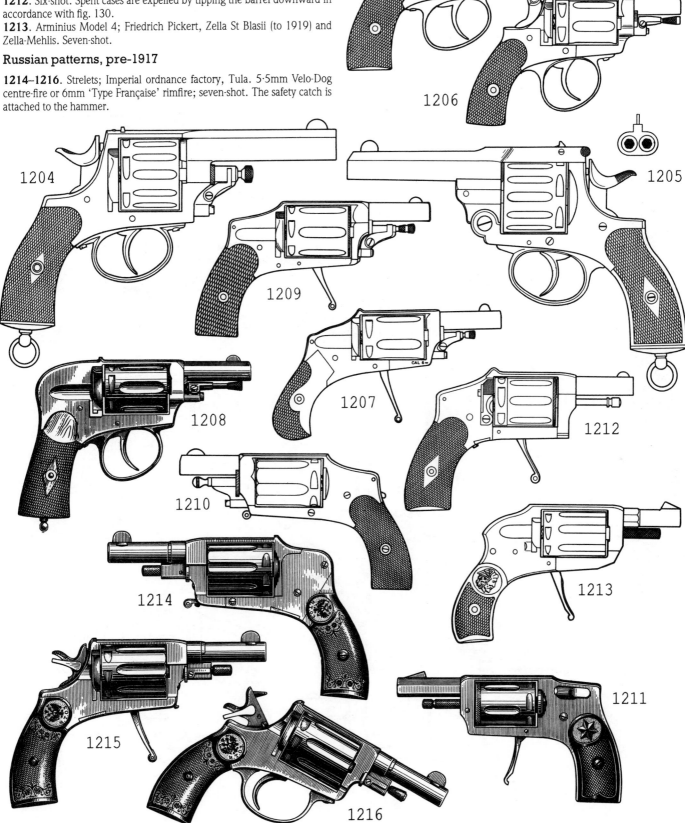

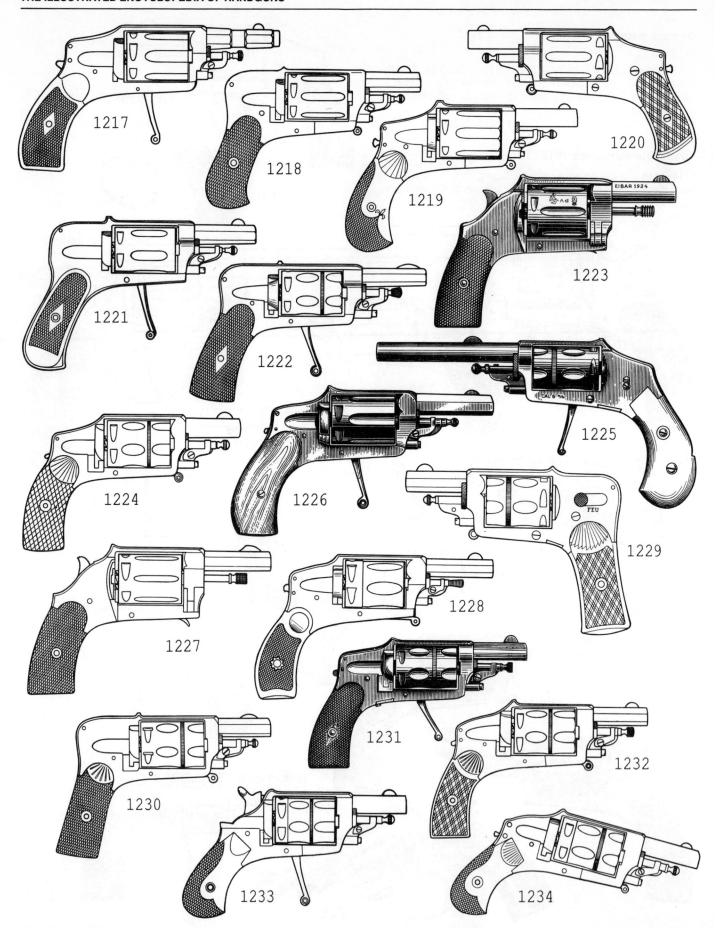

Spanish patterns

1217, 1218. Six-shot.
1219, 1220. Crucelegui Hermanos, Eibar. Six-shot.
1221, 1222. 'F.A.'; Francisco Arizmendi, Eibar. Five-shot.
1223. 'F.A.'; Francisco Arizmendi, Eibar. Six-shot. Spent cases are expelled by swinging the cylinder laterally and pressing the head of the extractor rod backward. Similar revolvers were made in Saint-Étienne
1224, 1225. 'F.A.G.'; Francisco Arizmendi y Goenaga, Eibar. Five-shot. The distinctive elongated barrel (fig. 1224) was intended for export to Austro-Hungary; see fig. 990.
1226. 'F.A.G.'; Francisco Arizmendi y Goenaga, Eibar. Six-shot.
1227. 'F.A.G.'; Francisco Arizmendi y Goenaga, Eibar. Six-shot. Spent cases are removed by swinging the cylinder laterally on its yoke and then pressing back on the head of the extractor rod.
1228. Retolaza Hermanos, Eibar. Five-shot.
1229. Velo-Brom; Retolaza Hermanos, Eibar. Five-shot.

Unknown patterns

1230–1234. Five-shot.
1235. Five-shot. Spent cases are ejected by tipping the barrel downward.

1236. Six-shot.
1237. Six-shot. Spent cases are extracted in accordance with fig. 131.
1238. Ten-shot. A tipping-barrel design.

5. HYBRID REVOLVERS

This section contains details of guns which, owing to their mixed construction, cannot be included in any of the previous categories. Obsolescent parts or old-fashioned designs were often perpetuated to keep production costs to a minimum, even though the resulting revolvers were less effectual than contemporaneous rivals.

Patterns based on the Lefaucheux system

In these, the characteristic—but obsolete Lefaucheux—construction was adapted for new centre- or rimfire cartridges which were not characteristic of the original pinfire system.
1239. ·22 Short rimfire; six-shot. German proofs.
1240–1243. ·22 Short rimfire; six-shot. Miniature revolvers of unknown make, all proved in Germany.
1244. 6mm Flobert or ·22 Winchester Central-Fire; six-shot. German proofs. The hammer is without a spur and the trigger is a ring.
1245. 7·5mm; six-shot.

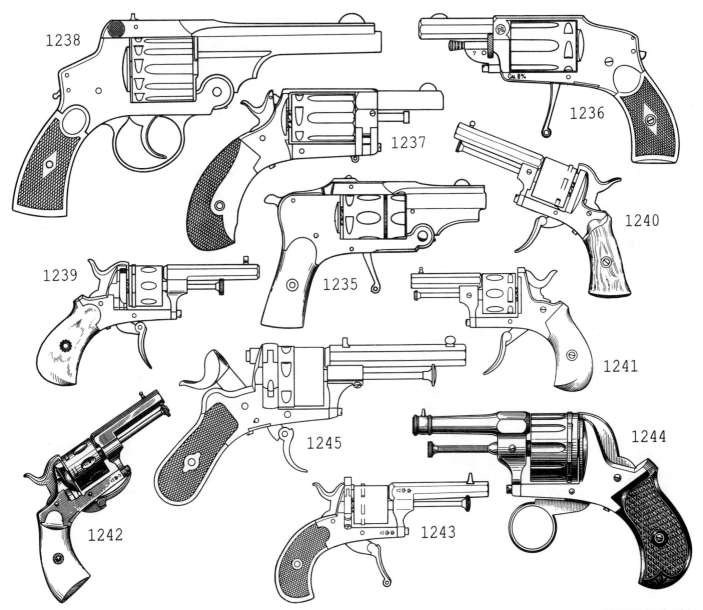

1246. ·320; six-shot. German proofs. Note the spurless hammer.

1247. ·320; six-shot. Possibly Spanish. The Smith & Wesson trade mark on the grips is spurious.

1248. ·44; six-shot. Probably made by Lefaucheux in Paris. Revolvers of this type, which was briefly used officially in France, were also made in Belgium. A smaller version appeared in ·38.

1249. ·44; six-shot. Probably made by Lefaucheux in Paris. This differs from the preceding revolver largely in the additional decoration. The grips are ivory.

1250. 'A.F.'; Auguste Francotte & Companie, Liége. ·380; six-shot.

1251. Arendt & Companie, Liége. ·380; six-shot. The loading gate opens backward, and the hammer can be cocked even with the safety catch applied.

1252. Guardian; Belgian. ·320; six-shot. Similar to fig. 1241, but smaller and lacking the swivel ring on the base of the butt.

1253. Guardian or 'American Model 1878'; Belgian. ·380; six-shot.

1254. Manufacture Française d'Armes et Cycles, Saint-Étienne. ·32; five-shot.

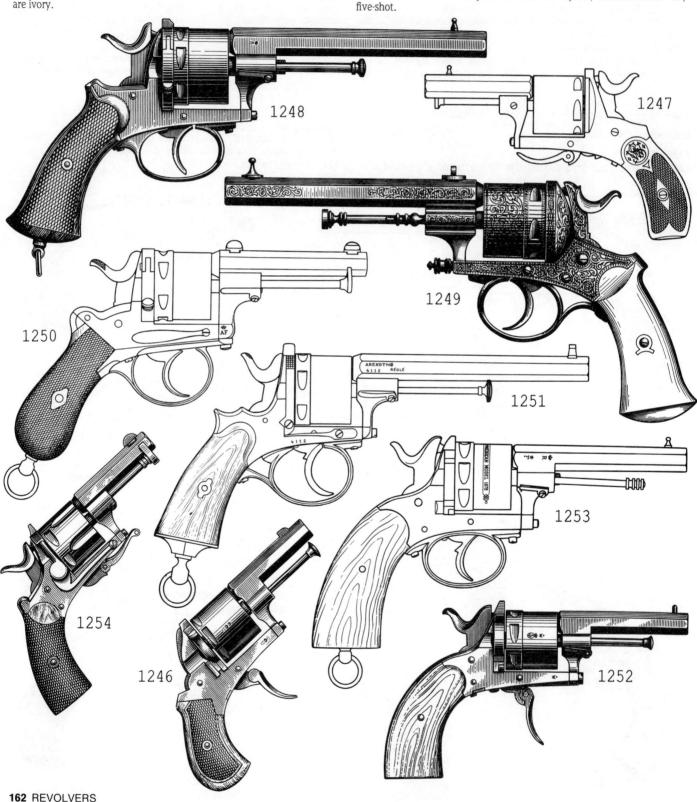

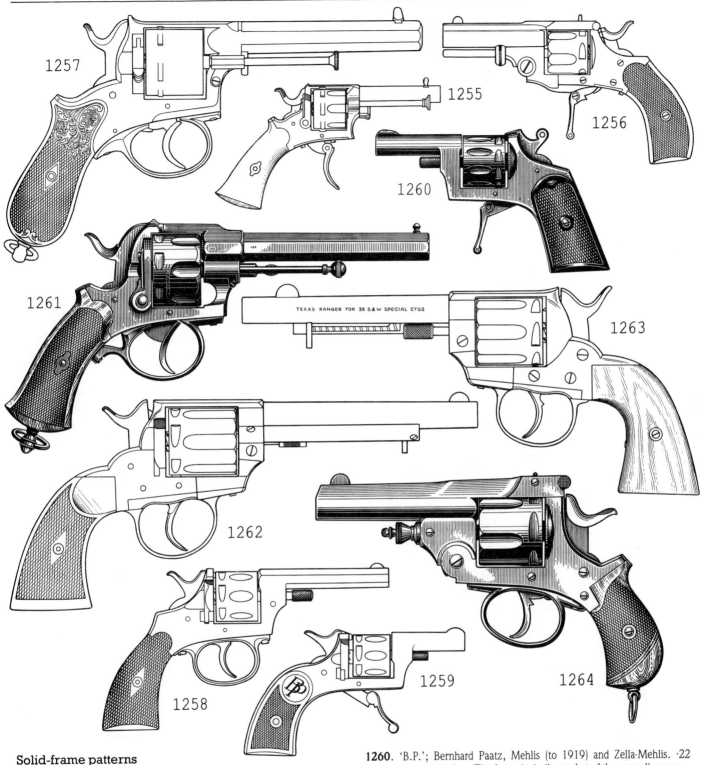

Solid-frame patterns

1255. ·22 Short rimfire; six-shot. French, Lefaucheux type.

1256. 6·35mm Auto; five-shot. Possibly Spanish. Folding trigger; no ejector. The cylinder must be removed for reloading. The constructional features are similar to those of a hinged-frame pattern; the 'hinge' is the button of the cylinder-axis spring catch.

1257. ·380; six-shot. An 'English Type' Lefaucheux.

1258. 'B.P.'; Bernhard Paatz, Mehlis (to 1919) and Zella-Mehlis. ·22; six-shot. The one-piece frame is open above the cylinder.

1259. 'B.P.'; Bernhard Paatz, Mehlis (to 1919) and Zella-Mehlis. ·22 Short rimfire; six-shot.

1260. 'B.P.'; Bernhard Paatz, Mehlis (to 1919) and Zella-Mehlis. ·22 Short rimfire; eight-shot. The frame is similar to that of the preceding gun.

1261. Model 1873; Rolland & Renault, Liége. ·380 Eley Rimfire; six-shot. An alteration of the pinfire gun shown in fig. 209.

1262. Model 1929; Spanish. Essentially similar to fig. 1263.

1263. Texas Ranger; Fabrique d'Armes Réunies, Liége. ·380; six-shot. This gun is based on the Colt Peacemaker, though the construction of the standing breech and firing mechanism follow European practice.

Hinged-frame patterns

1264. A Belgian-made five-shot revolver amalgamating clearly defined features of the Bulldog and Warnant patterns.

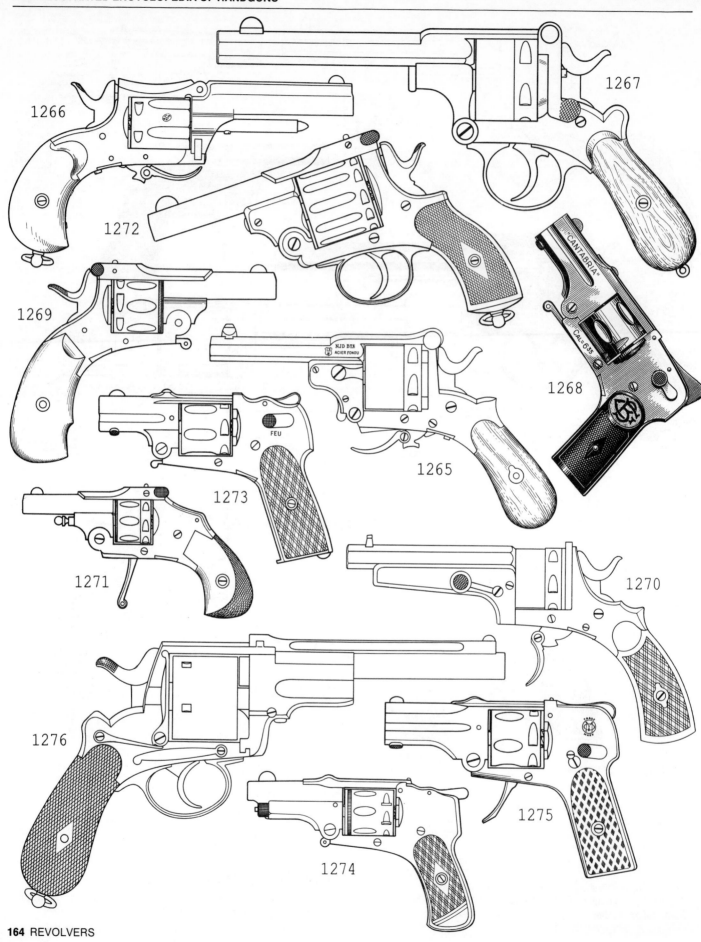

1265. 7·65mm Auto; six-shot. This Belgian-made gun resembles the Francotte system, though the breech-locking lever lies on only one side of the frame.

1266. ·320; five-shot. A Belgian Smith & Wesson imitation with an upward-tipping barrel. The barrel latch and the ejection system are typically S&W, but the double-action firing mechanism, rebounding hammer, folding trigger and the method of locking the cylinder are all European.

1267. 11mm; six-shot. This Belgian-made gun resembles the Francotte system, though the breech-locking lever lies on only one side of the frame.

1268. Cantabria; Garate Hermanos, Ermua. 6·35mm Auto; five-shot.

1269. 'H.D.H.'; Henrion, Dassy & Heuschen, Liége. ·320; six-shot. Similar to the preceding gun, but fitted with a folding trigger.

1270. La Rosa; Spanish. 7·65mm Auto; six-shot. The barrel and cylinder moves forward to load—similar to the Galand system, though the latter's lever is absent.

1271. Lepage & Companie, Liége, and other Belgian manufacturers. ·22 Short rimfire; six-shot.

1272. Puppy; Henrion, Dassy & Heuschen ('HDH'), Liége. 5·5mm Velo-Dog, 6·35mm Auto, 7·65mm Auto or 8mm Lebel; five- to ten-shot, depending on calibre.

1273. Velo-Mith; Crucelegui Hermanos or Retolaza Hermanos, Eibar. 7·65mm Auto; five-shot.

1274. Velo-Mith; Garate Hermanos, Ermua. 6·35mm Auto; six-shot.

1275. Velo-Mith; Ojanguren y Marcaido, Eibar. ·32 or ·38.

1276. Victor; possibly Belgian. ·450; five-shot. The extraction system is similar to that of the Merwin & Hulbert (q.v., see also fig. 129).

Swinging-cylinder patterns

Some of these offer original features and good quality, and thus lie on the boundary between proprietary and mixed construction. Thus the Henrion, Dassy & Heuschen 'Puppy', fig. 1283, differs from the original Francotte pattern (see 'Belgium') only in size. Owing to its small calibre, however, it also resembles the revolver of obviously mixed parentage shown in fig. 1281.

1277. ·22 or ·320; six-shot. Italian.

1278. 6·35mm Auto; five-shot. Probably made by Auguste Francotte & Companie or Établissements Lebeaux of Liége. Sold in pre-Revolutionary Russia as the 'Vityaz'.

1279. 6·35mm Auto; five-shot. Probably made by Auguste Francotte & Companie or Établissements Lebeaux of Liége.

1280. 'A.F.'; Auguste Francotte & Companie, Liége. 6·35mm Auto; five-shot.

1281. Browning type; Établissements Lebeaux. 7·65mm Auto; five-shot.

1282. Le Petit Formidable; French. 6·35mm Auto; five-shot.

1283. Puppy; Henrion, Dassy & Heuschen ('HDH'), Liége. 6·35mm Auto; five-shot.

1284. 'S.F.M.'; Société Française de Munitions, Paris. 7·65mm Auto; five-shot. Probably made in Saint-Étienne.

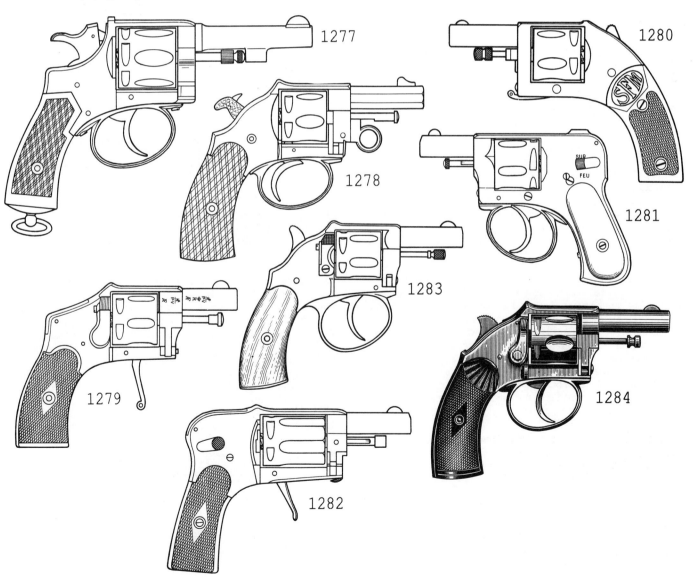

Pistol directory

The major differences between pistols and revolvers concern the way in which they operate, and, consequently, their major constructional features. To actuate the revolver mechanism, the shooter must exert physical force; conversely, energy generated by the cartridge is used to operate the mechanism of a pistol automatically.

In some firearms—e.g., machine-guns—the operating cycle includes the firing of the subsequent cartridge, allowing shooting to continue as long as the trigger is pressed and cartridges remain in the magazine. Pistols, however, are too light to control satisfactorily when firing in this way; thus they are generally semi-automatics, requiring the firer to press the trigger before each shot.

To be strictly accurate, the two classes should be differentiated as 'automatic' (or 'fully automatic') and 'semi-automatic' (or 'self-loading'). However, the distinctions have become blurred to a point where virtually *all* guns are known popularly as 'automatics'.

Guns which are capable of firing singly or continuously must embody a means of selecting whichever mode is required. These designs are termed 'selective fire'. The selector is generally an auxiliary lever, though attempts have been made to incorporate it in the trigger system.

Operating systems

Automatic pistols are much more diverse than revolvers, largely because of the differing ways in which the operating mechanism is arranged.

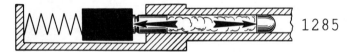

1285. The simplest form of operation—known as 'blowback'—is usually confined to guns chambering relatively weak cartridges. It relies simply on a heavy slide or breech block, a strong spring, and a stationary barrel. Blowback pistols are easy to make and effectual enough in their limited role.

When a cartridge is fired, the breech is held shut by the spring. As the bullet begins to move forward along the bore, a recoil reaction immediately tries to force the slide back. However, gas pressure delays the opening movement by holding the sides of the case against the walls of the chamber; in addition, as the bullet is much lighter than the slide, so the velocity with which the slide recoils is much less than that of the bullet. When the bullet emerges from the barrel, the pressure in the chamber immediately drops, the cartridge case is released, the slide is thrust back, and the spent case is ejected. The spring halts the backward movement of the slide, which then returns to push a fresh cartridge into the chamber.

Attempts have been made to adapt blowback principles to pistols chambering the most powerful military handgun cartridges (e.g., 9mm Bergmann-Bayard). However, the breech may start to open before residual pressure has dropped far enough to release the cartridge case from contact with the walls of the chamber. The extractor then often tears through the case-rim or rips the case-head from the body, causing a serious jam.

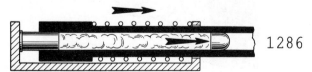

1286. Guns utilising the blow-forward system have been made, though few have appeared since 1914. They convert the energy created by friction between the bullet and the rifling to thrust the barrel *forward*. A spring then returns the barrel, and a new round enters the breech as it closes.

1287, 1288. Delayed, hesitation or retarded blowback systems (sometimes called 'semi-locked') attempt to combine the simplicity of the blowbacks

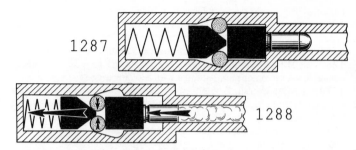

with the security of a locked breech. When a shot is fired, the opening movement of the slide is retarded by friction; the most popular methods involve levers or rollers, though rotating barrels have also been used. The roller-locked Heckler & Koch P-9S shown here is typical of modern practice.

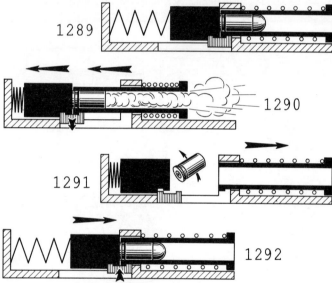

1289–1292. When a shot is fired in a typical long-recoil system (fig. 1289), the slide and barrel, securely locked together, are usually drawn back for almost the entire recoil stroke—certainly farther than the length of the cartridge case, creating a distinction between long- and short-recoil systems. When the moving parts reach their rearmost position (fig. 1290), the slide and barrel are unlocked. The barrel runs back first (fig. 1291), to be followed by the slide once sufficient gap has been created between them for the spent case to be ejected and a new cartridge stripped from the magazine. The slide finally catches up with the barrel, and the parts are re-locked as they are brought to a halt (fig. 1292).

1293, 1294. Short recoil is essentially similar to long recoil, excepting that the barrel and the slide are separated much more quickly—usually within a

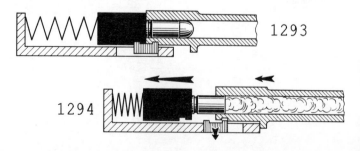

few millimetres, and certainly within the length of the cartridge case. The slide then reciprocates alone (fig. 1294), relying partly on its inertia and partly on the pressure of the return spring to reduce its velocity. The spent case is ejected on the backward stroke and a new round is stripped from the magazine as the slide runs forward again. Re-locking occurs during the short distance in which the slide and barrel travel forward together into battery.

Locking systems

Short recoil is the most popular operating system, being shared by all the locked-breech Brownings, the Parabellum (Luger), the Mauser C/96, the Nambu and countless others. The associated locking mechanism, however, varies greatly.

1295–1298. Pioneered by John Browning, the dropping barrel is locked by lugs inside the slide entering grooves on the upper surface of the barrel. When a shot is fired, the slide is thrust back by recoil and draws the barrel with it. A pivoting link attached to the frame lowers the barrel as it moves back, separating the grooves from the lugs. The barrel is then stopped whilst the slide reciprocates alone.

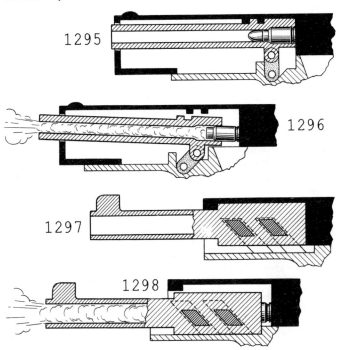

The original Brownings relied on two links between the barrel and the frame, which held the barrel parallel to the slide-top as it dropped. These were replaced by a simpler single-link system (figs. 1295, 1296) which tipped the breech downward, and ultimately by a cam-finger. The method of locking the barrel and slide together can also vary, as the lugs may lie on the surface of the barrel. Many modern guns of this class simply displace a large chamber-block into an enlarged ejection port in the slide. Alternatively, grooves in the slide or frame can be used in conjunction with lugs on the barrel-side, as in the British Webley & Scott pistol (figs. 1297, 1298).

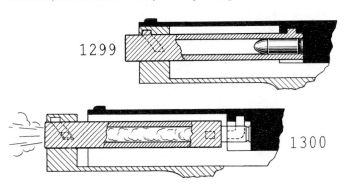

1299, 1300. Rotating-barrel locks are usually controlled by lugs on the outside of the barrel, one of which slides in a longitudinal cam-track in the frame and another in a transverse groove inside the slide. When a shot is fired (fig. 1299), the lug engaging the slide ensures a satisfactory lock. As the slide runs back, therefore, the barrel moves with it until the lug engaging the inclined frame-track rotates the barrel laterally. This releases the slide (fig. 1300). The barrel is then halted by the frame, the slide runs back, the spent case is ejected, and the slide returns to strip a new round out of the magazine. The locking lug on the barrel then re-enters its groove in the slide, and is rotated back into locking engagement (by the lug in the frame-track) as the barrel and slide move forward to battery.

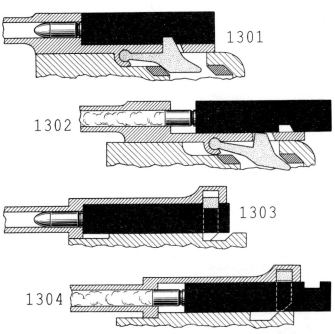

1301–1304. Pivoting or sliding levers, struts and wedges take many differing forms. All rely on the barrel and the slide being locked by a separate component which, after the initial backward movement, is disengaged by interaction of the moving parts with the stationary frame. This releases the slide. Locking systems of this type are found in the Mauser C/96 (a pivoting block, figs. 1301, 1302) and in the Finnish Lahti (a vertically sliding block, figs 1303, 1304).

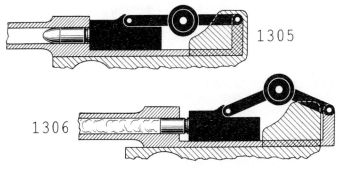

1305, 1306. The toggle- or knee-joint system, embodied in the Parabellum or Luger pistol, relies on levers connected with the breechblock to hold the transverse joint below the bore axis. When the gun is fired, the backward recoil force tends to force the joint downward into the solid floor of the barrel extension. As the barrel extension moves backward, however, the transverse joint is soon lifted above the bore axis by cam ramps on the frame. The barrel extension then stops, allowing the toggle-joint to continue upward. This retracts the breechblock far enough to eject the spent case, before a spring returns the parts to their original position. A new round is stripped from the magazine as the action closes, whereupon the joint drops below the bore axis and re-locks the breech.

Pistol construction

This depends greatly on the position of the recoil spring, which dictates the layout of many subsidiary parts. Most blowback pistols have the spring concentric with the barrel, whereas many locked-breech patterns carry it below the barrel on a separate guide rod. Alternatively, the spring may lie within the bolt, or in the grip.

The position of the magazine also governs the layout of a pistol. Many of the earliest guns held cartridges in a housing ahead of the trigger guard—e.g., the Bergmann-Schmeissers, Mauser C/96 or Charola y Anitua—but a detachable box in the butt, exemplified by the Borchardt of 1893, was more compact and had greater development potential.

The cartridges were usually arranged in a single column. However, some early Mausers staggered the cartridges to increase capacity, and double columns are now common. These were inspired by the Browning GP-35, which held thirteen rounds in the magazine and a fourteenth in the chamber. Whereas eight rounds were once the norm in military weapons, capacities as high as eighteen are now offered.

Virtually all modern pistols have detachable magazines. Prior to the First World War, however, fixed clip- or charger-loaded patterns were also popular.

A detachable magazine is essentially an open-top metallic box, containing a follower propelled by a spring. Cartridges inserted in the magazine push the follower downward, compressing the spring, and are held in place by ribs pressed into the magazine walls. Individual cartridges are forced forward out of the magazine on the return stroke of the slide, bolt or breechblock. Holes or slots in the magazine often enable the state of loading to be seen at a glance. To load a pistol of this type, the empty magazine is simply replaced by a full one; the first round is then fed into the chamber by cycling the slide by hand.

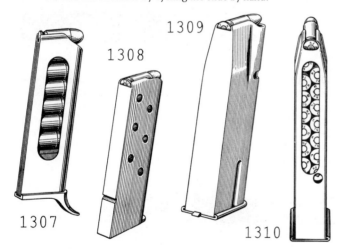

1307–1310. Typical magazines. Figs. 1307, 1308: single-column designs (Beretta M1934, FN-Browning M1900). Figs. 1309, 1310: staggered or double-column patterns (FN-Browning GP-35, Beretta M-92).

Most of the pistols with integral magazines—e.g, the Austrian Roth-Steyr and Steyr-Hahn—were loaded with a charger, which was inserted in special grooves cut in the receiver or slide. These lay above the rear of the open magazine well when the action was open. The cartridges were then pressed downward with the thumb, the empty charger was discarded, and the breech could be closed to strip a new round into the chamber. Though a few guns had a detachable magazine *and* charger-loading capability, they were never popular.

After the initial period of military enthusiasm, fixed magazines were abandoned. They were unnecessarily complicated and slow to load. A detachable magazine could be replenished in a fraction of time required to position the charger, strip the cartridges into the magazine and then close the breech.

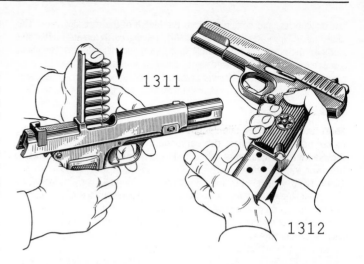

1311, 1312. Typical loading techniques. Fig. 1311: a charger system (Austro-Hungarian Steyr-Hahn). Fig. 1312: a detachable box magazine (Soviet Tokarev).

Many pistols incorporate a hold-open device, which keeps the slide in its retracted position after the last round has been fired and ejected. This shows the firer that he holds an empty gun. The magazine is then replaced and the slide can be run forward, either by pressing a separate catch or simply by arranging for the new magazine to release the slide as it is pushed home. The few seconds this saves could be critical, especially in the heat of battle.

Firing systems are also diverse. After some initial experimentation, preference was given to a concealed striker or an enclosed hammer. These were simple, reliable, well-protected from the elements, and (most importantly) extremely compact. However, firing systems of this type did not always operate smoothly and were rarely safe enough to risk carrying a cocked gun with a live round in the chamber. It was difficult to determine the state of cocking visually, and the constant compression of the mainspring—especially common in striker-fired patterns—invariably reduced durability.

Enclosed-hammer or concealed-striker pistols were almost always fitted with additional safety devices. The manual or non-automatic patterns were usually controlled by a small radial lever, which locked the firing mechanism; automatic safeties protruded from the grip-strap, disengaging only when the firer held the gun correctly. The safeties generally moved in opposition, which prevented a shot being fired accidentally by, for example, thrusting the gun into a pocket. It was virtually impossible for pressure to be applied in opposite directions simultaneously.

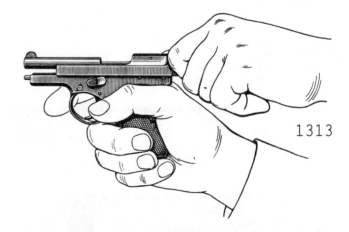

1313. Two hands are required to retract the slide of conventional guns—this is a Soviet 6·35mm TK—to chamber the first round.

Other forms of safety include trigger-locking buttons, catches to remove tension from the mainspring, bars which blocked the firing mechanism when the magazine was removed, and levers which could lower a cocked hammer safely onto a loaded chamber.

Many pistols, apart from pocketable designs, have had exposed hammers. These are particularly convenient to use, as they share many of the benefits of the revolver—for example, the hammer shows the state of cocking at a glance, and can be lowered smoothly under manual control when a shot is no longer required. Excepting designs with transfer-bar or similar safety systems, a pistol with its hammer down on a cartridge in the chamber is just as dangerous as a revolver in the same condition. However, the mainspring is relieved of tension when the hammer is dropped, and the firer can simply thumb it back again when the shot is required. As the ability to lower the hammer manually approximates with engaging the manual safety of an enclosed-hammer or striker-fired system, additional safety catches may be absent from exposed-hammer guns (e.g., the Tokarev).

The firing systems of the newest pistols share the most valuable advantage possessed by a revolver—the ability to fire the first shot simply by pulling the trigger—whilst avoiding the danger of igniting a chambered round either by an accidental blow on the hammer or simply by dropping the gun on a hard surface.

Some pistols are double-action-only, relying on recoil energy simply to eject the fired case and strip the next round into the chamber; the firer must actuate the trigger mechanism for each shot. Accuracy suffers, owing to the muscular effort involved, but the firing mechanism can be simple and reliable. In addition, the pistol is always ready for use. Safety catches are superfluous in these cases, and so the pistols handle like double-action enclosed-hammer revolvers.

As pistols are intended almost exclusively for use at short range, sights are essentially simple. The trajectory of the pistol bullet is flat enough for its effects to be disregarded. At their most primitive, therefore, particularly on the smallest pocket pistols, 'sights' may be nothing but a groove cut in the top of the frame. However, fixed sights generally comprise a blade and an open notch. Adjustable sights customarily comprise a blade at the muzzle and a leaf-and-slider pivoted in a frame attached to the top rear of the slide; they are normally confined to military weapons. Brightly coloured or luminous paint may be applied to the sights to improve performance in poor light.

The recent advent of improved production techniques—e.g., alloy or synthetic frames—has often led to changes in pistol design. Where appropriate, these are described in the individual captions

Fully automatic designs

Attempts were made from the earliest days to develop handguns which could fire automatically, among the most successful being an experimental Borchardt demonstrated in 1897. However, poor metallurgy, unreliable smokeless propellant, and the difficulties of controlling lightweight automatic weapons in one hand all caused interest to wane.

To ensure that only a single shot was fired for each press of the trigger, the semi-automatics were fitted with 'disconnectors'. The slide customarily depressed an auxiliary lever to separate the trigger and sear between shots. Thus the hammer remained cocked until the trigger was released to reconnect with the sear. Occasional returns were made to fully-automatic pistols—during the First World War, then again with the Mauser Schnellfeuerpistolen and Spanish copies of the C/96. In recent years, pistols have been offered with enlarged magazines, burst-firing capability, and detachable shoulder stocks to improve stability in automatic fire. None has been especially successful. A better approach has been to reduce the size of conventional submachine-guns (e.g., the Uzi) to the dimensions of a large pistol.

1314. The Chylewski-type cocking system, shown here on a Chinese Type 77, allowed only the firing hand to be used to chamber the first cartridge.

1315, 1316. These are typical of the modern ultra-compact blowback 'machine pistols', generally restricted to semi-automatic fire. Fig. 1315: the US 9mm Parabellum Wilkinson 'Linda', which is 12·2in overall with an 8·3in barrel, weighs 65oz, and has a detachable box magazine holding 31 rounds. The US Interdynamics KG-9 (fig. 1316), also chambering the 9mm Parabellum round, is 12·5in overall, has a 5in barrel and weighs about 46oz. The magazine holds 36 rounds. A compact version, the KG-99K, has a 3in barrel and a 25-round magazine.

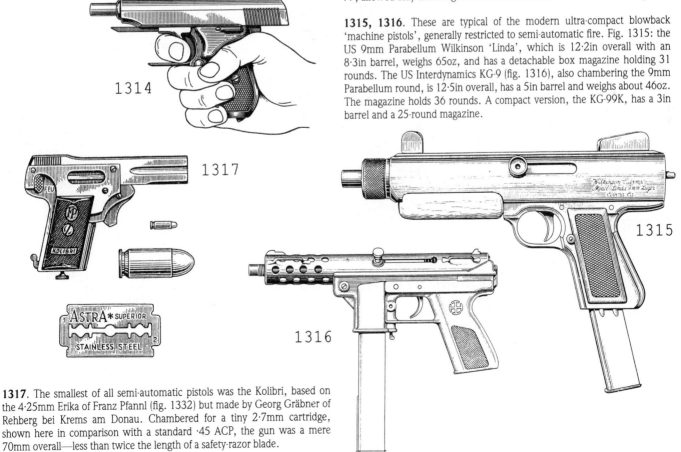

1317. The smallest of all semi-automatic pistols was the Kolibri, based on the 4·25mm Erika of Franz Pfannl (fig. 1332) but made by Georg Gräbner of Rehberg bei Krems am Donau. Chambered for a tiny 2·7mm cartridge, shown here in comparison with a standard ·45 ACP, the gun was a mere 70mm overall—less than twice the length of a safety-razor blade.

Argentina

Hispano-Argentina Fabricá de Automoviles SA ('HAFDASA') also once produced a large and heavy ·45-calibre pistol with a detachable 25-round magazine. It resembled a submachine-gun externally, but was smaller, lacked a stock, and could not fire fully automatically.

1318. Army Model 1905; Österreichische Waffenfabriks-Gesellschaft, Steyr. 7·65mm; 240mm overall, 160mm barrel. Ten rounds, charger-loaded. Early in the twentieth century, the 1905-pattern Austro-Hungarian Mannlicher pistol (fig. 1366) was adopted officially. The Argentine emblem appeared on the right side of the frame.

1319. Army Model 1927; Colt's Patent Fire Arms Manufacturing Company, Hartford, Connecticut. 11·25mm (·45 ACP); 216mm overall, 128mm barrel, 1106gm. Seven rounds. The Mannlicher was replaced with copies of the American Colt pistols, the 'M1916' being equivalent to the US M1911 and the 'M1927' to the M1911A1. Model 1927-type guns were subsequently made by the government-owned Fabricá Militar de Armas

Portatiles 'Domingo Matheu' of Rosario in 1947–66. An Argentine copy of the ·22 LR rimfire Colt Ace was also made in small numbers.

1320. Ballester-Rigaud and Ballester-Molina. 11·25mm (·45 ACP); 215mm overall, 127mm barel, 1020gm. Seven rounds. These guns, based on the 1911-type Colt-Browning, were apparently made for the Argentine military and police forces from c.1930 onward. The slide marks suggest that they were made for Hispano-Argentina Fabricá de Automoviles SA, Buenos Aires ('HAFDASA'), by subcontractors—i.e., first Ballester-Rigaud and later by Ballester-Molina. Work seems to have ceased in the 1940s, possibly when production of the 1927-pattern Colt copy began in Rosario. The guns were essentially similar to the Colt M1911, but lacked the automatic safety in the back strap. The retracting grooves in the slide have a most distinctive pattern and the trigger pivots on its axis instead of sliding backward.

1321. Bersa; Fabricá de Armas Bersa SA, Ramos Mejia. 7·65mm Auto; 165mm overall, 89mm barrel. Eight rounds.

1322, 1323. Bersa Model 83; Fabricá de Armas Bersa SA, Ramos Mejia, 1988 to date. 9mm Short; 695gm. Six rounds. A double-action blowback pistol derived from the Bernardelli patterns.

1324. Bersa Model 85; Fabricá de Armas Bersa SA, Ramos Mejia, 1988 to date. 9mm Short; 865gm. Twelve rounds. A conventional double-action blowback personal-defence pistol with a staggered-coloumn magazine. The Model 86 (introduced in 1991) is very similar but has a one-piece neoprene wraparound grip.

1325. Bersa Model 225; Fabricá de Armas Bersa SA, Ramos Mejia. ·22 LR rimfire; 127mm barrel, 737gm. Eleven rounds.

1326. Bersa Model 382; Fabricá de Armas Bersa SA, Ramos Mejia. 9mm Short; 165mm overall, 89mm barrel, 708gm. Seven rounds. This single-action gun was discontinued in 1987. The Model 383 was similar, but had a double-action trigger system.

1327. Bersa Model 622; Fabricá de Armas Bersa SA, Ramos Mejia. ·22 LR rimfire; 175mm overall, 100mm barrel. Greatly resembling the Beretta Model 70 (q.v.), this single-action blowback design has an exposed hammer and a single-column magazine.

1328. Bersa Model 644; Fabricá de Armas Bersa SA, Ramos Mejia. ·22 LR rimfire; 168mm overall, 90mm barrel. Eleven rounds.

1329. 'G.M.C.'; Garbi, Moretti y Compania, Mar del Plata. ·22 LR rimfire; 150mm overall, 78mm barrel. A blowback sporting pistol apparently dating from the 1940s.

1330, 1331. Hafdasa; Hispano-Argentina Fabricá de Automoviles SA, Buenos Aires. ·22 LR rimfire; 178mm overall, 70mm barrel. This gun—unusually for a pistol—embodies the 'slam fire' system more commonly encountered in submachine-guns. The striker is an integral part of the breechblock; consequently, pressure on the trigger releases the breech to run

forward, chamber a cartridge and fire the primer. The breech is then thrust backward, the fired case is ejected, and the breechblock remains held back on the sear. The receiver has elongated slits on both sides, allowing the firer to retract the breech block manually. The Zonda is similar to the Hafdasa, but the safety system differs in detail, only one slot appears in the receiver—on the right—and the front part of the slide has only a single notch for the finger instead of grooves.

Austria

In 1934, Österreichische Waffenfabriks-Gesellschaft amalgamated with other companies to form Steyr-Daimler-Puch. Production of some pre-1918 Steyr pistols continued in Austria virtually until the end of the Second World War. However, these had distinctive markings—in particular, an eagle lacking the imperial crown—and are included here. Guns made during the period of German annexation (1938–45) will often bear German markings.

1332–1334. Erika; Franz Pfannl, Krems am Donau. 4·25mm; 105mm or 125mm overall, 37mm or 57mm barrel, 225gm (37mm barrel). Six rounds. These small pistols were little more than dangerous toys, firing an ultra-low power cartridge containing a tiny jacketed bullet. Only when firing at point-blank range did the Erika pose any real threat, as the bullet would penetrate 4cm into pine board. The grip of the long-barrel variant, but not the magazine, was longer than that of the short-barrel gun.

1335–1337. Glock 17; Glock GmbH, Deutsch-Wagram, 1980 to date.

1339

1338

1337

1340

1341

1342

1344

1345

1343

1346

1347

1348

1349

9mm Parabellum; 188mm overall, 114mm barrel, 661gm (870gm loaded). Seventeen rounds. The Glock was the unexpected winner of the Austrian army handgun trials, being adopted in 1983 in preference to the Steyr GB-80. The frame and some parts of the mechanism are synthetic. The Glock 17L is a target-shooting derivative with an adjustable back sight, a 155mm barrel, and an elongated slide mounted on a standard-length frame. It weighs 750gm unladen. Glock pistols may be fitted with laser sights (in the recoil-spring rod tube) to enhance accuracy.

1338. Glock 18; Glock GmbH; Deutsch-Wagram, 1986 to date. 9mm Parabellum. This differs from the standard model largely in the addition of a fire-selector, a long barrel and a nineteen-round magazine. The standard seventeen-round and optional 33-round magazines can also be used.

1339, 1340. Glock 19; Glock GmbH; Deutsch-Wagram, 1989 to date. 9mm Parabellum; fifteen rounds. This is a compact version of the standard Glock 17, with a shorter barrel and a smaller magazine. A variant chambered for the ·40 S&W cartridge is known as the Glock 23.

1341. Glock 20; Glock GmbH; Deutsch-Wagram, 1990 to date. 10mm Auto. This differs from the Glock 17 principally in its calibre. The Glock 21 (·45 ACP) and Glock 22 (·40 S&W) are similar.

1342–1345. Little Tom; Wiener Waffenfabrik, Vienna. 6·35mm Auto or 7·65mm Auto; 115mm overall, 59mm barrel and 375gm (6·35mm), or 139mm overall, 79mm barrel and 580gm (7·65mm). Six 7·65mm or eight 6·35mm rounds. The first guns of this type were patented by Alois Tomiška, a Czech gunsmith, prior to 1914. Their characteristic feature was a double-action firing mechanism of a type subsequently employed in the Walther Polizei-Pistole and its successors. The Little Tom also has a curious magazine arrangement in which an empty box is forced out upward by the insertion of a loaded unit from the bottom.

1346, 1347. 'O.W.A.'; Österreichische Werke Anstalt, Vienna. 6·35mm Auto; 120mm overall, 50mm barrel, 410gm. Six rounds. The basic construction of these blowbacks was copied from the Clément (q.v.).

1348. Steyr GB-80; Steyr-Daimler-Puch AG, c.1981–6. 9mm Parabellum; 216mm overall, 137mm barrel, 930gm. Eighteen rounds. In the early 1970s, the Steyr company developed a pistol intended to compete for a military contract. Known as the Pi-18, it was a most distinctive delayed

blowback design with a staggered-column large capacity magazine and an exposed-hammer double action firing system. When a shot was fired, the backward movement of the slide was opposed by the pressure of propellant gas which had been bled from the bore—an adaption of an idea pioneered by the German Barnitzke toward the end of the Second World War.

Only prototypes of the Pi-18 were produced in Austria, though a substantial number of Rogak pistols, developed from blueprints supplied to Steyr's US importer, were made in the USA in 1977–82 in controversial circumstances. The perfected GB-80 appeared in 1981, but was beaten in the Austrian army trials by the Glock (q.v.) and rejected by the US Army when reliability fell short of the M1911A1 Colt-Browning. Unable to attract large-scale orders, Steyr terminated the project in the mid 1980s.

1349. Steyr Model 1909, post-war type; Österreichische Waffenfabriks-Gesellschaft, Steyr. 6·35mm Auto; 116mm or 169mm overall, 53mm or 116mm barrel, 350gm (53mm barrel). Six rounds.

1350–1353. Steyr Model 1934; Steyr-Daimler-Puch AG, Steyr. 7·65mm Auto; 166mm overall, 92mm barrel, 650gm. Eight rounds. This was based on the 1909-pattern Steyr pistol described above, though changes were made in the sights and the machining of the breech. Some guns (figs. 1352, 1353) will be found with the marks of Waffenfabrik Solothurn AG, an ostensibly neutral Swiss company designed to allow Austria and Germany to develop weapons by circumventing the provisions of the Treaty of Versailles.

1354. Steyr SP; Steyr-Daimler-Puch AG. 7·65mm Auto; 165mm overall. Eight rounds. Introduced in 1957, this was the first new pocket personal-defence pistol to be developed in Steyr since the original Pieper-designed pattern of 1909. The gun was a conventional blowback with an enclosed hammer and a double-action-only firing mechanism. Its most unusual feature was a cross-bolt safety catch set into the trigger lever.

Austria-Hungary

Austrian and Hungarian engineers played an important role in the development, distribution and military acceptance of the automatic pistol. Contributions were made in the 1890s by Kromar, Dormus, Schönberger, Krnka, Mannlicher and others, but the earliest guns were

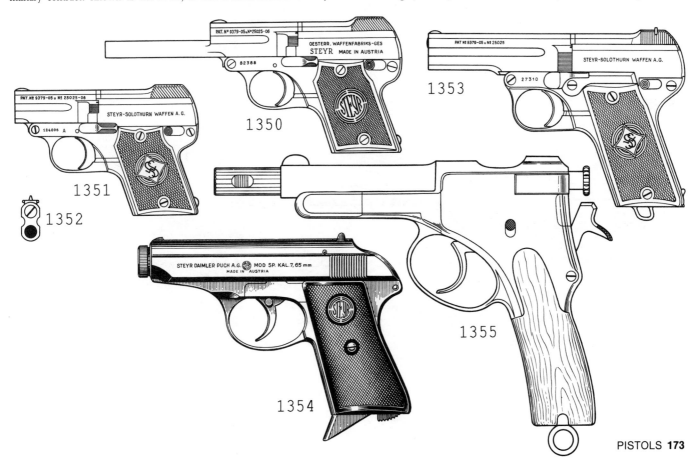

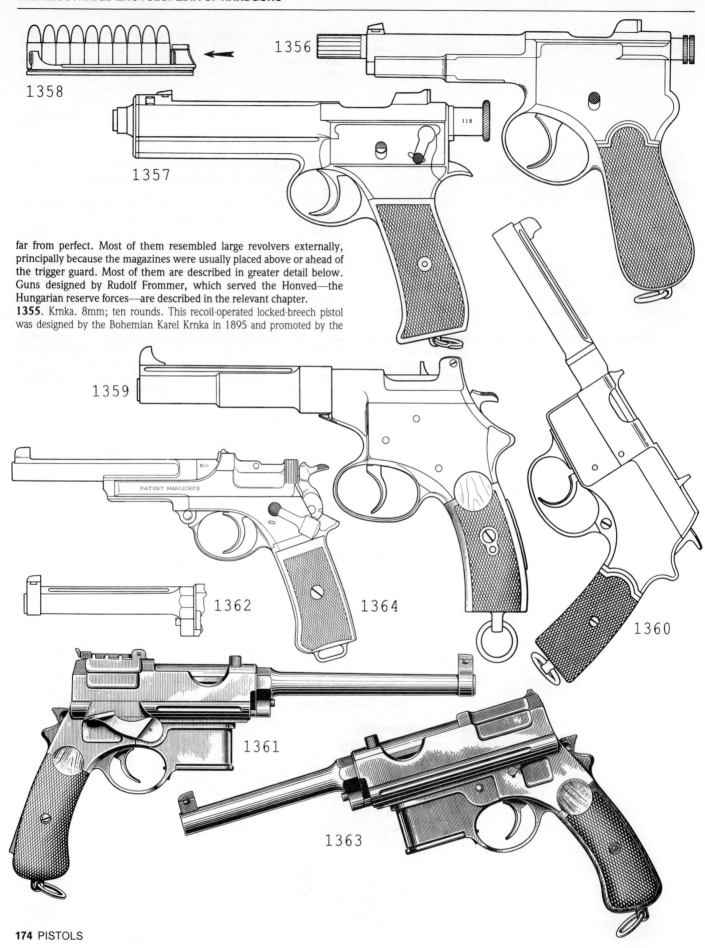

1358

1356

1357

118

far from perfect. Most of them resembled large revolvers externally, principally because the magazines were usually placed above or ahead of the trigger guard. Most of them are described in greater detail below. Guns designed by Rudolf Frommer, which served the Honved—the Hungarian reserve forces—are described in the relevant chapter.

1355. Krnka. 8mm; ten rounds. This recoil-operated locked-breech pistol was designed by the Bohemian Karel Krnka in 1895 and promoted by the

1359

PATENT MANLICHER

1362

1364

1360

1361

1363

ammunition-maker Georg Roth. The magazine in the grip was filled from a charger with a special slider.

1356. Krnka. 8mm; ten rounds. An improved model of 1899.

1357, 1358. Krnka. 8mm; 232mm overall, 128mm barrel. Ten rounds. The model of 1904 was extensively tested by the Austro-Hungarian army. It was the immediate precursor of the Roth-Steyr described below.

1359. Mannlicher, 1894 pattern; Schweizerische Industrie-Gesellschaft, Neuhausen, and others. 6·5mm or 7·6mm; (data for 6·5mm example) 215mm overall, 165mm barrel, 850gm. Five rounds. This pistol, unsuccessfully tested in several countries, fires from an unlocked breech. Most unusually, the barrel moves forward when a shot is fired. When the barrel reaches its farthest position, the spent case is ejected and the next cartridge moves up from the integral charger-loaded magazine to occupy the space behind the returning spring-propelled barrel. When the barrel stops against the standing breech, the gun is loaded but cannot be fired until the trigger of the revolver-type double-action firing mechanism has been pressed.

1360. Mannlicher, 1896 pattern. 7·65mm Mannlicher; six rounds. This unsuccessful prototype embodied a stationary barrel and a blowback-type breech mechanism.

1361–1363. Mannlicher, 1896 pattern ('Model 1903'); Österreichische Waffenfabriks-Gesellschaft, Steyr. 7·65mm Mannlicher; 276mm or 308mm overall, 120mm or 152mm barrel, 1070gm (152m barrel). Seven rounds. Widely known as the 'Austrian Mauser', this gun was patented in 1896. Several differing prototypes were made before series production began in the early 1900s. The detachable magazine ahead of the trigger guard contains cartridges in two rows. The ammunition shares the case dimensions of the 7·63mm Mauser, but contains less propellant and develops lower pressures; the construction of the Austrian pistol is appreciably weaker than its German

rival. The barrel of the Mannlicher recoils only about 2·5mm. A lever on the right side of the frame is used to cock the enclosed hammer. Some guns have fixed back sights, whilst others have a tangent-leaf type graduated to 500 metres. The grip often has a stock-attachment lug.

1364. Mannlicher, 1900 pattern; Waffenfabrik von Dreyse, Sömmerda. 7·63mm Mannlicher; 225mm overall, 140mm barrel. Eight rounds. The magazine, integral with the grip, is loaded from a special clip. The gun is an elegant blowback pattern with an exposed hammer.

1365. Mannlicher Model 1901; Österreichische Waffenfabriks-Gesellschaft, Steyr. 7·63mm Mannlicher; 205mm overall, 120mm barrel. Eight rounds. An improvement of the preceding gun.

1366–1368. Mannlicher Model 1905; Österreichische Waffenfabriks-Gesellschaft, Steyr. 7·63mm Mannlicher; 212mm or 240mm, 130mm or 160mm barrel, 920gm (160mm barrel). Eight or ten rounds. This was an improvement of the 1901 pattern. The safety catch was moved from the frame to the breech, the shape of the hammer was revised, and other lesser modifications were made. These pistols were easy to handle, effectual, shot acceptably accurately, and operated reliably enough to attract the attention of the Argentine army (see fig. 1318). However, they were not especially easy to make and were soon overtaken by more effectual designs.

1369, 1370. Roth-Steyr, or Repeating Pistol Model 1907 (Repetier-pistole M7); Österreichische Waffenfabriks-Gesellschaft, Steyr, and Fémaru Fegyver ës Gépgyár, Budapest. 8mm; 232mm overall, 128mm barrel, 990gm. Ten rounds. This incorporated the same charger-loading system as the 1895 Krnka pattern (fig. 1355) and was adopted by the Austro-Hungarian cavalry in 1907. Its distinguishing features included a fixed magazine, a 90° locking stroke, and an odd 'semi-double action' firing mechanism in which a pull on the trigger prior to each shot retracted the cocked striker by an additional

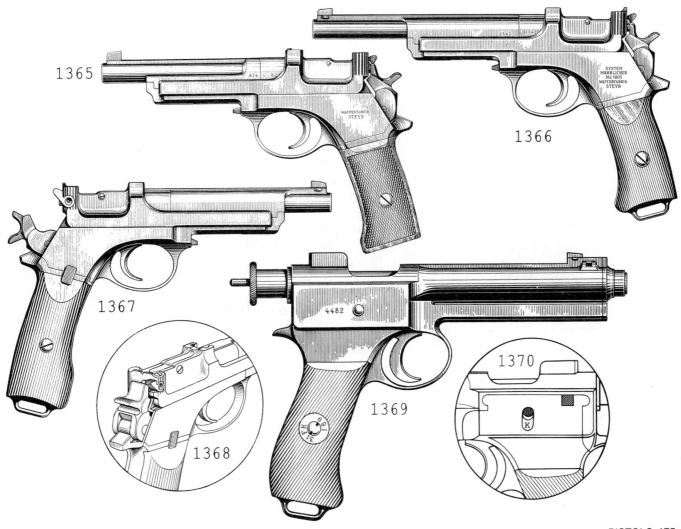

6mm before releasing it. This was regarded as a great safety feature for cavalrymen.

1371, 1372. Schönberger; Österreichische Waffenfabriks-Gesellschaft, Steyr. 8mm; five rounds, clip loaded. Probably dating from the mid 1890s, this pistol was based on patents granted to Josef Laumann in 1890–2. The action is basically blowback, but incorporates a friction-delay system to slow the opening stroke. Loading the chamber is accomplished by thumbing back the lever on the right side of the frame, which retracts the bolt, and then releasing it so that the breech can close on a fresh round. The cartridges are held in a metal clip, inspired by the contemporaneous Mannlicher service rifles. To unload the pistol, a button on the right side of the magazine can be pressed to eject the clip upward.

1373, 1374. Steyr, 1909; Österreichische Waffenfabriks-Gesellschaft, Steyr. 7·65mm Auto; 165mm overall, 90mm barrel, 650gm. Eight rounds. This pistol was designed by the Belgian Nicolas Pieper and is sometimes called 'Steyr-Pieper'. The cartridges can be loaded into the chamber either from the magazine—when the slide is retracted conventionally—or simply by tipping the barrel downward after the lever above the trigger on the left side of the frame has been pressed. The single-action firing mechanism has a concealed hammer, whilst the magazine catch lies on the rear side of the grip. The barrel must be tipped downward during unloading so that the chambered round can be removed manually; this round will not be ejected if the slide is drawn back owing to the lack of an ejector.

1375–1379. Steyr-Hahn, or Repeating Pistol Model 1911 (Repetierpistole M11); Österreichische Waffenfabriks-Gesellschaft, Steyr. 9mm; 215mm overall, 127mm barrel, 980 rounds. Eight rounds. This is by far the best known of the Austro-Hungarian military pistols, serving until the end of the Second World War. There were several differing variants of the basic design, beginning with the 1910 pattern (fig. 1375) and then progressing through the 1911 Austro-Hungarian army pistol (fig. 1376) to the 1912 export pattern (fig. 1377). The differences between these guns were comparatively

minor, e.g., the front sights of the two earlier models were integral with the slide whereas the 1912 type was a separate component retained in a dovetail slot. The notch cut in the slide to receive the tip of the breech catch was deeper on the 1912 model than its predecessors, and the shape of the slide-retaining pin differed. The Steyr factory also made an experimental M12/P16, which could fire automatically when the selector on the right side of the frame (fig. 1379) was raised. Some M12/P16 pistols had an elongated butt—oddly, still with ordinary grips—containing sixteen rounds. A wooden holster-stock could be attached when required.

The Steyr pistol relies on the barrel recoiling just far enough to rotate and unlock the breech (see figs. 1295–6). The fixed magazine contained a single row of cartridges, loaded through the top of the action from a special charger.

Guns sold to Romania had a large a crown above Md. 1912 on the front left side of the slide. Pistols issued to the Polish army from 1920 onward bore a large single-headed eagle; and those purchased by Chile were marked either with the national emblem or EJERCITO DE CHILE. After the assimilation of Austria into Germany in 1938, many M1911 pistols were altered for the 9mm Parabellum cartridge. There are marked P–08 to show that they chambered German 1908-type ammunition.

Belgium

The pistols designed by the American John Moses Browning achieved great popularity at the beginning of the twentieth century, though the designer had been forced to come to Europe to make progress. Browning was granted his original patents in 1897 and the first of these designs to be exploited—a simple blowback—appeared in 1899. This was soon replaced by the perfected 1900 pattern. This was a comparatively simple gun with a striker-type firing mechanism and a detachable box magazine in the grip, which allowed Browning to create a very compact design.

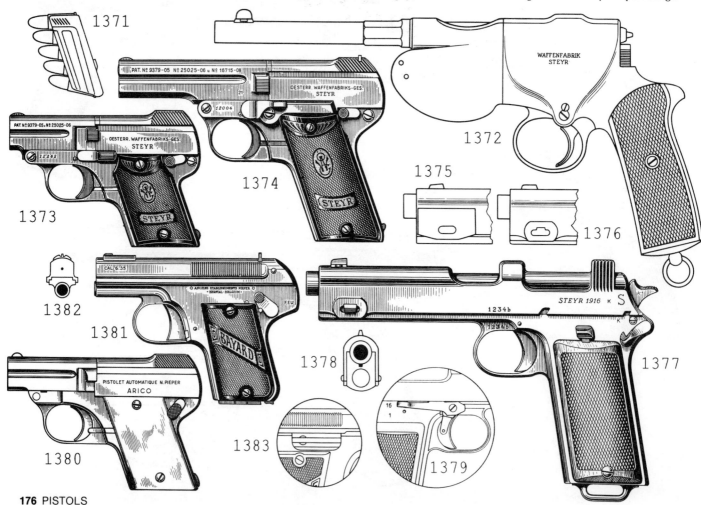

Though the 1900-type Browning was comparatively bulky, judged by modern standards, it was small and compact compared with its rivals. Few of the existing automatic pistols and revolvers could compete with it; at that time, there were no pocket firearms offering similar power and comparable convenience—as the FN-Browning was light and flat, had a comfortable grip containing a detachable box magazine, and balanced well. These features allied with excellent manufacturing standards to make the Brownings a runaway success. The millionth Model 1900 was made in 1912; more than a million examples of the Model 1906 were made in Belgium alone (there were innumerable Spanish imitations), whilst the Model 1903 was made for 37 years.

The name 'Browning' soon became synonymous with 'automatic pistol', even though most of the guns had nothing to do with John Browning himself. Genuine Browning-system guns were made in the USA by Colt's Patent Fire Arms Manufacturing Company of Hartford, Connecticut, in addition to those made in Belgium by Fabrique Nationale d'Armes de Guerre of Herstal-lèz-Liége. The Colt-made guns are included in the USA section. After the First World War, and the expiry of Browning's 1896-vintage patents, the basic operating principles were copied all over the world.

1380. Arico. 6·35mm Auto; 116mm overall, 53mm barrel, 350gm. Six rounds. These were simply standard Pieper-made guns (q.v.) marked with a distributor's brand-name.

1381–1385. Bayard; Anciens Établissements Pieper SA, Herstal-lèz-Liége, 1908. 6·35mm Auto, 7·65mm Auto or 9mm Short. Data for 6·35mm version: 124mm overall, 57mm barrel, 430gm. Data for 7·65mm and 9mm versions: 126mm overall, 57mm barrel, 470gm (7·65mm) or 460gm (9mm). Five 7·65mm or 9mm rounds, or six 6·35mm rounds. The smallest gun differs in construction from its larger cousins, which are difficult to distinguish externally. Designed and patented by Bernard Clarus, Bayard pistols exhibit several original features—e.g., the sprung base of the front sight can be pressed downward, and can then be removed to release the recoil spring and its guide rod

1386. Bayard Model 1923; Anciens Établissements Pieper SA, Herstal-lèz-Liége. 7·65mm Auto or 9mm Short; 148mm overall, 85mm barrel, 530gm (7·65mm) or 518gm (9mm). Six rounds. This is similar to the 1910-pattern FN-Browning.

1387. Bayard Model 1930; Anciens Établissements Pieper SA, Herstal-lèz-Liége. 6·35mm Auto; 113mm overall, 55mm barrel, 336gm. Six rounds. This is little more than a diminution of the Model 1923 described previously, incorporating minor improvements.

1388. Bergmann-Bayard; Anciens Établissements Pieper SA, Herstal-lèz-Liége. 9mm Bergmann-Bayard; 255mm overall, 100mm barrel, 1010gm. Six or ten rounds. The prototype of this pistol was the abortive German-made Bergmann-'Mars', work on which ceased in 1905. Owing to Spanish military interest, Bergmann licensed the project to Pieper in 1907 and production of the 'Model 1908' began in the Herstal factory. Guns were supplied to Spain, Denmark and possibly Greece by 1914. Work then ceased, though the Danes commenced production in Copenhagen in 1921. The magazine lies ahead of the trigger guard, reminiscent of the Mauser C/96. A wooden holster doubled as a shoulder stock.

1389, 1390. Browning Baby; Fabrique Nationale d'Armes de Guerre, Herstal-lèz-Liége. 6·35mm Auto; 103mm overall, 54mm barrel, 250gm. Six rounds. Though Browning died in 1926, his name still graced Fabrique Nationale guns. The Browning Baby was introduced in 1932; light and compact, it retained the basic construction and shooting qualities of the 1906-pattern pocket pistol.

1391–1393. Browning Double Action ('BDA'); FN Herstal SA, Herstal-lèz-Liége. 9mm Parabellum; 200mm overall (Standard Model), 118mm barrel, 920gm. Fifteen rounds. In recent years, realising that the popular GP-35 or High-Power pistol was approaching obsolescence, FN has made several improvements of the basic design. The BDA was introduced in 1983, differing from the previous pattern largely in substitution of a double-action firing mechanism for the single-action version. An ambidexterous safety catch appeared, the trigger guard was shaped to facilitate two-handed shooting, and the shape of the grips was refined. The BDA has been offered

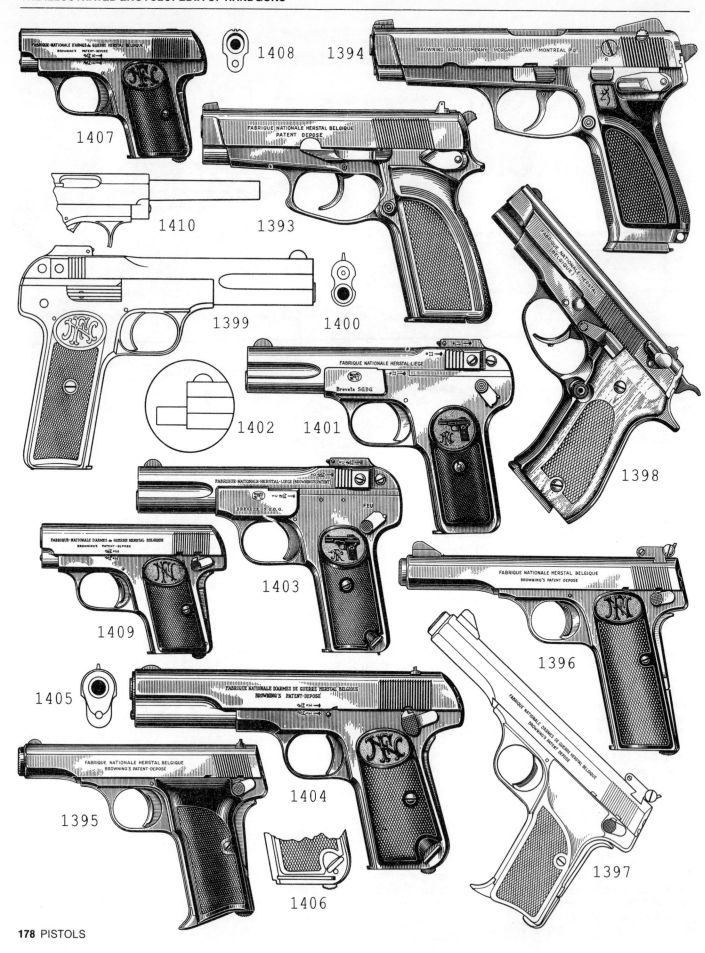

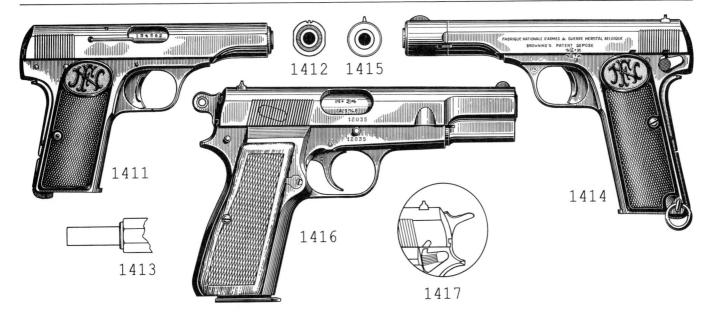

1412 1415

1411

1413

1416

1417

1414

in three basic versions: Standard (fig. 1391), Medium (BDA-9M, fig. 1392) and Compact (BDA-9C, fig. 1393). The BDA-9M has a standard-length grip, but is only 173mm overall and weighs 870gm. The BDA-9C is also 173mm long, but has a greatly abbreviated butt containing an eight-round magazine (the full-length fifteen round magazine will fit, but protrudes).

1394. Browning Double Mode ('BDM'); FN Herstal SA, Herstal-lèz-Liège. 9mm Parabellum; 200mm overall, 120mm barrel, 880gm. Fifteen rounds. This development of the BDA (q.v.) will be encountered with the marks of the Browning Arms Company of Morgan, Utah, or Montreal in Canada. It features ambidexterous controls and a selectable firing mechanism for conventional double action or double-action-only firing.

1395. Browning Model 115; FN Herstal SA, Herstal-lèz-Liège. 7·65mm Auto. This is similar to the Model 125 described below, but is shorter, lighter and has fixed sights.

1396. Browning Model 125; FN Herstal SA, Herstal-lèz-Liège. 7·65mm; nine rounds. This is a variant of the Model 130 (q.v.), differing in calibre and cartridge capacity. The length of the slide and the adjustable sights help to distinguish it from the Model 115.

1397. Browning Model 130; Fabrique Nationale d'Armes de Guerre, Herstal-lèz-Liège. 7·65mm Auto or 9mm Short; 178mm overall, 113mm barrel. Six 9mm or seven 7·65mm rounds. This was a modernised version of the Model 1910/22 (fig. 1414), though the slide was made in one piece, adjustable sights were customary, and the design of the grip was improved. It was intended principally for general-purpose use, including casual target shooting and personal defence.

1398. Browning Model 140-DA; FN Herstal SA, Herstal-lèz-Liège. 7·65mm Auto or 9mm Short; 170mm overall, 640gm. Twelve 9mm or thirteen 7·65mm rounds. This is a Belgian-made version of the Beretta Model 80-series double action ('DA') personal-defence pistols. A staggered-column magazine and an ambidexterous safety catch are amongst its features.

1399–1403. Browning Model 1900; Fabrique Nationale d'Armes de Guerre, Herstal-lèz-Liège. 7·65mm Auto; 164mm overall, 102mm barrel, 625gm. Seven rounds. Pistols of this type were originally offered in large (fig. 1403, 182mm overall, 765gm, eight rounds) or small sizes, though the former proved to be unpopular and were soon abandoned. The 1900-pattern FN-Brownings were distinguished by the barrel, which was firmly attached to the frame, and by the return spring above the barrel. The spring not only returned the slide to battery after firing, but powered the striker through a special intermediate lever. A safety catch lay on the left side of the frame, and a cocking indicator, part of the striker-actuating lever, broke the line of sight until the gun was ready to fire. Some guns were made with elongated barrels, often for sale in markets such as Austria-Hungary where barrel-length restrictions were enforced. These looked strange, as the barrel lay beneath the recoil spring and protruded from the bottom of the slide instead of the top (see fig. 1402).

1404–1406. Browning Model 1903; Fabrique Nationale d'Armes de Guerre, Herstal-lèz-Liège. 9mm Browning Long; 205mm overall, 128mm barrel, 980gm. Seven rounds. This was an improved form of the Model 1900, chambering a more powerful cartridge in an attempt to interest military authorities whilst retaining blowback operation. The lower part of the butt—particularly on the earliest guns—was often slotted to receive a holster-stock, when a special ten-round magazine could be substituted for the standard seven-round type. The return spring became concentric with the barrel, and the striker mechanism was replaced with an enclosed hammer. An automatic safety was let into the back strap of the grip.

Guns of this type were very popular. In addition to use in the Belgian armed forces, they were adopted in Sweden (where production was licensed to Husqvarna). They were purchased by gendarmerie in Russia—guns will be seen marked 'Moscow City Police' in Cyrillic on the right side of the slide—and in Turkey, when the top of the slide bears a Toughra (sultan's cypher) whilst the right side displays marks in Arabic.

The Model 1903 was sometimes listed as the 'Browning No. 2', 'No. 1' being retrospectively applied to the Model 1899. The advent of more FN-Brownings soon forced the abandonment of this system, whereupon a variation of it was applied to indicate calibre. Thus 'No. 1' came to signify 6·35mm, whilst 'No. 2' guns were all chambered for the 7·65mm Auto cartridge; 'No. 3', rarely encountered, was reserved for 9mm Short. Excepting in Spain, where the differentiation persisted into the 1920s, this system had been abandoned by the beginning of the First World War.

1407–1410. Browning Model 1906; Fabrique Nationale d'Armes de Guerre, Herstal-lèz-Liège. 6·35mm Auto; 114mm overall, 54mm barrel, 350gm. Six rounds. This was a diminution of the Model 1903, producing an ultra-compact, effectual and extremely popular pocket pistol. The reduction in size forced Browning to revert to a striker-type firing mechanism, though the concentric barrel-return spring was retained. The success of the Model 1906 was greatly helped by its cartridge which, though of small calibre, was loaded with smokeless propellant and developed more power than contemporaneous revolver patterns of similar size. Like its 7·65mm and 9mm cousins, the 6·35mm Browning cartridge was such a great success that its use soon became near-universal in pocket pistols. Fig. 1407 shows a gun with an automatic safety set into the back strap of the grip, whilst that shown in fig. 1409 has an additional manual safety catch on the left rear side of the frame. Fig. 1410 is a long-barrel variant destined for the Austro-Hungarian market, where short-barrel guns were banned.

1411–1415. Browning Models 1910 and 1910/22; Fabrique Nationale d'Armes de Guerre, Herstal-lèz-Liège. 7·65mm Auto or 9mm Short. Data for Model 1910: 153mm overall, 88mm barrel, 570–580gm, six 9mm or seven 7·65mm rounds. Data for Model 1910/22: 178mm overall, 113mm barrel, 685–705gm, eight 9mm or nine 7·65mm rounds. The first of the 7·65mm 'M1910' guns appeared at the end of 1909, intended to replace the Model

1900; the essentially similar 9mm version appeared two years later. Both types were phenomenally successful. A larger pattern—the M1910/22—was developed after the First World War to satisfy demands made by the army of the Kingdom of Serbs, Croats and Slovenes (subsequently Yugoslavia), to which a large number of FN-Mauser rifles had been sold. The butt was extended to accept a more capacious magazine and the barrel was lengthened. The addition of a distinctive extension shroud enabled the standard 1910-type slide to be used with only minor changes.

1416–1425. Browning Model 1935, GP-35 or High-Power; Fabrique Nationale d'Armes de Guerre and FN Herstal SA, Herstal-lèz-Liège. 9mm Parabellum; 197mm overall, 118mm barrel, 890gm. Thirteen rounds.

Patented in the early 1920s, perfected in 1928 but not placed in production until shortly before the Second World War began, this legendary pistol was seen as an improvement on the earlier Browning barrel-link system exemplified by the 1911-type Colt-Browning. The GP-35 remained recoil operated, but the breech was tipped by a cam finger instead of a link and a large-capacity staggered-column magazine was developed.

The gun has been offered with an adjustable back sight, graduated to 500 metres, or a simpler fixed pattern. The butts of adjustable-sight guns usually have a lug for a shoulder stock. A manual safety lever lies on the rear left side of the frame, though most guns have an additional internal safety to prevent the hammer being released if the magazine has been removed.

Browning High-Power pistols have been used by military and police forces throughout the world, having been the principal service weapons in more than fifty countries in addition to Belgium. The most recent guns show detail improvements—e.g., the hammer may have an elongated spur (fig. 1420) instead of a round head—but the operating principles have remained unchanged.

The High-Power Mark 2 (fig. 1421), popular with police forces, has an ambidexterous safety catch. The other drawings show High-Power pistols made in Argentina (fig. 1422), assembled in Portugal from Herstal-made parts (fig. 1423), and produced in the USA (figs. 1424, 1425). The HP Detective pictured in fig. 1425 has a 90mm barrel and weighs 865gm.

1426–1429. Clément; Charles Ph. Clément, Liége. 7·65mm Auto. Six rounds. Introduced in 1903 (fig. 1426), this gun features a recoil spring above the barrel in a stationary receiver, the front part of which fits over the barrel whilst the rear is held in the frame by a transverse bolt. The breech block reciprocates between the frame and the receiver. Guns of this type were also made in 5mm Clément (Charola y Anitua) and 6·35mm Auto— 135mm overall, 69mm barrel, 400gm, seven rounds. Figs. 1427 and 1429 show the perfected 'production' version of c.1905.

1430, 1431. Clément, 1907 pattern; Charles Ph. Clément, Liége. 7·65mm Auto; 150mm overall, 71mm barrel, 600gm. Six rounds. This shares the basic construction of the 1903 pattern described previously, but has been refined. A 6·35mm Auto version was also made; it was 118mm overall, had a 46mm barrel, and weighed 384gm.

1432. Clément, 1908 pattern; Charles Ph. Clément, Liége. 6·35mm Auto; 118mm overall, 50mm barrel. Six rounds. A minor variation of the M1907.

1433. Clément, 1909 pattern; Charles Ph. Clément, Liége. 7·65mm Auto; 150mm overall, 75mm barrel, 585gm. Seven rounds. The breech and slide of this gun were made in a single part.

1434–1436. Clément, 1909 pattern; Charles Ph. Clément, Liége. 6·35mm Auto; 120mm overall, 51mm barrel, 365gm. Six rounds. Some guns were made with elongated 118mm barrels, measuring 187mm overall.

1437, 1438. Clément, 1912 pattern (old); Charles Ph. Clément, Liége. 6·35mm Auto; 118mm overall, 57mm barrel, 385gm. Six rounds. A copy of the FN-Browning.

1439. Clément, 1912 pattern (new); Charles Ph. Clément, Liége. 6·35mm Auto; 115mm overall, 61mm barrel, 330gm. Six rounds. A modified version of the preceding gun, still based on the FN-Browning.

1440. Clément; Charles Ph. Clément, Liége. 7·65mm Auto; six rounds. Like figs. 1438 and 1439, this particular Clement pistol was copied from the FN-Browning.

1441, 1442. Delu; Fabrique d'Armes F. Delu & Companie, Liége. 6·35mm Auto; 108mm overall, 54mm barrel, 331gm. Six rounds. A characteristic feature of this pistol is its thinness. The ejection port lies in the top surface of the slide. Some guns lack the otherwise customary automatic safety.

1443, 1444. Dictator; Fabrique d'Armes Réunies SA, Liége, c.1910–14. 6·35mm Auto; 120mm overall, 58mm barrel, 403gm. Six rounds. The recoil spring is concentric with the barrel which, together with the breech, lies inside the stationary receiver. Also known as the 'Centaure'.

1445, 1446. Francotte; Auguste Francotte & Companie, Liége, c.1912–14. 6·35mm Auto; 109mm overall, 57mm barrel, 355gm. Six rounds. The rear of the frame has a shroud in which the slide reciprocates.

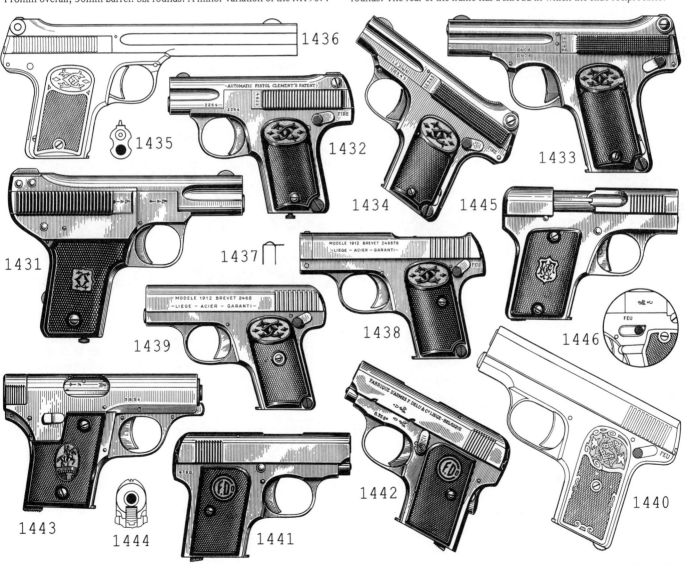

1447, 1448. Gavage; Fabrique d'Armes de Guerre de Haute Précision Armand Gavage, Liége. 7·65mm Auto. Apparently introduced about 1930.

1449. Hamal. This large recoil-operated pistol, patented by Victor Hamal about 1899 and reminiscent of the Mauser C/96, never progressed past the prototype stage. A few guns are said to have been made in England by Webley, whilst others may have been made in Liége.

1450. 'H. & D.'; Société d'Armes HDH, Henrion & Dassy, Liége, c.1912–14. 6·35mm Auto; six rounds.

1451. Herman; maker unknown. 6·35mm Auto. This gun is sometimes identified as Spanish.

1452–1454. Jieffeco; Janssen Fils & Co., Liége. 6·35mm Auto or 7·65mm Auto; (data for 6·35mm version) 116mm overall, 55mm barrel, 360gm. Six rounds. Designed by Henri Rosier c.1907 and made for Janssen by Robar & Companie (Manufacture Liégeoise d'Armes à Feu). These guns resemble the 1900-pattern FN-Browning externally, but differ in internal construction.

1455. Legia; Anciens Établissements Pieper SA. This is virtually the same as the gun drawn in fig. 1485. It was apparently made in a Pieper factory in Paris, though often encountered with Belgian proof marks.

1456. Le Martiny. 6·35mm Auto.

1457, 1458. Le Monobloc; Jules Jacquemart, Liége, 1911–14. 6·35mm Auto; 116mm overall, 53mm barrel, 390gm. Six rounds. Made in two basic patterns—old (fig. 1457) and new (fig. 1458)—this is distinguished by the one-piece frame and barrel unit.

1459, 1460. Lepage; Manufacture d'Armes Lepage SA, Liége, 1925–32. 7·65mm Auto; 147mm or 163mm overall, 81mm or 97mm barrel, 600gm (81mm barrel). Seven rounds. This pocket pistol is distinguished by its exposed hammer. In addition to the manual safety lever, it has an internal safety preventing a shot being fired if the magazine has been removed.

1461. Lepage; Manufacture d'Armes Lepage SA, Liége, c.1925–32. 6·35mm Auto; 110mm overall. Six rounds. The construction of this pocket pistol resembles that of the 1906-type FN-Browning pistol.

1462. Le Rapide; Manufacture Générale d'Armes & Munitions Jules Bertrand, Liége, c.1910. 6·35mm Auto. These frames of these guns are sometimes marked CONTINENTAL.

1463. Manufacture d'Armes à Feu, Liége. 7·65mm Auto; 114mm overall, 82mm barrel, 570gm. Seven rounds. Whether this is genuinely Belgian-made, or made in Spain for distribution in Belgium may be debated. The positioning of the safety catch is more typical of the Spanish 'Eibar' imitations of the 1906-type FN-Browning than the Belgian-made originals.

1464, 1465. Melior, old model; Manufacture Liégeoise d'Armes à Feu SA, Robar & Companie, Liége. This is virtually the same as the Jieffeco pistol described above, being made to the same Rosier patents. The Melior version—probably later—has additional retraction-grips on the front surface of the slide.

1466–1469. Melior, new model; Manufacture Liégeoise d'Armes à Feu SA, Robar & Companie, Liége. 7·65mm Auto or 9mm Short; 150–154mm overall, 90mm barrel, 595–635gm. Six 9mm or seven 7·65mm rounds. Introduced shortly after the end of the First World War, these resembled the 1910-pattern FN-Browning externally. However, their barrels are generally securely fixed into the frame (except for a few later modifications), whilst the breech block—which can be detached when the guns are stripped—is connected with the slide by an external bar retained by a sprung catch. Meliors were offered in several variants, including guns with automatic safeties.

1470. Melior, vest-pocket model; Manufacture Liégeoise d'Armes à Feu SA, Robar & Companie, Liége. 6·35mm Auto; 103mm overall, 48mm barrel, 235gm. Six rounds.

1471. Mercury; made for Tradewinds, Inc., Tacoma, Washington, by Manufacture Liégeoise d'Armes à Feu SA, Liége. 6·35mm Auto or ·22 LR rimfire; 114mm overall, 57mm barrel, 370gm. Six rounds. This is simply a modernised post-war version of the Melior pistol shown in fig. 1467.

1472. Mercury; made for Tradewinds, Inc., Tacoma, Washington, by Manufacture Liégeoise d'Armes à Feu SA, Liége. ·22 LR rimfire; 145mm overall, 89mm barrel, 590gm. Eight rounds. This is a refinement of the Melior pistol shown in fig. 1468. It was also made in 6·35mm Auto, and possibly in 7·65mm Auto.

1473, 1474. 'M.L.'; Manufacture Liégeoise d'Armes à Feu SA, Robar & Companie, Liége. 6·35mm Auto or 7·65mm Auto. These are basically modified versions of the 1906-type Browning. The position of the safety catch and the style of the slide-retracting grooves suggest that the guns may have been made in Spain shortly after the end of the First World War for sale in Belgium. Additionally, the 'patent number' on the slide is more typically

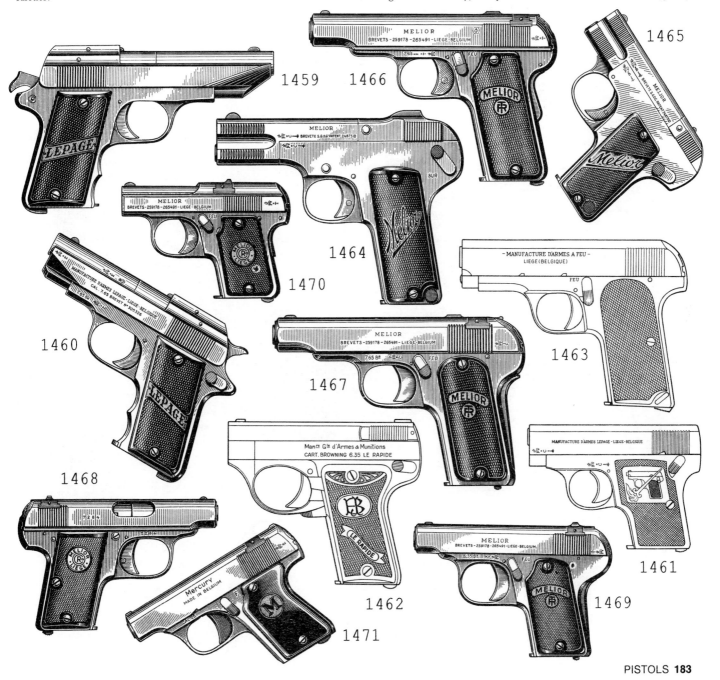

Spanish than Belgian. The elliptical depression on top surface of the slide contains a special indicator, which no longer aligns with bars on the slide when the chamber is loaded.

1475. Oyez Arms Company. A Pieper-type pocket pistol.

1476, 1477. Pieper Model C, Demontant type, 1907; Fabrique d'Armes Nicolas Pieper, Liége (probably made by Anciens Établissements Pieper, Herstal). 6·35mm Auto; 51mm barrel, 312gm. Six rounds. The earliest guns lacked the barrel-locking latch on the left side of the frame. There were several differing Piepers, differing only in chambering, magazine capacity and external appearance.

1478, 1479. Pieper Model N, Basculant or tipping-barrel type, 1908; Fabrique d'Armes Nicolas Pieper, Liége (probably made by Pieper of Herstal). 7·65mm Auto; 154mm overall, 81mm barrel, 600gm. Seven rounds. Guns of this pattern were licensed to Österreichische Waffenfabriks-Gesellschaft of Steyr in 1909 (see fig. 1373), but originated in Belgium. The 6·35mm Model P (125mm overall, 310gm) was similar.

1480. Pieper Model B ('Grande modèle'); Fabrique d'Armes Nicolas Pieper, Liége (probably made by Anciens Établissements Pieper, Herstal). 7·65mm Auto; 140mm overall, 64mm barrel.

1481. Pieper Model O, Basculant type, 1908; Fabrique d'Armes Nicolas Pieper, Liége (probably made by Anciens Établissements Pieper, Herstal). 7·65mm Auto; 145mm overall. 73mm barrel, 570gm. Six rounds.

1482. Pieper, 1909 type; Fabrique d'Armes Nicolas Pieper, Liége (probably made by Anciens Établissements Pieper, Herstal). 7·65mm Auto; 127mm overall, 53mm barrel.

1483. Pieper, 1909 type; Fabrique d'Armes Nicolas Pieper, Liége (probably made by Anciens Établissements Pieper, Herstal). 7·65mm Auto; 152mm overall, 76mm barrel.

1484. Pieper Model D, 1909 type; Fabrique d'Armes Nicolas Pieper, Liége (probably made by Anciens Établissements Pieper, Herstal). 6·35mm Auto;

116mm overall, 53mm barrel, 350gm. Six rounds. The post-war 'Model 1920' (Basculant type) was similar, but exhibited refinements such as diced retraction grips.

1485. Pieper, pocket model; Fabrique d'Armes Nicolas Pieper, Liége (probably made by Anciens Établissements Pieper, Herstal). 6·35mm Auto. Six rounds. Based on the French-made Légia pattern (see fig. 1455), this improvement on previous Piepers closely resembled the 1906-model FN-Browning—from which it differs principally in the way in which the barrel is connected with the frame. The Pieper barrel is screwed into a ring-shaped slot in the frame, whereas the Browning uses a sliding block. Placing the magazine catch in the rear of the butt allows an elongated ten-round magazine to be used.

1486. Pieper, pocket model; Fabrique d'Armes Nicolas Pieper, Liége (probably made by Anciens Établissements Pieper, Herstal). 6·35mm Auto.

1487. Teuf-Teuf; maker unknown. 6·35mm Auto. The original pattern is said to have been made in Belgium, but was subsequently copied in Spain by Arizmendi & Goenaga. The 'patent number' on the slide is more typically Spanish than Belgian.

1488. Vici; maker unknown. 6·35mm Auto.

1489. Warnant; L. & J. Warnant Frères, Hognée. 7·65mm Auto.

1490, 1491. Warnant; L. & J. Warnant Frères, Hognée, 1908–14. 6·35mm Auto; 110mm overall, 44mm barrel. Six rounds. The recoil spring lies above the barrel, the breech block being inside the stationary squared housing attached to the frame. Oddly, the magazine catch lies on the magazine body instead of the gun.

1492, 1493. Wilson; maker unknown. 6·35mm Auto.

1494. WS or 'Wegria-Charlier'; apparently made by Fabrique d'Armes Charlier & Companie, Liége. 6·35mm Auto. Patented by an inventor named Wegria in 1908, this pistol lacked a conventional trigger. It was fired by squeezing the pivoting lever set into the back strap of the butt.

Brazil The service handgun of the armed forces is a copy of the Colt M1911A1, chambered for the 9mm Parabellum round and known as the Imbel M973. The left side of the slide is marked FABRICA DE ITAJUBA—BRASIL. Shortened ·45-calibre Colts will also be encountered. These usually display the state emblem and EXERCITO BRASILIERO ('Brazilian army') on the left side of the slide. The PASAM machine-pistol is based on the 7·63mm German Mauser Schnellfeuerpistole M712, with a fire-selector switch to transform it into an embrionic submachine-gun. It is distinguished by a bulky fore-end with a sling swivel for a rifle-type strap, an auxiliary fore-grip, and a rod-pattern shoulder stock.

1495. Taurus PT-92; Forjas Taurus SA, Porto Alegre. 9mm Parabellum; 217mm overall, 125mm barrel, 960gm. Fifteen rounds. This military pistol is essentially similar to the Italian Beretta M92 (q.v.), made under licence in a factory erected with Italian aid. The PT-99 is a version of the PT-92 with an adjustable back sight, bright-finish nickel plating, and some minor changes to the parts. Its frame may be made of a light alloy. The PT-58 or 'Compact' model is chambered for the 9mm Short cartridge instead of 9mm Parabellum.

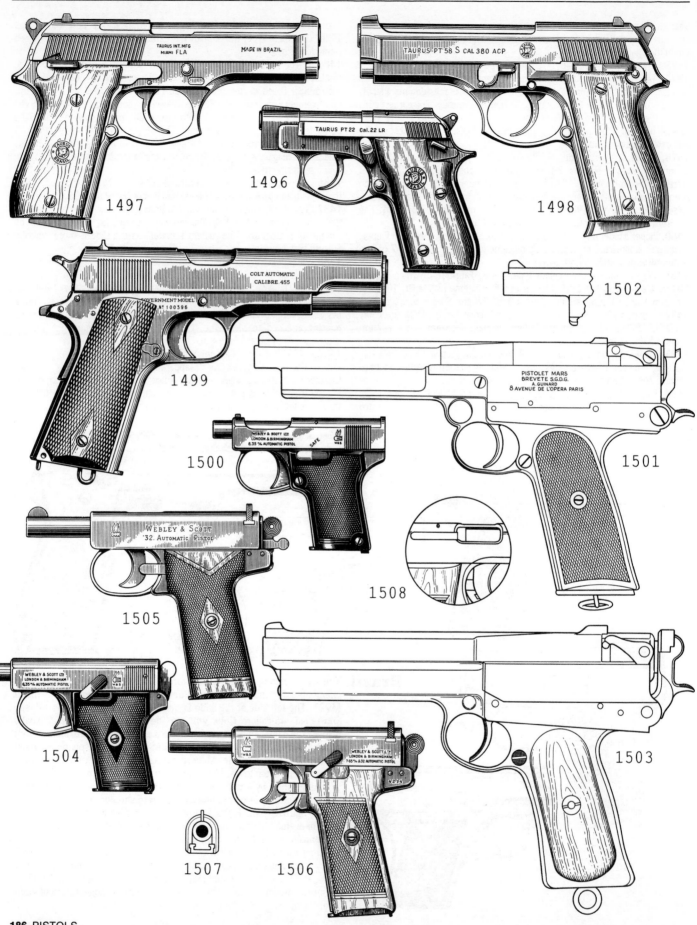

1513

1509

1510

1512

1511

1496. Taurus PT-22; Forjas Taurus SA, Porto Alegre. ·22 LR rimfire; 70mm barrel, 510gm. Ten rounds. Introduced in 1983, this was also derived from an Italian prototype. The PT-25 is similar, but is chambered for the 6·35mm Auto cartridge and has a smaller magazine.

1497. Taurus PT-92C (Compact); Forjas Taurus SA, Porto Alegre. 9mm Parabellum; 190mm overall, 108mm barrel, 880gm.

1498. Taurus PT-58S; Forjas Taurus SA, Porto Alegre. This is essentially similar to the PT-92C, but chambers 9mm Short ammunition.

Britain

The Browning GP-35 or High-Power first attained popularity with the British Army during the Second World War, being 'sealed'—officially approved for service—in 1944. The original guns were made by John Inglis of Toronto (fig. 1529); though they were retained after 1945, the Belgian-made GP-35 was adopted in 1957 as the 'Pistol 9mm, L9A1'. Depending on details, pre-1957 British guns were known as No. 1 Mk 1, No. 1 Mk 1*, No. 2 Mk 1 or No. 2 Mk 1*. The No. 1 pistols have adjustable back sights and stock lugs on the heel of the butt; No. 2 examples have fixed sights and lack the stock-attachment system. The addition of an asterisk (*) to the designation indicates modified extractors and raised back sights.

Browning-type pocket pistols will occasionally be encountered with Eley marks, but generally prove to have been made in Spain. The name 'Eley' was used in much the same way as 'Smith & Wesson', to make purchasers believe that the guns were of better than normal quality. 'Lepco'-brand pistols, distributed by Le Personne of London, were made in France (figs. 1673, 1674).

1499. Colt-Browning Model 1911; Colt's Patent Fire Arms Manufacturing Company, Hartford, Connecticut. ·455 W&S rimless; 8·5in overall, 5·05in barrel, 39oz. Seven rounds. Many US-made Colt pistols were acquired by the British forces during the First World War. They were particularly popular in the Royal Flying Corps and its successor, the Royal Air Force.

1500. Hammerless Pocket Model; Webley & Scott Ltd, Birmingham, 1910–39. 6·35mm Auto; 4·25in overall, 2·15in barrel, 11oz. Six rounds.

1501–1503. Mars; Webley & Scott Revolver & Arms Co. Ltd, Birmingham. 8·5mm, ·36 or ·45; 10·65in overall, 8·45in barrel, 52oz. Eight rounds. (Data for an 8·5mm example, fig. 1503.) These guns were patented in 1900 by Hugh Gabbett Fairfax, with whom Webley had negotiated a licence in 1899. Operating on long-recoil principles, Mars pistols had a distinctive rotating-bolt locking system and an elevator in the cartridge-feed system. When the moving parts ran backward, they took the next cartridge to be loaded; it was subsequently chambered as the barrel ran forward to battery.

Mars pistol cartridges—cylindrical or necked—were very powerful. For example, the muzzle velocity of the 8·5mm bullet was 1750 ft/sec, giving an energy of 940 ft.lb. However, owing to complexity and poor handling qualities, the guns never became popular. Gabbett Fairfax was bankrupted in 1902 and his successors, the Mars Automatic Pistol Syndicate, were liquidated in 1907.

1504. Pocket Model; Webley & Scott Ltd, Birmingham, c.1907–39. 6·35mm Auto; 4·35in overall, 2·15in barrel, 11oz. Six rounds.

1505–1509. Police Model; Webley & Scott Ltd, Birmingham, 1906–39. 7·65mm Auto or 9mm Short; 6·15in overall, 3·45in barrel, 20oz. Eight rounds. This simple blowback pistol was adopted by the Metropolitan Police, London, in 1911.

1510, 1511. South African Model; Webley & Scott Ltd, Birmingham, 1920–30. 9mm Browning Long; 8·1in overall, 5·5in barrel, 34oz. Eight rounds. Little more than the 1909-pattern ·38 pistol with an additional safety catch, this was adopted for colonial police service.

1512. Spitfire Mk 2; John Slough Ltd ('JSL'), Hereford. 9mm Parabellum or ·40 S&W. A modification of the Czech ČZ 75 (fig. 1586).

1513, 1514. Victory MC-5; Victory Arms Company, Brixworth. 9mm Parabellum, ·38 Super, ·41 AE or ·45 ACP; 4·4in, 5·9in or 7·5in barrel. Ten ·45 or seventeen 9mm Parabellum cartridges. Designed by David Smith and then made in small numbers in Britain in 1987–8, this exchangeable-barrel design has now been licensed to Magnum Research, Inc., of Minneapolis in the USA (fig. 1514).

1515. Webley-Whiting, 1904 pattern; Webley & Scott Revolver & Arms Co. Ltd, Birmingham. ·455 W&S rimless. This was the first pistol to embody the locking system designed by William Whiting, relying on the barrel-block sliding diagonally back and downward to release the slide. The 'V'-shaped recoil spring, concealed in the frame by the right grip-plate, transmits its force to the slide through an intermediate lever.

1516–1518. Webley-Whiting, Mk I and Mk I No. 2; Webley & Scott Ltd, Birmingham. ·455 W&S rimless; 8·5in overall, 5·0in barrel, 39oz. Seven rounds. The Mk I, introduced in 1912, was adopted by the Royal Navy in 1913. The Mk I No. 2 (fig. 1518) was adopted by the Royal Flying Corps in 1915, being distinguished by the design of its safety catch and back sight; it also had a slot on the back-strap to receive a shoulder stock.

1519. Webley-Whiting, 1909 pattern; Webley & Scott Ltd, Birmingham. 9mm Browning Long; 8·0in overall, 3·9in barrel, 32oz. Eight rounds. This embodied Whiting's breech-locking system, which relied on the barrel-block being cammed forward and upward as the slide ran back into battery.

1520. Webley-Whiting, high-velocity patterns, 1910 and 1913; Webley & Scott Ltd, Birmingham. 9mm Short; 8in overall, 5in barrel, 34oz. Eight rounds. Sharing the standard Webley breech-locking system, these have a distinctive enclosed hammer. The safety features provide the easiest means of distinguishing between them.

Bulgaria

1521. B-1300; State factory. 9mm. This is simply a Soviet Makarov pistol (q.v.) with a shortened grip.

Cambodia

1522. Asiatic-style pistol; maker unknown. 9mm; 195mm overall, 120mm barrel. Eight rounds. This is a distinctive hybrid of several Western designs.

1523. Colt-Browning copy; maker unknown. 9mm Parabellum; about 215mm overall, 125mm barrel. Eight rounds.

1524. FN-Browning High Power copy; maker unknown. 9mm Parabellum; 197mm overall, 118mm barrel, 950gm. Thirteen rounds.

Canada

1525. Colt-Browning Model 1911; North American Arms Co. Ltd, Quebec. ·45 ACP; 8·6in overall, 5·05in barrel, 39oz. Seven rounds. Small numbers of these pistols were made in the former Ross factory in 1918, but the production contract was cancelled before large-scale deliveries could begin.

1526–1528. P-12, P-13 and P-14; Para-Ordnance Company. ·45 ACP.

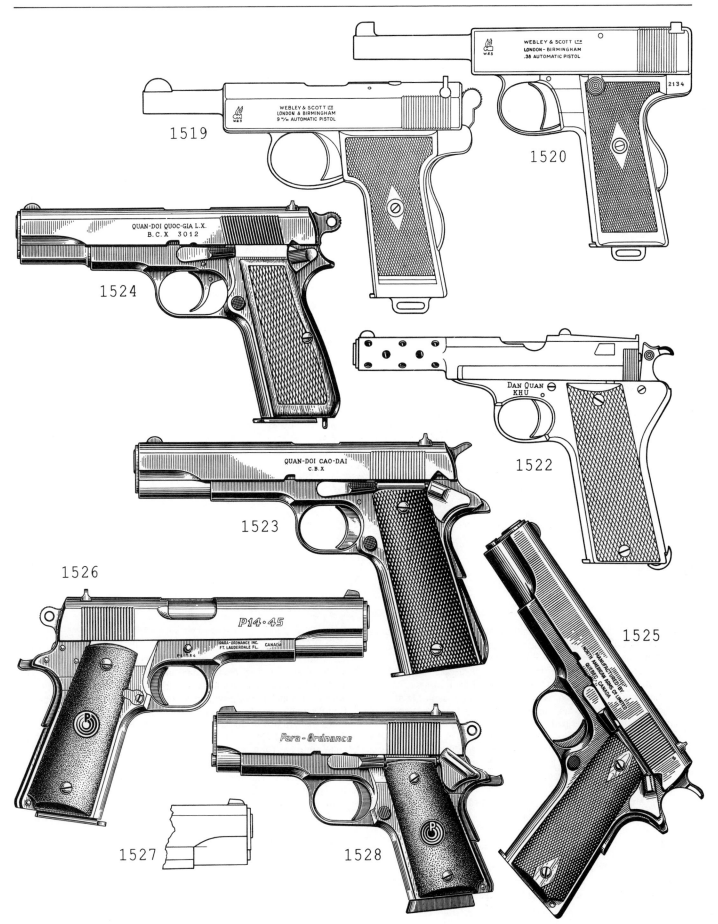

1529

1533

1530

1531

1532

1536

1537

1534

1535

Originally introduced in 1988, these are essentially Canadian derivatives of the M1911A1 Colt-Browning with staggered-column magazines. Capacity is revealed by the designation—the P-12 (3·5in barrel), for example, offers twelve shots: one in the chamber and eleven in the magazine. The P-13 has a 4·5in barrel and a twelve-round magazine, whilst the P-14 has a 5in barrel and a thirteen-round magazine. The P-1610 is externally similar to the P-14, but chambers 10mm Auto ammunition and offers sixteen shots (one in the chamber and fifteen rounds in the magazine).

1529–1532. Pistol No. 2; John Inglis & Company, Toronto. 9mm Parabellum; 197mm overall, 118mm barel. Thirteen rounds. These FN-style High-Power pistols were made in 1942–5, for China and Britain in addition to Canadian use. They differed from their Belgian prototypes in minor details; a lanyard ring is attached to the lower part of the grip, and the sights may vary. An experimental version with a lightened slide (figs. 1531, 1532) never progressed past the prototype stage.

Chile

1533. FAMAE; Fabrica de Material del Ejercito, Santiago. 6·35mm Auto; 114mm overall, 53mm barel, 350gm. Six rounds. This blowback pistol was based on the Browning of 1906. Later examples are marked 'Fabrica de Material de Guerra'.

China

The Chinese became enthusiastic purchasers of automatic pistols almost as soon as the first models had been perfected in Europe. The 1896-pattern Mauser was a particular favourite for paramilitary use, whilst the smaller FN-Brownings were popular commercially. The ·45 Colt-Brownings became popular in the 1920s.

China has also made large numbers of pistols, mostly in the period spanning the 1911 revolution to eventual seizure of power by the communists in 1949. Many of the guns are crude imitations of European systems, many being marked to give the impression that they were foreign imports. However, some bear the Mauser banner with the Browning name, or a jumbled series of letters. Many guns even have the same serial number!

Among the most important of the Chinese military weapons were C/96 copies, often made in the state arsenals, and FN-Browning High Powers made by Fabrique Nationale and Inglis.

1534–1545. Asiatic pistols; makers unknown. These are typical of the many hybrid designs encountered in the Far East, virtually no two of which are identical. The most popular chamberings are 7·63mm Mauser, 7·65mm Auto, 9mm Parabellum or ·45 ACP.

1546. Colt-Browning copy; maker unknown, possibly in Taiwan. Inspired

1538

1539

1540

1541

1542

1543

1544

1545

1546

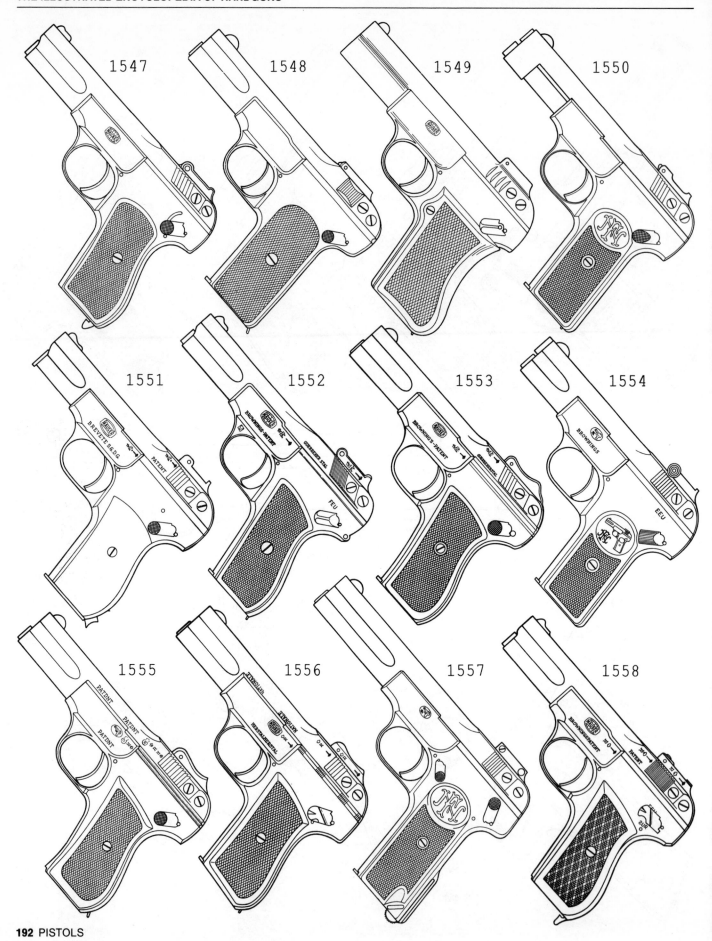

by the fully automatic Star pistols supplied to China from Spain in the 1930s, this gun is distinguished by its extended barrel and a fire-selector switch on the left side of the frame behind the grip.

1547–1560. FN-Browning copies; makers unknown. Usually chambered for the 7·65mm Auto cartridge—though alternatives exist—these are loosely based on the 1900-pattern blowback. They are inevitably distinguished by poor quality and exceedingly strange markings.

1561. FN-Browning GP-35; Fabrique Nationale d'Armes de Guerre, Herstal-lèz-Liége, and John Inglis Company, Toronto. 9mm Parabellum; 197mm overall, 118mm barrel, 890gm. Thirteen rounds. The original guns were supplied to the Chinese army by Fabrique Nationale, prior to 1940, and then by Inglis (1942–5). Modern FN-Brownings have been supplied to the Taiwanese.

1562–1564. Mauser copies; Shansei arsenal, 1929–32, and North China Industries Corporation, c.1970–80. ·45 ACP. The original indigenous C/96 variant (fig. 1562) was made in Shansei between the wars and offers good quality. However, much cruder copies are also known (e.g., fig. 1564). The recent Norinco Type 80 is based on the Mauser M712, can fire fully automatically when required, has a detachable twenty- or forty-round magazine, and will accept a metal stock.

1565. Model 213A; apparently made by State factory no. 66 for North China Industries Corporation ('Norinco'). 9mm Parabellum; 190mm overall, 112mm barrel, 910gm. Fourteen rounds. This is simply a variant of the Tokarev with a double-column magazine.

1566. North China Type 19; North China Engineering Company, c.1944–5. 8mm Nambu. This is basically a variant of the Japanese 14th Year

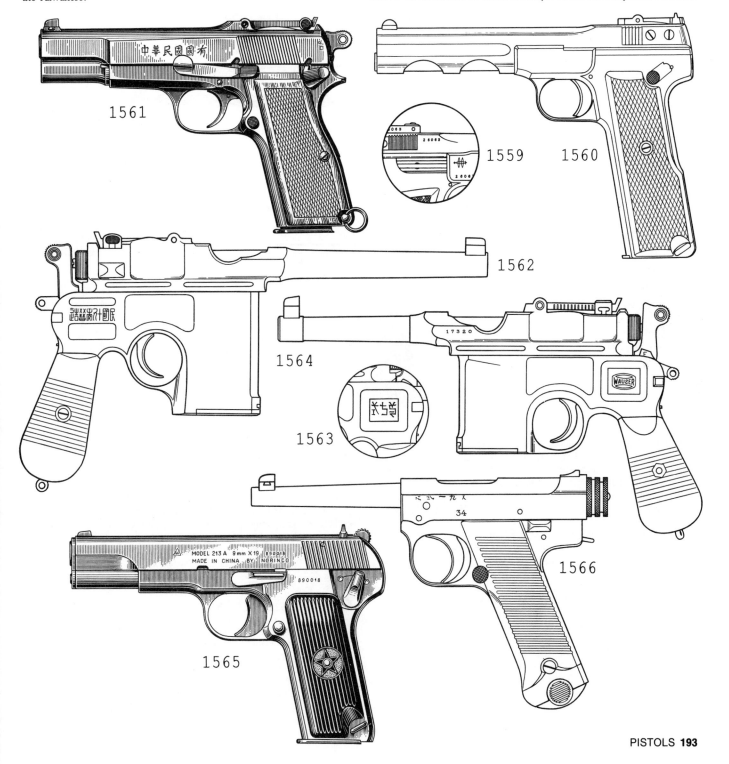

Type pistol (fig. 2032), produced on the Chinese mainland in the closing stages of the Second World War. The designation refers to the nineteenth year of the Japanese Showa era: 1944. Limited production of a revised pattern continued under Chinese control in 1945–6.

1567, 1568. Type 31, Year 31 or 31st Year Type. 7·65mm Auto. This simple blowback weapon was apparently adopted in 1942, the 31st year of the Chinese republic.

1569. Type 51; State factory no. 44. 7·62mm Tokarev; 185mm overall, 108mm barrel, 795gm. Eight rounds. This is a straightforward copy of the Soviet Tokarev pistol. It was replaced in Chinese service by the Type 59, a copy of the Makarov.

1570. Type 54-1; made by State factory no. 66 for the North China Industries Corporation ('Norinco'). 7·62mm Tokarev. The Model 213 is similar, but chambers the 9mm Parabellum cartridge.

1571. Type 67; State factory no. 66. 7·65mm Auto; 222mm overall, 89mm barrel. Nine rounds. The silencer of this pistol is an integral part of the slide, instead of a separate attachment. The gun can be fired as an ordinary semi-automatic, allowing the slide to reciprocate normally, but can also fire single shots. This is achieved by turning the breech around its longitudinal axis to lock the slide. When the shot is fired, therefore, the breech can only be opened manually. This not only eliminates the noise of the slide but also prevents an empty cartridge case being ejected at the scene

of an assassination. The silencer is comparatively clumsy, but the gun is effectual enough.

The earlier Type 64 was essentially similar, excepting that its silencer consisted of two superimposed cylinders fused together.

1572. Type 77B; made for North China Industries Corporation ('Norinco'). 9mm Parabellum; 127mm barrel, 965gm. Eight rounds. Note the one-hand cocking system, reminiscent of the Chylewski (fig. 2508) and the Bergmann/Lignose Einhand (fig. 1778). The original Type 77 was a blowback chambered for the 7·65mm Auto cartridge. It was 148mm overall, weighed 500g, and had a seven-round magazine.

Czechoslovakia

The first automatic pistols were made almost as soon as the country was created in the aftermath of the First World War. This was partly due to the efforts of Alois Tomiška and Josef Nickl, who had experienced success prior to 1918 with the Little Tom and the Nickl-Pistole respectively. Nickl, indeed, had worked for Waffenfabrik Mauser for some years. The first locked-breech pistol adopted by the Czechoslovak army—the 'Pistole N'—was a Nickl design. It was succeeded by a simplified version, known as vz. 24, whilst a blowback derivative (vz.

27) was adopted by the state police force. Large quantities of 6·35mm pocket pistols were also made prior to the Second World War.

During the period of German occupation (1938–45), manufacture of vz. 27, vz. 38, Duo and other guns continued. These are usually distinguished by three-letter manufacturer's codes (e.g., 'fnh' or 'aek').

Design work resumed in earnest after the end of the Second World War, resulting in a series of experimental models—e.g., ČZ-491, ČZ-531, ZK-524—based on either the Soviet Tokarev or the German Walther P.38. Eventually, the army adopted the 7·62mm ČZ-513, as the vz. 52, and the police accepted the 7·65mm vz. 50.

1573. Automaticka Pistole; Česká Zbrojovka, Prague. ·22 Short rimfire.

1574, 1575. ČSZ; Československe Statni Zbrojovka A.S., Brno (later Československá Zbrojovka). 6·35mm Auto; 113mm overall, 55mm barrel, 330gm. Six rounds. This small blowback was made in two differing patterns.

1576, 1577. ČZ vz. 24; Česká Zbrojovka A.S., Prague. 9mm Short; 155mm overall, 90mm barrel, 670gm. Eight rounds. The guns were made in a factory in Strakonice, despite their 'Prague' slide marks. Some will be found with slots in the back-strap of the grips to accept a shoulder stock. These were used by Polish frontier guards.

1578, 1579. ČZ vz. 27; Česká Zbrojovka A.S., Prague. 7·65mm Auto; 155mm overall, 99mm barrel, 670gm. Nine rounds. One of the guns produced under German supervision is shown in fig 1579. Note the manufacturer's code-group 'fnh' on the slide. Guns made after the

nationalisation of the Czechoslovakian firearms industry in 1950 were marked NARODNI PODNIK ('state enterprise').

1580. ČZ vz. 36; Česká Zbrojovka A.S., Prague. 6·35mm Auto; 127mm overall, 63mm barrel, 390gm. Eight rounds. A typical blowback pocket pistol, with a double-action-only trigger system.

1581. ČZ vz. 38; Česká Zbrojovka A.S., Prague. 9mm Short; 195mm overall, 120mm barrel, 885gm. Nine rounds. Designed by František Myška and made in the Strakonice factory, this service pistol incorporated a double-action-only trigger mechanism adapted from the vz. 36 (above). It was neither especially popular nor entirely successful.

1582. ČZ vz. 45; Česká Zbrojovka A.S., Prague. 6·35mm Auto; 127mm overall, 63mm barrel, 425gm. Eight rounds. This is simply a post-war version of the vz. 36, omitting the original safety catch.

1583. ČZ vz. 50; Česká Zbrojovka A.S., Prague. 7·65mm Auto; 170mm overall, 92mm barrel, 700gm. Eight rounds. This double-action blowback personal-defence pistol was clearly inspired by the Walther PP. It was made in the Strakonice factory.

1584. ČZ vz. 52; Česká Zbrojovka, Strakonice. 7·62mm; 210mm overall, 120mm barrel, 1050gm. Eight rounds. The service pistol of the Czechoslovak army until displaced by Soviet weapons, this interesting weapon incorporated a recoil-operated roller-lock breech. It is said to have been chambered for a cartridge dimensionally identical with the Tokarev type, but loaded to give higher velocity.

1577
1579
1578
1582
1583
1580
1576
1584
1581

1587

1586

1590

1588

1596

1585

1589

1595

1592

1591

1594

1593

1601

1597

1598

1600

1599

1585. ČZ 70; Česká Zbrojovka A.S., Prague. 7·65mm Auto; 170mm overall, 92mm barrel. Eight rounds. This is an improved version of the vz. 50 (fig. 1583).

1586, 1587. ČZ 75; Přesné Strojirentsvi, Uherský Brod. 9mm Parabellum; 210mm overall, 120mm barrel, 950gm. Fifteen rounds. Distinguished by its double-action firing mechanism and a large-capacity staggered-column magazine, this gun has been one of the greatest Eastern bloc successes of recent years, being copied in Britain (fig. 1512), Italy (fig. 2011), Switzerland (fig. 2521) and elsewhere. The commercial version has plastic grips, but military patterns are usually wooden. Spur or ring hammers may be encountered. The shape of the frame and slide of the latest guns is shown in the inset.

1588, 1589. ČZ 83; Přesné Strojirentsvi, Uherský Brod. 7·65mm Auto or 9mm Short; 173mm overall, 96mm barrel, 730gm. Thirteen 9mm or fifteen 7·65mm rounds. This gun has a double-action trigger and a double-column magazine. The safety, slide catch and magazine catch are all ambidexterous. Fig. 1588 shows a 7·65mm commercial version. The military version—ČZ 82—chamber either 9mm Short or 9mm Makarov cartridges

1590. ČZ 85; Přesné Strojirentsvi, Uhersky Brod. This is simply a development of the ČZ 75 with ambidexterous controls.

1591. ČZ 85 Auto; Přesné Strojirentsvi, Uhersky Brod. 9mm Parabellum; 206mm overall, 120mm barrel, 1020gm. Fifteen rounds. Introduced in 1992, this is a selective-fire modification of the standard ČZ 85 using the reserve magazine as a fore-grip. Similar modifications of the ČZ 75 have also been offered.

1592–1594. Duo; František Dušek, Opočno. 6·35mm Auto; 115mm overall, 54mm barrel, 370gm. Six rounds. This small blowback pistol was made in several patterns, differing in minor details.

1595. Fox, 1919 pattern; Alois Tomiška, Pilsen, or (from 1921) Jihočeská Zbrojovka, Prague. 6·35mm Auto; 124mm overall, 63mm barrel. Six rounds.

1596. Fox; Česká Zbrojovka A.S., Prague. 6·35mm Auto; 123mm overall, 63mm barrel, 405gm. Six rounds. A later version with a trigger guard is known as 'Model 1922'.

1597, 1598. Ideal; František Dušek, Opočno. 6·35mm Auto; 114mm overall, 54mm barrel, 400gm. Six rounds. The 'Singer' pistol is identical (see fig. 1598).

1599. Jaga; František Dušek, Opočno. 6·35mm Auto; 115mm overall, 54mm barrel, 385gm. Six rounds.

1600. Little Tom; Alois Tomiška, Pilsen. 6·35mm Auto; 115mm overall, 59mm barrel, 365gm. Six rounds. A blowback pistol distinguished by a double-action trigger system.

1601–1603. Mars; Pošumavská Zbrojovka, Kdyně. Fig. 1601: 6·35mm Auto, 116mm overall, 54mm barrel, 390gm, seven rounds. Fig. 1602: 7·65mm Auto, 124mm overall, 64mm barrel, 465gm, six rounds. Fig. 1603: 7·65mm Auto, 165mm overall, 91mm barrel, 705gm, eight rounds. These were all simple blowbacks derived from FN-Browning practice.

1604. Perla; František Dušek, Opočno. 6·35mm Auto; 103mm overall, 50mm barrel, 277gm. Six rounds.

1605, 1606. Pistol 'N', vz. 22; Československé Statni Zbrojovka, Brno. 9mm Short; 149mm overall, 87mm barrel, 635gm. Eight rounds. The prototypes of this pistol, designed by Josef Nickl, were made by Mauser prior to 1918. Fig. 1606 shows a gun marked by Mauser-Werke AG in 1922–3, apparently when attempts were being to market the weapon in Germany.

1607, 1608. Praga; Zbrojovka Praga, Vrsovice, 1920–5. 7·65mm Auto; 164mm overall, 95mm barrel, 645gm. Seven rounds. This was conventional blowback design based on the 1910-pattern FN-Browning, but lacking the grip safety and relying on the inner surface of the slide (instead of a separate bush) to retain the recoil spring. It was used in small numbers by the Czechoslovak army prior to the adoption of the Pistol 'N' (q.v.).

1609, 1610. Praga; Zbrojovka Praga, Vrsovice, c.1922–6. 6·35mm Auto; 107mm overall, 52mm barrel, 347gm. Six rounds. This gun has an interesting safety system. To make a loaded pistol safe, the trigger must be pressed *forward* as far as it will go and the slide must be drawn back slightly before being released. This locks the hinged trigger-lever into the frame. The depression in the front part of the slide must be retracted slightly with the forefinger of the firing hand to release the trigger, which immediately springs downward. The shape of the slide also facilitates one-hand cocking.

1611. PZK; Pošumavska Zbrojovka, Kdyně (formerly Kohout & Company). 6·35mm Auto; 97mm overall, 43mm barrel. Five rounds.

1612. Slavia; A. Vilimeč, Kdyně. 6·35mm Auto; 116mm overall, 54mm barrel, 415gm. Eight rounds.

1613. Zbrojovka Plzeň; A.S. dříve Škodovy Závody, Pilsen, 1919–20. 7·65mm Auto. This blowback general-purpose pistol was adapted from Browning blowback principles by Alois Tomiška and made in the former Škoda factory. The project was abandoned in 1920, however, and the contract was transferred to Praga Zbrojovka (see fig. 1607).

1614. Pistole 'Z'; Česká Zbrojovka, Prague. 6·35mm Auto; 115mm overall, 54mm barrel, 370gm. Six rounds. This is simply a version of the Duo (q.v.), made under state control after the Dušek factory was nationalised in 1950. It seems that guns were also made—or perhaps simply assembled—in Brno, being known as 'Brno Z'.

Denmark

The Danish police forces have made extensive use of the 1910- and 1922-type 9mm FN-Brownings. The army has used Swedish M40 Lahti pistols, Belgian FN-Browning High Powers and Swiss SP 47/8 (SIG P-210) pistols. These are marked M.40S, M1946 HV and M1949 HV respectively.

1615. M1910/21; Hærens Tøjhus (later Hærens Rustkammer), Copenhagen, 1922–35. 9mm Bergmann-Bayard; 255mm overall, 100mm barrel, 1010gm. Six rounds. This was a Danish-made version of the Belgian-made M1910, purchased from Anciens Établissements Pieper prior to 1914. The principal differences concerned the improved grips and the replacement of the frame-plate retaining catch with a large slotted-head bolt.

1616. Schouboe, first or 1902 pattern; Dansk Rekylriffel Syndikat A.S., Copenhagen. 11·35mm. This was the earliest of these interesting blowback pistols.

1617. Schouboe, 1907 pattern; Dansk Rekylriffel Syndikat A.S., Copenhagen. 11·35mm. An improved version of the preceding gun, this relied on special ammunition to function effectually. The standard bullet was aluminium with a wooden core and weighed only 3·1gm (later raised to 4gm). This permitted a high muzzle velocity, as high as 485 m/sec, but kept the recoil forces low enough so that a blowback breech could be used.

1618. Schouboe, 1912 pattern; Dansk Rekylriffel Syndikat A.S., Copenhagen. 9mm Parabellum, 11·35mm or ·45 ACP; 203mm overall, 130mm barrel, 890gm. Six rounds. Experiments with 9mm and ·45 ammunition were made in 1912, still relying on light bullets, but were not particularly successful; the 1916-pattern pistol reverted to the original 11·35mm calibre. The Schouboe was never widely used, though a few guns were apparently issued to Danish border guards. Total production does not seem to have exceeded two thousand.

1619. Schouboe; Dansk Rekylriffel Syndikat A.S., Copenhagen. 7·65mm; 170mm overall, 90mm barrel. Six rounds. A small-calibre version of the military weapons.

Egypt

The Helwan, a copy of the Italian Beretta M951 (fig. 1984) made by the Maadi company, is the standard service pistol. The Hungarian-made Tokagypt has also been widely distributed.

Finland

Prior to the adoption of the Lahti, the army was equipped with the 1923-pattern Parabellum. These were held in reserve until the 1960s.

1620, 1621. L-35; Valtions Kivääritedhas (VKT), Jyväskylä, 1937–58. 9mm Parabellum; 240mm overall, 120mm barrel, 1000gm. Eight rounds. Designed by Aimo Lahti in the late 1920s, this resembles the Parabellum externally. Internally, however, it bears a greater resemblance to the Bergmann-Bayard; the action is locked by a vertically-moving block in the rear of the receiver. The hammer is enclosed, the main spring lies in the grip, and the recoil spring is in the receiver. All but a few guns made during the Second World War were fitted with a pivoting accelerator to ensure the bolt opened properly in adverse conditions. The guns have butt-heel lugs to receive a shoulder stock, even though this accessory was quickly abandoned.

France

Excepting commercial designs imported from neighbouring Belgium, the first automatic pistols to be used in quantity in France were 7·65mm Ruby-type blowbacks purchased from Spain during the First World War.

In the 1920s, however, work began in earnest to develop indigenous patterns. Notable among these was the Le Francais (fig. 1625) and the SACM-Petter (fig. 1652), the latter being adopted by the French army. Manufacture d'Armes des Pyrénées Françaises of Hendaye ('Unique') and Manufacture d'Armes de Bayonne ('MAB') are the best known commercial pistol-making establishments. Both began by making copies of the 1906-pattern FN-Browning blowback, but eventually graduated to better and more powerful designs.

1622, 1623. Bernardon-Martin; Établissements Bernardon-Martin et Cie, Saint-Étienne, c.1906–12. 7·65mm Auto; 150mm overall, 95mm barrel. Seven rounds. Several variants of these blowback pistols were made. Accessories included a large-capacity U-shape magazine.

1624. Bernardon-Martin; Établissements Bernardon-Martin et Cie, Saint-Étienne. 6·35mm Auto. A small-calibre version of the preceding pistol.

1625–1627. Le Français, pocket model; Manufacture Française d'Armes et

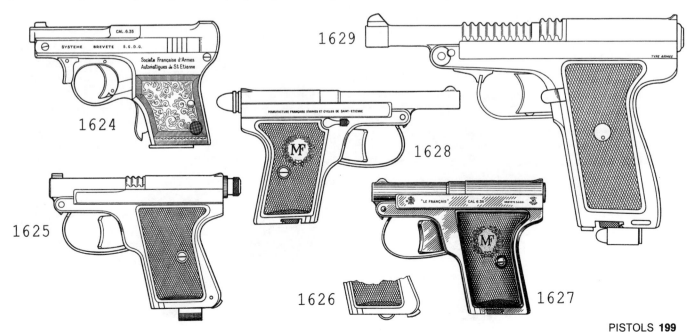

Cycles, Saint-Étienne, *c.*1926–39. 6·35mm Auto; 111mm overall, 60mm barrel, 320gm. Seven rounds. Made in accordance with a patent granted in 1913 to Étienne Minort.

1628. Le Français; Manufacture Française d'Armes et Cycles, Saint-Étienne, *c.*1926–39. 6·35mm Auto; 154mm overall, 89mm barrel, 350gm. Seven rounds. A miniature version of the standard pistol.

1629, 1630. Le Français, military model; Manufacture Française d'Armes et Cycles, Saint-Étienne, 1928–39. 9mm Browning Long; 203mm overall, 127mm barrel, 960gm. Eight rounds. These blowback pistols had very distinctive features. Pressing a lever on the right side of the frame allowed the barrel to tip downward under pressure from the spring-steel trigger guard. A cartridge could be inserted directly into the chamber without needing to retract the slide, then fired simply by activating the double-action striker-type trigger mechanism. Conventionally milled slide-ribs were customarily omitted from all but the 7·65mm guns. The Le Français lacks an ejector, relying instead on residual propellant gas to force spent cases out of the chamber. Owing to the double-action trigger, the pistol has no separate safety catch.

The recoil spring lies in the front of the grip and the magazine is allowed to pivot slightly in its well. The magazine is tipped slightly in its frame-well by a leaf spring in the back strap. This forces ribs on the back surface of the magazine into retaining grooves in the frame. The ribs must be pressed forward and down to remove the magazine. The floor-plate of many magazines has a loop into which a spare cartridge can be pressed; this round must be inserted manually into the chamber before firing can begin.

1631. Le Français 'Policeman'; Manufacture Française d'Armes et Cycles, Saint-Étienne, 1950–69. 7·65mm Auto; 152mm overall, 83mm barrel, 630gm. Eight rounds.

1632. Le Steph; Manufacture d'Armes Automatiques, Saint-Étienne. 6·35mm Auto; 111mm overall, 51mm barrel, 360gm. Six rounds. This blowback pistol is similar to the 1906-pattern FN-Browning, but has a detachable side-plate on the left side of the frame.

1633. MAB Model B; Manufacture d'Armes de Bayonne. 6·35mm Auto; 103mm overall, 50mm barrel. Six rounds. This blowback 'vest pocket' pistol is basically a copy of the Walther Model 9.

1634. MAB Model B; Manufacture d'Armes de Bayonne. 7·65mm Auto. A copy of the 1922-pattern FN-Browning, with an exposed hammer and a one-piece slide.

1635–1636. MAB Model C, or 'Cavalier'; Manufacture d'Armes de Bayonne, 1933–67 (7·65mm) or 1933–63 (9mm). 7·65mm Auto or 9mm Short; 154mm overall, 83mm barrel, 680gm. Six 9mm or seven 7·65mm rounds. These are basically Browning-type blowbacks, though differing in constructional details. The muzzle bush can usually be detached by operating the catch in the lower part of the slide.

1637, 1638. MAB Model D; Manufacture d'Armes de Bayonne, *c.*1935–65. 7·65mm Auto or 9mm Short; 178mm overall, 103mm barrel, 750gm. Eight 9mm or nine 7·65mm rounds.

1639. MAB Model E; Manufacture d'Armes de Bayonne. 6·35mm Auto; 158mm overall. Nine rounds. A conventional blowback pattern.

1640. MAB PA-8; Manufacture d'Armes de Bayonne, 1966–8. 9mm

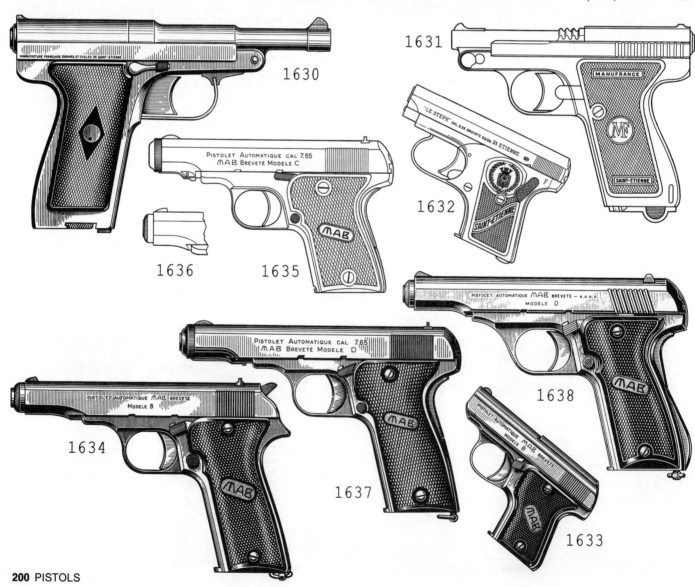

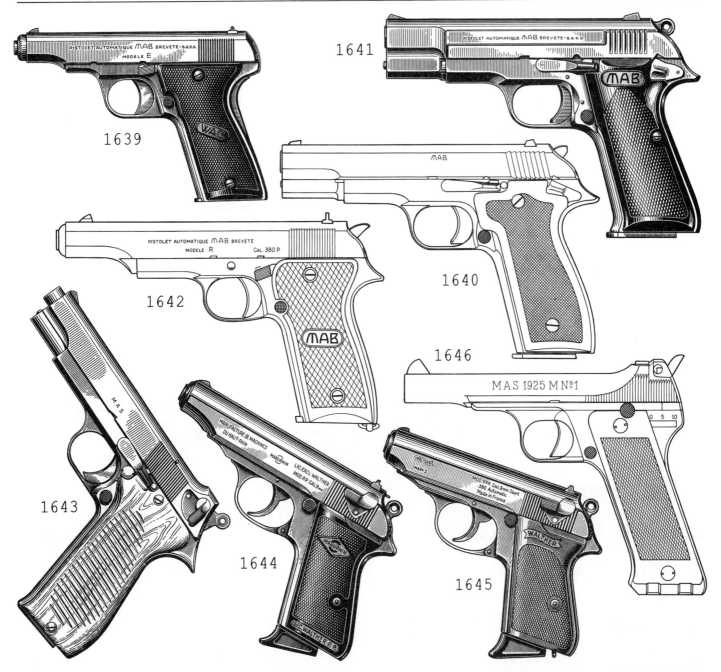

Parabellum; 202mm overall, 115mm barrel, 1080gm without magazine. Eight rounds. This is a derivative of the R Para.

1641. MAB PA-15; Manufacture d'Armes de Bayonne, 1966–85. 9mm Parabellum. This is similar to the PA-8, described above, excepting that it weighs 1110gm without its fifteen-round magazine.

1642. MAB Model R; Manufacture d'Armes de Bayonne, 1951–64. Data for ·22 LR rimfire, 7·65mm Auto or 9mm Short guns: 190mm overall, 100mm barrel, 750gm, eight 9mm, nine 7·65mm or ten ·22 rounds. Data for 7·65mm Long and 9mm Parabellum examples: 207mm overall, 120mm barrel, 1160gm, nine 7·65mm or eight 9mm rounds. Inserting a fresh magazine automatically trips the hold-open, allowing the slide to close on a new cartridge. The guns were blowbacks, excepting for the 7·65mm Long and 9mm Parabellum versions which incorporated a rotating-barrel delay system similar to that of the US Savage (q.v.).

1643. MAC Modèle 50; Manufactures d'Armes, Châtellerault (1953–63) and Saint-Étienne (1963 only). 9mm Parabellum; 193mm overall, 112mm barrel, 950gm with empty magazine. Nine rounds. This was essentially similar to the MAS Mle 35S (fig. 1648), but chambered NATO-standard

ammunition. Prior to the recent adoption of the Beretta 92-F, the MAC-50 was the principal French service pistol.

1644. Manurhin PP; Manufacture de Machines du Haut-Rhin, Mulhouse. ·22 LR rimfire, 7·65mm Auto or 9mm Short; 170mm overall, 98mm barrel. Seven 9mm, eight 7·65mm or ten ·22 rounds. These are licensed copies of the pre-war Polizei-Pistole (fig. 1839). Until recently, many of the guns bearing the marks of Carl Walther Sportwaffenfabrik of Ulm were actually made in France.

1645. Manurhin PPK; Manufacture de Machines du Haut-Rhin, Mulhouse. ·22 LR rimfire, 7·65mm Auto or 9mm Short; 155mm overall, 83mm barrel. Six 9mm, seven 7·65mm or nine ·22 rounds. A licensed copy of the pre-war Kriminal-Polizei-Pistole.

1646, 1647. MAS 1925 No. 1 and MAS 1932 Type A No 4; Manufacture d'Armes de Saint-Étienne. 7·65mm Long, ten rounds apiece. These blowback pistols were developed experimentally for military trials, but were unsuccessful. Their distinguishing features include a remaining-cartridge indicator on the frame behind the left grip.

1648. MAS Modèle 1935S; Manufacture d'Armes de Saint-Étienne, 1940 and 1946. Also made in the government factory in Châtellerault (1946 only) and by Société d'Applications Générales, Électriques et Mécaniques (1946–51). 7·65mm Long; 186mm overall, 106mm barrel, 915gm with loaded magazine. Eight rounds. This simplified Model 1935 (fig. 1652) was developed shortly before the Germans invaded France in 1940, but few guns were made until after the end of the war. The MAS 35S M1, introduced c.1947, had an improved safety system.

1649, 1650. Mikros; Manufacture d'Armes des Pyrénées Françaises, Hendaye. 6·35mm Auto or 7·65mm Auto. A copy of the Walther Model 9.

1651. PAP F-1; Manufacture d'Armes de Bayonne. 9mm Parabellum; 245mm overall, 152mm barrel, 990gm. Fifteen rounds. An elongated target version of the MAB PA-15 (fig. 1641), used by the army in small numbers.

1652. SACM Modèle 1935; Société Alsacienne de Constructions Mécaniques, Cholet, c.1937–46. 7·65mm Long; 193mm overall, 109mm barrel, 745gm with loaded magazine. Eight rounds. Designed by Charles Petter, this modification of the Browning dropping-barrel locking system was also popular in Switzerland (q.v.). It was adopted by the French army prior to the Second World War and was also made under German supervision. Survivors were still being retained for police use in the 1990s.

1653. Securitas. 6·35mm Auto. This interesting blowback pistol, lacking a conventional trigger system, may have been made by Manufacture d'Armes Automatiques of Saint-Étienne. See 'Le Steph', above.

1654. Union–France; M. Seytres, Saint-Étienne, c.1930–5. 7·63mm Mauser or 9mm Parabellum; 215mm overall, 125mm barrel, 1160gm. Nine rounds. A Colt-Browning copy, very similar to some of the Spanish Stars, apparently made for the Far East market between the world wars.

1655. Unique Bcf-66; Manufacture d'Armes des Pyrénées Françaises, Hendaye. 7·65mm Auto or 9mm Short; 168mm overall, 101mm barrel, 690gm.

1656, 1657. Unique C-2; Manufacture d'Armes des Pyrénées Françaises, Hendaye. 7·65mm Auto; 148mm overall, 78mm barrel, 655gm. Seven rounds. A distinguishing feature of this blowback pistol is an oval ejection port on the upper right side of the slide. The slide design of later guns (fig. 1657), however, exposes almost the entire length of the barrel.

1658. Unique D-1; Manufacture d'Armes des Pyrénées Françaises, Hendaye. ·22 LR rimfire; 148mm overall, 76mm barrel. Ten rounds.

1659. Unique D-2 and E-2; Manufacture d'Armes des Pyrénées Françaises, Hendaye. ·22 Short rimfire (E-2) or .22 LR rimfire (D-2); 180mm overall, 108mm barrel. Ten rounds.

1660. Unique Kriegsmodell; Manufacture d'Armes de Pyrénées Françaises, Hendaye. 7·65mm Auto; 148mm overall, 81mm barrel, 785gm. Nine rounds. This blowback automatic was produced under German supervision during the Vichy regime.

1661. Unique L; Manufacture d'Armes des Pyrénées Françaises, Hendaye. ·22 Long Rifle rimfire, 7·65mm Auto or 9mm Short; 148mm overall, 78mm barrel. Six 9mm, seven 7·65mm or ten ·22 rounds. Introduced in 1955.

1662. Unique Mikros, Model 5 or Model K; Manufacture d'Armes des Pyrénées Françaises, Hendaye. 6·35mm Auto; 112mm overall, 58mm barrel, 256gm. Six rounds.

1663, 1664. Unique Rr; Manufacture d'Armes des Pyrénées Françaises, Hendaye, c.1951–5. ·22 LR rimfire, 7·65mm Auto or 9mm Short; 146mm overall, 76mm barrel, 810gm. Eight 9mm, nine 7·65mm or ten ·22 rounds.

1647

1649

1648

1650

1651

1653

1652

1665. Ver-Car; Manufacture d'Armes Verney-Carron et Cie, Saint-Étienne. 7·65mm Auto. This Star-type blowback may have been supplied from Spain. **Not shown**. MAB Models G and G Z. ·22 LR rimfire or 7·65mm Auto. These are virtually identical with the Spanish Echasa or 'Fast' pistol (q.v.).

Imitations of the Browning M1906, 6·35mm

Doubtless helped by the proximity of the principal gunmaking districts to the Franco-Spanish border, many Spanish-made guns will be found with French proofmarks or French-language slide markings. These are included in the chapter devoted to Spain.

1666. Audax; Manufacture d'Armes des Pyrénées Françaises, Hendaye. 6·35mm Auto.

1667. EBAC; Manufacture d'Armes des Pyrénées Françaises, Hendaye, for Piot Lepage, Paris. 6·35mm Auto.

1668. Gallia; Manufacture d'Armes des Pyrénées Françaises, Hendaye. 6·35mm Auto; 119mm overall, 55mm barrel. Six rounds.

1669. H-V; Hourat et Vie, Pau. 6·35mm Auto.

1670. Kitu; maker unknown. 6·35mm Auto.

1671, 1672. Le Majestic; Manufacture d'Armes des Pyrénées Françaises, Hendaye. 6·35mm Auto. Similar to the Lepco guns described below.

1673, 1674. Lepco (or 'Helepco'); Manufacture d'Armes des Pyrénées Françaises, Hendaye. 6·35mm Auto. Made for H. Le Personne & Co. Ltd, well-known London distributors.

1675. Le Sans Pareil; Manufacture d'Armes des Pyrénées Françaises, Hendaye, for Piot Lepage, Paris. 6·35mm Auto.

1676. MAB Model A or 'Defender'; Manufacture d'Armes de Bayonne. 6·35mm Auto; 115mm overall, 53mm barrel, 380gm. Six rounds.

1677, 1678. SA; Société d'Armes, Paris. 6·35mm Auto.

1679. Triomphe Français; Manufacture d'Armes des Pyrénées Françaises, Hendaye. 6·35mm Auto.

1680. Union or Union–France; M. Seytres, Saint-Étienne. 6·35mm Auto.

1681–1683. Unique Model 10; Manufacture d'Armes des Pyrénées Françaises, Hendaye. 6·35mm Auto. Six or ten rounds. The version with a six-round magazine may have an automatic safety.

1684. Ver-Car; Manufacture d'Armes Verney-Carron et Cie. 6·35mm Auto; 118mm overall. Six rounds.

Imitations of the Browning M1906, 7·65mm

1685. Furor; Manufacture d'Armes des Pyrénées Françaises, Hendaye. 7·65mm Auto.

1686. Union or Union–France; M. Seytres, Saint-Étienne. 7·65mm Auto.

1687–1689. Unique; Manufacture d'Armes des Pyrénées Françaises, Hendaye. 7·65mm Auto; 150mm overall, 82mm barrel, 645gm. Nine rounds. The pistol shown in fig. 1689 was produced under German supervision during the Second World War.

Imitations of the M1910 Browning

1690. Audax; Manufacture d'Armes des Pyrénées Françaises, Hendaye. 7·65mm Auto.

1691. Unique Model 18 (?); Manufacture d'Armes des Pyrénées Françaises, Hendaye. 7·65mm Auto.

1680

1681

1682

1683

1684

1685

1686

1687

1688

1689

1690

1691

1692

1693

Germany

Germany has always been one of the leading manufacturers of automatic pistols and, notably prior to 1945, had achieved a justified reputation for quality. Names such as Mauser, Parabellum and Walther attained worldwide renown.

Soon after the German Democratic Republic was formed, Walther P.38 and PP were issued to the armed forces and police. Production of a 'Model 1001' facsimile of the PP began in the early 1950s, distinguished by the substitution of 1001-0-Cal. 7,65 for the Walther markings usually found on the left side of the slide. These guns were subsequently replaced by Soviet Tokarev and Stechkin patterns. Eventually, production of the Pistole M (Makarov) began in the former Sauer & Sohn factory in Suhl. Excepting markings, the East German Makarovs are difficult to distinguish from their Soviet counterparts.

Pre-1918 designs

1692, 1693. Adler; Adlerwaffenwerk Engelbrecht & Wolff, Zella St Blasii, 1905. 7·25mm Adler. An early design, this chambered a unique rimless cartridge with a slight neck.

1694. Beholla; Becker & Hollander, Suhl, c.1916–20. 7·65mm Auto; 140mm overall, 74mm barrel, 628gm. Seven rounds. This pistol was designed during the First World War specifically for military use, the intention apparently being to produce it in several factories simultaneously—see Leonhardt, Menta and Stenda. The Beholla was a simple blowback, easy to make, durable, reliable and compact.

1695. Bergmann-Schmeisser, 1894; made by Eisenwerke Gaggenau Gesellschaft for Theodor Bergmann. 5mm, 6·5mm, 7·5mm or 8mm. Data for an 8mm example: 280mm overall, 135mm barrel, 1080gm, five rounds.

Designed by Louis Schmeisser, this was the first of the Bergmann pistols to be produced in quantity (though the numbers involved were painfully small). The essence of the design was a blowback breech with a bolt reciprocating within an enveloping frame, and a fixed magazine ahead of the trigger aperture. To load the pistol, the magazine cover was opened and a clip was inserted. When the cover was replaced, a spring follower pressed the cartridges upward into the breech.

1696. Bergmann No. 2, 1896 pattern; made by V.C. Schilling of Suhl for Theodor Bergmann, Gaggenau. 5mm; 175mm overall, 80mm barrel, 470gm. Five rounds. This was a diminutive of the 6·5mm gun described below, originally made without an extractor. It deserves recognition as the first effectual pocket automatic.

1697. Bergmann No. 3, 1896 pattern; made by V.C. Schilling of Suhl for Theodor Bergmann, Gaggenau. 6·5mm; 255mm overall, 112mm barrel, 880gm. Five rounds. This was the first of the Schmeisser-designed pistols to be made in quantity. Mechanically similar to the preceding 1894 design, it retained the same clip-loaded internal magazine system. The earliest guns were made without an extractor, relying on residual propellant gas in the chamber to blow spent cases clear of the breech, but a conventional extractor was added about 1898.

1698. Bergmann M1897, Military Model or No. 5; made by V.C. Schilling of Suhl for Theodor Bergmann, Gaggenau. 7·8mm Bergmann No. 5; 270mm overall, 100mm barrel, 1155gm. Five rounds. The failure of the fixed-magazine Schmeisser designs to attract military attention encouraged Bergmann to offer a more powerful cartridge and a better magazine—doubtless inspired by the Borchardt. The 1897-pattern pistol superficially resembles the preceding 6·5mm blowback, but recoil displaced the bolt laterally into the receiver wall. The adjustable back sight was generally graduated to 1000 metres.

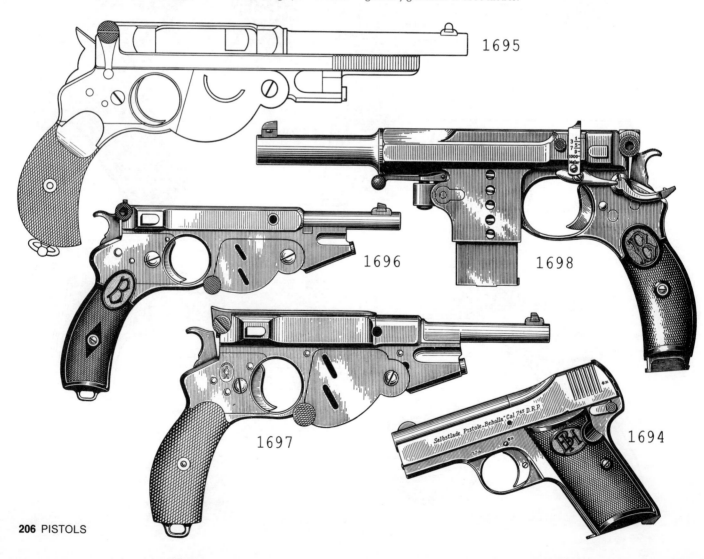

1695

1696

1698

1697

1694

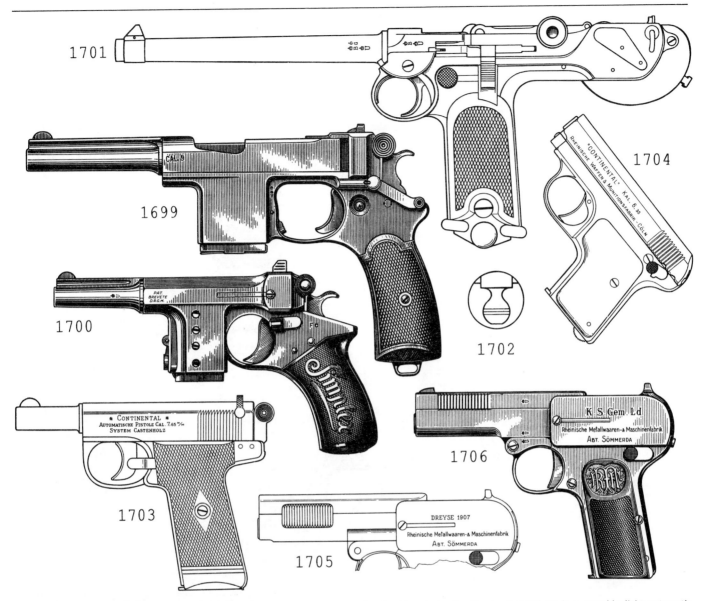

1699. Bergmann-Mars; made by V.C. Schilling of Suhl for Theodor Bergmann, Gaggenau. 7·65mm Auto, 7·8mm Bergmann No. 5 or 9mm Bergmann No. 6; 252mm overall, 104mm barrel, 910gm. Five rounds. Introduced in 1903, this powerful military pistol was especially popular in Spain and the Balkans. However, no sooner had the Spaniards adopted it officially than Schilling was purchased by Krieghoff and the liaison with Bergmann ended. The pistol was licensed in 1907 to Anciens Établissements Pieper and reappeared as the 'Bergmann-Bayard' (fig. 1388).

1700. Bergmann-Simplex; manufacturer unknown. 8mm; 196mm overall, 66mm barrel, 680gm. Five rounds. Introduced in the early 1900s, this was superficially similar to the Bergmann No. 5 of 1897 but was a simple blowback. The earliest examples were apparently made in Gemany—probably by Schilling—but most of them are thought to have emanated from Belgium after 1905.

1701, 1702. Borchardt; Ludwig Loewe & Companie, Berlin, c.1894–6, and Deutsche Waffen- und Munitionsfabriken, Berlin, 1897–9. 7·65mm; 353mm overall, 189mm barrel, 1310gm. Eight rounds. This unmistakable gun, patented by Hugo Borchardt in 1893, was the first commercially successful auto-loading design. It is now best known as the forerunner of the Parabellum. The Borchardt was locked by a toggle or 'knee-joint' system. When a shot was fired, the barrel and receiver recoiled far enough to lift the axis of the knee-joint above the bore. The breechblock and the toggle-links thereafter ran back alone. The necked cartridges, loaded with smokeless propellant, generated surprisingly high power for a handgun. Equipped with

its shoulder stock, the Borchardt pistol made a passable light automatic carbine. As a pistol, despite excellent performance when properly adjusted, it was too cumbersome and too delicate to achieve lasting success.

1703. Continental; Rheinische Waffen- und Munitionsfabriken, Cologne. 7·65mm Auto; 167mm overall, 99mm barrel, 630gm. Eight rounds. This was a copy of the Webley & Scott blowback pistol (fig. 1505), probably dating from 1912–13. The guns are often marked SYSTEM CASTENHOLZ, but the significance of this is unknown.

1704. Continental; Rheinische Waffen- und Munitionsfabriken, Cologne. 6·35mm Auto; 120mm overall. Seven rounds. This blowback pocket pistol was based on the 1906-pattern Browning. It was probably made in Spain in the early 1920s for distribution in Germany.

1705–1710. Dreyse; Rheinische Metallwaaren- und Maschinenfabriken, Sömmerda. 7·65mm Auto; 158mm overall, 91mm barrel, 650gm. Seven rounds. These guns were designed by Louis Schmeisser, who had previously worked with Theodor Bergmann (q.v.). Patented in 1907, the standard pistol was a simple blowback with the recoil spring concentric with the barrel and a striker-type trigger system. The barrel, receiver, breechblock and associated parts could be pivoted around a hinge on the lower front of the frame. The action was held closed by a sleeve under pressure from the recoil spring. This sleeve had to be moved slightly back to strip the gun, allowing the slide to be detached. The slide was held with a lug with grooved sides. To gain access to the lockwork, screws retaining the plate let into the left side of the frame were removed.

The 7·65mm Dreyse pistol was adopted by the Saxon gendarmerie and by police forces throughout Germany prior to 1914. Appropriate marks will often be found on the left side of the frame. Production continued into the First World War, many guns seeing military service.

1711–1714. Dreyse; Rheinische Metallwaaren- und Maschinenfabriken, Sömmerda. 6·35mm Auto; 115mm overall, 54mm barrel, 398gm. Six rounds. This was a diminutive of the 7·65mm Dreyse described previously. The detachable barrel was held by a special lug, connected with the slide.

1715–1719. Dreyse; Rheinische Metallwaaren- und Maschinenfabriken, Sömmerda. 9mm Parabellum; 213mm overall, 131mm barrel, 1100gm. Seven rounds. Apparently developed for military service late in 1914, this is structurally similar to the 7·65mm pistol described above—but has an unusually strong recoil spring to compensate for the absence of a locking mechanism. The 9mm Dreyse was made in large enough numbers to progress through several variants, but was not strong enough to withstand the battering of the powerful cartridge.

1720, 1721. Jäger; Franz Jäger & Companie, Suhl. 7·65mm Auto; 154mm overall, 94mm barrel, 650gm. Seven rounds. This interesting blowback pocket pistol—made largely of stampings—was patented shortly before the First World War began. Substantial numbers were made in 1915–18.

1722. Keszler; Friedrich Pickert, Zella St Blasii, c.1907. 7·65mm Auto; 164mm overall, 95mm barrel, 650gm. Seven rounds. This blowback design was an early, but comparatively unsuccessful German attempt to make a compact automatic pistol.

1723. Langenhan Army Model; Friedrich Langenhan, Suhl. 7·65mm Auto; 169mm overall, 105mm barrel, 650gm. Eight rounds. This individualistic blowback pistol was designed in 1913, though production did not begin until the First World War had started. The slide and breechblock were connected by a pivoting yoke. If the yoke-retaining screw loosened during firing, the breechblock could be blasted backward out of the gun on the next shot.

1724. Langenhan Model I; Friedrich Langenhan, Suhl. 7·65mm Auto; 137mm overall, 73mm barrel. Six rounds. Offered commercially after 1918, this was similar to the Army Model described previously, but smaller and lighter.

1725, 1726. Langenhan Models II and III; Friedrich Langenhan, Suhl, c.1920–5. 6·35mm Auto. Model II (fig. 1725): 145mm overall, 79mm barrel, 503gm, seven rounds. Model III (fig. 1726): 123mm overall, 59mm barrel, 439gm, six rounds. These were similar to the 7·65mm Langenhan listed previously, excepting for chambering, dimensions, and the replacement of the yoke with a sturdy cross-bolt catch.

1727. Mauser C/06-08; Waffenfabrik Mauser AG, Oberndorf. 9mm Mauser Export; six rounds. A few of these guns were made in c.1907–8, allegedly in a last attempt to challenge the Parabellum for lucrative German army contracts though they may have been subsequently offered to Brazil. The C/06-08 is short-recoil operated, relying on the outward displacement of two struts (one of each side of the breech) to release the bolt. The two-row detachable magazine lay in front of the trigger guard.

1728–1731. Mauser C/96 or M1896; Waffenfabrik Mauser AG,

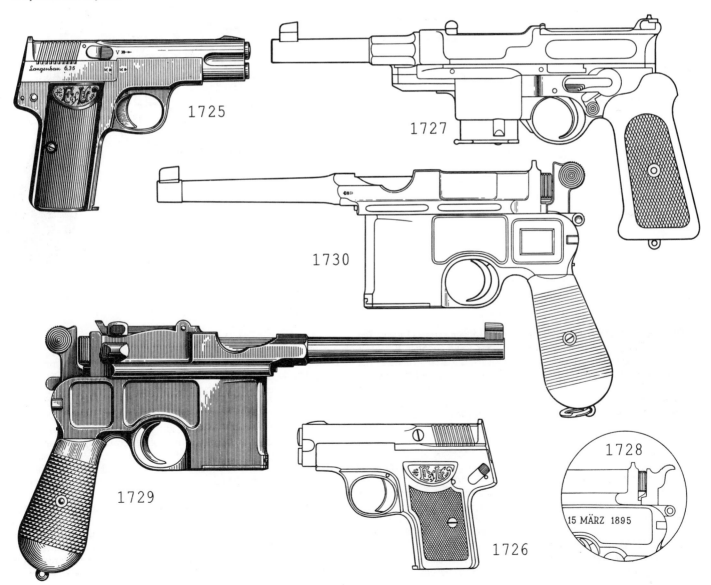

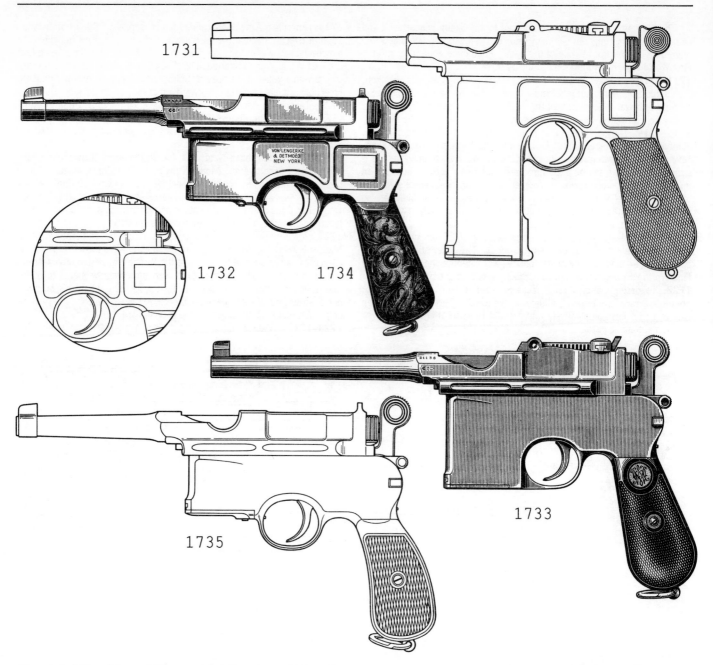

1731

1732   1734

1733

1735

Oberndorf. 7·63mm Mauser; 290mm overall, 140mm barrel, 1180gm. Ten rounds. This pistol apparently owes its success to the 7·65mm Borchardt cartridge, which Ludwig Loewe & Company allowed Mauser to purloin. The basis of the gun had been designed in c.1894 by the three Feederle brothers, as a private venture, but was ultimately patented in the Mauser name in the autumn of 1895. Fig. 1728 shows a detail of the perfected prototype, showing the date '15th March 1895'—apparently when it was fired for the first time.

The Mauser pistol, operated by allowing the barrel to recoil a short distance, was locked by a block rising into the underside of the bolt. The fixed staggered-row magazine lay in front of the trigger guard, and was charger-loaded through the top of the open breech. Though fixed-sight variants were made, most guns had a tangent-leaf sight optimistically graduated to 1000 metres. A special wooden holster doubled as a shoulder stock, transforming the pistol into an effectual light carbine. At 1000 metres, however, the spread of the bullets measured more than four metres wide by five metres high. At 100 metres, the bullets usually fell within a 30cm circle.

Many minor changes were made in the first few years of production, including adjustments to the rifling profile, the components of the firing

mechanism, and the disconnecting system. Fig. 1729 shows a cone-hammer gun with a ten-round magazine; fig. 1730 is a fixed-sight example; and fig. 1731 is a twenty-shot version with chequered rubber grips. All three date from 1898–9. The back-strap of the grip was generally slotted for the stock.

The 'Wonder Pistol-Carbine' was purchased privately by many British officers during the Second South African (Boer) War of 1899–1902, and became popular with travellers, hunters and gun collectors throughout the world. It was especially favoured in Russia, where the C/96 was one of the 'recommended pistol systems' that officers could use instead of the 1895-model service revolver. Officially, however, the C/96 was adopted only in Italy, Persia and Turkey prior to 1914. Field trials were undertaken in Germany in the early 1900s, but the C/96 was rejected in favour of the Parabellum (q.v.).

1732–1734. Mauser C/96, 1899–1905; Waffenfabrik Mauser AG, Oberndorf. 7·63mm Mauser; ten rounds. The first of these guns was distinguished by a hammer with a large pierced ring, but was otherwise similar to its cone-hammer predecessors and had panels milled out of the frame sides (fig. 1732). An order from the Italian navy in 1899 resulted in guns with flat-side frames (fig. 1733), which were then offered commercially until the panelled pattern reappeared in 1900. Fig. 1734 shows a six-shot short-barrelled pattern with a US distributor's name on the frame.

1735. Mauser C/96, c.1900; Waffenfabrik Mauser AG, Oberndorf. 7·63mm Mauser; six rounds. Often misleadingly known as the "Officer's Model", this curved-grip fixed-sight gun is simply one of several differing designs produced experimentally at the beginning of the twentieth century. Few were made.

1736. Mauser C/96, 1903–14; Waffenfabrik Mauser AG, Oberndorf. 7·63mm Mauser; ten rounds. A change to the safety system was made in 1903, accompanied by a small-ring hammer and a two-lug firing pin.

About 1909, Mauser introduced the first C/96 pistols chambered for the special 9mm cylindrical-case cartridge developed at least a year previously for the abortive C/06-08 (fig. 1727). The kinetic energy of the 9mm 'Mauser Export' bullet was greater than that of the 7·63mm type, registering 68kgm compared with 53kgm.

The C/96 safety was redesigned once again in 1912–13, so that it could be applied only after the hammer had been drawn back from full-cock to release the sear. A monogram consisting of the letters 'N' and 'S' (Neue Sicherung) appeared on the back surface of the hammer, and the head of the safety lever was solid. Concurrently, the ejector was made shorter and broader, and the power of the recoil spring was reduced.

1737. Mauser C/96, 1915 pattern; Waffenfabrik Mauser AG, Oberndorf. 9mm Parabellum; 290mm overall, 140mm barrel, 1150gm. Ten rounds. A contract for 150,000 of these guns was placed on behalf of the German army in 1915, though only about 135,000 had been delivered when the war ended. The guns were standard 'Neue Sicherung' examples, but had 500-metre back sights and a distinctive red-filled '9' branded into the grips to remind firers that they chambered the standard service cartridge.

1738. Mauser M1910; Waffenfabrik Mauser AG, Oberndorf. 6·35mm Auto; 136mm overall, 79mm barrel, 455gm. Nine rounds. This was the first of the small Mauser blowbacks, said to have been perfected by Josef Nickl (see 'Czechoslovakia'). Novelties included a spring-safety, activated with a button, and a slide that closed automatically on a new cartridge when the magazine was replaced. The guns could also be stripped without tools.

1739, 1740. Mauser M1910/14; Waffenfabrik Mauser AG (prior to 1922) and Mauser-Werke AG (1922–35), Oberndorf. 7·65mm Auto; 154mm or 174mm overall, 87mm or 107mm barrel, 650–685gm. Eight rounds. An example of the so-called 'Humpback' pattern is shown here, together with a long-barrel variant. The perfected guns had a flush-topped slide.

1741. Mauser M1912/14; Waffenfabrik Mauser AG, Oberndorf. 9mm; 185mm overall, 100mm barrel, 965gm. Eight rounds. The first Mauser pistol to incorporate a magazine in the grip was patented in 1907, with a locked breech, and was made experimentally as the 9mm 'M1909' blowback. It provided the basis for the 6·35mm M1910 and 7·65mm M1910/14 patterns described previously.

The M1912, offered for military service with fixed or adjustable sights, incorporated a delayed blowback system to handle a variant of the 9mm Mauser Export cartridge. Though the pistols were tried in Brazil and also possibly in Russia, they were not robust enough to handle the powerful ammunition. The project was abandoned after the failure of the M1912/14 (an M1912 with a stock-slot) and the outbreak of the First World War.

1742. Menta; August Menz, Suhl. 7·65mm Auto; 140mm overall, 74mm barrel, 625gm. Seven rounds. This was a variant of the Beholla, fig. 1694.

1743. Menta; August Menz, Suhl. 6·35mm Auto; 118mm overall, 63mm barrel, 384gm. Six rounds. A smaller version of the 7·65mm Menta described previously, probably dating from the early 1920s.

1751

„200"

1746

„100"
1747

1748

1744

DEUTSCHE SELBSTLADE PISTOLE
CAL 7.65 ZUM PATENT ANGEM.

1745

1755

128

1750

1749

1752

PATENT

S&S

1754

C.AL.7.65

S&S

1753

1744. Nordheim; G. von Nordheim, Suhl. 7·65mm Auto; 156mm overall, 93mm barrel, 600gm. Seven rounds. Apparently developed about 1912 and made in small quantities before the First World War, the chronology of this unusual blowback pistol is still disputed. Production may have continued after 1918, as guns have been reported with the later 'Vono' trademark.

1745. Parabellum M1900; Deutsche Waffen- und Munitionsfabriken, Berlin, 1900–7. 7·65mm Parabellum; 235mm overall, 120mm barrel, 880gm. Eight rounds. This legendary handgun was adapted by Georg Luger from the Borchardt of 1893 (fig. 1701), retaining the toggle-lock (or 'knee-joint;) principle but moving the recoil spring into the back of the grip behind the magazine well. The prototypes dated from 1898.

Originally known as the Borchardt-Luger, the pistol was soon renamed 'Parabellum'. This was inspired by the Latin phrase *Si vis pacem para bellum* ('if you seek peace, prepare for war'), which was DWM's telegraphic code-name. The 7·65mm necked-case cartridge was powerful and accurate, though a comparatively ineffectual man-stopper. However, as the pistol handled extremely well and could be stripped without tools, it was adopted in Switzerland in 1900 and subjected to lengthy testing in Germany, Britain, the USA and elsewhere. A 9mm-calibre version was developed in 1902.

1746, 1747. Parabellum M1904, navy pattern ('Pistole 1904'); Deutsche Waffen- und Munitionsfabriken, Berlin. 9mm Parabellum; 277mm overall, 150mm barrel. Eight rounds. This was the first Parabellum to feature an extractor doubling as a loaded-chamber indicator, though the riband-pattern main spring was initially retained. The toggle-grips had diced flat faces instead of the cutaway surfaces that had characterised the 1900 and 1902 patterns. The navy guns also had grip safeties, adjustable back sights, and a lug on the butt-heel for a shoulder stock.

1748. Parabellum M1906; Deutsche Waffen- und Munitionsfabriken, Berlin. 7·65mm Parabellum or 9mm Parabellum; 220mm or 240mm overall, 100mm or 120mm barrel. Eight rounds. This was an improved version of the 1900 (7·65mm) and 1902 (9mm) patterns, with the extractor doubling as a loaded-chamber indicator, diced flat-face toggle grips, and a coil-pattern recoil spring instead of a riband. The M1906 was sold in quantity to several armies—e.g., Bulgaria, Portugal, Switzerland—and proved equally successful commercially.

1749, 1750. Parabellum M1908, army pattern ('Pistole 1908' or 'Pistole 08'); Deutsche Waffen- und Munitionsfabriken, Berlin, 1908–18, and the Prussian royal gun factory, Erfurt, 1911–18. 9mm Parabellum; 217mm overall, 100mm barrel, 890gm. Eight rounds. The Luger-designed pistol was adopted by the German army owing to excellent accuracy, durability and reliability. It balanced well in the hand, whilst the angle of the grip to the bore promoted good snap-shooting. The Parabellum was adopted for infantry machine-gun units in 1907 and then, in 1908, for the entire army. It lacked a grip safety, stock lug and hold-open. However, the lug and the hold-open were restored in 1913.

1751. Parabellum M1908, long or 'artillery' pattern ('Lange Pistole 1908'); Deutsche Waffen- und Munitionsfabriken, Berlin, and the Prussian royal gun factory, Erfurt. 9mm Parabellum; 327mm overall, 200mm barrel, 1100gm. Eight or 32 rounds. This pistol was adopted in 1913 for artillerymen, and the NCOs and men of the munitions columns. The tangent-leaf back sight was graduated to 800 metres. Large-capacity spring-driven helical or 'snail' magazines, patented by Friedrich Blum in 1916, were issued from 1917 until the end of the First World War. They held twenty rounds in the drum and twelve more in the feedway.

1752. Roth-Sauer; J.P. Sauer & Sohn, Suhl, c.1906–1910. 7·65mm; 170mm overall, 99mm barrel, 650gm. Seven rounds. A distinguishing feature of this pistol, designed by Karel Krnka (see 'Austria-Hungary'), was the unique short-case cartridge. The Roth-Sauer used long-recoil principles to rotate the bolt out of engagement with the barrel, and was loaded from a charger with a sliding thumb-piece. The quirky firing mechanism was similar to that of the Roth-Steyr (fig. 1369).

1753. Sauer, old or 1913 pattern; J.P. Sauer & Sohn, Suhl. 7·65mm Auto; 144mm overall, 78mm barrel, 550gm. Seven rounds. The Roth-Sauer had been reasonably successful, but was soon overtaken by better designs. Consequently, Sauer embarked on a simpler blowback pistol. The recoil spring lay in the slide, concentric with the barrel; and the slide could be separated from the frame simply by turning the knurled collar at the rear. The position of the trigger indicated the status of the internal striker—when the striker was lowered, the trigger was in its rearmost position and comparatively rigid. The original pistols had an auxiliary spring-loaded lever in the trigger system, which was engaged only when the mechanism was being stripped. The post-war version of the Sauer pistol, described below, was somewhat refined and perceptibly smaller.

1754. Sauer, old or 1913 pattern; J.P. Sauer & Sohn, Suhl. 6·35mm Auto; 125mm overall, 64mm barrel, 400gm. Six rounds. This was a diminutive of the 7·65mm version.

1755. Schwarzlose, 1898 type; maker unknown, probably in Suhl. 7·63mm Mauser; 273mm overall, 163mm barrel, 940gm. Eight rounds. This was an early pistol design, operated by allowing the barrel to recoil approximately 12mm. A stud on the frame rotated the bolt out of engagement. The gun was well made, but may not have been sturdy enough to withstand prolonged use. It has been claimed that remaining manufacturer's stocks were sold to Russian revolutionaries in 1905.

1756–1759. Schwarzlose, 1908 type; A.W. Schwarzlose GmbH, Berlin. 7·65mm Auto; 142mm overall, 105mm barrel, 530gm. Seven rounds. The most unusual features were blow-forward operation and an enclosed hammer, but the guns were never popular in Europe. The tools, dies and surviving parts were subsequently sold to the Warner Arms Corporation of Brooklyn (see fig. 2591).

1760. Stenda; Stenda-Werke GmbH, Suhl. 7·65mm Auto; 141–145mm overall, 71–76mm barrel, 630–640gm. Seven shots. This was another of the many variants of the Beholla (fig. 1694), made after the end of the First World War. Stenda is sometimes said to have succeeded Becker & Hollander, which would date these guns to c.1920–5.

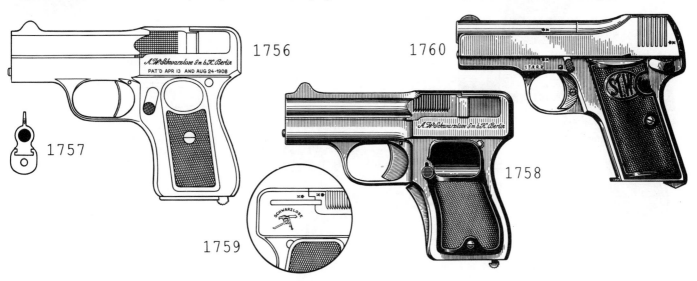

1761–1763. Walther Model 1; Carl Walther, Zella St Blasii, 1910–14. 6·35mm Auto; 112mm overall, 50mm barrel, 360gm. Six rounds. Patented in 1911, this was a small blowback-type pocket pistol with a concealed striker and a distinctive cross-bolt safety catch through the frame. The gun drawn in fig. 1763 has a flash-hider tube screwed to the barrel, possibly to comply with the laws of Austria-Hungary (q.v.).

1764. Walther Model 2; Carl Walther, Zella St Blasii, 1913–15. 6·35mm; 106mm overall, 54mm barrel, 277gm. Six rounds. A simplification of the Model 1, this had an ejection port on the right side of the slide, an internal hammer instead of a striker, and a back sight that doubled as a loaded-chamber indicator.

1765. Walther Model 3; Carl Walther, Zella St Blasii, 1913–14. 7·65mm Auto; 128mm overall, 66mm barrel, 470gm. Six rounds. This was structurally similar to the Model 2, though the ejection port was on the left side of the slide and the recoil spring was retained by a bush with a bayonet-joint.

1766–1768. Walther Model 4; Carl Walther, Zella St Blasii (c.1914–19) and Zella-Mehlis (1919–23). 7·65mm Auto; 150mm overall, 88mm barrel, 525gm. Eight rounds. The Model 4 was little more than the Model 3 with a longer barrel, an extended slide, and a butt accepting a larger magazine. The earliest guns had the indicator back sight, but this was changed in 1915 to a simpler fixed pattern.

1769. Walther Model 5; Carl Walther, Zella St Blasii (1915–19) and Zella-Mehlis (1919–23). 6·35mm Auto; 108mm overall, 54mm barrel, 275gm. Six rounds. This was an improved Model 2 with a fixed back sight and six-groove rifling instead of four.

1770. Walther Model 6; Carl Walther, Zella St Blasii, 1915–16. 9mm Parabellum; 209mm overall, 120mm barrel, 955gm. Eight rounds. This was developed during the First World as a potential service weapon, but was rejected when the blowback system proved unable to withstand the battering of powerful ammunition. Only small quantities were made.

1771. Walther Model 7; Carl Walther, Zella St Blasii, 1915–18. 6·35mm Auto; 135m overall, 78mm barrel, 355gm. Eight rounds. The Model 7 was a short-lived diminutive of the Model 4, with the ejection port on the right side of the Model 5-type slide.

1772–1776. Zehna; Eduard Zehner, Suhl. 6·35mm Auto; 121mm overall, 61mm barrel, 370–390gm. Six rounds. The dating of this blowback pistol is still the subject of dispute. It is suspected that it was designed either immediately prior to or during the First World War, but that production

may have been delayed until after 1918. There are two versions, one with the barrel pinned in place (fig. 1772) and the other retained by the recoil spring rod (fig. 1775). The external similarity between the Zehna and the Haenel (q.v.) is worthy of note, though no links between them have been discovered.

Guns made in 1919–45

1777. Armee-Pistole; Carl Walther, Zella-Mehlis, c.1937. 7·65mm Parabellum, 9mm Parabellum or ·45 ACP; 215mm overall, 120mm barrel, 790gm. Eight rounds. This was the enclosed-hammer predecessor of the Walther Heeres-Pistole and P.38, but production was barely two hundred.

1778. Bergmann Models 2 and 3; made in Suhl for Theodor Bergmann, Gaggenau. 6·35mm Auto. Model 3: 119mm overall, 55mm barrel, 450gm, nine rounds. Pocket pistols resembling the 1906-pattern FN-Browning were made in the Bergmann factories in Gaggenau and Suhl during the First World War, with single-action lockwork and cocking indicators. They were replaced after 1918 by the gun shown here. The Model 2 was similar, but had a short butt and a six-round magazine.

1779, 1780. Bergmann Models 2A and 3A; made in Suhl for Theodor Bergmann, Gaggenau. 6·35mm Auto. Model 2A: 119mm overall, 54mm barrel, 385gm, six rounds. After the end of the First World War, Bergmann produced distinctive pistols with a one-hand cocking system, originally patented by Witold Chylewski (see fig. 2508). The Model 3A was similar to the 2A, but had an extended butt accepting a nine-round magazine (fig. 1780). Bergmann's business was subsequently acquired by Lignose of Berlin, though the pistols retained their designations.

1781. Bergmann Special Model; Theodor Bergmann Erben, Suhl (Lignose AG), 1937–9. 7·65mm Auto; seven rounds. These were Menz PB Special pistols bearing the Bergmann name.

1782. DWM; Berlin-Karlsruher Industrie-Werke (formerly Deutsche Waffen- und Munitionsfabriken), Berlin, 1922–8. 7·65mm Auto; 154mm overall, 89mm barrel, 580gm. Seven rounds. Copied from the 1910-pattern FN-Browning, this was modified slightly in 1923 and remained available into the 1930s. Production is said to have ceased when Fabrique Nationale threatened to sue for patent infringement.

1783. Gecado; made for G.C. Dornheim AG, Suhl. 6·35mm Auto; 118mm overall. Six rounds. Despite its German marks, this is believed to have been made in Spain. It is a minor variant of the FN-Browning of 1906.

1784. Gustloff Werke, Suhl, c.1938–41. 7·65mm Auto; 168mm overall,

95mm barrel, 735gm. Eight rounds. The frame and slide of this unsuccessful blowback-type general purpose pistol were made of sintered metal. The action also embodied a lever which could be applied to relax the tension in the main spring when the hammer was cocked.

1785. Haenel Model I; C.G. Haenel Waffen- u. Fahrradfabrik, Suhl, c.1921–8. 7·65mm Auto; 118mm overall, 57mm barrel, 350gm. Six rounds. Usually credited to the Schmeissers, Louis and Hugo, this blowback pistol was made to patents granted in 1910 and 1921 to protect the method of securing the barrel and a means of preventing the magazine being removed whilst the safety catch was in the firing position.

1786. Haenel Model II; C.G. Haenel Waffen- u. Fahrradfabrik, Suhl, 1927–32. 6·35mm Auto; 102mm overall, 52mm barrel, 285gm. Six rounds. Designed by Hugo Schmeisser, this gun is similar externally to the Walther Model 9. Its most distinctive feature is the detachable barrel.

1787. Heeres-Pistole; Carl Walther, Zella-Mehlis, 1937–44. 7·65mm Parabellum or 9mm Parabellum; also advertised in ·38 Super and ·45 ACP. 212mm overall, 125mm barrel, 990gm. Eight rounds. This was a revision of the Armee-Pistole (q.v.) with an external hammer. Once perfected, it was little more than a commercial equivalent of the P.38.

1788. Heim; C.E. Heinzelmann, Plochingen am Neckar. 6·35mm Auto; 108mm overall, 55mm barrel, 310gm. Six rounds. A combination of FN-Browning and Mauser WTP features, this small blowback dates from about 1930.

1789–1791. Helfricht Model 2; Alfred Krauser, Zella-Mehlis, c.1921–9. 6·35mm Auto; 105mm overall, 51mm barrel, 323gm. Six rounds. This pistol, patented in 1920 by Hugo Helfricht, is also known as the Helkra. External appearance, internal construction and dismantling procedure are most unusual. The ejection port, which is split longitudinally between the slide and frame, only aligns at the moment of ejection. Models 2 and 3 (figs. 1789 and 1790) are similar externally, whereas the muzzle of the Model 4 (Fig. 1791) is virtually flush with the slide.

1792. He-Mo; Heinrich Moritz, Zella-Mehlis. 7·65mm Auto. Very little is known about this blowback pistol, sometimes listed as 'Hei-Mo', excepting that it post-dates 1919. FN-Browning and Spanish influences seem to be present in its construction.

1793. HSc; Mauser-Werke AG, Oberndorf, 1937–45. 7·65mm Auto or 9mm Short; 162mm overall, 86mm barrel, 585gm. Seven 9mm or eight 7·65mm rounds. Generally similar to the Walther PP, with which it was intended to compete, the HSc—'HS' represents 'Hahn, Selbstspanner' (hammer, self-cocking), 'c' signifies the third model—differed from its rival in many respects. For example, the detachable barrel was retained by a latch set into the trigger-guard web. A hold-open was disconnected as soon as a new magazine was inserted. The chamber had shallow longitudinal flutes, guarding against case-head separations caused by the breech opening too rapidly. The hammer was shaped to close the aperture in the rear of the slide whether cocked or lowered.

The HSc was originally intended for sale commercially, but, particularly after the Second World War began in earnest, was widely favoured by the military authorities. It was especially popular in the navy and the air force. Production stopped in 1945, but then recommenced under French supervision before finally ceasing in 1946. A slightly modified HSc reappeared in the 1970s and was licensed in the 1980s to Armi Renato Gamba of Gardone Val Trompia.

1794. Kaba Special; Karl Bauer, Berlin. 6·35mm Auto; 104mm overall, 53mm barrel. Six rounds. Possibly made for Bauer by Menz, this is similar to the Walther Model 9.

1795. Kobra; manufacturer unknown. 6·35mm Auto; 117mm overall, 59mm barrel, 367gm. Six rounds. This blowback pocket pistol has an exposed hammer. The back of the frame detaches during stripping, carrying the entire firing mechanism with it. Owing to the style of the patent mark, the gun probably dates from 1927–30—but confirmation is lacking.

1796. Kommer Model 1; Theodor Kommer, Zella-Mehlis. 6·35mm Auto;

111mm overall, 53mm barrel. Eight rounds. This is similar to the 1906-pattern Browning blowback, excepting for the longer grip. The sights may be the same as the Model 2, below. Emil Barthelmes of Zella-Mehlis is said to have produced a Kommer-like pistol, possibly in the early 1930s, but the relationship between the two (if any) has yet to be determined.

1797. Kommer Model 2; Theodor Kommer, Zella-Mehlis. 6·35mm Auto; 110mm overall, 51mm barrel, 344gm. Six rounds. A smaller version of the Model 1.

1798. Kommer Model 3; Theodor Kommer, Zella-Mehlis. 6·35mm Auto; 114mm overall, 55mm barrel. Eight rounds. This is much the same as the preceding guns, though the diameter of the barrel is increased near the muzzle. Knurling on the raised section facilitates removing the barrel, which must be turned during stripping.

1799. Kommer Model 4; Theodor Kommer, Zella-Mehlis. 7·65mm Auto; 150mm overall, 600gm. Seven rounds. The Model 4 is basically a copy of

the 1910-pattern Browning blowback, though the grip safety is absent and individual components—notably the sights—often differ in detail. Some, but by no means all guns have an indicator which protrudes from the slide when the striker is cocked.

1800, 1801. Leonhardt; said to have been made by Hans Gering of Arnstadt. 7·65mm; 142mm overall, 75mm barrel, 615gm. Seven rounds. A post-war variant of the Beholla (fig. 1694).

1802, 1803. Lignose Models 2 and 2A; Lignose AG, Berlin, c.1921–39. 6·35mm Auto. Model 2: 120mm overall, 54mm barrel, 395gm, six rounds. These were Bergmann-type blowback pocket pistols made after the original operations had been purchased by Lignose, the numerical designations being retained. The Model 2A was adapted for one-hand ('Einhand') cocking.

1804, 1805. Lignose Models 3 and 3A; Lignose AG, Berlin, c.1921–39. 6·35mm Auto. Model 3A: 120mm overall, 54mm barrel, 427gm, nine rounds. The 3A was an Einhand pattern.

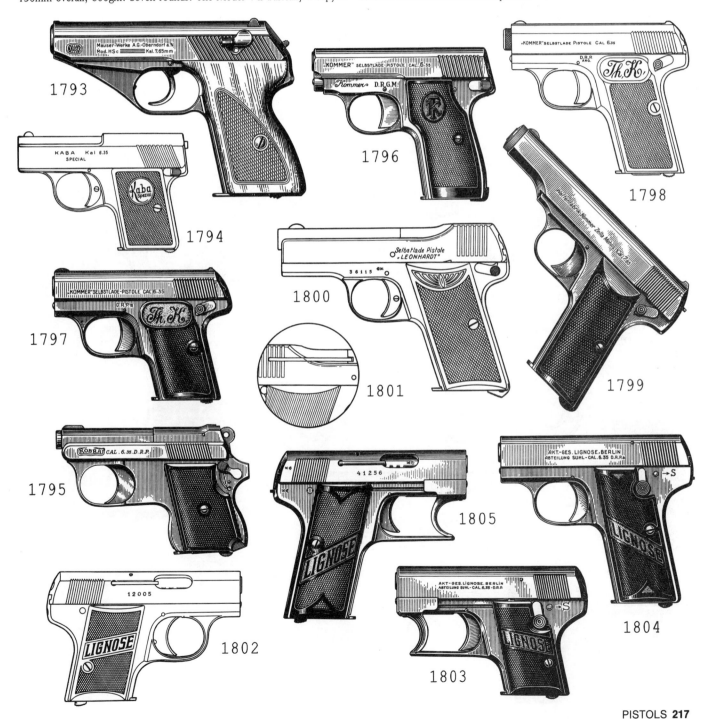

1806, 1807. Liliput M1925; August Menz, Suhl. 6·35mm Auto; 100mm overall, 51mm barrel, 270gm. Six rounds. The M1926 differs principally in the milling on the slide.

1808. Liliput M1927; August Menz, Suhl. 4·25mm; 91mm overall, 45mm barrel, 175gm. Six rounds. This tiny blowback pocket pistol fires a particularly ineffectual cartridge.

1809, 1810. Mann; Fritz Mann, Suhl, c.1920–4. 6·35mm Auto; 102mm overall, 45mm barrel, 250gm. Five rounds. The slide of this blowback pistol lies inside the frame, and the recoil spring lies above the barrel.

1811. Mann; Mann Werke AG, Suhl. 7·65mm Auto or 9mm Short; 122mm overall, 61mm barrel, 353gm. Five rounds. The recoil spring is concentric with the barrel. When the safety lever is applied, the magazine catch is disconnected.

1812, 1813. Mauser C/96, 1920 pattern; Waffenfabrik Mauser AG (prior to 1922) and Mauser-Werke AG (post-1922), Oberndorf. 7·63mm Mauser or 9mm Parabellum; 253mm overall, 98mm barrel, 1065gm. Ten rounds. Shortly after the end of the First World War, Mauser began to make so-called 'Police Models'—identical with the perfected pre-war 'NS' guns but with short barrels (to comply with the Versailles Treaty) and slightly abbreviated grips. Short-barrel Mausers had been so popular in revolutionary Russia that the genre is now often known as the 'Bolo-Mauser', deriving from the Russian *Bolshevik*. Many older guns were shortened in this era, but can usually be identified by their markings, full-length grips and signs of alteration.

1814, 1815. Mauser C/96, 1926 pattern; Mauser-Werke AG, Oberndorf. 7·63mm Mauser or 9mm Parabellum; 278mm or 296mm overall, 122mm or 140mm barrel. Ten rounds. This differed from the pre-war 'NS' type only in comparatively minor details; the most important was the advent of the Universal Safety, which allowed a cocked hammer to be lowered simply by pressing the trigger once the safety catch had been applied. Most guns were made with a stepped barrel and a full-depth grip.

1816–1818. Mauser M1930 and Schnellfeuerpistole; Mauser-Werke AG, Oberndorf. 7·63mm Mauser; 278mm or 296mm overall, 122mm or 140mm barrel. Ten or twenty rounds. The advent of Astra, Azul and Royal pistols in Spain, offering refinements such as detachable magazines and fire-selector systems, goaded Mauser into retaliation. The first selective-guns, known as Schnellfeuerpistolen, were made in 1931 to the designs of Josef Nickl. They were known in the USA as the Model 712—apparently a Stoeger designation. The standard M1930 semi-automatic, with a detachable magazine, was the M711.

The Schnellfeuerpistole had a two-position selector (fig. 1817) on the left side of the frame between the trigger-guard aperture and the grip. Markings 'N' ('Normale', single-shot) or 'R' ('Reihenfeuer', repetitive fire) showed the relevant lever positions. The Nickl design was replaced by that of Karl Westinger, patented in 1932–3. This had a distinctive selector plate, requiring the bottom corner of the frame panel to be abbreviated (fig. 1818).

The C/96 action was originally held open after the last shot had been fired by the magazine follower; this was not possible with the

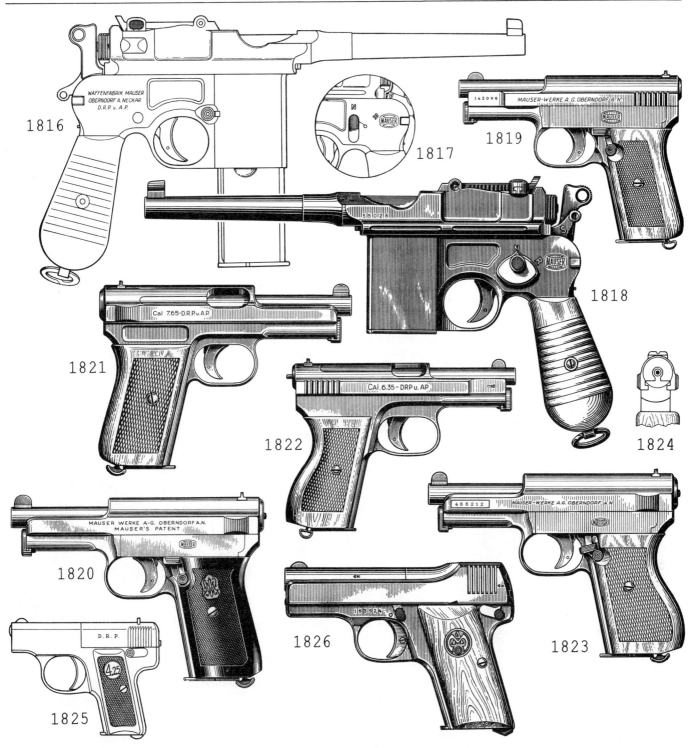

detachable-magazine patterns, so a separate hammer-operated catch was added. The hammer remained back after the last case had been ejected, and was thumbed past the full-cock position to release the bolt once a new magazine had been fitted. The bolts of most 'Spanish Mausers', conversely, closed on an empty chamber.

1819. Mauser M1910; Mauser-Werke AG, Oberndorf, c.1922–35. 6·35mm Auto; 136mm overall, 79mm barrel, 450gm. Nine rounds. The marks on the slide indicate that this blowback pistol dates later than 1922.

1820, 1821. Mauser M1910; Mauser-Werke AG, Oberndorf, c.1922–35. 7·65mm Auto; 154mm overall, 81mm barrel, 650gm. Eight rounds. Though based on the pre-1918 pattern, these guns date from the Weimar Republic.

1822. Mauser M1934; Mauser-Werke AG, Oberndorf, 1935–41. 6·35mm Auto; 136mm overall, 79mm barrel, 450gm. Nine rounds. This was simply a minor variant of the M1910 with a better grip.

1823, 1824. Mauser M1934. 7·65mm Auto; 154mm overall, 87mm barrel, 612gm. Eight rounds. A modernised version of the original M1910.

1825. Menz; August Menz, Suhl (unconfirmed). 4·25mm. The bore of this miniature pistol is drilled directly into the frame and the recoil spring lies in a chamber above the bore.

1826. Menz; August Menz, Suhl. 7·65mm Auto; 140mm overall, 74mm barrel. Seven rounds. This was another of the many versions of the blowback Beholla (fig. 1694), originating prior to 1918. Production continued into the 1920s.

1827. Menz; August Menz, Suhl. 6·35mm; six rounds. A diminutive of the gun described previously.

1828, 1829. Menz Model II, old pattern; August Menz, Suhl. 7·65mm Auto; 130mm overall, 68mm barrel, 495gm. Five rounds. This is one of many pocket pistols inspired by the Walther Model 9.

1830. Menz Model II, new pattern; August Menz, Suhl. 6·35mm Auto; 125mm overall, 61mm barrel, 330gm. Eight rounds. Similar guns will be found with the marks of Theodor Bergmann Erben (i.e., successors to Bergmann)—Lignose AG of Berlin, which purchased Bergmann in 1921 and Menz in 1937.

1831, 1832. Menz Models III and IIIA 'P&B'; August Menz, Suhl. 6·35mm Auto or 7·65mm Auto; 155mm overall, 88mm barrel, 700gm. Eight rounds. The Model III has an external affinity with the Walther PP and PPK models, but has a single-action trigger mechanism. A cartridge indicator is fitted in the slide. Model III A (fig. 1832, 163mm overall, 95mm barrel) is a pseudo-hammerless version.

1833. Militär-Pistole; Carl Walther, Zella-Mehlis. 9mm Parabellum; 222mm overall. Eight rounds. This enlargement of the Polizei-Pistole was produced experimentally for submission to the army. The MP was rejected owing to the lack of a breech-lock; most survivors bear numbers in the 5000s, but it is suspected that only a handful were made.

1834, 1835. Ortgies; Heinrich Ortgies & Companie (c.1920–2) or Deutsche-Werke AG (c.1922–32), Erfurt. 7·65mm Auto or 9mm Short. 7·65mm version: 163mm overall, 88mm barrel, 600gm, eight rounds. The 9mm pattern was similar, but had a seven-round magazine. Patented by Heinrich Ortgies in 1916–18 but only made in quantity after the end of the First World War, this blowback pistol is distinguished by its grip safety. Unlike most patterns, which spring back when hand pressure is relaxed, the Ortgies safety must be unlocked manually with a button on the left side of the frame—above the grip—which doubles as a stripping catch. Pressing the button allows the slide to be drawn back, lifted, then run forward and off the frame. The barrel may be detached simply by turning it around its vertical axis through 90°.

1836. Parabellum M1908, army pattern; Berlin-Karlsruher Industrie-Werke AG (formerly DWM), Berlin, 1922–30; Simson & Companie, Suhl, 1925–34; Mauser-Werke AG, Oberndorf, 1930–42; and Heinrich Krieghoff, Suhl, 1935–45. 7·65mm Parabellum or 9mm Parabellum; 217mm overall, 98mm barrel, 840gm. Eight rounds. The illustration shows a typical Weimar-period gun; many of those made during the Third Reich had plastic grips.

The Treaty of Versailles forbade commercial production of pistols greater than 8mm-calibre or with barrel lengths exceeding 100mm. Consequently, only 98mm-barrelled 7·65mm Parabellums were made in the BKIW (former DWM) factory until the late 1920s. In 1925, however, Simson & Companie was allowed to begin refurbishing 9mm P.08 for the armed forces. The BKIW production line was transferred to Oberndorf in 1930, and Krieghoff underbid everybody to obtain an air-force contract in the mid 1930s.

Parabellums were mass-produced in the Mauser factory until 1942, bearing the maker's codes 'S/42', '42' or 'byf'. The last batches of 9mm army-type guns were delivered to Portugal as the 'Pistola M943'. Small-scale assembly subsequently continued until 1945 even though the P.08 had been superseded by the Walther P.38.

1837. PB Special; August Menz, Suhl. 7·65mm Auto; 155mm overall. Seven rounds. This was a double-action blowback general-purpose pistol modelled on the Walther PP. Identical guns were marked by Theodor Bergmann Erben—see fig. 1781.

1838, 1839. Pistole 38 or P.38; Carl Walther, Zella-Mehlis, 1938–45; Mauser-Werke AG, Oberndorf, 1942–6; and Spreewerke GmbH, Berlin, 1942–5. 9mm Parabellum; 212mm overall, 125mm barrel, 990gm. Eight rounds. Issued from 1940 onward to replace the venerable Parabellum, this was a minor modification of the Heeres-Pistole (q.v.). The P.38 is locked by a pivoting block beneath the barrel, lugs on the edges of which are disengaged from the slide during the first stages of recoil. The double-action trigger mechanism has an exposed hammer and a de-cocking system which allows the cocked hammer to be safely dropped simply by pulling the trigger. An indicating pin protruded from the slide above the hammer when

the chamber was loaded. This was absent from the otherwise similar Heeres-Pistol, excepting for guns made in 1944–5.

The P.38 pistol was more effectual than the Parabellum, if somewhat less handy. Work in the Walther and Spreewerke factories ceased at the end of the Second World War, but production continued in Oberndorf under French supervision until 1946. Walther recommenced work in Ulm in 1957, continuing to make the P.38 (renamed 'Pistole 1') into the late 1980s. The P.38/P1 series has provided the basis for a series of Walther-made derivatives, in addition to most of the locked-breech Italian Berettas.

1840, 1841. PP or Polizei-Pistole; Carl Walther, Zella-Mehlis, 1930–45. ·22 LR rimfire, 6·35mm Auto, 7·65mm Auto or 9mm Short. Data for a 7·65mm example: 170mm overall, 98mm barrel, 690gm, eight rounds. This outstandingly successful blowback general-purpose pistol was patented in 1929. Though it had been preceded by several promising double-action designs—particularly by Alois Tomiška and Sergey Korovin prior to

1914—the PP was the first of this class to be an unqualified commercial success. The firing mechanism allowed the first shot to be fired without cocking the hammer manually, and the de-cocking system ensured that the hammer could be dropped on a loaded chamber in perfect safety. Production began again in France in the 1950s and is still continuing in Germany.

1842. PPK or Kriminalpolizei-Pistole; Carl Walther, Zella-Mehlis, 1931–45. ·22 LR rimfire, 6·35mm Auto, 7·65mm Auto or 9mm Short. Data for a 7·65mm example: 155mm overall, 83mm barrel, 560gm, seven rounds. This was identical mechanically with the Polizei-Polizei, but was smaller and lacked the solid back-strap to the frame. Guns have been made first in France and latterly in Germany since the 1950s.

1843, 1844. Rheinmetall GmbH, Sömmerda, c.1921–6. 7·65mm Auto; 165mm overall, 91mm barrel, 670gm. Eight rounds. This simple blowback pistol replaced the Dreyse (q.v.), work on which had stopped in 1918. The Rheinmetall bore a general resemblance to the 1910-pattern FN-Browning, though constructional details were quite different. Unlike the Browning, which had a detachable barrel, the barrel of the Rheinmetall was securely fixed in the frame. The German pistol was easily stripped, as it was necessary only to retract the slide and unscrew the rearmost portion whilst pressing the trigger. The sights were often simply a groove in the slide-top.

1845, 1846. Römerwerke AG, Suhl, c.1925–30. ·22 LR rimfire; 165mm barrel. Eight rounds. This blowback target pistol could be converted for self-defence simply by substituting a 6·35mm-calibre 63mm barrel.

1847–1850. Sauer, old or 1913 pattern; J.P. Sauer & Sohn, Suhl. 6·35mm Auto or 7·65mm Auto; 125–140mm ovrall, 400–530gm. These were minor variations of the pre-1918 patterns, made until the early 1930s.

1851. Sauer Behördenmodell, 1930; J.P. Sauer & Sohn, Suhl, c.1930–9. 7·65mm Auto; 145mm overall, 76mm barrel, 600gm. Seven rounds. A modernised form of the old 1913-type guns, these blowbacks were developed for semi-official use (Behörde, 'authorities').

1852. Sauer 38-H; J.P. Sauer & Sohn, Suhl, 1939–45. 7·65mm Auto or 9mm Short; 160mm overall, 85mm barrel, 620gm. Eight rounds. Developed to compete with the Walther PP and the Mauser HSc, this was an effectual double-action blowback pistol with an enclosed hammer and a cocking/de-cocking lever on the left side of the frame. Production ceased in 1945, but it is believed that 'Model 58' prototypes were made in the late 1950s in the new Eckenförde factory.

1853–1855. Simson, M1927; Simson & Companie, Suhl. 6·35mm Auto; 114mm overall, 55mm barrel, 372gm. Six rounds. This is an uncomplicated blowback pocket pistol. The M1922 had a different slide (fig. 1855).

1856. Stern; Albin Wahl, Zella-Mehlis. 6·35mm Auto; 126mm overall, 61mm barrel, 440gm. Ten rounds. A blowback dating from the 1920s.

1857, 1858. Stock; Franz Stock AG, Berlin, c.1925–35. 7·65mm Auto; 163mm or 170mm overall, 92mm or 100mm barrel, about 685gm. Eight

rounds. These sturdy and effectual blowbacks, made by one of Germany's leading machine-tool manufacturers, were popular with target shooters.

1859. Stock; Franz Stock AG, Berlin, c.1925–35. 6·35mm Auto; 120mm overall, 63mm barrel, 350gm. Seven rounds.

1860. Walther Model 8; Carl Walther, Zella-Mehlis, 1920–39. 6·35m Auto; 130mm overall, 74mm barrel, 364gm. Eight rounds. A hammer-fired blowback, this pistol could be dismantled (on all but the earliest guns) simply by pulling downward on the trigger guard to allow the slide to be pulled back, lifted upward and taken off the frame.

1861–1863. Walther Model 9; Carl Walther, Zella-Mehlis, 1921–40. 6·35mm Auto; 100mm overall, 51mm barrel, 254gm. Six rounds. This elegant little blowback pocket pistol, which inspired a legion of copies, is distinguished a unique '8'-shaped dismantling block retained by a spring-catch. The tail of the striker protrudes through the block to act as a cocking indicator.

1864. WTM or Westentaschenmodell, 1925 type; J.P. Sauer & Sohn, Suhl. 6·35mm Auto; 106mm overall, 56mm barrel, 400gm. Six rounds. These resembled the Walther Model 9 (fig. 1861) but differed in construction—e.g., the slide and barrel sleeve were separate parts.

1865. WTM, 1928 type; J.P. Sauer & Sohn, Suhl. 6·35mm Auto; 108mm overall, 50mm barrel, 300gm. Six rounds. A minor refinement of the preceding gun.

1866. WTP, later known as WTP-1; Mauser-Werke AG, Oberndorf, c.1922–39. 6·35mm Auto; 115mm overall, 61mm barrel, 329gm. Six rounds. Appreciably smaller than the 1910-pattern Mauser pistol, this was known as the 'Vest-pocket Pistol' (Westentaschenpistole, WTP).

1867. WTP-2; Mauser-Werke AG, Oberndorf, 1938–42. 6·35mm Auto; 103mm overall, 52mm barrel, 290gm. Six rounds. A diminution of the WTP-1 described above.

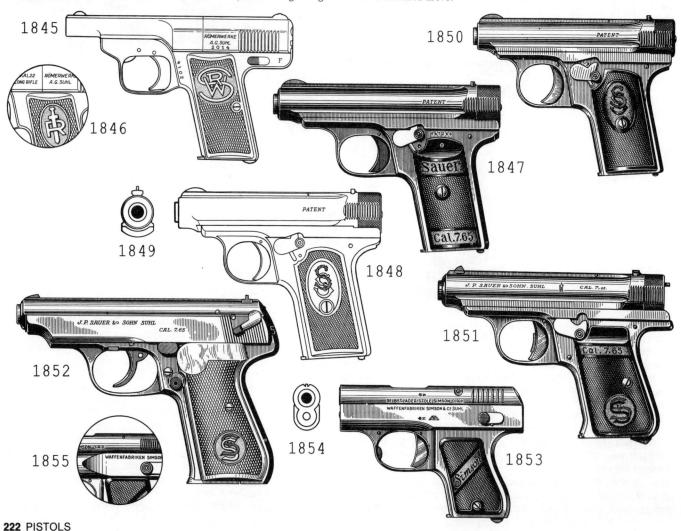

Post-war designs

1868. Erma KGP-68; Erma-Werke GmbH & Co. KG, München-Dachau. 7·65mm or 9mm Short; 187mm overall, 100mm barrel, 640gm. Five 9mm or six 7·65mm rounds. Superficially similar to the Parabellum, this is basically a simple blowback chambering low-pressure ammunition. The KGP-68A has an additional magazine safety to comply with the US Gun Control Act of 1968.

1869. Erma P-25; Erma-Werke GmbH & Co. KG, München-Dachau. 6·35mm Auto; 135mm overall, 70mm barrel, 380gm. Seven rounds. Loosely based on the pre-war Ortgies pistol, this blowback pistol has a different safety catch. Like many other guns in the series, it can also be obtained as a blank-firer.

1870. Erma P-459; Erma-Werke GmbH & Co. KG, München-Dachau. 9mm Short; 160mm overall, 89mm barrel, 675gm. Eight rounds. This blowback pistol is modelled, externally at least, on the 1911-pattern Colt-Browning.

1871. Erma P-552; Erma-Werke GmbH & Co. KG, München-Dachau. ·22 LR rimfire; 137mm overall, 73mm barrel, 410gm. A near-facsimile of the Walther PPK.

1872, 1873. Erma P-652; Erma-Werke GmbH & Co. KG, München-Dachau. ·22 LR rimfire, 135mm overall, 70mm barrel, 390gm. Seven rounds. A blowback pattern loosely modelled on the Walther TPH.

1874. Erma RX-22; Erma-Werke GmbH & Co. KG, München-Dachau. ·22 LR rimfire; 155mm overall, 83mm barrel, 565gm. Nine rounds. A copy of the Walther PP/PPK.

1875–1878. Gecado Model 11; Dynamit Nobel AG. 6·35mm. This is a Reck-made SM-11, typical of the new generation of pocket pistols. It is made largely of sintered metal alloy. Most of the lesser components are plastic, leaving only the barrel, springs, firing pin, etc., to be made of steel. The simplicity of construction has allowed guns of this general type to be made by several German manufacturers. A selection of slide-marks is also shown.

1879–1881. HK-4; Heckler & Koch GmbH, Oberndorf, c.1964–84. ·22 LR rimfire, 6·35mm Auto, 7·65mm Auto or 9mm Short. Typically 157mm overall, 85mm barrel, 520gm. Seven to ten rounds, depending on chambering. Introduced in the early 1960s and made in a one-time Mauser factory, this is distinguished by the ease with which its barrel/recoil spring assembly can be changed. A rotating striker adapts to rim- or centre-fire ammunition as required.

1882. HK P-7 or PSP (Polizei-Selbstlade-Pistole); Heckler & Koch GmbH, Oberndorf. 9mm Parabellum; 166mm overall, 105mm barrel, 950gm. Eight rounds. This pistol was developed in 1973–5 to satisfy the rquirements of

the West German police. When a shot is fired, the backward motion of the slide is opposed by propellant gas bled from the bore to act on a piston under the barrel. The striker is cocked automatically as hand pressure forces the lever on the front of the grip backward. The original PSP, which had a small trigger guard and lacked the ambidexterous magazine catch of its successors, was discontinued in 1986.

1883. HK P-7 M8 and P-7 M13; Heckler & Koch GmbH, Oberndorf, introduced in 1983. 9mm Parabellum; 171mm overall, 105mm barrel, 950gm. Eight or thirteen rounds. This was an improved form of the PSP, with cartridges arranged in a single (M8) or staggered row (M13). The P-7 K3 blowback, in ·22 LR rimfire or 9mm Short, relies on an oil-filled buffer to suppress recoil.

1884. HK P-7 M10; Heckler & Koch GmbH & Co KG, Oberndorf, introduced in 1991. ·40 S&W; ten rounds. This is a minor variant of the standard P-7 M8 (q.v.).

1885, 1886. HK P-9S; Heckler & Koch GmbH, Oberndorf, c.1972–84. 7·65mm Parabellum, 9mm Parabellum or ·45 ACP. Data for a 9mm example: 192mm overall, 102mm barrel, 875gm. Nine rounds. This unique pistol incorporates several interesting features, including a delayed-blowback mechanism in which rollers retract under backward pressure into the breechblock, allowing the slide to reciprocate only when the chamber pressure has dropped to a safe level. The polygonal rifling lacks sharply

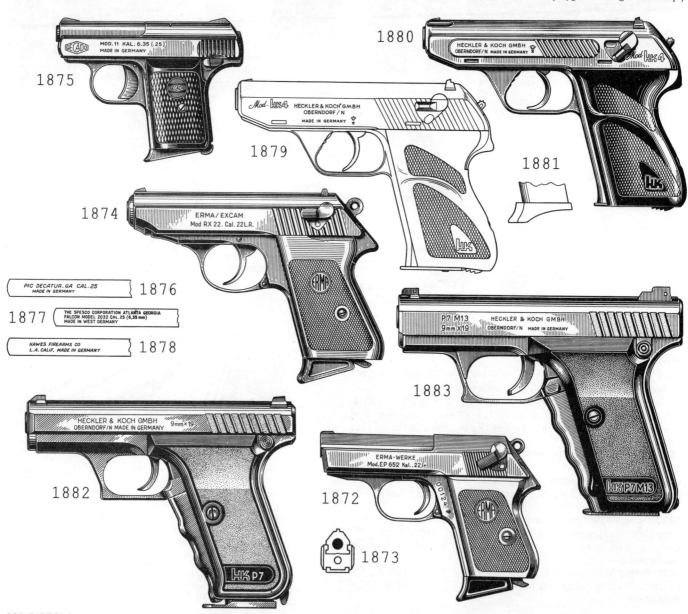

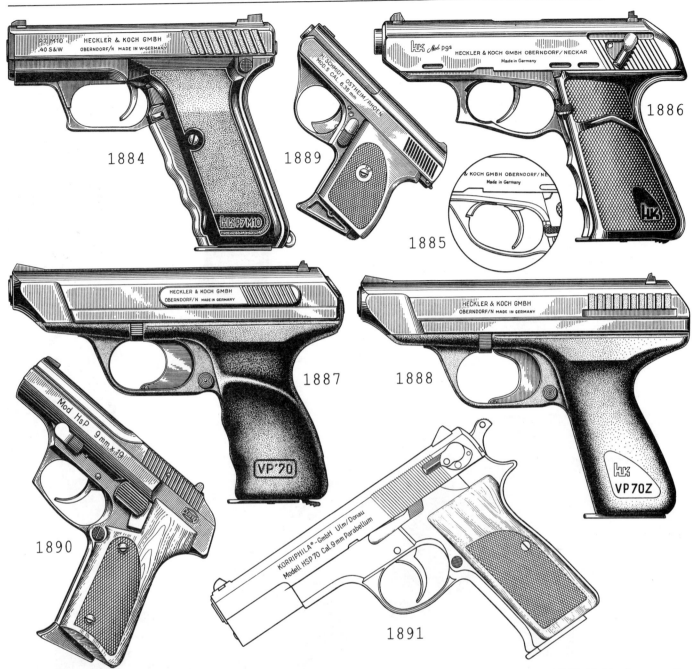

1884

1889

1886

1885

1887

1888

1890

1891

defined edges, minimising wear and the deposition of fouling. The trigger is double-action. A cocking/de-cocking lever lies on the left side of the frame, whilst an indicator pin protrudes from the back of the slide when the hammer is cocked.

Manufacture of the P-9S incorporated the newest techniques, such as forged barrel-bores and a largely synthetic receiver. The ·45 version appeared in 1977, the original P-9 of 1969, with a small trigger guard and a single-action trigger, being discarded at about the same time. Many guns have the front surface of the trigger guard adapted to facilitate a two-hand grip. Sport and target-shooting variants were offered with longer barrels, barrel weights, special sights and adjustable grips. These were all discontinued in 1984, though new guns were available for many years.

1887. HK VP-70; Heckler & Koch GmbH, Oberndorf, c.1970–84. 9mm Parabellum; 204mm overall, 116mm barrel, 920gm. Eighteen rounds. This was a large selective-fire blowback design, with ordinary rifling, a double-row magazine, double-action-only lockwork, an enclosed striker, and a push-button safety. The frame was made almost entirely of plastic, whilst a shock absorber reduced the recoil sensation. The pistol was simple, robust

and easily operated. The essentially similar VP-70 A1 (also known as the VP-70M), with a holster-stock of peculiar shape, had an additional three-shot burst-firing system. It was discontinued in the early 1980s.

1888. HK VP-70 Z; Heckler & Koch GmbH, Oberndorf, c.1974–84. 9mm Parabellum; eighteen rounds. This was a semi-automatic modification of the VP-70, lacking the stock and burst-firing attachment.

1889. HS Model 5; Herbert Schmidt GmbH, Ostheim/Rhön. 6·35mm Auto; six rounds. Introduced in the late 1970s, this is similar to the Reck SM-11 and other inexpensive pocket pistols. It is also made as a blank-firer.

1890. HsP; Mauser-Werke GmbH, Oberndorf, 1976–83. 9mm Parabellum; eight rounds. Designed by Walter Ludwig, this was developed to compete with the Walther, Heckler & Koch and SIG-Sauer pistols in the German police trials of the 1970s. Unfortunately, the recoil-operated HsP was perfected too late to compete and was unable to find any long-term success. Few were made.

1891. HSP-70; Korriphila-Präzisionsmechanik GmbH, Ulm. 7·65mm or 9mm Parabellum; 205mm overall. Twenty rounds. This was a short-lived roller-locked design.

1892. HSP-701, Type I Defense; Korriphila-Präzisionsmechanik GmbH, Ulm. 7·65mm Parabellum, ·38 Special, 9mm Police, 9mm Parabellum, 9mm Steyr, 10mm or ·45 ACP; 182mm overall, 100mm barrel, 990gm. Nine rounds. This was introduced in 1983 to replace the unsuccessful HSP-70. Recoil enables the slide to depress a transverse roller into the floor of the frame behind the magazine well, releasing the slide/breechblock assembly to reciprocate. The trigger is a double-action-only pattern. The HSP-701 was also offered as the Type II Compact with a 127mm barrel and a conventional double-action trigger, or in Type III Competition form with a single-action trigger.

1893. Korth GmbH, Ratzeburg/Holstein. 9mm Parabellum and others; 206mm overall, 102mm barrel, 1240gm. Ten rounds. Introduced in the late 1980s, this particularly well-made, but also unusually expensive recoil-operated semi-automatic pistol incorporates a special buffer to absorb the shock of firing.

1894. Mauser 90-DA; Mauser-Werke Oberndorf GmbH. 9mm Parabellum. Despite its marks, this is a Hungarian-made FÉG P9R (q.v.) distributed by Umarex, licensees of the well-known Mauser banner trademark.

1895. Mauser-Parabellum 29/70; Mauser-Jagdwaffen GmbH, Oberndorf. 7·65mm Parabellum or 9mm Parabellum; 100mm or 150mm barrel. Eight rounds. Production of this well-known gun resumed in Oberndorf in the early 1970s, on the basis of the Swiss 06/29 pattern (fig. 2509). Special commemorative patterns have also been made in addition to the standard 29/70 and 06/73 sporting guns, the latter being based on the P.08.

1896. PPK; Carl Walther Sportwaffenfabrik, Ulm/Donau. 7·65mm Auto. This is a typical post-war version of the original design, made in France by Manurhin but proved and marked in Germany.

1897. PP Super; Carl Walther Sportwaffenfabrik, Ulm/Donau, 1975–81. 9mm Police; 170mm overall, 92mm barrel, 760gm. Seven rounds. This was adapted from the basic double-action PP to chamber a new 9mm round designed to investigate the limits of blowback operation. The cartridge lies between the 9mm Short and 9mm Parabellum in size and power, and has a noticeably rebated rim.

1898. Reck P-8 or La Fury 8; Karl Arndt Reck, Lauf bei Nürnberg. 6·35mm Auto; 115mm overall, 56mm barrel, 360gm. Eight rounds. Only the most important parts of this gun are steel—e.g., the barrel, striker, springs and pins. The remaining parts are sintered metal.

1899. Reck SM-11; Karl Arndt Reck, Lauf bei Nürnberg. 6·35mm Auto; 115mm overall, 55mm barrel, 325gm. Five rounds. This is similar to the Reck P-8, but has a shorter grip, the safety lever is placed differently, and the stripping procedure has been changed. Its construction also parallels that of the P-8, excepting that plastic is used for the grips, the magazine floor-plate, the safety catch and the trigger lever.

1900. Rhöner Model 115; Rhöner Sportwaffen GmbH. 6·35mm Auto; 116mm overall, 55mm barrel, 390gm. Six rounds. This simple blowback pocket pistol is similar to the Reck SM-11 described previously.

1901. RSM Stingray. 6·35mm Auto; 114mm overall, 57mm barrel, 280gm. Six rounds. This is believed to have been made by Reck.

1902. TP or Taschenpistole; Carl Walther Sportwaffenfabrik, Ulm/Donau, 1961–71. ·22 LR rimfire or 6·35mm Auto. A post-war version of the Walther Model 9, this was soon replaced by the more effectual TPH.

1903. TP-70; Korriphila-Präzisionsmechanik GmbH, Ulm. 6·35mm Auto; 66mm barrel, 340gm. Six rounds. Designed by Edgar Budischowsky, this is basically an amalgam of Colt and Walther features.

1904. TPH (Taschenpistole mit Hahn); Carl Walther Sportwaffenfabrik, Ulm/Donau, introduced in 1968. ·22 LR rimfire or 6·35mm Auto; 135mm overall, 71mm barrel, 310gm. Six 6·35mm or seven ·22 rounds. A refined diminutive of the PP series, this replaced the TP (fig. 1902).

1905. Walther P1A1; Carl Walther GmbH, Ulm, 1989 to date. 9mm Parabellum; 179mm overall, 90mm barrel, 810gm. Eight rounds.

1906. Walther P4; Carl Walther Sportwaffenfabrik, Ulm/Donau, 1974–82. 9mm Parabellum; 200mm overall, 110mm barrel, 800gm. Eight rounds. This was a compact version of the P1 (P.38) with an alloy frame. The de-cocking lever on the slide merely lowers the hammer, blocking the firing pin only as it does so. A separate safety system is incorporated in the trigger.

1907. Walther P5; Carl Walther Sportwaffenfabrik, Ulm/Donau. 9mm Parabellum; eight rounds. Introduced in 1975, this modernised P1 incorporates the well-tried locking system in a streamlined full-length slide.

1908. Walther P5 Compact; Carl Walther GmbH, Ulm. 9mm Parabellum; 168mm overall, 79mm barrel, 780gm. Eight rounds. Dating from 1988, this is simply a shortened version of the standard pattern.

1909. Walther P5 Target; Carl Walther GmbH, Ulm. Introduced in 1991, this is intended for sports-target shooting. It is 63mm longer than the standard P5, and its rifling makes a turn in 476mm instead of 250mm.

1905

1908

1906

1907

1910. Walther P38K; Carl Walther Sportwaffenfabrik, Ulm/Donau, 1974–80. 9mm Parabellum; 70mm barrel. Eight rounds. This short-lived variant of the P1 differs from the standard gun only in barrel-length and the repositioning of the front sight on the slide.

1911, 1912. Walther P88; Carl Walther Sportwaffenfabrik, Ulm/Donau. Announced in 1986, but not made in quantity until 1988, this military pistol has a staggered-column magazine and a Browning-type tipping-barrel breech lock. The double-action firing mechanism incorporates a de-cocking mechanism and an exposed hammer. A P88 Compact appeared in 1991.

Hungary

Regaining independence after the end of the First World War, Hungary was initially armed with a combination of Austro-Hungarian weapons—e.g., Roth-Steyr, Steyr-Hahn—and the indigenous Frommer, work on which had begun in the early 1900s. Made in Budapest, the perfected Frommer had been adopted as the service pistol of the Honved (the Hungarian reserve forces) in 1912. The recoil-operated patterns were superseded in the 1920s by the first of the simpler blowbacks. These were in their turn succeeded by pistols based on the Tokarev and the Walther PP.

The standard 7·62mm 48.M Tokarev copy is essentially similar to its Soviet counterpart, but bears the Hungarian state emblem on the grips. In addition to guns made for the armed forces, Hungary has maintained a healthy export trade in recent years. With a few exceptions, the guns have been based on the Walther PP or the FN-Browning GP-35. They are often seen with the marks of Western European retailers, particularly German companies such as Hebsacker ('Hege-Waffen').

1913. Army M1929, or Pisztoly 29.M; Fémáru Feyver és Gépgyár Részvénytarsaság, Budapest, 1929–35. 7·65mm Auto or 9mm Short; 173mm overall, 100mm barrel, 720gm. Seven rounds. Adopted by the Hungarian army and patented in Frommer's name, this was a blowback derivation of the 'Stop' design.

1914. Army M1929, modified. ·22 LR rimfire. A target pistol adapted from the standard service pistol described above.

1915–1918. Army M1937, or Pisztoly 37.M; Fémáru Feyver és Gépgyár Részvénytarsaság, Budapest, 1937–44. 7·65mm Auto or 9mm Short; 173mm overall, 100mm barrel, 700–750gm. Seven rounds. A simplification of the 29.M pattern, developed to facilitate manufacture, this was a popular gun. Large numbers of the 9mm version were supplied to the German army during the Second World War ('Pistole Modell 37 [u]'), distinguished by their markings and an additional manual safety catch.

1919. Attila Pistole, or AP; Fémáru és Szerszamgépgyár NV, Budapest. 7·65mm Auto or 9mm Short; 177mm overall, 100mm barrel, 600gm. Eight rounds. This is a minor variant of the 48.M pistol described below, with a bright-finish alloy frame and a blued steel slide. A short-barrelled compact version is known as the 'AKP'.

1920. Eiler. 6·35mm Auto; 113mm overall, 58mm barrel. Six rounds. A blowback pocket pistol, similar to the Nalava.

1921. FÉG FP-9; Fémáru és Szerszamgépgyár NV, Budapest. 9mm Parabellum; 198mm overall, 118mm barrel, 950gm. Thirteen rounds. This near-facsimile of the FN-Browning GP-35 High Power—easily distinguished by markings and the ventilated slide rib—was specifically intended for the export market.

1922, 1923. FÉG FP-9R; Fémáru és Szerszamgépgyár NV, Budapest. 9mm Parabellum. Fourteen rounds. This was a modification of the standard FP-9

1910

1909

1911

1913

1912

1920

described above, with a double-action firing mechanism and a modified magazine.

1924. FÉG Model R; Fémáru és Szerszamgépyár NV, Budapest. 7·65mm Auto; 140mm overall, 72mm barrel, 450gm. Six rounds. A typical modern double-action pocket pistol.

1925. Frommer, 1901 pattern; Fegyvergyár Részvénytarsaság, Budapest. 8mm Roth. Operated by long recoil, this gun featured an integral magazine in the butt. Loading was accomplished with a special charger.

1926. Frommer, 1906 pattern; Fegyvergyár Részvénytarsaság, Budapest. 7·65mm Roth(-Sauer). This was similar to the 1901 version, but had a detachable magazine.

1927. Frommer, 1910 pattern; Fegyvergyár Részvénytarsaság, Budapest. 7·65mm Auto or 9mm Short; 187mm overall, 100mm barrel, 630gm. Eight rounds. Refinement of the components and smaller size distinguished this gun from the preceding version. Some examples had a grip safety.

1928. Frommer-'Baby'; Fegyvergyár Részvénytarsaság, Budapest. 7·65mm Auto or 9mm Short; 123mm overall, 55mm barrel, 500gm (7·65mm) or 440gm (9mm). Five 9mm or six 7·65mm rounds. This was very similar to the standard pattern described previously, excepting for size.

1929. Frommer-'Liliput'; Fémáru Feyver és Gépgyár Részvénytarsaság, Budapest, *c.*1928–40. 6·35mm Auto; 111mm overall, 53mm barrel, 320gm. Six rounds. This small-calibre blowback is basically a diminutive of the 29.M (fig. 1913).

1930, 1931. Frommer-'Stop'; Fegyvergyár Részvénytarsaság, Budapest, *c.*1912–20. 7·65mm or 9mm Short; 165mm overall, 98mm barrel, 620gm. Seven rounds. Adopted in 1912 to arm the Honved, or army reserve, this was locked by rotating the barrel; two studs at the muzzle engage lateral seats cut inside the slide. The return and barrel springs lie in a separate chamber in the top of the slide.

1932. Nalava. 6·35mm Auto. A small blowback pocket pistol based on the 1906-type FN-Browning.

1933. Tokagypt 58; Fémáru és Szerszamgépyár NV, Budapest. 9mm Parabellum; 195mm overall, 116mm barrel, 910gm. Eight rounds. This modification of the Tokarev was ordered for the Egyptian army. It had a manual safety catch and a one-piece wraparound grip, and was widely advertised commercially as the Firebird.

1934, 1935. Walam-48 or 48.M; Fémáru és Szerszamgépyár NV, Budapest. 7·65mm Auto or 9mm Short. Data for 9mm R-61. 157mm overall, 86mm barrel, 530gm. Six rounds. This was a copy of the Walther Polizei-Pistole, retaining the blued steel frame. Commercial examples were usually marked in English and lacked the national emblem moulded into the grips of the police-issue guns. The RK-69, R-61 (9mm Makarov, fig. 1935) and PA-63 versions were similar, but were smaller and had alloy frames.

Indonesia

1936. Pi.A; Fabrik Sendjata Ringan Pindad, Bandung. 9mm Parabellum; 197mm overall, 118mm barrel, 890gm. Thirteen rounds. This was a copy—apparently unlicensed—of the FN-Browning GP-35 High Power, many of which had previously been supplied by Fabrique Nationale.

Israel

The Beretta M1951 and M92 (figs. 1984, 1973) are the principal service pistols of the Israeli armed forces.

1937, 1938. Desert Eagle; Israeli Military Industries, Ramat ha-Sharon. ·357 Magnum, ·44 Magnum or ·50 AE; 260mm overall, 152mm barrel, 1500gm. Nine rounds. This pistol, introduced in 1983, was originally conceived as the 'Eagle' target pistol. It is not only gas-operated, but also chambers revolver-type Magnum cartridges. Barrels may measure 6in, 8in,

10in or even 14in (152–355mm). The Desert Eagle is a general-purpose variant of the target-pistol design, intended for self-defence.

1939–1941. Jericho 941; Israeli Military Industries, Ramat ha-Sharon. 9mm Parabellum ·40 S&W or ·41 AE; 207mm overall, 112mm barrel, 906gm. Ten (·41), eleven (·40) or fifteen (9mm) rounds. Derived from the popular Czech-made ČZ 75, this pistol offers an optional ambidexterous safety catch on the slide or ('F' patterns only) on the frame.

1942. Jericho 941-FS; Israeli Military Industries, Ramat ha-Sharon. 9mm Parabellum ·40 S&W or ·41 AE; 195mm overall, 100mm barrel, 900gm.

1943. Jericho 941-FB; Israeli Military Industries, Ramat ha-Sharon. 9mm Parabellum, ·40 S&W or ·41 AE; 184mm overall, 90mm barrel, 860gm.

1944. Sirkis. 9mm Parabellum; 176mm overall, 100mm barrel, 890gm. An Israeli-made but US-distributed double-action personal-defence pistol.

1945. Uzi; Israeli Military Industries, Ramat ha-Sharon. 9mm Parabellum; 240mm overall, 115mm barrel, 1890gm without the magazine (2·14kg laden). Twenty rounds. This was based on the well-known submachine gun, relying on pressing and similar manufacturing techniques. Thus it is angular, rough, bulky and heavy.

Italy

The Italians have a lengthy tradition of gunmaking, particularly in the area around Brescia, yet have made few contributions to handgun design. The success of the Beretta 92 series notwithstanding, almost all of the current generation of guns are derivatives of non-Italian patterns.

Pre-1945 designs

1946. Army M1906 and M1910 (Glisenti); Società Siderugica Glisenti (M1906), Metallurgica Bresciana gia Temprini (M1906, M1910). 7·65mm Parabellum or 9mm Glisenti. Data for M1910: 206mm overall, 94mm barrel, 900gm. Eight rounds. Based on a design by Bethel Revelli, offered for trials in 1902, this was the first automatic pistol adopted by the Italian Army. The barrel was allowed to recoil a short distance, disengaging a dropping block to release the breechbolt. The M1906 was made in small numbers, but the calibre was soon enlarged; it was apparently intended to copy the German 9mm Parabellum round, but this proved to be too powerful for the

comparatively weak breech-lock and the weaker '9mm Glisenti' pattern was substituted. The principal contractor for the later gun was Metallurgica Bresciana, which had apparently acquired the rights from Glisenti.

1947–1949. Beretta M1915; Pietro Beretta, Gardone Val Trompia. 7·65mm Auto or 9mm Glisenti. Data for 7·65mm version: 149mm overall, 84mm barrel, 568gm, eight rounds. Data for 9mm version: 170mm overall, 96mm barrel, 780gm, seven rounds. The first 9mm striker-fired blowback pistols were produced for military service during the First World War, soon proving effectual. They were distinguished by a safety lever on the rear of the frame, the second being shown in fig. 1948. An oval ejection port was cut in the top right side of the slide, the front part of which was cut away from the barrel. The front sight lay on the slide bridge and the grips were wooden. The 7·65mm diminutive was essentially similar, but lacked the distinctive safety catch.

1950. Beretta M1919; Pietro Beretta SpA, Gardone Val Trompia. 7·65mm Auto; 149mm overall, 84mm barrel, 560gm. Eight rounds. This was a streamlined form of the M1915, with stamped-metal grips and a modified safety catch.

1951. Beretta M1919 and M-318; Pietro Beretta SpA, Gardone Val Trompia. 6·35mm Auto. Data for M318: 114mm overall, 60mm barrel, 355gm. Eight rounds. This was simply a small-calibre version of the standard Beretta blowback pistol. Cosmetic alterations made during its long life have created several recognisable sub-varieties.

1955

1960

1959

1961

1958

1957

1952. Beretta M1923; Pietro Beretta SpA, Gardone Val Trompia. 9mm Glisenti; 162mm overall, 97mm barrel, 870gm. Eight rounds. This was little more than the 1919 pattern with an exposed hammer substituted for the concealed striker.

1953. Beretta M1931; Pietro Beretta SpA, Gardone Val Trompia. 7·65mm Auto; 158mm overall, 86mm barrel. Eight rounds. The gun shown was used by the Italian navy.

1954. Beretta M1934; Pietro Beretta SpA, Gardone Val Trompia. 9mm Short; 150mm overall, 86mm barrel, 730gm. Seven rounds. This was the official service pistol of the Italian Army during the Second World War. The 1935 pattern was similar, but chambered the 7·65mm Auto cartridge. Commercial variants in both 7·65mm and 9mm have been marketed since the Second World War as the 'Puma'.

1955. Brixia M1912; Metallurgica Bresciana gia Temprini SA, Brescia. 9mm Glisenti; 206mm overall, 94mm barrel. Eight rounds. This pistol was a strengthened refinement of the standard army M1910 or Glisenti pistol, lacking the original grip safety and detachable side-plate. It was apparently offered to the Italian army shortly before the First World War. Carrying the Roman name for Brescia, the Brixia was only ever made in small numbers.

1956. Galesi M1923; Industria Armi Galesi, Collobeato/Brescia. ·22 Short rimfire, ·22 LR rimfire or 6·35mm Auto; 121mm overall, 59mm barrel, 350gm. Seven rounds. The first of these blowback pocket pistols was made

prior to 1914, but the design did not gain popularity until after the end of the First World War. The earliest guns had automatic (grip), manual and magazine safety catches. Beginning with the 1920 pattern, however, the grip safety was discarded. Many versions of the basic design have been made, differing in barrel length, grips, sights, or the shape of individual parts. Guns will be seen with a selection of slide markings, including Industria Armi Galesi (IAG), Armi Galesi (AG) and Rino Galesi (RG).

1957, 1958. Galesi M1930; Industria Armi Galesi, Collobeato/Brescia. 6·35mm Auto or 7·65mm Auto. Data for 6·35mm version: 110mm overall, 310gm, six rounds.

1959, 1960. Sosso; Guilio Sosso, Turin. 9mm Parabellum. Data for Model II: 227mm overall, 145mm barrel, 990gm, twenty rounds. The original Sosso Model I appeared in 1934, but was replaced by the Model II of 1938–40; production was meagre. Sosso pistols were operated by recoil and locked by a swinging lever beneath the barrel. A distinguishing feature is provided by the curved magazine, which contains an endless metal-link band which can rotate around two longitudinal pins inside the magazine body. The back sight was generally a fixed notch, though some guns had adjustable tangent-leaf sights graduated to 400 metres.

1961. Sosso-FNA; Fabbrica Nazionale d'Armi, Brescia. 9mm Parabellum; 242mm overall, 150mm barrel, 1150gm. Twenty rounds. This was produced in small numbers during the Second World War.

Post-1945 designs

1962. Benelli M76 DA or B-76 DA; Benelli Armi SpA, Urbino. 9mm Parabellum; 205mm overall, 108mm barrel, 965gm. Eight rounds. This pistol was developed in the late 1970s for the US market, but has not been made in large numbers. It embodies a form of delayed blowback.

1963, 1964. BDA-380; Pietro Beretta SpA, Gardone Val Trompia. 7·65mm Auto or 9mm Short; 170mm overall, 640gm. Twelve 9mm or thirteen 7·65mm rounds. These guns were made in Italy for FN Herstal of Belgium, but will often be found with the marks of the Browning Arms Company of Morgan, Utah.

1965. Beretta M-20; Pietro Beretta SpA, Gardone Val Trompia. 6·35mm Auto; 118mm overall, 60mm barrel. Seven rounds. This is similar to the M-950B, but has a double-action trigger system. The M-21A (·22 LR rimfire or 6·35mm Auto) is comparable, but has smooth-surface grips with 'PB' in an oval. The rimfire version has an eight-round magazine.

1966. Beretta M-70; Pietro Beretta SpA, Gardone Val Trompia. 7·65mm Auto; 165mm overall, 90mm barrel, 490gm. Eight rounds. Similar structurally to the M1934, this presents a much more modern appearance. Small-calibre variants are known as M-71, M-72, M-73 and M-74.

1967. Beretta M-70S; Pietro Beretta SpA, Gardone Val Trompia. 9mm Short; 165mm overall, 90mm barrel, 670gm. Seven rounds. This is a minor variant of the M-70 with a steel frame instead of alloy.

1968. Beretta M-70T; Pietro Beretta SpA, Gardone Val Trompia. 7·65mm Auto; 240mm overall, 152mm barrel, 540gm. Nine rounds. The M-101 is a ·22 rimfire version with a ten-round magazine.

1969. Beretta M-84; Pietro Beretta SpA, Gardone Val Trompia. 9mm Short; 172mm overall, 97mm barrel, 640gm. Thirteen hounds. This is an effectual blowback personal-defence pistol with a double-action firing mechanism, a double-column magazine and an ambidexterous safety catch.

The M-81 is similar, but chambered for the 7·65mm Auto cartridge; M-81BB (7·65mm) and M-84BB (9mm S) have an additional magazine safety; M-82BB (7·65mm), M-85BB (9mm S) and M-87BB (·22 LR) have loaded-chamber indicators. The 7·65mm pistols have twelve-round magazines.

1970. Beretta M-85F; Pietro Beretta SpA, Gardone Val Trompia. 9mm Short; 97mm barrel, 620gm. Eight rounds. This is similar to the Model 84 (fig. 1969) but the recurved trigger guard facilitates a two-hand grip.

1971. Beretta M-86; Pietro Beretta SpA, Gardone Val Trompia. 9mm Short; 185mm overall, 111mm barrel, 660gm. Eight rounds. This is much the same as the preceding guns, but the barrel pivots on a hinge to give access to the chamber.

1972. Beretta M-90; Pietro Beretta SpA, Rome. 7·65mm Auto; 168mm overall, 92mm barrel, 550gm. Eight rounds. A blowback personal-defence pistol with a double-action trigger system.

1973. Beretta M-92; Pietro Beretta SpA, Gardone Val Trompia. 9mm Parabellum; 217mm overall, 125mm barrel, 950gm. Fifteen rounds. This is basically a modernised version of the M1951 (fig. 1984), sharing recoil operation and a breech lock adapted from that of the Walther P.38. The double-action firing system and the staggered-column magazine were new,

whilst the safety catch lay on the left side of the frame. The magazine catch appeared in the lower part of the grip, the stocks generally being wooden.

1974. Beretta M-92S; Pietro Beretta SpA, Gardone Val Trompia. 9mm Parabellum; 217mm overall, 125mm barrel, 950gm. Fifteen rounds. This is a version of the M-92 with an additional safety catch on the left side of the slide. The M-92SB has the catch on both sides.

1975. Beretta M-92SB-C; Pietro Beretta SpA, Gardone Val Trompia. 9mm Parabellum; 195mm overall, 105mm barrel. Fourteen rounds. A shortened 'Compact' version of the M-92; M-92SB-C Tipo M is similar, but has an eight-round single-column magazine.

1976. Beretta M-92F; Pietro Beretta SpA, Gardone Val Trompia. 9mm Parabellum; 217mm overall, 125mm barrel. Fifteen rounds. Developed to satisfy the demands of the armed forces of the USA, this features a broader trigger than normal, a recurved trigger guard, matted finish, and plastic grips. The M-92F-C is a shortened version. Model 92-D is basically an M-92F with its hammer recessed into the slide. It also lacks a safety catch.

Pistols have also been chambered for the 7·65mm Parabellum cartridge. The M-98 and M-98F correspond with the M-92 and M-92F respectively, whilst the M-99 is similar to the M-92SB-C.

1977, 1978. Beretta M-949, or Cougar; Pietro Beretta SpA, Gardone Val Trompia. 9mm Short; 150mm overall, 86mm barrel. Seven rounds. This is a modernised version of the M1934 (q.v.). The ·22 LR 'Plinker' is similar but

has an alloy frame, and the M·948 (also ·22) has an elongated barrel.

1979. Beretta M·950; Pietro Beretta SpA, Gardone Val Trompia. 6·35mm Auto; 118mm overall, 60mm barrel, 285gm. Seven rounds. This blowback pocket pistol incorporates an exposed hammer, but lacks an ejector. Spent cases are projected from the chamber by residual gas pressure, a method pioneered by Theodor Bergmann in the 1890s. To unload the Beretta, therefore, the barrel must be tipped up in the manner of many pre-1914 Pieper pistols. The externally similar M·950B, introduced in the 1970s, embodied a conventional ejector.

1980. Beretta M·950BS; Pietro Beretta SpA, Gardone Val Trompia. ·22 LR rimfire or ·25 Auto; 280gm. Six ·25 or eight ·22 rounds.

1981. Beretta M·951, or Jetfire; Pietro Beretta SpA, Gardone Val Trompia. ·22 LR rimfire; 158mm overall, 102mm barrel. This was similar to the M·950BS, but has a longer barrel. The M-2 and M-4 had barrels of 66mm and 102mm respectively. Excepting for chambering, the M·951 Minx (·22 Short rimfire) was similar to the M·951.

1982, 1983. Beretta M1934, or Bantam; Pietro Beretta SpA, Gardone Val Trompia. 6·35mm Auto; 116mm overall, 60mm barrel, 370gm. Eight rounds. Engraved versions were designated M-420 (standard) or M-421 (deluxe). The M-418 or Panther was a later modification.

1984, 1985. Beretta M1951 or Brigadier; Pietro Beretta SpA, Gardone Val Trompia. 9mm Parabellum; 210mm overall, 114mm barrel, 930gm. Eight rounds. Developed shortly after the end of the Second World War, incorporating a pivoting locking block inspired by that of the Walther P.38, this was adopted by the Italian army after initial teething troubles had been overcome. It has also served the forces of Egypt and Israel. The earliest guns had a short slide from which a short section of muzzle protruded.

1986. Bernardelli M-60; Vincenzo Bernardelli & Co. SNC, Gardone Val Trompia. ·22 LR rimfire or 7·65mm Auto; 165mm overall, 89mm barrel, 570gm (alloy frame) or 610gm (steel frame).

1987. Bernardelli M-68; Vincenzo Bernadelli & Co. SNC, Gardone Val Trompia. 6·35mm Auto; 104mm overall, 55mm barrel, 255gm. Five 6·35mm or eight ·22 rounds.

1988. Bernardelli M-68; Vincenzo Bernardelli & Co. SNC, Gardone Val Trompia. ·22 Short; 104mm overall, 55mm barrel. Six rounds.

1989. Bernardelli USA model (or M-80); Vincenzo Bernadelli & Co. SNC, Gardone Val Trompia. ·22 LR rimfire, 7·65mm Auto or 9mm Short; 165mm overall, 89mm barrel. This is a post-1969 version of the M-60, made specifically for the US market with a safety catch on the slide.

1990. Bernardelli P-018; Vincenzo Bernardelli & Co. SNC, Gardone Val Trompia. 9mm Parabellum; 213mm overall, 122mm barrel, 998gm. Fifteen rounds. This recoil-operated military-style pistol is locked by a tipping-barrel system, has a double-action firing mechanism, and utilises a high capacity staggered-column magazine.

1991. Bernardelli P-018 Compact; Vincenzo Bernardelli & Co. SNC, Gardone Val Trompia. 9mm Parabellum; 190mm overall, 102mm barrel, 950gm. Fourteen rounds. A shortened version of the previous gun.

1992, 1993. Bernardelli PA ('Pistola automatica'); Vincenzo Bernardelli & Co. SNC, Gardone Val Trompia, c.1947–61. 7·65mm Auto or 9mm Short. Data for the standard model: 158mm overall, 89mm barrel, 725gm, seven 9mm or eight 7·65mm rounds. The guns were also made with a 150, 200 or 250mm barrel with the front sight on the slide-bridge. An elongated seventeen-round magazine may also be encountered. Fig. 1993 shows a short-lived 'Model UB' variant (178mm overall) chambered for 9mm Browning Long or 9mm Parabellum cartridges.

1994. Bernardelli PA 'Baby'; Vincenzo Bernardelli & Co. SNC, Gardone Val Trompia, 1949-62. ·22 Long rimfire; 104mm overall, 55mm barrel, 262gm. Six rounds.

1995–1998. Galesi Model 6; Industria Armi Galesi, Collobeato/Brescia. 6·35mm Auto or 7·65mm Auto. Data for 6·35mm version: 121mm overall,

1988

1991 1990

1989

1994

1992 1993

1995

1996

1997

59mm barrel, 350gm, seven rounds. Data for 7·65mm version: 155mm overall, 85mm barrel, eight rounds.

1999. Galesi Model 9. 6·35mm Auto. The M503 is very similar.

2000. Galesi Model 506. 6·35mm Auto; 130mm overall, 72mm barrel, 450gm. Eight rounds. The M512 is the same as Model 6 (fig. 1995), excepting that it has 500-series grips.

2001. Galesi Model 515. 7·65mm Auto.

1998

2001

1999

2000

2002. GT-21 Baby; Giuseppe Tanfoglio, Gardone Val Trompia. 9x21mm; 175mm overall, 90mm barrel, 850gm. Twelve rounds. A reduced-scale version of the gun drawn in fig. 2026.

2003. GT-21 Combat; Giuseppe Tanfoglio, Gardone Val Trompia. 9 × 21mm; 210mm overall, 120mm barrel, 1015gm. Fifteen rounds. Holes in the top surface of the muzzle coincide with holes in the top of the slide, acting as a compensator to keep the muzzle down during the firing cycle. The GT-41 is similar, but chambers ·41 AE cartridges.

2004, 2005. GT-25. Giuseppe Tanfoglio. 6·35mm Auto; 121mm overall, 63mm barrel, 330gm. Seven rounds. Tanfoglio makes a range of Beretta-type blowbacks, many of which have been sold (by FIE, Inc.) as 'Titans' in North America. The gun shown in fig. 2005 has a frame and barrel of oxidised steel, whilst the slide is gold-finished and the grips are brown plastic. It was sold in the USA as the 'Gold Titan'.

2006. GT-32 and GT-380; Giuseppe Tanfoglio, Gardone Val Trompia. ·22 LR rimfire, 7·65mm Auto or 9mm Short; 172mm overall, 98mm barrel, 730gm. Six to ten rounds, depending on chambering. These pistols are sold in the USA as 'Titan'.

2007, 2008. GT-32 XEB and GT-380 XEB; Giuseppe Tanfoglio, Gardone Val Trompia. 7·65mm Auto or 9mm Short; 186mm overall, 98mm barrel. Eleven 9mm or twelve 7·65mm rounds. Also known as the Super Titan.

2009. GT-32 Targa and GT-380 Targa; Giuseppe Tanfoglio, Gardone Val Trompia. 7·65mm Auto or 9mm Auto; 98mm barrel, 735gm, Seven 9mm or eight 7·65mm rounds. Distrbuted in the USA by FIE of Hialeah, Florida, and often so marked.

2010. GT-38P; Giuseppe Tanfoglio, Gardone Val Trompia. 9mm Short (·380 Auto); 80mm barrel, 600gm. Made for distribution by FIE in the USA.

2011, 2012. GT-90 (also known as Tanarmi TA-90); Giuseppe Tanfoglio, Gardone Val Trompia. 9mm Parabellum; 210mm overall, 120mm barrel,

1015gm. Fifteen rounds. This is a copy of the Czech ČZ 75. The TA-90 Baby (fig. 2012) is only 175mm overall, has a 90mm barrel and weighs 850gm. Its magazine contains twelve rounds. The ST-30 and TA-18 are similar, but chamber 9mm Police (9 × 18mm) and 7·65mm Parabellum ammunition respectively.

2013. GT-380 HE Targa; Giuseppe Tanfoglio, Gardone Val Trompia. 9mm Short; 98mm barrel, 800gm. Eleven rounds. Distributed in the USA prior to 1991 by FIE of Hialeah, Florida.

2014. GT-380 SSP; Giuseppe Tanfoglio, Gardone Val Trompia. 9mm Short. Otherwise similar to the GT-380, this is made of stainless steel and is often encountered with the marks of the pre-1991 US distributor, FIE, Inc.

2015. Hijo Militar; Rigarmi–Rino Galesi. ·22 LR rimfire or 7·65mm Auto; 160mm overall.

2016. Lercker. 6·35mm Auto; 184mm overall, 102mm barrel, 930gm. Twenty rounds. Introduced shortly after the end of the Second World War, this selective-fire design was soon banned by the authorities as it was essentially a pocketable submachine-gun. Even its first shot was fired from an open breech.

2017, 2018. RGP-80 (Fig. 2017) and RGP-81 (Fig. 2018); Armi Renato Gamba, Gardone Val Trompia. 7·65mm Auto, 9mm Short or 9mm Police (9 × 18mm). Data for RGP-80: 160mm overall, 85mm barrel, thirteen 9mm Police or fourteen 7·65mm/9mm Short rounds. Introduced in the early 1980s, these were based on the Mauser HSc. The principal differences were external styling and the use of staggered-column magazines.

2019, 2020. Rigarmi; Rino Galesi. 6·35mm Auto. This small-calibre blowback is distinguished by the sizeable ejection port (fig. 2020).

2021. Sata; Sabatti & Tafaglio company. 6·35mm Auto; 116mm overall, 64mm barrel. Eight rounds. Introduced in 1954.

2022. Ultra; Giuseppe Tanfoglio, Gardone Val Trompia. ·41 AE. A modified

version of the standard GT-90 series, intended for practical pistol shooting.

2023. Zoli pistols; A. Zoli & Co., Gardone Val Trompia. 6·35mm Auto. A variant of the Sata (fig. 2021).

Japan

2024. Hamada; Japan Gun Company, Tokyo, 1941–4. 7·65mm Auto; 160mm overall, 88mm barrel, 680gm. Nine rounds. The original Hamada pistol, retrospectively designated 'Type 1', was basically a copy of the 1910-type blowback Browning, a few thousand being made for the Japanese forces. A greatly modified version was developed for the standard service-pistol cartridge in 1942 by a team led by Major Yato, whose name is now often attached to this 8mm Type 2 pistol. Production in Notobe in 1944–5 was meagre.

2025. Hino; Komuro Gun Factory, Tokyo, c.1908–11. 7·65mm Auto; 237mm overall, 194mm barrel, 815gm. Eight rounds. Patented by Kumaso Hino and Tomojiro Komuro in 1903, this pistol featured blow-forward operation, projecting the barrel away from the standing breech when the gun was fired. It was not successful and only a few hundred were made.

2026. Nambu Type, Model A; Imperial artillery arsenal, Koishikawa, Tokyo (c.1903–23), and the Tokyo Gas & Electric Light Company (c.1910–27). 8mm; 229mm overall, 117mm barrel, 870gm. Eight rounds. Developed in 1899–1902, this gun was placed in limited production in 1903—for sale to army officers—and was formally adopted by the Japanese navy in 1909. Work continued until the 1920s. It was recoil operated, relying on short barrel travel, and was locked with a pivoting block. An automatic safety was set into the front grip-strap, a tangent-leaf back sight was fitted on top of the breech, and the return spring was placed in a special housing offset on the left side of the receiver.

2027, 2028. Nambu Type, Model B; Imperial artillery arsenal, Koishikawa, Tokyo (c.1909–23), and the Tokyo Gas & Electric Light Company (c.1924–7). 7mm; 170mm overall, 83mm barrel, 580gm. Seven rounds. Made in prototype form as early as 1903, this diminutive Type A was apparently destined for senior officers as a badge of rank. Sales were comparatively poor. It was widely known as the 'Baby', its larger brother being 'Papa'.

2029. New Nambu Model 57; Shin Chuo Kogyo, Tokyo. 9mm Parabellum; 200mm overall, 116mm barrel, 960gm. Eight rounds. This is based on the M1911A1 Colt-Browning.

2030. New Nambu Model 57A; Shin Chuo Kogyo, Tokyo. 9mm Parabellum; 198mm overall, 118mm barrel, 890gm. Eight rounds. Another copy of the Colt M1911A1.

2031. New Nambu Model 57B; Shin Chuo Kogyo, Tokyo. 7·65mm Auto; 160mm overall, 90mm barrel, 600gm. Eight rounds. This is a conventional exposed-hammer blowback general-purpose pistol.

2032–2035. Taisho 14th Year Type, 1925; Imperial arsenals in Koishikawa (Tokyo), Atsuta (Nagoya) and Kokura, plus the Nambu Rifle Manufacturing Company (later Chuo Kogyo), Tokyo. 8mm; 231mm overall, 117mm barrel, 900gm. Eight rounds. This was a refinement of the Nambu (fig. 2026) undertaken in Koishikawa arsenal in 1922–4. The twin return springs were placed symmetrically, one on each side of the frame.

A modified 14th Year Type is shown in fig. 2034. The enlarged trigger guard allowed the pistol to be operated with a gloved hand, and an additional leaf spring in the front grip-strap halped to retain the magazine in place. The breechbolt-nut on guns made in 1944–5 may be cylindrical, lacking the knurling on earlier examples. Shortened guns are also known, the barrel usually being cut to about 65mm.

2036–2038. Type 94; Nambu Rifle Manufacturing Company (later Chuo Kogyo), Tokyo. 8mm; 186mm overall, 97mm barrel, 783gm. Six rounds. Introduced in 1934, this compact (if quirky) pistol was apparently designed by Kijiro Nambu in 1929–32 for airmen and tank crews. The breech, controlled by short barrel recoil, is locked by a vertically-moving block. The quality of the pistols produced during the Second World War declined appreciably, the last examples (e.g., fig. 2038) being very crude.

Korea

NORTH (PEOPLE'S DEMOCRATIC REPUBLIC)
The standard service pistols are indigenous variants of the Soviet Tokarev—Type 51 and Type 54, with coarse and fine slide-retraction grooves respectively.

2039. Type 68; state factories. 7·62mm Tokarev; 195mm overall, 108mm barrel, 795gm. Eight rounds. A somewhat modified Tokarev.

2040. Type 70 or M1970; state factories. 7·65mm Auto. A single-action blowback, modelled externally on the Tokarev.

2038

2037   2036

2039

2040

Korea

SOUTH (REPUBLIC OF)

The US Colt M1911A1 remains the principal service pistol of the South Korean armed forces.

2041. A Colt-Browning M1911A1 copy; ·45 ACP.

2042. A copy of the Colt-Browning pocket model of 1903; 7·65mm Auto.

Mexico

2043. Corla; Fábrica de Armas Zaragoza. ·22 LR rimfire; 162mm overall, 89mm barrel. This simple blowback is modelled externally on the M1911A1 Colt-Browning, though greatly reduced in scale.

2044. Obregon; Fabrica Nacional de Armas, Mexico City. ·45 ACP; 216mm overall, 125mm barrel, 1060gm. Seven rounds. Patented by Alejandro Obregon in 1933–5, this also resembles the 1911 type of Colt-Browning externally—but operates quite differently, relying on recoil to rotate the barrel until it releases the slide. The Obregon served the Mexican army in small numbers.

2045. Trejo Model 3; Armas Trejo SA, Zacatlan. 9mm Short; 170mm overall. Eight rounds.

2046. Trejo Tipo Rafaga; Armas Trejo SA, Zacatlan. ·22 LR rimfire; 165mm overall. A blowback modelled on the Colt-Browning, this was capable of firing automatically when the selector was set accordingly.

2047. Zaragoza; Fábrica de Armas Zaragoza. ·22 LR rimfire; 190mm overall, 115mm barrel, 700gm. Ten rounds. Another of the many blowback sporting pistols modelled on the Colt M1911A1.

Norway

2048. Army M1914; Kongsberg Våpenfabrik. 11·25mm (·45 ACP); 216mm overall, 128mm barrel, 1100gm. Seven rounds. This is a licence-built variant of the Colt M1911, previous guns being purchased from the USA and issued as the 'M/1912'.

Persia

2049. Model 1317; Carl Walther Waffenfabrik, Zella-Mehlis. 9mm Short; 170mm overall, 98mm barrel. Seven rounds. These variations of the Walther Polizei-Pistole were distinguished by Arabic marks on the slide; Hegira year 1317 corresponds to 1939.

Poland

2050. P-64; Zaklady Metalowe 'Lucznik', Radom. 9mm Makarov; 160mm overall, 87mm barrel, 620gm. Six rounds. this pistol was initially designated 'Czak'—the initial letters of the surnames of its designers, Polish army officers Czepukaitis, Zymni, Adamczyk and Koczmarski—but was subsequently renamed '9mm pistol, model of 1964' (P-64). It is a typical modern blowback with a double-action firing mechanism.

2051. P-83; Zaklady Metalowe 'Lucznik', Radom. 9mm Makarov; 160mm overall, 90mm barrel. Eight rounds. A modernised version of the P-64 described previously.

2052. Smok; Fabryka Nakulski, Gniezno. 6·35mm Auto; 102mm overall, 52mm barrel. Six rounds. A small pocket pistol similar to Walther Model 9.

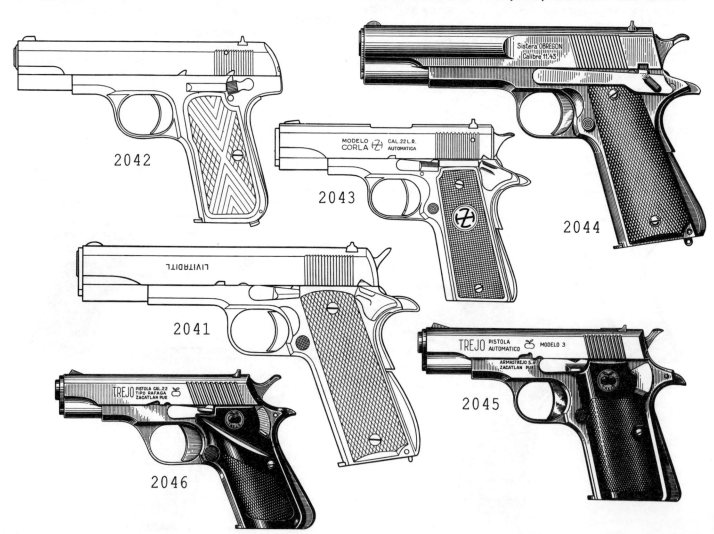

2053, 2054. VIS-35; Fabryka Broni, Radom. 9mm Parabellum; 208mm overall, 120mm barrel, 1030gm. Eight rounds. This variant of the Colt-Browning breech-locking system is credited to Wilniewczyc and Skrzypinski, but is sometimes called 'Radom' owing to the place of manufacture. A special lever on the left side of the slide can be used to drop the hammer even if a live round was chambered. The back strap of the grip is slotted to receive a stock. Fig. 2054 shows a gun made during the German occupation of Poland (1939–45), being issued to the Wehrmacht as the 'Pistole 35 (p)'. These guns were often crudely made, quite unlike the high-quality pre-war Polish products. Wartime guns may have differing grips, and often lack the stock-slot or the stripping catch.

South Africa

2055. Mamba; apparently made by Viper Manufacturing Company for the Sandock-Austral Small Arms Company, Boksburg, c.1977–82. 9mm Parabellum. Data for Model I: 220mm overall, 125mm barrel, 1070gm. Fourteen rounds. This military-style pistol, made entirely of stainless steel, had a double-action trigger system and a staggered-column magazine.

2056. PAF Junior; State arms factory, Pretoria. 6·35mm Auto; 112mm overall, 53mm barrel, 375gm. Six rounds. Made in the 1950s, this small pocket pistol is similar to the 1906-type FN-Browning. A later version lacked separate sights, a simple channel in the slide sufficing.

Spain

Prior to 1914, the long-established Spanish gunmaking industry was renowned chiefly for legions of copies—principally Colt and Smith & Wesson-type revolvers—which were distinguished, more often than not, by poor quality. The advent of the FN-Browning pocket automatic in 1906 was a godsend to the many small manufacturers in the Eibar district, the first of hundreds of differing copies being made prior to 1914. Comparatively little development work was undertaken in Spain throughout this period, though the Charola y Anitua pistol of 1897 was a pioneering semi-automatic, and the Jo-Lo-Ar had, if nothing else, the merits of a one-hand cocking mechanism.

The abilities of the Spanish gunmaking fraternity were tested to the limit during the First World War, when hundreds of thousands of handguns were purchased by France and Italy, whose own industries proved incapable of meeting demand. Even the British purchased Smith & Wesson-style ·455 revolvers from Garate, Anitua y Cia and Trocaola, Aranzabal y Cia.

This process established the best-known of the Spanish gunmakers internationally. In addition to the Browning-type and 'Ruby' blowbacks, therefore, copies of the Colt-Browning, Mauser C/96 and other military-style guns were being marketed by the 1920s. Success was greatly facilitated by the Treaty of Versailles, which effectively hamstrung the German firearms industry.

The Civil War proved a disaster for the gunmakers, few of whom were allowed to recommence work after the hostilities ceased in 1939. Since then, however, Gabilondo ('Llama' brand), Echeverria ('Star') and Unceta ('Astra') have established themselves amongst the world's leading manufacturers, and the reputation of Spanish firearms, once so low, has been largely rehabilitated.

Pre-Civil War patterns

2057. Alkar; Fábrica de Armas Alkartasuna SA, Eibar. 7·65mm Auto; 154mm overall, 80mm barrel. Seven rounds. This blowback design superficially resembles the 1910-pattern FN-Browning, though the return spring lies under the barrel instead of around it, and the manual safety will be found on the left side of the frame above the trigger.

2058. Astra Model 300; Esperanza y Compañía (to 1926) and Unceta y Compañía, Guernica, 1922–47. 7·65mm Auto or 9mm Short; 159mm overall, 99mm barrel, 700gm. Six 9mm or seven 7·65mm rounds. This blowback pistol, similar in some respects to the 1910-type FN-Browning, has the return spring concentric with the barrel and a detachable muzzle collar. The barrel is held in the frame by a sliding catch, whilst an automatic safety is set into the back strap of the grip.

2059. Astra Model 400; Esperanza y Compañía (to 1926) and Unceta y Compañía, Guernica, 1921–46. 9mm Largo (9mm Bergmann-Bayard); 226mm overall, 150mm barrel, 992gm. Eight rounds. Adapted from the Campo-Giro, this military-style blowback pistol relies on the strength of the return spring and the weight of the recoiling parts to slow the opening of the breech until chamber pressure has dropped sufficiently.

2060. Astra Model 900; Unceta y Compañia, Guernica, 1927–36. 7·63mm Mauser; 296mm overall, 140mm barrel, 1300gm. Ten rounds. Derived from the Mauser C/96, these were among the best of the Spanish copies. The Astra differs from its German prototype only in minor respects.

2061. Astra Model 901; Unceta y Compañia, Guernica, 1928–36. 7·63mm Mauser; 316mm overall, 160mm barrel, 1380gm. Twenty rounds. Adapted from the Astra 900 described previously, this had a fire-selector on the side of the frame, allowing automatic fire when necessary.

2062. Astra Model 902; Unceta y Compañia, Guernica, 1928–36. 7·63mm Mauser; 316mm overall, 160mm barel. Ten or twenty rounds. An improved version of the Astra 901, this featured a detachable magazine.

2063. Astra Model 903; Unceta y Compañia, Guernica, 1932–6. 7·63mm Mauser; 316mm overall, 160mm barrel. Ten or twenty rounds. Realising that pistols were difficult to control when firing automatically, Unceta modified the basic Astra 902 to accept a rate-reducer mechanism in the grip.

Though the rate of fire was reduced, it was still too high to promote effectual shooting.

2064. Astra Model 3000; Unceta y Compañia, Guernica, c.1947–56. ·22 LR rimfire, 7·65mm Auto or 9mm Short; 159mm overall, 100mm barrel, 700gm. The Model 3003 was similar, but decoratively etched.

2065. Azul; Eulogio Arostegui, Eibar. 6·35mm Auto. This was a typical exposed-hammer pocket pistol.

2066. Azul MM31; made by Beistegui Hermanos for Eulogio Arostegui, Eibar, 1931–8. 7·63mm Mauser; 296mm overall, 140mm barrel. Ten rounds. A copy of the Mauser pistol, with a selector for single-shot or automatic fire.

2067. Bernedo; Victor Bernedo y Compañia, Eibar. 6·35mm Auto. A pocket pistol exhibiting some original design features.

2068, 2069. Boltun; Francisco Arizmendi, Eibar. 6·35mm Auto or 7·65mm Auto. Pocket pistols based on the Belgian Piepers.

2070. Bulwark; Beistegui Hermanos, Eibar. 6·35mm Auto. A typically Mannlicher-type pocket pistol.

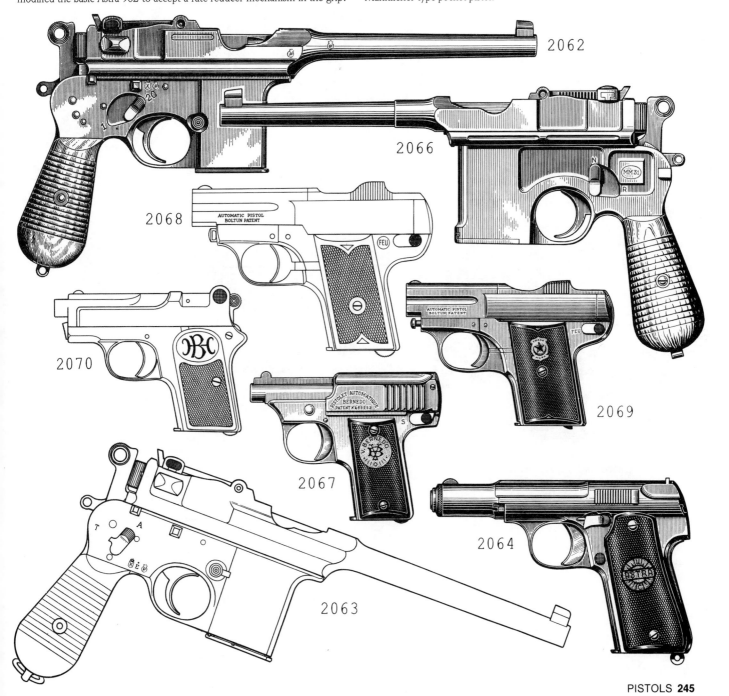

2071, 2072. Campo Giro, M1913 and M1913/16; Esperanza y Unceta, Guernica. 9mm Largo (9mm Bergmann-Bayard); 237mm overall, 165mm barrel, 950gm. Seven rounds. Designed by Venancio López de Ceballos y Aguirre, Count of Campo-Giro, the first of these pistols was tested by the Spanish army in 1904. The 1912 pattern was the first to be issued, with a locking wedge beneath the barrel, but teething troubles led to the substitution of a simplied blowback M1913. The detachable stock was made of thick wire. This was replaced by the M1913/16, with the magazine catch on the butt instead of under the back of the trigger guard. The safety catch was altered so that it could be applied with the hammer cocked, and the grips were held with two bolts instead of one. The Campo-Giro was superseded by the Astra M1921 (Astra 400).

2073, 2074. Charola y Anitua; made by Anitua, Charola y Compañia of Eibar, and then possibly by Garate, Anitua y Compañia, c.1897–1905. 5mm Charola y Anitua (5mm Clément); 205mm overall, 84mm barrel, 570gm. Six rounds. This, the earliest Spanish semi-automatic pistol—indeed, one of the first to be marketed commercially anywhere—was operated by short barrel-recoil and loaded from a charger. A few Spanish-made guns chambered a 7mm cartridge, whilst a few Belgian copies were made for the 7·65mm Auto cartridge.

2075, 2076. Colonial; Fabrique d'Armes de Grande Précision, Eibar. 7·65mm Auto; 175mm overall, 101mm barrel, 879gm. Nine rounds. This blowback is similar to the Alkar (q.v.), but somewhat larger.

2077. Continental; made for Tómas de Urizar of Barcelona. 6·35mm Auto. An exposed-hammer blowback pocket pistol.

2078. Eley M1912; maker unknown. 6·35mm Auto.

2079, 2080. Express; made for Tómas de Urizar of Barcelona. 6·35mm Auto or 7·65mm Auto. An assortment of guns bearing this name was made in the 1920s and 1930s. Most of them were imitations of the 1906-type FN-Browning, described in the relevant chapter below.

2081, 2082. Express; made for Tómas de Urizar of Barcelona. 6·35mm Auto; 113mm overall, 50mm barrel, 420gm. Eight rounds. The front sight of the pistol shown in fig. 2082 doubles as a loaded-chamber indicator.

2083. Fiel; Erquiaga, Muguruzu y Compañia, Eibar. 6·35mm Auto; 116mm overall, 41mm barrel, 375gm. Eight rounds.

2084, 2085. Jo-Lo-Ar; Hijos de Calixto Arrizabalaga, Eibar. 7·65mm Auto or 9mm Short. Data for 7·65mm version: 166mm overall, 97mm barrel, nine rounds. Data for 9mm version: 226mm overall, 155mm barrel, nine rounds. The barrel of the Jo-Lo-Ar tips downwards, similar to the Pieper or Steyr pistols, and a special one-hand cocking lever is pivoted on the right side of the frame. Unusually for an automatic pistol, a sheathed trigger is used.

2086. La Lira; Garate, Anitua y Compañia, Eibar, c.1910–14. 7·65mm Auto; 205mm overall, 125mm barrel. Alternatively marketed as the Triumph, this is basically a copy of the 1905-pattern Mannlicher pistol with a detachable magazine.

2087. Llama Models 1 and 2; Gabilondo y Compañia, Elgoeibar, introduced in 1933. 7·65mm Auto (Model 1) or 9mm Short (Model 2); 160mm overall, 94mm barrel. Eight 9mm or nine 7·65mm rounds. These are blowback pistols, lacking automatic safeties.

The Llama Model 4, introduced in 1931, is a locked-breech Colt-Browning copy chambered for the 9mm Largo (9mm Bergmann-Bayard) cartridge. It was claimed to have a 'tolerant chamber', accepting several differing long-case 9mm cartridges—e.g., 9mm Parabellum or 9mm Steyr. Variants chambering the 7·65mm Parabellum and ·45 ACP rounds have also been offered. The Model 5 is an export version of Model 4, whilst the Model 7 is identical excepting for chambering (·38 Super).

The 9mm Parabellum Llama Model 11 Special ('Especial'), made by Gabilondo y Compañia in 1936–54, is identical with the Mugica pistol shown in fig. 2094.

2088. Longines; Cooperativa Obrera, Eibar. 7·65mm Auto; 177mm overall, 101mm barel. Nine rounds. A near-facsimile of the Alkar and Colonial pistols.

2089. Looking-Glass; Acha Hermanos, Eibar. 6·35mm Auto. The elevating front sight doubles as a loaded-chamber indicator.

2090–2092. Martian; Martin Bascaran, Eibar. 6·35mm Auto or 7·65mm Auto. Data for 6·35mm version (fig. 2090): 112mm overall, 50mm barrel,

2097

2099

PATENT "RUBY" CAL.45

"ROYAL"
PATENT 16561

2094

"MUGICA"-EIBAR (SPAIN)
CAL.9% PARABELLUM

2093

MANUFACTURE OF FIRE ARMS
CAL. 6.35
FIRE

2100

SEAM PATENT № 11.627
Pocket Model Cal. 6.35

2095

2101

SHARP-SHOOTER PATENT № 68027
EIBAR-1924
CAL 6⅓
PV
NORMAL

2098

2102

SHARP-SHOOTER PATENT № 68027

2096

Phoenix Arms Patent
PHOENIX

2103

AUTOMATIC PISTOL STAR PATENT

«STAR»
CAL 6⅓

2104

315gm, six rounds. Data for 7·65mm version (fig. 2092): 144mm overall, 74mm barrel, 600gm, seven rounds. A pocket pistol with characteristic flutes in the slide.

2093. Mondial; Gaspar Arizaga, Eibar. 6·35mm Auto; 120mm overall, 62mm barrel, 340gm. Seven rounds. This is essentially similar to the US Savage pistol.

2094. Mugica; José Mugica. 9mm Parabellum; 193mm overall, 122mm barrel, 900gm. Eight rounds. Based on the 1911-pattern Colt-Browning, this was a standard Llama-brand gun made by Gabilondo y Compañia of Elgoeibar.

2095. Orbea y Compañia, Eibar. 6·35mm Auto; 112mm overall, 50mm barrel. Six rounds.

2096. Phoenix; made for Tómas de Urizar of Barcelona. 6·35mm Auto; 118mm overall, 58mm barrel, 327gm. Six rounds. This particular brand of gun was apparently quite popular in the USA.

2097, 2098. Royal; Beistegui Hermanos y Compañia, Eibar (often mistakenly attributed to Zulaica y Compañia, which acted as distributor). 7·63mm Mauser; 320mm or 340mm overall, 160mm or 180mm barrel, 2000–2060gm. Twenty rounds. A version with a ten-round magazine was also made, often with a 140mm barrel. Royal pistols were either self-loading (fig. 2097) or capable of automatic fire (fig. 2098).

2099. Ruby; Gabilondo y Urresti, Elgoeibar. ·45 ACP. An imitation of the 1911-type Colt-Browning.

2100. S.E.A.M.; Sociedad Española de Armas y Municiones, Eibar. 6·35mm Auto; 110mm overall, 51mm barrel.

2101, 2102. Sharp-Shooter; Hijos de Calixto Arrizabalaga, Eibar. 6·35mm Auto or 7·65mm Auto. Data for 6·35mm version: 134mm overall, 76mm barrel. Data for 7·65mm version: 163mm overall, 99mm barrel, 760gm, nine rounds. A modified Jo-Lo-Ar (fig. 2084, 2085), with a conventional trigger guard.

2103. Star, 1906 type; Bonifacio Echeverria y Compañia, Eibar. 6·35mm Auto; 115mm overall, 67mm barrel.

2104. Star, 1908 type; Bonifacio Echeverria y Compañia, Eibar. 6·35mm Auto.

2105. Star, 1914 type; Bonifacio Echeverria y Compañia, Eibar. 7·65mm Auto.

2106–2108. Star Model 1; Bonifacio Echeverria y Compañia, Eibar. 7·65mm Auto.

2109. Star M1919; Bonifacio Echeverria y Compañia, Eibar. 6·35mm Auto; 121mm overall, 66mm barrel. Eight rounds.

2110, 2111. Star M1920; Bonifacio Echeverria y Compañia, Eibar. 6·35mm Auto; 128mm overall, 68mm barrel, 445gm. Eight rounds.

2112. Star M1922 or New Model; Bonifacio Echeverria y Compañia, Eibar. 9mm Short.

2113. Star, Model A; Bonifacio Echeverria y Compañia, Eibar, introduced in 1921. 7·63mm Mauser; 255mm overall, 169mm barrel, 1020gm. Eight

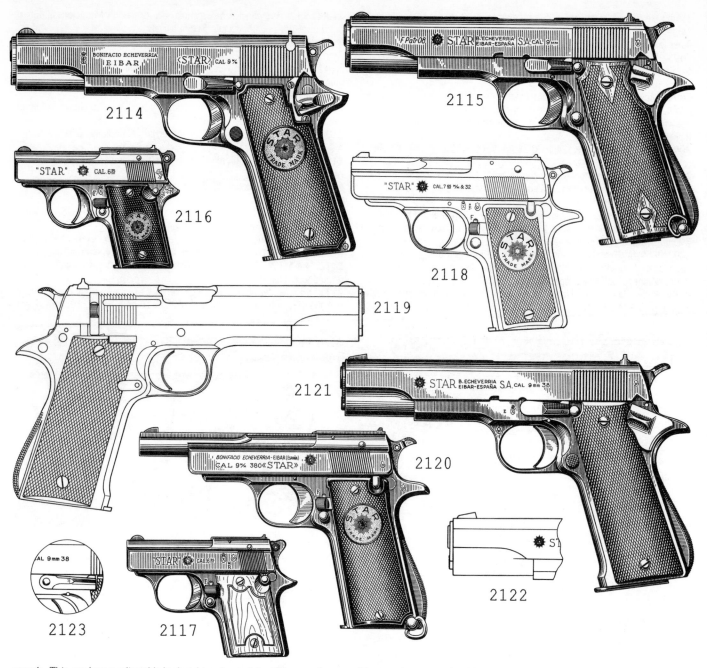

rounds. This gun has an adjustable back sight and a stock-lug. The muzzle on some examples does not protrude from the slide in the manner drawn here.

2114. Star Models A and AS; Bonifacio Echeverria y Compañia, Eibar. 9mm Largo (9mm Bergmann-Bayard); 210mm overall, 125mm barrel, 1000gm. Eight rounds. The improved AS differs only in minor details. Both patterns have been used by the Spanish armed forces and police.

2115. Star Models B and BS; Bonifacio Echeverria y Compañia, Eibar, c.1927–84. 9mm Parabellum; 215mm overall, 125mm barrel. Eight rounds. Similar to the A and AS, these differ principally in chambering. Models P and PS are also similar, but chamber for the ·45 ACP round and have seven-round magazines. Some of the earliest guns had a fire-selector on the right side of the slide.

2116, 2117. Star Model E; Bonifacio Echeverria y Compañia, Eibar, 1932–4. 6·35mm Auto; 106mm overall, 52mm barrel, 282gm. Six rounds.

2118. Star Models H and HN; Bonifacio Echeverria y Compañia, Eibar, 1934–41. 7·65mm Auto (H) or 9mm Short (HN).

2119. Star Model HD; Bonifacio Echeverria y Compañia, Eibar. 9mm Largo (9mm Bergmann-Bayard); 215mm overall, 125mm barrel. Eight rounds.

These guns are capable of firing fully automatically, owing to the inclusion of a selector switch in the mechanism.

2120. Star Models I and IN; Star–Bonifacio Echeverria SA, Eibar, 1934–41. 7·65mm Auto (I) or 9mm Short (IN). Data for 9mm version: 178mm or 193mm overall, 110mm or 125mm barrel, 730–765gm, eight rounds.

2121–2123. Star, Model M; Bonifacio Echeverria y Compañia, Eibar, introduced in 1932. 9mm Largo (9mm Bergmann-Bayard); 215mm overall, 125mm barrel, 1065gm. Nine rounds. Components of the Super Star, which is longer by 5mm, are drawn in fig. 2123. The 9mm Parabellum Model MB and the 7·63mm Mauser Model MM are similar to the Model M externally, excepting for the sights—which are often—and the chambering. Elongated single-column magazines holding sixteen or 32 rounds could be obtained, and some guns were adapted to accept wooden holster-stocks. A selective-fire version was known as the 'MD', but the cyclic rate of 800 shots per minute was too high to promote accuracy—even when the stock was attached.

2124. Star, military model; Bonifacio Echeverria y Compañia, Eibar, introduced in 1920. 9mm Largo (9mm Bergmann-Bayard) or ·45 ACP. The shape of the hammer and the rear part of the slide, with the manual safety, was inherited from earlier models. Later Stars looked much more like the Colt-Browning M1911A1.

2125. Super Destroyer; Gaztañaga, Trocaola y Compañia, Eibar. 7·65mm Auto; 145mm overall. Eight rounds.

2126. Tanque; Ojanguren y Vidosa, Eibar. 6·35mm Auto.

2127, 2128. Tauler, Models II and III; made by Gabilondo y Compañia, Elgoeibar, for Tauler y Compania of Madrid. 7·65mm Auto or 9mm Short.

2129. Tauler, Models IV, V and P; Tauler y Compania, Madrid. 9mm Largo (9mm Bergmann-Bayard) or 9mm Parabellum; 216mm overall, 128mm barrel. Nine rounds. The slide-mark of the Model P is also shown. The Colt-Browning-type Tauler pistols were made by Gabilondo y Compañia (Llama brand) in Elgoibar.

2130. Thunder M1919; Martin Bascaran, Eibar. 6·35mm Auto; 112mm overall, 50mm barrel, 375gm. Six rounds.

2131. Unknown. 6·35mm Auto.

2132. Victoria M1911; Unceta y Compañia, Guernica. 6·35mm Auto. A typical exposed-hammer pocket pistol.

2133. Warwink; Gaspar Arizaga, Eibar. 7·65mm Auto; 156mm overall. Eight rounds. A copy of the US Savage.

2134. Webley & Scott Type; maker unknown. 7·65mm Auto.

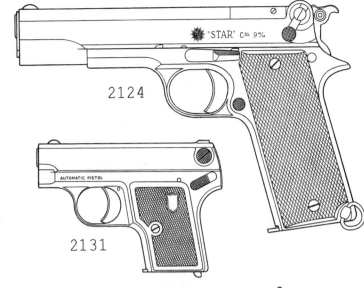

Post-Civil War patterns

2135. Astra A-60; Astra–Unceta Compañia, Guernica, 1987–92. 7·65mm or 9mm Short; 168mm overall, 89mm barrel, 720gm. Magazine: twelve (7·65mm) or thirteen (9mm) rounds. The preceding A-50 is similar, excepting that the safety lever lies on the frame.

2136. Astra A-70; Astra–Unceta Compañia, Guernica. 9mm Parabellum; 166mm overall.

2137. Astra Model A-80; Astra–Unceta Compañia, Guernica, 1982–9. 9mm Parabellum or ·45 ACP; 180mm overall, 98mm barrel, 955–985gm. Nine ·45 or fifteen 9mm rounds. This military-style locked-breech pistol offers a double-action trigger system and a staggered-column magazine.

2138. Astra A-90; Astra–Unceta Compañia, Guernica, 1985–90. 9mm Parabellum; 180mm overall, 98mm barrel, 985gm. Fifteen rounds. A variant of the A-80 with the satefy catch on the slide instead of the frame.

2139. Astra Model 600; Unceta y Compañia, Guernica, 1943–6. 9mm Parabellum; 206mm overall, 135mm barrel, 900gm. Eight rounds. A compact version of the Model 400, originally made for the German army during the Second World War.

2140. Astra Model 800 or Condor; Unceta y Compañia, Guernica, 1958–69. 9mm Parabellum; 210mm overall, 135mm barrel, 910gm. Eight rounds.

2141, 2142. Astra Model 2000, or Cub; Unceta y Compañia, Guernica, introduced in 1954. ·22 LR rimfire or 6·35mm Auto; 112mm overall, 57mm barrel, 315–340gm. Six 6·35mm or seven ·22 rounds. Variants include the chrome-plated 2001 and the etched, silver-plated 2003. A long-barrelled derivative was known as the Astra Camper. The rimfire version can usually be distinguished from the cantre-fire gun by milling on the slide (fig. 2142).

2143. Astra Model 4000 or Falcon; Unceta y Compañia, Guernica, 1956–86. ·22 LR rimfire, 7·65mm Auto or 9mm Short; 164mm overall, 98mm barrel. Seven 9mm, eight 7·65mm or ten ·22 rounds.

2144. Astra Model 7000; Unceta y Compañia and Astra–Unceta Compañia, Guernica. ·22 LR rimfire; 125mm overall, 60mm barrel, 415gm. Eight rounds.

2145, 2146. Constable, or Astra Model 5000; Unceta y Compañia and Astra–Unceta Compañia, Guernica, 1969–91. ·22 LR rimfire, 7·65mm Auto or 9mm Short; 168mm overall, 108mm barrel, 648–680gm. Seven 9mm, eight 7·65mm or ten ·22 rounds. Based on the Walther PP, this gun may have the safety catch on the slide (fig. 2145) or the frame (fig. 2146).

2147. Echasa Model Fast; Echave y Arizmendi, Eibar. ·22 LR rimfire, 6·35mm Auto, 7·65mm Auto or 9mm Short; 157mm overall, 80mm barrel, 400gm. Seven to ten rounds, depending on calibre. Models 221 and 222 are ·22 rimfire versions; Models 631 and 633 are 6·35mm; Model 761 is 7·65mm; whilst Model 902 chambers 9mm Short ammunition. The grips of the Models 221 and 631 are plastic, whereas those of the 222 and 633 sub-variants are wooden. Guns of this type, encountered under the tradenames Dickson Special Agent or Basque, were distributed in the USA.

2148. Firestar M40; Star–Bonifacio Echeverria SA, Eibar, Introduced in 1990. ·40 S&W.

2149, 2150. Firestar M43; Star–Bonifacio Echeverria SA, Eibar, 1990 to date. 9mm Parabellum; 163mm overall, 86mm barrel, 798gm. Seven rounds. A compact locked-breech Star, based on the Colt-Browning.

2151. Firestar M45; Star–Bonifacio Echeverria SA, Eibar, 1992 to date. ·45 ACP. Seven rounds.

2152. Llama; Gabilondo y Compañia, Elgoeibar. ·45 ACP.

2153. Llama Model 3A; Gabilondo y Compañia, Elgoeibar, 1955–85. 9mm Short; 160mm overall, 94mm barrel, 585gm. Eight rounds. Locked breech. The Model 3 of 1936–54 was identical, but lacked the grip safety. Model 6 was identical with the Model 3, but was slightly heavier. The Models 10 and 10A chambered the 7·65mm Auto cartridge, and the Model 15 was a ·22 LR rimfire derivative. The guns were all blowbacks.

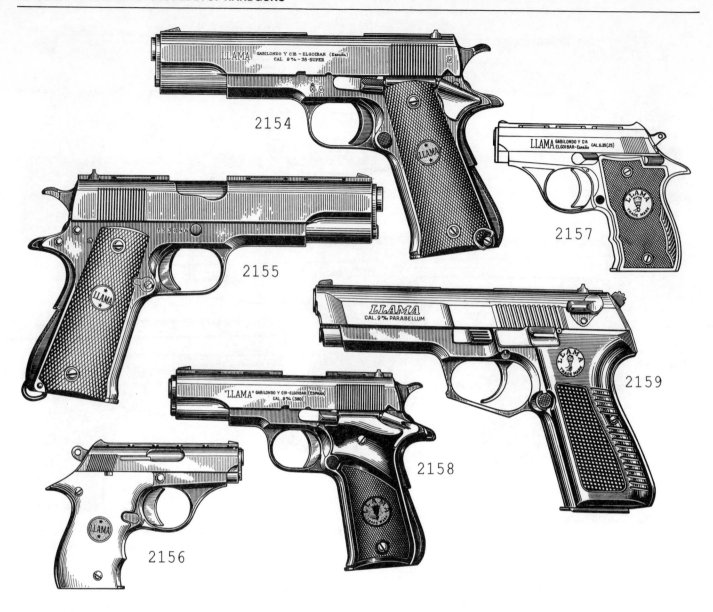

2154. Llama Model 8; Gabilondo y Compañia, Elgoibar, 1955–85. 9mm Largo (9mm Bergmann-Bayard); 216mm overall, 128mm barrel, 1000gm. Nine rounds. This is a minor variant of the Model 7. The Llama 21 and 22 were similar to the Model 8, but chambered for 9mm Largo and ·45 ACP respectively. They had an adjustable back sight and a raised front sight, whilst the muzzle of the lengthened barrel protruded from the standard slide by about 7mm.

2155. Llama Model 9A; Gabilondo y Compañia, Elgoibar, c.1954–85. ·45 ACP; 216mm overall, 128mm barrel, 1100gm. Seven rounds. The Llama 9 of 1936–54 was essentially similar.

2156, 2157. Llama Model 17 (Fig. 2156) and Model 18 (Fig. 2157); Gabilondo y Compañia, Elgoeibar. 6·35mm Auto; 120mm overall, 60mm barrel, 350gm. Six rounds. This blowback pattern was also apparently offered in ·22 Short rimfire.

2158. Llama Model 19; Gabilondo y Compañia, Elgoeibar. 9mm Short; 160mm overall, 94mm barrel, 465gm. Eight rounds. This is much the same as the Llama Model 3, excepting that the frame is made of alloy and some parts have been refined. Later examples have a raised ventilated rib on top of the slide, and the slide retraction grooves may be vertical or inclined.

2159. Llama M82; Llama–Gabilondo y Compañia, Vitoria, 1985 to date. 9mm Parabellum; 209mm overall, 98mm barrel, 865gm. Fifteen rounds. A powerful pistol suited to modern requirements, this has a double-action trigger system and a staggered-column magazine.

2160, 2161. Llama Omni; Llama–Gabilondo y Compañia, Vitoria, 1982–6. 9mm Parabellum (Omni II, III) or ·45 ACP (Omni I); 203mm or 197mm overall respectively, 1140gm. Seven ·45, nine 9mm (Omni II) or thirteen 9mm (Omni III) rounds. Featuring a double-action trigger system, this was the first locked-breech Llama to abandon the Colt-Browning locking system. It was not an outstanding success, however, and has been replaced by more conventional designs.

2162. Megastar; Star–Bonifacio Echeverria SA, Eibar, 1992 to date. ·45 ACP; 215mm overall, 114mm barrel, 1350gm. Twelve rounds.

2163. Star Model 28 DA; Star–Bonifacio Echeverria SA, Eibar, 1983–4. 9mm Parabellum; 205mm overall, 110mm barrel, 1140gm. Fifteen rounds. This military-pattern pistol has a double-action trigger system and a staggered-column magazine. The safety is ambidexterous, and the recurved trigger-guard bow facilitates a two-handed grip.

2164, 2165. Star M30 PK; Star–Bonifacio Echeverria SA, Eibar, 1985–9. 9mm Parabellum; 193mm overall, 98mm barrel, 860gm. Fifteen rounds. The 30M is identical, but 12mm longer.

2166. Star M31; Star–Bonifacio Echeverria SA, Eibar, 1990 to date. 9mm Parabellum; 193mm overall, 98mm barrel, 1110gm. Fifteen rounds. A variant with an alloy frame weighs merely 850gm.

2167. Star Model BKM (alloy frame) and BM (steel frame); Star–Bonifacio Echeverria SA, Eibar. 9mm Parabellum; 180mm overall, 99mm barrel, 725gm. Eight rounds.

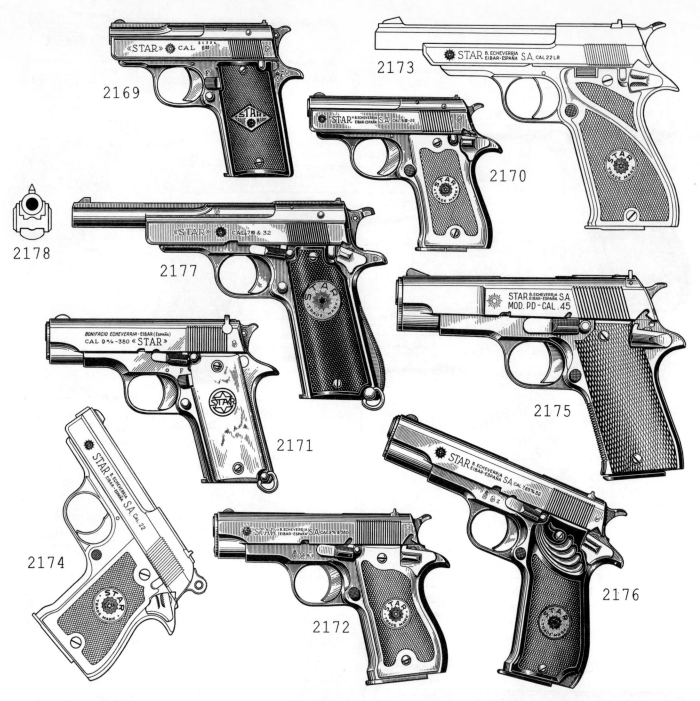

2168. Star Model BKS, Starlight; Star–Bonifacio Echeverria SA, Eibar, 1970–81. 9mm Parabellum. Made with a lightweight alloy frame.

2169. Star Model CO; Star–Bonifacio Echeverria SA, Eibar, 1941–57. 6·35mm Auto, 120mm overall, 60mm barrel, 400gm. Eight rounds.

2170. Star Model CU, Starlet; Star–Bonifacio Echeverria SA, Eibar, introduced in 1957. 6·35mm Auto; 120mm overall, 60mm barrel, 295gm. Seven rounds. The latest pistols are known as 'Model CK'.

2171. Star Model D; Bonifacio Echeverria y Compañia, Eibar, c.1941–57. 9mm Short.

2172. Star Model DK, Starfire; Star–Bonifacio Echeverria SA, Eibar, introduced in 1957. 9mm Short; 146mm overall, 80mm barrel, 430gm. Six rounds. Now known as 'DKL'. A 7·65mm Auto equivalent is the 'DKI'.

2173. Star Models FR (1967–72) and IR (introduced c.1955); Star–Bonifacio Echeverria SA, Eibar. ·22 LR rimfire (FR) or 7·65mm Auto (IR); 185mm overall, 110mm barrel, 790gm. Nine 7·65mm or ten ·22 rounds. Rimfire guns may be encountered with long barrels.

2174. Star Model HK, Lancer; Star–Bonifacio Echeverria SA, Eibar, 1955–68. ·22 LR rimfire; 140mm overall, 75mm barrel, 410gm. Eight rounds.

2175. Star Model PD; Star–Bonifacio Echeverria SA, Eibar, 1975 to date. ·45 ACP; 180mm overall, 110mm barrel, 710gm. Six rounds. Featuring an alloy frame, this is the smallest Spanish pistol made in this chambering.

2176. Star Model S (1946–72) and SI (1946–56); Star–Bonifacio Echeverria SA, Eibar. 7·65mm Auto or 9mm Short; 165mm overall, 120mm barrel, 620gm. Nine 7·65mm or eight 9mm rounds. The Super S had 125mm barrel. Modernised post-1970s versions are designated 'SS' and 'SIS'.

2177, 2178. Star, officer's model; Bonifacio Echeverria y Compañia, Eibar. 7·65mm Auto; 178mm or 193mm overall, 110mm or 125mm barrel. Nine rounds. Similar to the Models I and IN, this has a different safety system and an additional slide-retaining catch.

Browning copies

Many gunmakers made pocket pistols copied from the 1906-type FN-Browning. Some of these were facsimiles of their Belgian-made prototypes, but most have characteristic features of their own. The most obvious of these are the manual safety, which almost invariably lies on the left side of the frame above the trigger instead of behind the grip. Many guns were hammer-fired instead of relying on a striker mechanism, though this is not usually obvious externally. Some have elongated grips, increasing the magazine capacity, whilst many chamber 7·65mm ammunition instead of 6·35mm.

Identifying these Spanish-made guns is often complicated by the markings, which may be in English or French. French-style marks were popular owing to the proximity of the Franco-Spanish border to Eibar.

1. 6·35mm Imitations of the 1906 Browning

Note: all guns are chambered for the ·25 ACP (6·35mm Auto) cartridge.

2179. AAA M1919; A. Aldazabal, Eibar. Six rounds. Hammer fired.

2180. Action; Modesto Santos, Eibar. Six rounds. Striker fired.

2181. Allies; Bersaluce Arietio-Aurtena y Compañía, Eibar.

2182–2185. Alkar; Fábrica de Armas Alkartasuna SA, Eibar. Fig. 2182: seven rounds, hammer fired. Fig. 2183: six rounds, hammer fired. Fig. 2184: six rounds, hammer fired. Fig. 2185: details unknown.

2186, 2187. Apache; Ojanguren y Vidosa, Eibar. Seven rounds. Generally hammer fired.

2188. Asiatic; maker unknown.

2189. Astra Model 200 (1924); Esperanza y Unceta, Guernica. Six rounds. Hammer fired. There is also a version with an automatic safety.

2190. Astra Firecat; Unceta y Compañia, Guernica. Six rounds. Usually hammer fired.

2191, 2192. Atlas; Acha Hermanos y Compañía, Ermua. Six rounds. Hammer fired (fig. 2191) or striker fired (fig. 2192).

2193. Aurora; maker unknown. Six rounds. Hammer fired.

2194–2200. Automatic Pistol. Fig. 2194: Six rounds. Hammer fired. Fig. 2195: Model 1911, six rounds, hammer fired. Fig. 2196: six rounds, hammer fired. Fig. 2197: Model 1916, six rounds, hammer fired. Fig. 2198: six rounds, hammer fired. Figs. 2199, 2200: details unknown.

2201, 2202. Avion; Azpiri y Compañia, Eibar. Six rounds. Fired by a striker (fig. 2201) or hammer (fig. 2202).

2203. Azul; Eulogio Arostegui, Eibar. Six rounds. Hammer fired.

2204. Beistegui Hermanos, Eibar. Six rounds. Hammer fired.

2205. Benemerita M1918; D.F. Ortega de Seija, Madrid. Seven rounds. Hammer fired.

2206. Bronco M1918; Echave y Arzimendi, Eibar. Six rounds. Usually hammer fired.

2207. Bufalo; Gregorio Bolumburu, Eibar. Six rounds. Hammer fired.

2208. Bulwark; Beistegui Hermanos, Eibar. Six rounds. Striker fired. Sometimes marked by Fabrique d'Armes de Grande Précision of Eibar.

2209. Campeon M1919; Crucelegui Hermanos, Eibar. Six rounds?

2210. Cantabria M1918; Garate Hermanos, Ermua. Seven rounds. Hammer fired. Usually marked by Fabrique d'Armes de Grande Précision.

2211. Celta; made for Tómas de Urizar of Barcelona.

2212. Colon; Azpiri y Compañia, Eibar. Six rounds. Hammer fired.

2213–2216. Colonial; Fabrique d'Armes de Grande Précision, Eibar. Six rounds. Fired by hammer (fig. 2213) or striker (fig. 2214). Fig. 2215 shows a hammer-fired seven-round example. Details of fig. 2216 are unknown.

2217–2220. Continental; made for Tómas de Urizar of Barcelona. Six (fig. 2217) or seven (figs. 2218, 2219) rounds. Striker fired. Often marked by Fabrique d'Armes de Grande Précision, Eibar. Fig. 2220 shows the hammer-fired M1920.

2221, 2222. Cow Boy; maker unknown. Six rounds, hammer fire. Spanish-made, despite the 'Fabrication Française' slide mark on fig. 2221.

2223. Crucelegui Hermanos. Eight rounds. Hammer fired.

2224. Danton; Gabilondo y Compañia, Elgoeibar.

2225. Defense; maker unknown.

2226. Demon; Manufactura de Armas 'Demon', Eibar.

2227–2229. Destroyer; Isidro Gaztañaga, Eibar. Six rounds. Fig. 2227 shows the M1913, and fig. 2239 the M1918.

2230. Dewaf Model VI; maker unknown.

2231. Diana; Sociedad Española de Armas y Municiones, Eibar. Possibly made by Erquiaga, Muguruzu y Compañia, Eibar.

2232. Douglas Model 1914; Lasagabaster Hermanos, Eibar. Seven rounds. Hammer fired.

2233. Duan; F. Ormachea, Eibar. Six rounds. Hammer fired.

2234, 2235. EA; Eulogio Arostegui, Eibar. Six rounds. Hammer fired. Fig. 2235 shows the Model 1916.

2236. El Cid M1915; Casimir Santos, Eibar.

2237. Ermua M1924; possibly made by Acha Hermanos of Ermua.

2238. Ermua M1925 (Duan); made by F. Ormachea, Eibar, for Tómas de Urizar of Barcelona.

2239, 2240. Errasti; Antonio Errasti, Eibar. Six rounds. Hammer fired.

2241. E.S.A.; Fábrica de Armas Automaticas 'E.S.A.', Eibar.

2242. Etna; Santiago Salaberrin, Eibar. Six rounds. Hammer fired.

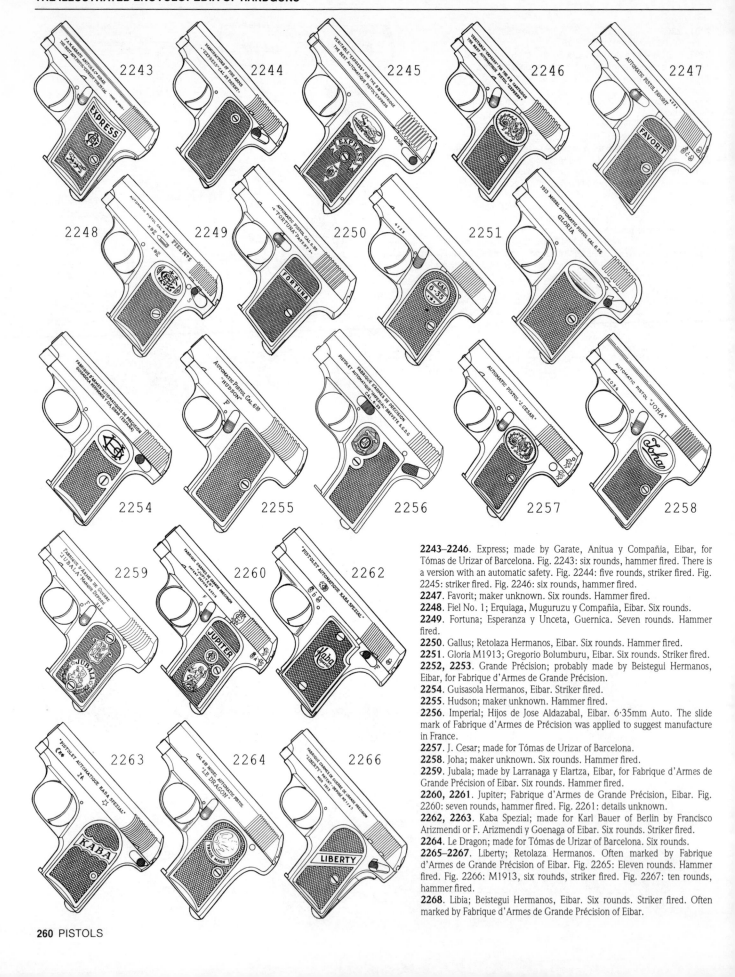

2243–2246. Express; made by Garate, Anitua y Compañia, Eibar, for Tómas de Urizar of Barcelona. Fig. 2243: six rounds, hammer fired. There is a version with an automatic safety. Fig. 2244: five rounds, striker fired. Fig. 2245: striker fired. Fig. 2246: six rounds, hammer fired.

2247. Favorit; maker unknown. Six rounds. Hammer fired.

2248. Fiel No. 1; Erquiaga, Muguruzu y Compañia, Eibar. Six rounds.

2249. Fortuna; Esperanza y Unceta, Guernica. Seven rounds. Hammer fired.

2250. Gallus; Retolaza Hermanos, Eibar. Six rounds. Hammer fired.

2251. Gloria M1913; Gregorio Bolumburu, Eibar. Six rounds. Striker fired.

2252, 2253. Grande Précision; probably made by Beistegui Hermanos, Eibar, for Fabrique d'Armes de Grande Précision.

2254. Guisasola Hermanos, Eibar. Striker fired.

2255. Hudson; maker unknown. Hammer fired.

2256. Imperial; Hijos de Jose Aldazabal, Eibar. 6·35mm Auto. The slide mark of Fabrique d'Armes de Précision was applied to suggest manufacture in France.

2257. J. Cesar; made for Tómas de Urizar of Barcelona.

2258. Joha; maker unknown. Six rounds. Hammer fired.

2259. Jubala; made by Larranaga y Elartza, Eibar, for Fabrique d'Armes de Grande Précision of Eibar. Six rounds. Hammer fired.

2260, 2261. Jupiter; Fabrique d'Armes de Grande Précision, Eibar. Fig. 2260: seven rounds, hammer fired. Fig. 2261: details unknown.

2262, 2263. Kaba Spezial; made for Karl Bauer of Berlin by Francisco Arizmendi or F. Arizmendi y Goenaga of Eibar. Six rounds. Striker fired.

2264. Le Dragon; made for Tómas de Urizar of Barcelona. Six rounds.

2265–2267. Liberty; Retolaza Hermanos. Often marked by Fabrique d'Armes de Grande Précision of Eibar. Fig. 2265: Eleven rounds. Hammer fired. Fig. 2266: M1913, six rounds, striker fired. Fig. 2267: ten rounds, hammer fired.

2268. Libia; Beistegui Hermanos, Eibar. Six rounds. Striker fired. Often marked by Fabrique d'Armes de Grande Précision of Eibar.

2269, 2270. Looking Glass; Acha Hermanos, Eibar. Six rounds. Hammer fired; its barrel can be elongated, as in Fig. 2317. Often distributed by Fabrique d'Armes de Grande Précision of Eibar.

2271, 2272. Marina; Gregorio Bolumburu, Eibar. Six rounds. Hammer fired.

2273, 2274. Marte; Erquiaga, Muguruzu y Compañia, Eibar. Six rounds. Hammer fired.

2275. Martian; Martin Bascaran, Eibar. Six rounds. Striker fired.

2276. Merke; F. Ormachea, Eibar. Six rounds. Hammer fired.

2277. Minerva; Fabrique d'Armes de Grande Précision, Eibar. Seven rounds. Hammer fired.

2278, 2279. MS; Modesto Santos, Eibar. Six rounds. Hammer fired.

2280. Olympia; maker unknown.

2281. Omega; Armero Especialistas, Eibar. Six rounds. Hammer fired.

2282. Orbea; Orbea y Compañia, Eibar. Six rounds. Hammer fired.

2283, 2284. Paramount; Apaolozo Hermanos, Eibar. Six rounds. Hammer fired.

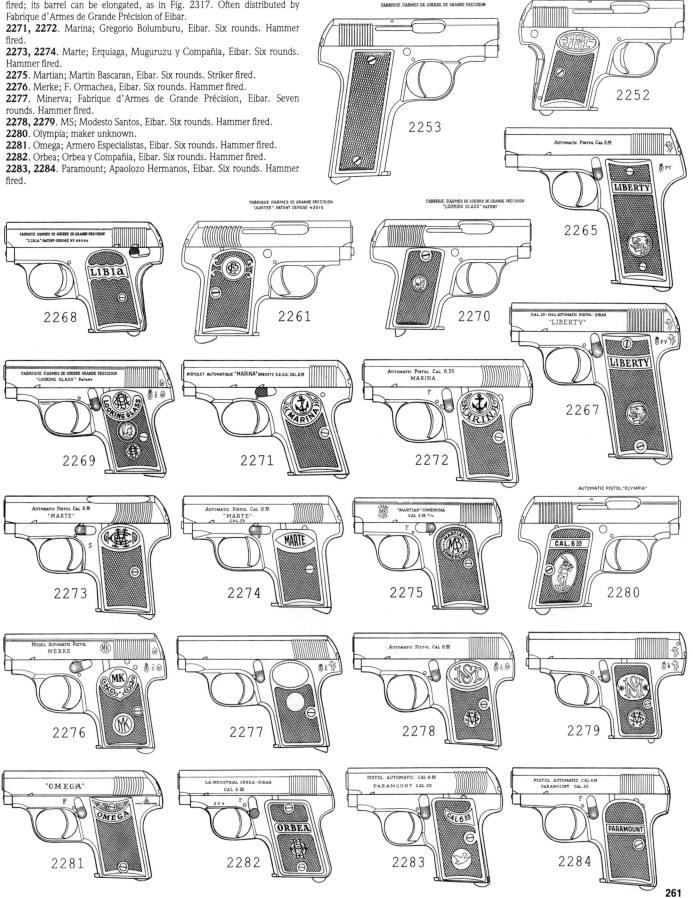

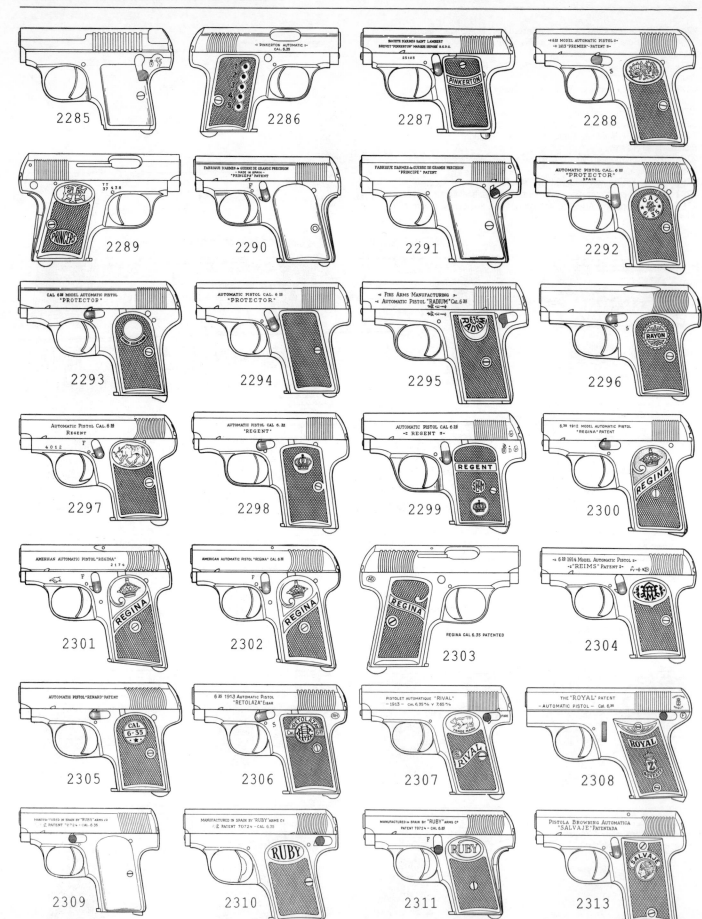

2285

2286

2287

2288

2289

2290

2291

2292

2293

2294

2295

2296

2297

2298

2299

2300

2301

2302

2303

2304

2305

2306

2307

2308

2309

2310

2311

2313

2285–2287. Pinkerton; Gaspar Arizaga, Eibar. Fig. 2285: six rounds, striker fired. Fig. 2286: five rounds. Fig. 2287: often marked 'Société d'Armes . . .', but undoubtedly made in Spain.

2288. Premier M1913; made for Tómas de Urizar of Barcelona. Six rounds. Hammer fired.

2289, 2290. Princeps; made for Tómas de Urizar of Barcelona. Six rounds. Hammer fired. Often marked by Fabrique d'Armes de Grande Précision.

2291. Principe; possibly made for Tómas de Urizar, Barcelona. Often marked by Fabrique d'Armes de Grande Précision. Six rounds. Striker fired.

2292–2294. Protector; Santiago Salaberrin or Echave y Arzimendi, Eibar. Six rounds. Hammer fired.

2295. Radium. Six rounds. Made in Spain, in spite of its Belgian proofmrks.

2296. Rayon; maker unknown. Six rounds. Hammer fired.

2297–2299. Regent; Gregorio Bolumburu, Eibar. Often marked by Sociedad Española de Armas y Municiones. Six rounds. Hammer fired.

2300–2303. Regina; Gregorio Bolumburu, Eibar. Seven rounds. Hammer fired. Fig. 2300 is marked 'M1912'. The details of fig. 2303 are not known.

2304. Reims; Azanza y Arrizabalaga, Eibar. Six rounds. Hammer fired.

2305. Renard; Echave y Arizmendi, Eibar. Six rounds. Hammer fired.

2306. Retolaza; Retolaza Hermanos y Compañia, Eibar.

2307. Rival; Fábrica de Armas 'Union', Eibar.

2308. Royal; M. Zulaica y Compañia, Eibar.

2309–2312. Ruby Arms Co.; Gabilondo y Urresti, Elgoeibar. Six rounds, usually striker fired. Some versions lack the automatic safety in the back strap of the grip.

2313. Salvaje; Ojanguren y Vidosa, Eibar. Seven rounds. Hammer fired.

2314, 2315. 'S.E.A.M.'; Sociedad Española de Armas y Municiones, Eibar. Six rounds. Hammer fired. The barrels may be elongated.

2316. Selecta Model 1918; Echave y Arizmendi, Eibar. Seven rounds. Hammer fired. There is a version with an automatic safety.

2317–2319. Singer; Francisco Arizmendi, Eibar. Six rounds. Striker fired.

2320. Sivispacem Parabellum; Thieme y Edeler, Eibar.

2321. Sprinter; Garate, Anitua y Compañia, Eibar. Striker fired.

2322–2324. Stosel; Retolaza Hermanos, Eibar. Six rounds. Hammer fired. Fig. 2322 shows the Stosel No. 1 and fig. 2324 is the M1912.

2325, 2326. Tatra; maker unknown. Six rounds. Hammer fired.

2327. The Victory, 1914 model; Zulaica y Compañia, Eibar. Seven rounds. Hammer fired.

2328. Tisan; Santiago Salaberrin, Eibar. Six rounds. Hammer fired.

2329. Titan; Retolaza Hermanos, Eibar.

2330, 2331. Titanic; Retolaza Hermanos, Eibar. Hammer fired. Fig. 2331 shows the M1914.

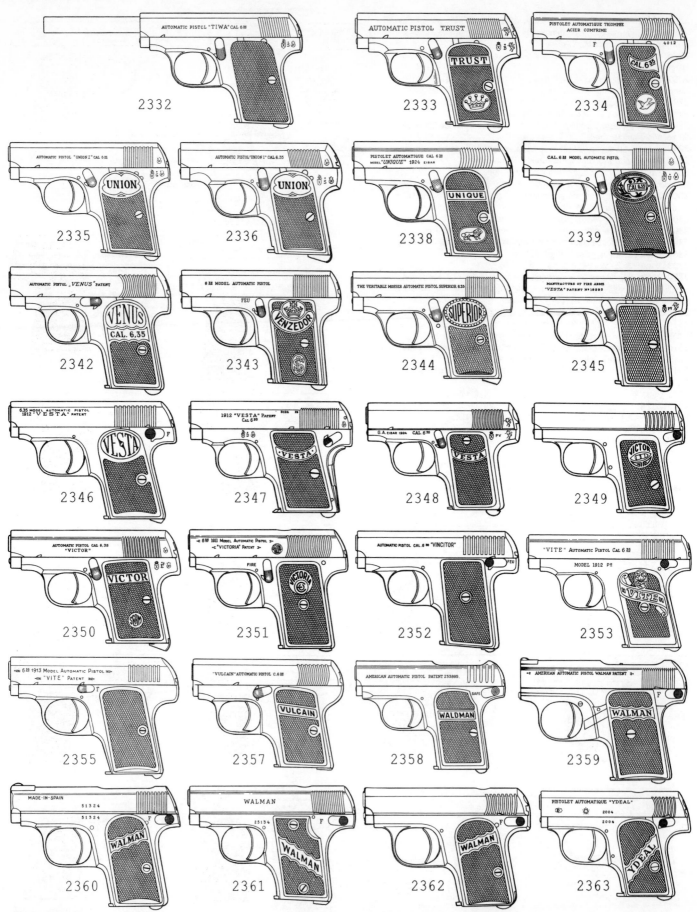

2332. Tiwa; maker unknown. Six rounds. Hammer fired.

2333. Trust; Fabrique d'Armes de Grande Précision, Eibar. Six rounds. Hammer fired.

2334. Triomphe; Apaolozo Hermanos, Zumorraga. Six rounds. Usually hammer fired.

2335–2337. Union; made by Esperanza y Unceta and Unceta y Compañia of Guernica, possibly for Seytres of Saint-Étienne. Six rounds. Hammer fired.

2338. Unique Model 1924; made by Unceta y Compañia for Manufacture d'Armes des Pyrénées Françaises of Hendaye. Six rounds. Hammer fired.

2339. Unknown. Six rounds. Hammer fired. Similar to 'Zaldun' (q.v.).

2340, 2341. Unknown. Twelve rounds. Hammer fired.

2342. Venus; made for Tómas de Urizar. Six rounds. Hammer fired.

2343. Venzedor; Casimir Santos, Eibar. Six rounds. Hammer fired.

2344. Veritable Mosser Superior; possibly made by Gabilondo y Cia, Eibar.

2345–2348. Vesta. Fig. 2345: by Garate, Anitua y Compañia of Eibar, six rounds, hammer fired. Figs. 2346, 2347: M1912, possibly made by Hijos de A. Echeverria of Eibar, six rounds, striker fired. Fig. 2348: M1924 by Garate, Anitua y Compañia, six rounds, striker fired. There is also a version of the M1924 with the safety in the rear part of the receiver.

2349, 2350. Victor; Francisco Arizmendi, Eibar. Fig. 2349: six rounds, striker fired. Fig. 2350: six rounds, hammer fired. Often marked by Fabrique d'Armes de Précision of Eibar.

2351. Victoria M1911 and M1916; Esperanza y Unceta, Guernica. Six rounds. Hammer fired. The 1916 pattern has an indicator showing the presence of a cartridge in the firing chamber.

2352. Vincitor; M. Zulaica y Compañia, Eibar. Six rounds. Striker fired.

2353–2356. Vite; Esperanza y Unceta, Guernica. Fig. 2353: M1912, six rounds, striker fired. Fig. 2354: M1912, eight rounds, striker fired. Fig. 2355: M1913, six rounds, striker fired. Fig. 2356: M1913, eight rounds, striker fired.

2357. Vulcain; maker unknown. Five rounds. Hammer fired.

2358. Waldman; F. Arizmendi y Goenaga, Eibar. Six rounds. Striker fired.

2359–2362. Walman; F. Arizmendi y Goenaga, Eibar. Usually six rounds. Striker fired.

2363, 2364. Ydeal; Francisco Arizmendi, Eibar. Striker fired. (Fig. 2364 shows the second version).

2365. Zaldun; maker unknown.

2. 7·65mm Imitations of the 1906 Browning.

Note: all guns are chambered for the ·32 ACP (7·65mm Auto) cartridge.

2366. AA M1916; Azanza y Arrizabalaga, Eibar. Nine rounds. Hammer fired.

2367. AAA M1916; A. Aldazabal, Eibar. Seven rounds. Hammer fired.

2368. Acha Hermanos, Ermua. Nine rounds. Hammer fired.

2369. Aldazabal, Leturiondo y Cia, Eibar. Nine rounds. Hammer fired.

2370, 2371. Allies; Bersaluce Arietio-Aurtena y Compañia, Eibar. Fig.

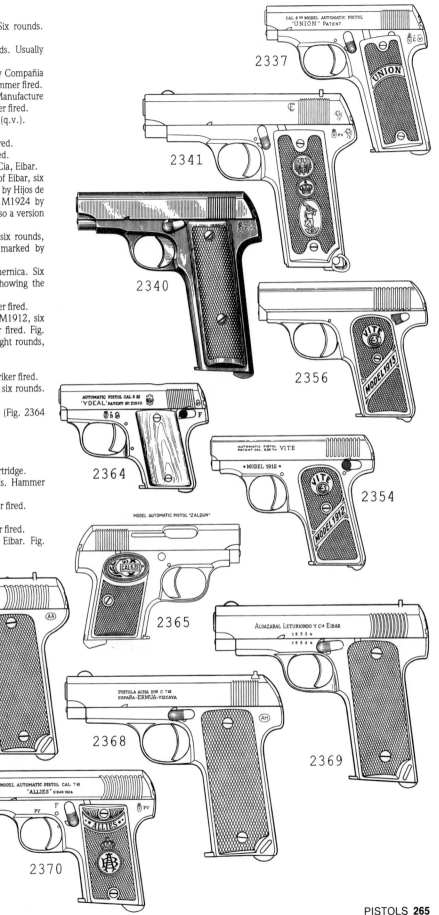

2370: M1924, six rounds, hammer fired. Fig. 2371: nine rounds, hammer fired.

2372–2374. Alkar; Fábrica de Armas Alkartasuna SA, Eibar. Fig. 2372: seven rounds, hammer fired. Fig. 2373: nine rounds, hammer fired. Fig. 2374: seven rounds, hammer fired.

2375. Arizaga; Gaspar Arizaga, Eibar. Nine rounds. Hammer fired.

2376–2378. Arrizabalaga; Hijos de Calixto Arrizabalaga, Eibar. Nine rounds. Hammer fired.

2379. Asiatic; maker unknown.

2380–2383. Astra; Esperanza y Unceta, Guernica. Fig. 2380: nine rounds, hammer fired. Fig. 2381: M1911, seven rounds, hammer fired. Fig. 2382: twelve rounds, hammer fired. Fig. 2383: 1915 and 1916 models, nine rounds, hammer fired. There is a version of the M1915 with a shortened grip; its magazine holds seven cartridges.

2384, 2385. Astra; Unceta y Compañia, Guernica. 7·65mm Auto. Ten (fig. 2384) or thirteen (fig. 2385) rounds. Hammer fired.

2386–2389. Automatic Pistol, anonymous. All hammer fired. Figs. 2386–2388: nine rounds. Fig. 2389: eleven rounds.

2390. Automatische Selbstlade-Pistole. Manufacturer unknown.

2391. Azul; Eulogio Arostegui, Eibar. Seven rounds. Hammer fired.

2392. Beistegui Hermanos M1914. Nine rounds. Hammer fired.

2393. Bernedo; Victor Bernedo y Compañia, Eibar.

2394. Bolumburu; Gregorio Bolumburu, Eibar. Nine rounds. Generally hammer fired.

2395. Bristol; Gregorio Bolumburu, Eibar. Nine rounds. Hammer fired.

2396. Bronco M1918; Echave y Arizmendi, Eibar. Six rounds. Hammer fired.

2397. Brunswig M1916; Esperanza y Unceta, Guernica. Nine rounds. Hammer fired.

2398. Campeon M1919; Crucelegui Hermanos, Eibar. Six rounds. Hammer fired.

2399. Ca-Si; Fabrique d'Armes de Grande Précision, Eibar. Six rounds. Hammer fired.

2400, 2401. Cebra. Nine rounds. Hammer fired. Fig. 2400: made by Beistegui Hermanos, Eibar, for Arizmendi, Zulaica y Compañia of Eibar. Fig. 2401: made by Arizmendi, Zulaica y Compañia of Eibar.

2402. Cobra; made for Arizmendi, Zulaica y Compañia, Eibar. Nine rounds. Hammer fired.

2403. Continental; made for Tómas de Urizar of Barcelona.

2404. Demon; Manufactura de Armas 'Demon', Eibar. Twelve rounds. Hammer fired.

2405. Destructor; Iraola Salaverria y Compañia, Eibar. Six rounds. Invariably hammer fired.

2406, 2407. Destroyer; Isidro Gaztañaga, Eibar. Fig. 2406: nine rounds, hammer fired. Fig. 2407: M1914, seven rounds, hammer fired.

2408. Diana; Erquiaga, Muguruzu y Compañia, Eibar.

2409. Echave y Arizmendi, Eibar. Nine rounds. Hammer fired.

2410. Echeverria; Hijos de A. Echeverria, Eibar. Nine rounds.

2411. E.S.A.; Fábrica de Armas Automaticas 'E.S.A.', Eibar.

2412–2418. Express; made by Garate, Anitua y Compañia, Eibar, for Tómas de Urizar of Barcelona. Fig. 2412: eight rounds, hammer fired. Fig. 2413: six rounds. Figs. 2414, 2415: six rounds, hammer fired. Fig. 2416: seven rounds, hammer fired. Fig. 2417: eight rounds, hammer fired. Fig. 2418: six rounds, striker fired.

2419, 2420. Errasti; Antonio Errasti, Eibar. Seven rounds. Hammer fired.

2421. Fabrique d'Armes de Guerre, Eibar. Nine rounds. Hammer fired. Probably the same as 'Fabrique d'Armes [de Guerre] de Précision'

2422, 2423. Fiel; Erquiaga, Muguruzu y Compañia, Eibar. Fig. 2422: seven rounds, hammer fired. Fig. 2423: nine rounds, hammer fired.

2424. Garate, Anitua y Compañia, Eibar. Nine rounds. Hammer fired.

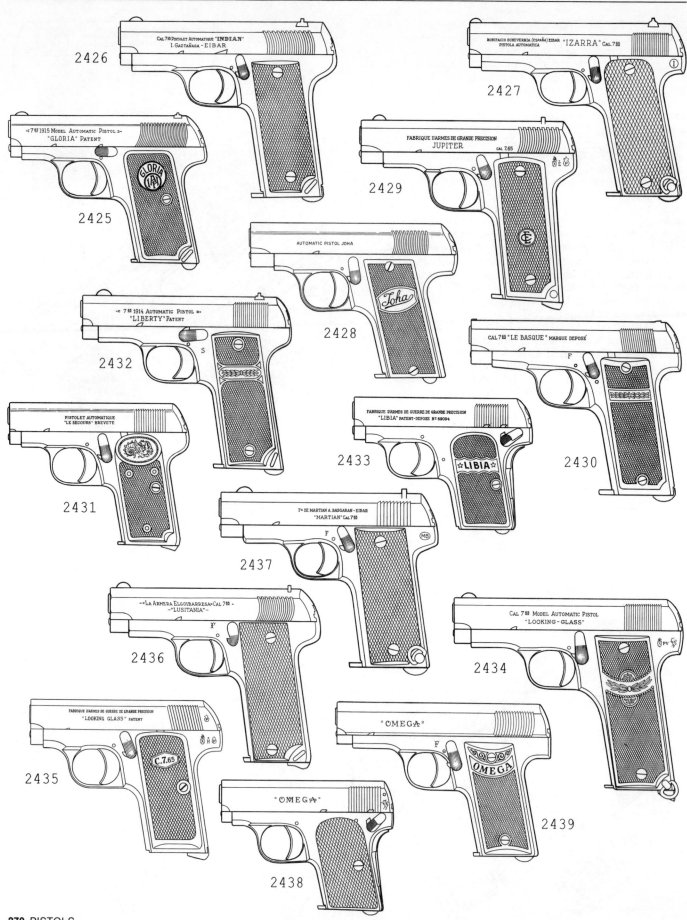

2425. Gloria M1915; Gregorio Bolumburu, Eibar. Seven rounds. Usually Hammer fired.

2426. Indian; Isidro Gaztañaga, Eibar. Nine rounds. Hammer fired.

2427. Izarra; Bonifacio Echeverria, Eibar. Nine rounds. Hammer fired.

2428. Joha; maker unknown. Seven rounds. Striker fired.

2429. Jupiter; Fabrique d'Armes de Grande Précision, Eibar. Nine rounds. Hammer fired.

2430. Le Basque; Eulogio Arostegui or possibly Echave y Arizmendi, Eibar. Nine rounds. Hammer fired.

2431. Le Secours; made for Tómas de Urizar of Barcelona. Seven rounds. Hammer fired.

2432. Liberty M1914; Retolaza Hermanos or Gregorio Bolumburu, Eibar. Nine rounds. Hammer fired.

2433. Libia; Beistegui Hermanos, Eibar. Six rounds. Striker fired.

2434, 2435. Looking-Glass; Acha Hermanos, Eibar. Nine rounds. Hammer fired. Often marked by Fabrique d'Armes de Grande Précision.

2436. Lusitania; La Armera Elgoeibarresa, Elgoeibar. Six or nine rounds. Hammer fired.

2437. Martian; Martin Bascaran, Eibar. Nine rounds. Hammer fired.

2438, 2439. Omega; Armero Especialistas, Eibar. Usually six rounds, striker fired.

2440–2442. Paramount; Apaolozo Hermanos, Eibar. Nine rounds. Hammer fired.

2443, 2444. Plus Ultra, M1932; Gabilondo y Compañia, Elgoeibar. Twelve rounds. Hammer fired. Note the 'Ruby' mark on fig. 2444.

2445. Praga; Sociedad Española de Armas y Municiones, Eibar. Seven rounds. Hammer fired.

2446. Precision; made by or for Fabrique d'Armes de Grande Précision, Eibar. Six rounds. Hammer fired.

2447, 2448. Princeps; Fabrique d'Armes de Grande Précision of Eibar. Six rounds. Hammer fired. Fig. 2448: possibly made by Thieme y Edeler, Eibar, for distribution by Fabrique d'Armes de Grande Précision of Eibar.

2449. Puma; Fabrique d'Armes de Grande Précision, Eibar.

2450. Puppel; Ojanguren y Vidosa, Eibar. Seven rounds. Hammer fired.

2451. Regent; made by Gregorio Bolumburu for Sociedad Española de Armas y Municiones of Eibar.

2452–2454. Regina; Gregorio Bolumburu, Eibar. Fig. 2452: seven rounds, hammer fired. Fig. 2453: nine rounds, hammer fired. Fig. 2454: six rounds, hammer fired.

2455. Republic; possibly made by Arrizabalaga of Eibar. Nine rounds. Hammer fired.

2456. Reims M1914; Azanza y Arrizabalaga, Eibar. Generally six rounds. Hammer fired.

2457. Retolaza M1914; Retolaza Hermanos, Eibar. Nine rounds.

2458. Roland; Francisco Arizmendi, Eibar. Six rounds. Striker fired.

2459–2461. Royal; M. Zulaica y Compañia, Eibar. Fig. 2459: seven rounds, hammer fired. Fig. 2460: nine rounds, hammer fired. Fig. 2461: twelve rounds, hammer fired.

2462, 2463. Ruby Arms Co.; Gabilondo y Urresti, Elgoeibar. Nine rounds. Hammer fired.

2464. Salaverria; Iraola Salaverria y Compañia, Eibar. Nine rounds. Hammer fired.

2465. 'S.E.A.M.'; Sociedad Española de Armas y Municiones, Eibar.

2466. Selecta M1919; Echave y Arizmendi, Eibar. Hammer fired.

2467, 2468. Singer. Striker fired. Fig. 2367: by F. Arizmendi y Goenaga of Eibar, seven rounds. Fig. 2368: by Francisco Arizmendi of Eibar, six rounds.

2469, 2470. Stosel; Retolaza Hermanos, Eibar. Fig. 2469: M1912, striker fired. Fig. 2470: M1914 No. 1, nine rounds, hammer fired. The 1913 pattern has a shortened grip and a seven-cartridge magazine.

2471. Teuf-Teuf; Arizmendi y Goenaga, Eibar.

2472, 2473. Titanic, 1914 model; Retolaza Hermanos, Eibar. Six rounds. Hammer fired.

2474, 2475. Trust; Fabrique d'Armes de Grande Précision, Eibar. Nine rounds (fig. 2475). Hammer fired.

2476. Trust-Supra; Fabrique d'Armes de Grande Précision, Eibar. This gun has grips bearing the mark of Tómas de Urizar of Barcelona.

2477. Union; Unceta y Compañia, Guernica. Six rounds. Hammer fired. Possibly made for M. Seytres of Saint-Étienne.

2478, 2479. Unknown. Nine rounds. Hammer fired. Fig. 2479 has a switch for automatic fire.

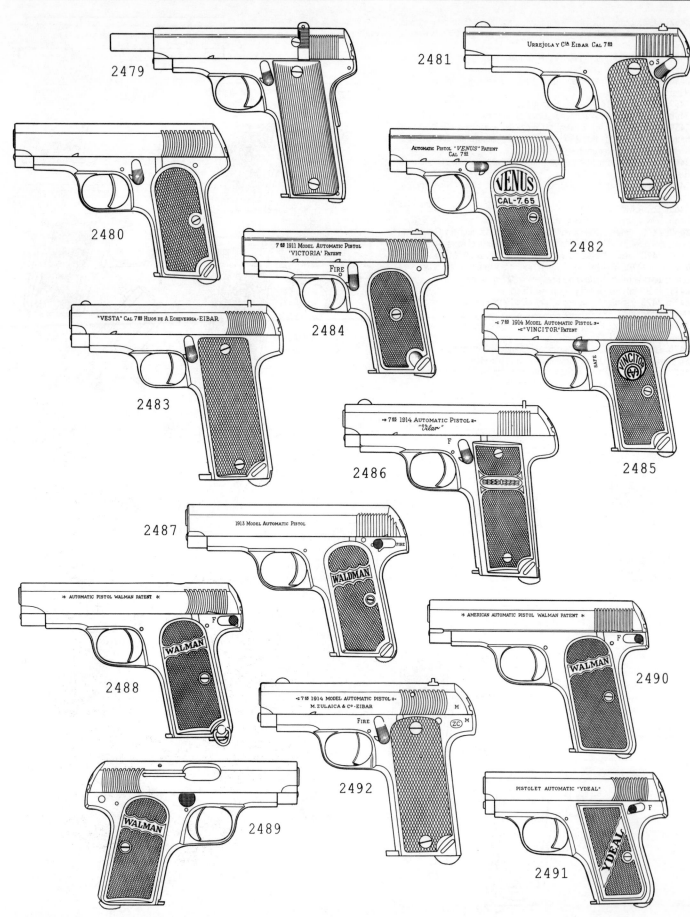

2480. Unknown. Seven rounds. Hammer fired.

2481. Urrejola y Compañía, Eibar. Nine rounds. Hammer fired.

2482. Venus; made for Tómas de Urizar of Barcelona. Six rounds. Hammer fired.

2483. Vesta; Hijos de A. Echeverria, Eibar. Nine rounds. Hammer fired.

2484. Victoria M1911; Unceta y Compañia, Guernica. Seven rounds. Hammer fired.

2485. Vincitor M1914; M. Zulaica y Compañia, Eibar. Seven rounds. Hammer fired.

2486. Vilar M1914; Retolaza Hermanos or Gregorio Bolumburu, Eibar. Nine rounds. Hammer fired. Virtually the same as 'Liberty', above.

2487. Waldman M1913; F. Arizmendi y Goenaga, Eibar. Seven rounds. Hammer fired.

2488–2490. Walman M1914; F. Arizmendi y Goenaga, Eibar. All striker fired. Fig. 2488: M1914. Fig. 2489: seven rounds. Fig. 2490: details not known.

2491. Ydeal; Francisco Arizmendi, Eibar. Six rounds. Striker fired.

2492. Zulaica M1914; M. Zulaica y Compañia, Eibar. Nine rounds. Hammer fired.

3. Imitations of the 1910 Browning.

2493. Astra, Model 700; Unceta y Compañía, Guernica. 7·65mm Auto. Ten rounds. Striker fired.

2494. Boltun; Francisco Arizmendi, Eibar. 7·65mm Auto. Seven rounds. Striker fired.

2495. Bufalo; Gregorio Bolumburu, Eibar. 7·65mm Auto. Seven rounds. Striker fired.

2496, 2497. Danton; Gabilondo y Compañía, Elgoeibar. 7·65mm Auto. Fig. 2496: nine rounds. Fig. 2497: thirteen rounds. Both are hammer fired.

2498. Destroyer, 1919 model; Isidro Gaztañaga, Eibar. 7·65mm Auto. Seven rounds.

2499. Handy, M1917; maker unknown. 9mm Short. Seven rounds.

2500. Rex; Gregorio Bolumburu, Eibar. The slide marking 'Manufacture d'Armes à Feu' and the Belgian proofmarks cannot disguise the Spanish origins of this gun.

2501. Ruby Arms Co.; Gabilondo y Urresti, Elgoeibar. 7·65mm Auto. Seven rounds. Striker fired.

2502. Walman; Arizmendi y Goenaga, Eibar. 7·65mm Auto. Seven rounds. Striker fired.

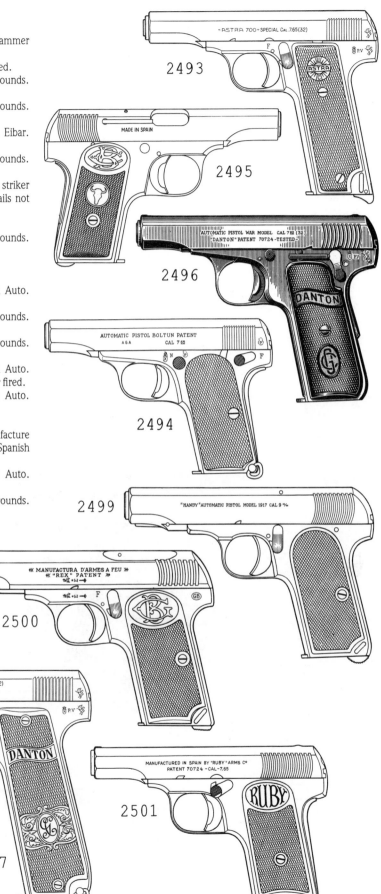

Sweden

2503. Hamilton Model 1901; J. Thorssin & Sons, Alingsås. 6·5mm; 267mm overall, 105mm barrel, 1225gm. Six rounds. An early blowback pistol design. When the breechblock is thrust back, it follows a curved path downward towards the butt in an attempt to slow the opening of the breech by friction.

2504. M/07; Husqvarna Våpenfabriks Ab, Huskvarna. 9mm Browning Long; 205mm overall, 128mm barrel, 930gm. Seven rounds. A version of the Belgian FN-Browning Mle 1903 pistol (q.v.) made under licence for the Swedish army until c.1941.

2505. M/40; Husqvarna Våpenfabriks Ab, Huskvarna. 9mm Parabellum; 240mm overall, 120mm barrel, 1265gm. Eight rounds. A version of the Finnish L-35 Lahti pistol, made for the Swedish armed forces in 1942–6.

Switzerland

Copies of the Austrian 1909-pattern Steyr pocket pistols were marketed in the 1930s by Waffenfabrik Solothurn AG. Details of the guns will be found in the Austrian section.

Between-war designs

2506, 2507. Arquebusier; Ernest & François Mayor, Lausanne. 6·35mm Auto; 118mm overall, 55mm barrel, 325gm. Five rounds. Made to a 1919-vintage patent of Ernst Rochat.

2508. Chylewski; Schweizerische Industrie-Gesellschaft, Neuhausen. 6·35mm Auto; 117mm overall, 53mm barrel, 373gm. Six rounds. Allegedly made in 1910–13, but more probably immediately after the end of the First World War. Chylewski's patent for chambering a cartridge with one hand was subsequently acquired by Bergmann (see German Bergmann and Lignose pistols).

2509. Ordonnanzpistole 06/29 W + F; Eidgenössische Waffenfabrik, Bern. 7·65mm Parabellum; 235mm overall, 120mm barrel, 880gm. Eight rounds. A Parabellum (Luger) adopted by the Swiss army to replace similar 1900- and 1906-pattern guns. Manufactured from 1933 until 1947.

2510. Petter; Schweizerische Industrie-Gesellschaft (SIG), Neuhausen. 7·65mm or 9mm Parabellum. This system provided the basis for the French MAS-35 in addition to several Swiss target and military models.

2511. SP 44/16; Schweizerische Industrie-Gesellschaft (SIG), Neuhausen. 9mm Parabellum; 215mm overall, 120mm barrel, 1090gm. Sixteen rounds.

A military pistol with a large-capacity staggered column magazine. A short-lived postwar version was known as 'SP 47/16'.

Post-1945 designs

2512, 2513. SP 47/8 or P 210; Schweizerische Industrie-Gesellschaft (SIG), Neuhausen. 7·65mm Parabellum or 9mm Parabellum; 215mm overall, 120mm barrel, 865gm. Eight rounds. Developed from the SP 44/16 (see fig. 2511), this gun was adopted by the Swiss army as the Ordonnanzpistole 49. It is now known commercially as P 210-1 (wooden grips) or P 210-2 (plastic grips). The P 210-5 target versions have improved sights, whilst the P 210-6 is chambered for ·22 LR rimfire ammunition.

2514. P220; Schweizerische Industrie-Gesellschaft (SIG), Neuhausen, and J.P. Sauer & Sohn GmbH, Eckenförde. 7·65mm Parabellum, 9mm Parabellum, ·38 Super or ·45 ACP; 198mm overall, 112mm barrel, 830–880gm. Seven (·45 ACP) or nine rounds (7·65mm, 9mm and ·38). Issued to the Swiss army as the Model 75. The locking shoulder on the barrel rises into the ejection port when the slide is closed and the action is locked.

The 7·65mm and 9mm models were introduced in 1975, followed by ·45 version early in 1976. Blowback derivatives have also been made in ·22 LR rimfire, with ten-round magazines. The firing mechanism is double-action for the first shot only, whilst the shaped front surface of the trigger guard supports the forefinger of the left hand when a two-hand grip is used.

2515. P225; Schweizerische Industrie-Gesellschaft (SIG), Neuhausen, and J.P. Sauer & Sohn GmbH, Eckenförde. 9mm Parabellum; 180mm overall, 98mm barrel, 820gm. Eight rounds. This greatly resembles the SIG-Sauer P220, but is shorter. It has served police in West Germany as the 'P6'.

2516. P226; Schweizerische Industrie-Gesellschaft (SIG), Neuhausen, and J.P. Sauer & Sohn GmbH, Eckenförde. 9mm Parabellum; 196mm overall, 112mm barrel, 845gm. Similar to the P225 described previously, but with a fifteen-round staggered-column magazine.

2517. P228; Schweizerische Industrie-Gesellschaft (SIG), Neuhausen, and J.P. Sauer & Sohn GmbH, Eckenförde. 9mm Parabellum. Thirteen rounds. A derivative of the P226 (q.v.) shortened by 16mm.

2518, 2519. P229; Schweizerische Industrie-Gesellschaft (SIG),

Neuhausen, and J.P. Sauer & Sohn GmbH, Eckenförde. ·40 S&W. Twelve rounds. A modification of the P228, chambered for differing ammunition. Changes have also been made to the contours of the slide.

2520. P230; Schweizerische Industrie-Gesellschaft (SIG), Neuhausen, and J.P. Sauer & Sohn GmbH, Eckenförde. ·22 LR rimfire, 7·65mm Auto, 9mm Short or 9mm Police (9 × 18); 168mm overall, 92mm barrel, 440–535gm. Seven (9mm) or eight rounds (7·65mm). Introduced commercially in 1974. Also offered in ·22 LR rimfire, with a ten-round magazine.

2521. AT-84P; International Technology & Machines AG (ITM, now part of Sphinx Industries), Solothurn. 9mm Parabellum; 184mm overall, 93mm barrel, 900gm. Ten rounds. This pistol is based on the Czech ČZ 75 (fig. 1611). The AT-84S is similar, but larger: 206mm overall, 120mm barrel, 1000gm.

2522. AT-88H; International Technology & Machines AG (ITM, now part of Sphinx Industries), Solothurn. 9mm Parabellum, 9mm AE or ·41 AE; 172mm overall, 87mm barrel, 740gm. A variant of the preceding gun.

2523. AT-2000 Sphinx; International Technology & Machines AG (ITM, now part of Sphinx Industries), Solothurn. 9mm Parabellum or ·41 AE; 206mm (SDA version), 184mm (PDA) or 172mm (HDA) overall. Double-action for every shot. The AT-380 is outwardly similar, but chambers 9mm Short ammunition.

Turkey

In addition to indigenous copies of the Walther Polizei-Pistole, the Turkish forces have also used the M1911A1 Colt-Browning.

2524, 2525. Kirikkale; Kirikkale Tüfek Fabricasi, 1948–52. 7·65mm Auto or 9mm Short; 170mm overall, 98mm barrel, 690gm. Seven (9mm) or eight (7·65mm) rounds. A copy of the Walther PP, named after the town in which it was made. It deviates from the German prototype in purely minor respects: e.g., the magazine-release catch is arranged differently, and the magazine base-plate has an extended finger rest. The left grip displays 'F.j.M' whilst the right one bears the crescent-and-star national emblem.

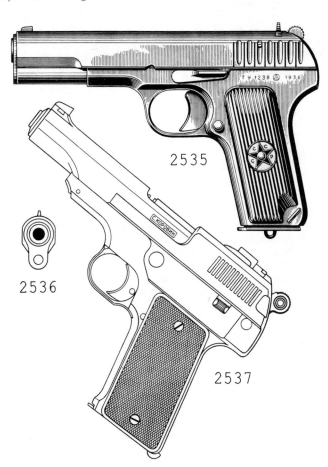

2535

2536

2537

2526. MKE; Makina ve Kimya Endustrisi, Kirrikale, 1952–3. 9mm Short; 170mm overall, 98mm barrel, 650gm. Seven rounds. A later variant of the pistol described previously, differing from it only in minor details.

Union of Soviet Socialist Republics

Details of the 1895-pattern 7·62mm 'gas-seal' Nagant revolver, production of which continued well into Soviet days, will be found in the section devoted to Russia.

Between-war designs

2527–2529. TK; Tula ordnance factory, introduced in 1926. 6·35mm TK; 127mm overall, 68mm barrel, 400gm. Eight rounds. Designed by Sergey Korovin, this was intended as a target pistol but became popular among commanders of the Red Army in the course of time. The cartridge contained a more powerful powder charge than that of the dimensionally comparable 6·35mm Auto (·25 ACP), which was used as a standard of comparison for the new Soviet pistol. The initial velocity of the TK bullet was about 228 m/sec compared with 200 m/sec for the 6·35mm Auto pattern. In addition, the TK pistol held a larger number of cartridges in the magazine than the 1906-pattern FN-Browning, had more effectual sights, a longer sight radius, a more convenient grip, and a better positioned safety catch. An improved TK appeared in the early 1930s, without the flutes alongside the ejector that had characterised the slide of the original pattern. The retraction grooves on the new slide were milled diagonally instead of vertically, and the grips were retained by internal quick-release plates instead of screws.

2530, 2531. Korovin; Tula ordnance factory. An experimental 7·65mm pistol designed by Sergey Korovin. Double-action for the first shot.

2532. Prilutskiy; Tula ordnance factory. An experimental 7·65mm pistol designed by Sergey Prilutskiy in the early 1930s.

2533, 2534. TT, 1930 pattern; Tula ordnance factory. 7·62mm; 195mm overall, 116mm barrel, 850gm. Eight rounds. Designed by Fedor Tokarev, this pistol replaced the obsolescent 1895-model Nagant revolver in the Red Army (though the revolvers remained in the army inventory and production did not stop immediately). The TT was an effectual design, though flaws in detail initially obscured success. Prior to the advent of the TT pistol, in addition to the Nagant revolvers, the Red Army had a selection of foreign weapons of differing systems and calibres, hindering repairs and ammunition supply. Adopting the TT put an end to this unpractical diversity.

Technically, the TT pistol was superior to many of the leading pistols of the day in some respects. It was distinguished by simple design, durability and reliability. It operated on a variation of the Browning dropping-link system (see introduction). Recesses inside the top of the slide interlocked with grooves on the barrel. The pistol had no manual safety, though there was a half-cock notch on the hammer. The components of the firing mechanism were all combined in a detachable sub-frame, and the pistol could be field-stripped without tools.

The powerful bottle-necked cartridge was adapted from the 7·63mm Mauser pattern, as the German pistol had been particularly popular with Tsarist army officers. Though the lethality of the small-diameter bullet was poor, it had been selected specifically to allow the same rifling machinery to be used for pistol, rifle or machine-gun barrels alike and, secondly, to allow the standard pistol cartridge to be used in a submachine-gun.

2535, 2536. TT, 1933 pattern; Tula ordnance factory. 7·62mm. Eight rounds. The original TT was improved shortly after it had been introduced. Detail changes were made in the trigger mechanism; the grip back-strap, originally a seperate component, was forged integrally with the frame; and the locking lugs encircled the barrel to facilitate production. Although the TT was the first Soviet military self-loading pistol, it proved to be powerful and reliable during the Great Patriotic War, remaining in service after 1945. Issue in many other countries indicates the soundness of its design.

2537–2542. Experimental designs, 1938–41. Problems with the Tokarev pistol led to a series of trials, the initial competition for which was announced as early as 1938. None of the guns were perfected prior to the German invasion of the USSR in the summer of 1941. They included submissions by Korovin (7·62mm, figs. 2537 and 2538), Rakov (7·62mm, figs. 2539 and 2540), Tokarev (7·62mm, fig. 2541) and Voevodin (7·62mm, fig 2542).

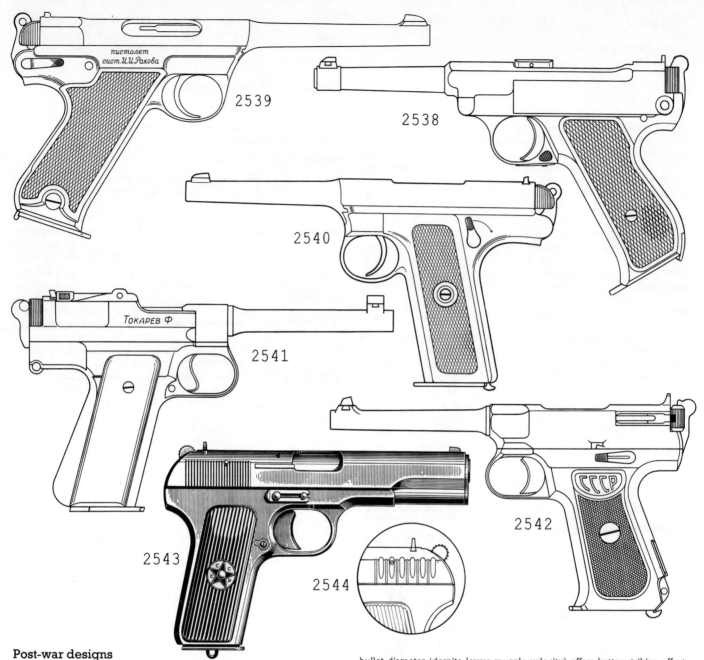

пистолет сист.И.И.Ракова 2539

2538

2540

Токарев Ф 2541

2543

2544

CCCP 2542

Post-war designs

2543. TT, 1951 pattern; state ordnance factories. 7·62mm. Eight rounds. The modifications concerned the retraction grooves on the slides, which were milled much more finely than the pre-war segments.

2544. P-3; believed to have been made in the Izhevsk ordnance factory. 5·6mm (·22 LR rimfire). Ten rounds. Shortly after the end of the Great Patriotic War, Sevryugin created this blowback target pistol from the basic TT. The most obvious external identification feature is that fewer retraction grooves were milled in the slide.

2545–2549. Experimental designs, 1945–51. Pistol trials continued after the end of the war, with an assortment of submissions—Sergey Simonov (7·65mm fig. 2545), Sergey Korovin (7·65mm, fig. 2546), Igor Stechkin (fig. 2547) and Konstantin Baryshev (9mm experimental pistol, 1947, figs. 2548 and 2549). Voevodin, Rakov and Makarov also submitted designs.

2550, 2551. PM; Izhevsk ordnance factory. 9mm Makarov; 160mm overall, 93mm barrel, 730gm. Eight rounds. The work of Nikolay Makarov, this blowback design was adopted after an extensive series of trials to replace the TT. An early example is shown in fig. 2549, and a later one in fig. 2550. The PM handles better than the Tokarev and, largely owing to the larger

bullet diameter (despite lower muzzle velocity) offers better striking effect. The main structural advantages of the Makarov pistol lie in its firing mechanism, double-action for the first shot, and in the safety lever on the left side of the slide that facilitates handling.

2552–2554. PB; Izhevsk ordnance factory. 9mm. Eight rounds. This is a silenced adaption of the Makarov, the muzzle and the detachable silencer being shown alongside the main illustration.

2555–2558. APS; Izhevsk ordnance factory. 9mm Makarov; 225mm overall, 138mm barrel, 1,020gm. Twenty rounds. The work of Igor Stechkin, this large blowback design, with a double-action trigger system, was introduced concurrently with the PM to fulfil the dual functions of pistol and submachine-gun. It was intended for officers engaged in combat as well as NCOs and men of some special units. The safety lever, which doubled as a selector, had three positions: safety, single shots and automatic fire. Cyclic rate of fire was about 700–750 rounds per minute, the back sight was adjustable for ranges of 25–200 metres, and the pistol was carried in a wooden or plastic holster doubling as a shoulder-stock. Owing to the moderate power of the 9mm Soviet cartridge, the recoil of the APS was substantially less than that of the Mauser M712 pistol; automatic fire from

2545

2546

2547

2550

2548

2555

2551

2549

2558

2553 2552

2557

2554

2556

the Stechkin was possible in exceptional cases without the stock attached, all but impossible with the Mauser. However, although the APS apparently worked satisfactorily, it was judged to be too heavy and too cumbersome to be issued in large quantities.

2559-2561. APB; Izhevsk ordnance factory. 9mm. Twenty rounds. This is simply a version of the Stechkin pistol (see above) with an elongated barrel, a silencer and a shoulder-stock.

2562, 2563. PSM; Izhevsk ordnance factory. 5·45mm; about 155mm overall, 85mm barrel. Eight rounds. This unusually small-calibre pistol was developed by Tikhon Lashnev, Anatoliy Simarin and Lev Kulikov. It operates on blowback principles, and has a hammer-type firing system that is double-action for the first shot. The safety is so situated that the hammer can be cocked whilst the safety is switched off. The pistol has no protruding parts, being flat and only 18mm wide; the grips are made of a light alloy.

2564. Margolin. 5·6mm (·22 LR rimfire). A target pistol designed by Mikhail Margolin.

2565. MTsM-K or Margo. 5·6mm (·22 LR rimfire); 190mm overall, 700gm. Seven rounds. A sporting version of the popular Margolin target pistols. The Drel is essentially similar, but in 5·45mm calibre and has an ambidexterous safety lever. Its magazine contains ten rounds.

United States of America

Automatic pistols were patented by George Luce in the United States as early as 1874, though the experiments had no lasting success. Not until substantial progress had been made in Europe did American-born inventors make their mark on the self-loading handgun. Hiram Maxim, best known for his machine-guns, produced an effectual pistol design in 1896. The magazine was contained in a sharply raked grip, but the gun was never successful. Much more was achieved by John M. Browning, whose first relevant patents were filed in 1897.

Pre-1918 designs—i) Colt-Browning patterns

The appearance of Browning pistols in the United States stimulated the development of automatic pistols. The first guns were made in the Colt factory in Hartford, Connecticut; they were initially called 'Colt-Browning', but later became best known simply as Colts.

2566. ·38 Model 1900; Colt's Patent Fire Arms Manufacturing Company, Hartford, Connecticut. ·38; 9·25in overall, 6in barrel, 36oz. Seven rounds. Made in accordance with the 1897 Browning patent, the slide and barrel are unlocked after recoiling by two links, one at the muzzle and the other at the breech. The barrel, therefore, remains parallel with the barrel during the unlocking movement.

2567. ·38 Military Model, 1902; Colt's Patent Fire Arms Manufacturing Company, Hartford, Connecticut. Dimensions generally as Model 1900, above. The hammer and the milling on the slide can be the same as that on the 1903 model.

2568. ·38 Pocket Model, 1903; Colt's Patent Fire Arms Manufacturing Company, Hartford, Connecticut. ·38; 7in overall, 4·5in barrel, 30oz. Eight rounds.

2569, 2570. ·45 Model 1905; Colt's Patent Fire Arms Manufacturing Company, Hartford, Connecticut. ·45; 8in overall, 5in barrel. Seven rounds. Fig. 2570 shows a later model with a grip safety.

2571, 2572. ·45 Model 1909; Colt's Patent Fire Arms Manufacturing Company, Hartford, Connecticut. This was the first of the Colt-Browning series to use only a single link in the locking system. Consequently, the breech tipped downward during recoil.

2573, 2574. ·45 M1911; Colt's Patent Fire Arms Manufacturing Company, Hartford, Connecticut. ·45 ACP; 8·59in overall, 5·03in barrel, 39oz. The 1909-pattern pistol, which had proved effectual, was soon refined. The most obvious change concerned the grip, which was raked more steeply; the perfected Model 1911 was adopted by the US armed forces. As a 'Government Model', it was produced not only in Hartford but also at other arms plants in the United States. Therefore, military Colts made prior to 1918 may bear the marks of Springfield Armory, the Remington

Arms Company or, much more rarely, the North American Arms Company of Montreal.

ii) Personal-defence and pocket patterns

2575. ·25 Hammerless Pocket Model; Colt's Patent Fire Arms Manufacturing Company, Hartford, Connecticut. ·25 ACP; 4·45in overall, 2·13in barrel, 13oz. Six rounds. Introduced in 1908, this was a minor variant of the FN-Browning Mle 1906.

2576, 2577. ·32 Hammerless Pocket Model; Colt's Patent Fire Arms Manufacturing Company, Hartford, Connecticut. ·32 ACP; 7in overall, 3·25in barrel, 19·5oz. Eight rounds. Introduced in 1903, this was basically a reduced-scale version of the Belgian FN-Browning of the same year. The ·32 model was produced in several sub-patterns differing in purely minor respects. For instance, the second (1911–26) and third versions (1926–45) had a differing muzzle from the original shown in fig. 2577, whilst the second modification had an additional magazine safety. A ·380 seven-shot variant was also made.

2578. H&R; Harrington & Richardson Arms Company, Worcester, Massachusetts, c.1912–14. ·25 ACP; 4·45in overall, 2·15in barrel, 12·3oz. Seven rounds. Patented in 1907, these guns were modelled on the British Webley pistols, though the firing mechanism differs in detail and they use a recoil spring instead of a V-shaped plate spring.

2579. H&R; Harrington & Richardson Arms Company, Worcester, Massachusetts, c.1916–22. ·32 ACP; 6·5in overall, 3·5in barrel, 21·9oz.

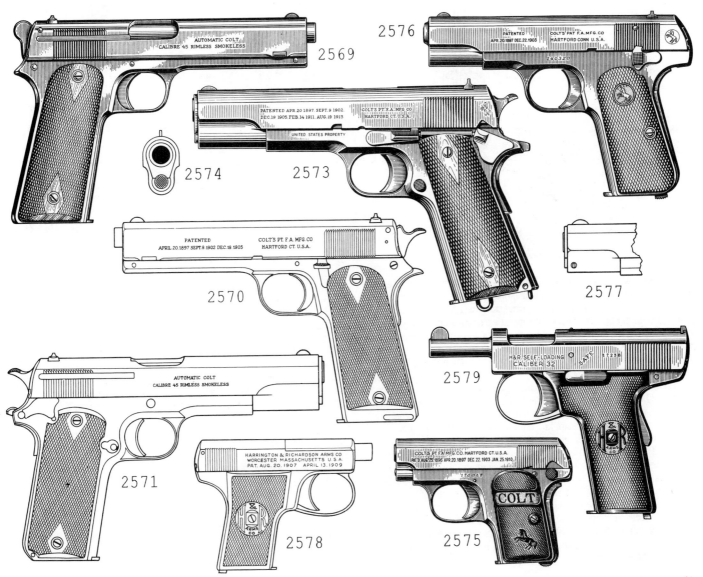

Eight rounds. This was essentially similar to the ·25-calibre version described previously, but had a coil-pattern recoil spring instead of a V-shaped riband. New guns were still being sold from dealers' stocks as late as 1939.

2580. Phoenix; Phoenix Arms Company, Lowell, Massachusetts. ·25 ACP; 4·6in overall, 2·2in barrel, 13·1oz. Six rounds. A copy of the Belgian Melior pistol (q.v.), produced early in the twentieth century.

2581. Model 1907; Savage Arms Company, Utica, New York, 1907–17. ·32 ACP; 6·6in overall, 3·75in barrel, 22oz. Ten rounds. In 1905, Savage acquired the rights to a breech-locking system patented by Elbert Searle. When a shot was fired, the bullet was spun by the rifling; as the bullet turned, it created an opposing reaction in the fabric of the barrel. This opposing force pressed a cam-lug on the barrel against the edge of a slightly-curved longitudinal groove inside the slide, retarding the initial backward movement of the breech. Once the bullet had left the muzzle, engagement between the cam lug and the slide groove ceased and the action reciprocated normally. The staggered-column arrangement of cartridges in the detachable magazine was also a distinguishing feature of the Savage pistol. An experimental ·45 pistol was tested by the US Army, but failed to defeat the Colt-Browning in the race for military adoption. The ·32 version announced in the summer of 1907 was much more successful. A somewhat larger ·380 version was introduced in 1913—7·1in overall instead of 6·6in. This size differential applied to virtually all Savage pistols of this type.

2582. Model 1915 Hammerless; Savage Arms Company, Utica, New York, 1915–19. ·380 ACP; 7·1in overall, 4·25in barrel, 23·1oz. Nine rounds. The slide catch lies on the front right side of the receiver. A ·32 ACP version was also made. The last guns made after the introduction of the Model 1917 had finer retraction grooves on the slide (see fig. 2584).

2583, 2584. Model 1917; Savage Arms Company, Utica, New York, 1917–26. ·32 ACP; 6·6in overall, 3·8in barrel, 22oz. Ten rounds. Distinguished by the spur-hammer, this was introduced to replace the unsuccessful Model 1915. The earliest examples had the coarsely grooved slides shown in fig. 2583, but these were rapidly superseded by the perfected fine-groove pattern. A ·380 ACP version was also made in small numbers in 1918–28. The ·32 version was purchased by the French during the First World War and by the Portuguese army in 1916–17.

2585, 2586. ·25 Pocket Model; Savage Arms Company, Utica, New York. ·25 ACP; 4·7in overall, 2·45in barrel, 12·2oz. Six rounds. The larger pattern is 5·8in overall and has a 3·55in barrel. Small numbers of these simple blowback pistols were made from about 1914 until 1919.

2587, 2588. S&W Automatic Pistol; Smith & Wesson, Springfield, Massachusetts. ·35 S&W; 6·5in overall, 3·5in barrel, 22oz. Seven rounds. Introduced in 1913, this unusual but unsuccessful pistol was a modification of the Belgian Clément (q.v.) of 1909 and had a distinctive automatic safety on the front grip-strap. It was discontinued in 1921.

2589. The Infallible; Warner Arms Corporation, Norwich, Connecticut. ·32 ACP; 6·6in overall, 3·75in barrel, 25oz. Seven rounds. This was patented in 1914–15 by Andrew Fyrberg, but was delicate and unreliable. Pistols made from 1917 until production was abandoned in 1919 were marked by the Davis-Warner Arms Corporation of Assonet, Massachusetts.

2590. Union Automatic Pistol; Union Arms Company, Toledo, Ohio. ·32 S&W or ·38 S&W. Patented in 1903–8 by Joseph Reifgraber of St Louis, this unusual pistol—which chambered rimmed revolver cartridges—was operated by a combination of gas and recoil. A few were manufactured in c.1910–12, without lasting success.

2591. W.A.C. or Warner Automatic Pistol; Warner Arms Corporation, Brooklyn, New York. ·32 ACP; 5·6in overall, 4·15in barrel, 18·7oz. Eight rounds. This was a variant of the Schwarzlose (q.v.) blow-forward pistol, apparently assembled in the USA in c.1911–13 from stocks of obsolescent parts imported from Germany.

Between-war designs

2592, 2593. ·45 M1911A1; Colt's Patent Fire Arms Manufacturing Company, Hartford, Connecticut. Data as M1911 (fig. 2573). A minor improvement of the original 1911-pattern ·45 pistol—easily recognisable by the arched grip back-strap—this was officially adopted by the US Army in 1926. During the Second World War, pistols were produced by contractors other than Colt and can be found bearing the names of the Ithaca Gun Company of Ithaca, New York State; Remington-Rand, Inc., of Syracuse, New York; and the Union Switch & Signal Company of Swissvale, Pennsylvania. The M1911A1 has been extremely successful, equipping the armies of more than twenty armies throughout the world. The pistol still provides the basis for a wide range of commercial and target versions made by many differing gunmakers, including Colt. These are listed separately in the post-1945 section below. A ·22 LR rimfire blowback target pistol based on the M1911A1, the Ace, appeared in 1931.

2594. Remington Model 51; Remington Arms Company, Ilion, New York. ·32 ACP or ·380 ACP; 6·63in overall, 3·5in barrel, 21·2oz. Eight rounds (·32 version). Designed by John Pedersen, this delayed-blowback pistol was introduced in 1919 (·380) or 1921 (·32). It was discontinued in 1927.

2595, 2596. S&W Automatic Pistol; Smith & Wesson, Springfield, Massachusetts. ·32 ACP; 6·55in overall, 3·45in barrel, 25·8oz. Seven rounds. Introduced in 1924 to replace the unsuccessful 1913 pattern described previously, this resembles its predecessor in many respects. However, the breech block and the slide were fused into a single reciprocating component and the barrel was forged integrally with the frame. The automatic safety duplicated that of the previous model. The pistol was discontinued in 1936.

Post-1945 guns—i) Colt-Browning and associated types

2597. American MX-9; American Arms, Inc., North Kansas City, Missouri. 9mm Parabellum; 3·75in barrel, 27oz. Nine rounds. A commercial model based on the Yugoslavian variant of the TT. Similar developments sold by US distributors are shown elsewhere below.

2598, 2599. Bren Ten Combat Model; Dornaus & Dixon Enterprises, Inc., Huntington Beach, California. 10mm Auto; 8·75in overall, 5in barrel, 37·7oz. Eleven rounds. This powerful military-style pistol, derived from the Czech ČZ 75 by Jeff Cooper, was introduced in 1983. It was made entirely of stainless steel and had a double-action firing mechanism for the first shot; the safety catch was ambidexterous. The Bren Ten Pocket Model (fig. 2599) was identical in all respects excepting length, weight and a nine-round magazine. The promoters failed in the late 1980s, ultimately being replaced by Peregrine Industries; the gun became the 'Falcon' (q.v.).

2600. CAC 45·1 Combat Model. This pistol is based on the Colt M1911A1, from which it differs principally in considerably reduced size, the location of the safety on the slide, and the omission of the automatic grip safety.

2601. Combatmaster; New Detonics Manufacturing Corporation, Phoenix, Arizona. ·45 ACP; 3·5in barrel, 25·6oz. Six rounds.

2602. Commander; Colt's Manufacturing Co., Inc., Hartford, Connecticut. 9mm Parabellum, ·38 Super or ·45 ACP; 7·85in overall, 4·4in barrel, 26·5oz. Seven (·45) or nine rounds (9mm and ·38). M1911A1-type or 'Government Model' pistols introduced commercially after the end of the Second World War generally had a rounded hammer, the 'Commander' being shown here. Full-length and shortened versions were offered, whilst, simultaneously, Colt promoted guns with improved sights and better grips.

MK IV/Series 70 guns were introduced in the early 1970s, followed by the improved MK IV/Series 80 in 1982. The principal improvements have been made in the hope of overcoming the poor accuracy that arose in tipping-barrel guns when they became excessively worn; vibration of the muzzle, arising from the gap between the outside of the barrel and the inside of the slide-mouth, generally increased bullet scatter. The specially shaped bush of the Series 70 Colts engages an expanded muzzle to reduce the effects of wear appreciably. Series 80 guns feature an improved form of this bush and a striker which can only reach the primer of a chambered round when the shooter presses the trigger. New Colt models often have receivers made of light alloy.

Various US companies have imitated the M1911A1, among them the Auto Ordnance Corporation, the Arcadia Machine & Tool Company (AMT), Essex Arms Corporation, L.A.R. Manufacturing, Inc. (which produces

Grizzly pistols), Crown City Arms (Condor, Eagle, Falcon, Hawk and Swift), M-S Safari Arms and Randall. Additional details will be found in alphabetical model/manufacturer order.

2603, 2604. Coonan 357 Magnum; Coonan Arms, Inc., St Paul, Minnesota. ·357 Magnum, or a ·357 rimless equivalent; 8·27in overall, 5in barrel, 42oz. Seven rounds. The insert shows the alternative spur hammer.

2605. Delta Elite; Colt Industries, Inc., Hartford, Connecticut. 10mm Auto. Introduced in 1987. Identical mechanically with the standard M1911A1.

2606. Detonics 45 ACP; Detonics, Inc, Seattle (later Bellevue), Washington. 9mm Parabellum, ·38 Super, ·45 ACP or ·451 Magnum. Introduced in 1977 and made until the late 1980s, this is a shortened version of the M1911A1 Colt. The Scoremaster was a target-shooting derivative measuring 8·75in overall.

2607. Detonics Mk VI; Detonics, Inc, Seattle (later Bellevue), Washington. ·45 ACP; 6·73in overall, 3·5in barrel, 29oz. Six rounds. Made on the basis of the Colt M1911A1.

2608. Double Action Officer's ACP; Colt's Manufacturing Co., Inc., Hartford, Connecticut. ·45 ACP; 7·25in overall, 3·5in barrel, 34oz. A shortened version of the standard Double Eagle, introduced in 1991.

2609. Double Eagle; Colt's Manufacturing Co., Inc., Hartford, Connecticut. ·45 ACP, plus (from 1990) 9mm Parabellum, ·38 Super or 10mm Auto; 8·5in overall, 5in barrel, 39oz. Eight rounds. Introduced in 1988 (Mk I/Series 90) or 1989 (Mk II/Series 90), this is a development of the perfected Series 80 Colt-Browning system, with a double-action trigger system for the first shot.

2610. Falcon, Peregrine Industries, Huntington Beach, California. 10mm Auto, ·40 S&W or ·45 ACP. A revision of the Bren Ten (q.v.), introduced in 1991. The promoter became 'Falcon Industries, Inc.' in 1993.

2611. General Officer Model (M1911A1, also known as 'Colt, ·45 Model 15'), Rock Island Arsenal. A bronze plate let into the left grip is intended to receive the owner's name.

2612. Government Model 380; Colt's Manufacturing Co., Inc., Hartford, Connecticut. ·380 ACP; 6in overall, 3·25in barrel, 22oz. Seven rounds. A compact pistol of the Mk IV/Series 80, introduced in 1983.

2613, 2614. Grizzly Win-Mag Mk I; L.A.R. Manufacturing, Inc., West Jordan, Utah. ·357 Magnum, ·357 Winchester Magnum, ·357/45, 10mm Auto, ·44 Magnum, ·45 Winchester Magnum or ·45 ACP; typically 10·5in overall, 6·5in barrel, 51oz. Seven rounds. A powerful and heavy pistol developed in 1983 from the Colt M1911A1.

2615. Lightweight Officer's Mk IV/Series 80; Colt's Manufacturing Co., Inc., Hartford, Connecticut. ·45 ACP; 7·25in overall, 3·5in barrel, 24oz. Six rounds. A variant of the M1911A1 introduced in 1985; also made in a steel-frame version, which weighs about 34oz.

2616. Mitchell Model 88; Mitchell Arms, Inc., Santa Ana, California. 9mm Parabellum; 3.75in barrel, 28·2oz. Eight rounds. Made in Yugoslavia.

2617. Mustang 380; Colt's Manufacturing Co., Inc., Hartford, Connecticut. ·380 ACP; 5·5in overall, 2·75in barrel, 18·5oz. Five rounds. A compact pistol in the Mk IV/Series 80, introduced in 1987.

2618. Mustang Plus II; Colt's Manufacturing Co., Inc., Hartford, Connecticut. ·380 ACP; 5·63in overall, 2·75in barrel, 20oz. Seven rounds.

Basically a combination of the Mustang and Government models, announced in 1988. It mates the dimensions of the former and the grip shape of the latter—allowing two additional cartridges to be carried in the magazine.

2619. Nova; La France Specialties, Inc., San Diego, California. 9mm Parabellum; 6·18in overall, 3in barrel, 21·2oz. Six rounds. Based on the Spanish-made Star BKM.

2620. On Duty; AMT, Irwindale, California. ·40 S&W; 4·4in barrel, 32oz. Twelve rounds. Made of either carbon or stainless steel. Apparently adapted from the well-proven Smith & Wesson action.

2621. Omega. A double-action pistol based on M1911A1.

2622, 2623. Parker Model GS; Wyoming Arms Manufacturing

Corporation, Thermopolis, Wyoming. 9mm Parabellum, 10mm Auto, ·40 S&W, ·45 ACP or ·357 Magnum; 3·4in or 5in barrel, 28·9oz or 35·3oz. Nine rounds. A target-shooting version with improved sights and a 7in barrel was also offered. Discontinued in 1992.

2624. Pit Bull ZG-51; Auto-Ordnance Corporation, West Hurley, New York. ·45 ACP; 7·25in overall, 3·5in barrel, 36oz. Seven rounds. A shortened M1911A1 Colt, introduced in 1989.

2625. Randall; Randall Firearms Research, Lomita, California. A left-handed version of the standard Colt M1911A1, with all the operating controls on the right and the ejection port on the left.

2626, 2627. Ruger P-85 DC; Sturm, Ruger & Co., Inc., Southport, Connecticut. 9mm Parabellum; 7·85in overall, 4·5in barrel, 32oz. Fifteen rounds. Fitted with ambidexterous de-cocking ('DC') levers. The P-89 DC is

essentially similar (see fig. 2627).

2628. Ruger P-91 DC; Sturm, Ruger & Co., Inc., Southport, Connecticut. ·40 S&W. The P-90 DC is identical, but chambered for ·45 ACP.

2629. Seecamp; L.W. Seecamp Co., Inc., New Haven, Connecticut. An adaption of the M1911A1 Colt. It has a double-action firing mechanism for the first shot.

2630, 2631. Servicemaster; New Detonics Manufacturing Corporation, Phoenix, Arizona. ·45 ACP; 4in barrel, 32oz. Seven or eight rounds. Similar but longer pistols include the Scoremaster (4·75in barrel) and Compmaster (5·5in). The Scoremaster muzzle is shown in fig. 2631.

2632, 2633. S&W Model 39; Smith & Wesson, Springfield, Massachusetts. 9mm Parabellum; 7·5in overall, 4in barrel, 27·5oz. Eight rounds. The firing mechanism is generally double-action for the first shot, though some single-

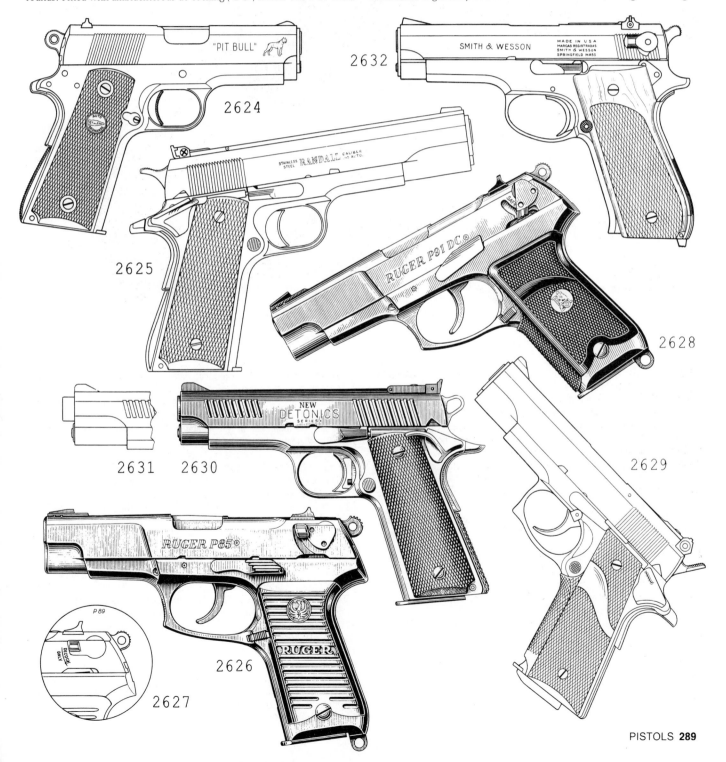

action guns have been made. The Model 52 target version has a longer barrel and adjustable sights.

2634. S&W Model 39 and other full-size guns have often been altered in accordance with individual requests. One such pistol, the 'Snake' produced in West Germany, is shown here. It may chamber either 7·65mm Parabellum or 9mm Parabellum cartridges, magazines holding seven or thirteen rounds depending on the type of gun selected for conversion.

2635. S&W Model 59; Smith & Wesson, Springfield, Massachusetts. 9mm Parabellum; 7·5in overall, 4in barrel, 29·6oz. Similar to the M39, but with a fourteen-round staggered column magazine. These pistols are used mainly by the US Air Force.

2636. S&W Model 59 SS; Smith & Wesson, Springfield, Massachusetts. 9mm Parabellum. Fourteen rounds. Model 39 SS is similar, but has an eight-round magazine.

2637. S&W Model 459; Smith & Wesson, Springfield, Massachusetts. 9mm Parabellum; 7·4in overall, 4in barrel, 29·6oz. ·Fourteen rounds. A new version of the Model 59, introduced in 1980. Improvements included the back sight, which became a distinguishing feature. The Model 439 is a similar adaption of the original Model 39.

2638. S&W Model 469; Smith & Wesson, Springfield, Massachusetts. 9mm Parabellum; 6·9in overall, 3·5in barrel. Twelve or fourteen rounds. A shortened version of the Model 459, introduced in 1983.

2639. S&W Model 645; Smith & Wesson, Springfield, Massachusetts. ·45 ACP; 8·9in overall, 5in barrel. Longer and heavier than the otherwise similar Model 459.

2640. S&W Model 1006; Smith & Wesson, Springfield, Massachusetts, 1990 to date. 10mm Auto; 8·5in overall, 5in barrel, 38oz. Nine rounds.

Smith & Wesson has produced several new pistols in the 1990s. Developed from the original Models 39 and 59 by way of the Model 469 (compact) or Model 645 (full-size), they share similar structure, dimensions and appearance. Novelties include the use of 10mm and ·40 S&W cartridges; refinements in the shape of the trigger guard to improve handling characteristics whilst firing two-handed; a differently shaped grip; ambidexterous safety levers; a spurless hammer; and luminous night sights. The trigger has usually been altered to be double-action for every shot.

The new designations are often based on barely discernible differences. For example, guns of the earlier pattern—e.g., Models 39 and 59—now have six separate designations: 439, 539 and 639, then 459, 559 and 659. The initial number indicates the material of the receiver ('4' is aluminium alloy, '5' is steel and '6' is stainless steel). In addition, there are designations pertaining specifically to low-volume production runs of 1,000–2,500 units.

In new four-digit designations, the first two figures indicate the series, differing principally in calibre—the 3900 and 5900 series chamber 9mm Parabellum, 1000-series guns are 10mm Auto; 4000 indicates ·40 S&W; 4500 represents ·45 ACP. The last two digits indicate other features. Consequently, Model 3904 has ordinary sights, 3906 has adjustable sights, 3953 is made of stainless steel, and 3954 is made of carbon steel.

2641. S&W Model 1066 NS; Smith & Wesson, Springfield, Massachusetts. 10mm Auto. Double-action for every shot; fitted with night sights ('NS'). Only a thousand of these guns were made.

2642, 2643. S&W Model 1076; Smith & Wesson, Springfield, Massachusetts. 10mm Auto; 7·84in overall, 4·25in barrel. Used by the FBI, this pistol has a de-cocking lever on the left side of the frame and a special spurless hammer. Owing to the absence of a manual safety catch, the Model

1076 does not meet US standards for a commercially saleable handgun. An optional straight-back grip may be obtained to order.

2644. S&W Model 3904; Smith & Wesson, Springfield, Massachusetts. 9mm Parabellum; 7·5in overall, 4in barrel. Eight rounds. Model 3906 is similar, but has adjustable sights.

2645. S&W Model 3913; Smith & Wesson, Springfield, Massachusetts. 9mm Parabellum; 6·8in overall, 3·5in barrel, 26oz. Eight rounds. Model 3914 is similar, but made of carbon steel.

2646. S&W Model 3913 LS; Smith & Wesson, Springfield, Massachusetts. This differs from the standard Model 3913 in the shape of the hammer. The Model 3314 LS is similar, but made of carbon steel.

2647. S&W Model 3953; Smith & Wesson, Springfield, Massachusetts. 9mm Parabellum. Stainless steel construction; double-action for every shot. Model 3954 is identical, excepting that it is made of carbon steel.

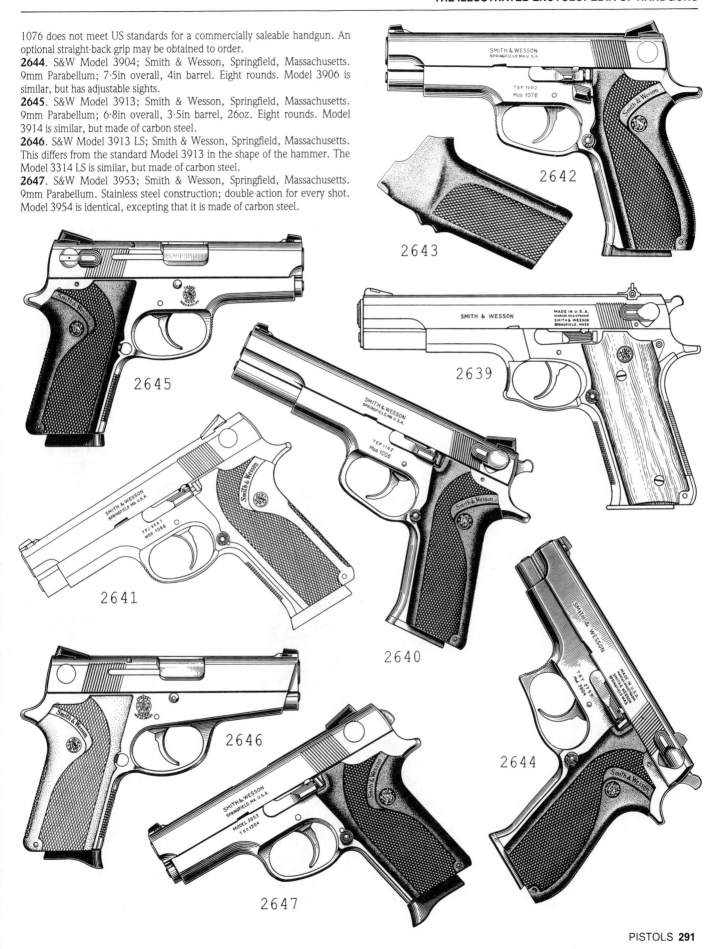

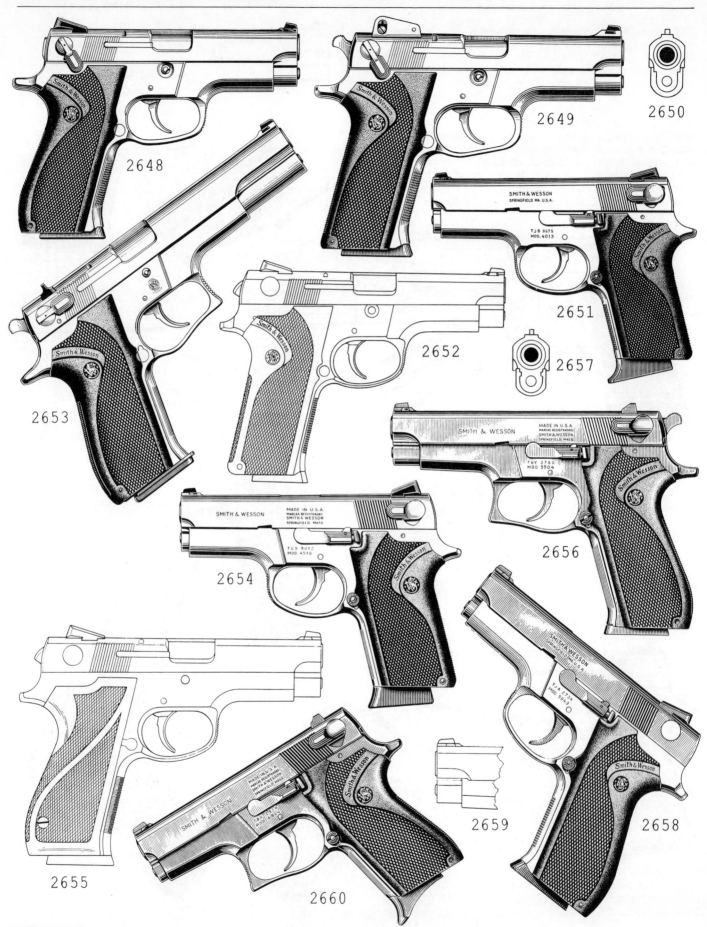

2648

2649

2650

2651

2657

2652

2653

2654

2656

2655

2659

2658

2660

2661

2662

2663

2664

2665

2666

2648–2650. S&W Model 4006; Smith & Wesson, Springfield, Massachusetts. ·40 S&W; 7·5in overall, 4in barrel, 36oz. Eleven rounds.

2651. S&W Model 4013; Smith & Wesson, Springfield, Massachusetts. ·40 S&W. Built on the frame of the Model 4516 (q.v.).

2652. S&W Model 4046; Smith & Wesson, Springfield, Massachusetts. ·40 S&W. Double-action for every shot.

2653. S&W Model 4504; Smith & Wesson, Springfield, Massachusetts. ·45 ACP; 8·5in overall, 5in barrel, 36oz. Eight rounds. Model 4506 is similar, but has adjustable sights (see fig. 2649).

2654. S&W Model 4516; Smith & Wesson, Springfield, Massachusetts. ·45 ACP; 7·13in overall, 3·75in barrel, 33·8oz. Seven rounds. Model 4567 NS is similar to the preceding gun, but with a short hammer spur and night sights. The slide is blued and the frame is bright. Only 2500 were made.

2655. S&W Model 4586; Smith & Wesson, Springfield, Massachusetts. ·45 ACP; double-action for every shot.

2656, 2657. S&W Model 5904; Smith & Wesson, Springfield, Massachusetts. 9mm Parabellum; 7·5in overall, 4in barrel, 28·5oz. Fifteen rounds. Model 5906 is similar, but has adjustable sights and is slightly heavier.

2658, 2659. S&W Model 5943; Smith & Wesson, Springfield, Massachusetts. 9mm Parabellum. Fifteen rounds. Made of stainless steel; double-action for every shot. Model 5944 is similar, excepting that it is made of carbon steel and slightly longer overall. The recurved front surface of the trigger guard, facilitating a two-hand grip, is optional.

2660. S&W Model 6904; Smith & Wesson, Springfield, Massachusetts.

9mm Parabellum; 7in overall, 3·5in barrel. Twelve rounds. Model 6906 is similar, but made of stainless steel.

2661. Springfield P-9; Springfield Armory (now Springfield, Inc.), Geneseo and Colona, Illinois. 9mm Parabellum, ·38 Super, ·40 S&W or ·45 ACP; 8·1in overall, 4·72in barrel, 35·3oz. Fifteen rounds (9mm Parabellum). A copy of the Czech ČZ 75. The P-9C is a 'Compact' version of the preceding pistol, structurally identical but measuring 7·25in overall.

2662. Springfield M1911A1 Compact; Springfield Armory (now Springfield, Inc.), Geneseo and Colona, Illinois. ·45 ACP; 7·25in overall, 4·25in barrel. Six rounds. A shortened version of the popular M1911A1 Colt-Browning.

2663. Thompson M1911A1; Auto-Ordnance Corporation, West Hurley, New York. A faithful copy of the standard full-size M1911A1.

2664. Trifire; Arminex Ltd, Scottsdale, Arizona. 9mm Parabellum, ·38 Super or ·45 ACP. The pistol has a two-way safety on the slide. Barrel lengths 5in (illustrated), 6in, 7in and 8in. The slide is extended in accordance with the barrel length. The promoter moved to Las Vegas in 1988, but the guns were discontinued in the early 1990s.

2665. Viking Combat. 9mm Parabellum or ·45 ACP; 7·8in overall, 4·25in barrel, 36oz. Seven ·45 or nine 9mm rounds. Double-action trigger mechanism, but otherwise based on the Colt M1911A1.

2666. Witness DA, or DA 45; European-American Armory ('E.A.A. Corporation'), Hialeah, Florida. ·45 ACP (9mm Parabellum, ·38 Super, 10mm Auto or ·40 S&W optional); 8·13in overall, 4·72in barrel, 35oz. Ten rounds in ·45 ACP. Made in Italy, apparently by Tanfoglio (q.v.); based on the Czech ČZ 75. There is also a eight-shot Compact Witness DA 45.

ii) Other locked-breech pistols

2667. Air Crew; Kimball Arms Company, Detroit, Michigan. ·30 M1 Carbine; 7·9in overall, 3·55in barrel, 28·9oz. Seven rounds. Also offered with a 5in barrel. After the Second World War, Kimball produced what was claimed—with justification—to be the world's most powerful pocket pistol. Unfortunately, the breech mechanism was a supposedly delayed blowback relying on lateral grooves in the chamber to slow case ejection by increasing friction whilst the barrel moved back by about ·2in. The strength of the slide-retaining lugs on the frame was insufficient, and so the Kimball rapidly gained the reputation of being potentially dangerous to fire. It was soon discontinued, though derivatives had been touted in ·22 Hornet, ·357 Magnum and ·38 Special.

2668. All-American Model 2000 (AA 2000); Colt's Manufacturing Co., Inc., Hartford, Connecticut. 9mm Parabellum; 7·5in overall, 4·5in barrel, 29oz. Fifteen rounds. Polymer frame; double-action for every shot. Introduced in 1991.

2669. American Arms Sabre. 9mm Parabellum or ·40 S&W; 3·75in barrel, 25·1oz. Nine rounds. Double-action for every shot. Basically an Italian Sites pistol completed to US specifications.

2670. Armscorp SD9; Armscorp USA, Baltimore, Maryland. 9mm; 3·07in barrel, 28·2oz. Six rounds.

2671. AMT-IV (Automag IV); AMT, Irwindale, California. ·45 Winchester Magnum; 10·7in overall, 6·61in barrel, 52·2oz. Six rounds. AMT-III is almost identical, excepting for the front part of the slide. 9mm Winchester Magnum; 10·62in overall, 6·54in barrel, 44·8oz. Seven rounds.

2672. Auto Mag Pistol (AMP) Model 180; Auto-Mag Corporation, Pasadena, California. ·357 AMP or ·44 AMP; 11·5in overall, 6·5in barrel, 57oz. Seven rounds. This extraordinarily powerful pistol was designed in the late 1960s by Max Gera of Sanford Arms, Pasadena, and marketed by Auto-Mag from 1970 until the company failed in 1972. Despite a succession of interested parties—including the TDE Corporation, High Standard and AMT—the project failed to prosper and the last guns were assembled in the early 1980s. They were recoil-operated and locked by rotating the bolt head into the barrel extension.

2673. Iver Johnson's Arms, Inc., Jacksonville, Arkansas. 9mm Parabellum. A double-action pistol developed in 1985–6 but never produced in quantity.

2674. KAC; Knight Armament Company. 9mm Parabellum; 6·73in overall, 3·68in barrel, 29oz. Thirteen rounds. Made of stainless steel.

2675. Thomas; A. James, Covina, California. ·45 ACP; 6·4in overall, 3·35in barrel, 33·5oz. Six rounds. A 1970s pocket/personal defence pistol, small in comparison with guns of such a large calibre. Double-action for every shot.

iii) Personal defence and pocket pistols

2676. AT-32 and AT-380; Accu-Tek, Chino, California. ·32 ACP or ·380 ACP; 2·75in barrel, 16oz. Five rounds.

2677. AFM Mark X Stainless Steel; American Firearms Manufacturing Co., Inc., San Antonio, Texas. ·25 ACP; 4·55in overall, 2·2in barrel. Eight rounds. Practically identical with the Guardian (q.v.), made of stainless or carbon steel.

2678. Auto Nine; Auto Nine Corporation, Parma, Idaho. ·22 LR rimfire; 4·35in overall, 2·2in barrel. Five rounds. A small pocket pistol. A variation has a slide similar to that shown in fig. 2686. The inscription FTL MKTG CORP. lies on the right side of the frame.

2679. Bauer 25; Bauer Firearms Corporation, Fraser, Michigan. ·25 ACP; 4·05in overall, 2·15in barrel, 8·8oz. Six rounds. A copy of the FN-Browning 'Baby' pistol made from 1973 until 1981. The Bauer was copied by companies such as KDI and PSP in 1985–9, but is now being marketed as the 'Fraser' (see below).

2680. Back Up; OMC, El Monte, California. ·380 ACP; 4·75in overall, 2·5in barrel, 17·7oz. Five rounds. Made of stainless steel, this was introduced in the mid 1970s.

2681. Davis P-380; Davis Industries, Mira Loma, California. ·380 ACP; 2·8in barrel, 22oz. Five rounds. A similar pistol in ·32 ACP, known as the P-32, has a six-round magazine.

2682. Derringer Automatic; American Derringer Corporation, Waco, Texas. ·25 ACP; 4·55in overall, 2in barrel, 15oz. Eight rounds. This is

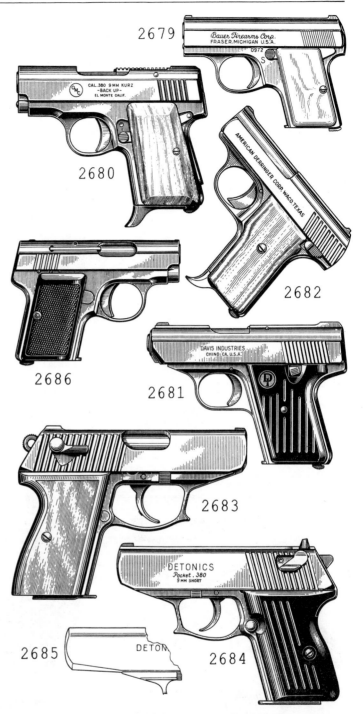

essentially similar to European pistols such as the Reck and SM, produced either as a firearm or a starting pistol. It is made of stainless steel; a Baby version has a shorter grip containing a five-round magazine.

2683. Detonics Pocket 9; Detonics, Inc., Seattle and Bellevue, Washington. 9mm; 5·7in overall, 3in barrel, 26oz. Six rounds. Derived from the Walther PPK, this has distinctive features of its own: safety levers lie on both sides of the slide, whilst the fixed trigger guard has a recurved front surface to facilitate two-handed use.

2684, 2685. Detonics Pocket 380; Detonics, Inc., Seattle and Bellevue, Washington. ·380 ACP; 5·75in overall, 3in barrel, 22·9oz. The same pistol with an extended barrel and slide is known as the Pocket 9LS: 6·77in overall, 4in barrel, 28·2oz (fig. 2685).

2686. Diana; Wilkinson Arms Company, Parma, Idaho. ·22 LR rimfire or ·25 ACP; 4·2in overall, 12oz. Six rounds. Introduced in 1982, this is very similar to FN-Browning of 1906.

2687. Double Deuce; Steel City Arms, Inc., Pittsburgh, Pennsylvania. ·22 LR rimfire. A modernised Walther TPH, introduced in the early 1980s. Features include ambidexterous safety levers and a trigger guard designed to support the finger in two-handed fire.

2688. Escort M-61; Smith & Wesson, Springfield, Massachusetts. ·22 LR rimfire or ·25 ACP. A pocket pistol produced only in 1969–74.

2689. Fraser. A later version of the Bauer pistol described above; a copy of the FN-made Baby Browning.

2690. FTL; FTL Marketing Corporation. A pocket pistol based on the 1906-model FN-Browning. See also Auto Nine, fig. 2678.

2691. Grendel P-10; Grendel, Inc., Rockledge, Florida. ·380 ACP; 3in barrel, 15oz. Ten rounds. Double-action for every shot.

2692. Guardian Model 270; FAI or Michigan Armament, Inc. ·25 ACP; 4·7in overall, 2·3in barrel, 12·5oz. Six rounds. Also known as the G27C—'G' for Guardian, '2' for calibre .25, '7' for the date of introduction (1977?) and 'C' for chrome plating—this is a variant of the Italian Galesi (q.v.). The Guardian SS ('Stainless Steel') is very similar to the Indian Arms Corporation pistol shown in fig. 2694. The inscription MICHIGAN ARMAMENT INC. lies on the left side of the receiver.

2693. IJ TP22B and TP25B; Iver Johnson's Arms, Inc., Jacksonville, Arkansas. ·22 LR rimfire and ·25 ACP respectively; 5·39in overall, 2·83in barrel, 14·5oz. Seven rounds. Introduced in 1981 on the basis of the Walther TPH. The first few guns were made in Middlesex, New Jersey, and marked as drawn here.

2694. Indian 380; Indian Arms Corporation, Detroit, Michigan. ·380 ACP; 6·1in overall, 3·25in barrel, 22·2oz. Six rounds. This pistol, made of stainless steel, was based on the Walther PPK. It differs from its prototype principally in the shape of the slide, which has a ventilated rib. Production began in 1982. The American Arms Eagle of 1984 is essentially similar, excepting that the ventilated rib is absent and the retraction grooves milled into the slide are coarser.

2695. Intratec, Miami, Florida. ·22 LR rimfire or ·25 ACP. Ten (·22) or eight (·25) rounds. Double-action for every shot.

2696. Iver Johnson Compact; Iver Johnson Division of AMAC, Jacksonville, Arkansas. ·25 ACP; 2in barrel, 9·3oz. Six rounds. Introduced in 1991.

2697, 2698. Jennings J-22 and J-25; Jennings Firearms, Inc., Stateline, Nevada, and Irvine, California. ·22 LR rimfire and ·25 ACP respectively; 4·93in overall, 2·5in barrel, 13oz (·22 version). Six rounds. Introduced in 1981 (fig. 2697), but subsequently modernised (fig. 2698). The Jennings Firearms/Bryco Arms M-38 (·22 LR rimfire, ·32 ACP or ·380 ACP) is similar, but larger—2·75in barrel, 16·1oz. Six rounds in all chamberings.

2699. Jennings Firearms/Bryco Arms M-48. ·22 LR rimfire, ·32 ACP or ·380 ACP; 6·7in overall, 4in barrel, 19oz. Six rounds.

2700. Junior Colt; Colt Industries, Inc., Hartford, Connecticut. ·25 ACP; 4·7in overall, 2·35in barrel, 10·6oz. Six rounds. This was made by Astra (q.v.) from 1957 until 1969; thereafter, a few were assembled in Hartford from Spanish-made parts (1970–2). The Colt 380 was identical with the Spanish Starfire (q.v.), excepting for the Colt trademark on the grips and COLT ·380, CAL ·380 or, alternatively, COLT'S POCKET AUTOMATIC CALIBRE ·380 AUTOMATIC PISTOL on the slide.

2701. Lorcin L-25; Lorcin Engineering Co., Inc., Mira Loma, California. ·25 ACP; 2·4in barrel, 13·4oz. Six rounds.

2702. Raven P-25; Raven Arms, Industry, California. ·25 ACP; 4·75in overall, 2·4in barrel, 15oz. Six rounds. Now being made by Phoenix Arms of Ontario, California, as the HP25 (·25 ACP) or HP22 (·22 LR rimfire).

2703. Seecamp LWS-32; L.W. Seecamp Co., Inc., New Haven, Connecticut. ·32 ACP; 4·13in overall, 2in barrel, 10·5oz. Six rounds. The firing mechanism is double-action only. Introduced in 1985.

2704. S&W Model 422; Smith & Wesson, Springfield, Massachusetts. ·22 LR rimfire; 4·5in barrel, 22·9oz. Ten rounds. A derivative with a 6in barrel is designated 'Model 622'.

2705. S&W Model 2214; Smith & Wesson, Springfield, Massachusetts. ·22 LR rimfire; 3in barrel. Eight rounds.

2706. Sterling Model PPL; Sterling Arms Corporation, Gasport and Lockport, New York. ·380 ACP. This pistol was similar to the pre-war Colt Woodsman target pistol (or, perhaps, the High Standard Model HB) but fired centre-fire ammunition.

2707. Sterling Model 300; Sterling Arms Corporation, Gasport and Lockport, New York. ·25 ACP; 4·8in overall, 2in barrel, 13oz. Six rounds. A single-action pocket pistol based on European practice, this resembles the Italian Galesi. Model 302 is similar, but chambered for ·22 LR rimfire ammunition.

2708. Sterling Model 400 Mk II; Sterling Arms Corporation, Gasport and Lockport, New York. ·380 ACP; 6·5in overall, 26oz. Seven rounds. This double-action design, derived from the Walther PP, appeared in 1976 (Mk I) and improved in 1979 (Mk II). The Model 402 was similar, but chambered ·32 ACP ammunition. Models 400S and 402S were made of stainless steel. From 1973 onward, a variant of the Model 402 was made in ·22 LR rimfire.

2709. Stoeger-Luger Model STLL; Stoeger Industries, South Hackensack, New Jersey. ·22 LR rimfire; 8·9in overall, 4·5in barrel, 30oz. Eleven rounds. Introduced in 1976, this is a blowback 're-creation' of the fabled German Parabellum. The TL pattern is identical, but has a 5·5in barrel. Frames were

2709

2706

2705

2708

2707

made of steel from 1982 onward, whilst the safety lever may lie on either the left (STLR, TLR) or right (STLL, TLL) side of the frame. Some guns will be encountered with the marks of Navy Arms of Ridgefield, New Jersey, whose Replica Arms subsidiary made them for Stoeger.

2710. Sundance A-23; Sundance Industries, Valencia, California. ·25 ACP; 4·88in overall, 2·5in barrel, 16oz. Seven rounds.

2711. Walther Model PPK/S; Interarms, Alexandria, Virginia. ·22 LR rimfire, ·32 ACP or ·380 ACP; 6·1in overall, 3·27in barrel, 22oz. Seven rounds. This is basically a PPK with the deeper frame and grip of the standard PP, satisfying import regulations imposed by the US Gun Control Act of 1968. Production began in the USA in 1980.

Other US handguns

● BDA-380. Made in Italy by Beretta and then delivered to the United States (fig. 2017).
● Norton TP-70. A variant of the West German pistol TP-70 (fig. 1846), manufactured by American Arms, Inc., in Provo, Utah.
● Rogak. A short-lived, possibly unlicensed variant of the Austrian Steyr Pi-18 made by Rogak, Inc., in the late 1970s. Quality was poor, causing jams and breakages; clearing a misfire was particularly difficult, as the action lacked an ejector. The receiver was an investment casting and the firing mechanism sub-assembly was synthetic.
● F.I. Model D; Firearms International. Spanish Star pistols, practically identical with fig. 2140. Similar examples were also sold in the USA by Iver Johnson.
● Charter Arms Model 79K. The Erma EP-459 (fig. 1907) in ·32 ACP or ·380 ACP. A ·22 LR rimfire version was known as Model 40.

Vietnam

Pistols made in this country before the revolution in August 1945 and the formation of the Democratic Republic of Vietnam (renamed 'Socialist Republic of Vietnam' in 1976) were either crude copies of existing weapons or hybrids incorporating features taken from several European pistols; most are difficult to distinguish from guns considered here as being made in China (q.v.). A Tokarev-type pistol was the service weapon of the army of the Democratic Republic.

Yugoslavia

Prior to the Second World War, Belgian 9mm Short (·380 ACP) FN-Browning Mle 1922 pistols were issued to the army and police forces in Yugoslavia. In addition to the manufacturer's marks, the slides bore the state emblem and inscriptions in Serbo-Croatian. In more recent times, the armed forces have used the M57 (Tokarev) and M67 (Makarov) pistols in 7·62mm and 9mm respectively.

2712, 2713. Model 1931; Kragujevač arsenal. 9mm Short; 183mm overall, 102mm barrel. Seven rounds. A Jovanovič-system blowback design, the first indigenous handgun to be made in Yugoslavia.

2714. Model 57; Zavodi Crvena Zastava, Kragujevač. 7·62mm; 195mm overall, 116mm barrel, 900gm. Nine rounds. This copy of the Tokarev, produced in the Socialist Federal Republic, can be identified by its elongated grip. A variant chambered for the 9mm Parabellum is designated 'M65'.

2715. Model 70; Zavodi Crvena Zastava, Kragujevač. 7·65mm Auto; 165mm overall, 94mm barrel, 675gm. Eight rounds. Similar externally to the Tokarev, this is a simple blowback. The Model 70K chambers the 9mm Short (·380 ACP) cartridge, its magazine containing seven rounds only.

2716. Model 70A; Zavodi Crvena Zastava, Kragujevač. 9mm Parabellum; 200mm overall, 116mm barrel, 900gm. Nine rounds. A derivative of the Soviet Tokarev pistol with a safety catch on the left side of the slide.

2717. ZCZ-40; Zavodi Crvena Zastava, Kragujevač. ·40 S&W; 108mm barrel, 850gm. Thirteen rounds? A double-action military pattern pistol inspired by the SIG-Sauer P220 (q.v.). The ZCZ-99 is similar, excepting that it chambers 9mm Parabellum and has a fifteen-round magazine.

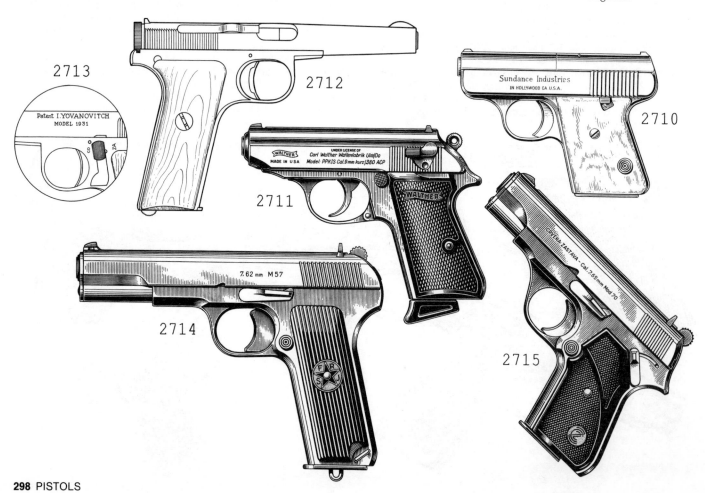

Miscellaneous patterns

Non-automatic pistols

2719, 2720. COP; C.O.P., Inc., Torrance, California. ·357 Magnum; four rounds. This gun has a four-barrel cluster, each barrel being fired sequentially.

2721. LM-4; Semmerling Corporation. ·45 ACP; four rounds. Designed by an American engineer named Lightman, this has the general appearance of an automatic pistol—but is reloaded manually by pulling forward and then releasing the barrel.

2722, 2723. S-4M. A twin-barrelled Russian design, loaded by tipping the barrel downward.

2724, 2725. MSP. Two rounds. Another of the compact Russian-made pistols, this also loads by tipping the barrel block downward.

2726. PSS-1; probably made in Izhevsk or Tula. 7.62mm. Chambered for a special silenced cartridge.

Shoulder stocks

2727. Steyr-Hahn, 1911 and most subsequent patterns; Austria-Hungary.
2728. FN-Browning M1903; Belgium.
2729–2731. FN-Browning GP-35 or High Power. Figs. 2729 and 2730 show Belgian-made stocks; fig. 2731 is Canadian.
2732. Bergmann-Bayard; Anciens Établissements Pieper. Belgium.

2733. Lepage, 9mm Bergmann-Bayard. Belgium.
2734, 2735. Parabellum; Germany. Fig. 2734 shows a wood-body holster stock attached to a 1904-type navy pistol; fig. 2735 shows the standard board-type stock, with a separate leather holster, attached to a long-barrelled 1908-type gun. Note the drum magazine inserted in the latter.
2736–2739. Mauser C/96; Germany. Figs. 2736 and 2739 are the most common types. Fig. 2737 is an early pattern, whilst fig. 2738 accepts a gun with a fixed twenty-round magazine.
2740. Heckler & Koch VP70A1; Germany.
2741. Star, various patterns; Spain.
2742. Astra, twenty-shot patterns; Spain. The holster-stock accompanying the ten-round guns is similar, but lacks the leather magazine shroud.
2743. Brixia, 1920 type; Italy.
2744. APS or Stechkin; USSR.
2745. Colt-Browning M1905; USA.
2746. Nambu Type A or 'Papa' model; Japan.

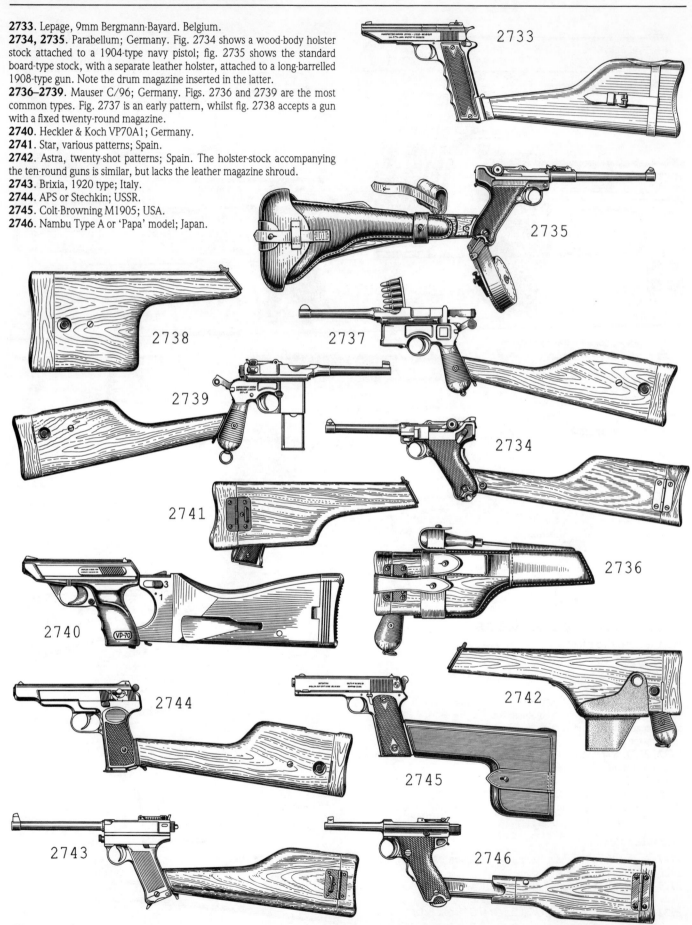

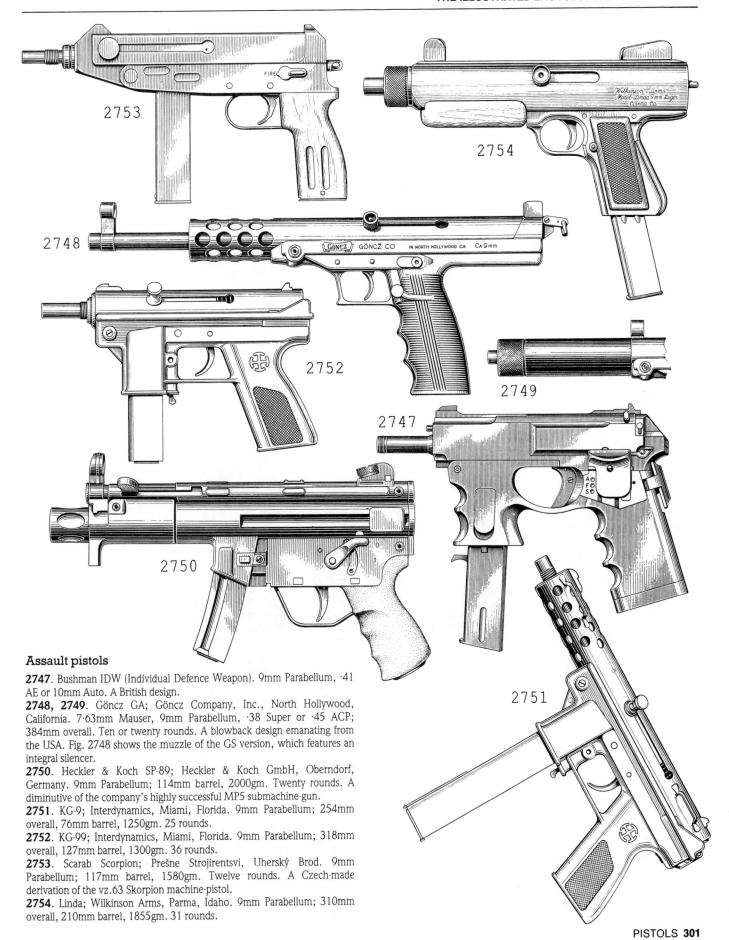

Assault pistols

2747. Bushman IDW (Individual Defence Weapon). 9mm Parabellum, ·41 AE or 10mm Auto. A British design.

2748, 2749. Göncz GA; Göncz Company, Inc., North Hollywood, California. 7·63mm Mauser, 9mm Parabellum, ·38 Super or ·45 ACP; 384mm overall. Ten or twenty rounds. A blowback design emanating from the USA. Fig. 2748 shows the muzzle of the GS version, which features an integral silencer.

2750. Heckler & Koch SP-89; Heckler & Koch GmbH, Oberndorf, Germany. 9mm Parabellum; 114mm barrel, 2000gm. Twenty rounds. A diminutive of the company's highly successful MP5 submachine-gun.

2751. KG-9; Interdynamics, Miami, Florida. 9mm Parabellum; 254mm overall, 76mm barrel, 1250gm. 25 rounds.

2752. KG-99; Interdynamics, Miami, Florida. 9mm Parabellum; 318mm overall, 127mm barrel, 1300gm. 36 rounds.

2753. Scarab Scorpion; Prešne Strojirentsvi, Uherský Brod. 9mm Parabellum; 117mm barrel, 1580gm. Twelve rounds. A Czech-made derivation of the vz.63 Skorpion machine-pistol.

2754. Linda; Wilkinson Arms, Parma, Idaho. 9mm Parabellum; 310mm overall, 210mm barrel, 1855gm. 31 rounds.

Other patterns

2755. Calico 950; American Industries, Cleveland, Ohio. 9mm Parabellum. Fifty rounds. The manufacturer claims that this gun can be used in perfect safety under water.

2756. Calico M·100; American Industries, Cleveland, Ohio. ·22 LR rimfire. 100 rounds. A rimfire chambering makes this weapon easier to control, and the size of the magazine compensates for the reduction in the striking power of individual bullets.

2757. Mars; Russian state factory, Tula. ·410 (10·4mm × 65mm); 350mm overall, 260mm barrel. Five rounds. Developed by a team that included Aleksandr Zhuk—for cosmonauts, pilots, geologists, prospectors and others who must survive under extreme conditions—this unique gun contains cartridges in a revolving cylinder above the breech. The striker is cocked by a lever as the cylinder turns, spent cases being extracted as the barrel (which lies beneath the cylinder axis) is tipped downward. Accessories include a telescope sights and a shoulder-stock doubling as an emergency ejector. Cartridges may be loaded with shot or a flechette.

2756

2755

2757

Ammunition

0 1 2 3 4 5 CM

Plain lead bullets are shaded horizontally; jacketed examples are shaded vertically.

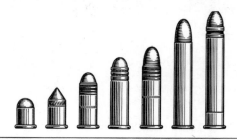

2758–2762. Lefaucheux pin-fire cartridges.

2758: 5mm.
2759: 7mm.
2760, 2761: 9mm (fig. 2761 contains a charge of small-diameter shot).
2762: 12mm.

2763–2769. Small-calibre rimfire cartridges.

2763: ·22 Flobert 'Monte Cristo'.
2764: ·22 Bousquet.
2765: ·22 Short (or 'Kurz').
2766: ·22 Long ('Lang').
2767: ·22 Long Rifle ('LfB', 'Lang für Buchse').
2768: ·22 Magnum.
2769: ·22 or 6mm 'Type Française'.

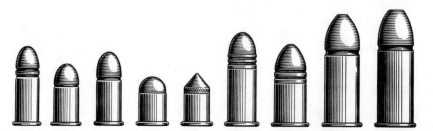

2770–2778. Medium-calibre rimfire cartridges.

2770: ·30 Long.
2771: ·32 Extra Short.
2772: ·32 Short.
2773: 9mm Flobert 'Monte Cristo'.
2774: 9mm Bousquet.
2775: ·38.
2776: ·41 Short.
2777: ·44.
2778: ·46.